Encouraging Transport Alternatives:
Good Practice in Reducing Travel

Encouraging Transport Alternatives: Good Practice in Reducing Travel

David Banister and Stephen Marshall

London: The Stationery Office

Applications for reproduction should be made in writing to The Stationery Office Limited, St Crispins, Duke Street, Norwich NR3 1PD.

The information contained in this publication is believed to be correct at the time of manufacture. Whilst care has been taken to ensure that the information is accurate, the publisher can accept no responsibility for any errors or omissions or for changes to the details given.

David Banister and Stephen Marshall have asserted their moral rights under the Copyright, Designs and Patents Act 1988, to be identified as the authors of this work.

A CIP catalogue record for this book is available from the British Library.

A Library of Congress CIP catalogue record has been applied for.

First published 2000

ISBN 0117 023 884

Printed in the United Kingdom by The Stationery Office Limited
TJ002269   C7.5   08/00   542733   19585

Published by The Stationery Office and available from:

The Stationery Office
(mail, telephone and fax orders only)
PO Box 29, Norwich NR3 1GN
Telephone orders/General enquiries 0870 600 5522
Fax orders 0870 600 5533

www.thestationeryoffice.com

The Stationery Office Bookshops
123 Kingsway, London WC2B 6PQ
020 7242 6393 Fax 020 7242 6412
68–69 Bull Street, Birmingham B4 6AD
0121 236 9696 Fax 0121 236 9699
33 Wine Street, Bristol BS1 2BQ
0117 926 4306 Fax 0117 929 4515
9–21 Princess Street, Manchester M60 8AS
0161 834 7201 Fax 0161 833 0634
16 Arthur Street, Belfast BT1 4GD
028 9023 8451 Fax 028 9023 5401
The Stationery Office Oriel Bookshop
18–19 High Street, Cardiff CF1 2BZ
029 2039 5548 Fax 029 2038 4347
71 Lothian Road, Edinburgh EH3 9AZ
0870 606 5566 Fax 0870 606 5588

The Stationery Office's Accredited Agents
(see Yellow Pages)

and through good booksellers

Contents

List of figures

List of tables

Acknowledgements

This book has drawn on research undertaken over a considerable period of time. There has been a history of interest in the application of measures from planning, land use and development to supplement direct actions in the transport sector to reduce levels or proportions of car-based travel. The main trigger for the book was the European Commission Directorate General VII – Transport's project DANTE (Designs to Avoid the Need to Travel in Europe), carried out over a two-year period ending in December 1998. The main output from that project was the *DANTE Good Practice Guide*, which has provided the starting point for this book. We are grateful to the European Commission for funding this project and allowing us to work together.

In particular, we thank Kees Maat and Erik Louw, both of Delft University of Technology, for contributing Chapters 5 and 11, respectively, and we are grateful to Daniel Mittler of the Bartlett School of Planning for undertaking additional research and supplying material for the Edinburgh case study.

We also thank Alan McLellan and Nick Green of the Bartlett School of Planning, University College London, who contributed research and graphical material, and who together with other colleagues have provided comment and constructive criticism about the venture. We are grateful to our partners in the DANTE team who have also supported the book and provided much of the case study material from their respective countries: Sandra Mathers and Laurie Pickup of Transport and Travel Research Ltd, UK; Jens Peder Kristensen of PLS Consult A/S, Aarhus; Massimo Marciani of FIT Consulting, Rome; Madalina Cotorogea and Ovidiu Romosan of Regia Autonoma de Transport Bucuresti; and Rico Maggi and Juerg Maegerle of Zürich University. As usual, any errors or misinterpretation of advice remain the responsibility of the authors.

Where illustrations are not the property of the authors, every effort has been made to contact the original copyright holders and we apologise for any omissions.

CHAPTER 1

Travel Reduction: Means and Ends

1.1 Introduction

The amount of travel worldwide is on a steady upward trajectory. In Europe, this 'mobility explosion' is outstripping the growth in population by a factor of over ten: for example, while population increased by 3.4% in a decade, there has been a 40% increase in car travel, measured in passenger kilometres (Marshall *et al.*, 1997). This considerable increase in travel might be regarded positively as a reflection of increasing personal mobility and economic growth. However, it is less than welcome when the side-effects are observed in increasing congestion on the roads and in the skies, and tangibly experienced in increased levels of air pollution, the consumption of land and other environmental consequences.

This concern over the adverse environmental impacts of transport is shared by politicians, professionals and the public. Various policies are available to mitigate these consequences through strategies such as the design of appropriate transport infrastructure or the development of 'clean' technology to make vehicles less polluting. Yet while such measures can be valuable, they can only make a limited contribution. The careful design of infrastructure, e.g., to deflect noise and pollutants away from their immediate environs, may be seen merely as a local means of treating the symptoms, but not the causes, of the problem. Similarly, making the vehicle cleaner may assist to some extent, but even zero-emission cars cause pollution and use resources in their construction, operation and disposal (Wackernagel and Rees, 1996).

Perhaps more ominously, if the availability of such partial solutions continues to encourage more travel and more car use – fuelling the problem – these solutions may actually help to exacerbate the damage done to the environment overall.

A more fundamental approach to tackling the problem is to attempt to reduce the amount of travel itself. Travel reduction may be regarded as a worthy objective not only for environmental reasons, but for economic efficiency (travel *per se* is not a productive activity) and social equity (for example, reducing travel distances can maximise accessibility for those without cars). Other factors being equal, the shorter the journey length, the more likely it is that a journey will be made on foot or bicycle, or by public transport (Banister, 1997).

The aspiration to reduce travel – and particularly car travel – is increasingly finding its way on to the policy agenda across Europe (CEC, 1998), and is being addressed on all scales, from the national level to that of city and local authority initiatives. In the UK the recent White Paper on Transport has placed a strong emphasis on reducing travel and encouraging alternatives to the use of the car where possible (DETR, 1998a). Travel reduction policies also appear as part not only of transport policy, but of land-use policy (DoE and DoT, 1994; DoE, 1995; DETR, 1999) and guidelines for the design of new development (DETR, 1998b).

Yet, in the right circumstances, people like to travel. Travel is a leisure activity in its own right, whether in the form of motoring, backpacking or any other mode. Mobility can be a valued 'commodity', or represent a sense of opportunity, or it may even be a 'perk' of the job. To be going places is to be getting on. People also like their own vehicles. The attachment of the owner to a car (or motorbike, or bicycle) is demonstrated in the amount of time and money annually invested in it. The inevitable consequence of vehicle ownership is vehicle use.

Accordingly, any attempt to curb use of that favoured vehicle, or to restrain mobility, is liable to provoke a hostile response. On closer inspection, the public's concern for the environment may lag behind that of policy makers. In a recent survey of motorists, when asked to choose between some 'motoring fantasies', only 8% opted for congestion-free streets. The most popular choice was 'a year's supply of free fuel' (*NCE*, 1999).

Naturally, people value the benefits and convenience of using their own car (Banister, 1997). How, then, can policy makers moderate demand for car travel so as to minimise the disbenefits of unrestrained car use – pollution, noise, accidents and so on – which are shared by both users and non-users? Whereas it may be in each person's interest individually to use the most convenient means of transport possible (and that often means the private car), there would be communal benefits if, collectively, we travelled less. The challenge is to reconcile the immediate desire for mobility with the longer-term and more distant consequences.

Whichever solutions are proposed, it is never going to be an easy task to make substantial reductions in travel, as this would imply effecting 'sea-changes' in behaviour. It is not simply a matter of managing to 'get people out of their cars and back on to public transport', as most journeys now made by car were never undertaken on public transport (Adams, 1997). This reflects the fact that journeys are now made by a new generation of people, between new places and for new purposes.

The policy balancing act has been described by Abraham and Rosenkrantz (1995) thus: 'We cannot force people to walk, cycle or use trains or even live at higher densities. We can, however, remove barriers to choosing alternate transport modes and housing types and promote more livable environments through debate, demonstration and negotiation...'. The implication is that each 'push' must be balanced with a sufficient degree of 'pull'. If motorists are to be encouraged to leave their cars behind, a convenient alternative must be available, and if mobility is to be restrained, there must be some alternative means of maintaining accessibility for travel reduction to be successful.

How, then, might this be achieved? One might start by refraining from increasing capacity. Ever since the link

Figure 1.1 A residential street in Woonerf, Enschede: people want both a good environment and the mobility offered by cars

between expanded traffic capacity and traffic generation was convincingly expressed (SACTRA, 1994), the option of 'doing nothing' has had a certain pragmatic appeal to policy makers. In other words, if you are in a hole, stop digging!

However, more proactive policies for reducing travel should also be examined. There is a need to consider the exact meaning of 'travel reduction', and how it may be achieved. Before any policy recommendations may be made, it is necessary to discern existing good practice in reducing travel. To achieve this, it is necessary first to identify travel reduction policies already operating, and secondly to establish that these are good practice in the sense that they are actually seen to reduce travel.

1.2 What does travel reduction mean, and how may it be achieved?

Travel reduction can take a variety of forms (see Figure 1.2), for example:

- a reduction in the *number of trips* made;
- a reduction in vehicle kilometres, by reducing the *distance* involved in trips;
- a reduction in vehicle kilometres, by reducing the *number of vehicles* involved in trips, e.g., by changing from low-occupancy cars to high-occupancy public transport.

A reduction in vehicle hours or minutes, e.g., by travelling at off-peak times to avoid the time and energy spent in congestion, also constitutes travel reduction.

In each of these cases the amount of travel involved is in some way reduced, while the purpose of the trip is still fulfilled. Thus, one may reduce travel by shortening or cutting out, say, the journey to work, but the work activity itself can still take place. The current strong focus of Government policy (and possibly public thinking) is to switch the mode of transport, but this does not necessarily reduce travel, and it may even encourage more. The other options (i.e., to reduce the number of trips or distance travelled) are less important in Government thinking, but these are the areas where real change *can* take place.

Travel reduction as envisaged here does not restrict an individual's mobility, in the sense of restricting accessibility to activities and services or confining one's locus of movement. Rather, it means undertaking existing activities in such a way that alternative means of travel, or alternatives to travel, can be pursued.

Figure 1.2 Travel Reduction Options

Travel may be represented by a variety of quantitative parameters. If we consider travel in terms of vehicle kilometres, then we can represent the volume of travel as the product of the number of trips, the trip distance (km/trip) and the number of vehicles involved:

$$\text{Travel (vehicle km)} = \text{trips} \times \frac{\text{km}}{\text{trip}} \times \text{vehicles}$$

Travel may be represented diagrammatically by a block aligned along mutually perpendicular three-dimensional axes. We may therefore *reduce travel* by reducing any of these parameters (all else being equal).

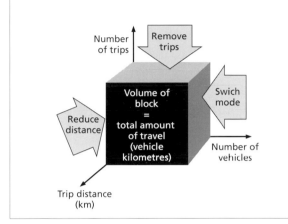

Transport is traditionally viewed as a derived demand: this means that the travel itself has no intrinsic value, but the costs of travel are outweighed by the benefits derived from other activities undertaken at the destination, e.g., work or leisure. However, it is now becoming clear that although the urban and inter-urban road systems will not be able to cope with the expected growth in traffic, the building of new roads will only serve to increase the demand for the roadspace available. This will in turn exacerbate the negative effects on the environment. As a result, policy makers are now moving away from traditional 'predict and provide' policies (Goodwin *et al.*, 1991).

Accompanying this policy shift has been a growing realisation that the solutions to today's transport problems are no longer restricted to what would traditionally be regarded as 'transport policy'. Traditional measures such as the promotion of public transport or the restriction of road capacity do continue to provide valuable solutions, but there are other approaches that may lie outside the traditional scope of transport engineering, such as the application of technology or land-use planning.

For example, developments in computer and communication technologies have made possible the introduction of 'teleworking' to replace the need to travel to work. Land-use planning techniques can also reduce the need for car travel. For example, the introduction of mixed-use

developments encouraging linking of journeys to fulfil multiple purposes, or planning the layout of urban areas to encourage short trips that could conveniently be made by bicycle or on foot (Figure 1.3), could reduce travel by car travel. In both of these cases, congestion problems are addressed by reducing the demand for transport rather than increasing the supply.

This move away from traditional transport solutions has also emphasised the need for involvement of non-transport bodies in travel reduction. Whereas most traditional transport policy solutions are the responsibility of national and local authorities, the responsibility for travel reduction is spreading increasingly to other organisations, for example, in company commuter plans and car-sharing schemes operated by private employers, awareness campaigns led by pressure groups or land-use measures implemented by developers. It is vital to obtain input from all the relevant agents and decision makers, and to encourage these bodies to work together in achieving travel reduction and hence to arrive at sustainable solutions.

So far we have discussed both the abstract parameters of travel reduction (e.g., vehicle kilometres) and the more concrete policy instruments (e.g., mixed-use development). It is possible to link these conceptually by considering the travel reduction process in terms of six mechanisms of substitution or switching. This set of mechanisms provides the framework within which many of the travel reduction measures in this book have been evaluated (Table 1.1).

As will be seen in this book, the travel reduction policies to activate these mechanisms may be 'push' policies – making conditions more unfavourable for car drivers – or 'pull' policies – making conditions more favourable for the alternative modes. Policies may include elements of both push and pull: they may include components which

Figure 1.3 Mews in central London: this form of development and land-use mix can assist in creating travel alternatives

essentially *restrict* mobility (such as road closures) as well as components which inherently *promote* mobility in one form or another (albeit mobility of a more efficient or environmentally benign nature), such as travel by public transport or by bicycle.

This explains how it is possible for a somewhat eclectic range of measures, from the supply of free bicycles to the construction of heavy rail systems, to be numbered among travel-reducing policies, even though at first sight they might appear to be promoting mobility. The point is that they should promote mobility in a way that gives rise to a reduction in the overall amount of motorised travel. For example, ten commuters in a bus instead of in ten single-occupancy cars would achieve a reduction in vehicle kilometres for the same number of passenger kilometres. Thus, initiatives intending to boost bus patronage can contribute to reducing travel overall.

The diversity of these 'travel reduction' measures means that they fall within a large proportion of contemporary policies coming under the general category of 'sustainable mobility', from the organisation of lift-sharing to the planning of compact cities. The topics covered in this book are therefore of significance to transport policy in general, and are not merely some minority 'anti-mobility' concern – although the concept of reducing travel does turn against some traditional tendencies of transport planning (for example, the concern for making travel easier and faster, and generally encouraging more of it).

Far from being a minority concern, travel reduction may now be seen as a useful 'umbrella' under which a comprehensive and consistent range of policies may be organised. It also provides a concrete criterion for successful evaluation of policies. Thus, each of those varied policies – from lift-sharing to the creation of compact cities – may be evaluated according to a common criterion: the extent to which it contributes to travel reduction.

1.3 The scale of the problem and the necessary conditions

The logic of the argument is clear: the amount of traffic is on a rapidly increasing path, while the growth in the amount of roadspace available is increasing at only a fraction of that pace. For example, 85% of all journeys made in the European Union (EU) occur on the road network. The last 30 years have seen a five-fold increase in European car ownership levels, with a further 30% increase expected over the next 20 years as households move towards multiple car ownership. In the 15 European Union (EU15) countries, between 1985 and 1995 population increased marginally (+3.4%) and the road network length increased by 10%. The real growth has come in car ownership (+31%) and in car travel (+40% in passenger kilometres). The increase in bus patronage (+6%) and rail (+3%) over the same period has been relatively modest (Marshall *et al.*, 1997).

Table 1.1 Substitution and switching mechanisms which can contribute to travel reduction

Mechanism	Example	Travel reduction contribution
Substitution		
By linking trips	A series of single purpose trips is replaced by a single trip combining different purposes	Reduced no. of trips
By technology	The trip itself is removed, while the activity takes place via electronic communication	
By trip modification	The type of trip is modified – for example, a series of shoppers' trips replaced by a single goods delivery round	
Switching		
Mode switching	A series of single occupancy vehicle trips is replaced by one higher occupancy vehicle trip (or, simply, a car trip is replaced by a trip by other mode)	Reduced no. of vehicles per person (or, simply, reduced number of car trips)
Destination switching	An activity is switched from a remote to a more local destination	Reduced no. of kilometres per trip
Time switching	Trips at congested periods are avoided	Reduced vehicle hours per trip

When these considerations are taken together, certain clear messages emerge. Firstly, there is increased usage of and dependence on the car, and hence there is a need to focus on reducing car travel. Secondly, the option of switching to public transport is always politically attractive, as it is seen as being a positive (pull) factor. However, public transport is already working near to capacity at certain times of the day, so additional demand can only be met by substantial new investment in capacity. Many governments do not seem prepared to make this kind of investment. Indeed, it could be argued that the tendency is away from investment, as more countries liberalise and privatise their public transport systems. Again, the conclusion here is that car use has to be reduced.

Thirdly, even if the car is seen as the solution to the problem and not the cause of it, the consequences of this 'solution' are unacceptable. To accommodate today's levels of demand, to ease congestion and to cope with expected increases in car-based demand would mean massive new investment in roads. Few governments are prepared even to contemplate such a policy as it is seen as being expensive and politically unattractive. Indeed, most governments are looking at the means to reduce all forms of public expenditure. This convergence requirement, where national public expenditure does not exceed predetermined levels, is central both to the establishment of a strong single European currency and to the achievement of a single market in Europe. All EU countries have signed up to the Maastricht Treaty, which sets strict limits on public expenditure as a total proportion of national income, on inflation rates and other convergence criteria necessary to the achievement of the single market. Within the macro-economic issues, transport is seen as one area where public expenditure can be quite easily cut, particularly on controversial road projects (Banister, 1994).

On these three important grounds then, it is important to look at the means by which travel reduction can take place, particularly by car. Car dependence has to be reduced. Although the public transport system can help through some modal switching, other measures are necessary to reduce trip distances and the numbers of trips (Figure 1.2). It is unlikely that there will be substantial new investment in roads, as this is politically undesirable. The scale of the problem is already vast and increasing.

To achieve change on the scale identified here, it is argued that there are two other necessary conditions that must be met. Even if the first of these, i.e., the transport case for reducing car dependence, is widely accepted, this alone is not sufficient to bring about real change. There must also be strong environmental arguments: this is the second

necessary condition. The environmental impact of transport ranges from the consumption of fuel and land to the effects of pollution, noise and vibration, as well as accidents, visual intrusion and community severance. As the transport sector is a significant contributor to the consumption of scarce resources and overall environmental damage, it is necessary for transport policy to address ways of reducing these adverse environmental impacts (Banister, 1998b) and their wider externalities (Table 1.2).

Within the EU and nationally, the new transport debate is about sustainability and sustainable mobility. At the heart of the emerging consensus is recognition that in the past there has been a direct link between economic growth and transport growth. As economies grow, people benefit through higher incomes, which encourage expenditure on consumer durables, including cars. As car ownership grows, so does the use of cars and car dependence. The acquisition of a car is the single most important event in changing the travel patterns of households (Banister, 1997).

The new debate concerns how to break this assumed link between economic growth and transport growth. The key is to reduce the transport intensity of the economy through decoupling transport growth from economic growth

Table 1.2 Road transport: quantified environmental and social costs in Great Britain

	Annual cost, £ billion (1994 prices)
Air pollution	2.0–5.2
Climate change	1.5–3.1
Noise and vibration	1.0–4.6
Total costs	4.6–12.9
Road accidents	5.4
Quantified social and environmental costs, other than congestion costs	10.0–18.3
Congestion costs*	10.9–20.5
Total road transport externalities	**20.9–38.8**

Congestion costs are the costs of delays to road users and operators and increased running costs at low speeds in congested conditions. Quantified social and environmental costs include the full costs to the community of pollution, noise and other intrusive social effects.

Notes: Some costs could not be quantified, for example the loss of habitat, degradation of landscape, destruction of cultural assets and disruption of communities.

The huge range of uncertainty over the values used give a total range of £21 billion to £38 billion.

Source: Royal Commission on Environmental Pollution (1997)

(Banister and Steen, 1999; Stead and Banister, 1999). There are many means by which economic growth can be maintained (or enhanced) with less use of resources in transport (Banister *et al.*, 2000). This argument is central to the notion of sustainable transport, where the imperative of economic growth is matched by an equal concern over the use of resources (land and energy), the reduction of externalities (pollution, noise and accidents) and the promotion of strong social and spatial equity priorities in transport.

Although the arguments for travel reduction may be strong in transport and environmental terms, these are still not sufficient on their own to result in substantial change. There is a third necessary condition, the strong political commitment to positive action. This in turn requires an equal commitment of support from the electorate, industry, commercial activities and other stakeholders.

Travel reduction policies may be implemented in order to achieve environmental benefits for society as a whole. The political responsibility for such policies requires foresight and long-term planning in order to compete with concerns of an apparently more urgent nature. Consequently, there is a danger of losing sight of or even avoiding decisions which may require people to change their behaviour, especially where this might involve individuals having to sacrifice some element of their current lifestyle. If short-term pragmatism always prevails then there is a danger that these environmental problems will magnify as they are perpetuated further into the future.

The task of tackling travel reduction is not made easier by the fact that the priorities and preferences of different sections of society may be divergent. For example, there

Figure 1.4 Walking and cycling in Amsterdam; this car-free street is also served by trams

are differences in priorities between the more mobile and less mobile, between the more affluent and the less affluent, and between the polluter and the polluted. Indeed, there may be conflict even for individuals, who may wish to see further support for public transport and promotion of non-motorised modes, and at the same time also to continue driving whenever it suits them, and resisting any attempts to make it more difficult to do so.

Although the main argument throughout this book concerns encouraging alternatives to travel, particularly by car, it is not 'anti-car'. For the reasons stated here, there is no alternative path that can be followed, particularly in European cities. At present there are unacceptable levels of congestion and delay, the environmental and external costs are too high and transport is contributing directly to the lowering of the quality of city life. To create attractive, sustainable cities requires new thinking about the role of transport and the car in the city. The argument is not that the car has no role, but rather that through creative combinations of measures its role can be redefined as part of a clear strategy for sustainable mobility. This means making the best use of available technology. It means linking land use, development and transport. It means a more limited use of the car. It means reallocation of space to priority users (Figure 1.4). It means involvement of all parties in the discussion, debate and action. And it means strong political commitment. There are clear opportunities to create the sustainable and liveable city that will attract people back to urban dwelling. This is the clear message recently reinforced by the Urban Task Force (1999) in its recommendations to the UK Government.

How, then, is it possible to resolve these conflicting demands and desires? How can we know the best way of achieving travel reduction? The approach taken by this book is to examine existing good practice in the application of travel reduction strategies. In doing so it gives examples of strategies which have been implemented, and evaluates the results of their success to demonstrate the extent to which these, indeed, represent good practice in achieving travel reduction.

Only by studying real cases in depth can we appreciate the context, the complexity of interactions and the implications of the scale of actual reduction in travel. It is thus possible to take account of potential barriers to implementation and also barriers which might prevent those implemented measures from realising the desired travel reduction outcomes. From a wide range of case studies it is possible to make a comparative evaluation between countries, and hence draw conclusions about the potential transferability of results.

The examination of good practice allows the identification of the travel situations which may be most amenable to substitution or switching away from the car to more environmentally friendly alternatives. This will provide a foundation from which those charged with transport and environmental policy making may choose the most appropriate action for addressing their own circumstances.

This book is directed towards those who are responsible for or concerned with tackling the issue of travel reduction. It is intended to be both a stimulus and a resource, encouraging the reader to access and explore material from which to gain an understanding of the travel reduction issues involved.

1.4 The structure of the book

This book does not have all the answers, and it is not intended to be prescriptive. The problems are well known, yet the scale of change necessary to achieve sustainable transport and the difficulties confronting decision makers are often underestimated. There are no ready-made solutions that can be applied in all situations or even in one city (Figure 1.5). Here we systematically review the policy measures available to reduce dependence on the car and to encourage travel alternatives. We offer a range of examples of what has been accomplished and how this has been achieved, backed up with evaluative findings. In drawing attention to both the principles lying behind the successes and the context in which they were achieved, we aim to lay a foundation from which readers may generate their own solutions.

Much of the empirical research for this book has been based on the six cities at the heart of the EU DGVII DANTE project (Figure 1.6).* These cities spanned a range of different sizes, locations, countries, policies, organisations and strategies for transport. Some measures were common to more than one city, others were unique to particular cities; some measures were applied on their own, whilst others were packaged together.

The main focus of the book is on measures that may be implemented at the local authority level. Although urban areas are given prominence because it is there that the problems of congestion and pollution are most keenly felt

*The DANTE (Designs to Avoid the Need to Travel in Europe) project has been funded by the European Commission Directorate General VII – Transport. This project has examined a comprehensive range of measures across Europe, and evaluated their contribution to and potential for travel reduction (DANTE Consortium, 1999).

– and correspondingly where the majority of innovations and the application of travel reduction strategies have taken place so far (Figure 1.6) – some cases from inter-urban corridors and other rural areas have also been included.

Of course, the principles on which existing practice is based may also be applied in rural areas and on national and indeed international scales – as in the case of substitution of travel by telecommunications. The evidence we cite is based primarily on travel in terms of the movement of people; the issue of freight transport lies outside the scope of the book.

Part I of this book describes the most important categories of policy measures to reduce travel, with evidence taken from a range of case studies – although individual measures do not always easily fall into one category or another, and successful implementation usually requires a mixture of them. First, the focus is on organisational and operational measures (Chapter 2), then on the means by which infrastructure can be better used to reduce car use (Chapter 3). Chapter 4 covers the range of financial measures available, which are complemented by the land-use measures (Chapter 5). The final chapter in Part I explores the role that technology can have in reducing travel. These chapter divisions very broadly reflect the different interests of the professions to the travel reduction issue and the very wide range of measures that are available. Many go beyond the sphere of interest of conventional transport policy.

Part II turns to the means by which policy can be converted into action, by interpreting the knowledge and experience of good practice (Part I). The combination of measures

Figure 1.5 Street in central London: congestion problems are most keenly felt in urban areas

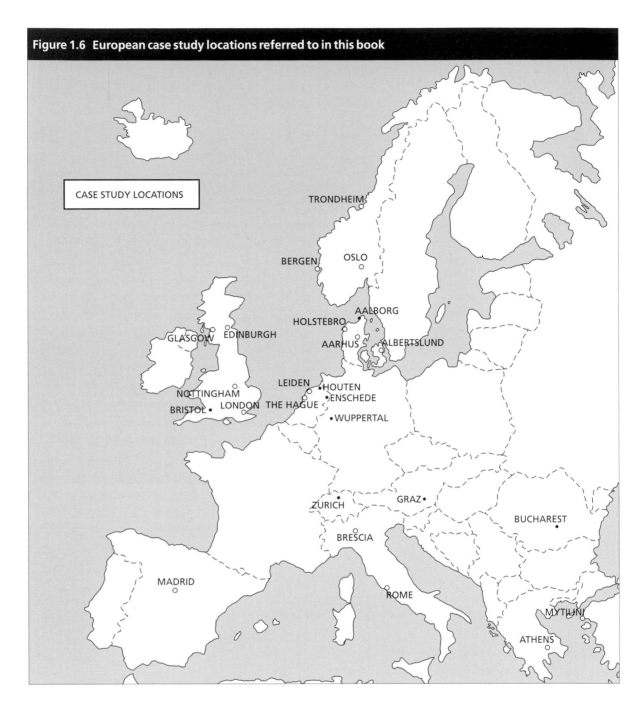

Figure 1.6 European case study locations referred to in this book

CASE STUDY LOCATIONS

and how these may realise success is central to the second part of the book.

Individually, the measures discussed in Part I are not sufficient to be effective. To achieve a real reduction in travel, it is essential to combine several of them as a package of mutually supporting actions which achieve the overall strategy for the city (Chapter 7). In Chapter 8 the underlying mechanisms of switching and substitution are explored. Crucial here, and in assessing the scale of success (Chapter 9), are the identification and measurement of travel reduction. This is important, as evaluation of travel reduction is not a straightforward task: it will be seen that it is easier to detect travel than to detect 'non-travel' or to prove that travel reduction has taken place.

Other complexities arise from the fact that the effects of measures may not match their intended outcomes. In some cases there may be a clear demonstration that travel has not been reduced, or that it has even increased. In others, however, the relative desirability of the outcomes may not be so clear. For example, a measure may be aimed primarily at objectives other than travel reduction, and may thus be successful in its own terms, although it does not reduce travel.

One of the perceived limitations of all schemes is that even though they may achieve substantial levels of traffic reduction in one location, this success would not translate elsewhere. This issue of transferability is central to Chapter 10. Two important chapters then examine the barriers to implementation and the difficulties in realising the travel reduction outcomes. An attempt is made to pinpoint the very real issues of translating good intention into practice, and then obtaining the anticipated behavioural response from people and companies. It is here that the transport and environmental arguments, which are often strong and accepted (our first two necessary conditions), meet with the required political commitment and public support (the third necessary condition). Any good practice in travel reduction must address all three conditions. The concluding chapter provides an interpretation of the preceding chapters and summarises the main messages emerging from them on the potential for achieving real and significant levels of travel reduction.

Part I: Policy Measures

Reducing Travel Through Organisational and Operational Measures

2.1 Introduction

The measures in this group are all relatively easy to introduce and many have a long history of success. They require better use of the available forms of transport through increased occupancy levels and through improved use of the available network, hence avoiding the need for the substantial capital investment in infrastructure or rolling stock which typically accompanies conventional transport supply solutions. Additionally, in contrast to many traditional large-scale transport schemes which require city or national government initiative, activation of these measures is possible through personal action, or at the scale of workplaces or local neighbourhoods.

An essential part of travel reduction is to place the responsibility for action on the residents, employers and others (e.g., schools, retailers and hospitals). These agents all contribute to the problems of city congestion and they should be actively involved in seeking solutions. A key requirement of policy is therefore not simply to provide transport alternatives, but to engender in the public the motivation to change their travel behaviour in the first place.

Organisational and operational measures are fundamentally concerned with changing behaviour and encouraging more flexible practices to make the best use of existing resources. Flexibility in shopping and work is already part of everyday life, with shops being open for 24 hours a day and many people working flexitime or shifts. Technology (Chapter 6) also offers huge potential benefits for trip substitution and new patterns of activity. However, that flexibility is often used as a means to increase car dependence rather than to reduce it. Individuals will naturally take advantage of the longer opening hours or flexitime at work to reorganise their own activities so that the use of the car is increased. This dilemma is often at the heart of many travel reduction strategies which are formulated with good intentions, but have the net result of increasing travel rather than decreasing it. Flexibility may also make it harder for individuals to participate in a car-pooling or car-sharing scheme.

More positive examples of flexibility include the development of demand-responsive transport which deviates from fixed routes, and transport optimisation where real-time information can be used to give priority routing to particular (high-occupancy) forms of transport. Companies do seem to be prepared to participate in both the organisation of innovative schemes and their financing, often through commuted payments. Even here, however, there is often strong opposition from city centre businesses to the possibility of paying for a scheme which involves having no parking spaces at the destination point, even though the payments are then used to enhance access more generally to the city centre.

At the heart of the discussion is the necessity to move away from the objective of maximising individual benefits, towards a wider notion of community good. Commuted payments are a good example, as the payments are used to the benefit of the community as a whole through financing the travel alternative, such as the Park and Ride scheme in Bristol. The companies paying for this do not profit directly in proportion to the payments made, but Bristol as a whole benefits, as fewer cars come into the city centre and the environmental quality improves. Similarly, car pooling, car sharing and the use of demand-responsive services are all suboptimal if the individual's benefits are to be maximised. If the situation is viewed on a citywide basis, then the balance shifts with the individual's loss being more than outweighed by the community gain. The importance of media campaigns and the raising of awareness of the costs must therefore be emphasised. It is only when large numbers of stakeholders (including individuals) realise the scale and nature of the problem, and then make a strong commitment to the collective benefits, that change will take place.

In the following discussion, each of the measures under the organisational and operational headings is introduced with a short description, supplemented by comments on complementary measures and barriers. Examples of implementation are given, together with information on the difficulties and lessons learned from the case studies. In many cases, there is no single 'best' way to introduce a measure (or a combination of measures), and much of the most useful information has come from practical experience.

2.2 Car pooling

Car pooling occurs when two or more people share one car ride for several trips (usually commuting), where previously each individual had made their own car trip. This substitution by linking several trips into a single one reduces the overall number of vehicle kilometres. Car pooling can be arranged informally between colleagues, although more formal schemes are operated at a regional level through city and company travel initiatives, which try to match supply and demand in any given area. A car-pooling package may include dedicated car-pooling parking spaces at employment locations, as well as financial incentives such as reduced parking charges. Car pooling is different from car sharing (Section 2.3), where individuals share ownership or access to a car to make their own individual journeys.

Either switching or substitution can take place by implementing this measure. To encourage car pooling and ensure that this travel reduction is not negated by the effects of freed-up capacity encouraging new generation, the presence of high-occupancy vehicle (HOV) priority and roadspace gives car drivers an incentive to share their trips, at the same time reducing the overall roadspace occupied.

One of the main challenges facing car-pooling schemes is the lack of public acceptability because of the restrictions that individuals perceive to be imposed on their personal freedom. Both the driver and the passenger(s) lose flexibility in the route that is taken, in any additional destinations (e.g., for shopping) that may be incorporated into the trip and in the timing of the journey. A study in Rome suggests that media campaigns highlighting the environmental benefits of car pooling, together with an organised body which matches potential poolers according to their professional, social and even musical interests (car radio), can encourage individuals to participate in such schemes.

The Netherlands

As part of the Second Transport Structure Plan – the national strategic transport plan and policy – the Dutch Government is seeking to encourage car pooling. Car pooling is encouraged in several ways:

- cuts in the tax rate for car pooling;
- media campaigns;
- building car-pool car parks;
- founding car-pool registers (databases to register who is interested in car pooling, to assist in matching supply and demand).

In the Netherlands, on an average day 2.7 million cars are used for commuting purposes. Almost 320,000 of these (approximately 12%) are used for car pooling with an average occupancy of 2.4 people, giving a total of 770,000 commuting by car pool.

Car pooling does not necessarily reduce the number of cars used in commuting in those cases (45%) where car-pool passengers do not already own a car. However, those passengers would have had to make their journey by some other mode – or considered buying a car – if car pooling were not available. In the other cases, where more than one car owner shares a single car, overall travel in terms of vehicle kilometres can certainly be reduced (Kropman and Neeskens, 1997; Molnar, 1997).

2.3 Car sharing

Car sharing is one of the few measures which reduces travel by influencing car ownership. It gives individuals access to a car without ownership, through the mechanism of collective provision, whereby individuals can use a car from a pool. It is believed that a lack of ownership will lead to the more selective use of the car by combining car trips and using other means of transport. Therefore car-sharing schemes encourage substitution by linking trips and mode switching to achieve travel reduction.

In principle there are two methods of car sharing: one is to share a car informally with neighbours, friends or relatives; the more formal alternative is to have joint access to a fleet of cars owned by a car-sharing organisation and supported by city or company travel policies at a regional level. There are subscription- or card/voucher-based schemes, some of which have additional services such as pick-up and delivery, or a discount on taxis and public transport. Another type of scheme provides car sharing as an integral part of a car-free residential development. Business car sharing also exists, in the form of shared company cars that can be used by several employees.

Car sharing is different from car renting because in the case of car sharing there is a commitment (the subscription or voucher) to use the car several times during a certain period, so one has to be a 'member' of a car-sharing scheme in order to be eligible to use one of the cars. Car renting has no such restrictions (but incurs higher financial costs).

Evidence from the Dutch case studies suggests that car sharing can lead to travel reduction. Car sharing is suitable for individuals or households with a low level of travel (less than approximately 10,000 km a year), and a high frequency of car use for short trips. Car sharing is a particularly good alternative to car ownership in urban areas, because other modes of transport are readily available for short trips. Owning a car in some urban situations can be an inefficient use of financial resources, because the purchase and running costs are relatively high. Car sharing is not suitable for commuter travel, for which there is a peak demand for cars followed by long periods of inactivity. It is also unsuitable for implementation in areas where there is a lack of space to park the car-pool fleet, which is often the case in the higher-density areas where car pooling is most effective.

Leiden and Culemborg, the Netherlands

Car sharing is growing in popularity in the Netherlands, where around 60,000 people now participate in private car-sharing schemes. It is interesting to note that car pooling has always been regarded as a business in the Netherlands (the implementors are generally car dealers or renters), whereas in Germany and Switzerland the measure has an ideological background of environmental transport.

Several car-sharing schemes in Leiden and Culemborg have been analysed for their impact on travel reduction (AGV, 1996). Participants in both schemes tend to be those who already used public transport frequently. The decision to participate in the scheme might be made when considering the purchase or replacement of a car.

Scheme participants included those who formerly owned a car – 31% in Leiden, 22% in Culemborg – and those who did not previously have a car – 64% in Leiden, 61% in Culemborg (Figure 2.1). On average there has been a decrease in car use per person annually by 500 and 2,200 km in Leiden and Culemborg, respectively, with former car owners recording the biggest decrease.

City Car Club, Edinburgh, UK

In Spring 1999, 30 Edinburgh residents joined the UK's first pay-as-you-drive car-sharing scheme. The scheme was started in the high-density middle-class area of

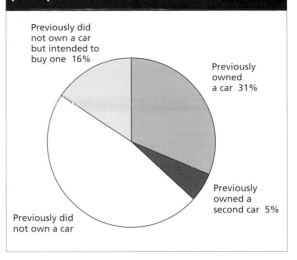

Figure 2.1 Characteristics of car-sharing scheme participants in Leiden, the Netherlands

Previously did not own a car but intended to buy one 16%

Previously owned a car 31%

Previously owned a second car 5%

Previously did not own a car

Marchmont, some 2 km from the city centre. The Club, run by the car rental firm Budget, is expected to be extended citywide over the coming years. Budget estimates that each car club vehicle replaces between four and six private cars (Birch, 1999). The scheme is targeted at relatively infrequent drivers who travel no more than 12,800 km per annum. Such drivers can save themselves up to £1,500 (2,250 euros) a year by joining the club. Drivers have to pay £99 (150 euros) in membership dues annually, they have to pay for petrol on their journeys and they are charged £5 for the first hour and £2.50 for every subsequent hour for which they use the Club's cars. This pricing structure compares favourably with many existing schemes in continental Europe.

The real attraction of the Edinburgh scheme, however, is its convenience: it is run with a sophisticated software package that allows easy booking over the phone, and that keeps track of where the vehicles are and who is supposed to have access to them. The Club's cars are therefore available 24 hours a day and at minimum notice. Membership of the Club can provide almost the same level of convenience as outright car ownership. The members only have to be willing to walk to the dedicated car parking spaces of the Club, which are located throughout the Marchmont area.

Carriba – car sharing in Wuppertal, Germany

The local power company (owned by the city council) in Wuppertal, Germany, runs its own very successful car-sharing scheme. This scheme not only targets individual car owners but also provides local companies with cheap mobility services. For example, the major central shopping centre (Rathaus Galerie) is one of the corporate members of the scheme. Carriba, like the Edinburgh car-sharing scheme, is operated through a call centre, making cars (none of which is older than one year) available 24 hours a day. Carriba had 270 members at the end of 1998 and operated more than 20 cars at 18 designated parking places. Carriba has a policy of opening a new parking place in every area that has at least five customers. It thus ensures that customers are never more than a short walk away from their nearest Carriba parking bay.

Carriba so far has mainly been a success in middle-class areas of Wuppertal. Carriba cars therefore often replace second cars rather than first cars. Nonetheless, the evidence for Carriba directly contributing to travel reduction is conclusive. Members who were interviewed by the operating company recorded a reduction in mileage of between 30 and 50%. Some individual members even managed to cut their monthly mileage by two-thirds, from 1,500 to 500 km (WSW, 1998)!

2.4 Commuted payments

Developers of new city centre sites can be required to make contributions towards new Park and Ride provision in lieu of on-site parking spaces. Commuted payment schemes are generally aimed at commuting trips, encouraging car-based workers to mode-switch, but they can also be targeted at non-commuters through application to a range of developments, including retail and leisure. This measure can be implemented by local authorities at the regional level, as strategic decisions can be taken on the location of parking restrictions and Park and Ride provision.

There has been a positive reaction to this measure, as the number of commuted payment agreements in the example of Bristol indicates. It is a valuable method of controlling private non-residential parking in countries where legal restrictions constrain the use of more radical measures to reduce existing parking provision and overcome resource barriers. Experience from Bristol suggests that commuted payment schemes can successfully restrict new private non-residential parking in urban centres. Further analysis is required, however, to assess the true impact of this measure on mode switching.

When measures restricting car use are being implemented, it is essential that complementary policies are in place to ensure adequate alternative transport provision. It can be valuable to have a Park and Ride site already in operation when implementing commuted payments, as this provides an immediate alternative to car-based

commuting and reassures developers of local authority commitment to Park and Ride provision. The case study highlights the importance of payments becoming due on completion of development, allowing for some flexibility and consultation with local businesses, and taking care not to limit the practical applications of funds collected.

Bristol, UK

In Bristol, the City Council's commuted payment scheme requires developers of new city centre offices to make contributions towards additional Park and Ride provision in lieu of on-site parking spaces. The measure aims to encourage people working in the centre of Bristol to travel on the Park and Ride buses instead of driving to work, and provides a good example of making a car restraint measure viable by providing attractive alternatives to the car. The policy originally related to all city centre development, but was later restricted to office-based sites because of opposition from developers.

Agreements have been signed, or payments have been agreed, with 22 city centre office developments. On the basis of the monetary value of these agreements, it can be estimated that some 780 parking spaces will be provided by Park and Ride rather than in the city centre (Figure 2.2). However, it is difficult to quantify exactly the car journeys into the centre that have been, or will be, saved through the scheme.

Careful planning is required when setting up the legal agreements, to avoid future difficulties in using the funds collected. In Bristol, payments are specifically for the 'development of new Park and Ride provision', and cannot be used to enhance existing services and sites. However, insufficient payments have been collected to date to enable the local authority to build a new site. It is stated in recent legal agreements that the payments can be returned to the developers if not used within three years.

Bristol City Council is currently planning to make payments due on completion of development, rather than on occupation. Many sums are still outstanding where sites have not been occupied, and it is often difficult to establish when occupation takes place.

Restriction of parking can be a controversial issue, and some consultation with local businesses and developers may be necessary. The Bristol commuted payment scheme allows some room for flexibility, and on certain occasions charges have been waived or reduced in lieu of payments for other requirements such as improved lighting at the site (Mathers, 1999).

2.5 Company work hours policy

Organisations can adjust the daily time period within which business takes place, in order to diffuse trips throughout the day and avoid peak-hour congestion. Company work hours policies are not designed to reduce the overall rates of trips, but to encourage time switching to avoid peak-hour periods, and hence to reduce the amount of travel (vehicle hours) in congested conditions. Such policies may also obviate the need for further investment in transport capacity, which might generate additional trips through capacity release. These flexible business hours can be complemented by teleactivities and teleworking measures (Chapter 6) that can build further flexibility into the travel needs of employees and customers of the organisation.

Flexible working hours have already been adopted in many workplaces, where there is evidence that switching or substitution has taken place, and are most effective when implemented and coordinated across a range of organisations. Although these changes alone may not lead to any improvement, diffusion of trips throughout the day reduces the need to build more capacity into the system to accommodate excessive peak demand.

Rome, Italy

In 1995, the Council of Rome implemented a work hours policy which introduced differentiated opening times of municipal offices in pilot areas with the aim of creating a more flexible working day for employees and service users. This measure encouraged trips to be made outside the congested peak period, with more efficient use of the public transport system. Telecommunications and computing infrastructure has also been provided to encourage teleworking and the decentralised dissemination of information and services to residents (using smart cards and interactive kiosks). Time switching occurred, with groups of people accessing municipal facilities at different times at their own convenience. From a user analysis, it was established that retired people preferred an early morning extension to opening hours, whereas those in employment preferred facilities to be open at lunchtime. A significant minority of residents was also keen to visit council offices in the evening through an extension of opening hours (Commune di Roma, 1997; Commune di Roma and CISPEL, 1997).

2.6 Demand-responsive transport

In traditional public transport, relatively large vehicles typically follow fixed routes and schedules. Demand-responsive transport makes use of information technologies to adjust routes and schedules according to individual requests from passengers who can call in advance and reserve places on these routes. This often allows demand-responsive transport to be provided by smaller vehicles, and may result in reduced aggregate route distances being travelled.

The aim of demand-responsive transport solutions is to improve the attractiveness of public transport while improving the efficiency and capacity utilisation, and thus to encourage mode switching. Typically, demand-responsive transport is introduced on routes with a low patronage, in off-peak hours when capacity utilisation would have been poor, or when the service would otherwise have been less frequent.

There has been a positive reaction to demand-responsive transport, and it is a useful tool for improving the attractiveness of public transport and so increasing patronage. This is done by improving the service frequency, schedule, network and location of stops, which are targeted to the individual user's needs and are more flexible than a traditional public transport system. The result is often a more efficient utilisation of capacity, and thus reduced energy consumption. Thus, demand-responsive transport can reduce the total travel distance and increase service and quality. However, when it represents an improvement in public transport service provision, it may also provide an incentive to travel more.

Figure 2.2 Brislington Park and Ride car park, Bristol, where developers have paid for some 780 parking spaces in lieu of providing on-site parking in the city centre

Holstebro, Denmark

In 1993, the Municipality of Holstebro took over the operation of local public bus services. As part of a series of structural changes in the bus network it was decided to implement a bus-taxi system on selected routes. The bus-taxi can be booked by telephone, at least 30 minutes in advance, for pick-up at the home address in nine different zones of the city. On the return trip from the city centre the bus-taxi has regular scheduled departure times for the nine different zones. It is operated in the evenings when occupancy on the scheduled service is low. This operation costs approximately 62,000 euros/year, but the savings in ordinary bus operation in the period have been 40,000 euros/year, so the net annual cost of the service is 22,000 euros/year. The energy consumption of the bus-taxi is 40% lower than that on the routes that were replaced by the service, although greater distances are driven. The number of passengers per weekday night has increased by 150% since the introduction of the service (DANTE consortium, 1997: Appendix 12, pp. 29–32)

2.7 Media campaigns

Media campaigns disseminate information to individuals to encourage them to change their travel behaviour, often by encouraging mode switching. Thus attempts are made to inform and influence people by emphasising the negative impacts of car travel (e.g. environmental effects) and the benefits of other forms of travel (e.g., the time benefits of using public transport). The information is packaged so as to be consumer-friendly, and is often targeted at a particular group of people, using media such as television, radio, newspapers and even roadshow-style exhibitions. Neighbourhood groups may also become involved, to encourage local participation.

Typically, these campaigns take place for a specific period of time and often in conjunction with other transport initiatives. For instance, the provision of a new public transport route may be accompanied by a media campaign focusing on the households along the route to encourage them to switch transport modes. Financial incentives, such as fare reductions, may even be offered in conjunction with the campaign.

As the case studies below suggest, media campaigns can facilitate travel reduction by helping to overcome the social and cultural barriers affecting other measures. They work particularly well when certain segments of the car-using population are targeted, e.g., in a particular neighbourhood or workplace. Media campaigns are a useful tool when run in conjunction with other measures, such as publicising improvements to non-car transport networks. They can also be used to foster closer links with external organisations, in order to influence travel behaviour more effectively in the future. However, neither the long-term nor the wider travel impacts have been monitored, so it is not known what the overall contribution of such measures to long-term travel reduction might be.

Enschede, Netherlands

This project aimed to reduce car use through raising public awareness, and was linked to a nationwide campaign whose slogan was 'The car can manage a day without you'. It occurred after several years' investment in the cycle network and traffic reduction schemes in the city centre, with the aim of encouraging people to use more sustainable forms of transport than their cars. One experiment was carried out in a particular neighbourhood in Enschede, and a control area in the nearby town of Hengelo in 1992–1993.

The rationale was based on the idea of trying firstly to create awareness, secondly to change attitude and thirdly to change behaviour. This translated into a comprehensive package of information and incentives to reach target users which included:

- press releases;
- kick-off meetings in neighbourhoods;
- information stands at local events;
- information packages for participants (a leaflet about the negative effects of car use, information about alternatives to the car, kilometre reduction cards, booklets with references to the nationwide campaign to reduce car use, information about local organisations who deal with traffic and transport);
- cooperation with community associations;
- publication of good examples of desirable travel behaviour;
- rewards for good behaviour (reduced fares for travel by public transport, discounts at shops when travelling by bicycle);
- feedback to participants.

The effects of the experiment were assessed by means of travel diaries and questionnaires, which addressed travel behaviour and the residents' attitudes. For control purposes, an identical survey was conducted in another neighbourhood (in Hengelo) which had not been targeted by the campaign. Of the respondents in the neighbourhoods targeted by the campaign, 20% stated that they used the car less often after the campaign than before. In the control neighbourhood, by contrast, the corresponding proportion was 11%. In the experimental neighbourhoods, 12% of respondents stated that they had switched from car to another mode of transport (generally the bicycle), whereas in the control neighbourhood this was 7%. It was found that mode switching occurred mainly for trips up to 5 km. This evidence suggests that raising awareness in itself can make a difference to travel behaviour and contribute to reduction in car travel, although in this case the overall travel impact of the scheme, measured across the city, was not monitored (Naber, 1994; DANTE Consortium, 1997: Appendix 12).

Bristol, UK

As part of the annual 'Don't Choke Bristol' campaign, the city coordinated a 'Bike to Work Day'. This was part of a series of events involving a variety of local organisations, from schools to private companies. 'Don't Choke Bristol' is part of a national 'Don't Choke Britain' campaign, coordinated by the new Local Governmental Association, and acting as an umbrella under which local authorities and organisations can run their own campaigns. The aim of 'Bike to Work Day' (Figure 2.3) was to provide a promotional and practical focus for the council to encourage people to replace car trips by bicycle for their journeys to and from work.

In 1997 the campaign was structured in the following way. Firstly, companies who had participated in 1996 were contacted by telephone to see if they wished to do so again (all agreed). Telephone calls then targeted other employers in Bristol, starting with the largest and working down the scale as far as resources permitted. A total of 77 companies agreed to participate, more than a threefold increase on the previous year, when only mailshots had been sent out. Interested companies were sent an information pack containing a cycling leaflet, promotional poster and re-order form. Five days after the event, a follow-up questionnaire was sent to all participants to monitor the impact and establish longer-term links. Of the 25 who responded, 21 requested further information about becoming a cycle-friendly employer.

Monitoring has shown a significant increase in the number of cyclists recorded around the city on 'Bike to Work Day', albeit from a small base (Bristol City Council, 1996a). In 1996, 190 cyclists were recorded at one monitoring point, compared with 91 on a typical non-campaign day (a 109% increase). Of the companies participating in the 1997 campaign, eight reported an increase in cyclists on the

Figure 2.3 Media campaigns can highlight the benefits to be gained by the individual, quite apart from the wider environmental gains

day, with around the same number reporting no increase. The campaign was particularly effective when companies themselves encouraged their employees to cycle to work.

However, the decline (if any) in car use was not monitored, so it is difficult to judge the overall travel impact of this initiative. It is also difficult to assess whether the additional cyclists continued to cycle to work after the campaign. Although the long-term impacts have not been monitored, valuable links have been established with several companies, many of which have requested further information on cycling issues. The council recognised that if additional time and resources were available, the impact could be increased by providing continuous practical support and advice to employers, with more events held throughout the year and a greater emphasis on promoting commuter plans.

2.8 Peak congestion avoidance

Peak congestion avoidance measures can reduce the amount of time spent on travel, by encouraging time switching to avoid peak-hour periods. They may also negate the need for further investment in transport capacity, which may otherwise generate additional trips through capacity release. Peak congestion avoidance can be achieved in a variety of ways, and by a variety of implementors. For example, central or local government may achieve peak spreading by implementing a form of time-based road pricing – charging for road use in peak periods and thus encouraging non-essential road users to travel during off-peak periods. Work, study or operating hours can also be altered directly, for example, by introducing flexitime for employees within an organisation, staggering university or school hours and the starting and finishing times of large organisations within a particular area, or staggering freight and passenger deliveries to avoid peak periods.

Switching or substitution can take place through the implementation of this measure, as at least one of the case studies demonstrates. These examples illustrate the potential for simple administrative measures to achieve peak spreading and improve traffic flows, provided they can be incorporated into people's activity schedules or that individuals can adapt to those schedules. People on the 'front line', such as business employers or suppliers of transport services, can have a significant impact on the adoption of peak congestion avoidance measures. In some cases, the spreading of activities to avoid peak periods can affect the potential of other complementary measures targeting the workplace. For example, the introduction of employees' flexitime within an organisation can present a barrier to the introduction of a coordinated lift-sharing scheme.

Athens, Greece

The Ministry of Environment and Public Works introduced a staggered work hours scheme for the city of Athens in 1994, with the aim of reducing peak period congestion and improving environmental conditions (DANTE Consortium, 1997: Appendix 12, pp. 301–302). In 1995, a special ministerial decree was passed to fix staggered opening hours for all land uses during the summer period (June–September). Employer and labour unions were consulted regarding the acceptability of the scheme, and opening hours were set (Table 2.1).

In autumn 1997, the strategy was applied for an entire year, again setting opening hours according to discussions between the Ministry, employers' unions and specific industry unions, and basing the decision on previous experience of application during the summer months.

The Ministry is assessing the impact of the scheme in Athens, and is planning to refine the measure for transfer to other large Greek cities, possibly Thessaloniki and Patra. In Athens, peak spreading measures work in

Table 2.1 Opening times for Athens businesses and offices

	Opening time
Public corporations	07.00
Public and local authorities	07.30
Retail trade (supermarkets, bakeries, building materials)	07.30
Banks and insurance companies	08.15
All other retail shops	09.15

conjunction with a variety of other environmental schemes, for example, the restriction of access by private cars to the central area of Athens.

Lesvos, Greece

The port of Mytilini is the main gateway to the Greek island of Lesvos for passengers, cars and freight delivery vehicles, which unload in the main street of the city – a two-way street with only one lane in each direction. As car use and the capacity of the ships arriving at the port have all grown substantially, traffic congestion has also increased.

Ship arrivals give rise to a large number of vehicles unloading in a short time, augmented by the traffic created by people travelling to the port to pick up passengers. Lack of resources and space limited the options for introducing new infrastructure, so the port authority collaborated with the shipping company NEL Lines (Figure 2.4) to coordinate ship schedules, avoiding peak congestion periods. This has been introduced over a five-year period and, although some ships arrive during peak hours, the majority reach port at off-peak times. Peak traffic occurs between midday and 15.00, when shops and services close. Arrival times for the peak season (August) show that the majority of ship unloadings are now concentrated in the early morning hours until around 09.00, or after 16.00 – thus avoiding the peak period congestion.

The measure has been well received for a number of reasons. Local merchants were already lobbying to be supplied early in the day with produce, and travelling on night-time ferries is attractive to travellers, who can then sleep during the trip. In addition, worsening traffic conditions during the afternoon were causing severe problems in unloading ships, so the ship operators welcomed a measure that would avoid this problem period. Benefits to the service providers and local traders were decisive in adopting the strategy, but it has also shifted traffic away from the peak, improving traffic conditions (DANTE Consortium, 1997: Appendix 12, pp. 297–300).

2.9 Transport optimisation

The efficiency of passenger transport operations can be increased without changing the purpose of the journey. The same number of passengers can be delivered to the same destinations, but with a reduced number of vehicle kilometres travelled, because the vehicle's trip is modified to take account of a more efficient route or scheduling arrangement. Mode switching may also occur as a result of improvements to the transport service. Various tools are used to achieve this: typically, a transport optimisation measure comprises the use of route-planning software, the use of planning and assignment practices and the hiring of planning staff or transport coordinators.

This measure has had a positive reaction in terms of improving the utilisation of public transport services. Because operators have a strong financial incentive to optimise the use of their fleets – in the example below transport costs were cut by 30% – they are likely to receive the measure favourably and implement it.

However, changing entrenched schedules and route plans may meet some public opposition, particularly from passengers who have to change their travel routines. Such

Figure 2.4 NEL Line ferries at Mytilini: careful scheduling of shipping services can minimise congestion of road traffic in port towns

schemes may also take time to implement fully, since there is likely to be a period of adjustment and readjustment during which time the changes will be revised in the light of experience.

Albertslund, Denmark

The transport optimisation measure was implemented by the municipality in Albertslund in 1993. The aim of the measure was to provide better municipal transport services through increased coordination, without increasing the number of vehicles. A transport coordinator was employed, and route planning and other computer tools were used. The measure was run on a trial basis from 1993, before becoming permanent in 1995. As a result, the Municipality managed to improve the service and reduce the number of vehicles. There was also a positive environmental impact. The CO_2 emissions per passenger kilometre were reduced from 70 g in 1994 to 60 g in 1995. Furthermore, the measure resulted in annual net financial savings to the municipality of 9,000 euros. There were some initial difficulties, however, because the measure resulted in changed routines and organisational structures (Rambøll *et al.*, 1997).

2.10 Conclusion

In many European cities, these organisational and operational measures have already been introduced, not necessarily with the aim to reduce travel. More often, the objective has been to encourage mode switching to public transport and to some extent to encourage a more rational use of the car, particularly for the journey to and from work. So the main aim has been to make more efficient use of the available road network, in particular to use any spare capacity on the bus system. In Table 2.2 the eight different measures are summarised, together with their travel reduction aim, and lessons and limitations from the case studies. On their own these measures are unlikely to have a major impact, but if they are implemented on a citywide scale, in conjunction with the other groups of measures, then their impact on mode switching may become significant. The impacts measured are detailed in the sections on the case studies and are also summarised in Chapter 9.

The other main conclusion from this group of measures is that they often require the active cooperation and participation of different stakeholders. The empirical evidence suggests that this support is often not fulsome, as many interest groups try (successfully) to weaken the scale of the introduction of the measure. This limitation

Table 2.2 Summary of organisational and operational measures

Measure	Travel reduction	Lessons and limitations
Car pooling	Mode switching Substitution	Combine with HOV priority Limitations of personal freedom and privacy
Car sharing	Linking trips Mode switching	Best where annual mileage is low and for high-frequency short trips. Not so suitable for commuting
Commuted payments	Mode switching	Can be used in city centres, particularly for new private non-residential parking Must be clear that the payments are used to promote public transport Timing of payment and implementation is important
Company work hours policy	Time switching Flexibility and trip substitution	Not explicitly designed to reduce travel Reduces need to build more capacity and facilitates complementary measures being taken
Demand-responsive transport	Time flexibility Mode switching	Improves the attractiveness of public transport Best on routes with low levels of patronage Attractive to particular users (e.g., the elderly)
Media campaigns	Direct impact unclear: may influence any form of switching or substitution	Overcome some of the social and cultural barriers Need to be targeted at particular users or activity (e.g., workers, shoppers) Often complementary to other measures
Peak congestion avoidance	Time switching Mode switching	Needs to be coordinated at the city level Support required from major employers and institutions May work against other measures such as car pooling and car sharing
Transport optimisation	Trip modification Mode switching	Mainly directed at optimising public transport Real-time routing Some resentment from existing users if routes are changed

must be overcome, as it is often through a citywide scheme that the full benefits will be realised. As with many travel reduction measures, partial implementation is likely to produce poor and often unmeasurable results, whereas full implementation has a measurable impact. In addition, high-quality demonstration projects can be used as exemplars of good practice so that more widespread implementation can take place.

Infrastructure Interventions to Reduce Travel

3.1 Introduction

Infrastructure intervention measures are not directed at investment in new road infrastructures in our cities – rather the reverse. One of the main opportunities that arise in creating high-quality liveable cities is to reassess what roadspace should be made available to different users. Traditionally, most road systems have been set up as a hierarchy, and only motorised modes of transport (subject to certain qualifications) can have access to motorway-standard infrastructure, the top member; and as one comes further down the hierarchy, the range of users increases. In urban areas, most of the space is still allocated to the car, either for movement or for parking. But separate space (footways) is available for pedestrians, and this increases in proportion nearer the city centre and in other locations where pedestrian flows are high. Cyclists, buses and delivery vehicles often have to share space with the car. This sharing often leads to delay, and the potential for accidents (particularly for cyclists) is increased.

This group of measures reassesses the priorities for roadspace allocation to different users. It is argued that to achieve a reduction in travel by car, it is necessary to reduce the amount of roadspace available to the car, particularly where other modes are to be encouraged (e.g., in city centres and residential areas). Dedicated routes for cyclists, pedestrians and public transport are necessary, to give these modes a 'fair crack of the whip', if substantial mode switching is to take place. This can overcome the drawbacks of the traditional situation where the more efficient movers of people (public transport) and non-polluting modes (pedestrians and cyclists) either have to take their place in queues of traffic along with everyone else, or are left standing on the pavement. This situation disadvantages them even further.

The argument for reallocation of priority (of time and space) is successfully illustrated by the high levels of tram use in many European cities, not just in the centre, but along the main corridors, and in residential, commercial and subcentres at the periphery. When space is allocated to particular modes (shared as necessary), it is possible to have several networks superimposed on the existing road system. At present, with areas allocated to pedestrians and non-pedestrians, all vehicular users compete for the scarce amount of space available. Allocation to priority users allows this situation to change and even offers the opportunity to reduce the amount of space available to the car. The question here is whether car traffic degeneration takes place.

3.2 Bicycle priority and roadspace

Physical infrastructure provision and traffic management schemes along bicycle routes can be designed so as to minimise journey times, improve the efficiency and enhance the safety of individuals using this mode. The intention is to make cycling more attractive, to encourage mode switching. Components of this measure include:

- junction priorities and facilities (e.g., advanced stop lines, staggered stop lines, bicycle bypasses, signal priority);
- allocation/segregation of roadspace to provide cycle lanes (e.g., widening of nearside lanes, introduction of bicycle lanes, bus/bicycle lanes, segregated bicycle tracks) (Figure 3.1);
- traffic management solutions such as contraflow bicycle lanes;

Figure 3.1 Cycle lanes can run either on a dedicated alignment or along an existing carriageway

- off-road bicycle routes;
- bicycle networks, combining all or some of the above.

The components chosen will depend on circumstances. For example, segregation of cyclists from motor vehicles may not be necessary on low-flow roads. In some cases it may be possible to modify existing infrastructure to provide bicycle priority or roadspace. Citywide network provision is not always possible, and measures can be implemented steadily on a corridor basis. Since the bicycle is most suitable for short journeys of under 5 km, other important complementary measures include land-use measures which reduce travel distances between activities, such as urban concentration and the design of new developments (see Chapter 5).

The case studies suggest that the provision of citywide bicycle priorities and roadspace can facilitate switching or substitution, although it is difficult to pinpoint the impacts of individual measures. Both in Bristol and Enschede, recent citywide increases in bicycle flows have been achieved. Although the profile of cycling is now rising, in many countries low usage, because of a lack of a cycling tradition, can make it difficult to justify a large-scale programme for improvements to bicycle access. As a result, many bicycle networks are being introduced on a step-by-step basis. When considering cycling provision, it is important not to restrict the focus to bicycle lanes, as all aspects of road design and management have the ability to affect the actual and perceived safety of cyclists.

Enschede, the Netherlands

Since 1978, the Municipality of Enschede has been extending and improving the city bicycle network. The area Structuurplan states that all main roads should be provided with on-road bicycle 'strips' or segregated bicycle lanes; by 1992, 152 km of cycle network existed within the built-up area.

From 1984, a series of new bicycle facilities were introduced to promote bicycle safety and travel time. These included advanced stop lanes at traffic lights to clarify priority in favour of bicycles (cars have to wait behind the cyclists); bicycle paths behind bus stop bays to allow bicycles to pass stopping buses easily, and keep buses from cutting off cyclists on their way to or from the stop; small additional bicycle paths at intersections by which cyclists turning right can bypass the traffic lights; a new design of roundabout with a separate circumferential bicycle lane; intersections with green lights for cyclists in all directions (twice during a complete cycle); bicycle priority by detection loops in the pavement; guidance on

cycling provided for schoolchildren; and guarded bicycle parking (funded in part from parking charges).

Since the introduction of the measures the modal share of cycling has increased, reversing earlier trends in the 1960s and 1970s. The modal share in Enschede is higher than the national average, and it is increasing for journeys of all distances (Table 3.1). The conclusion is that targeting particular modes can help maintain or improve modal shares through investment and improvement of facilities, and it can create favourable circumstances for bicycle use in general, citywide.

Table 3.1 Modal share of trips by bicycle by residents (%)

	All trips		Trips up to 5 km	
	1982–84	1995	1982–84	1995
Enschede	34.2	35.6	42.9	44.7
Dutch average	28.9	27.8	37.7	39.2

Source: DANTE Consortium (1997: Appendix 12)

Bristol, UK

Both on- and off-road cycle lanes have been implemented in Bristol, in conjunction with a variety of cycling priority and traffic management measures. For example, on one major radial route a section of inbound on-street cycle lane has been introduced, in conjunction with bicycle priorities. Traffic counts taken before and after implementation show an increase in both numbers and modal share of bicycles, and a small reduction in numbers and modal share of cars. Traffic count data from the later years suggest that implementation of individual stretches of bicycle lane should be followed up with further measures to maintain high levels of bicycle use. However, with such small numbers of vehicles being recorded, further analysis is required to establish the true impacts of individual bicycle priority/roadspace measures in Bristol. Only 5–10% of the total proposed bicycle network has been implemented in Bristol so far, so visible impacts are still small. However, although the extent of modal shift is not known, bicycle flows recorded at the Bristol Central Cordon have been increasing since 1987. A model has shown a target of 12% bicycle use to be realistic for Bristol.

National Cycle Network, UK

The long-distance National Cycle Network (NCN) being developed in the UK is considered to be a valuable asset and very important in catering for and encouraging bicycle use. The NCN is a partnership coordinated by the non-governmental organisation SUSTRANS and involving hundreds of local authorities and landowners in the UK. It will be a combination of traffic-free paths on disused railways, towpaths and tracks, and traffic-calmed and minor roads. Around 5,000 km are scheduled to be open in June 2000, and the aim is to complete approximately 10,500 km by 2005. It is intended that the network will reach into the centre of each urban area it passes, providing a major attraction for utility cycling in those areas. Few sections of the National Cycle Network have been open for a long period of time, and so few evaluation data are available. However, the highly tourist-based sea-to-sea route across the Pennines – the first section opened in 1995 – attracts around 15,000 users a year. The successful Bristol–Bath bicycle route forms part of the National Cycle Network, and runs on the former Midland Railway line.

3.3 High-occupancy vehicle priority and roadspace

High-occupancy vehicle (HOV) lanes and priorities can be introduced to encourage the linking of car trips through multiple-passenger journeys (e.g., by car pooling). This may involve mode switching, if individuals change from single-occupancy cars to multiple-occupancy buses for the journey. HOV lanes are physical roadspace measures in the form of dedicated lanes for high-occupancy vehicles, which can include both buses and cars with several passengers. The lanes may be separated from the main flow of traffic by a fence or barrier, or marked out in some way, e.g., with coloured road surfaces. Enforcement is generally an important and complex part of such a scheme, and may require police or video surveillance to identify abusers of the HOV roadspace. HOV measures can also take the form of junction or traffic-light priorities.

HOV priority and roadspace can increase vehicle occupancy through the presence of switching or substitution. However, it is important that incentives to travel more are not included in any such scheme. This problem is well illustrated by the construction of additional motorway lanes, as in the case of the HOV-bus facility in Madrid, which in turn has increased the overall capacity of the corridor and is therefore unlikely to achieve an overall reduction in travel.

Madrid, Spain

The Madrid HOV scheme involves the construction and operation of lanes for HOVs and buses along a major corridor in the city, i.e., on a section of motorway in the north-west of Madrid, extending from the urban village of Las Rozas (some 18 km from the urban core) to the urban district of Moncloa, and ending in a new interchange station.

The HOV-bus lane is physically separated from the remaining all-purpose lanes by concrete barriers. It comprises two different sections – two reversible lanes for buses and HOVs followed by a single lane for buses only. The existing motorway was widened to provide the additional lanes, thus increasing overall capacity on the corridor. The total length of the HOV provision is 12.3 km and the bus lane is 3.8 km long. The facility operates on a reversible-flow basis, inbound in the morning and outbound in the evening. Implementation was completed in 1995, with the total capital cost of infrastructure estimated at 57.7 million euros (1994).

The main goals of the Madrid HOV-bus lane are:

- to carry more people using fewer vehicles, thus increasing motorway capacity;
- to reduce congestion and provide improved services for bus and HOV users;
- to reduce travel times on the corridor, particularly for buses and HOV users;
- to achieve a reduction in vehicle numbers, so reducing overall energy consumption and emissions.

The Madrid scheme has been successful in encouraging people to use the HOV-bus lane. Numbers of HOV-lane users are increasing. Of all the people travelling on the corridor during the morning peak period, 64% were found to be travelling in the two HOV-bus lanes, with only 36% travelling in the three all-purpose vehicle lanes (November 1995). Of these HOV-bus-lane users, 45% were bus passengers. The HOV-bus facility carries one-third of all vehicles on the corridor and two-thirds of all passengers, suggesting that the scheme is having a positive influence on vehicle occupancy. The average occupancy of private cars increased from 1.36 in 1991 to 1.47 in March 1996, and the number of one-passenger vehicles fell during this period. However, it is unlikely that the scheme is reducing overall travel, as the capacity of the motorway has been increased by the addition of extra lanes (CAPTURE Consortium, 1998).

3.4 Park and Ride

Park and Ride schemes generally involve the provision of free car parking on the outskirts or suburbs of a town or city, and regular alternative-mode transport from that site into the urban centre. Mode switching is encouraged by persuading car-based travellers entering an urban area to park their cars and travel into the centre by public transport. This reduces vehicle kilometres by replacing individual car trips with a smaller number of high-occupancy public transport trips.

A regional Park and Ride strategy may be implemented gradually, resulting in a ring of sites serving an urban centre. Where this involves several local authorities, collaboration may be required. Some element of collaboration between the local authority and public transport providers may also be required, where these are not the same body. Public sector investment may be necessary to obtain land for parking facilities and set up the public transport provision, but during the initial period a Park and Ride site can often be built up to run as a commercial entity.

The evidence shows that Park and Ride schemes can reduce travel, by encouraging car-based travellers to park on the outskirts of a town or city and travel to the centre by bus or rail. The choice of scheme should depend on the context and problems being addressed. For example, in Zürich the Park and Ride schemes based around S-Bahn stations have proved much more successful than systems based on buses and trams, partly due to the faster speed of the S-Bahn. Care must be taken when choosing the site location, service provision and pricing structures to ensure success and avoid potential negative side effects, for example:

- non-acceptance, through low patronage and lack of switching from private cars due to access difficulties (e.g., the site is not located on a major route into the city; access routes become congested if the site is too close to the city centre) or relatively high Park and Ride costs;
- change without improvement, where switching from other public transport modes is due to relatively low Park and Ride costs;

Figure 3.2 This double-decker bus for the Park and Ride service in Bristol runs between peripheral car parks and the city centre

- contradictory outcomes, where additional travel generation takes place (e.g., additional journeys are made to the urban centre; additional mileage is travelled to the Park and Ride site).

Bristol, UK

The bus-based Brislington scheme in Bristol was the first purpose-built Park and Ride site serving Bristol. The service currently provides 1,300 free parking spaces on the outskirts of Bristol and regular bus services (Figure 3.2) from the site into the city centre. Factors contributing to its success include extensive bus priorities allowing fast and reliable service provision, and a high-profile marketing campaign. The service is seen as a 'package' including bus priority, quality of service and security. Bristol is working towards the provision of a ring of bus-based Park and Ride sites around the city, and a second site is now in operation.

The site has been well patronised since opening in October 1993, mainly by commuters and shoppers, and a large proportion of users (between 56 and 72%) would previously have travelled to the city centre by car or van. In 1996 around 500 car journeys (round trips to/from the centre of Bristol) to the centre of Bristol were saved each weekday, and over 460 each Saturday, due to Park and Ride provision. The modal share of car journeys to and from the centre of Bristol has fallen since the introduction of Park and Ride and bus priorities. However, there is also evidence that the Park and Ride scheme has attracted passengers from other public transport services such as buses (15–34%) and trains (0.8–12%), and may generate a certain amount of additional travel (Table 3.2).

Enschede, the Netherlands

The *Parkeerbus* (Park and Ride) service in Enschede was implemented in 1986 and, in contrast to the Bristol scheme, operated only on Saturdays. It was introduced specifically to relieve heavy weekend parking problems resulting from shoppers travelling to Enschede from outside the city – only 51% of passengers were residents of Enschede. Free parking and regular free buses into the city centre were provided, with costs covered by retailers and the Municipality. The service was abolished after only six months, as a result of over-use by local residents, although a shoppers' service on German Bank Holidays remains. Enschede now operates a cheap return-ticket system for all city buses. Although some car trips to the centre were saved, general patronage was much lower than in Bristol. However, on German public holidays up to 4,700 passengers were attracted (removing 2,000 cars

Table 3.2 Previous mode of transport used by Park and Ride users in Bristol (%)

Previous mode of travel	Thursday		Saturday	
	1994	1996	1994	1996
Car/van	55.5	54.0	72.1	69.9
Bus/coach	28.1	33.9	15.0	17.1
Train	11.9	7.8	0.8	0.8
Walk	0.6	—	—	—
Cycle	0.7	0.4	—	—
Would have travelled elsewhere	1.3	0.7	7.7	3.6
Would not otherwise have travelled	2.0	2.3	4.5	8.3

Source: DANTE Consortium (1997: Appendix 12), after Bristol City Council (1996b), Avon County Council (1994a)

from a city centre with 10,000 parking spaces), and the service has generated significant income for the city (Greaf, 1995; Weger, 1987).

3.5 Parking capacity

The overall number and availability of parking spaces can be reduced in a target district, in order to restrict car use. Car drivers will respond to such reductions by switching their mode of travel, switching the time of their journey or switching their destination to one more amenable to their needs as a driver. Typically, the number of parking spaces is reduced, and access to the remainder is restricted through either a time limit per visit, parking charges or permits for certain user groups.

There has been a positive reaction to parking capacity reductions and restrictions. This measure has been successful in decreasing the overall use of parking spaces, and the restrictions can be targeted at certain car drivers (in this case commuters) to encourage them to change modes.

Potential barriers to implementation include legal problems and the long-term implications of attempts to effect changes to private parking. The lack of control over private parking spaces can allow a growth in overall levels of traffic to continue, despite a reduction in the use of public spaces.

Zürich, Switzerland

The Municipality of Zürich sought to reduce the number of car commuters in the city by restricting the supply and attractiveness of parking spaces available to them.

Between 1984 and 1994 the overall number of public parking spaces in the city was reduced from 52,000 to 49,000; parking charges were introduced or increased; and residents' needs were favoured over those of commuters, by allowing them to purchase special parking cards giving them greater parking priority.

The management of residential neighbourhood spaces had a significant impact on parking (Figure 3.3). After implementation of the card scheme, the total number of cars parked in the area decreased by 19%, with a shift from commuter to shopping and leisure traffic. Generally, residents (inhabitants as well as traders) judged the measure positively, largely because they were the main beneficiaries of the scheme.

However, overall levels of traffic are not thought to have decreased, although they did remain stable. This may be because the parking strategy related to public, rather than private, spaces. In fact, the number of private spaces in the city increased during this period. The government has placed a restriction on the number of private parking spaces in new developments, but the impacts of this will take a long time to be felt. Because private parking spaces account for such a large share of the total number of spaces in the city, it is felt that this strategy is not as effective as it could have been in achieving travel reduction (Planungsbüro Jud AG, 1990; Stadtplanungsamt Zürich, 1991; Anon., 1997).

3.6 Public transport priority and roadspace

Physical infrastructure provision and traffic management schemes along public transport routes can be designed in such a way as to minimise journey times and maximise service reliability of this mode. The intention is to make

Figure 3.3 Parking in a residential street in Zürich: parking supply may be used to influence parking demand and hence travel behaviour

public transport more attractive, to encourage individuals to mode-switch. Typically, this measure would include dedicated lanes on roads and priority traffic-signal settings at intersections, where public transport vehicles are given a green light whenever they approach. New information technologies can enhance the effectiveness of priority schemes through the application of informatics; public transport subsidies and capacity investment are often an integral part of the implementation of this measure.

Implementation of priority schemes for public transport have an immediate effect on service quality, which increases the relative attractiveness of this mode of travel, particularly if roadspace is reduced for other users (i.e., car drivers), enabling switching or substitution to take place. The case studies below demonstrate how improvements to the quality of a service can lead to an increase in public transport patronage and modal share. However, it is more difficult to determine whether this leads to overall travel reduction or simply creates incentives to travel more.

Bristol, UK

Since 1991 a series of bus priority measures have been introduced in the Bristol area. Bus lanes have been introduced on several routes in Bristol, primarily for travel into the city, while inbound and outbound bus lanes on the A4 Bath Road accommodate both Park and Ride and regular services (Figure 3.4). New bus lanes introduced between 1991 and 1994 have reduced bus journey times by up to two-thirds, and decreased the variability of journey times by as much as 89%. This has had a positive impact on modal switching, particularly during the morning peak period, and the data indicate that bus patronage on corridors where bus lanes have been introduced has increased faster than traffic growth. For example, after one particular bus lane was introduced in 1993 on a radial road into Bristol, the modal share of cars during the morning peak decreased from 88% to 72% while numbers and modal share of buses increased slightly and patronage increased by 9%. However, mode switching during the afternoon peak has proved harder to achieve.

The effectiveness of bus priority measures can be severely affected by parking and moving-vehicle violations. Parking violations have a highly detrimental effect on the functioning of a bus lane. Violations by moving vehicles impose only minor delays, but problems can occur if queuing traffic spreads into the bus lane. The violation rate in Bristol is relatively low, but varies among locations: at one point on the Westbury Road it reached 15.2%, but the application of a red surface coating has reduced the rate to 1.8% (Avon County Council, 1994b).

Bucharest, Romania

From 1990 onwards, the Municipality of Bucharest implemented a traffic plan with the objectives of reducing public transport congestion in the city centre, increasing levels of service and improving safety conditions. As part of this plan, dedicated public transport contraflow lanes were constructed in 1997 on the busiest sections of Elisabeta and Kogalniceanu Boulevards. After this measure, the level of overall traffic was reduced by 30%, the travel speed increased by 50%, the number of passengers rose by 39% and accidents decreased by 60%. However, much of the traffic decrease can be accounted for by an increase in traffic in surrounding streets, which immediately became very congested. Besides this route switching, some mode switching to public transport took place, although the overall growth in travel in Bucharest obscures these statistics (PROED SA, 1997; RATB, 1996/1997a,b).

Zürich, Switzerland

Since 1977, the Municipality of Zürich has implemented a package of measures (*Beschleunigungs Programm*) which has the aim of increasing the speed of public transport vehicles in order to reduce both journey and waiting times. Dedicated public transport lanes were created, which were supported by a series of complementary

Figure 3.4 The A4 Bath Road bus service, Bristol, makes use of bus lanes to boost its competitiveness

measures. These included the prohibition of parking and waiting on a number of roads; banning of left turns at junctions where roadspace is shared with trams; car- and taxi-free zones; and the presence of sufficient uniformed police to enforce the restrictions.

In 1985 a computer-guided traffic-light signalling system, using a state-of-the-art selective vehicle-detection system, was introduced in the city, giving public transport vehicles priority at intersections. Of the 270 traffic lights positioned along bus and tram routes, 217 respond to transmitters in the vehicles via one of the 2,000 detectors embedded in the road surface, which allow the vehicles to cross at these intersections with a substantial reduction in waiting time. The average waiting time for public transport at intersections during the evening rush hour has decreased by 38% since 1985 (Pharoah and Apel, 1995; Stadelmann et al., 1996).

3.7 Road capacity restraint and reduction

The supply of roadspace available to cars can be reduced, or roads completely closed, in order to reduce the attractiveness of car travel and encourage mode switching. The concept behind this measure is based on a reversal of the proposition that increasing road capacity generates additional demand, i.e., a 'degeneration' of car travel will take place as capacity is reduced. It can be implemented in various ways:

- reduction in the number of lanes;
- street closures or introduction of one-way streets;
- lowering of speed limits;
- overall reduction in the number of parking places;
- alterations at traffic lights (signal delays or changes in priority).

HOV lanes, roadspace dedicated to public transport or to bicycles and parking capacity reduction are measures that are all complementary; together they can reduce the roadspace available for cars, and improve the attractiveness of other modes at the same time.

There has been a positive reaction to road capacity restraint and reduction where schemes have been implemented, but the associated travel reduction is difficult to measure. Although there will be less traffic on streets that have been closed, this may simply be a change without improvement because cars may simply be displaced to other streets rather than removed altogether. However, there do seem to be 'degenerational' effects of road closures on car traffic, as a recent collation of case study material demonstrates.

Evidence from 100 locations was collected, and summaries were produced for the 49 worldwide schemes where road capacity had been reduced and where there were sufficient data to make a 'before-and-after' comparison. The schemes ranged from town centre traffic management, bus priority measures and bridge closures, to earthquake-induced changes. The data had to be available for two points in time and included road-based and cordon based traffic counts, roadside interviews, repeated cross-sectional travel surveys and panel surveys. It is clearly acknowledged that the methodology used has severe limitations (Goodwin et al., 1998).

The data showed a wide range of results. For the sample where complete traffic information was provided (the 49 cases), the average reduction in traffic was 41%. Less than half of this reduction was diverted to other routes or times of travel. The net reduction was 25%. In seven cases there was an increase in travel after road capacity reduction. The median results indicated that 50% of cases showed an overall traffic reduction greater than 14%.

The conclusions reached by the authors were that: 'the balance of evidence is that measures which reduce or reallocate road capacity, when well-designed and favoured by strong reasons of policy, need not automatically be rejected for fear that they will inevitably cause unacceptable congestion. The effects of particular schemes will be reinforced or undermined by network conditions, and by the sticks and carrots of other policies, in a time-scale which is continually determined by wider choices about home, work and social activities. The most important responses to a scheme may be governed by the extent to which the scheme tilts the balance in decisions that many people will be making anyway, during the natural development of their lives' (Goodwin et al., 1998).

Perhaps the main barrier to the implementation of road capacity restraint and reduction measures is public resistance from both local residents and businesses, concerned about the reduction in car accessibility and its indirect effects; similar arguments were raised in opposition to area access controls. In such cases it is important to highlight the positive impact on the liveability of their neighbourhoods, as a result of (for instance) a reduction in rat-running or nuisance caused by (illegally) parked cars.

Edinburgh, UK

Princes Street is Edinburgh's premier shopping area and it has long been the site of a fierce battle over roadspace. Several proposals for partial or full pedestrianisation have been put forward over the years, yet not until 1997 were any travel alterations put into place. Then, cars (but not buses) were banned from travelling eastwards; the pedestrian walkway was widened and bicycle lanes were put in place (Figure 3.5). In an attempt to avoid simply shifting cars to the parallel street, George Street, it too was closed to through-traffic. Only customers of George Street shops are now allowed to drive and park there. The verdict on these changes is still undecided. Whilst road accident rates on Princes Street have fallen by an impressive 14%, there is no evidence so far of travel reduction taking place. Instead, traffic may have been diverted elsewhere: an extra one million cars reportedly travel through Stockbridge annually (Lord Provost's Commission, 1998).

London, UK

Hammersmith Bridge, a long-established river crossing in west London, was recently closed to cars and taxis by the local authority because it was never built to carry the growing volume of traffic crossing it. Public transport and emergency vehicles continue to use the bridge, but a smart card/intercom system operates barrier gates, which stop all other vehicles. Cyclists and pedestrians also have free access to the bridge.

After the bridge closed, traffic volumes on the local approach roads declined from 31,000 to 3,000 vehicles per day (i.e., a decrease of 28,000). At the same time, the volume of traffic on the adjacent bridges and routes increased from 105,000 to 122,000 vehicles per day (i.e., an increase of 17,000). This suggests that although some traffic was simply displaced as a result of the closure, there was a net decline in traffic of around 11,000 vehicles per day, which was one-third of the total (Cairns et al., 1998).

Figure 3.5 The reallocation of roadspace on Princes Street, Edinburgh, showing widened footways, a bicycle lane (far side) and bus lane (near side)

Although this measure has had some success in reducing traffic, it has not been entirely popular with local residents, who feel that their loss of accessibility is not outweighed by the improvements to their quality of life. A campaign has been waged to have the bridge reopened to all vehicular traffic with the result that it reopened to all traffic under 7.5 tonnes in autumn 1999.

3.8 Traffic calming

Roadspace can be designed so as to minimise car use and its impact in a target area. By reducing the capacity of a street and positioning physical barriers such as speed humps or bollards to reduce car speeds, mode switching can be induced, particularly if the design incorporates other complementary measures such as public transport/cycling priority and roadspace. Traffic-calming schemes are usually aimed at removing through-traffic from a particular street or network of streets, typically in residential areas.

As the case study demonstrates, traffic calming can have a positive impact by reducing the level of traffic in a target area, although change without improvement may take place if the traffic is just displaced elsewhere. It is popular in the residential areas where most schemes are to be found, but difficult to implement on public transport routes and in commercial districts, for some traffic-calming features may restrict the access of large vehicles.

Bristol, UK

Kingsdown is a residential area of Bristol with largely unrestricted on-street parking. Problems were being experienced with commuter parking (Figure 3.6) in the neighbourhood, as it is within walking distance of the city centre. Implementation of environmental traffic-calming measures designed to discourage commuter access was completed in July 1992, and included the introduction of one-way streets, road closures, speed humps and road narrowings.

Overall daily recorded traffic flows in the Kingsdown area were reduced by 10% following implementation. Although the traffic counts were not classified by type of vehicle, it is thought that much of the overall reduction resulted from a decrease in car-based commuter access and parking. Traffic has been displaced slightly to other routes as a result of the scheme. However, this is in the nature of traffic calming, where the main priority is not necessarily to reduce overall traffic but to shift it away from sensitive areas. Since the scheme was introduced, a dramatic and sustained reduction in Kingsdown accident rates has been experienced (Avon County Council, 1993).

Other restriction measures have also been found to be effective. Traffic calming restricts roadspace physically and, with the resulting 'cost' or 'hindrance' to car users, redistributes the benefits directly in favour of vulnerable road users such as cyclists or pedestrians. Physical control of area access in the city centre of Enschede (see Chapter 5) has achieved a reduction in vehicles within the cordoned area – and, more importantly, a 90% reduction in car traffic.

3.9 Area access control

Car access and use can be restricted in a designated area in order to encourage mode switching, and sometimes time switching, by making car use less attractive than other modes. At a district level, cars may be restricted permanently through the use of physical barriers (e.g., forming pedestrianised zones). Alternatively, controls may be more flexible, closing specific areas at certain times (see Section 2.8) with the assistance of various technologies, such as automated gates, video controls and electronic access cards. Access controls are frequently combined with parking measures, since car trips are often intended to terminate beyond the restricted zone in adjoining neighbourhoods.

Access controls are often found in the centres of towns and cities where high levels of car traffic and congestion are contributing to the decline in the local economy and the 'liveability' of the area for residents and pedestrians. If sufficient controls are in place, implementation of access restrictions will have an immediate impact on car traffic in a designated area. A positive reaction to implementation is exemplified by the experiences of Enschede, where a 90% decline in car traffic was recorded after the introduction of a restricted zone. However, there may be a displacement effect, as car drivers change their destination to areas with better parking facilities; if these destinations are at a greater distance, there may even be a contradictory outcome of increased travel. This destination switching may be controlled by regulating parking provision in the affected areas through parking charges, or by encouraging the car driver to switch to another mode of travel to the restricted area through Park and Ride provision.

Access control may encounter a lack of public acceptability. Therefore, in order for implementation to be successful, it is important that the restrictions proposed for a particular area meet the needs of the local residents and businesses, who are in many cases most affected by this measure but are often not the cause of the problem.

Figure 3.6 Commuter parking in Kingsdown, Bristol, before traffic calming was introduced

This can be done by awarding them a dedicated parking place or a special access card, and in the case of businesses ensuring that there is access for delivery and service vehicles. Businesses are often concerned with the commercial impact of restrictions on cars, although evidence from the Netherlands suggests that the impact of such measures is neutral, or even beneficial to the local economy, with improvements to the environment offsetting loss of accessibility. Such concerns may be addressed through involvement of the public in media campaigns.

Enschede, the Netherlands

Car access to the centre of Enschede has been restricted since 1980, when a pedestrian area was introduced. In 1990 this area was extended with the creation of a stadserf, or 'town yard' (Figure 3.7). When restrictions are in place, cars can access the centre on only one road. These controls are in place all night, and through the weekend; during weekdays, when entry controls do not apply, car traffic is discouraged by heavy parking restrictions and streets designed to give pedestrians priority. Monitoring of the scheme has demonstrated that there has been a positive reaction to the scheme and the number of cars in the stadserf area has decreased by 90%.

The issue of commercial impact was significant during the implementation process. The first attempt of the city council to close a larger part of the city centre in 1989 failed because of lack of support from local entrepreneurs. A consultation group (consisting of local retailers, residents, police, hotels and caterers, culture agencies, disabled persons and the municipal economic development department) was then formed to examine the issues and generate proposals. After a public hearing, a six-month pilot scheme was approved, the success of which led to the implementation in 1991 of a much more ambitious permanent scheme than originally proposed. The lesson to be learned about the Enschede case is that public support can be won, by involving local people and businesses in the implementation process, and by demonstrating to them the problems cars cause in their neighbourhood (Meijs and Himmels, 1994; Mulder and Hillen, 1991, 1992; Wel, 1995).

Rome, Italy

To reduce the number of vehicles using the inner city, the Municipality of Rome has created a restricted access area in the historic centre – the Zona Traffico Limitato (ZTL). Access to this area is controlled by ten gates, with an entry and payment system using electronic smart cards. Residents within the ZTL area can obtain this access card free of charge (for one car per family), whilst for owners of a public transport season ticket the price is cheaper than for others. Each authorised vehicle has an on-board unit to identify the vehicle and to check the availability of money on the smart card. In combination with the access controls, parking charges have been introduced across the central area and public transport provision has been improved. Although empirical data of the effects of this measure are limited, it was observed that there was an increase in car traffic during a period when controls were temporarily suspended, suggesting a positive reaction to the scheme when implemented (Giovenali, 1995; Municipality of Rome, 1997).

3.10 Conclusion

Some of the main features of the eight measures considered in this chapter have been summarised (Table 3.3). One general point, not yet mentioned, is that imposition

Figure 3.7 Entrance to the stadserf, Enschede, with an access control sign in both Dutch and German

of a series of networks with different priorities on the current road network increases the potential conflict points. The network intersection points where the various modes have to cross each other need careful consideration. The Netherlands, Denmark and Germany have all been successful in integrating the different networks, but in other countries less thought has been given to the priorities and mechanisms needed (e.g., sensitive local design and more complex phasing on intersections controlled by traffic lights). In this extended conclusion, comments are made on the potential for transferability and factors of success, as they relate to each mode (individually and in combination).

Cycling

For cycling, there is no universal set of measures, and each scheme needs to be considered as part of a citywide programme. It is very desirable to design networks for cyclists, preferably where traffic flows are high. There is a strong cultural element in attitudes to cycling which needs to be developed so that high levels of bicycle use can be guaranteed. Perhaps cycling can first be introduced as a leisure activity (e.g., by promoting the SUSTRANS National Cycle Network), and then for journeys to school (high potential) and work (some potential).

Evidence from the Netherlands suggests that cycling can be considered a viable alternative to the car for trips of up to 7.5 km. Longer bicycle journeys are made mainly for leisure purposes. Cycling measures are particularly appropriate for an area where many short trips are made by car (and are therefore potentially replaceable by cycling trips). Citywide network provision of cycle roadspace and priority measures would be ideal for encouraging cycling, but is not always possible; measures can also be implemented progressively, on a corridor basis.

In short, there is substantial potential for greater use of bicycles to reduce travel by car. Cyclists represent a wide cross-section of people, and there are many opportunities for companies and schools to take the lead. The supporting infrastructure is not expensive, and cycling measures work well with appropriate spatial planning and restrictions on car use in residential areas. Attention must be given to the perceived safety and security issues throughout all the aspects of road design and management, and through education and training programmes in schools and workplaces.

Table 3.3 Summary of infrastructure intervention measures

Measure	Travel reduction	Lessons and limitations
Cycle priority and roadspace	Mode switching	Substantial potential in many cities, as distances are short Safety and security often perceived as problems Network essential to encourage high levels of use
HOV priority and roadspace	Increasing occupancy Mode switching Linking trips	Enforcement important for success Can be used on many different types of road Can be used on bridges
Park and Ride	Mode switching Increased occupancy	Needs to be linked with other forms of priority, and restraint on city centre parking May encourage longer journeys to reach Park and Ride car park
Parking capacity	Mode switching Destination switching Time switching	This measure is already used frequently, but often lacks control over parking Needs to be combined with positive measures to encourage change
Public transport priority and roadspace	Mode switching Increased occupancy	An important part of most packages, as the intention is to raise public transport use and efficiency Quality of service improvements result in increased patronage
Road capacity restraint and reduction	Mode switching	The outcome from the implementation of the other measures is less space available for the car Traffic degeneration is 'not yet proven'
Traffic calming	Mode switching	Less traffic in residential and other areas Needs to be part of a citywide strategy Public resentment in adjacent areas from displaced traffic
Area access control	Mode switching Destination switching Time switching	Substantial potential, particularly when seen as part of an area-wide treatment Care over traffic diversion affects roads around the control area Some problems with public acceptability

Park and Ride

Park and Ride is now a major component of many cities' transport strategies, but it is often not considered along with the other necessary supporting measures. The success of a Park and Ride service will depend partly on the speed and efficiency of the corridor. For example, a bus-based Park and Ride scheme may require a bus priority network where traffic congestion poses a threat to service speed and reliability. In Zürich, the Park and Ride schemes based around S-Bahn stations have proved much more successful than bus and tram-based schemes, partly due to the faster speed of the S-Bahn. The introduction of Park and Ride generally requires the presence of an implementing body able to coordinate activities. Where more than one local authority is involved, for example where the service will serve several administrative areas, cooperation may be required. Park and Ride is ideal for implementation in close proximity to an 'attractive' area, such as an urban centre or work location. This need not be a city centre, as Park and Ride can also be used to serve other locations, such as peripheral business parks. When serving an urban centre, a ring of Park and Ride sites may be more effective in terms of containing the volume of traffic against a rising tide of car use.

Park and Ride sites are often implemented to serve peak-period commuter journeys. However, off-peak shopping journeys can also be targeted, particularly as shoppers tend to have a higher turnover on site, so there is a greater potential for reducing journeys. Park and Ride can be appropriate for both regular and seasonal use, as with the Enschede visitor Park and Ride service.

Although the implementation of a first Park and Ride site in a city may cause some problems, these initial setbacks can be overcome: when a ring of sites has been constructed, a long-term reduction in congestion levels can eventually be achieved.

As already noted with many travel reduction measures, it is important to consider the whole transport system in a city. Park and Ride can only be effective if is perceived as a more attractive option than travelling by car. For example, if parking in the city centre is cheap and available, then Park and Ride patronage will be affected. Bus-based Park and Ride works well in combination with bus priority measures, particularly where traffic congestion on the approach to a Park and Ride site, or between the site and the urban centre, is likely to be a problem.

Traffic calming and area access control

These measures are self-enforcing, perhaps implying increased public acceptance of the need to curtail car use, in contrast with measures such as road pricing which remain controversial in many countries. This can perhaps be linked with the immediate and visible benefits to pedestrians offered by both traffic calming and area access control (Figure 3.8), without an evident 'up-front' financial penalty on car users.

Car restraint measures are often controversial, and implementation of radical measures may be problematic due to low public and political acceptability. For example, when implementing area access control in a city centre, opposition may be encountered from local businesses concerned that they will lose trade. It may be possible to overcome some of these barriers through consultation: in Bristol, the Kingsdown traffic calming scheme was initially rejected by local residents and the emergency services, following concerns over access restrictions, but an acceptable compromise was eventually reached and implemented. Often it is important to remain responsive

to the needs of local residents and business in order to win their support. For example, when implementing area access control it may be necessary to make special arrangements for access by local residents and delivery vehicles. Media campaign measures may also be valuable in raising support and awareness.

Enforcement is an important aspect of many measures to restrain car use, particularly in the cases of area access control, road pricing and parking restrictions. It will often be necessary to develop an effective means of enforcement and reducing violations, in order to ensure the measure's success in discouraging car use.

Combinations of measures

When implementing measures restricting car use, it is essential to provide adequate alternative transport provision, for reasons of both capacity and public acceptability. For example, it can be valuable to have a Park and Ride site already in operation when implementing commuted payments, as this provides an immediate alternative to car-based commuting. When introducing area access control, it is often necessary to implement complementary parking measures to avoid the spread of traffic and parking into adjoining areas. Combination with Park and Ride is another option. By their nature, many of the above measures to restrain car use are appropriate for implementation in a particular area or corridor. For example, traffic calming is generally applied to sensitive zones such as residential areas or outside schools.

The set of measures discussed in this chapter offers considerable potential for real change as they can be 'easily' introduced with the current range of powers available to city authorities. Many partial schemes have been implemented, but no city seems to have systematically reviewed its priorities for the allocation of roadspace to priority users. When this opportunity is taken, together with direct action to promote the use of the new networks (by schools, employers, residents' groups, etc.), then travel alternatives will become much more important and a substantial step towards the sustainable and liveable city will have been taken.

Figure 3.8 A cheap and simple, but effective measure in Zürich: prohibition of driving, but cycling permitted

Financial Levers to Reduce Travel

4.1 Introduction

Pricing underlies the group of measures most fiercely debated in the literature. It is widely accepted that the motorists do not pay the full costs of their travel, particularly if externalities are included.* In addition, there is a concerted effort in Europe to meet the challenging targets set at the 1998 Kyoto Conference on reducing the levels of CO_2 emissions. The EU15 have accepted a reduction of 8% on 1990 levels by 2010, but some countries (e.g., the UK, the Netherlands and Germany) have committed themselves to much more difficult targets. Transport is one sector that is expected to make a substantial contribution to the achievement of the targets. The principal means by which the targets will be met is through the application of the best available technology so that vehicle engines become more efficient, through the use of alternative fuels (e.g., ethanol or methanol), and through substantially raising the tax on fuel.

In the UK, there is a continuing commitment to raise fuel taxes by at least 6% per annum in real terms; this means a doubling of real fuel prices every 13–14 years. In 2000, the tax and duty on petrol and diesel in the UK amounts to 80% of the pump price. This change is in line with a gradual change in thinking by many national governments as taxation is switched from labour (production) to consumption. At the centre of an ecological tax reform is the argument that consumers should pay the full resource costs (including externalities and costs related to intergenerational concerns) of the products they use.†

The focus here, though, is not on the role of national (and international) governments, but on the supporting role that city and local governments can play in reducing

travel. In this chapter, five local pricing measures are discussed. Within this group, there are two alternative complementary paths, one based on promoting alternatives to the car through subsidy and investment, and the other on making the car less attractive through increases in the costs of bringing it into the city.

Of all the measures discussed in this book, the issue of pricing is the most controversial and complex. The economic case for road pricing is clear as it permits marginal social cost pricing, including the internalisation of the external costs (Newbery, 1990). However, there are still many unresolved questions over its effectiveness in achieving change. Peirson and Vickerman (1998) constructed a model for London passenger travel, from which they concluded that efficient pricing does not result in substantial shifts away from the use of road transport. Similar analysis in Belgium suggested that a reduction of 15% in car demand would result from efficient pricing of transport externalities (De Borger et al., 1996). Both models were mainly driven by income and the assumption that demand for car travel continues to grow. Over a relatively short period of time, the impact of road pricing would be diluted by income effects.

These uncertainties still exist, even among the economists and even though the estimates for the external costs of transport have risen substantially in the recent past (Maddison et al., 1996). Questions have been raised about the responses of transport users to road pricing, particularly about the reliability of the crucial assumptions on elasticities, and there is uncertainty over whether the cost of air pollution is nearer to 0.4% or 3% of GDP (Maddison et al., 1996). Nevertheless, there has been a consistent and growing belief (e.g., Royal Commission on Environmental Pollution, 1994; CEC, 1995) that road pricing must form the essential core of any travel reduction policy in cities. This debate has not ended: it has only just begun. Many other issues, such as the impact on city business and prosperity, the effects on rent and property prices, the diversion effects (to other cities) and public acceptability,

---

* Externalities cover costs such as congestion, pollution, noise, accidents and community severance, which are imposed by road users (e.g., car drivers and public transport travellers) on non-users of the road systems or on other road users (see Table 1.2).

† Intergenerational effects relate to the impacts on future generations and forms the basis of the standard WCED definition of sustainable development. See WCED (1987) Our Common Future (The Brundtland Report), The World Commission on Environment and Development, Oxford: Oxford University Press.

have not yet been tested. Some local authorities are gradually moving towards considering the introduction of road pricing as a demonstration project (e.g., in Edinburgh and Leeds). These demonstration projects are critical to the future of road pricing as one or two poorly implemented schemes would mean that such policies become more difficult to introduce elsewhere. In particular, the response of the residents, employers and other groups based in city centres needs to be carefully monitored.

In this chapter, road pricing is only covered briefly as there is no example in Europe of a full electronic road pricing scheme. Details are given of the cordon pricing schemes implemented in the major cities in Norway. The other financial levers presented explore the role of subsidy and investment in cycling and public transport, as well as the pricing of parking, which is probably the most important action currently available to raise the perceived costs of using the car in the city.

4.2 Bicycle subsidy

Public (or private) funds can be used to enhance the attractiveness of cycling, and so to encourage mode switching with the effect of reducing vehicle kilometres. This can be achieved through planning at a regional level using a range of tools such as:

• investment in bicycle infrastructure;

• enhancement of bicycle safety and accessibility;

• introduction of company or city bicycles.

Furthermore, direct or indirect cycle subsidies can be used to promote the attractiveness of bicycles, for example, by provision of free bicycles and bus passes as a compensation for agreeing not to own a car.

Figure 4.1 Company cycle scheme, Aalborg

Since the bicycle is most suitable for short journeys of under 5 km, other complementary measures are those which reduce travel distances between activities, including land-use measures such as urban concentration and the design of new development (see Chapter 5).

Bicycle subsidies are a useful tool to influence individual behaviour to achieve switching or substitution. As the case studies demonstrate, they can be particularly effective in areas where cycling already accounts for a significant proportion of trips, because local conditions (e.g., existing infrastructure and built environment) and a cycling 'tradition' (through social and cultural acceptability) are important factors of success. However, in areas where bicycle use is historically low, the cost of implementing an integrated package of cycling measures, ranging from physical infrastructure through to safety awareness campaigns, can be expensive relative to the magnitude of modal switching achieved. Resource constraints in the public sector may limit the availability of funds for this measure.

Aalborg, Denmark

A company bicycle scheme (Figure 4.1), designed to increase modal share and safety for cyclists, was implemented by Aalborg Municipality and the Danish National Roads Directorate. Aalborg Municipality also participated as users of the scheme, in conjunction with participating companies Ramboll A/S, Berner A/S, Post Danmark, Aalborg Technical College, Aalborg School of Arts, Craft and Design and Aalborg Hospital.

The scheme is part of a larger group of measures running from 1995 to 1998 to increase the modal share of the bicycle and improve bicycle safety. In May 1996, nine local companies and organisations were given 35 bicycles, with the condition that if they used them to travel more than 300 km they could keep them free of charge. Otherwise they would pay a small fee. In the six-month trial period, the 35 company bicycles were used to travel nearly 21,700 km. Table 4.1 illustrates the number of trips and trip lengths distributed by trip purpose.

As part of the scheme, participants kept a logbook, where they registered whether the trip replaced one that would have been taken using other modes of transport. Out of the 21,669 km travelled by the bicycles, 18,188 km replaced another transport mode. This means that the bicycle trips replaced another mode in 84% of the total distance cycled, and in 85% of all trips. Table 4.2 shows the trips replaced by bicycle, listed by mode.

Table 4.1 Company bicycle scheme: trip characteristics

Trip purpose	No. of trips	Average trip length (km)	Total distance travelled (km)
Commuting	1253	9.8	12330
Shopping	384	4.8	1856
Post office	66	4.7	308
Meeting	649	4.8	3137
Others	532	6.8	3640
Not Indicated	56	7.1	398
Total	2940	7.4	21669

Source: Aalborg Kommune (1997)

Table 4.2 Company bicycle scheme: modes replaced

Mode	No. of trips	Distance (km)
Taxi	305	1552
Bus	524	6645
Company car	187	1162
Private car	922	5975
Bicycle	182	1102
Others	302	1359
Not indicated	71	393
Total	2493	18188

Source: Aalborg Kommune (1997)

Significantly, a relatively high proportion of switching was observed from car to company cycle: 44% of all trips and 39% of the total travel distance. Because the measure had a high profile in the local media, it created general awareness of the concept of company bicycles. During the project period, several interested parties enquired into the possibility of acquiring company bicycles. This measure has been shown to be successful in encouraging switching from car to bicycles. In the strictest sense it has encouraged travel, by promoting bicycle use, but overall it has assisted in the drive towards sustainable mobility, and therefore it is complementary to travel reduction objectives. The scheme was also successful in raising awareness about both company bicycles and other bicycle projects in Aalborg.

Aarhus, Denmark

In 1995 the Municipality of Aarhus and the Danish National Agency for Environmental Protection initiated the CykelBuster project which aimed to increase significantly the modal share of bicycles by targeting individuals who were thought to be most amenable to cycling. The project participants were given the free use of a high-quality bicycle, as well as one year's free subscription to public transport services in Aarhus. In return, participants signed a contract agreeing not to use their cars during this period.

Before the implementation of the measure (April 1995) car travel accounted for 80% of trips made by participants, with cycling accounting for 8.5%. After one year (March 1996) the proportion of journeys made by car had halved to 40%, whilst those made by bicycle had more than trebled to 28%. Other modes of travel also significantly increased their share of overall travel. This measure therefore proved to be very effective in encouraging a shift from the car to other modes of travel, among individuals who already used the bicycle for a reasonable proportion of trips (DANTE Consortium, 1997: Appendix 12, pp.25–29).

4.3 Parking charges

Pricing mechanisms can be used to influence the demand for parking spaces at a district level. If the cost of parking is increased, driving to a particular destination becomes less attractive, and so drivers switch to alternative modes to reach their destination, or switch destination altogether. Typically, commuters are the target of such a pricing policy, by making the cost of long-stay parking prohibitive. This measure may be complemented by others promoting public transport alternatives.

There has been a positive reaction to parking charges, which can influence travel behaviour by changing the types of users of parking spaces, as the Zürich example (below) demonstrates. However, there is no empirical evidence that travel reduction takes place as a result of parking charges alone, because non-commuters are prepared to pay a relatively high cost to park for a short length of time. Indeed, short-term parking increases the turnover of cars per space, and this improvement in system efficiency can encourage car travel as a result of increased space availability at any one time. Nevertheless, there is evidence to suggest that parking charges can be effective when combined with other parking measures, namely parking restrictions and capacity reduction. Although local authorities may be able to regulate parking charges for public spaces only, they can exert influence indirectly on privately developed spaces through commuted payments. With both public and private spaces, legal barriers may restrict a local authority's ability to change radically the cost of parking provision, as in the case of Zürich.

Zürich, Switzerland

In recent years the number of free public parking spaces in Zürich has been reduced from around 75% of the total to zero, and parking charges have been doubled. Roadside parking spaces in the city are equipped with parking meters. They permit a maximum parking time of between 30 minutes and two hours. In the city centre the 30- and 60-minute limits predominate.

The aim of this measure was to reduce the number of car commuters, and encourage people to travel to work by alternative modes. As a result, there has been a shift from long- to short-term parking, with a concomitant shift to shopping and leisure purposes from commuter use. To this extent, the measure may have been successful in encouraging a modal shift for commuter travel.

However, by increasing short-term demand for parking, there is greater use of spaces because of a higher turnover of parked cars. In effect, an increase in parking space capacity has occurred, leading to a growth in travel. Research suggests that parking charges would have to be significantly higher in Zürich to discourage this additional car parking, even though higher parking charges are prohibited by federal law, so in this case there is a legal barrier. The authorities in Zürich have therefore focused their efforts on reducing the number of parking spaces and improving public transport to achieve travel reduction (Maeder, 1993).

4.4 Public transport investment

Investment in public transport infrastructure and services can expand the passenger-carrying potential of the system. Mode switching takes place when individuals choose to use an improved public transport system in place of their cars. This investment involves capital expenditure, which differs from funds devoted to running costs in the form of public transport subsidies.

Investment in public transport capacity is a powerful tool for encouraging use of public transport and reducing that of cars by facilitating switching or substitution. However, creating an attractive public transport network, with increased system capacity, creates incentives for individuals to travel more, which can lead to an increase in overall

levels of travel. Considerable resource barriers also exist, because the cost of constructing public transport networks and the longer-term operational costs can be high.

Zürich, Switzerland

In Zürich a regional S-Bahn system provides public transport services into the city from up to 50 km away. By 1990, investment of about 1.2 billion euros had created a 400-km integrated network, by upgrading existing railway lines, constructing 12 km of new tunnels in the inner and central city, building stations and acquiring new rolling stock (e.g., double-decker carriages). This upgraded system served new destinations in the region and improved accessibility to a number of city centre destinations (Figure 4.2) with a high level of service frequency. At the same time, a new regional ticketing system and a zonal fare structure were introduced. The stated objective of this investment was to increase travel on the rail network by 20%, and to reduce car traffic at the city boundary by a similar amount through mode switching between car and tram.

Since the upgraded S-Bahn opened, there has been a significant increase in public transport use, and car use has remained constant at 1990 levels. Three years after opening (1993–94), the S-Bahn was carrying 31% more passengers than before (up to 90% on upgraded lines), while the use of regional and rural buses (often 'feeding' the S-Bahn) had increased by 53%. In other words, the modal share of public transport has risen while that of cars has fallen, although there has been overall travel growth.

Further improvements still have to be made to certain operational aspects of the improved system, in particular feeder bus and tram services. The smaller municipalities around Zürich do not have the resources to support these innovations. At a time of growing public fiscal restraint, resource issues may impede the future development of the network, which has proved costly to build and operate (Massnahmenplan Lufthygiene Kanton Zürich, 1988; Statistische Berichte des Kantons Zürich, 1995, 1996; Züricher Verkehrsverbund, 1995).

4.5 Public transport subsidy

Public (or private) funds can be used to ensure that high levels of public transport services can be provided and accessibility to such services maintained, even if they are not commercially viable. If it is ensured that public transport services are operational and affordable, individuals may be attracted to mode-switch. This source of funding typically accounts for between 20 and 90% of the overall costs of running public transport services in Europe. Subsidies are paid either to the user – through cheap season tickets, for example – or to the operator. A complementary range of financial incentives can also be used to make car travel less attractive, such as parking charges and road pricing.

This measure can therefore facilitate switching or substitution. Subsidies for public transport exist explicitly to promote this mode of transport. In areas of high car ownership the measure is used to encourage modal switching from the car, whilst in areas of low car ownership it is used to stop modal switching away from public transport to the car. As the Enschede case study demonstrates, financial incentives are successful in attracting people to public transport from other modes. However, this example also illustrates the main drawback: subsidies can create incentives to travel by attracting passengers who are making new journeys, or are switching from other favourable modes, such as cycling. Resource constraints in the public sector may limit the availability of funds to subsidise public transport.

Enschede, the Netherlands

In March 1997, Oostnet/TET, the bus operator for the Enschede area, introduced subsidised off-peak fares on services to the city centre in order to encourage local residents to use public transport instead of the car for such journeys. For trips taking place on Saturdays between 09.00 and 18.00, a ticket can be purchased for Dfl.1.75, significantly less than the standard price. The introduction of this subsidised ticket led to an increase of 7.5% in the number of passengers during these periods in the short term, and 15% over a longer time period. A survey of these new passengers found that over one-third of them had previously made the same journey by car, thus demonstrating that modal switching occurred. However, just over half of the new passengers had previously travelled by bicycle: a classic case of 'change without improvement' (DANTE Consortium, 1997: Appendix 12, pp. 254–255).

4.6 Road pricing

Road pricing seeks to moderate demand for roadspace, and may therefore be applied to reduce the volume of vehicle traffic travelling on specific roads at a particular time, or into certain areas. Thus destination and time switching of a car journey can be encouraged; ultimately public transport may become relatively more attractive, thus encouraging mode switching.

Financial levers can be used to control demand: vehicles using affected roads or areas pay a toll according to the time or location. Different systems have been tested for road pricing, ranging from relatively cheap ticketing systems to expensive automated payment systems using Global Positioning Systems (GPS) to determine the location of a vehicle at any given time. In both cases, the toll can be varied according to the particular need for travel reduction on a road or in an area at any given time.

Road pricing can facilitate switching or substitution within a target route or area, with the added advantage of raising valuable financial resources (see the Norwegian case study). It is important that these resources are not used to fund new infrastructure (as is often the case to overcome public opposition) – any gain in capacity creates incentives to travel more. As the technology for running such systems continues to improve, it is likely that in the future more sophisticated schemes will be implemented which will minimise delay to the user at the tollbooth.

However, there are several concerns for such schemes. Although they can lead to travel reduction in the cordoned area, they may displace traffic to other (free) roads and locations, and some journey lengths may increase as a result. Beyond these direct impacts, broader concerns are equity issues affecting the user (tariffs will affect lower-income users disproportionately), the impacts upon the spatial economy (cordoned areas may become less attractive commercial/residential locations) and the lack of public acceptability of a potentially unpopular tax on mobility (although public awareness and media campaigns are essential to increase public awareness).

Figure 4.2 High-quality public transport interchange in Zürich

Cordon road pricing in Norway

Information on three Norwegian schemes has been given by Hervick and Braathen (1994) and the CEC (1997).

Trondheim

There has been a cordon toll, with differentiated tariffs, in operation since 1991. The charging period is from 06.00 until 17.00, with a high tariff from 06.00 to 10.00 and a low tariff from 10.00 to 17.00. At other times and at weekends there is no charge. About 21 million vehicles passed through the toll ring in 1992 during the charging period, or about 50% of all vehicles. For manual payment, the charge is NOK 15 (Norwegian kroner) per car, with no discounts or charges for passengers; trucks are charged at twice this rate.

The electronic system charges for each trip, either through prepayment on an electronic card or direct transfer from the driver's bank account. Within the high-tariff period the prepayment charge is NOK 12, and during the low-tariff period the discount varies between 30 and 50%, depending on the size of the prepayment (30% if it was low, or 50% high), whilst the discount for the direct transfer method is at a standard 30%.

The objectives of the Trondheim system have been to raise funds to build a new road to bypass the city and to improve public transport. Public support for the scheme has grown and some 42% of respondents claim to have changed their travel patterns. Commuters have changed to different modes or different times of travel, but shoppers are more likely to make changes in their time of travel, followed by changes to their destination and frequency of travel. About 80% of drivers use one of the electronic charging systems, with 70% of these using the direct transfer rather than the prepayment scheme.

The revenues from the toll ring were about 8.75 million euros (in 1992) per annum, which more than covered the debt on projects already constructed in the Trondheim area. Additional revenue is required if new projects are to be undertaken. A more sophisticated system has been discussed, with the number of toll stations being increased from 12 to 20 (1996), so that a higher proportion of motorists can be charged. The city is now being divided into six charging zones (Langmyhr, 1999).

Bergen

A cordon toll has been in operation since January 1986; the tolls are in force on weekdays from 06.00 to 22.00. Paper vignettes are stuck to the windscreen, but monthly and weekly subscribers obtain electronic tags. The objectives were to introduce comprehensive demand management regimes and to raise funds to finance the road infrastructure and to cover the costs of public transport. The number of cars in Bergen was reduced by 10% after the first year in operation.

Oslo

A cordon toll and road levy have been in operation since 1990, with discounted season tickets and special lanes for occasional users paying cash. The charges are in force for 24 hours a day for seven days a week. The principal objective is to raise funds for infrastructure financing (mainly roads); 20% is reserved for public transport improvements. There have been 5–10% reductions in the number of vehicles crossing the cordon.

4.7 Conclusion

The pricing and financial levers available to reduce the travel are powerful, but they have not been fully or consistently exploited. Pricing has been used to raise revenue for general expenditure, and investment (and subsidy) in public transport has often been very variable over time. Tremendous opportunities are available, particularly in road pricing, provided that the introduction of such measures forms part of a coherent citywide strategy to reduce the use of the car (Table 4.3). However, evidence from the past seems to indicate that the integration of the different policy measures has not been addressed. Even in Norway, where cordon pricing has been introduced, it has been seen as a means to finance more roads and to act as a lever for matching funding from the State. Such a strategy is short-term and makes it much more difficult to introduce a policy that tackles the city as a whole. There is evidence that development pressures are now operating outside the cordon area, and new road construction is likely to increase car dependence and travel distances. In addition, the expectation that demand increases with rising income implies that, over the longer term, pricing strategies may have a decreasing impact. City centre parking is already costing more than £30 a day in some cities, yet (some) people are prepared to pay this price.

The distributional impacts of pricing strategies have to be addressed, as the argument that pricing is a means of allowing the rich to continue to use their cars has not been countered. More importantly, as enshrined in French law, there are certain rights to mobility. All users should have the right to travel and the freedom of choice of mode, with reasonable access and at a reasonable cost. Subsidy of and investment in public transport (and cycling facilities) are means by which that right can be ensured, but even here there is the possibility of two types of transport systems – one for the rich and one for the poor.

Table 4.3 Summary of financial levers

Measure	Travel reduction	Lessons and limitations
Cycle subsidy	Mode switching	Potential to issue free bicycles is an incentive to use Investment in the complete network is important to maximise use
Parking charges	Mode switching Destination switching	Needs to be part of an areawide strategy Control of parking is a problem
Public transport investment	Mode switching Raising occupancy	Essential part of any politically acceptable package Major investment necessary if large numbers are going to use public transport
Public transport subsidy	Mode switching Raising occupancy	It is not necessary to subsidise public transport (or any transport) on sustainability criteria Subsidy should be carefully targeted at particular groups (social and spatial equity)
Road pricing	Mode switching Time switching Destination switching	Must form part of a clear citywide strategy Concern over particular groups (e.g., residents and local businesses) A major proportion of revenues should be returned to the city for transport-related investment – to improve public acceptability

Pricing and distributional questions form one of the basic dilemmas in transport. If transport is a means to an end (i.e., a derived demand), then everyone needs a basic minimum level of transport to access the requirements of daily life. The sustainable mobility arguments suggest that there should be no subsidy to any form of transport (public or private) and that the user should pay the full costs (including any externalities). These two perspectives are not compatible in every case, and so subsidy of particular users under particular conditions may be appropriate. Similarly, much investment in transport is still undertaken by the public sector, with the road budget taking the major share. New priorities may imply that the private sector should become responsible for the construction and maintenance of the road network, with costs being recouped through charges. The public sector should concentrate on investment in the public transport and bicycle networks, but even here there may be a strong case for private-sector investment as public budgets are reduced.

One possible means to resolve the distributional issues related to pricing would be to introduce tradable mobility credits (Sorrell and Skea, 1999). As individual motorised transport is at the same time a basic need and a luxury good, the tax system should lower the fixed costs of car use and raise the variable costs. As discussed earlier, effective incentives for not further increasing but for decreasing overall mileage cannot directly be coupled with monetary costs, for social reasons. Tradable mobility credits can solve the distributional problem. Every person obtains a limited number of road-free credits and other mobility services at reasonable prices. Establishing a market for these credits will lead to higher costs for those who travel further, and to extra income for those driving less. Such a system was discussed in detail in Switzerland about 10 years ago.

Encouraging the use of public transport may be coupled with the same system of tradable mobility credits (TMCs), as they could be used for paying for public transport services. This would effectively decrease car mileage if public transport were attractive. Technically, smart cards would present an easy means by which TMCs could be realised. The cards could be sold (or recharged) by public authorities according to the respective personal quota, and they could be used for payment of fees on the car or of public transport fares, or be traded between individuals or over electronic systems. With increasing flexibility of working hours and the use of information technology services, there would be a clear incentive to time-switch and peak-spread according to the charges being levied. This would in turn reduce the costs of public transport. Such a system could also be linked with the pollution profile of the vehicle so that 'clean' cars were charged much less than 'polluting' cars (POSSUM, 1999).

Pricing and financial levers are central to much thinking in Europe about reducing travel distance and car dependence. Further debate is still needed on mixing together the available measures in creative packages of both financial and other measures. A free-standing financial package is unlikely to be successful on its own, either in achieving travel reductions and sustainable mobility, or in being politically and publicly acceptable.

CHAPTER 5

Travel Reduction 'Built In': The Role of Land-Use Planning

5.1 Introduction

Transport and land use are fundamentally linked. Transport itself constitutes a significant land use, as well as providing the framework for accessibility for all other land uses. This chapter concentrates on the potential contribution of land-use policies towards the objectives of sustainable mobility and travel reduction.

Since activities such as housing, working, shopping and leisure are separated in space, travel is essential. Growing prosperity has been the major factor behind the increase in mobility. As people became more affluent, they were able to buy a car and to travel more. Households moved out of the cities to live in villages and suburbs, and this process was facilitated by better infrastructure (Salomon et al., 1993). This spatial deconcentration of housing and employment gives rise to many undesirable consequences. Longer distances lead to increases in the amount of overall travel and encourage people to take the car rather than travelling by foot or by bicycle. Moreover, a scattered urbanisation pattern encourages criss-cross travelling, which is not easy to serve by public transport.

However, it is possible that reversal of urban sprawl could have a great potential in reducing the need to travel, especially by car. Land-use solutions may be applied where there is a need to modify the demand for transport, in contrast to supply-side solutions reliant on the provision of transport infrastructure, traffic control systems, etc. Land use is an important influence on transport demand, as the use and geographical distribution of activities and buildings affect the pattern and overall amount of travel by different modes of transport. This is manifested through trip generation rates for different land-use activities, the resultant patterns of movement between origins and destinations, the relative accessibility of these destinations, and hence the relative convenience of using different modes. The design of built form may also encourage sustainable modes and discourage car use.

Thus land-use policy seeks to reduce travel distances in order to achieve an overall reduction in mobility, and it seeks to improve the base for public transport and soft modes (e.g., walking or cycling) in order to promote a modal shift. With land-use planning measures, it should be possible to 'build in' travel reduction, in the sense that once a settlement has been laid out in a manner which encourages walking, cycling and accessing public transport, this pattern may be expected to prevail for a long time without further need for proactive travel reduction policies.

A variety of land-use solutions is available to influence travel behaviour and the need to travel. The measures involved encompass, firstly, the location of land uses and activities; secondly, the spatial layout and structure of settlements; and, thirdly, the design of the infrastructure to support walking activity. Measures concerning the choice of location include the location of new housing developments, the location of companies (such as the Dutch ABC policy) and, in a way, mixed-use development, which can also be seen as a way to structure settlements. Measures concerning the design and layout of settlements include the use of higher densities and public transport as well as bicycle or walk-oriented design.

The implementation of land-use planning measures is typically carried out by local authorities, although some measures may be coordinated at a national level by central government – for example, policies for urban concentration or integrated planning. In such a way, the Netherlands has national policies, which set out an overall framework in which local policies can operate. In the UK, innovative solutions such as car-free areas tend to be one-off initiatives promoted by local authorities, as opposed to being part of a wider national strategy.

Development at public transport nodes combines aspects of transport operation, planning coordination and development, and this is reflected in the range of possible implementing bodies: for example, in Denmark, responsibility is shared between local and central government, transport companies and other private companies.

The current extent of implementation of land-use measures varies somewhat between the countries studied, with the Netherlands having the highest level of implementation. Of individual types of measure, location of companies and design of locations (to facilitate walking, cycling, etc.) have the highest implementation levels across all the countries studied. These measures are useful in their own right to suit particular local objectives, as well as combining to form an integrated transport strategy.

5.2 Location of new developments

Since the growth of travel is strongly related to the increasing distances that exist as a consequence of sub-urban sprawl, there could be a great potential to reverse this trend through urban concentration. This policy uses instruments at a regional level to develop housing, employment and service localities in close proximity to each other, and to the central city, in order to reduce the distances people travel between them. It seeks to prevent the dispersal of urban functions and activities over a large area, thus limiting the urban sprawl that would increase travel distances and car dependence. By focusing new development within or adjacent to the fabric of existing urban areas, travel distances can be reduced by switching to more local destinations, creating a built form which facilitates mode switching while also making best use of existing transport infrastructure and hence negating the need for capacity expansion. Complementary to urban concentration is a restrictive policy that prohibits building outside the urban area. Moreover, the policy is often implemented in conjunction with higher densities, mixed-use development and measures to improve public transport as well as cycling and walking. Other options involved in choice of location concern the connection of new developments to the public transport infrastructure.

The urban concentration concept seeks to reverse suburbanisation, and in so doing replicates the spatial configuration of older cities in order to support the same high modal share that walking, cycling and public transport enjoy in these areas (due to shorter trip lengths) relative to conventional suburban development. The following case study demonstrates that travel reduction has taken place where this measure has been implemented, although the impact may be relatively small.

The Netherlands

In the Netherlands, new construction is to be directed to the so-called VINEX locations (named after the acronym for the Fourth Report on Physical Planning Extra).

According to the compact city policy contained within VINEX, new housing development areas have to be sited in accordance with the urban concentration principle. A limited amount of residential development under the urban concentration principle has taken place so far. Empirical research has been generated in case studies of similar housing developments in two locations.

Hollander et al. (1996) have evaluated the impact of the proximity principle on the commuting rate, by comparing behaviour before and after moves to new residential locations, which resembled the VINEX locations in the Randstad, all being accessible by public transport. The research showed that with a use rate of 60%, the car was and has remained the preferred mode of transport. Furthermore, the use of the car showed hardly any tendency to decrease. The average journey to work has become slightly shorter. However, any reductions were entirely accounted for by a small number of households who had moved over a very long distance and had reduced their commuting substantially. The other households proved to have increased the distances they covered.

Konings et al. (1996) investigated 25 new residential locations in the province of Noord-Brabant. They compared the travel behaviour before and after the moves. They distinguished between three classes of locations (intra-urban, urban extensions and rural) and three density classes. That exercise revealed that after the moves, there was no reduction in the length of the journeys to work. Just as in the Randstad, the only reduction was brought about by a limited number of long-distance movers, while the others travelled further. Their study also showed that the usage of the car remained at a very high level. Even in combination with a residential relocation, travel behaviour proves hard to change. Nonetheless, a weak yet significant relationship between car travel and residential density did show up – the use of the car declines slightly where the density of the development increases. Yet the use of public transport remains disappointingly low. The bicycle, however, plays a remarkably large role, especially in the rural areas (Table 5.1).

The concept of proximity is a plausible assumption because it seeks to reduce travel at its source: if distances between activities are reduced, then travel distances may also reduce. However, complex socio-economic and demographic factors determine travel patterns as well as urban form. This may be the major cause of the poor results of the studies described above. Nevertheless, it is conceivable that continuing urban sprawl will result in a higher level of car use than would have been the case if no land-use policy to reduce travel had been implemented in

Table 5.1 Modal split (%) in the journey to work by location type and density in Noord-Brabant

Mode	Location type/Density					Total
	Rural/ ≤20	Rural/ 20–30	Urban extension/≤20	Urban extension/20–30	Urban concentration/>30	
Cyclist, pedestrian	24	31	21	23	27	**25**
Car	74	66	76	67	61	**69**
Public transport	2	3	3	10	12	**6**
Total	100	100	100	100	100	**100**

Note: Density figures are given in dwellings per hectare
Source: Konings et al., 1996

the first place. Moreover, a study of all travel (including shopping, leisure and social trips) with a longer time horizon may yield different results, as the built environment changes at a relatively slow pace, and its effects will only be felt over a long period of time.

5.3 Location of companies

Spatial planning tools such as land-use controls may be used at a district level to coordinate, facilitate and focus urban development at points of high public transport accessibility, namely nodes or interchanges. In doing so, it aims to enhance the attractiveness of public transport relative to the car, and so encourage mode and destination switching. In particular, large-scale generators of trips, such as shopping centres, are encouraged to locate at such points on the public transport network, so that this mode can 'capture' a large share of these trips.

This measure can achieve travel reduction, although this may be difficult to demonstrate. Like other land-use measures, it is implemented over a long period of time, with many of its effects becoming apparent only in the long term. The effects are greatest at the points on the public transport system with the greatest accessibility. The example of The Hague described below shows clearly what is achievable in good, accessible locations. Likewise, the greater the accessibility of the transport system as a whole, the larger the impacts will be through a 'network' effect. Good public transport accessibility is needed, not only at the destination (companies), but also at the origins (dwellings). However, this requires large-scale investment in public transport. It should be noted that investing in public transport may have the unwelcome effect of creating incentives to travel more, if improved capacity or service levels attract a new set of passengers. Improving the transport network and focusing development at nodal points may also lead to change without improvement, if

journey lengths increase as people switch destinations in response to the concentration of development at a limited number of key nodes.

The Netherlands

The Dutch ABC location policy sets conditions on where businesses can locate in order to control mobility. The mobility characteristics of the business have to match the accessibility characteristics of the area where it wishes to locate (Figure 5.1). Locations have been categorised as follows:

- A: highly accessible by public transport and tight restrictions on parking (10 spaces per 100 employees in the Randstad, 20 elsewhere); the target group involves labour- or visitor-intensive companies, such as offices or public facilities;

- B: good accessibility by both car (fewer parking restrictions, namely 20 spaces per 100 employees in the Randstad, 40 elsewhere) and public transport;

Figure 5.1 The principles of the Dutch ABC location policy

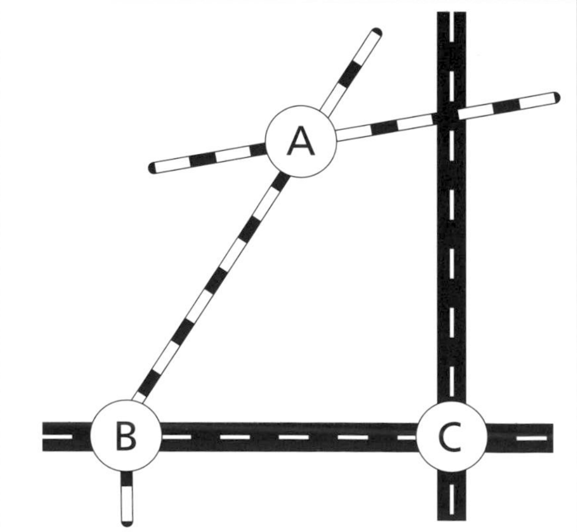

- C: highly accessible by car and less reachable by public transport, no parking restrictions; the target group are companies that need to be accessible by car or truck.

All new or amended local plans must grade development sites according to the above categories, while the mobility effects of new development must reflect their location. Municipalities have a range of objectives, and often attach considerable importance to the economic advantages that companies can provide, such as employment, revenues from land development and local taxes. As a consequence, they often grade development sites using the most flexible 'B' type to maximise the opportunity for development, trading off the mobility effects (Priemus and Maat, 1998).

Despite this, there are recorded examples of the policy having worked (MVROM, 1994). As a result of the ABC policy, in 1992 the Dutch Ministry of Housing, Spatial Planning and the Environment located its new offices beside the Central Station in The Hague, which is highly accessible by public transport and clearly an A-type location. The switch in travel destination induced a modal shift for commuting in favour of public transport (from 34 to 77% of all trips), whereas the car's share dropped from 41 to 4%, with a corresponding decrease in

distance travelled by car of 69% (Figure 5.2). However, the average commuting distance (all modes) increased by 8% to 20.6 km, while the share of cycle and walking trips decreased from 25 to 19%, as good public transport encouraged a modal switch. These effects are changing over time as employees change the location of their homes. In addition to the move to the new location, the Ministry implemented various other measures such as demand management and parking policy.

5.4 Mixed-use development

Different land uses may be mixed together in close proximity to encourage individuals to link trips (because several activities can be found in the one location), or change mode. The shorter trip lengths that can be generated in a mixed-use development are more amenable to walking, cycling and public transport. Mixed-use development can be found on all spatial scales, from a single building containing several different activities to entire urban areas (Figure 5.3). One example is introduction of a living/work space, which removes the need to commute. The mixing of land uses is commonly measured in terms of job ratio, which is the ratio of jobs in an area to workers resident in that area.

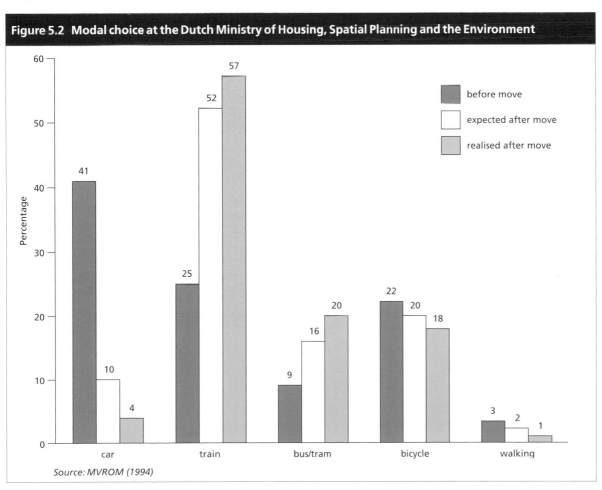

Figure 5.2 Modal choice at the Dutch Ministry of Housing, Spatial Planning and the Environment

before move
expected after move
realised after move

Source: MVROM (1994)

There has been a positive reaction to mixed-use development in the form of uptake and use of premises. However, as with other land-use measures it is difficult to find evidence of long-term change. Although the job ratio has been used as an indicator, little empirical research has examined its effect on travel patterns. Job ratios can have a statistical impact upon travel times, energy use per trip and modal split, although these impacts may be small.

Some problems may be encountered when implementing mixed-use development. Often the land-use planning system and the development process favour single-use developments, such as shopping malls and office parks. Institutional and policy barriers may exist, and a suitable package of land-use policies and tools must be in place to facilitate a change in the development to favour mixed-use development, such as the changes to planning regulations in the living/work example below.

London, UK

Living/work development is the provision of integrated living and working accommodation within a single self-contained unit. In Hackney, inner London, the local council has been promoting such units in recent years, and around 500 units have been built. A catalyst for this recent activity has been the development of new information and communication technologies, which allow people to run a home office or telecommute to a remote office elsewhere. Although there has been no empirical evidence yet, each of these units has the potential to remove at least one return home-to-work commuting journey per day.

The local council has had to amend the land-use regulatory system to allow these living/work units to be developed. Previously, the planning system would not have allowed residential and employment uses to coexist in the same unit. This increased flexibility in the regulation of land use has been matched by stricter controls on the parking provision for such units. Because of the potential for travel reduction, the council has allowed a maximum of only one parking space per unit, which is substantially less than the 1.5 spaces which are normally provided for a residential unit alone, without considering the spaces provided at employment units (Hackney Borough Council, 1996).

Glasgow, UK

Since 1991, public authorities in Glasgow have been developing a mixed-use urban neighbourhood in the

Figure 5.3 Mixed-use frontage in central London: uses can be mixed horizontally along a block, or vertically with different uses on different storeys

inner city. The project is an attempt to build a 'walkable neighbourhood unit', and it has been argued that a high pedestrian modal share of travel can be achieved by developing a mixed-use area, with a 1 km radius from the centre to the edge (25–35 ha in total). Eight hundred housing units are being clustered around Crown Street – a new public-transport-oriented road, lined with buildings containing a mixture of apartments, retail outlets, local facilities, offices and workshops, as well as a park (Urban Villages Forum, 1997).

Bucharest, Romania

After 1989, the private sector in Romania started to develop at a rapid rate, and in Bucharest various developments went ahead which were haphazardly located in the area of Iuliu Maniu Boulevard, where the existing public transport network is relatively good. Alongside existing businesses, a theatre, a commercial centre (METRO) and a petrol station have all been built. Many temporary commercial kiosks have been erected adjacent to footpaths, making retail outlets more accessible to commuters. The city authority decided to consolidate the development that was already taking place at this site by implementing a locational policy targeting the area, improving its public transport accessibility and introducing traffic management measures to restrain car use. This package of measures included a fourfold increase in the operational capacity of public transport vehicles in the period 1990–1997; the implementation of an environmentally friendly trolley-bus route in 1996; the installation of traffic signals and the reconfiguration of the main crossroads; and parking restrictions on the carriageway. Other measures will be implemented in the near future, including the relocation of a bus stop closer to the metro station (which will decrease the distance between the stops by 100 m and the transfer time by 1.6 min) and the implementation of an exclusive lane 3.5 m wide for public transport, together with priority traffic lights at successive intersections.

Although public transport passenger numbers increased by 41%, travelling conditions were better as load factors (i.e., the number of passengers on a bus, tram or train) decreased by 2% to 85% as a result of increased capacity. In 1997, 8% of car drivers used public transport more frequently than they had in 1996. Although these data show a mixed set of results in terms of overall travel reduction, they demonstrate that positive changes in behaviour do take place as the use of public transport can be dramatically increased through transport and land-use policies. Alongside these changes, there may also be an increase in the number of multipurpose trips (shopping, job, education, leisure) to this mixed-use area, which might otherwise have generated further single trips elsewhere (RATB, 1997).

5.5 Design of locations

New development is often highly car-dependent. Changing the way in which we develop land on a site-by-site basis offers the opportunity to influence travel behaviour positively. This measure is essentially concerned with the application of urban design and other spatial planning tools at a very local level so as to encourage mode switching by increasing the attractiveness of favoured modes. The main components of such a measure are:

- a layout that discourages car use, e.g., with a low speed limit and a reduced number of parking spaces per dwelling/business;
- a layout that promotes walking and cycling, e.g., with dedicated carriageways, and direct routes;
- high-density land use to increase the potential local customer base for public transport.

The impact of this measure is difficult to evaluate in the short term, since changes to urban form and its impacts are incremental in character. However, the case study described here does demonstrate long-term travel reduction. Its level of success depends on the strategic spatial framework within which it is implemented. For instance, a new suburb designed to promote cycling, but located at a great distance from the city centre (Figure 5.4), will have less effect on the level of cycling than a new residential area close to the city centre.

Empirical evidence also challenges the utility of certain key components of the measure. Dutch research has found only a small increase in the use of public transport in various new higher-densitiy residential neighbourhoods (Maat, 1999a). This small positive effect might not be enough to offset considerable social/cultural barriers to living at higher densities. Elsewhere, it has been concluded that higher densities may help to reduce the need to travel, but that this has to be balanced against the availability of open space (Banister et al., 1997). Therefore, developers and investors are unwilling in general to build high-density housing on a large scale (Maat, 1999b).

Figure 5.4 Greenfield development at Ypenburg: both the location and form of new developments may reduce the attractiveness of using green modes of transport

A rather successful example of a design measure is the new town of Houten. The built-up area of Houten has a green and suburban 'look' and is not built to a high density. It is clearly the domain of pedestrians and cyclists.

Houten, the Netherlands

Houten is situated near the city of Utrecht in the Netherlands and has a population of approximately 30,000. It was built in the 1970s and 1980s around a small existing village, and designed to minimise car use and to encourage other modes of travel. The layout of Houten (Figure 5.5) is bicycle-friendly, and there is a direct railway service to central Utrecht. The shopping centre and offices are located near the railway station(s), in the middle of the town. All residential neighbourhoods are within approximately 1.5 km of the city centre. A dense network of amenable cycle routes forms the backbone of the system, and there are direct cycle routes to the city centre as well as secondary routes connecting all neighbourhoods and other destinations generating cycle traffic. However, access by car to most of the neighbourhoods requires a more circuitous route to the city centre by way of the ring road just outside the built-up area, and this also discourages through-traffic. It is striking that Houten does not need parking measures to discourage car use as there is only a limited role for the car.

Car trip generation in Houten is about 10% less than the Dutch average, despite car ownership levels being among the highest. Cycle use for shopping and commuting is high, with a frequent rail service to Utrecht and large cycle storage facilities at the railway station (Bach, 1996).

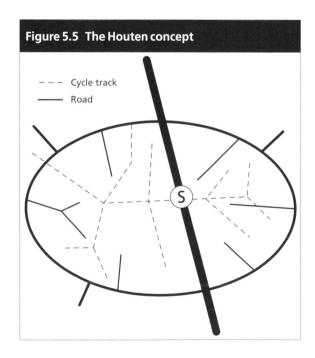

Figure 5.5 The Houten concept

- – – Cycle track
- —— Road

Figure 5.6 shows that compared with similar villages, walking and cycling in particular are higher in the zones more than 500 m from the centre. However, the radical design of Houten does have some drawbacks. Although few cars are used for shopping purposes, the distances travelled by these cars is high, because there are no direct routes from the neighbourhoods to the shopping centre. The overall travel distances for shopping by car in Houten are therefore more or less the same as in comparable cities (Brükx et al., 1993). The same principles behind the built form have been used in other proposals for developments around the Netherlands, but not at the same level. Consequently, Houten is rather a unique case, even in the Netherlands.

5.6 Car-free developments

By restricting people's ability to use a car in some way, they may be encouraged to mode-switch. Implementation takes place on a site-by-site basis using land-use planning policy tools, such as planning regulations, which remove parking provision in new developments. However, contractual control can also be exerted: the user of the development agrees (with the developer/local authority) not to own and operate a car from the site, in return for occupation rights. In conjunction with this restriction on ownership, car-sharing schemes involving a car pool can meet the occasional needs of the occupier (Section 2.3).

This is a relatively new measure; there are few examples of car-free developments in practice, so their impact on travel behaviour is unrecorded. However, Dutch evidence suggests that giving up ownership of a car can be an effective way to reduce travel by this mode. A survey of the participants in four car-sharing schemes found that people who gave up personal car ownership reduced the distance they drove each year by 65%.

There has been a positive reaction to the measure, and a small but growing number of car-free housing schemes are being proposed, are under construction or have been built, particularly in urban areas. These range in size from single-building developments in London through to large estates, such as the 600-dwelling GWL area in Westerpark, Amsterdam. Urban design initiatives in the form of the removal of parking provision are more commonly used in such schemes than contractual controls. Schemes with contractual controls are proving more difficult to develop, perhaps because they more explicitly restrict an individual's liberty than the 'softer' urban design-led schemes. For instance, the 220-unit Hollerland project in Bremen failed through non-acceptance, with

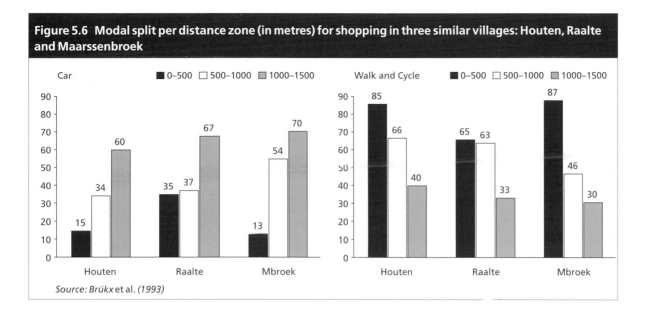

Figure 5.6 Modal split per distance zone (in metres) for shopping in three similar villages: Houten, Raalte and Maarssenbroek

Source: Brükx et al. (1993)

potential occupiers citing (among other things) concern about the lack of flexibility with contracts should their mobility needs change over time. Beyond such individual concerns, there are also potential institutional and legal barriers to car-free development regarding the legality of a no-car ownership agreement. Moreover, local authority regulations often stipulate that a minimum number of parking spaces must be provided per dwelling.

London, UK

The London Borough of Camden has recently incorporated the promotion of car-free housing into its Green Transport Strategy for this part of inner London. To achieve this goal, it has identified the parts of the Borough most amenable to this type of development (the district closest to central London with the best public transport links), and has set a target that at least 25% of new housing in this area should be car-free. It is using the planning system and urban design as a mechanism to achieve car-free housing, and has changed local regulations on parking provision to encourage developers to design car-free schemes: controls stipulating maximum, and not minimum, numbers of spaces per dwelling controls now apply. There has been a positive reaction to the strategy, and developers seem willing to accept these changes, as do homebuyers. Three schemes are currently under construction, with housing units selling well.

Edinburgh, UK

In December 1995, Edinburgh became the first council in Britain to grant outline planning consent to a car-free housing development. It took until June 1998 for detailed planning permission to be granted, and the development will become available in April 2000. It is being built by the Canmore Housing Association and will provide for 120 flats (Figure 5.7). It is situated just west of the city centre with an excellent provision of public transport at the site (see Section 7.5). Plans to make residents sign a pledge not to own a car (Mittler, 1999a) did, in the end, prove impossible to implement. But there will be no provision for car parking at the site and the concierge at the development will have control over the vehicle in- and out-flow. Access will be allowed only for essential deliveries, removal vans and the emergency services. Normally, access will be via footpaths and a dedicated cycle route, which skirts the entire scheme. The development has a number of desirable features from a sustainable development point of view, not least its (re-)use of waste heat from a brewery across the road.

Its travel reduction impact, meanwhile, will be real but limited. Most residents who move into the flats would not own a car, regardless of where they lived (only 17% of residents in other Canmore Housing Association properties own cars). However, 26 flats are developed for shared ownership and 25 are being sold in the private sector. The residents moving into these 51 flats will be most likely to have made a conscious decision not to own a car. The scheme has generated considerable interest. It aims to demonstrate the financial viability of car-free housing developments, and thus it contributes to travel reduction as a symbol and example, as much as being a functioning housing scheme.

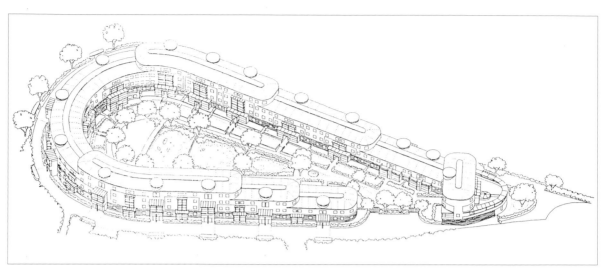

Figure 5.7 Car-free housing development in Edinburgh

5.7 Conclusion

Reducing the need to travel, in particular by car, requires consideration of certain basic conditions, which are shaped by the urban form and structure. Travel is derived from the requirement to bridge the gap between activities. The shorter the distances between living, working and leisure facilities, the shorter the distance to be travelled, because more activities can be linked in one trip. Furthermore, shorter distances are easier to carry out on foot or by bicycle (soft modes). The second reason for using urban form is in the design of locations that discourage car use and encourage the use of, firstly, soft modes and, secondly, public transport. Travel reduction can be built up by using an appropriate urban form.

However, although urban form shapes the conditions, socio-economic, demographic and lifestyle are additional factors that determine travel patterns. For instance, dual-income households make longer trips on average, since they are oriented towards two places of work. Moreover, because these families have a more complex activity pattern, they will increasingly use the car, as this is the fastest and most flexible mode. Although physical design cannot cause changes in behaviour, it may at least support or assist the choice of change (Table 5.2).

Land-use planning measures may work best for specific types of trip with a fixed spatial dimension, such as commuting or local shopping. For other trip purposes, land-use planning has less potential to provide alternatives. There is a need to recognise that the solutions offered, such as high-density living and mixed-use zoning, may cater for the tastes of only a limited proportion of the population. These solutions would not accommodate those individuals in search of more open space or exclusively residential neighbourhoods.

Land-use planning measures can be applied at a variety of levels, from regional policy down to an individual plot or even a single building. The spatial limitation of any individual land-use measure means that, for a particular trip, both origin and destination need to be favourable for use of public transport or non-motorised modes. If only one of these end points is favourable, there may be a tendency to persist with use of the car on grounds of convenience. This implies that it would be beneficial to apply policies consistently at the regional, or even national, level.

However, land-use solutions applied to particular localities may not necessarily discourage car use in general. Thus, if conditions are made too unfavourable for car use in one location, individuals may simply take their car elsewhere. There is some degree of self-selectivity among users: those who choose to live in developments which are pedestrian- or bicycle-friendly, or where cars are explicitly banned, may be that segment of the population who do not choose to use or own a car in the first place. However, without the availability of such developments, those individuals may have no alternative but to own and use a car.

In comparison with other types of travel-reduction measures, land-use solutions can take a long time to be effective. The built environment is renewed only slowly, and new developments intended to promote particular travel outcomes will represent only a marginal addition to the travel reduction potential of the total built environment. However, once 'built in' to an area, the underlying

Table 5.2 Summary of land-use measures

Measure	Travel reduction	Lessons and limitations
Location of new developments	Mode switching Destination switching	The right location is a major condition for travel distance (reducing trip length) and mode choice (basis for bicycle and public transport), but, socio-economic and demographic factors have greater effects
Location of companies	Mode switching Destination switching	Right company at the right location: in particular, labour- and visitor-intensive companies should be located at nodal points of public transport (modal switch) Accessibility from origins is important, as well as parking restrictions, although most companies prefer car accessibility without parking restrictions
Mixed-use development	Mode switching Linking trips	Mixed use encourages trip linking and switching to soft modes, and provides a better basis for public transport Mixed use development at interchange on the public transport network, but such development is not always allowed by the planning system (environmental nuisance, such as noise and air pollution, as well as safety risk)
Design of locations	Mode switching	Combination of suburban preferences and mode switching to soft modes and public transport has good potential Cycle tracks and public transport facilities should be combined with discouraging car use Reduced car use can mean fewer but longer car trips
Car-free development	Mode switching	Combined with design of location Legal barrier: in some countries, prohibiting car ownership may be illegal

travel reduction potential should remain in place, passively, over the long term (i.e., without the need for further proactive policies). Urban planning, in particular mixed-use development, can also promote urban vitality over longer periods of the day.

Finally, it may be noted that land-use planning measures often overlap in scope and tend to be complementary to each other. There is also good potential for combination with other types of measures, both restraining car use and

promoting alternatives. Thus, high-density developments featuring urban concentration are commensurate with public transport promotion; high-density and mixed-use developments can mean that destinations are close together, hence promoting walking and cycling. Land-use policies can also restrict parking availability or ban the use of cars. Similarly, mixed-use development is commensurate with bringing homes and workplaces together (see Section 6.5) and with promoting activities outside the normal working day.

Technological Means of Reducing Travel

6.1 Introduction

Technology is one of the most powerful influences in society, and its contemporary impacts are likely to be as profound as those arising from the Industrial Revolution 200 years ago. Technology now influences all aspects of production, consumption and life.

In transport, technology is influential in at least three different ways. It is used to improve the efficiency with which production of vehicles takes place and the design of the vehicles themselves, together with development of new fuels. It also has a major impact on the organisation and management of transport systems, such as distribution (e.g., logistics, just-in-time deliveries, inventory databases), information exchange, control (e.g., area traffic control and air traffic control systems) and more recently route guidance systems (in vehicles). The third major application of technology is directly to change travel patterns. Technology has a potentially powerful role in allowing activities to be undertaken with little or no travel, where travel was previously required.

However, the substitution of technology for transport is not a simple effect. In the past, all forms of new technology (e.g., the telephone) facilitated additional travel as contact networks were widened and as arrangements for meetings could be made spontaneously. It would seem that the new technologies, including the new communication forms (e.g., fax, e-mail, the Internet, mobile phones), allow even greater flexibility and may add substantially to the demand for travel. In addition, if these new forms of technology are to be truly portable, it is likely that they may be fitted as options (or even as standard equipment) in new cars. The opportunity to substitute technology for travel is available, but the actual impact is likely to be complex and subject to change over a very short time period. Its main advantage is that it allows a huge new flexibility in travel and for arrangements to be undertaken with much shorter lead times. Established patterns of activities are becoming less standard as new patterns emerge which are both tailored to individual requirements and adaptable to short-term changes in circumstance.

This chapter describes four possibilities for positive applications of technology to reduce travel. They relate mainly to the direct impact on travel patterns (the third group of technological impacts mentioned above), but route guidance systems are also covered. It is clear from the examples that the possibilities of technological means to change travel patterns are enormous as they impact on all areas (both rural and urban), on all types of activities and apply to all groups of users. However, judgement must be cautious when claims are made about the actual reductions in travel. Even if the direct influence of technology leads to the reduction (or elimination) of one set of trips, it often means that the vehicle and the time are released for other types of use. The indirect effects must also be included in any assessment of the real changes resulting from technological innovation.

6.2 Home delivery of goods and services

With this measure, the providers of goods and services deliver their products directly to their customers, rather than requiring each customer to travel to the provider. Generally, this involves a service provider or delivery vehicle making multiple-stop journeys to customers at their homes or businesses. This substitutes for travel by trip modification, removing the need for a trip by each customer, and making the provider's trip more efficient by linking trips to several customers. Where a large number of delivery trips are required, scheduling software may be used to increase the efficiency of trips.

Home delivery services may be implemented with the explicit aim of reducing travel. Alternatively, however, the primary aim may be to improve access to services and facilities in isolated areas. Among the measures considered in this book, home delivery is unusual in that it does not rely on implementation by central government or local authorities, but can be put in place by the manufacturers and/or providers of goods and services themselves.

Evidence from the Lesvos case study below suggests that mobile goods and service provision can facilitate travel reduction by limiting the number of trips necessary to meet the needs of isolated island customers for goods and services. Home delivery can also improve access to services and facilities in isolated areas, particularly rural ones. However, as with the mobile shops on the island of Lesvos, the high costs involved in delivering goods and services can mean that the goods themselves are more expensive than those purchased in central areas.

Lesvos, Greece

A variety of mobile services is available on the rural Greek island of Lesvos. They have not been planned by a central authority, but have evolved to meet the accessibility needs of the island's rural population. They also have the potential to reduce car use in the island capital of Mytilini, by reducing travel to the city.

Three of the island's banks operate a mobile banking service to serve villages and small towns. In all, 27 of the island's 72 settlements (representing around 40% of the rural population of Lesvos) are served by these mobile banking outlets, on average around three or four times per week. In the summer months, four additional villages are included on the route, to serve tourist needs.

As the banking vans are not able to communicate with the central headquarters, the majority of transactions that they conduct are simple; yet an average of 110,000 transactions are performed by the mobile banks each year, representing around 10% of the total number carried out in the central banks of Mytilini. This banking activity corresponds to approximately 47,000 people (or 30,000 households) eligible to hold an account. It has been calculated that the provision of mobile banking services saves around 400 trips per day to Mytilini, based on the assumption that all transactions would otherwise have been carried out in that city. However, as it is possible that not all of these trips would have been made to Mytilini in the absence of a mobile banking service, this estimate should be regarded as an upper limit.

The island currently has 71 licences for mobile shops, 46 of which concern food-related trades. The average income of these mobile shops has been estimated at around 150,000 euros per year. Negative aspects include the time spent travelling by the service provider between customers, and the space limitations of trading from a van. These factors, coupled with rising fuel prices, mean the cost of goods from mobile shops is generally higher than those in central village shops. Service and freight-transport agents

are among the other mobile providers. Service agents gather requests for services or official documents which are only available centrally, travel to Mytilini as official representatives of their customers to collect the documents and then return to the villages for distribution. Freight agents offer a similar service for heavy or bulky goods. It is thought that these services, as with the mobile banking service, reduce travel by limiting the number of trips necessary to meet the needs of isolated island customers (DANTE Consortium, 1997: Appendix 12, pp. 304–307).

6.3 Informatics

Informatics are electronic information systems which are used in transport in various ways to optimise and guide the flow of traffic in order to improve efficiency and relieve congestion, by encouraging car users to switch their destination or time of travel. They can be used to monitor traffic, to act as a means of communication and to disseminate information. The application of these technology measures has grown rapidly in the last few years with the development of powerful computers. They are used by traffic management and planning authorities, who implement them at a regional level, as well as by individuals, users who are provided with travel information and guidance. Informatics systems range from in-vehicle technology to large-scale traffic management systems.

Examples of informatics system applications in the context of travel reduction strategies are:

- traffic information systems, providing users with information on road conditions, weather or congestion;

- route guidance systems, providing information on the most efficient route or alternative routes in case of congestion, accidents or roadworks;

- parking information systems, advising drivers on the location of, and route to, available parking facilities;

- strategic traffic management systems, providing authorities with information on congestion, weather or traffic incidents.

Informatics systems are typically used to improve the efficiency of flow of traffic in and around cities, and can facilitate travel reduction. However, this increased efficiency can result in additional capacity being released, which in turn increases the attractiveness of car travel and thus may generate additional traffic. Informatics systems can also help car drivers to choose more efficient routes, which can reduce the total trip length and the transit time. Furthermore, an optimal utilisation of capacity and reduced congestion will have derived benefits for surrounding routes.

Aalborg, Denmark

In 1995 a parking information system was installed in the city of Aalborg, with the aim of applying telematics to reduce the traffic generated by vehicle drivers looking for parking space, as well as improving conditions for those parking in the city. The system provides information on the availability of vacant parking spaces and on the optimal route to parking locations (Figure 6.1). The measure contributes to the overall city policy through a more efficient utilisation of the parking facilities, in order to reduce traffic volumes in the city centre

In evaluating the effects of the measure, ten gates were set up along the outer perimeter of the city. Drivers were asked which gate they used, and which route they took to the parking facility. Based on this, 'before' and 'after' matrices were set up to describe the distribution of trips between the parking facilities and the gates, and the average trip lengths. The number of vehicles in each of the parking facilities per day was registered by means of the parking information system (Table 6.1).

In terms of attitudes towards the system and its general acceptance, 67% of all respondents felt that the parking information system was an improvement. In terms of behavioural changes it was concluded that:

- 7% of respondents believed they had changed their parking habits;
- fewer searched in vain for parking space – parking search activity had been reduced by 12% in the four highest-load parking facilities;

Figure 6.1 Aalborg: P-info variable message sign showing availability of parking spaces

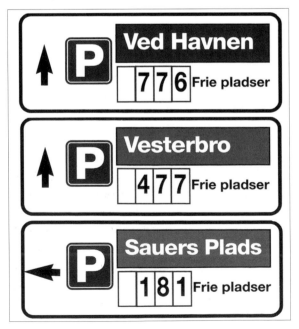

Table 6.1 Parking information system: traffic effects

Parameter	Effect
Reduction in average trip length from gate to parking (m)	115
Total reduction (vehicle km/day)	930
Annual total reduction (vehicle km)	280 000
Reduction in total traffic in city centre (%)	0.3

Note: Data are for weekdays and Saturdays; exludes Sundays.
Source: Hansen (1996)

- the number of drivers who decided where to park before the trip was increased by 14%.

The city centre business community is positive towards the system because it is an improvement of the service to their customers. Moreover, the system provides information on parking facilities in the city centre, which is important in terms of competition with larger shopping centres elsewhere.

The effects of the measure are more or less in line with what was expected in the city of Aalborg: the users of the system are positive, and it has become easier to locate parking space in the city. There are, however, some adverse effects that may undermine the benefits. More people may go to the city centre by car because parking has become easier. This is highlighted in the survey, which revealed that 3% of respondents believed they made more trips to the city centre after the system was established.

6.4 Teleactivities

Information and communication technologies can be used by individuals and organisations to interact electronically, rather than physically. This electronic contact can take the form of social interactions, such as e-mail and newsgroups, or transactions for commercial and public goods or services, such as telebanking. The need to make a trip is removed by substitution of technology. Teleactivities are aspatial, and can therefore be provided at any location where there is access to the necessary equipment.

Teleactivities can be used to realise travel-reduction objectives. Although relatively new, this measure is growing in significance, and a large number of organisations, from retailers through to municipalities, now operate interactive electronic services. As the case study below demonstrates, teleactivities can successfully remove the need to travel, without affecting the purpose of the trip.

However, the wider effects are a little less clear and contradictory outcomes may exist. It is difficult to determine the possible consequences of enabling people to undertake Internet activities, for which their physical location is insignificant. For instance, long-distance relationships initiated on the Internet (which might not have otherwise existed) may create additional trips, should this tele-activity be converted subsequently into physical travel.

Environment97 Conference

In November 1997 an environmental conference (organised by the UK Institute for Chemical Engineers) was held on the Internet, for interested professionals and academics, with a view to reducing the impact of conferences on the environment. It took place over several days; the website contained many of the features of a conventional conference, including the presentation of papers, which were released onto the website at specific times, subsequent discussions and even exhibition stands (Figure 6.2). The facilities of the website were accessed by clicking on electronically generated images of familiar sites (e.g., participants enrolled by clicking on a picture of a reception desk in a lobby).

Records were kept of the people using the site, from which a travel impact analysis was made. According to a questionnaire filled in by participants from around the world, 9,000 of them would have attended the conference if it had taken place physically (in London). It was calculated that had these people actually attended a conventional conference in this city, they would have travelled a total of 32 million kilometres, generating almost 1,000 tonnes of CO_2. In reality, the only energy consumed by attendance at the conference was that used by computing and telecommunications equipment.

6.5 Teleworking

Telecommunications can be used to allow an individual to work at a location remote from their normal place of work, thereby replacing commuter journeys with electronic communication. As part of a broader group of measures which substitute travel with technology, the measure can be implemented anywhere that the necessary computing and telecommunication equipment is available.

The nature of teleworking depends on the place from which the electronic connection takes place. Some individuals work from home, whereas others pay to use special collective facilities at telecentres. Teleworking can even take place on the move; for example, an employee may work on a train journey between two clients, negating the need to make a trip back to the office.

Teleworking is becoming more widespread because technological advances and new organisational practices allow individuals to plan their own work schedule more flexibly.

Figure 6.2 The Environment97 website home page: non-travel in hyper-reality

This increased interest is reflected in the number of studies investigating the potential of this measure. In Europe as a whole, it has been predicted that in the year 2000, one in 10 of the working population will be connected to their office computer systems from their homes (Graham and Marvin, 1996).

At least one of the case studies shows that teleworking can reduce travel by a small amount. However, one of the continuing barriers to the development of teleworking in Europe is a lack of information on successful models and development strategies, which are important for a relatively new and innovative measure. One resource barrier is the potential cost of the necessary equipment, which both employers and employees may be reluctant to pay. Furthermore, the case study illustrates that there may be some social implications of working in isolation from home. To overcome these barriers, the following guidelines for employees have been developed:

- teleworkers should be company employees and not deemed self-employed;
- to avoid isolation, contracts of employment should require home workers to work periodically from the office;
- there should be a separate room available at home for teleworking, with a dedicated telephone line, and payment for additional costs such as heating and lighting;
- there should be regular meetings between teleworkers, and electronic mail and telephone links should be provided to other teleworkers at the employer's expense;
- there should be a regular weekly liaison discussions between a teleworker and his or her supervisor/manager;
- teleworkers should enjoy the same rates of pay and employment benefits as office-based workers, including child care provision and family leave, and should be included in career development and appraisal schemes with training opportunities;
- there should be a defined number of working hours.

The Netherlands

The Netherlands Ministry of Transport introduced a range of measures aimed at restraining mobility in the Netherlands, one of which was to stimulate teleworking in order to substitute telecommunications for travel. Teleworking could offer flexibility such that, where travel was required, it could be made outside peak periods, thereby avoiding congestion. The Netherlands Structure Plan set a target of reducing all peak-hour traffic by 5% (1995–2015) by the use of teleworking. Three experiments in the period 1990–1994 involved surveys of teleworkers

and also covered other household members by means of travel diaries and periodic questionnaires. The results of the experiments are summarised below.

In Experiment 1 (30 workers; some self-selectivity), teleworkers made 17% fewer trips, and travelled 16% less distance than before. Car use by teleworkers decreased, especially for car passengers, for whom it fell by 27%. Meanwhile, others in the household made 9% fewer trips, but in some cases the distance they travelled increased.

In Experiment 2 (30 workers; some self-selectivity), teleworkers made 10% fewer trips, with travel distance down 14%. Travel by public transport was reduced by 63%, but travel by car did not decrease. The distance travelled for others in the household increased in several cases, while the distance travelled at weekends increased, both for teleworkers (73%) and others (137%).

In Experiment 3 (204 workers), the average number of trips on a teleworking day was about half that of a normal working day. The average distance on a teleworking day was under one tenth of that on a normal day, while the average travelling time on a teleworking day was about 40% of that on a normal day.

It can be seen that in Experiments 1 and 2 there was a clear reduction in the total number of trips made by teleworkers, while for other household members there were some increases in travel. The reduction in travel for teleworkers applied to all modes (except for the car in Experiment 2). Experiment 3 also supported the result that teleworkers made fewer trips, travelled considerably less distance, and also spent less time travelling. In terms of travel reduction parameters, there was a decrease in trips, vehicle kilometres and vehicle hours (TUD, 1997).

Rome, Italy

The TRADE pilot project created telecentres and related infrastructure in Rome, in order to encourage teleworking, thereby reducing the need to commute and improving the quality of life for participants. The project involved 33.6% of the municipal workers who included teleworking as part of their daily routine. On average, the reduction in the level of travel for participants amounted to 0.8 km per trip. It has been calculated that full-scale implementation would have led to a reduction in travel of 3,000,000 km per year in the short term, with a 0.7% reduction in vehicle emissions. However, although 91% of participants were satisfied overall with teleworking, 14% expressed concern about the lack of human contact, and 5% encountered more domestic problems (Municipality of Rome, 1996).

Table 6.2 Summary of technological measures

Measure	Travel reduction	Lessons and limitations
Home delivery of goods and services	Trip modification Trip linkages	Often used to improve access to services and facilities in isolated areas Potential for introduction by public authorities or the private sector
Informatics	Destination switch Time switching Trip modification	Huge potential now being realised in management, monitoring, information Improved efficiency in the system may lead to more, rather than less, travel
Teleactivities	Trip substitution	Access to telefacilities is strongly related to income and knowledge, together with the necessary skills Reduces the impact of distance as the technology is aspatial May substantially increase the contact network of individuals, or eventually generate more trips
Teleworking	Trip substitution	Already common practice with many companies Estimates have often been very optimistic Actual patterns of teleworking are very complex

6.6 Conclusion

As noted in Section 6.1 and from the evidence cited here, it is clearly agreed that technology has an enormous potential for changing travel patterns. It is also agreed that this potential will be realised, but whether the net effect is a travel reduction is much less certain. History and some recent evidence suggests that technology in all its forms will increase, not decrease, travel as it facilitates moving around. The more specific applications of technology outlined here (Table 6.2) give some hope that, under certain conditions, travel reduction will take place. It seems that two conditions will have to be met. Firstly, technological innovation must be introduced as part of a set of measures. Home deliveries from supermarkets, for example, could be combined with public transport services to the supermarkets (as no shopping then has to be carried), free Internet access to the shop (so that there is no need to travel to shop), and parking charges at the supermarket (to discourage car trips).

Secondly, as with many of the measures outlined in these last five chapters, a clear level of support and commitment from the general public is essential. People have to be convinced about both the necessity and desirability of travel reduction strategies, and they have to be prepared to take positive action themselves. Without that commitment to support and action, no real change will take place. This requires the public to reassess their personal priorities so that notions of the common good come first. This is an essential prerequisite to any form of sustainable transport system.

Part II: Policy into Action

Combining Measures

7.1 Introduction

The list of policies that have the potential to reduce travel is substantial. Some 30 measures have been discussed in Part I of this book, and they could easily be subdivided further into more specialised policy instruments. As pointed out in Chapter 1, these travel reduction measures include a host of conventional transport policies – such as the promotion of public transport – as well as more dedicated or radical measures such as capacity reduction.

In the right circumstances such measures may reduce travel effectively. In most cases, however, their success will depend on the influence of other policies, which may either complement and hence reinforce the travel-reducing potential of an individual measure, or detract from its success. In particular, we have observed how some measures, such as promoting public transport, are normally associated with increasing travel to some extent, unless accompanied by mode switching away from lower-occupancy vehicles such as the private car. Similarly, some travel reduction mechanisms may combine beneficially to amplify the travel-reducing impact (Chapter 8). When implementing travel reduction policies, therefore, it will normally be advantageous to combine complementary measures into packages.

Studying those cities that are trying to reduce travel, we see that in most cases a number of different measures are implemented, whether this is deliberately planned or occurs coincidentally. As a first step in analysing the combination of measures, we first examine some of the reasons for it.

Reasons for combining measures

To provide prerequisites for successful implementation

For a certain measure to work, it may be necessary to have first implemented other measures; this would apply where it is necessary to provide capacity by means of an alternative corridor or an alternative mode. For example, if a bicycle promotion campaign is to be effective, it may be necessary to establish a sufficient bicycle infrastructure, or some other visible investment in conditions for cyclists. Also, it would almost certainly apply to the general case of media campaigns, where some prior material implementation of measures is likely to be necessary as the basis for promotion.

To enhance or boost the effects of measures already implemented

A measure may increase the positive effects of another measure that is already implemented, possibly capitalising on the investment already made in implementing the original measure. For example, improving the frequency or speed of a bus service could increase the use of a Park and Ride facility.

To serve a variety of stakeholders

In the political process it is often necessary to balance the interests of a variety of stakeholders. Implementation of combinations of measures that are not necessarily directly related can be a tool for policy makers to serve these different stakeholders. It may be easier to implement a package that contains both 'popular' and 'unpopular' components, and that is seen to be fair, even where travel-reducing components are only present in some of the measures, than to introduce the 'unpopular' measures alone.

Thus, for example, if a city decides to close certain streets to private cars, it may be necessary to invest in improved parking facilities, so as not to disbenefit car drivers.

To achieve a greater visible impact

A simple reason for combining measures can be that a greater number of measures will most probably result in a more significant and visible impact. A successful package can therefore be a good advertisement for the behaviour patterns being promoted, and hence may lead to more success. For example, the combination of closure of a shopping street to general traffic and introduction of a light rail route along it would present the street users with

Table 7.1 Summary of packaged measures

City/Case	Measure	Location	Switching mechanism	Push/Pull
Enschede	Stadserf (central area access control)	City centre	Mode, destination	Push
	Parking control	City centre	Mode	Push
	Cycle network	City	Mode	Pull
	Park and Ride	Radial	Mode	Pull
	Bus lanes	Various	Mode	Pull
	Bus priority	Various	Mode	Pull
	Traffic calming and road closure	City	Mode	Push
	Media campaign	Selected neighbourhoods	Mode	Push and Pull
Zürich	'Speed-up' measure (public transport priority)	City	Mode	Pull
	Restricted roadspace for cars	City	Mode	Push
	S-Bahn	City and to/from hinterland	Mode	Pull
	Park and Ride	City and to/from hinterland	Mode	Pull
	Parking restriction	Inner city	Mode	Push
	Public transport-oriented development	City	Mode	Pull
Aarhus	Road closure	City centre	Mode, route/destination	Push
	Bus axis	City centre	Mode	Pull
	Bicycle paths	City centre	Mode	Pull
	Pedestrian space	City centre	Mode	Pull
Edinburgh	Roadspace reallocation	Urban corridor	Mode	Push/Pull
	Bus lanes	Urban corridor	Mode	Pull
	Bus priority at 'smart' traffic lights	Urban corridor	Mode	Pull
	Cycle lanes	Urban corridor	Mode	Pull
	Car-free housing	Inner city	Mode	Pull
Bristol–Bath	Bus lanes	Corridor	Mode	Pull
	Park and Ride	Corridor	Mode	Pull
	Cycle route	Corridor	Mode	Pull
	Rail service	Corridor	Mode	Pull
	New development permission	Corridor Area	Mode	Pull
Nottingham	Car pooling	Site	Mode, linking trips	Push/Pull
	Cycle initiatives	Site	Mode	Pull
	Works buses	Site	Mode	Pull
	Promotion and information	Site	Mode, linking trips	Push/Pull

tangible evidence of a way in which good public transport access can be coupled with a car-free shopping environment. Additionally, the identity of a series of measures as a 'package' could assist in the promotion of those measures as a whole.

Unintentional or accidental combinations

In some cases the conjunction of measures may not have an explicit 'reason', but may occur accidentally or coincidentally. In some cases the resulting combination might be counterproductive (see Chapter 12), and by definition 'unintentional' combination would not be the aim of the policy-making process. However, where fortuitous combinations do occur, these can be numbered among the cases of good practice, and lessons may be learned from them for future policy making.

Method of combination

With these possibilities in mind, we turn to the question of how the measures should be optimally packaged to achieve policy objectives. It would be theoretically possible to model a multitude of combinations of measures to test which were most beneficial. However, there may be little enough data available to establish whether travel reduction has taken place in a particular situation, let alone to isolate individual components of cause and effect (see Chapter 9). The approach adopted here is therefore to examine case

studies where combinations have been applied in practice, and to observe the aggregated effects. From this analysis some general conclusions may be drawn.

Cities, then, typically use combinations of measures to achieve results. Even though they cannot prove precisely which measure achieved the desired effect, it is clear whether the combination of measures as a whole has worked. To illustrate how this can be done, in Sections 7.2–7.7 we will present some examples of how measures have been combined successfully.

The background transport situation and policies in the locations concerned are described briefly, with demonstrations of how different measures have been combined and conclusions about the eventual travel reduction effect (Table 7.1).

7.2 A citywide package: Enschede, the Netherlands

Background

In 1996 the Municipality of Enschede (Figure 7.1) introduced its new Mobility Plan which will run from 1996 to 2005 (Geemente Enschede, 1996). This new plan was necessary because car traffic was still growing

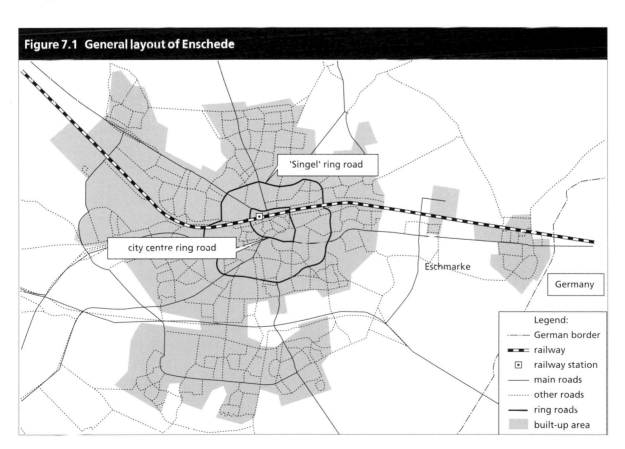

Figure 7.1 General layout of Enschede

'Singel' ring road

city centre ring road

Eschmarke

Germany

Legend:
- German border
- railway
- railway station
- main roads
- other roads
- ring roads
- built-up area

(despite all kinds of measures in the past), resulting in an ongoing negative impact on the capacity of the road network, traffic safety and the city environment. The main objective of the Mobility Plan is the reduction of the continual growth of intra-urban car use by making cycling and public transport more attractive. Compared with the previous Road Structure Plan, the emphasis is more on intra-urban traffic, and both public transport and cycling are seen as equally acceptable alternatives to the car. According to the Mobility Plan, the residents of Enschede are encouraged to travel by bicycle and public transport for their trips within the city. This allows the limited road capacity to be used by visitors from outside, who are more dependent on the car and who are important to the economy of the city centre. Accordingly, the first priority is to deal with mobility in and around the city centre, which is followed by improvement of the liveability of residential areas by reducing speed and eliminating rat-running (Figure 7.2).

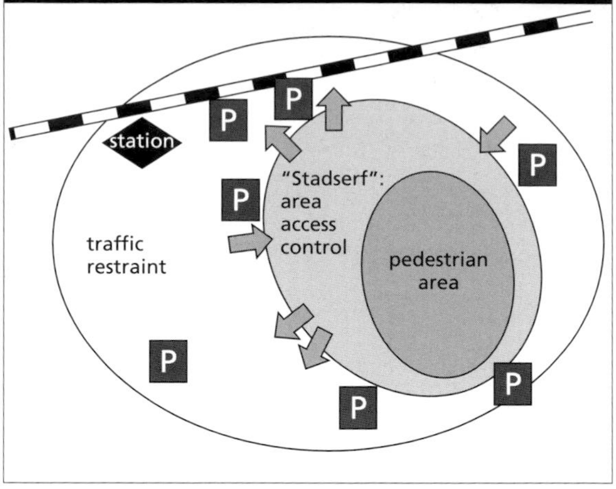

Measures implemented

To implement the policy, the Municipality of Enschede has been introducing various measures in an integrated way since 1993. At first, the city centre was restricted to cars. This was not implemented all at once, but in two stages. As the restricted area was expanded, parking was gradually removed from the city centre and concentrated in car parks adjacent to the city centre ring road. The number of car parks with charges increased; on-street parking was reduced, parking control was extended to surrounding residential neighbourhoods (by parking permit schemes) and charges for long-stay parking were increased. However, the total number of parking places was not reduced, in order to maintain the attractiveness of the city centre as a shopping and leisure destination.

At the same time, the city's bicycle network was extended and more cycle storage facilities were built in the city centre. All the main cycle routes are oriented towards the city centre (see Section 3.2). In Enschede there were several experiments with Park and Ride schemes aimed at shoppers from the surrounding region and Germany. At present there is one highly successful Park and Ride scheme on certain days, targeted especially towards German visitors, while for the Enschede residents special cheap tickets for the city buses have been introduced. During the 1980s, public transport gradually received more attention. In several new residential areas, bus lanes were built. Also, various bus priority measures at traffic lights were implemented. All of these measures had the same aim: to restrict intra-urban car use by making cycling and public transport more attractive to the citizens (see Section 3.4).

Figure 7.2 Enschede: areas of traffic restraint and access control

During the 1980s and 1990s the link between traffic planning and land-use planning became closer, particularly in the case of new residential areas. At first new residential areas were equipped with separate bicycle tracks and bus lanes. Later, the designs changed: not only were residential areas designed to promote cycling and public transport, but also to discourage car use. Traffic calming is now a usual feature in new residential areas, while older neighbourhoods are also being provided gradually with road closures, speed humps, one-way streets, etc. All of these measures are aimed at discouraging through-traffic which has no intentional destination within the residential areas (see Section 4.5).

The 1990s also saw an increase in public participation in transport policy. Although it may not be regarded as a measure in itself, it is nevertheless an important strategy to obtain public support for the implementation of the transport policy. The implementation process of the stadserf (central area access control – see Section 3.9) in Enschede is a good example. Additionally, public hearings were involved in the preparation of the Mobility Plan. In Enschede there is also a special municipality by-law which states that, in the decision-making process, there should be a consultation with the public affected by traffic engineering schemes such as road closures, the introduction of one-way streets, the reduction of parking places and so on.

There have been media campaigns in particular neighbourhoods to encourage modal switching away from the car (see Section 2.7). These necessarily build on the fact that alternatives have been provided, as there is good public transport provision and visible improvements for cyclists across the city.

Results and conclusions

Several surveys show that the policy in Enschede has had some success in achieving mode switching. In 1995, 38% of trips with their origin and/or destination within Enschede by citizens were made by bicycle or moped, and 42% by car. Compared with 1987–1989, the bicycle share increased by 7% and the share of car trips decreased by 9%. The usage of public transport is low (4%), so it is difficult to assess the level of success for mode switching to public transport (Table 7.2).

However, the total number of trips between 1987–1989 and 1995 increased by 24%, so there has been no travel reduction overall. With regard to the policy for the city centre, traffic counts show a stable number of cars in and around the city centre, while there has been a major increase in the numbers of cars in the outer parts of the built-up area. For bicycles the pattern is the same, except that the increase in the outer neighbourhoods is lower.

In Enschede, then, a package of complementary measures has been implemented which includes restriction of car travel while promoting the alternatives, backed up by physical design of neighbourhoods. Some travel reduction and some stabilisation of car traffic have been observed, so it may be regarded as a moderate success. This assessment of success must be seen in the context of a citywide set of measures and citywide evaluation of results, implemented and monitored over eight years. As we shall see, as the scale of evaluation reduces to focus on particular routes or user groups, a higher level of success may be identifiable.

7.3 A city within its hinterland: Zürich, Switzerland

Background

The city of Zürich has 361,000 inhabitants; however, a further 500,000 people live in the suburbs outside the city proper. Many of these people work in the city or visit Zürich several times a week for shopping or leisure activities.

The city forms one commune within the canton of Zürich, and because of its size, is also one of the seven regional planning authorities (which are usually a union of communes). The canton has strategic control of land use and the road and rail networks, and coordinates and funds public transport services. The regional authority then produces more detailed zoning plans, which show whether land allocated for building should be used for

Table 7.2 Modal split (%) of trips made by the residents of Enschede

	1987–89	1992–94	1995
Car (driver + passenger)	51	44	42
Public transport	3	3	4
Bicycle or moped	31	38	38
Walking	14	14	17
Other	1	0	1
Total	100	100	100

Source: CBS (1996)

residential, commercial or industrial development. The canton prepares a plan for land-use and transport policy that is designed to guide the development over a 25–30-year period. The two elements of land-use and transport planning are seen as closely related. Population and employment projections, but not forecasts for car ownership or traffic levels, form part of the official plan.

This split between canton and city of the ownership and responsibility for roads in particular limits the achievement of the city in some areas, and has led to policy conflicts (e.g., over the degree to which road capacity can be taken away from general road traffic). The canton has the final say on both national and cantonal roads, as well as on others that it designates as being of regional significance; this power of decision now includes land-use approvals that might affect these roads.

Measures implemented

In Zürich, the transport policy characteristically involves a combination of measures. For example, a 'speed-up' measure (public transport prioritisation at traffic signals) was designed from the outset as a package of measures, including on the one hand a dynamic traffic-light system and on the other hand a restriction of roadspace for private transport in order to create separate lanes for public transport (see Section 3.6). Both of these measures help to increase the speed and punctuality of public transport and at the same time they restrict the roadspace used by private transport. Further measures for restricting private roadspace are the implementation of pedestrian priority, provision of separate lanes for cyclists and an increase in the space allocated for footways.

Other measures work only because of the restriction of parking spaces in the city of Zürich – for example, the public transport investment into the opening of the

S-Bahn together with Park and Ride spaces at the S-Bahn stations (see Section 4.4). In the city centre this means that spaces are normally time-restricted by parking meters (normally for one hour) or have progressive tariffs in multi-storey car parks, which for commuters makes it extremely expensive or even impossible to park legally. In the residential district, 'blue zone' parking is implemented which restricts the use of a space to two hours. Also, the doubling of parking charges and the doubling of illegal parking penalties has contributed to the success of the public transport investment by further discouraging car use (see Sections 3.5 and 4.3).

The land-use planning measure works only in combination with overall transport policy: settlement density can be increased only in areas well served by transport, and the success of this policy is related to the level of the public transport service provided in those areas, among other factors.

Results and conclusions

It has been estimated that, 100 days after opening the new S-Bahn system, the number of passengers was 21% higher than in to the previous year. The largest rates of increase (up to 90%) recorded on those S-Bahn corridors with improved services (Züricher Tages Anzeiger, 4 September 1990). Another two years later the number of passengers had increased by a further 7%, without any reduction in local tram and bus services. Use of regional and rural buses had also increased by 53% between 1989 and 1992. The S-Bahn increases were remarkable, considering that the use of the Swiss railway Schweizerische-Bundes Bahn (SBB) was already at a high level before 1990 (it was used by 50% of the commuters to Zürich).

There has been no discernible reduction in traffic levels in the city as a result of the opening of the S-Bahn or of the other public transport measures. However, what has been achieved is a stabilisation of traffic flows, despite an increase in city employment and a general increase in mobility. In the inner city, traffic flows have increased very little since 1980, though there has been some growth in the inter-peak period and a general shift of the working day to earlier times. Further from the centre, traffic growth rates have been much higher, particularly on the motorways, although on the city streets traffic has largely stabilised in the last few years.

Overall one could say that the transport policy of the city of Zürich was quite successful. One explanation is the direct democratic element of Swiss politics and the partial political autonomy of the city. Another reason is the

historic city structure: space for traffic is very scarce and it is necessary for policy-makers to address the issue of mass transportation seriously.

The high use of public transport is clearly influenced by the supply-side policy, which means that the public transport network service is very frequent, geographically dense, fast and punctual all over the city and even in the outskirts. The problem which can arise with this kind of policy is the very high cost of construction and operation of the network. Until the recent budget crises in the city this was no problem, but in general this kind of policy could only be recommended for municipalities with sufficient resources.

There are probably too many 'pull' measures supporting public transport, in the sense that subsidies do not restrict car use and therefore may lead overall to mobility increases. In contrast, 'push' measures (e.g., implementation of fuel taxes or road pricing) would discourage car use more significantly. Of course, car users favour the pull measures which do not restrict car use. Because more than half of the households are car users, it is more difficult for push measures to be accepted in a direct democratic process.

The case of Zürich shows that it is possible to combine measures in a way which discriminates between the inhabitants of the city and those from outside. In practical terms, this means that it is possible to encourage modal switching for outsiders (especially commuters), by restricting car access within the city centre, while boosting the capacity of radial public transport routes. Taken together, these measures can be effective in reducing the overall amount of travel.

7.4 A city centre: Aarhus, Denmark

Background

Aarhus is one of the largest cities in Denmark, located in the western part of the country, with 250,000 inhabitants. The city is the main educational and economic centre of Jutland, so there is a large number of commuters and tourists every day. With a steady increase in both the workforce and the number of cars per inhabitant, the roads in and around Aarhus are becoming increasingly congested and the environmental impacts are becoming significant. This has led the Aarhus Municipality to implement a number of measures to regulate the traffic, the most significant being the regulation in the city centre by means of an integrated package of measures.

Measures implemented

In the period between Autumn 1993 and Spring 1995 considerable changes were made to the traffic structure of the city of Aarhus with the purpose of improving the city environment (Figure 7.3) and improve its accessibility. Traffic rearrangement has been achieved by blocking car through-traffic, improving the bus network and improving facilities for bicycles (see Section 4.2).

More specifically, the following measures have been implemented:

- central roads in the city centres have been blocked to car traffic and one-way traffic has been introduced on some roads, in order to direct car traffic around the core of the city;

- accessibility by bus has been improved by establishing a 'bus axis' through the city centre, improving transit times and routes;

- a series of bicycle paths has been established in the city centre to improve bicycle accessibility and safety in the city centre;

- some city centre areas have been reconstructed, blocking all motorised traffic and improving attractiveness, safety and accessibility for pedestrians.

Results and conclusions

The total amount of traffic in Aarhus has not changed as a result of the measure, but there have been considerable geographical shifts in traffic. The restructuring of traffic in the city has made it possible to improve and rebuild certain streets and squares in the city centre, thus improving the visual environment there.

Traffic has been reduced by 30% (approximately 9,000 vehicle kilometres/day) in the city, comprising reductions of nearly 60% in the central areas and 15% on the perimeter. Traffic has increased on some of the bigger ring roads around the city. Before implementation of the measures, approximately 70% of the traffic used the ring around the city, but, after implementation of the measure, this figure increased to 80%.

The barrier effects and pedestrian safety were calculated from the volume of traffic, the street width and a sensitivity factor based on the number of pedestrians on the street. The barrier effects of traffic were found to have been reduced by approximately 40% in the central parts of Aarhus, while on the ring the barrier effect increased by 10%. There has also been a very positive safety impact. In the city, the annual reduction of accidents has been around 20–25%, whereas the increase in accidents is expected to be around 10% on the ring. Overall, therefore, the measure has contributed to a small net improvement in safety (DANTE Consortium, 1997: Appendix 12, pp. 23–25).

In this case it has been possible to target a combination of measures to achieve travel reduction in a particular area – the city centre. The basic complementary mechanisms of 'push' and 'pull' have been used, with the focus on the city centre, where car traffic is discouraged, while walking, cycling and use of the bus have been promoted.

7.5 An urban corridor: Edinburgh, UK

Background

Edinburgh remains a centralised city with jobs and services as well as residential functions all focused on the city centre. Of Edinburgh's 252,000 jobs, 40% are located in the city centre, where residential densities are also extremely high (from 4,000 to over 10,000 persons/km²). Easy access to the city centre is thus essential to any travel reduction strategy for the city. If car travel to (and within) the city centre can be discouraged, a large proportion of Edinburgh's traffic problems will be solved. Based on this insight, the City of Edinburgh Council has focused its bus priority scheme (Greenways) on the urban corridors leading into and through Edinburgh's city centre.

Figure 7.3 Aarhus city centre, where reduction of traffic has improved the environment for pedestrians

Measures implemented

The most visible feature of the Greenways, as the name suggests, is that road lanes are painted green. These green lanes are only to be used by buses, taxis and cyclists. Crucially, Greenways are therefore more than simply bus lanes: they are lanes reserved for all road-based sustainable transport modes (Figure 7.4). By being situated on existing roads, they reduce the amount of roadspace available to cars.

All radial roads leading to the city centre (Glasgow Road, Leith Walk, Gorgie Road, Slateford Road and Lothian Road) now have Greenways in place. So does Princes Street, the major shopping spine which links different parts of the city centre with each other. Greenways operate during the day (usually between 07.30 and 18.30 on weekdays and 08.30 and 18.30 on Saturdays). Some are operational only during peak hours on weekdays (from 07.30 to 09.30 and 16.00 to 18.30).

Strict parking restrictions operate on all Greenway routes. Stopping is never allowed at bus stops and corners. Elsewhere, stopping is forbidden during the times at which Greenways are in operation, but parking is permitted at night. Drivers and delivery vehicles are also allowed to load or park on Greenways for short periods (up to an hour), as long as they use only the dedicated parking and loading spaces, of which 1,143 are operational along the routes. Disabled drivers, furthermore, are allowed to park without time restriction at any bay.

The introduction of the Greenways scheme was linked with the implementation of 'smart traffic lights' in Edinburgh. Using IT technology, buses can 'force a green light' for themselves as they approach a traffic light. This measure has helped buses to speed up their travel times

Figure 7.4 Bus lanes in Edinburgh have sped up services and boosted patronage

by more than the anticipated 10% on most Greenways routes, and by up to 25% on some (Begg, 1998). To prevent car drivers from rushing through streets parallel to the Greenways in an attempt to avoid the restrictions imposed upon them, the Greenways scheme was also linked with traffic-calming measures on side streets along the route, to discourage 'rat runs' there. Raised-table crossing points were introduced at the entrances to side streets, forcing drivers to slow down if they wanted to leave the major radial roads (see Section 3.8). Speed restrictions of 20 mph (32 km/h) are also planned for zones in the city centre, including all areas affected by Greenways.

The pedestrian environment along Greenways was also improved. Lowered kerbs were introduced at crossing points. As Greenways take up the lanes closest to pedestrians, they have also removed cars from the immediate pedestrian environment. This must have slightly reduced the amount of pollution to which pedestrians are exposed (no hard data are yet available to confirm this). It has certainly reduced the number of road accidents. In the case of Princes Street, which is highly frequented by pedestrians, the number of accidents has fallen by 14%.

This beneficial result is also attributable to several complementary changes in the road design and access rights on Princes Street. The pedestrian walkway has been widened and car traffic has been banned entirely on the lanes taking traffic from west to east. In that direction at least, all of Princes Street is, in effect, a Greenway. Cyclists, too, have benefited from the Greenways. Not only is it safer to cycle along routes that are (more or less) clear of parked cars and have fewer vehicles travelling on them, the Greenway routes also offer cyclists advanced cycle stop lines at most traffic lights and special cycle lanes for turning (right) off Princes Street.

Furthermore, the Greenways network is to be linked with the first-ever guided busway in Edinburgh, which will become operational in 2000. This busway, dubbed Central Edinburgh Rapid Transit (CERT), will link the city centre with Edinburgh airport, some six miles to the west. It will cut journey times to less than 20 min. Even before it has become operational, its promotion has already raised the profile of public transport as an attractive and reliable alternative to the car.

Finally, though this is coincidental rather than planned, the Greenways network increases the attraction of Edinburgh's first car-free housing scheme (see Section 5.5) which will open on Slateford Road in the Spring of 2000. This car-free housing scheme will have a bus stop right on its doorstep. Due to the Greenways, it will take no more than five minutes to travel from there to the city centre or to Haymarket railway station, which serves all rail routes leaving Edinburgh towards the west.

Results and conclusions

The Greenways system is more than a simple bus priority scheme. It is a comprehensive package of measures which promotes the use of modes other than the car. It redistributes roadspace away from cars, to cyclists and taxis as well as buses. It has been welcomed by Edinburgh taxi drivers as well as by the cycling pressure group SPOKES. Greenways are complemented by parking restrictions, 'smart traffic lights', which give buses priority at intersections and traffic calming in streets off the main routes. They make positve changes to the pedestrian environment, and produce a general enhancement of the environment for non-motorised users of Edinburgh's central shopping area along Princes Street.

All of these measures in combination have worked well. Bus times have improved (see above) and road accidents have decreased (a 14% reduction in Princes Street; road accidents have also been halved since 1994 across the city as a whole). During the first six months of the scheme an extra 250,000 bus passengers were recorded on Greenways routes alone. In 1998, 750,000 more bus passenger trips were recorded than in 1997. However, despite the traffic-calming measures in side streets, there have been problems with traffic being diverted to other parts of the inner city road network. The inner suburb of Stockbridge now records one million more car journeys on its streets than before the Greenways scheme was introduced (Lord Provost's Commission, 1998). Although most people welcome the Greenways scheme, opposition remains fierce in some quarters, particularly from shop owners (see 'overcoming barriers', Chapter 11). Edinburgh residents were extremely sceptical about Greenways when they were first proposed, even though these same people regularly cite the excessive traffic on the roads as Edinburgh's foremost problem (Mittler, 1999b).

All in all, however, the Greenways scheme does confirm the insight that traffic reduction measures work best when they are implemented in conjunction with several other measures, as a policy package. Greenways have achieved and even surpassed their target of 10% time reduction on bus journeys, and have increased the number of bus passenger trips. They have established the bus as the most efficient mode of transport, at least for trips into the city centre. This has helped Edinburgh to maintain a high proportion of bus commuter trips to (town centre) jobs.

Across the city, 49.5% of all commuter trips are made by bus. Other cities with a clear focal structure can learn from this experience. The creation of urban corridors in which the hierarchy of road users is weighted in favour of buses, cyclists and taxis can achieve a modal shift towards more sustainable transport modes, but to achieve the implementation of such a far-reaching scheme does require considerable political will.

7.6 An inter-urban corridor: Bristol–Bath, UK

Background

The valley formed by the River Avon between Bristol and Bath has been a focus for movement for many centuries. The corridor between the two cities is approximately 19 km long, with the A4 road closely paralleled by the main Bristol–London railway line. The city of Bristol, with an urban area population of approximately half a million, is the focus of employment, government, business, shopping, leisure, cultural and social activities for the region. Bath has a smaller population of 80,000, but is also a distinct centre in its own right, with large numbers of tourists visiting its historic attractions.

The corridor (Figure 7.5) is heavily used for commuter traffic, particularly for people commuting to Bristol and Bath from rural areas. For example, 79,000 people living outside Bristol travel to work in the city daily. Car use in the region is running approximately 10 years ahead of the UK average. In 1991, 73% of households in the former administrative area of Avon had access to a car, compared with a national average of 63%, and the proportion of people using cars to travel to work is increasing at the expense of all other modes of transport.

The authorities responsible for the two corridor cities are, respectively, Bristol City Council and Bath and North East Somerset Council; Wansdyke Council is responsible for the corridor area between the two cities. The local integrated transport strategy seeks to develop attractive and viable alternatives to the car, discourage car use where alternatives are available and reduce the adverse impact of motor vehicle use.

Measures implemented

A wide range of traffic and travel reduction measures have been implemented on the Bristol–Bath corridor, as follows.

- Bus services and priorities: bus services on the corridor are frequent, with bus-based Park and Ride sites at either end serving Bristol and Bath (see Section 3.4). Services in the rural parishes are less comprehensive. Local councils produce yearly publicity material to promote local public transport services (see Section 2.7). Bus priority measures, including bus lanes (Figure 7.6), have been implemented at various points along the A4 (see Section 3.6).

- Cycle provision: a Bristol–Bath cycle route forms part of the National Cycle Network, and runs on the former Midland Railway line. Cyclists and motorcyclists are able to use bus lanes on the A4 (see Section 3.2).

- Rail provision: the A4 is closely paralleled by the main Bristol–London railway line, with stations at Keynsham and Oldfield Park providing access to both cities.

- Land-use planning: proposals for new development are assessed in terms of provision of public transport facilities, safe routes for cyclists and cycle parking, and safe and convenient access for pedestrians (see Sections 2.4 and 3.8).

These measures are used in combination as part of the integrated transport strategy.

Results and conclusions

The evidence suggests that a combination of bus-based Park and Ride and bus priority lanes have been successful in reducing car modal share on the A4 Bristol–Bath corridor, and achieving some switching from cars to buses. During the case study period the car modal share recorded at the Bristol end of the corridor rose from 87% to 88% between 1990 and 1991, but then fell to 79% in 1993, continuing to fall over the next few years and reaching 77% by 1996. Further east on the corridor, between the Brislington Park and Ride site and the Avon ring road, modal share remained high until 1994, but then fell from 85% to reach 74% by 1996. Meanwhile, recorded patronage of Bristol-bound buses on the A4 during the morning peak increased significantly, and both Park and Ride services have been well patronised since opening. This suggests

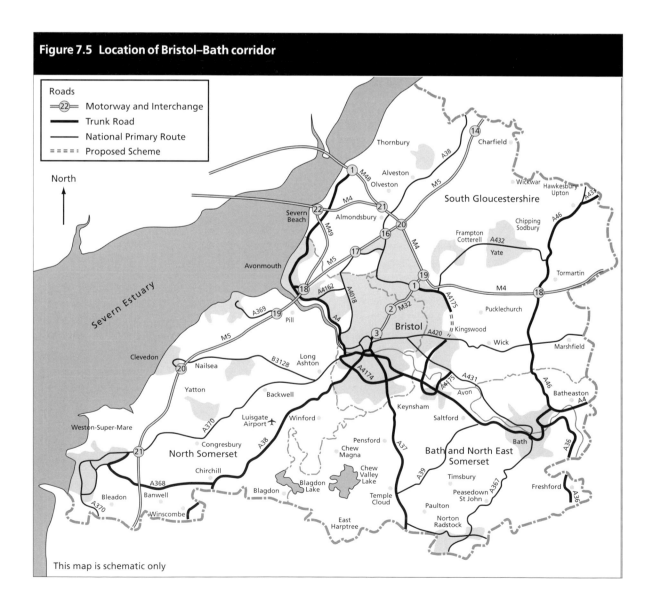

Figure 7.5 Location of Bristol–Bath corridor

This map is schematic only

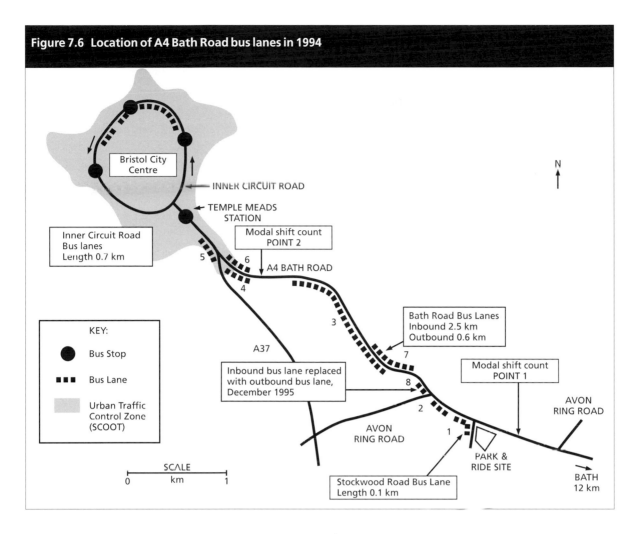

Figure 7.6 Location of A4 Bath Road bus lanes in 1994

that a significant proportion of car users have switched to public transport.

As there were major infrastructural changes on and around the A4 during the period evaluated, it is difficult to assess the impacts on overall corridor traffic flows. These instances of new road building can hardly be regarded as complementary to travel reduction, and probably reduce the effectiveness of sustainable transport strategies. However, the overall impact on traffic levels in the A4 corridor appears to have been positive, as traffic levels are rising more slowly than the national average.

7.7 Access to a company site: Boots, Nottingham, UK

Background

The city of Nottingham has a population of approximately 284,000 and a workforce of around 122,000 according to the 1991 Census. In 1991, 36% of city workers in Nottingham owned two or more cars, 47% owned one car, and only 17% did not own a car at all. Approximately 60%

commuted by car, and 25% by bus. The real costs of car use are falling, and public transport fares have been rising faster than income levels since 1974. Car travel has doubled since 1970, and 20% of car journeys made are under 8 km. Projected traffic growth in the city is unsustainable, and there is a need for measures to reduce travel in the city.

Boots is the largest employer in Nottingham, with 6,500 employees at the Beeston site on the outskirts of the city centre. The site is self-contained, and constitutes the centre of the company's administrative headquarters, and manufacturing and warehouse functions. Due to the location of the site, access by public transport is severely restricted. Traffic in and out of the site becomes congested, especially at peak times. The current plan to transfer a further 1,000 employees to the Beeston site has led to concern that the existing access to the site would be inadequate unless measures are taken to reduce car traffic.

The Boots Commuter Plan

The main aim of the Boots Commuter Plan is to reduce car travel, thus reducing congestion and improving the

71

accessibility of the site. The Plan is also consciously formulated to reduce car travel and vehicle emissions in line with UK Government and European Union guidelines.

The targets of the current Boots Commuter Plan have been:

- to reduce peak commuter traffic by 10% by 2000, and another 10% by the year 2005;
- to increase cycle use by 50% by 2000;
- to increase works bus usage.

Specifically, the Plan aims to reduce the amount of business car travel between Beeston and Nottingham office buildings by up to 400 journeys per day.

The Commuter Plan consists of a series of individual measures, which are described in turn below:

- Car pooling: a computer system matches people in terms of location and start and finish times (this is particularly important for shift workers), for sharing car journeys to and from work. A free £5 gift voucher is offered on registration, and a free taxi home for stranded participants is provided as an incentive. However, this service has been used only infrequently. Boots does not wish to make their car-pooling scheme 'over-successful', as it may start to attract custom from public transport. The Beeston site car-pooling scheme is now being extended to other Boots sites. Each new member of staff is invited to join the scheme. Participants either share costs on a reciprocal basis, or charge rates for shared journeys depending on fuel, depreciation and servicing costs.

- Bicycle initiatives: Boots has provided additional bicycle sheds, showers, lockers and changing facilities. The local authority has also provided a bicycle track extension to the site from Clifton Bridge, along Thane Road.

- Works buses: daily works bus provision has been increased from 56 to 63, including a shuttle link to the local railway station. These cover peak, off-peak and lunchtime periods, and run to and from all major residential sites around the city centre. The buses are subsidised by the company at an annual cost of £250,000 – the staff can buy Easy Rider bus discount tickets. An independently run bus service also operates between Beeston and the city centre throughout the day.

- Promotions and information: a Boots Travel-to-Work fair, attended by approximately 600–800 people over three days, included free bike safety checks by a 'bike doctor' and a police security coding team; bus information and promotional displays; free gifts with car-sharing registration; and a focus on the health issues of walking or cycling to work. Company bus service and other timetable details are provided in the main restaurant, and individual route cards and booklets are available to staff. A help desk function has also been established.

Results and conclusions

With almost 11,400 vehicles recorded entering and leaving the Beeston site each day, the car-pooling scheme achieved a reduction in overall traffic flows of only 0.7%. However, more significant impacts occur during peak hours, with a 2% reduction in vehicles entering the site between 08.00 and 09.00, and a 1.5% reduction in the number of vehicles leaving the site between 16.00 and 17.00. The evidence therefore suggests that the car-pooling scheme has achieved a small but positive reduction in vehicle flows and congestion in the vicinity of the Boots Beeston site, particularly at peak times. The car-pooling scheme was an important element in the company's transport plan.

7.8 Conclusion

In all the preceding examples there is a combination of restraint of travel (particularly car use) and the promotion of the alternatives. Thus, restrictive measures such as area access control or parking restrictions are combined with promotional measures such as public transport or cycle priority. Additionally, a further layer, that of media campaigns, can be used to encourage the desired behavioural change. This may be in the form either of a citywide campaign, or of awareness being raised among commuters at a particular place of employment.

As a conclusion, then, it may generally be recommended that when combining measures into strategy packages, all three forms of measure should be present to gain maximum effect:

- restraint on less-favoured travel behaviour (e.g., car use);
- promotion of the favoured alternatives;
- creation of awareness regarding travel reduction means and ends.

In a sense these are interdependent: it is no use preventing access by car if no alternatives are available. Similarly, providing a good public transport supply will not reduce travel if any increase in patronage is not tied to a switch away from car use. Finally, if the public are not aware of the existence of the alternatives to car travel, or are not convinced of the need to reduce travel, then the desired changes in behaviour are unlikely to materialise.

Good practice in packaging measures involves:

- a combination of push and pull policies, ensuring that some appreciable restriction on current patterns

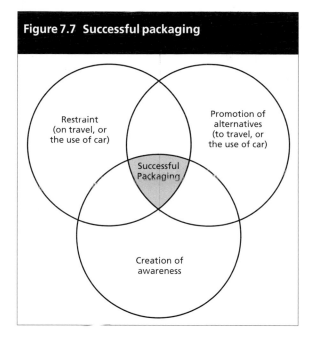

Figure 7.7 Successful packaging

Restraint (on travel, or the use of car)

Promotion of alternatives (to travel, or the use of car)

Successful Packaging

Creation of awareness

- the promotion of the push and pull measures together as a package, to highlight the existence of choice in travel behaviour (which is otherwise so often a matter of habit) and where the choices between the alternatives available are made explicit.

Overall, the concept of *packaging* can therefore be understood not only in terms of the assembly of complementary measures, but in terms of the 'fronting' or 'selling' of the contents as an attractive product. To make the most of the investment, the contents and promotion must do justice to each other. The packaging itself could thus be seen as a promotional measure in its own right.

Too often, policies are introduced which include only one or two of the approaches (Figure 7.7). Restraint policies on their own are unpopular and difficult to implement unless accompanied by explanation and complementary actions. Similarly, awareness programmes that are very general only raise levels of knowledge (e.g., about the environment), are ineffective. They should be targeted at the travel reduction objectives of the policy and involve all relevant stakeholders in that process so that responsibilities for action can be allocated. Even actions to promote alternatives will be less effective if introduced in isolation. It is only when all three components are packaged together, with a clear strategy on the overall objectives of the transport and land-use policy, that effective travel reduction may take place.

of car use is felt (pull policies alone may simply increase travel overall);

- a range of *alternative* pull policies, so that individuals are presented with a series of choices; when faced with a restriction regarding their original first choice, they will not then feel they are, for example, being 'forced out their car', but rather, that they are being given the opportunity to exercise their preference, whether this is to switch mode or destination, or choose some other trip modification (the car continues to be an option, albeit a less favourable one);

Underlying Mechanisms

8.1 Introduction

A substantial number of individual travel reduction measures have been identified in Part I, but in essence they can be considered in terms of a much smaller number of underlying mechanisms. In this chapter, six basic travel reduction mechanisms are considered: switching mode, destination or time; and substitution by linking trips, technology or trip modification (see Table 1.1).

Measures utilising a switching mechanism do not impact upon the overall number of journeys that are undertaken, but rather seek to change certain components of each journey to achieve travel reduction. However, measures involving a substitution mechanism do have an impact upon the number of journeys made, because they seek to replace one set of trips with another requiring less travel, or to make use of new forms of communication that remove any need for a trip.

Considering travel reduction in terms of these basic mechanisms can assist understanding of the travel reduction potential of particular measures, and hence identification of appropriate policy strategies. For example:

- some measures may appear superficially different, but may behave according to the same fundamental mechanism – hence, where one measure may be inappropriate or unavailable locally, another measure using the same basic mechanism may be tried instead;

- some measures may reinforce or complement each other according to these mechanisms, and therefore an appropriate package of measures may be assembled;

- policy makers may be able to prioritise the different mobility implications of each mechanism (e.g., reduction in passenger kilometres, reduction in vehicle trips, reduction in traffic, etc.).

Each of the 30 measures presented in Part I may be related to one or more of these six mechanisms (Table 1.1). They are discussed, together with their differing impacts upon travel behaviour, in more detail in the following section, to evaluate their travel reduction potentials (Table 8.1).

8.2 The six basic mechanisms

Mode switching

Mode switching involves the transfer from one mode of travel to other more environmentally friendly modes, with incentives to discourage one mode and/or encourage others. The most successful schemes encompass both. For example, a Park and Ride policy can provide secure, accessible parking facilities, at the same time reducing roadspace for cars (by reallocating existing roadspace for bus lanes), and it can also be combined with a reliable, high-frequency public transport service with better journey times than cars (Figure 8.1).

Mode switching is by far the most prevalent mechanism for travel reduction measures, and is present in approximately two-thirds of all measures considered. It is a particularly important mechanism for measures applied through transport policy measures. (By contrast, mode switching is not so heavily relied upon by land-use and technology measures, which focus on non-transport solutions to problems.) In many ways, therefore, mode switching can be seen as a 'traditional' tool for influencing

Figure 8.1 Bicycle racks and bus stops next to the central railway station in Almere, the Netherlands: convenient interchange facilities can assist in switching between modes

Table 8.1 Measures categorised by the underlying mechanisms

Mechanism	Measures (over two columns)	
Mode switching	Car sharing (2.3)	Commuted payments (2.4)
	Demand-responsive transport (2.6)	Media campaigns (2.7)
	Transport optimisation (2.9)	Cycle priority and roadspace (3.2)
	Park and Ride (3.4)	Parking capacity (3.5)
	Public transport priority and roadspace (3.6)	Road capacity restraint and reduction (3.7)
	Traffic calming (3.8)	Area access control (3.9)
	Cycle subsidy (4.2)	Parking charges (4.3)
	Public transport investment (4.4)	Public transport subsidy (4.5)
	Road pricing (4.6)	Location of new developments (5.2)
	Location of companies (5.3)	
Destination switching	Media campaigns (2.7)	Parking capacity (3.5)
	Area access control (3.9)	Parking charges (4.3)
	Road pricing (4.6)	Location of companies (5.3)
	Design of locations (5.5)	Informatics (6.3)
Time switching	Company work hours policy (2.5)	Media campaigns (2.7)
	Peak congestion avoidance (2.8)	Parking capacity (3.5)
	Area access control (3.9)	Road pricing (4.6)
	Informatics (6.3)	
Substitution by linking trips	Car pooling (2.2)	Media campaigns (2.7)
	HOV priority and roadspace (3.3)	Mixed use development (5.4)
Substitution by technology	Media campaigns (2.7)	Teleactivities (6.4)
	Teleworking (6.5)	
Substitution by trip modification	Media campaigns (2.7)	Transport optimisation (2.9)
	Car-free developments (5.6)	Home delivery of goods and services (6.2)

Note: Figures in parentheses refer to the appropriate section in Part I.

travel behaviour, because it is favoured by conventional, transport-oriented solutions. Mode switching is also popular because it can maintain or increase the volume of people entering a city (hence boosting economic activity) without necessarily increasing travel.

Although popular among policy makers, mode switching is not necessarily the most effective mechanism for encouraging travel reduction. By switching from one mode to another without changing the destination or purpose of the journey, the same amount of travel (in terms of passenger kilometres) still takes place. There is also the potential for adverse modal switching, which is difficult to control; for example, evidence suggests that improving public transport encourages cyclists and pedestrians to switch to motorised, less sustainable modes. However, the number of vehicle kilometres may be reduced (e.g., one bus journey may be substituted for a larger number of individual car journeys), thus achieving a reduction in travel in terms of vehicle kilometres.

Another factor to be borne in mind is the relative reluctance of individuals to give up using cars. Evidence suggests that people would choose first to switch time, destination or purpose (by linking trips) before switching mode (Salomon, 1997). Therefore, even where this mechanism is theoretically suitable for application in a particular case, its uptake by the public may be disappointing.

Destination switching

Destination switching involves changing from the normal trip destination to an alternative, closer destination, in order to reduce trip lengths. It may also facilitate a modal shift if it encourages a switch to a destination that is more accessible by environmentally sustainable modes of travel.

This mechanism requires changes to be made in the location of activities, in order to impact upon travel behaviour. It is therefore not surprising that it is commonly involved in about half of all land-use measures to secure travel reduction.

Destination switching seeks to influence journey length, but not the number of trips undertaken. Therefore there is less travel in terms of both vehicle kilometres and passenger kilometres. It can also lead to a reduction in the negative externalities of travel, if positive modal switching can be induced. Thus destination switching is an effective mechanism for achieving travel reduction.

Time switching

This mechanism influences the times when travellers make their journeys, to avoid peak periods when congestion is at its greatest and also periods when air quality is poor (Figure 8.2). For example, road pricing might seek to adjust the level of traffic on selected routes or areas at certain times of day by varying the cost to drivers of undertaking journeys accordingly.

Time switching is used in a relatively small number of the measures under consideration. Although it does not necessarily contribute directly to travel reduction in terms of the number of trips or vehicle kilometres, travel may be reduced in terms of passenger and vehicle hours and there may be an overall reduction in energy consumption. However, there are also potential contradictory effects if transport systems are used more extensively during off-peak periods, thus freeing capacity at peak times for new travellers. In theory, existing journeys can take place more efficiently when congestion and travel times are reduced; this leads to a reduction in the negative externalities of travel such as air pollution.

Figure 8.2 Traffic queue in Marylebone, London: travel can be reduced by avoiding time spent in congestion

Substitution by linking trips

With this mechanism, a single trip combining different activities and purposes replaces a series of single-purpose trips, hence reducing the number of journeys and overall distance travelled. This mechanism is involved in a small number of measures, mostly those relating to land use. Attempts are made to combine a range of activities at one location so that multipurpose single trips can be made by an individual. The mechanism can also apply to non-locational components, such as combining several individuals' potential journeys in one trip, e.g., by car pooling.

This can lead successfully to a reduction in travel in several ways. Firstly there can be a reduction in the number of trips (and also passenger and vehicle kilometres, since one trip can be made for several activities). Secondly, with car pooling or the use of high-occupancy vehicles, individuals can maintain the number of journeys they make, but make less vehicle-intensive trips by sharing vehicles (constant passenger kilometres, with a decline in vehicle kilometres). If destination switching is involved in this process of linking trips, and the new destination involves shorter trip lengths, then there is also the potential for modal switching to occur. As in the case of destination switching, this mechanism could be used to facilitate change in the long term if land-use measures are applied.

Substitution by technology

By this mechanism a potential activity-related journey never takes place, because the activity is undertaken through some form of electronic communication. For example, many consumer financial transactions can now be made by telephoning a call centre; the need to make a journey to a bank, insurance broker, etc., is then eliminated (see Section 6.4).

The deliberate replacement of travel by technology has only developed as a significant force in recent years, following the introduction of the necessary information and communication technologies, and their growing uptake among producers and consumers of goods and services. As a relatively new mechanism, it is therefore applied in only a small number of measures to influence travel behaviour (or, rather, few conventionally recognised categories have evolved in which to place these technologies).

It can be very straightforward to use technology as a tool for travel reduction. By substituting travel with electronic communication the need to make a trip is removed and no passenger or vehicle kilometres are recorded.

Substitution by trip modification

Here the nature or number of journeys is changed by replacing them with another kind of trip, without affecting their purpose. For example, a series of shoppers' trips may be replaced by a single delivery run with the same volume of goods to several homes. Similarly, car-free developments require individuals and households to reassess and modify their travel patterns (see Section 5.6).

To be found in only a small number of measures, trip modification can have a variety of impacts upon travel, depending upon the way in which the trip is modified. For instance, the goods delivery run mentioned above will involve fewer vehicle kilometres by linking the goods delivery to several households. This measure can also eliminate trips completely, if the goods have been ordered electronically (substitution by technology: see above).

8.3 Outcomes of the basic mechanisms

As noted in Chapter 1, the above set of mechanisms may be seen as providing a link between policy measures (e.g., in a bus priority scheme) and travel reduction outcomes (e.g., reduction in vehicle kilometres). This is illustrated in Figure 8.3, which is a development of Figure 1.2. The volume of the block, which represents overall travel in terms of vehicle kilometres, may be reduced by a decrease in the number of vehicles, the number of kilometres or the number of trips.

Combinations are also possible which may increase one or more of these parameters while reducing travel overall. For example, with mode switching, several individual car trips may be replaced by a single trip by public transport. The result of this mechanism may be that *additional* trip making (and travel in terms of passenger kilometres) can be accommodated, while travel in terms of vehicle kilometres is still reduced. (Here, the height of the block in Figure 8.3 could remain the same or even increase, while it is squeezed so that the breadth, and hence the overall volume, is reduced.) This mechanism may therefore be popular with city authorities because it can allow increased access to cities and a boost to economic activity, while reducing the number of vehicles, hence causing a visible reduction in traffic.

8.4 Linking the mechanisms

We have earlier suggested that combining measures can be the most effective way to realise travel reduction (Chapter 7), and demonstrated how the diversity of policy

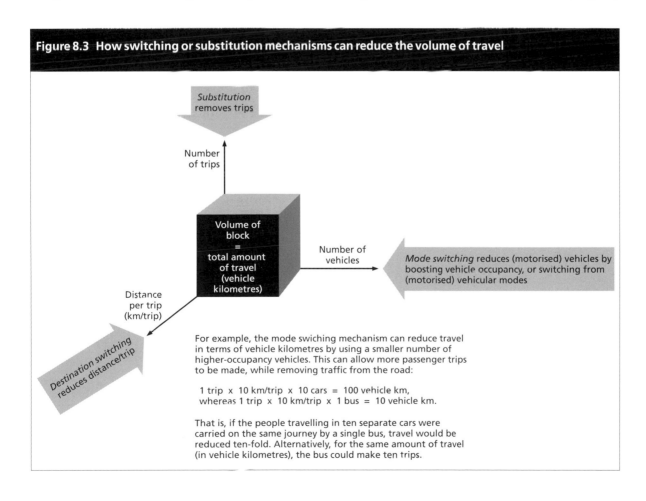

Figure 8.3 How switching or substitution mechanisms can reduce the volume of travel

Substitution removes trips

Number of trips

Volume of block = total amount of travel (vehicle kilometres)

Number of vehicles

Mode switching reduces (motorised) vehicles by boosting vehicle occupancy, or switching from (motorised) vehicular modes

Distance per trip (km/trip)

Destination switching reduces distance/trip

For example, the mode swiching mechanism can reduce travel in terms of vehicle kilometres by using a smaller number of higher-occupancy vehicles. This can allow more passenger trips to be made, while removing traffic from the road:

1 trip x 10 km/trip x 10 cars = 100 vehicle km,
whereas 1 trip x 10 km/trip x 1 bus = 10 vehicle km.

That is, if the people travelling in ten separate cars were carried on the same journey by a single bus, travel would be reduced ten-fold. Alternatively, for the same amount of travel (in vehicle kilometres), the bus could make ten trips.

measures can be related to six basic mechanisms which explain the terms in which travel is reduced. We shall now explore how these different mechanisms may be combined.

For the purposes of these examples we presuppose that a candidate traveller has previously been making a multitude of separate trips, by car, to a multitude of different locations, to carry out various activities, and that this behaviour can be replaced by equivalent activities with less travelling. The example of substitution used here is that of linking trips, since this best illustrates the intermediate stages of a combination of mechanisms (rather than an outright cessation of trip-making).

In this section we concentrate on travel reduction in terms of vehicle kilometres, which may be activated by mode switching, destination switching or substitution (Figure 8.4). Where these overlap, they reinforce their travel reduction potentials; the innermost section of the

diagram, which encompasses all three mechanisms, theoretically has the greatest potential.

However, some trips may be constrained by external factors related to mode, destination or particular trip circumstances, which mitigate against the corresponding switching or substitution mechanisms being practicable. The greater the number of these (external) constraints, the more likely it is that a single, non-overlapping mechanism would have to suffice to achieve travel reduction (Figure 8.5).

Examples illustrating the seven possible combinations (I–VII in Figure 8.4) are:

I   switching mode only: travel to work or shops by bus instead of by car;

II switching destination only: travel to a local shop instead of an out-of-town superstore;

III substitution (by linking trips) only: visit the town centre, combining all trip purposes, instead of

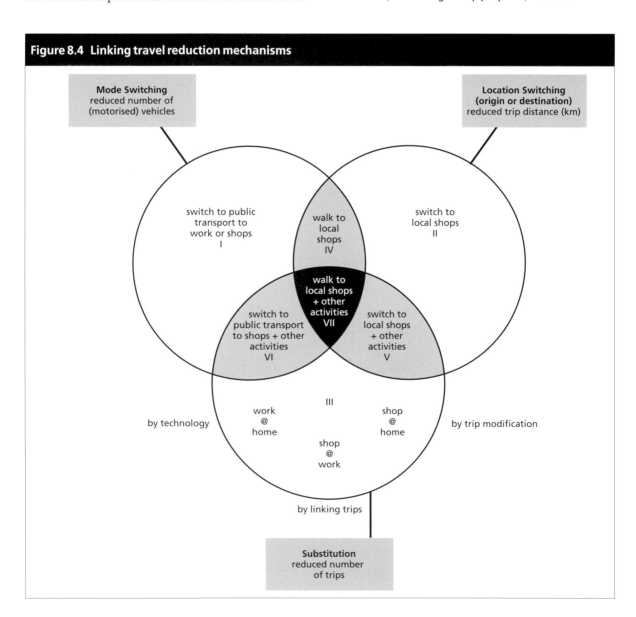

Figure 8.4 Linking travel reduction mechanisms

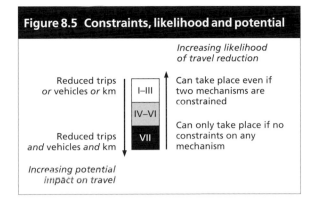

Figure 8.5 Constraints, likelihood and potential

making separate trips for work, shopping, leisure and other activities;

IV switching both destination and mode: walk to local shop instead of driving to the out-of-town superstore;

V substitution (linking trips) while also switching destination: visit the town centre to do all the shopping, instead of making separate trips to different out-of-town stores, and combining this with personal business or leisure activities;

VI substitution (linking trips) while switching mode: take bus to the town centre, combining all trip purposes, instead of making separate (car) trips for shopping, leisure and other activities;

VII linking trips while also switching destination and mode: walk to town centre to do all shopping, instead of making separate car trips to different out-of-town superstores, and combining this with personal business or leisure activities.

Note that the following circumstances are assumed in these examples:

• the traveller currently favours driving;

• the work location is at a distant and fixed destination;

• 'shopping, leisure and other activities' are provided for at various distances and locations;

• there is choice of where to go for 'shopping, leisure and other activities';

• the traveller might switch to public transport (or a car pool) for long journeys;

• the traveller might switch to walking (or cycling) for short journeys.

The first two reflect *contributory factors* which give rise to the need to consider reducing travel in the first place, while the final four are conditions that are required in order for the proposed travel-reducing mechanisms to work. It is these latter conditions that policy can usefully address.

In these examples, the 'work' trip could be any locationally constrained trip, and be made for other purposes: for

example, it could be a social trip to visit a particular house, or a shopping trip to a particular store. Similarly, the reference to 'shopping, leisure and other activities' could represent any purposes where a variety of locational options is possible (as typified by the proliferation of food shops or banking outlets in an urban area). But it may also apply to trips made for other reasons, including company business.

In reality, not all mechanisms would apply in all circumstances. It is possible to separate out the different circumstances by considering the constraints which would rule out particular mechanisms.

Broadly, therefore:

• destination switching strategies would not be effective for trips with a fixed location, such as work trips (although the provision of 'telecentres' at intermediate locations between home and work might be considered under the combination of switching destination and substitution by technology);

• mode-switching strategies would not be effective in cases where journeys to facilities were sufficiently long or otherwise adverse to deter travel on foot or bicycle, or where public transport was poor (for journeys of any significant length), as might typically arise in rural areas, where often the only practicable means of travel is by car;

• trip-linking strategies would not be effective in cases where individual travellers (or journeys) were constrained, for example by time or through the need for escorting, so that separate trips were required for different purposes.

For these three cases, only travel possibilities not dependent on releasing the associated constraints would be amenable for change. The travel reduction mechanisms that are feasible in circumstances with specific constraints are I–VI (see Figure 8.4 and discussion above). In summary, they may be applicable as follows:

• For locationally constrained trips (e.g., work trips), assuming that these must apply to travel to a fixed, distant destination, there are transport alternatives where:
  I public transport is good between the home and the workplace;
  III shops, etc., can be located close to the workplace;
  VI public transport is good and shops are close to the workplace.

• For modally constrained trips (e.g., in rural areas) for which, due to long distances and poor public transport, a car is likely to be used, there are transport alternatives where:
  II shops are located close to the home;
  III shops are located close to the workplace;
  V a variety of shops are located close to the home.

- For individually constrained trips for which, due to time or escort constraints, separate trips are required, there are transport alternatives where:
  - I   public transport is good between the home and the workplace;
  - II shops are located close to the home
  - IV shops are located sufficiently close to the home to allow non-motorised trips.

The preceding discussion has demonstrated how various policy options overlap and are complementary to various degrees. This means that for any given situation it is likely that more than one policy would be appropriate, but not all are required simultaneously. The actual policies implemented would depend on a trade-off between, firstly, the likely *applicability* of a policy, and, secondly, its likely *effectiveness* in reducing travel (assuming that it is applicable).

Thus, the more constraints applying (e.g., journey purpose, location, available mode), the fewer types of mechanism will be available, and the more likely a single (non-overlapping) mechanism will be appropriate. This is shown in the upper part of Figure 8.5, where the most heavily constrained options can only hope to reduce travel by one mechanism – reducing trips *or* vehicles *or* vehicle kilometres (i.e., VII).

For less constrained trips, however, there is the greatest potential for reducing travel by applying a combination of overlapping mechanisms, which have the potential to reduce trips and vehicles and vehicle kilometres (Figure 8.5).

8.5 Implications for policy

Following consideration of the above mechanisms (Table 8.1) and their possible combinations (Figures 8.4 and 8.5), a number of policy implications emerge which would be required to tackle travel reduction. These policies comprise:

- provision of feasible alternative 'long distance' travel, i.e., public transport;
- provision of attractive, safe and convenient local routes for walking and cycling for access to shops and services, and to access the public transport;
- location of shopping and other facilities close to homes;
- location of a sufficient *variety* of shopping and other facilities close to homes;
- location of shopping and other facilities close to workplaces;
- location of workplaces close to homes.

It can be seen that two of these policies relate to transport provision, while four relate to location. This points to the potential contribution of land-use planning policies towards solving transport problems, and clearly demonstrates the importance of land-use planning for the success of these travel reduction mechanisms (Chapter 5). It also points to some specific policy implications (Figure 8.6).

Firstly, whereas the first option – attempting universal provision of public transport to cater for all journeys – would be unrealistic because of the dispersed nature of travel patterns, the second – attempting comprehensive provision of good local networks of pedestrian and cycle friendly routes – is certainly feasible, and can assist both with access to public transport and with local movement needs themselves.

Secondly, the fact that proximity between origins and destinations features in all four of the 'location' policies above points to the importance of land-use policies such as location of development and location of companies (which can also be assisted by the layout of urban structure). Thirdly, the four 'location' cases implicitly (and in the case of the fourth option, explicitly) suggest mixed-use development.

In general, mixed-use policies may be used to encourage linking of trips, whether this is linking trips by individuals, by time, by destination or by purpose. That said, the more that simultaneous linking of trips is envisaged, paradoxically, the more likely a car would arguably be the most convenient vehicle for the purpose, as it can accommodate several people, transport passengers or goods and cover long distances on extended door-to-door trip chains. And, as noted before, there is no guarantee that the existence of mixed uses – or activities located in proximity – will mean that particular individuals will actually live, work and shop locally.

Nevertheless, it is important to consider all these possibilities afforded by the different mechanisms and their potential combination, rather than simply to consider travel reduction by mode switching alone, or traditional traffic restraint devices.

8.6 Activation of travel reduction mechanisms

A further consideration to be taken into account is the order of activation of travel reduction mechanisms, in terms the willingness of travellers to change their behaviour in response to policies. For example, Salomon (1997) has suggested that travellers are more likely to change their time of travel or their route before they would be prepared to change mode, or to change their destination (e.g., their workplace) before changing their origin (e.g., their home).

This approach is essentially a sequential procedure; in practice, the ordering of activation of mechanisms might be, for example, to link trips, then switch destination, then switch mode. In other words, a traveller who undertook a multitude of car trips to distant destinations could reach the more desired state of fewer non-motorised trips to near locations by:

- first reducing the number of trips (i.e., III);
- then switching to a closer destination (i.e., V);
- and finally switching mode (i.e., VII).

The actual ordering would depend on the relative flexibility of activities and locations. In the preceding analysis it has been assumed that activities like shopping are relatively flexible, while the location of workplace and home have been considered 'fixed'. Thus, for shopping trips people might be prepared to switch destination to avoid changing mode (e.g., switching from one shopping centre where car parking became constrained to another where parking was freely available). Conversely for work, people might be more prepared to switch mode (e.g., switching to public transport if workplace parking became constrained). Indeed, 'flexible' activities or locations

could be *defined* as those which would be switched in preference to switching mode, whereas 'fixed' activities or locations would be those which would trigger a change in mode first (Figure 8.7).

An alternative approach might be the simultaneous decision, where critical trigger mechanisms result in changes in mode, location and time: each situation is treated differently, but an external (or internal) change would have to be on a sufficiently large scale to precipitate change. This suggests that decisions are changed when critical thresholds are reached, rather than decisions being made on the basis of marginal change. Examples of large-scale internal change would be the decision to give up the car (or acquire a car), or a large-scale external change could be the closure of the city centre to cars and the implementation of a high-quality Park and Ride scheme.

A third approach could suggest that the propensity to change behaviour is dependent on individual circumstances. For some, it may be easier to change route than to change time, or to change job rather than change mode. In the long term, it is possible for people to make life-cycle changes which would allow for both changes of jobs and changes in home location. These changes would not be independent of travel decisions. However, in the short term any change in one parameter (e.g., one household member changing to a job out of town) could lead to an increase in travel.

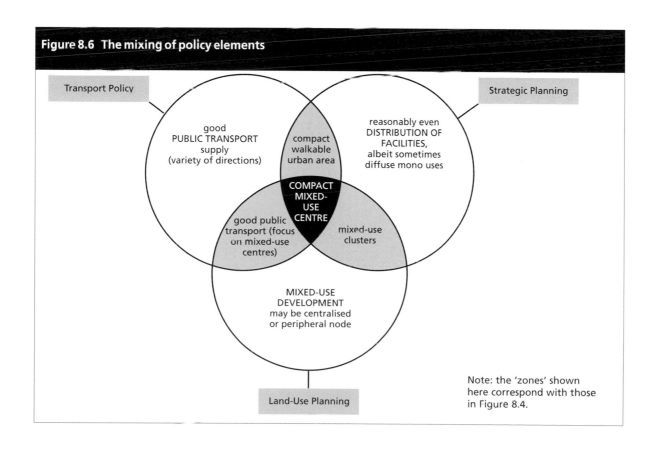

Figure 8.6 The mixing of policy elements

Transport Policy

Strategic Planning

good
PUBLIC TRANSPORT
supply
(variety of directions)

compact
walkable
urban area

reasonably even
DISTRIBUTION OF
FACILITIES,
albeit sometimes
diffuse mono uses

COMPACT
MIXED-
USE
CENTRE

good public
transport (focus
on mixed-use
centres)

mixed-use
clusters

MIXED-USE
DEVELOPMENT
may be centralised
or peripheral node

Land-Use Planning

Note: the 'zones' shown
here correspond with those
in Figure 8.4.

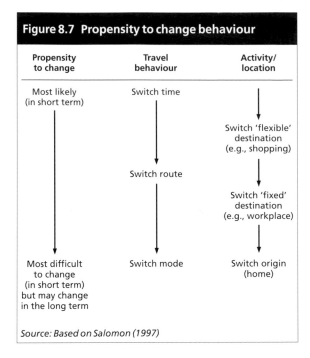

Figure 8.7 Propensity to change behaviour

Propensity to change	Travel behaviour	Activity/ location
Most likely (in short term)	Switch time	
		Switch 'flexible' destination (e.g., shopping)
	Switch route	
		Switch 'fixed' destination (e.g., workplace)
Most difficult to change (in short term) but may change in the long term	Switch mode	Switch origin (home)

Source: Based on Salomon (1997)

The significance of the foregoing discussion lies in the identification and exploration of the underlying mechanisms which relate to travel behaviour and the potential to reduce travel. This provides a framework within which it would be possible to investigate actual cases of policy intentions and behavioural outcomes. Without such a degree of resolution, there is a danger that crude application of 'off-the-shelf' policies will miss their intended target of travel reduction.

8.7 Conclusion

In this chapter we have tried to impose a structure on the different measures outlined in Part I of the book. Such a structure helps in examining the exact nature of the travel reduction strategy and the means by which alternatives can be packaged together (Chapter 7). The argument that there is a simple cause (policy action) and effect (travel reduction) has been dismissed as being unrealistic. What policy makers should be looking for is a range of combinations of measures that are mutually supporting – hence the extensive discussion of activation issues. If policy makers are not aware of the complexity of the issues being discussed, then actions may actually create more travel rather than producing less travel. Rather than having a self-fulfilling policy we have a self-defeating one (Marshall and Banister, 2000).

Certain clear messages come out of this chapter:

- The number of measures currently identifiable for mode switching is much greater than those for the other five mechanisms highlighted (Table 8.1 and Figure 8.4).

- Paths can be identified to move towards the centre of the diagram (in Figures 8.4, 8.5 and 8.6) which combine several of the travel reduction mechanisms. This process is important as it is likely to have greater public support than attempts to achieve the most difficult changes instantaneously.

- A clear distinction needs to be drawn between the different factors that are operating (longer-term or given constraints) and the conditions necessary for the travel reduction mechanisms to work. Many decisions are made under heavily constrained circumstances. As the number of constraints increases, so the range of options decreases and their likely impacts are reduced.

- There seems to be some argument for the uniqueness of each situation in terms of the appropriate measures available (this issue is taken up in Chapter 10). It is argued here that the measures are transferable, but that their impacts will be different in different situations.

- Propensity to change travel behaviour varies according to the individual, their location, the activity being considered and the actual mechanism of change. Some changes can be made instantaneously, but others will only be identified over a longer period of time (Figure 8.7).

By understanding the basic mechanisms at work and through the categorisation of trip reduction measures, we can now explore the key issues of identification and evaluation of successful travel reduction.

Evaluating Success

9.1 Introduction

Evaluating the success of travel reduction policies is not straightforward. Unlike the quantification of travel, whose parameters – such as traffic volumes or public transport patronage – may be directly observed and measured, travel reduction must be inferred or deduced indirectly. In other words, it is easier to detect travel than to detect 'non-travel' or to prove that travel reduction has taken place (Figure 9.1).

For example, a decrease in traffic on a particular route may not necessarily demonstrate travel reduction, as that traffic may simply have transferred to another route. Similarly, an observed increase in the use of a public transport service does not necessarily imply that there has been a switch away from use of the car, as the extra patronage may represent additional journeys. Likewise, the recorded incidence of telecommuting might demonstrate the removal of the journey to work, but this may be accompanied by additional trips for other purposes or by other household members.

In this chapter we examine the quantified effects of travel reduction measures in an attempt to evaluate their success by collating the results of the case study examples presented in Part I. The scale of success is also considered in terms of the geographical scale of impact and is related to the cost. Further considerations for evaluating the success of travel reduction policies are then discussed.

9.2 Indicators of travel reduction

Since travel reduction is not directly measurable, it is necessary to approach the evaluation by means of intermediate parameters and processes. First, it is necessary to generate indicators that relate to our conception of successful travel reduction. In Chapter 8, we considered travel reduction in terms of six underlying mechanisms. These can be used as a starting point for generating indicators of travel reduction success. The six mechanisms imply travel reduction outcomes, such as:

- reduction in car trips (from mode switching away from the car);

- reduction in car kilometres (from mode switching away from the car);

- reduction in vehicle kilometres per passenger kilometre (from mode switching from low-occupancy to high-occupancy vehicle);

- reduction in vehicle kilometres per trip (from destination switching, or from time switching if off-peak routes are shorter);

- reduction in vehicle hours spent travelling (from time switching);

- reduction in total number of trips (from substitution by linking trips, substitution by technology, substitution by trip modification);

- reduction in passenger kilometres (from any case where trips are removed).

Figure 9.1 Measuring travel reduction is not straightforward: it requires a combination of counting of what is there (e.g., bicycles) and deducing what is not there (e.g., riders)

In all cases, the evaluation parameters involve the relative term 'reduction', and hence, at least, require the availability of 'before' and 'after' data (i.e., at least two sets of data, or one data set viewed longitudinally). If we were only concerned with *traffic* reduction, we could stop here, since a single calculation would enumerate the differences in traffic volumes for a particular location, and hence divulge the reduction in traffic.

However, *travel* reduction requires consideration of different modes and destinations and the tracing of individuals' journeys and purposes, and therefore we may require not only these longitudinal data, but 'lateral' data to find out what is happening with regard to other routes, other times, other vehicles and other travellers. This would require more than two sets of data, but ideally a series of compatible data sets. However, such detail is not always available. So a broad three-step approach has been taken here, by which data are assembled incrementally, building towards the conclusion of travel reduction success.

The three steps, or criteria, tend to be realised in the order in which they are described in detail below: in most cases, a positive reaction is identifiable, while only in a smaller subset of cases are all three criteria demonstrable, in which case it is possible to conclude convincingly that travel has been reduced. In simple terms, the greater the number of steps achieved, the more demonstrably successful is the measure.

However, the number of steps observed may be a function of the availability of data, so it is possible that measures which are seen to have achieved only one step may in reality have achieved all three. In this sense the steps may be seen not simply as outright degrees of success, but as 'degree of resolution' of evidence for travel reduction. This has implications for assessment (Section 9.6).

Step 1: Positive reaction

A positive reaction is an indication that the measure has resulted in the desired positive behaviour, in terms of travellers' uptake and use of services (or, in the case of technology, products). The positive reaction builds upon the creation of the favourable circumstances in the first place – an essential 'foundation' stage, which cannot necessarily be taken for granted. An example of a 'positive foundation' would be an improvement in, say, bus journey times, by a measure designed for this purpose. An example of a positive reaction by travellers would be increased patronage observed on the route. At this level of success, it is not known if this evidence reflects any actual travel reduction.

Step 2: Switching or substitution

Activation of switching or substitution mechanisms may be directly observed by means of surveys of individuals' behaviour, comparing trip making before and after the measures are implemented. Alternatively, and with less certainty, the occurrence of switching or substitution may be deduced from evidence of aggregate changes in travel patterns. As examples, a workplace survey may reveal that certain employees are working at home instead of making a daily commuting trip; or, from modal split figures, it may be deduced that switching between modes has taken place on a travel corridor.

Establishment of switching or substitution, however, does not necessarily imply that overall travel has been reduced. This requires the final step.

Step 3: Travel reduction

To reach the conclusion that travel reduction has indeed taken place, according to one or other of the specified travel reduction parameters (e.g., vehicle kilometres), ideally there would be direct evidence. This might be obtained from a household survey where it is clear that individually and collectively less travel is being pursued by any particular household. For example, a commuter may have given up travelling to work on certain days, with their car remaining totally unused on those days.

Alternatively, it may be necessary to rely on more circumstantial evidence, such as aggregate data, from which there are reasonable grounds to conclude that travel reduction in one form or another has actually taken place. For example, a new Park and Ride site may be established on the edge of a town. If the Park and Ride service is well patronised, with a corresponding reduction in flows of cars on the route into town, it is reasonable to conclude that both modal switching and travel reduction have taken place.

9.3 Evaluation of success: case study results

The travel reduction outcomes of the case studies discussed in Part I are tabulated according to their level of success: Table 9.1 shows those measures which have attained the first level of success – positive reaction; Table 9.2 those which demonstrate switching or substitution as well as positive reaction; and Table 9.3 those which demonstrate positive reaction, switching or substitution, *and* travel reduction.

Table 9.1 Case studies showing positive reaction only

Section	Measure	Case study	Positive reaction
3.9	Area access control	Rome	Reduction in cars during operation of zone
3.9	Area access control	Enschede	Number of cars in zone reduced by 90%
5.6	Car-free development	London	Uptake of scheme (i.e., non-car-using residence established)
2.3	Car sharing	Edinburgh	Each car club vehicle replaced by four to six private cars
2.4	Commuted payments	Bristol	22 city centre offices participating in schemes
2.6	Demand-responsive transport	Holstebro	Number of passengers increased by 150%
2.7	Media campaigns	Bristol	Increased number of cyclists recorded on 'Bike to Work' day
5.4	Mixed-use development	London	Uptake of scheme
3.4	Park and Ride	Enschede	47 000 passengers on German Bank Holiday
3.5	Parking restrictions and capacity reduction	Zürich	Spaces reduced from 52 000 to 49 000 (down 5.8%); number of cars parked reduced by 19%
2.8	Peak congestion avoidance	Athens	Uptake of scheme
3.7	Road capacity restraint and reduction	London	One-third of traffic 'disappeared'
6.5	Teleworking	Rome	Participation in experiment
3.8	Traffic calming	Bristol	Traffic flows in area down 10%
2.9	Traffic optimisation	Albertslund	Reduction in numbers of vehicles used

The cases in Table 9.1 are the most tentative 'successes'. Evidence is available to suggest that, at least, the positive side of the travel reduction behaviour has taken place. Without evidence of a reduction in car travel or travel overall, however, it is not possible to conclude that these cases represent actual travel reduction.

From the case studies considered, there are no clear correlations between the success of the measures and their particular classifications. For example, the 12 cases exhibiting explicit travel reduction (Table 9.3) fall into a range of policy categories and represent a variety of travel reduction mechanisms.

However, with reference to Tables 9.1 to 9.3, the following points may be noted:

- restraint measures can be used progressively to reduce traffic in an area, leading to large proportional decreases in particular locations;
- assessment of schemes targeting individuals or groups can reveal direct switches in behaviour – e.g., former car users who switch to cycling or car sharing, or commuters who switch their time of travel, in each case as part of a specific scheme;
- scheme-based data may demonstrate good relative levels of switching or travel reduction, but the absolute numbers may be small;

- most of the cases of explicit travel reduction (Table 9.3) refer to removal of car trips or reduction in car travel distance, perhaps reflecting the current emphasis of measures which aim to target car use; in these cases, the total amount of travel may be reduced, if switching from car to higher-occupancy modes leads to fewer vehicle kilometres.

The first three of these points relate in some way to geographical scale, whether in terms of scale of implementation or scale of impact assessment. These issues of scale are addressed in the next section.

9.4 Geographical scale

Measures can be implemented on various geographical scales. In the broadest sense it is possible to identify four of these: national, regional, city and neighbourhood scales. When assessing the overall scale of success of measures, both the relative impact (e.g., percentage travel reduction) and the geographical scale will determine the overall impact in absolute terms. Thus, a neighbourhood measure with a low level of impact individually could have the same overall impact if applied nationally, as a regional or citywide measure with a higher individual impact.

Table 9.2 Case studies showing positive reaction plus switching or substitution

Section	Measure	Case	Positive reaction	Switching or substitution
2.2	Car pooling	Netherlands	12% of commuter journeys made by car poolers	55% transfer from single-person car trips
2.5	Company work hours policy	Rome	Uptake of scheme	Time switching occurred
3.2	Cycle priority and roadspace	Bristol	Increase in number of cyclists; decrease in number of cars	Increase in modal share of cyclists; decrease in modal share of cars
3.2	Cycle priority and roadspace	Enschede	Increased cycle use	Modal share for bicycles increased from 34.2% to 35.6%
4.2	Cycle subsidy	Aalborg	22 000 bicycle km cycled	18 000 bicycle km had previously been by a different mode
5.4	Mixed-use development	Bucharest	Passenger numbers increased by 41%	8% of car drivers used public transport more frequently
3.3	HOV priority and roadspace	Madrid	HOV bus lane carries one-third of all vehicles and two-thirds of all passengers on the corridor	Average occupancy of private cars increased from 1.36 to 1.47 persons
2.8	Peak congestion avoidance	Lesvos	Uptake of scheme	Timings have shifted, reducing congestion around port
4.4	Public transport capacity investment	Zürich	S-Bahn carries 51% more passengers (and up to 90% more on upgraded lines)	Modal share for public transport has increased; that for car has fallen
3.6	Public transport priority and roadspace	Bucharest	Number of passengers increased by 39%; traffic on boulevards concerned decreased by 30%	Some mode switching to public transport
3.6	Public transport priority and roadspace	Bristol	Patronage increased by 9%	Modal share for car decreased from 88% to 72% (morning peak)
4.5	Public transport subsidy	Enschede	7.5–15% increase in patronage	Over one-third of new passengers had previously used car
3.7	Road capacity restraint and reduction	Edinburgh	Traffic levels reduced on routes affected (accident rates down 14%)	Traffic switched away from target route and parallel route
4.6	Road pricing	Norway	Number of vehicles entering cordon decreased by 5–10% (Oslo), 10% reduction in cars (Bergen)	42% of interviewees changed travel behaviour (switching mode, time or destination) (Trondheim)

Examples of measures implemented on a national scale are public transport deregulation (as in the UK) and fuel pricing (as in each EU country). Other measures vary in their geographical scale of implementation in different countries. For example, public transport subsidies are allocated nationally in the Netherlands, but by region or city in the UK and Romania.

The measures mentioned above are implemented uniformly throughout their geographical area. However, other measures may be operated on a wide geographical scale but not uniformly, i.e., they are implemented in different ways so that they fit local circumstances.

Most of the measures discussed in this book belong to this last category. A good example is the case of different traffic-calming schemes. Broadly speaking, in the city centre itself one can find the strictest measures (e.g., car-free city centres), while further out the form of traffic calming may become more relaxed (e.g., one-way streets, speed humps). Similarly, the most rigorous parking policies are normally found in central areas.

Traffic-calming schemes are fairly specific to residential or other sensitive areas. These are areas where space for roads cannot be expanded (city centre) or cars have a negative effect the liveability (e.g., in case of rat running

Table 9.3 Case studies showing positive reaction, switching or substitution and travel reduction

Section	Measure	Case	Positive reaction	Switching or substitution	Travel reduction
2.3	Car sharing	Leiden	In the Netherlands as a whole there are 60 000 people participating in car-sharing schemes	31% of car sharers were former car owners	Car use reduced by 500 km per person per annum
2.3	Car sharing	Culemborg	(see above)	22% of car sharers were former car owners	Car use reduced by 2 200 km per person per annum
2.3	Car sharing	Wuppertal	Uptake of scheme	Use of shared cars replaced private vehicle trips and trip-making rate	Reduction in distance travelled between 30 and 50%
5.5	Design of locations	Houten	Use of cycle lanes and pedestrian routes	Higher modal share for bicycles in the town	Car trip generation rate 10% less than Dutch average; less car use than for comparable towns
5.3	Location of companies	The Hague	Commuting to central offices by central station	Modal share for public transport up from 34 to 77%; modal share for car down from 41 to 4%	Distance travelled by car decreased by 69%
6.2	Home delivery of goods and services	Lesvos	110 000 transactions per year (10% of total)	Substitution of trips	Estimated saving of 400 trips per day
6.3	Informatics	Aalborg	Use of parking information system	Switching of route and destination in search of parking spaces	City centre traffic down marginally (0.3%); parking trip length down by 115 km per trip; reduction of 930 vehicle km /day (280 000 veh km/year)
2.7	Media campaigns	Enschede	Greater use of cycling among target group	12% of target group switched from car	20% of target group used car less
3.4	Park and Ride	Bristol	Uptake of Park and Ride service	56% of users would previously have travelled by car; modal share for car fell	500 car journeys to city centre saved per weekday
6.4	Teleactivities	London	9 000 tele-delegates participated	Telepresence substituted for travel	Estimated saving of 32 million km
6.5	Teleworking	Netherlands	Teleworking experiment uptake (200 workers)	Teleworking substituted for commuting trips	Average number of trips on teleworking day about half compared with normal day; distance under one-tenth; travel time about 40%.
5.2	Location of new development	Netherlands	Location of housing at 'VINEX' locations	Destination switching (on a limited scale)	Modest reduction in commuting distance; fewer car km/week

Note: Horizontal comparison shows how the additional data in successive columns give more convincing resolution of the travel reduction outcome.

and overspill parking from the city centre to residential areas). These are the areas where there will be public support for these measures. In areas where these difficulties do not occur, in most cases public protest will be a real barrier to implementation, because local residents do not feel the necessity for restricting car use.

In the Netherlands, new residential areas are designed as traffic-calming areas by preventing through-traffic from infiltrating the neighbourhood, whereas in the future whole neighbourhoods will have a speed limit of 30 km/h. In the city of Graz, Austria, the introduction of the same speed limit has been introduced on three-quarters of the city's road network (775 km) has resulted in fewer traffic accidents and an increased use of bicycles. Initially there was no majority in the population to support the measure, but now there is. In Zürich, there is a high degree of political autonomy for individual communes. This allows residents of a particular district to vote for measures which may disbenefit outsiders. For example, the 'Blue Zone parking restrictions' favour residents over commuters.

A general trend is thus seen to emerge from the case study cities: the most restrictive measures are applied in the central areas, whereas 'pull' measures are applied more uniformly across the cities. This results in a balancing of 'push' and 'pull' in the inner city. Traffic reduction or stabilisation can be realised in the city centre, while travel growth may continue unchecked in the suburbs, where the pull policies (encouraging use of public transport, cycling and so on) are not balanced by restrictions against car use.

Arising from consideration of the geographical scale of impact is the question of the most effective geographical scale for implementation. Improvements in public transport are most (cost-) effective in urban areas. Since roadspace in cities is limited, travel by car is already more difficult than in rural areas, and consequently demand for public transport is relatively high. For public transport priority measures, a certain amount of congestion is necessary to make the investment reasonable.

For most other measures there is no 'most effective' geographical scale, for example, they may be implemented in certain neighbourhoods, but could be extended to the whole city. The only limit to application then becomes the amount of resources available, e.g., to meet the expense of applying a company bicycle measure to the whole city.

Planning and land-use policies are mostly implemented on the city or regional level. In some cases there are strict guidelines from the national government. A drawback of these policies is that they deal mainly with new developments, and have less effect on the existing built-up area. This limits the effective geographical impact of such measures.

9.5 Benefits of measures relative to costs

The relative benefits of the implementation of a measure may be considered in relation to their costs. There are several difficulties in carrying out a classical cost-benefit analysis as a means of evaluating success: there are problems in evaluating the environmental benefits of reduced travel, as well as in determining good indicators of the costs of the measures themselves.

The costs of the individual measures are not difficult to calculate, but there are substantive variations in the costing methods used. For example, some measures are evaluated on basis of the full implementation costs of the measure as a whole, whereas some are based on partial or marginal costing, and others are evaluated using a cost-per-unit or cost-per-user basis. As a result, it is difficult to compare directly the costs of implemented measures.

Measures may also be financed in several different ways, ranging from full financing by the implementing body, through mixed or joint financing, to user-payer models of financing. The mixed models of financing may further confuse the assessments of costs of measures, both because it can be difficult to evaluate how much has been spent on the measure, but also because the financing of the measure can be distributed over time.

In addition to the economic costs, there are also the environmental costs relating to the externalities. In measures designed to encourage travel alternatives, much of the rationale is based on estimating the full costs of the proposal. This implies that the priorities central to cost-benefit analysis need to be broadened from a primary concern over travel-time savings to alleviation of the environmental costs.

As noted in Chapter 1 (Table 1.2), the external costs of transport are substantial and all forms of road tax (this amounted to £16.4 billion in 1993 in the UK) cover only 30–50% of these costs, which include air pollution, climate change, noise, vibration, accidents, and congestion. International researchers (e.g., DeLucchi, 1995; Schipper, 1995; Small and Kazimi, 1995) argue that these figures for external costs are too high and that the motorist pays about 70% of their full external costs. Maddison et al. (1996) conclude that the current taxes paid by road users amount to 3.1p/km. To internalise fully the externalities, this tax should be increased with an additional environmental tax of between 8.1 and 9.8p/km to give a total charge of between 11.2 and 12.9p/km.

There is substantial uncertainty over the values and assumptions used (e.g., the discount rates and the importance of global warming). Given this uncertainty, local air pollution accounts for about 4.8p per vehicle kilometre for car travel, whilst noise (0.78p), road damage (0.36p), accidents (1.5p) and congestion (4.6p) are the other main components. Global warming is insignificant in these calculations at only 0.024p per vehicle kilometre.

When the impact of a measure is being assessed, the benefits are rarely expressed in monetary terms. For a classical cost-benefit analysis it is necessary to translate both the costs and benefits into comparable units. Benefits of travel reduction measures are typically expressed in some modal-switching, trip-reduction or similar parameters. Assigning a monetary unit to these effects is difficult, as they are complex combinations of a variety of factors: reduced congestion can mean reduced emissions and an improved environment, as well as reduced journey times and the potential for greater efficiency and economic performance.

As noted above, the main benefits may lie in reducing vehicle kilometres, particularly by car, as this reduction will have substantial environmental benefits. Ironically, the external costs of using the car have been calculated with a view to charging the motorists more for driving their cars into the city (e.g., through road pricing and parking charges), but the same figures can be used to calculate the benefits from travel avoidance policies. In addition to the savings to the user, there are substantial environmental benefits, and there may also be benefits (quantifiable and unquantifiable) to the local economy and in the creation of quality neighbourhoods in cities.

Therefore, when comparing the cost-benefits of various measures it would be useful to establish some common form of benefits measure. This could be achieved, for example, by assigning a weighted average monetary benefit to switched mode or reduced-distance trip, or the benefit could be calculated from the number of switched or reduced-distance trips, giving a cost-benefit measure in, say euro/trip reduction. Alternatively, a more qualitative approach could consider broad categories of level of investment as opposed to precise cost-benefit calculations.

It is often possible to evaluate the relationship between the investment and the resulting reduction in car kilometres per inhabitant without precise data, because the difference between the effect of the measures is often very large. Table 9.4 shows how this might be done, grouping together some examples of measures. This is only an example of the more qualitative method; the location of the different measures may vary according to conditions in individual cities, and measures implemented on a small scale for a small outlay can achieve useful benefits.

Table 9.4 Travel reduction impact compared with cost of investment

		Investment	
		Small	**Large**
Impact	**Small**	Media campaign Car sharing	Public transport scheme (targeting existing public transport users)
	Large	Road pricing (implementation cost less revenue stream)	Traffic-free zone

The units of impact measurement and the scale of financing can be adjusted to the specific circumstances where they are to be applied. The term 'investment' is appropriate for a one-off payment, but in the cases where the financing is prolonged over a period of several years it is more correct to use 'net present value'. An estimate of net present value is also recommended where there is an income stream to take into consideration, for example, in the case of road pricing, as the revenue generated thereby would offset to some extent the investment or operating cost.

This kind of analysis demonstrates the benefits of travel reduction relative to its costs. Moreover, it draws attention to the fact that travel reduction is a means to an end. The reduction in trips and vehicle kilometres – and especially in car trips and car kilometres – is not pursued for its own sake, but to achieve wider environmental benefits (and in some cases, societal benefits or benefits of economic efficiency). Accordingly, beyond the 'third step' of evaluation of travel reduction there lies another set of evaluations, which will include the assessment of environmental and other benefits.

9.6 Considerations in evaluating success

If a city gives priority to travel reduction, it is necessary to collect detailed data to allow an explicit evaluation of each measure implemented. Without this detailed evaluation it is difficult to demonstrate and attribute the success of particular measures.

For a full assessment of the success of a measure, then, it would be necessary to take into account various parameters relating to travel reduction impact, while bearing in mind the geographical scale of impact and the relative cost effectiveness of the measure, and the wider environmental, economic and community benefits.

Evaluation data ideally allow precise calculation of the total reduction in numbers of trips and in passenger and vehicle kilometres in the area influenced by the measure. However, such detailed evaluation data are very seldom found, for a number of reasons; as we have seen earlier, one is that, unlike travel itself, it is difficult to measure 'travel reduction' directly.

Another reason is that the evaluation of measures does not always relate primarily to travel reduction, because travel reduction is often only one component – and possibly a secondary one – of the overall objective of a particular policy. For example, a parking information system may be established with the main objective of facilitating parking in city centres, but it could also be described in terms of attempting to reduce travel as this measure can reduce the distance and time taken to search for a parking space. A thorough evaluation of the success of a measure often becomes impossible because there are not enough evaluation data available relating to travel reduction. In particular, in some cases the measure may be perceived to be successful to the satisfaction of its promoters, and evaluation is considered unnecessary or too costly.

The availability of evaluation data on travel reduction can be treated by the three steps towards travel reduction introduced earlier, plus an additional level relating to objectives of the measure not related to travel reduction. The result is a graduation according to the quality pyramid in Figure 9.2.

Here, the higher they reach in the pyramid, the more useful the travel reduction evaluation data will be to establish travel reduction. In reality, the higher they appear up in the pyramid, the less likely it is that there will be data available. For most measures that are implemented, some evaluation data are collected about their success in terms of their own objectives, but for very few measures is a wider range of data obtained – e.g., on the growth in non-car travel as well as the reduction in car travel – thereby allowing a total view of the overall change in travel.

Furthermore, the higher levels in the pyramid often require the availability of data at the lower levels. In this interpre-

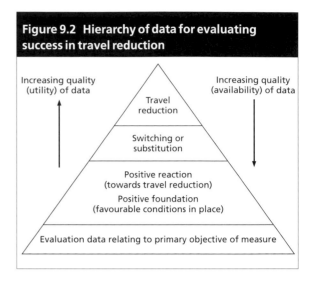

Figure 9.2 Hierarchy of data for evaluating success in travel reduction

Increasing quality (utility) of data

Increasing quality (availability) of data

Travel reduction

Switching or substitution

Positive reaction (towards travel reduction)

Positive foundation (favourable conditions in place)

Evaluation data relating to primary objective of measure

tation, the relative 'scarcity' of data at any particular level is related to the probability of all requisite data at the lower levels being available. In other words, it is first necessary to obtain data on use (positive reaction) before it is possible to deduce that switching or substitution has taken place, and only then is it possible to deduce that travel reduction has taken place.

In this respect it is possible to break down the levels shown into intermediate steps, equating with individual evaluation parameters or data requirements. A selection of evaluation parameters is presented in Table 9.5 which illustrates parameters applicable to the mode-switching mechanism; alternative or equivalent parameters would apply for different forms of switching or substitution. For example, substitution by technology would have parameters such as availability of telecommunications hardware and software (0.1.1); uptake and use of telecommunications (1.1, 1.2); evidence for substitution of telecommunications for travel (2.1). The final 'travel reduction' parameters (3) would, however, be the same.

Table 9.5 clearly demonstrates the potential extent and complexity of the data required for evaluating whether travel has been reduced. A combination of quality (utility) and quantity (availability) is required to demonstrate properly that travel reduction has taken place.

It can be seen that user surveys or household travel surveys can identify changes in travel behaviour and therefore directly account for the removal of trips or the reduction in distances. However, these do not necessarily give an indication of the overall scale of effects. Conversely, aggregate surveys of traffic volumes or patronage can give the overall scale of changes in travel, but cannot attribute causes or prove travel reduction. For the best estimate of travel reduction, some combination of these approaches

Table 9.5 Examples of evaluation parameters and data required

Degree of success	Parameter	Data required
	The result may be: (1) yes; (2) no; (3) no evidence from available data; (4) no data	Each data item typically requires both 'before' and 'after' data, and in some cases may also require trend data, or projections of what would have happened had the policy not been implemented
0 Positive foundation (while normally a prerequisite for successful travel reduction, the data used here does not contribute directly to the travel reduction evaluation)	0.1 Improved level of service for favoured mode (walk, cycle, public transport)	0.1.1 Availability of route or access to area for favoured mode 0.1.2 Capacity of route section for favoured mode (veh/h) 0.1.3 Transit time for route section for favoured mode (min) 0.1.4 Quality/comfort of journey by favoured mode 0.1.5 Frequency of public transport service (veh/h)
	0.2 Decreased level of service for car?	0.2.1 Availability of route or access to area by car, etc.
1 Positive reaction	1.1 Increased use of favoured mode by individuals?	1.1.1 Trips per person per day by favoured mode (walk, cycle, public transport) 1.1.2 Distance per person per day by favoured mode (walk, cycle, public transport)
	1.2 Increased use of favoured mode or patronage of service (aggregate)?	1.2.1 Pedestrian flows (ped/h) 1.2.2 Bicycle flows (cycle/h) 1.2.3 Public transport flows (passengers/h along route/corridor) 1.2.4 Public transport patronage (passenger boardings, passenger km)
2 Switching or substitution	2.1 Direct evidence of individuals switching mode	2.1.1 Stated evidence that trips formerly made by car have been replaced by trips made by favoured mode
	2.2 Increase in non-car modal share?	2.2.1 Modal share of favoured mode (walk, cycle, public transport) by numbers of persons (e.g., passing a cordon point) by number of person trips (e.g., generated in a zone) by numbers of person km (e.g., evaluated for a given city/network) 2.2.2 Modal share of favoured mode (public transport) by numbers of vehicles by numbers of vehicle trips by numbers of vehicle km
	2.3 Decrease in modal share of car?	2.3.1 Modal share of car by numbers of persons by numbers of person trips by numbers of person km 2.3.2 Modal share of car by numbers of vehicles by numbers if vehicle trips by numbers of vehicle km
	2.4 Increase in vehicle occupancy?	2.4.1 Vehicle occupancy of cars of buses, etc.
	2.5 Deduction that modal switching has occurred?	2.5.1 Combination of evidence from 1, 2.2 and 2.3

Table continues overleaf

Table 9.5 (continued)   Examples of evaluation parameters and data required

Degree of success	Parameter	Data required
3 Travel reduction	3.1 Reduction in car trips	
	3.2 Reduction in car km	
	3.3 Reduction in total number of trips	Deduced or calculated from combination of above data
	3.4 Reduction in total number of vehicle km	
	3.5 Reduction in total number of passenger km	

Note: This table addresses parameters and data requirements for the mode-switching case. Equivalent parameters would apply for the other switching or substitution mechanisms.

Table 9.6   Evaluation factors and their outcomes

Evaluation factor	Evaluation outcome
Primary purpose of measure	If the primary purpose of the measure is explicitly to reduce travel, the data collected are more likely to be useful; if a measure is directed at only one mode or one location, there may not be enough data to prove travel reduction.
Scale of target user group	Measures targeted at a contained set of users, e.g., company commuters or home workers, may have more detailed data on individuals' travel behaviour
Automatic data collection	Some technologically based measures, such as road tolling, may automatically collect data on traffic throughput
Timescale of application	Some measures, e.g., land-use measures, may take a long time to implement, and require long-term evaluation of their effects
Attribution of cause and effect	Some measures can demonstrate their effects clearly – e.g., pedestrianisation and the removal of all traffic from a street; others – e.g., commuted payments policies – are not 'visible' and only indirectly attributable to changes in travel
Positive side-effects	Apart from the availability of travel reduction results, many measures will have other benefits, such as environmental improvements, which may be tangible and appreciated by the public

would be ideal. This implies that more data, and a greater resolution of data, may be required to demonstrate convincingly the true extent of travel reduction.

9.6 Conclusion

This chapter has demonstrated the relative scale of success of the case studies in terms of travel reduction outcomes: as far as can be determined from the available data, they do indeed represent good practice. We can see that the estimated degree of success is dependent on the degree of resolution of the data available. We cannot always be sure exactly how successful a measure has been, but we can gain a broad impression of its minimum performance. At the most basic level, success must include a positive user reaction. The next level of success is demonstrable when some switching or substitution is observed. Finally, travel reduction itself may be observed or deduced via parameters such as a reduction in number of trips or a reduction in vehicle kilometres. Additionally, these travel reduction benefits may be closely related to various environmental benefits and if appropriate translated into monetary benefits.

Although success may be evaluated in this way, it seems that it will not always be possible to isolate the causes and effects of travel patterns, which in some cases are quite complex. For example, where a travel reduction measure is implemented at the same time as an improvement in capacity of the road infrastructure, the reductions in existing travel by car may be obscured by new travel generation or rerouting due to the improvement. Also, the apparent success of a measure may obscure an adverse mechanism. For example, a Park and Ride scheme may encourage longer trips or higher proportions of trips by car, or circuitous road layouts designed to deter car use may increase travel distances for those journeys made by car.

It is therefore possible that even if travel has not apparently been reduced, the measure may yet have played a role in helping to curb the growth in travel which may otherwise have occurred. This may make the scheme's assessment – and hence justification – difficult. Moreover, some measures may take a long time to implement (e.g., the building up of a bicycle network over a number of years) and an even longer time to take effect (such a network may only be influential in encouraging bicycle use once it is substantially completed). In the longer term, any travel reduction tendencies may be obscured amid the generally increasing trends in travel.

Overall, there is a range of factors affecting the likelihood of obtaining good evaluation data and positive results by which to demonstrate travel reduction success. Some typical factors are summarised in Table 9.6.

Transferability and Compatibility Analysis

10.1 Introduction

So far we have seen examples of a variety of travel reduction measures and how these have been applied in combination in particular cities. The question then arises: is it possible to transfer successful traffic reduction strategies to other cities or situations? Although case study data may show that a particular measure has been successfully implemented in one city, that same measure may not prove successful in another one. Yet it is vital for transport planners and decision makers to have a feel for the likelihood of its success in their city before making the decision to implement it.

This chapter presents a general approach to assessing the transferability of measures between cities. To judge the potential for the transferability of a travel reduction measure, it is necessary to consider the nature of the measures applied, and their travel reduction results, together with the basic characteristics of the cities involved and hence the differences between the circumstances in which the policies were to be realised. For example, it should be borne in mind that both problems and solutions may differ between large and small cities, and between different parts of Europe. Nevertheless, some useful comparisons may be observed.

Inter-city comparisons can help to clarify some of these questions. Comparative data, although unable to provide a complete solution, offer the opportunity to study what other cities are doing and to compare a particular city with a range of others. Which cities have similar characteristics to the one under consideration? Have they successfully reduced traffic levels using a measure which could be suitably transferred? Is it possible to learn from their mistakes?

This chapter allows comparison of equivalent data from a range of European cities. It allows interpretation of the data, showing the comparatively strong and weak points of any particular town or city, making it possible to assess the likely impacts of implementing the travel reduction measures. It therefore analyses the evidence by city, rather than by measure or policy package.

10.2 The seven case-study cities

In this chapter, seven case-study cities are explored in more depth. These cities are described in outline in the text, but more detailed comparative data are given in Tables 10.1–10.4. These cities have been selected to give a geographical range of city sizes, locations, different political contexts and policy priorities. They are not representative of European cities, but illustrative of the wide range of situations that have to be addressed when exploring the possibilities of travel reduction. The four tables give data for each city on a range of geographical scales, and they summarise the principal transport problems and policies. This presentation facilitates basic inter-city comparisons and identification of cities with similar characteristics. These comparative data act as the framework within which the transferability analysis can be carried out.

Aalborg, Denmark

Aalborg is the regional capital of North Jutland, and with some 125,000 inhabitants is the fourth-largest city in Denmark. The city of Aalborg's recorded history dates back to the beginning of the second millennium, but only in the last century has the city grown to be of some size and importance, with many industries and a university with approximately 10,000 students. Host to the Aalborg Charter of sustainable cities, the city has an attractive pedestrianised core and an extensive bicycle network.

Aalborg actually consists of two cities located on either side of the Limfjord Channel (Figure 10.1). Aalborg proper is on the southern side of this channel, while on the north side lies Nörresundby. Administratively, both cities are located in Aalborg Municipality; nevertheless, their separation by the channel presents an important physical barrier to movement.

A road bridge and a railway bridge currently connect the two city centres, and a tunnel links the southern and

Table 10.1 Comparative data: transport features of the seven case-study cities

City	Cars per 1 000 inhabitants	Cars per 1 000 inhabitants for country	Trips by public transport (millions/yr)	Trips by public transport (per inhabitant/yr)	Total length of cycle tracks (km)	Total length of cycle tracks per person (m)
Aalborg	399	310	15.3[a]	96	160	1.0
Bristol (former Avon area)	425 (1991)	374[b]	58	n/a[c]	n/a	n/a
Bucharest	162	93	924	454	5[d]	n/a
Edinburgh	289[a]	374[b,e]	148.5	330.85	128 (off-road 64)	
Enschede	361 (1994)	361 (1994)	6	41	152[f]	1.0
Rome	623	543	247	89	3	0.001
Zürich	364	450	341[g]	947	205	0.6

Notes: Data for 1995 unless stated otherwise.
a: calculated; b: UK figure; c: not available; d: not in use; e: 42.6% of households were without a car in Scotland in 1991; f: in built-up area only; g: weekend trips by S-Bahn and inner-city S-Bahn trips not included

Table 10.2 Comparative data: modal split (%) in the seven case-study cities

	Aalborg	Bristol[a]	Bucharest[b]	Edinburgh[a]	Enschede[c]	Rome	Zürich[d]
Car	54	55	4	49.5	42	53	28
Bicycle	15	3		1.5	38[e]	0	7
Walking	9	11	6	11.8	17	20	28
Public transport	10	27	90	34.5	4	27	37
Other	12	4	0	2.7	1	0	0

Notes: Data for 1995 unless stated otherwise.
a: trip to work (1991); b: preferred mode; c: residents only; d: Social data (1995); e: bicycle and moped.

Table 10.3 Comparative data: geographical features of the seven case-study cities

	No. of inhabitants: admin area	built-up area	Administrative area (km²)	Population density in administrative area (inhabitants/km²)	No. of people in employment in catchment area	No. of jobs in administrative area	No. of commuters inflow	outflow
Aalborg	160 000	125 000	552	290	300 000	85 303	21 300	9,600 (1994)
Bristol	400 000	550 000	110	3 650	980 000	210 000[a]	80 000	30 000
Bucharest	2 037 278 (1996)	n/a	228	8 935	278 541[b]	878 200 (1994)	300 000 (1992)	n/a
Edinburgh		448 850	260	1 698	767 800[c] (plus 30 000 self-employed)	252 000	71 500 (1991)	17 200 (1991)
Enschede	147,832	129 086	141	1 046	600 000	64 260 (1995)	17 818 (1994)	9 322 (1994)
Rome	3 660,000	2 760 000	1 307	2 800	5 185 316	1 033 253	66 728	15 628
Zürich	360 848	360 848	91	4 174	469 800	311 897	160 284	49 481

Notes: Data for 1995 unless stated otherwise.
a: built-up area; b: Sectorul Agricol Ilfov – area surrounding Bucharest and two other counties in the south of Bucharest; c: Lothian area.

Table 10.4 Comparative data: main transport problems and policies in the seven case-study cities

	Main transport problems	Main transport policies
Aalborg	High levels of traffic in the city centre Traffic forecasts show that there may be a need for a third crossing facility of the Limfjord channel	Ensure a transport supply which is satisfactory to citizens The public transportation system should serve community groups who do not have access to cars Public transport should help reduce the harmful effects generated by transport, without a significant reduction in accessibility to the city centre Conditions for weaker modes of transport should be improved Support and promote sustainable and environmentally friendly modes of transport The public transport system should be an alternative to the private car in the city centre
Bristol	Increasing traffic flows and congestion Traffic-related air pollution The adverse impact of motor vehicle use on vulnerable road users Relatively low public transport usage and concerns about accessibility	Break the pattern of increased car use Encourage alternatives to the car Discourage car use where alternatives are available Integrate transport, particularly public transport, with urban renewal and planned development Improve national and international links
Bucharest	Crossing the city by public transport is possible only by several transfers Radial tram network offers a low commercial speed Lack of proper behaviour and development connected with non-motorised travel modes Despite a network of large roads across the city, there are no exclusive public transport lanes High operating cost and low capacity of the public transportation system Obsolete traffic management The traffic capacity of roads is reduced by chaotic parking	Enforce restrictions on city centre parking Sustaining the investors interested in revitalising the historic commercial area Introduce a new economic policy to bring fuel and energy prices in line with international prices Implement physical measures for surface public transport Introduce socially-oriented subsidies for public transport Renew public transport fleet through purchase of new vehicles
Edinburgh	Fast rise in car ownership and car use (twice national average) Air pollution resulting from transport is responsible for over 100 premature deaths per year Decline in use of public transport overall since bus deregulation (135 million passenger journeys in 1992 compared to 177 million bus journeys in 1980) Lack of local rail and tram network Increasing suburbanisation and resulting commuter inflows (29% of people working in the city live outside its boundaries) Rise of out-of-town shopping centres which generate further traffic (one such centre, the South Gyle, is responsible for 200 000 extra car kilometres being travelled every day)	Introduce integrated strategy to increase public transport use, walking and cycling while reducing car use at the same time (Moving Forward Strategy) Greenway bus priority routes on key roads leading into city centre to speed up bus travel (see Section 7.5) Redistribute roadspace, privileging pedestrians, cyclists and buses, and restrict car access (in selected areas) Guided busway to the airport City Car Club to provide an attractive alternative to car ownership Restrictive parking policy (enforced by private company); metered parking as well as upper limit of number of car parking spaces allowed at new developments Build Car Free Housing Scheme for 120 households (supported by City Planning Department) Introduce road pricing (and by 2005) trial charge for bringing car into city centre (planned for 1999/2000) Reactivate disused railway lines, starting with Crossrail project connecting the city centre to the south-east of the city
Enschede	Growth of intra-urban car traffic Quality of life in residential areas is at risk due to problems with road safety, noise and air pollution	Increase the economic development and house-building in the city centre Reduce continual growth of intra-urban car use Make public transport more attractive Improve the bicycle infrastructure Discourage unnecessary traffic on city centre road network Create car-restrained (city centre and residential) areas

Table continues

Table 10.4 (continued) Comparative data: main transport problems and policies in the seven case-study cities

	Main transport problems	Main transport policies
Rome	Increasing congestion and difficulties in traffic flow management Increase in number of road accidents Traffic-related air and acoustic pollution The need to save more energy Inadequate public transport Residents' migration from the central area to the suburban areas and surroundings	Increase focus on vulnerable road users Introduce additional pedestrian reserved paths in the city centre, pedestrian areas and restrictions to private cars (ZTL) Plan land-use planning to favour a new citywide organisation according to the characteristics of each area Make public transport more attractive Increase priority management of road junctions Improve parking charge system and restrictions in free parking use Introduce additional Park and Ride infrastructure
Zürich	No additional space for significant traffic expansion	Adjust the existing space reserved for traffic Motivate people to switch from private car to public transport Reserve parking for inhabitants in their home district, as well as for the local traders Supply parking for short-term visitors Force soft mobility

northern highways, situated to the east side of the built-up area. The need for a third road-crossing has been subject to debate, although other alternatives, such as travel reduction strategies, are also under consideration. The potential for travel reduction strategies to obviate major new infrastructure construction therefore makes Aalborg an interesting case study.

Bristol, UK

With a population of around 450,000, the city of Bristol is the largest urban area in the south-west region of the UK, and one of the ten largest cities in England. The city has its origins as a port and river-crossing at the confluence of the Rivers Avon and Frome. It is expanding rapidly, particularly on the outer fringes, in terms of housing, employment, shopping and leisure developments. Bristol has experienced the national trend for declining traditional industries and a sustained growth in office development, 'hi-tech' servicing industry and warehousing distribution, and demands for out-of-town sites are rising.

These factors have contributed to growing levels of traffic entering the city, particularly car-based commuter flows. Car ownership in the region as a whole is running approximately 10 years ahead of the national figure, and the city has the highest level of car ownership and one of the highest levels of car use of all the large UK cities. These high levels of car ownership, coupled with high levels of

Figure 10.1 Aerial view of Aalborg, showing Limfjord Channel and crossings

in-commuting, relatively low public transport usage and increasingly dispersed workplaces and shops, mean that congestion is a continuing problem. As a response to this, the city has undetaken a series of measures to combat the increasing growth in travel and encourage alternatives to car use.

Bucharest, Romania

Bucharest is situated in south-eastern Romania, by the banks of the Colentina and Dambovita rivers and 64 km north of the River Danube. As the capital, Bucharest is the political, cultural, scientific and economic centre of the country. It is also the main focal point of the country's national road and rail networks. With over 2 million inhabitants, Bucharest occupies an area of 228 km², about 70% of which is the built-up area of the city.

In terms of urban form, Bucharest has three well-defined ring-shaped zones: the central zone, comprising public, political and administrative institutions and residential areas; the middle zone, with mainly residential areas and some industrial and commercial areas; and the peripheral zone, comprising large areas of blocks of flats and important industrial sites.

The major streets in Bucharest are laid out in a broad radial-concentric pattern. Many of these routes are formed by wide boulevards, with 15% of the network constituted of roads with six or more lanes. The city is well served by public transport, with a metro system, trams, buses and trolleybuses. Public transport use is high, running at about 90% of trips. However, car ownership and use have been increasing from a low base. Car ownership, especially, has shown rapid growth since 1990, with an average increase of 9% per year between 1990 and 1995 (DANTE Consortium, 1997: Appendix 12, pp. 183–189).

Edinburgh, UK

Edinburgh, the capital of Scotland, has a population of 450,000. It is one of the fastest-growing city locations in the UK and has an above-average growth in car ownership. The re-establishment of the Scottish Parliament in 1999 has given an additional boost to the status of the city, and it is anticipated that increased activity as a result of the parliament may well fuel the growth in travel to and within the city.

Unlike many other British cities, Edinburgh escaped the blight of large-scale road building and comprehensive redevelopment in the 1960s and 1970s, and has managed to preserve an attractive medieval and Georgian core more or less intact. The city centre therefore remains an attractive location for business and tourism, although the traffic and congestion generated as a result of this success is threatening to compromise this attractiveness.

The city is therefore having to balance the need to accommodate growth in travel demanded by business and tourism with the need to protect its historic centre and maintain its attractiveness to residents and visitors alike. The city has set ambitious travel reduction targets and has embarked on some innovative schemes to reduce car use.

Enschede, the Netherlands

Enschede is the central city of the Twente region, located in the eastern part of the Netherlands near the German border. With a population of 148 000, it is the tenth-largest city in the Netherlands. Along with Almelo and Hengelo, Enschede is part of the 'Bandstad Twente' (Corridor City Twente) in which urbanisation is being concentrated along the railway in order to optimise mobility and public transport accessibility. The built-up area of Enschede forms a quarter of the total area of the municipality, with the majority of the remainder being farmland or nature reserve.

Enschede was traditionally an industrial city, with employment concentrated in the textile and engineering fields, but more recently it has been shifting towards a service economy. A characteristic of the travel patterns in the city is the influx of visitors from Germany, especially at weekends and holidays.

The main road network of Enschede consists of three ring roads and various radial routes. Enschede has direct rail services to Amsterdam (including Schiphol Airport) and The Hague. Within the city, the bus provides the main form of public transport, with services focused on the bus station, which is adjacent to the central railway station. There is good provision of bicycle facilities within the city, and bicycle use is high.

Rome, Italy

Rome is the largest city and capital of Italy, with a population of around 3 million inhabitants. Internationally, Rome is a city of outstanding international significance as a historic and religious centre. Within Italy, it is an important centre of public administration and education with over 20 ministries and eight universities, including La Sapienza, the largest university in Europe with nearly 300,000 students. Overall, therefore, the city has an important role as a service centre and tourist destination.

Rome is served by three airports (the most important being Leonardo da Vinci Airport at Fiumicino) and it is a major railway hub (centred on Stazione Termini). The city has a subway system with two lines, and an extensive bus network. The road network is divided into several categories of route, including 80 km of urban motorways

Figure 10.2 Traffic in inner-city Rome

as well as main roads, inter-borough streets and local streets. The main routes for through-traffic avoid the most sensitive part of the city's historic centre, as part of a specific policy to protect the most vulnerable areas of the city which are of artistic, architectural and archaeological importance.

Rome has a metropolitan area of over 400,000 ha, comprising 65 municipalities and 19 districts. In recent decades there has been a shift in population towards the suburban and peripheral areas, with a decline in the inner-city population. This has led to greater travel demand in the outer areas of the city and increasing journey lengths. There has also been an increase in travel by private transport relative to public transport (Figure 10.2) (DANTE Consortium, 1997: Appendix 12, pp. 313–317).

Zürich, Switzerland

Zürich is the largest city and most important business centre of Switzerland. The city and its suburban hinterland are under separate political administrations, with 361,000 inhabitants in the city proper and a further 500,000 in the suburbs and outlying areas.

The average income of the inhabitants of the city and its hinterland is high compared with other European cities. This may be one reason why Zürich and its conurbation can afford what is considered an excellent (though expensive) public transport system, with a very high spatial density of services. This system includes buses, trams and the suburban railway, the S-Bahn, which was recently modernised with new lines, including underground links.

A high proportion of travel in Zürich is by commuters and others from outside the city proper. Although some 60% of trips in the city are made by inhabitants, they account for

less than half the travel in terms of passenger kilometres. The remainder is by those from the suburban areas and the rest of the canton.

10.3 Transferability analysis

Tables 10.5 and 10.6 show a selection of travel reduction measures implemented in each of the case-study cities, their suitability for each city and their potential for transfer to other cities. Eight different measures (or groups of measures) are presented from the 30 individual measures considered in Part I of the book. The main factors of success are identified, together with the necessary conditions. Using the city data (Tables 10.1–10.4) with the transferability analysis (Tables 10.5 and 10.6), it is possible to make a series of judgements on the likely applicability and the impacts of implementation in a different context. Where similar measures have been implemented in two or more of the case-study cities, it is possible to consider the appropriateness and relative success with a higher degree of confidence. Where a case-study city has not yet implemented a particular measure, the reasons behind this decision are explored.

This presentation is not intended to be prescriptive; rather, it is indicative of the careful analysis that is required before transferring the experiences from one city to another. We have tried to allow for variance between cities as each is unique, but it is important to be able to draw on the rich experiences of European cities which have already implemented travel reduction measures. The city data tables and the transferability analysis should not be carried out in isolation. They are part of the decision process and could be used by policy makers as a starting point so that new measures could be considered, particularly as parts of a package of measures that help achieve a citywide transport strategy or vision.

The city data (Tables 10.1–10.4) can also be used with the information presented in Chapter 9 on the scale of success of travel reduction measures. For each measure featured in the case-study cities, the three scales of success can be discussed:

- success in encouraging favoured behaviour (e.g., in the use of public transport or cycling);
- success in achieving a switching or substitution effect (e.g., a switch from the car to public transport);
- success in achieving measurable travel reduction.

The means by which this can be achieved is best illustrated with a flow diagram (Figure 10.3), which follows the course of events when different situations are

Table 10.5 Transferability analysis: policies one to four

City	Restrictions on city centre parking? (Section 3.5)	Area access control? (Section 3.9)	Land-use planning (various measures)? (Sections 5.2–5.6)	Telecommunications (various measures)? (Chapter 6)
Aalborg	**No** Attempts to collect developer contributions were unsuccessful; delays meant funds had to be returned	**Yes** Aalborg is continually extending its pedestrianised areas, and is now also implementing 'non-car roads' (i.e., for use by buses, bicycles and pedestrians)	**Yes** Aalborg has an extensive land-use planning scheme (and is starting to use an integrated planning approach similar to that of Aarhus) **But** A national system like the ABC system does not apply, so travel implications of land-use policy are not so fully addressed	*No formal schemes evaluated* A Danish study from 1996 showed that there is a possibility of travel reduction, but as many teleworkers tend to move further from their workplace (or take jobs further from their home), the total amount of travel may increase Similarly, teleconferencing and telecommunications in general may stimulate as well as substitute for travel
Bristol	MEASURE CASE (Section 2.4): Commuted payments scheme *Necessary conditions:* Legal framework *Other factors of success:* It may be helpful to have a successful Park and Ride site already in operation, to provide both an immediate alternative to car-based commuting and visible proof of an alternative	**Yes** Some pedestrianisation has been introduced in the city centre shopping areas Area access control measures linked to technological solutions may be promoted through the Clear Zones Project **But** Further extensive pedestrianisation would adversely affect central area accessibility, particularly for public transport vehicles Area-based temporal access restrictions have not been considered due to likely problems of implementation, legal constraints, administrative costs and issues of enforcement	**Yes** Planning policies focus development relative to transport but not in a formalised system like the Dutch ABC system Parking provision for new city centre development is restricted in accordance with the high levels of public transport accessibility found there	*No formal schemes evaluated* Some informal teleworking would occur amongst those in appropriate occupations, and a trial project involving a limited number of city council staff has been undertaken Widespread implementation would be likely to require enhanced IT/communications provision, together with a change in organisational practices and a full consideration of the impact on quality of life (loss of social interaction, health and safety issues, etc.)
Bucharest	**Yes** Parking restrictions by time and user are mainly in the central area of the city Restrictions are backed up by clamping/removal operations; good enforcement has led to good observance Needs to be accompanied by improvements to public transport	**Yes** In the city centre, access for goods vehicles over 5 t is limited; only vehicles with an entry pass and supply shops are allowed to enter The pass is free if used during the night; the rule does not apply to infrastructure service operators A project to reorganise the historical	**Yes** The Bucharest development plan for the next 25 years stipulates the concentration of new residential buildings in the north of the city, separate from business sites **But** An urbanism certificate is required for a new building, relating to its function; this may require parking to	**Yes** There is large-scale use of phone-based teleconferences by large companies and central government, which can reduce time and distance travelled **But** In other areas such as teleworking, uptake is hindered by lack of network infrastructure and limited

organisational experience

be provided, and hence contribute to the convenience of car use

centre is at the design stage; this will include banning car access and creating a pedestrian area

Needs to overcome objections from the car-owning lobby

Edinburgh

Yes There are strict restrictions on Greenway bus priority routes

A large proportion of city centre parking spaces are reserved for residential parking only (2 561 of 5 902 city centre on-street car parking spaces)

Parking meters are in operation for all non-residential parking places, strictly enforced by a private company

The number of car parking spaces permitted for new office developments in centre is limited by local planning rules

Parking restrictions have proved a very effective tool but there have been serious problems with local shopkeepers along Greenways routes complaining about loss of passing trade

Yes But pedestrianisation is only very limited so far; it is reserved to small side-streets off main shopping streets, although there are plenty of exceptions for people living locally and for local firms

Pedestrianisation of the main shopping street (Princes Street) is planned but has proven politically difficult

There has been some success with restricting access to buses, taxis and cyclists only, implemented on Princes Street and planned for the Royal Mile, the spine of the Old Town

No information available on formal schemes

However, given the prevalence of IT jobs in the city, teleworking (on an informal basis) is probably quite common

Meanwhile, the development of Edinburgh's IT sector in general has led to traffic generation, with many firms based at new out-of-town business parks or near Edinburgh Airport

Enschede

Yes A parking card scheme for residents in areas around the city centre is already in operation

The number of parking spaces is not being reduced, but the number of free spaces will be reduced and the parking charges increased

There is no legal basis for a commuted payments scheme

MEASURE CASE (Section 3.9)
Restriction of car use in city centre
Necessary conditions:
Participation of city centre businesses and inhabitants in the preparation of the measure
Other factors of success:
Enthusiastic project leader

Yes Development along public transport corridors encouraged

Public transport access improvements demanded from developers in return for expansion rights at shopping centres (recent examples: South Gyle west of the centre and Kinnaird Park, south-east of the centre)

Brownfield development encouraged over greenfield development, e.g., major regeneration of brownfield site in north-central part of the city, called Waterfront Edinburgh

But Patchy implementation (see non-complementary measures, Chapter 12)

MEASURE CASE (Section 5.3)
Influencing firm location (ABC classification)
Necessary conditions:
Good public transport network and a strict implementation of land-use plans (these are compulsory in the Netherlands)
Other factors of success:
This is the Dutch national policy, applied in Enschede by the local authority

MEASURE CASE (Section 6.5)
Teleworking, Netherlands
Necessary conditions:
The type of work must be suitable for telecommuting
The employee should be used to working independently
Most telework jobs require a personal computer at home, but in many cases some data communication is also required

Table continues overleaf

Table 10.5 (continued) Transferability analysis: policies one to four

City	Restrictions on city centre parking? (Section 3.5)	Area access control? (Section 3.9)	Land-use planning (various measures)? (Sections 5.2–5.6)	Telecommunications (various measures)? (Chapter 6)
Rome	**Yes** Parking and access restrictions for non-residents Further implementation of road pricing scheme	MEASURE CASE (Section 3.9) Restricted access zone *Necessary conditions:* Regulation and management of mobility in surrounding districts, to avoid 'congestion shift' from city centre to suburban areas *Other factors of success:* Extensive bus priorities allowing fast and reliable service provision Involvement of interest groups and organisations Extensive public awareness campaign	**Yes** The Municipality is undertaking initiatives to increase the overall quality of life and the best ways of using areas in accordance with the aim of overall sustainability **But** Difficulties in long-term land-use planning are encountered in Rome, mainly due to the 'anarchic development' experienced in the city centre from the 1950s to the late 1970s	MEASURE CASE (Section 6.5) Traffic decongestion teleworking (TRADE) *Necessary conditions:* Necessary telematic infrastructure, Affordable network access charges Employment flexibility and legal accommodation of issues such as safety, insurance, etc *Other factors of success:* A wide consensus towards developing teleworking from central government to local bodies, involving key actors such as new firms, public/private bodies and trade unions
Zürich	MEASURE CASE (Section 3.5) Parking restriction and capacity reduction *Necessary conditions:* Control of parking duration Additional enforcement required to guarantee success *Other factors of success:* No alternative free parking possibilities Good public transport supply as an alternative to using the car	**No** There are few pedestrian zones where car use is prohibited It is difficult to have a car-free city centre due to the topography: the space for roads in the inner area is limited	Since 1985 the canton of Zürich has had a masterplan of land use, whose key concept is that of mixed land use The city administration uses this law to oblige the land-owners to define the intended use of zones in a framework including public and private transport accessibility, the facilities for pedestrians and cyclists, parking space, sewerage and waste, water, energy and emissions The government must have the authority to implement the measure; barriers exist between the different levels of authority, e.g., the city level and the canton level	No information available

102

presented to planners in two different cities. The important messages are that transferability is a central part of any emerging view on the general application of travel reduction strategies, but that it must be tackled in a non-simplistic way, as there are many differences between cities. It should be seen as one part of the assessment process in which planners review experience elsewhere and learn from it. Transferability without consideration and modification is not likely to prove successful.

10.4 Compatibility analysis

As part of the transferability analysis, it may also be appropriate to carry out a compatibility analysis, which relates to whether the policy objectives being pursued in the different cities are consistent with each other. There seems to be an inherent contradiction between the desire of politicians to restrain (motorised) mobility but at the same time to maintain accessibility (and by implication economic competitiveness). In many cases, this contradiction has been reformulated as part of the sustainability debate or desire for sustainable mobility, which itself may be a contradiction of terms. The following examples illustrate some of the situations that have arisen.

- In Aalborg, the aim of the public transport policy is 'to reduce the harmful effects generated by transport, but without significant reduction in accessibility to the city centre'.

- The city of Bristol, while advocating a series of mobility restraining measures, moderates this by aiming for a 'balanced' approach, ensuring that the economic viability of the city is maintained and/or enhanced through the introduction of new transport measures. Indeed, it is reported elsewhere that one of Bristol's other key transport policies is to improve national and international links, which presumably implies promoting more travel, perhaps air travel.

- The city of Edinburgh aims to promote a healthy and sustainable environment. It has set ambitious targets to cut the share of journeys by car while reducing travel overall. Yet the city is simultaneously forging ahead with schemes that will result in more car travel, and it has had difficulty in resisting the temptation to grant planning permission to major new traffic-generating developments. It also aims to attract more international visitors, many of whom arrive by air.

- In Enschede, a major influence informing the city's transport policy has been the desire to 'keep the city centre accessible and increase its economic viability, while at the same time to improve the city's liveability'.

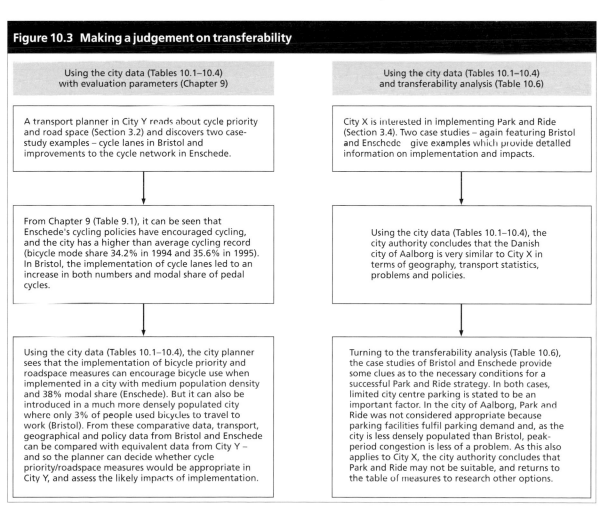

Figure 10.3 Making a judgement on transferability

Using the city data (Tables 10.1–10.4) with evaluation parameters (Chapter 9)	Using the city data (Tables 10.1–10.4) and transferability analysis (Table 10.6)
A transport planner in City Y reads about cycle priority and road space (Section 3.2) and discovers two case-study examples – cycle lanes in Bristol and improvements to the cycle network in Enschede.	City X is interested in implementing Park and Ride (Section 3.4). Two case studies – again featuring Bristol and Enschede – give examples which provide detailed information on implementation and impacts.
From Chapter 9 (Table 9.1), it can be seen that Enschede's cycling policies have encouraged cycling, and the city has a higher than average cycling record (bicycle mode share 34.2% in 1994 and 35.6% in 1995). In Bristol, the implementation of cycle lanes led to an increase in both numbers and modal share of pedal cycles.	Using the city data (Tables 10.1–10.4), the city authority concludes that the Danish city of Aalborg is very similar to City X in terms of geography, transport statistics, problems and policies.
Using the city data (Tables 10.1–10.4), the city planner sees that the implementation of bicycle priority and roadspace measures can encourage bicycle use when implemented in a city with medium population density and 38% modal share (Enschede). But it can also be introduced in a much more densely populated city where only 3% of people used bicycles to travel to work (Bristol). From these comparative data, transport, geographical and policy data from Bristol and Enschede can be compared with equivalent data from City Y – and so the planner can decide whether cycle priority/roadspace measures would be appropriate in City Y, and assess the likely impacts of implementation.	Turning to the transferability analysis (Table 10.6), the case studies of Bristol and Enschede provide some clues as to the necessary conditions for a successful Park and Ride strategy. In both cases, limited city centre parking is stated to be an important factor. In the city of Aalborg, Park and Ride was not considered appropriate because parking facilities fulfil parking demand and, as the city is less densely populated than Bristol, peak-period congestion is less of a problem. As this also applies to City X, the city authority concludes that Park and Ride may not be suitable, and returns to the table of measures to research other options.

Table 10.6 Transferability analysis: policies five to eight

City	Park and Ride? (Section 3.4)	Public transport investment? (Section 3.6 and 4.4)	Cycle priority and roadspace? (Section 3.2)	Cycle subsidy? (Section 4.2)
Aalborg	**No** There is already sufficient city-centre parking to fulfil demand. There is not enough congestion in the city at peak hours to justify such a scheme	**Yes** Bus priority lanes along several bus routes. Allows buses to keep to timetable, even at congested times. In central area, buses are allowed where car access is restricted	**Yes** University city with tradition of high modal share for cyclists. Facilities continue to be developed by provision of new bicycle lanes and paths	MEASURE CASE (Chapter 4.2) Company bicycle scheme. *Necessary conditions:* An awareness campaign is important to 'sell' the idea. The bicycles were given free to participants, but had to be used for a specified distance. *Other factors of success:* Bicycle-friendly environment
Bristol	MEASURE CASE (Section 3.4) Park and Ride. *Necessary conditions:* Bodies able to fund and carry out the implementation. Parking restrictions: Park and Ride must be a more attractive option than driving. *Other factors of success:* Extensive bus priorities allowing fast and reliable service provision. A high-profile marketing campaign	MEASURE CASE (Sections 3.6 and 7.6) Bus priority on Bristol–Bath corridor. *Necessary conditions:* Enforcement to prevent violation. Bus lane violation was reduced markedly when treated with red surfacing	MEASURE CASE (Section 3.2) Cycle lanes. *Necessary conditions:* Policy support and follow-up measures. *Other factors of success:* Existence of cycle culture is important. Bicycle measures can be introduced as a leisure activity, then extended to other journey purposes. Promotional strategies can be valuable	**Yes** E.g., City Council Employee Scheme: which gives a tax-free allowance for business travel by bicycle, a loan for purchase of a bicycle, pool bicycles and secure parking at many offices. Bristol also supports the introduction of workplace-based Bicycle User Groups which seek to promote cycling
Bucharest	**No** Lack of financial resources. Congested public transport network: demand currently exceeds supply, so any Park and Ride scheme would contribute to overcrowding	MEASURE CASE (Section 3.6) Bus lanes. *Necessary conditions:* Obtaining authorisation from the municipality and other agents. The allocation of exclusive lanes requires adequate street width and capacity. *Other factors of success:* Prolonged green signal phase at traffic lights in the direction of the exclusive lane. Restraint on stopping and parking. Clear road markings and traffic signs. Enforcement by the traffic police. Creating awareness among car drivers	**No** Low level of cycling demand and poor use of the few bicycle lanes provided (one converted to a parking area). Perception of cycling as a leisure activity, not a transport mode. Lack of funding, perceived lack of value for money. Bicycle lanes are unpopular with car users because road capacity will be reduced	**No** Lack of resources

Edinburgh	**No, but** Two schemes to the west of the city are planned to become operational by 2000 and several smaller schemes do exist in the outer commuter belt, particularly in the Fife area, across the River Forth	**Yes** Bus priority lanes along all major routes leading in and out of the city centre Greenways show that determined bus prioritisation can make a difference, as 250,000 extra passenger trips were recorded within the first 6 months of the new scheme alone	**Yes** Substantial increase in bicycle lanes on and off roads (128 km overall) On-road bicycle paths targeted around Edinburgh University Major programme of creating advanced bicycle stop lines at traffic lights Cycle priority measures linked with 'Greenways' bus priority scheme Cycling policy success largely due to very effective campaigning by local cycling pressure group, SPOKES, so that cycling is a high-profile policy issue at all levels	**Yes** Council staff are paid a mileage allowance if they commute by bicycle or use their bicycle on council business The council has a dedicated four-person team on cycling acting as cycling advocates within the administration The local Chamber of Commerce supports green commuter plans and payment of a mileage allowance to cyclists
Enschede	MEASURE CASE (Section 3.4) Park and Ride *Necessary conditions:* Police directing visitors' cars to parking area Limited number of parking places available in city centre *Other factors of success:* Dedicated service, with low level of access to residents	**Yes** Bus priority lanes are currently limited to the city centre and some new residential areas Two new high-grade bus lanes are planned, to link the outer residential areas with the city centre Buses are given priority at traffic lights	MEASURE CASE (Section 3.2) Cycle route improvements *Necessary conditions:* Existence of bicycle culture: infrastructure provision alone will not lead to more cycling Measure must be built over several decades *Other factors of success:* Travel distances should not exceed 8 km Purpose of trips should not be limited to leisure activities	**Yes** In the Netherlands almost every person has at least one bicycle Company bicycle schemes are being expanded Around 100 000 bicycles have been provided by companies to their employees Reduced taxes and exemption from VAT It is also possible to hire bicycles
Rome	**Yes** Parking spaces located at interchange points	**Yes** Required public funding and commitment from the municipality Introduction of new ticketing system Introduction of new services accompanied by a large advertising campaign Accompanied by restrictions on access by car and the introduction of parking charges Creation of Park and Ride areas (free of charge with a bus season ticket)	**Yes** Pilot measures have been introduced: bicycle paths, bicycle lanes, and public transport/bicycle interchanges are planned	No information available

Table continues overleaf

Table 10.6 (continued) Transferability analysis: policies five to eight

City	Park and Ride? (Section 3.4)	Public transport investment? (Section 3.6 and 4.4)	Cycle priority and roadspace? (Section 3.2)	Cycle subsidy? (Section 4.2)
Zürich	**Yes** Swift transfer to fast S-Bahn service direct to city makes Park and Ride an attractive alternative to other modes Restrictive parking policy for the city centre	MEASURE CASE (Sections 3.6, 4.4 and 7.3) Public transport capacity investment and priority *Necessary conditions:* Running a dense and frequent public transport service is expensive Coordination with local feeder services is essential Adequate roadspace to create separate lanes *Other factors of success:* Parking restrictions in the city centre significantly aid mode switching	**Yes** Provision of cycle lanes and other facilities **But** Cycling is in competition with excellent and inexpensive public transport Topographic and climatic conditions are not conducive to cycling – only a limited part of the city is flat	No information available

- In Zürich, there are policies for promoting public transport while restraining car traffic. However, the parking management policy, which makes it difficult for commuters to park, has the effect of making more parking spaces available for shoppers and other visitors, thereby encouraging more trips of this type.

Economic competitiveness is the key to this drive to maintain accessibility. Thus, in the case of Aalborg, a parking information system makes it *easier* for shoppers to park in the city centre. The system is supported by the business community, as it allows the city centre to compete with larger shopping centres elsewhere. Meanwhile, in Enschede the purpose of the transport policy is to combat congestion because it jeopardises the accessibility of the city centre and hence economic development. The strategy is quite explicit: to free up capacity on the main roads to allow visitors from the surrounding region to visit Enschede.

Therefore, while the policies outlined above may assist with travel reduction objectives, they appear to be driven by economic considerations. It would appear that as long as travel reduction policies are in line with these wider city objectives, they have a chance of promotion and implementation. Where they do not, however, those policies are likely to suffer.

Thus, in Edinburgh, proposals for road pricing have met a hostile response in some quarters. The City Council's transport convenor was accused of 'killing' Edinburgh and its business community. The plans are being delayed. Elsewhere, the city's policy of opposing new out-of-town shopping developments has been overturned in the case of a recent superstore proposal, due to the fear of the loss of jobs and competition from other nearby centres such as Livingston (Mittler, 1999b).

We have seen that there is sometimes a policy paradox because of the conflicting objectives of reducing mobility while maintaining accessibility. Yet, in the case studies reported here, we have also seen that a wide range of policies has been implemented with some degree of success. The extent to which travel reduction has been successful has been seen in Chapter 9; it includes shifts in modal share, replacement of car trips and overall reductions in vehicle kilometres. The question then becomes: how have these cities managed to achieve this travel reduction, without compromising accessibility or other policy objectives?

On closer inspection of the cases, it is seen that there has not been a uniform application of travel restraint. The cities studied have achieved their results largely by means of targeting. This is done mainly on two fronts: user group and location. As we shall see now, these are often closely related.

Targeting by user group

In many cases travel reduction policies are targeted towards particular user groups, defined by journey purpose. The main target in the cases studied is the commuter.

In Bristol, travellers commuting by car have been the main target. Commuters are encouraged to switch to public transport, by leaving their cars at home or transferring to the bus at Park and Ride sites, or by cycling (Figure 10.4). As the Park and Ride scheme has succeeded for work journeys, the shopping and leisure markets are also being targeted.

In Enschede, it is the city's own inhabitants, especially car travellers, who are the main target. In the city centre, however, access restrictions do not apply to residents or business proprietors, and so in practice it is local commuters or shoppers who are affected. The Park and Ride scheme targets German visitors.

In Rome, also, commuters are the target and residents and local businesses are exempt from central access restrictions.

In Zürich, the restrictive parking policy is aimed mainly at commuters. This has freed up space for short-stay parking, leading to increases in shopping and leisure trips.

Figure 10.4 Competition for roadspace along a radial corridor in Bristol, where commuting by car is discouraged in favour of commuting by bike or public transport

Parking is also made easier for residents, by a residents' parking scheme. Indeed, the car mobility of residents has increased.

In the case of Aalborg, policy is directed at a more general range of travellers. The parking information system is devised to assist shoppers. The other policies also tend to promote travel – by bicycle or bus – or make it easier to negotiate congestion, for traffic in general.

Similarly, in Edinburgh, the general policies of promoting public transport and cycling potentially apply to any traveller. However, the car-free housing and car club schemes there are directed at (inner-city) residents, while improvements in the pedestrian environment on Princes Street and the Royal Mile would no doubt particularly benefit shoppers and visitors.

The targeting of user groups has been successful. This makes certain types of (car) travel sufficiently inconvenient for trip switching or substitution to take place. Thus, the Park and Ride system in Zürich is reckoned to have led to a 4.5% reduction in car commuting, and it is estimated that at full capacity a 10% reduction could be achieved. The implementation of the company bicycle scheme in Aalborg targeted specific employees; this was successful in that it encouraged bicycle use among scheme participants, where 44% of trips by bicycle replaced car trips.

Targeting can also be more clearly demonstrated to be successful because it permits sufficiently disaggregated monitoring for mode switching and travel reduction to be detected. For travel reduction, then, targeting of users seems to be a successful strategy, although it leaves open the question of whom is being encouraged to change their behaviour, and who is able to 'carry on regardless'.

Targeting by location

The other key area of targeting is location. While many of the policies may aim generally to reduce travel and traffic overall, there is a distinct tendency to concentrate on the central areas of the cities concerned.

In Aalborg, the main focus is to reduce the overall volume of traffic in the city centre; for example, the aim of the public transport policy is to make public transport a convincing alternative to the private car in the central area. The parking information scheme is aimed at reducing city centre traffic by reducing the time and distance spent searching for a parking space. The central area is also the focus for environmental improvements such as pedestrianisation.

In Bristol, while no areas are targeted explicitly in the cases under consideration here, the main emphasis appears to be on radial transport to and from the city centre, implicitly aimed at maintaining accessibility to the centre. This applies to commuting, shopping and leisure journeys alike.

In Edinburgh, a variety of locations are included. The central area does feature prominently, in the improvements to Princes Street and the Royal Mile. As in Bristol, promotion of public transport on radial routes affects many parts of the city – and reaches out to the airport – but these routes are themselves focused on the city centre.

In Enschede, much attention is paid to the city centre, with pedestrianisation and other restrictions to vehicular access; however, other measures such as traffic calming and bicycle facilities are applied across the town, including the outlying areas.

In the case of Zürich, transport policies formulated in the city affect the travellers from the rest of the conurbation. The promotion of public transport and the provision of Park and Ride serves those from across the conurbation, while there is a reduced parking supply in the inner areas. Parking is restricted in the inner city – except for residents, who benefit from spaces being more available.

As with targeting of users, the targeting of locations can be seen to be successful, as traffic volumes have often been successfully reduced in the inner areas. At the very least, the results of policies, such as the removal of traffic in central streets, can be clearly seen on the ground (while the corresponding increases in traffic elsewhere may not be so visible). Targeting by location is also closely linked to targeting by user group, such as commuters and shoppers, who typically live outside the central areas but travel there to fulfil their journey purpose.

It is implicit in Park and Ride, where there is no complementary roadspace restraint, that as more existing car drivers switch to public transport, more roadspace is freed up for other car drivers. Some of these drivers would not have visited the city centre without this encouragement. Because of the efficiency of public transport (more passengers per vehicle or passengers per hour), the total potential throughput of travellers to the city centre is increased.

This increased throughput by public transport would not normally be reflected in increased traffic levels on the corridor. Indeed, traffic levels may go down, as the increased number of passenger trips is accommodated in higher-occupancy vehicles. It appears that traffic has been restrained or reduced, although travel (at least in terms of passenger trips) has increased. As far as the city (and particularly its economy) is concerned, this is a win–win situation. It is indeed the fulfilment of the policy of restraining mobility while maintaining accessibility.

Seen in this light, it is not surprising that measures that aim to switch trips from cars to public transport are popular. Indeed, public transport measures as a means of 'travel reduction' are present in all the city cases studied. This is also in accord with the general observation that the 'mode switching' category is clearly the most popular form of travel reduction mechanism (Marshall *et al.*, 1997).

10.5 Conclusion

Each city and each application of travel reduction measures is unique. But it is still important to establish the necessary conditions and constraints for successful implementation. In this chapter, we have used transferability analysis to try to control for as much of the possible differences between cities. It also allows decisions to be based not just on the evidence of the travel reduction measure, but also on the city context within which it is placed. The transferability analysis is also based on a matrix of measures versus cities, so that one can review the alternatives by measure or by city (Tables 10.5 and 10.6). Alternatively, the transferability analysis can be problem-related and linked to the illustrative flow diagram (Figure 10.3).

In addition to the transferability analysis, we have described a compatibility analysis where the broader context of the transport strategy of the city is examined. Here, it is suggested that there are many common elements among the policies being adopted within the case-study cities, but that there are also important differences and inconsistencies. This is where that the real dilemmas facing policy makers become apparent. There is the inherent problem that travel reduction measures might lead to counter-productive results (i.e., an increase in

travel). These issues have been addressed in the previous three chapters. More fundamentally, there is often a basic inconsistency in policy making. Many cities aspire to a sustainable transport strategy, but most actions taken tend to reduce its sustainability rather than increase it, particularly when viewed in the citywide and regional context. The city centre may be sustainable, but the suburbs and peripheral business parks and retail centres are the new generators of unsustainable transport.

Our conclusions on this inconsistency are twofold. First, it is important that good practice is subject to careful scrutiny and analysis before being transferred to another city (or even elsewhere in the same city). It should be subject to careful discussion between those who have implemented the measure and those who have yet to implement it. The design of all travel reduction measures needs to be carefully assessed, as good demonstrations are likely to encourage further implementation. Poorly thought-out demonstrations, particularly of controversial measures, are likely to have further negative repercussions, as no city will be willing to take the risk of re-introduction or to try the extension of an unpopular measure. High-quality monitoring is required before, during and after the implementation, so that fine-tuning can take place.

Secondly, a compatibility analysis should also be carried out to ensure that the measures being transferred fit into the overall policy strategy of the city. This compatibility analysis is crucial, as it provides the necessary conditions for success. As noted in Chapter 1, many cities have similar broad policy objectives on transport and the environment. However, we have also pointed out differences in both interpretation and detail, but more importantly in levels of political and public support for action. The measures being transferred must be appropriate, but equal importance should be allocated to the exact form of measure implementation, its scale, timing, compatibility with the policy of the city and popularity with the city's residents.

Barriers to Implementation

11.1 Introduction

When the effects of transport policies are studied, most attention is paid to policy making and policy effects. The outcome of a political decision is a set of measures to tackle a particular problem. Policy makers then sit and relax, and wait for the results. It is more or less taken for granted that once a policy decision has been made, the policy will be implemented and the people will respond with the expected changes in behaviour. When the results of a policy fall short of their expectation, the people are blamed. Individuals regularly refuse to behave in ways that the policy makers would prefer. This gap between the assumptions underlying policy measures on the one hand, and the behavioural responses by individuals on the other, is normally referred to as the policy–behaviour gap. In reference to the gap between policy measures and behavioural responses to congestion, Salomon and Mokhtarian (1997) point to the large set of alternative strategies that individuals have at their disposal to avoid the expected behaviour.

However, unexpected or unintended behaviour by the public is only one explanation. Another is that something went wrong during the implementation so that the measure has not accomplished what was intended. This may even occur with a potentially promising measure that seems likely to achieve a clear policy goal. During policy making, there are not only expectations about the behaviour of the public, but also about the way a measure can be implemented. According to Smith (1973: p. 199), 'problems of policy implementation may be more widespread than commonly acknowledged'. If the programmes are of a new, non-incremental nature, difficulties with implementation may occur. This has been the case with attempts to reduce car use. The old response to increased car use was to provide more infrastructure. However, increased accessibility and capacity gave rise to more traffic. Many cities could scarcely cope with more cars and a policy shift towards traffic restraint was made.

In this chapter we will discuss the implementation of measures with the objective of reducing car use in cities,

in Section 11.3 on the measure level, and in Section 11.4 with a broader policy level in mind. But first we will outline the importance of implementation and the relationship between implementation and the success of the measure and/or policy.

11.2 The importance of implementation

The term 'implementation' can have several meanings. It may refer to the operating routines of an organisation that is responsible for the implementation of policy, or to empirical details that reflect the application of a policy principle, such as the amount of a tax rise. In this sense implementation can be seen as a process. According to Quade (1989: p. 338), 'implementation is a directed change that follows a policy mandate, the process of rearranging patterns of social conduct so as to honour the prescriptions set forth in some policy mandate'. By this definition, implementation starts after the decision to adopt a specific course of action is made, and continues until this course is well established and integrated into the activities of the system.

However, this does not mean that the political decision level, at which objectives are set and measures to achieve these targets are chosen from a set of alternatives, is not important to implementation. Good decision making takes account of the difficulties which might appear during the implementation process. If, for example, it is clear that a proposed measure will encounter difficulties during implementation, policy makers should address those difficulties or not implement the measure at all. The implementability is of even greater importance, as is the potential of the measure to influence behaviour. A measure's success may therefore depend on the manner of its implementation. Good implementation is important because bad implementation:

- increases the risk of obtaining unintended results (side-effects);

- will lower public support (and also for measures to be implemented in the future);
- will use unnecessarily, or waste, the resources of the implementor.

It is therefore important to recognise that some measures have a better chance than others of being successfully installed and implemented. The measure that is to be implemented 'should not necessarily be the one with the greatest potential for an excess of benefits over costs unless the probabilities of successful initiation and implementation have been estimated and the expected costs that would be incurred by failure have been taken into account' (Quade, 1989: p. 341).

In theory, the distinction between policy making and policy implementation is clear. In practice, however, this distinction is not always explicit because policy is shaped as it is put into practice (Ringeling, 1987). During implementation there is always something that does not perform according to plan. For instance, conditions occur that differ from those anticipated. These unforeseen barriers may threaten the optimal implementation of a measure, or make it necessary to implement the measure differently from the way initially intended. In addition, measures are often adjusted on the basis of experience or changed circumstances. Sometimes, demonstration projects are set up just to gain relevant experience, before full implementation. Therefore the process should be seen not as a linear model in which policy decision making is followed by direct implementation, but rather as a circular process in which some kind of negotiation is involved. Negotiation takes place both in the stage of detailed scheme definition and during the implementation itself.

The implementation process of a particular policy or measure cannot be analysed in isolation. There are always adjoining policies and situations that influence the policy under consideration (Figure 11.1). In evaluation studies, the normal practice is to look at the policy under consideration and the intended results or the behavioural response of the public. When we evaluate the policy implementation, we analyse the creation of a measure, such as a bicycle path, a Park and Ride scheme or traffic calming. Maat and Louw (1999) call this the policy output, and the resulting behaviour the policy effect. This chapter deals with the policy output exclusively. We look at how an implementor has created or produced the measure in relation to the original plan, and which obstacles are met.

For the implementation of a measure, other policies and variables are important and should be taken into account. It is important to realise that policy variables are under the control of the implementor, whereas situation

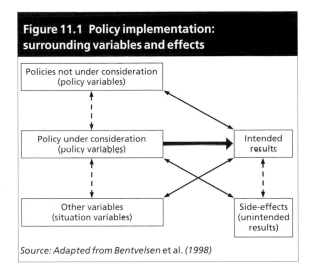

Figure 11.1 Policy implementation: surrounding variables and effects

Source: Adapted from Bentvelsen et al. (1998)

variables are not. The meaning of policy and situation variables can best be explained by an example.

Let us suppose that a city administration wants to introduce a Park and Ride scheme to reduce the number of cars entering the city. The intended result of the implementation is a large car park on the fringe of the built-up area, and a frequent bus service between the car park and the city centre with the exclusive use of bus lanes. The policy under consideration is the transport policy. A policy not under consideration but of equal importance to the implementation is spatial planning. A site has to be found for the car park, in a way that is appropriate from the transport point of view. That is, the site has to be located where a large number of customers are expected. At the same time, this location has to be available from the planners' point of view. For instance, if the site is designated for a new residential neighbourhood, planners will be opposed to that location.

Other variables may differ considerably, depending on the measure involved. In the case of the Park and Ride scheme, the price can be important. If the price for entering the city is low compared with the price of the Park and Ride scheme, the scheme is at a disadvantage. Why should one buy an expensive ticket, just to enter the city? Additional measures may be necessary, such as introduction of high parking fees in the city or restriction of the number of parking spaces. The side-effects of Park and Ride schemes are not unknown. Congestion may occur near the site, or levels of traffic in the hinterland may increase. Also, the construction of a bus lane may reduce the number of parking spaces in neighbourhoods through which this bus lane runs. These side-effects may take the form of an uncomfortable consequence, and a policy-driven outcome that was not foreseen at all (Hallsworth et al., 1998). Both foreseen and unforeseen side-effects may influence the implementation of measures. Foreseen side-effects are to be taken into account during the stage of (political) decision making, while unforeseen side effects may lead to adjustments of a measure that has already been implemented.

11.3 Barriers to implementation of measures

There are several forces that prevent a measure from being implemented in its most ideal form. They could either reduce its potential once implemented, or even make implementation impossible. Barriers may vary from country to country, and even from region to region. Also, there may be variations in time, because situational variables change.

Barriers can be divided into five main categories: institutional/policy, legal, resources, social/cultural and side-effects.

Institutional and policy barriers

These include problems over coordinated actions between different organisations or levels of government, and conflicts with other policies. The large number of public and private bodies involved in transport provision in most countries often leads to difficulty in achieving coordination of action by the implementors (see the Bucharest case study, below). Sometimes this is due to differences in cultures between departments (e.g., bureaucratic versus market-orientated). In other cases, differences in the distribution of legal powers between governmental bodies affects the implementation of measures and schemes. Also, the implementing organisation itself has to be well equipped to accomplish the implementation properly. An unstable administrative organisation and unqualified personnel may reduce the capacity to implement (Smith, 1973).

Institutions and priorities: Bucharest, Romania

Due to the high level of traffic congestion in the central area of Bucharest, the Technical Commission for Traffic Safety and Fluency proposed the implementation of a one-way traffic system including exclusive lanes for buses and trolleybuses. This scheme encountered institutional and policy barriers which were also linked to legal and resource barriers.

Firstly, there is no transport authority, at either the national or the local level, even in Bucharest. This means that it is difficult to coordinate and integrate all transport operators' activities, which can sometimes lead to side-effects that reduce the effectiveness of the measures.

Secondly, the process of project approval and procurement is complicated by the number of decision-making agents involved at different stages in the project approval. This can lead to a long and laborious process before the measure can finally be implemented (Figure 11.2).

Thirdly, the institutional context in Bucharest also affects regulation of transport; the absence of a transportation law that allows allocation of priority to public transport results in a legal barrier to the introduction of bus lanes.

Fourthly, there is a lack of autonomy in the Municipality of Bucharest, resulting in prolonged processes at the local level. The implementation of transport projects requires the investment of significant sums which are hardly covered by the municipality budget, due to its dependence on the state budget. This is also a resource barrier.

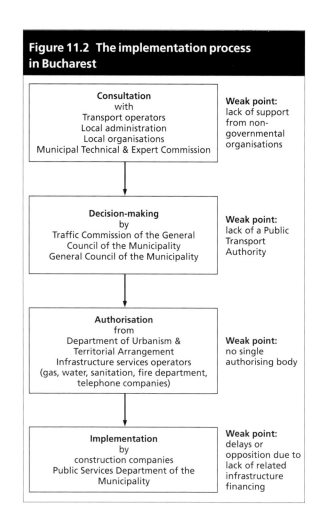

Figure 11.2 The implementation process in Bucharest

Consultation with Transport operators Local administration Local organisations Municipal Technical & Expert Commission	Weak point: lack of support from non-governmental organisations
Decision-making by Traffic Commission of the General Council of the Municipality General Council of the Municipality	Weak point: lack of a Public Transport Authority
Authorisation from Department of Urbanism & Territorial Arrangement Infrastructure services operators (gas, water, sanitation, fire department, telephone companies)	Weak point: no single authorising body
Implementation by construction companies Public Services Department of the Municipality	Weak point: delays or opposition due to lack of related infrastructure financing

Legal barriers

Many transport policies and measures necessitate adjustment of laws and regulations, within or outside the realm of transport. If implementation is complicated by legal requirements or even made impossible by law, legal barriers are raised (see the London case study, below). They can occur at several levels. For example, the design and signposting of transport schemes in almost all countries is circumscribed by government regulations and directives. Although many of these are beneficial in ensuring reasonable standards, others can impose restraints on innovative solutions. When good implementation requires changes in rules or regulations outside the transport domain, one can expect that more effort will be needed to facilitate these changes, as compared to changes that concern an alteration to the transport rules alone.

Changing the rules: London, UK

As part of a 'live/work' initiative in the inner London borough of Hackney, proposals were drawn up for a mixed-use zone integrating housing and business uses. However, the existing planning regulations did not allow residential and employment uses to be located in the same unit. Therefore, in this case, in order to allow the development to take place, the borough council has changed planning and building regulations, thus enabling the scheme to be realised.

Resource barriers

The principle is very simple. To implement a measure, adequate financial or physical resources have to be available. If these resources are not available in time and in the right amount, implementation will be delayed (see the first Enschede case study, below). Lack of funds for implementation is closely linked to institutional barriers, as local, regional and governmental authorities are unlikely to provide money for schemes that do not concur with policy.

Public purchase – private lease: Enschede, the Netherlands

In Enschede, a new electronic bus priority system was introduced, which required the installation of a special device in the buses. One of the reasons why the bus company was reluctant to invest in this equipment was that the forthcoming deregulation of public transport would not allow them to gain a return on their 'upfront' investment, as it was possible that within a few years the company would lose the concession to provide bus services in the region to another operator. Therefore this investment for the improvement of the public transport service was at risk.

This barrier was overcome by means of a financial mechanism whereby the municipality would bear the upfront costs of the devices and lease them to whichever bus company is running the concession.

Earmarking money: Enschede, the Netherlands

The municipality of Enschede has created a mobility fund, the money from which may be used only for the implementation of the transport policy and is funded by the revenues from parking fees.

Within the category of resource barriers, physical barriers could take the form of space restrictions or they could be related to the topography of an area. For example, there may not be adequate space on the outskirts of an urban area for the introduction of Park and Ride facilities and the large parking areas they require. Hilly terrain may be an impractical area in which to promote travelling by bicycle.

Social and cultural barriers

The public acceptability of measures is important to their effectiveness: while some measures may theoretically be effective at reducing car use, their effectiveness is minimal if people do not accept their introduction or implementation (see the Rome case studies, below). Social acceptability may often depend on whether the proposed strategy comprises 'push' or 'pull' measures (i.e., whether it is a strategy of discouragement or encouragement). On the whole, pull measures tend to be popular, and may encourage an increase in, for example, the use of alternative modes of transport. But they are not likely to achieve a comparable reduction in car use, as many people are reluctant to give up the perceived freedom associated with owning and using a car. However, although push strategies may have more direct effect on criteria such as car use, they tend to be unpopular (Stokes, 1996). Social acceptability involves the travelling public, local businesses and other organisations that will be affected by the implementation of a new measure.

Demonstrating that the medicine works: Rome, Italy

The Municipality of Rome intended to introduce a measure to create a restricted access zone (Zono Traffico Limito; ZTL) in the central area of the city. At first the public did not accept the measure and the residents set up a committee to prevent even a pilot application in restricted areas. The mayor, looking for a popular consensus, delayed the full-scale implementation, and for some months tests were run at weekends only. Only after the Municipality published pollution statistics, showing a better air quality in sample areas of the city where the measure had been adopted, was public consensus reached – and thus the measure was fully accepted.

Refining measures to gain acceptance: Rome, Italy

The proposed introduction of parking charges as part of the ZTL also met resistance, as it was not usual in Rome for car drivers to pay for use of public facilities. After many complaints in the press, accusing the Municipality of abusing of their role by impinging on private freedom, free parking permits were issued to all the residents and shopkeepers in the ZTL. After this, complaints became weaker, although the package of measures only gained acceptance as a normal aspect of daily life in Rome after more than a year of operation.

Cultural barriers (e.g., differences in culture between countries, or even regions) can have a significant effect on the potential for transferability of travel avoidance measures (see Chapter 10). Cycling provides a good example. In Denmark and the Netherlands, the bicycle is a socially acceptable form of transport, being ridden daily and routinely by all strata of society. In other countries there are a differences in attitudes to cycling, which can relate to the perceived danger of accidents or the social status of cyclists. This was certainly true in the UK in the 1980s, where research found that the low social status of cycling was at least as big a deterrent as its perceived dangers. It is frequently argued that since then the image of cycling in the UK has improved but, for the most part, this relates not to utilitarian cycling, but to leisure cycling. The difference appears to be one of habit (Tolley, 1997).

Side-effects

Almost every measure has one or more side-effects. If implementation of a measure has serious side-effects, this may hinder other activities to such an extent that implementation becomes too complicated, although these side-effects may only have a limited influence on the success of the measure itself. For instance, traffic calming not only reduces the speed of cars, but it also causes inconvenience to public transport, and it may bring about a change in the nature of traffic injuries (as was noticed in Zürich; see the case study below).

It is often difficult to foresee side-effects. This is especially the case when they occur outside the scope of the implementing agency or when they only become clear after implementation. Strictly speaking, in the latter case a side-effect is not a barrier to implementation, because it was not anticipated before or during implementation. However, if the same measure is to be implemented elsewhere, this possibility should be taken into account during the decision-making process.

Traffic calming produces noise: Zürich, Switzerland

The implementation of speed humps created a stop-and-go behaviour among car drivers which induced noise and sometimes led to excessive speeds between the humps, rather than the desired steady but slow speed. This desired outcome could be reached more satisfactorily with soft measures, e.g., the arrangement of (displaced) on-street parking. Also, the chance was missed to create an area with trees, benches or small spaces which could be used by the residents. Of course, this solution would be quite expensive.

Another side-effect of traffic calming is the potential effect on the number and seriousness of road accidents. In Zurich the number of minor accidents increased, whereas the more serious ones declined in frequency. This particular side-effect may be seen as a positive one.

Investigation of barriers and the implementation process

Barriers can be linked to the implementation process (Figure 11.1), as the policy under consideration is the measure of the scheme. Institutional, policy, legal and financial resource barriers are all policy variables. They are essentially under the control of the government, which means that the levels at which these barriers occur depend on actions or (political) decisions made by the government. Social, cultural and physical barriers are situational barriers, over which the government or implementor has no control; the measure can only be adjusted according to these circumstances. Side-effects can be due to policy variables, situation variables or to both. Sometimes measures can be adapted in such a way that negative side-effects do not occur. In other cases, negative side-effects have been anticipated and can be seen as an inevitable cost of the measure. The costs of preventing the side-effects are too high, or the intended results are so essential that side-effects are acceptable.

An empirical investigation of a wide range of policy measures has been undertaken (DANTE Consortium, 1998) to assess the scale of the barriers to implementation. Barriers which occurred during policy making, and prevented measures from being implemented, are excluded from this analysis. Information was gathered by interviews with decision-makers and implementors. In a few cases, studies on the implementation process were available. These studies were either on pilot projects implemented to gather information about the implementability of a measure and its results, or they were on successful measures which can be demonstrated as examples of good practice to other cities.

It was found that only one measure was implemented without any form of barrier (Figure 11.3), namely the introduction of 'accessible' (e.g., to wheelchair users) bus stops in Aalborg (Figure 11.4) – a good example of a very cheap 'pull' measure. The other measures had to cope with one or more barriers. There are two measures that encountered all barrier types: the (mixed-use) development at public transport nodes in Bucharest, and traffic calming in Zürich.

Barriers may occur in various forms. Sometimes they are of limited importance, but in other situations they can seriously hinder implementation. For each measure and barrier type, the influence of the barriers on the implementation process was assessed as to whether barriers have occurred or not, and if so whether they were:

- of limited importance;
- real, but overcome satisfactorily;
- real in such a way that they could not be overcome satisfactorily and the measure was implemented badly.

The histogram presents the frequencies of occurrence of each type of barrier. This visual representation shows us the relative seriousness of the various barriers to implementation (Figure 11.5).

The results show that resource barriers occurred most frequently, followed by institutional/policy and social/cultural barriers. Side-effects and physical/other barriers were the categories with the fewest entries. Looking at the seriousness of the barriers, it appears that most of them are real but were overcome. Within the resource category, in 18% of the measures the seriousness of the barrier hindered good implementation. Side-effects hardly affected the implementation process.

It should be noted that this analysis has only considered those projects that were actually implemented in the case-study cities. So, despite substantial barriers to implementation (Figures 11.3 and 11.5), it demonstrates that they can be overcome, even though implementation may not be ideal (e.g., due to resource constraints). Those projects that were not implemented because the barriers were too high have not been considered. Further analysis of the data has investigated the scale of seriousness of the barriers according to the type of measure being introduced (Figure 11.6), and the policy objectives of:

- pull measures that promote alternative modes;
- push measures that restrict travel by car;
- combined pull and push measures.

For each category two indicators are calculated: the first is the barrier probability, i.e., the mean frequency of barriers for all measures, regardless of their seriousness; the second indicator is the barrier seriousness (or weight), which is the mean importance (limited, real, or real and not overcome) of barriers for all measures, regardless of the frequency of the barriers. The difference between the two indicators should be interpreted in relative terms. A large difference between probability and seriousness means that there may be a large number of small barriers, but a small difference means that the level of seriousness is relatively high and that the barriers are all important.

Figure 11.4 Wheelchair-accessible bus stop, Aalborg

Figure 11.3 Frequency of barriers

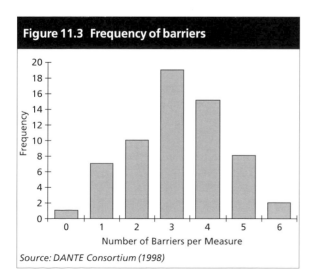

Source: DANTE Consortium (1998)

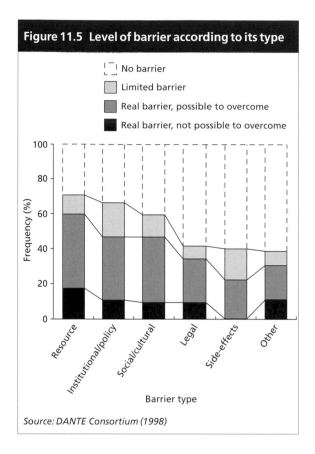

Figure 11.5 Level of barrier according to its type

Source: DANTE Consortium (1998)

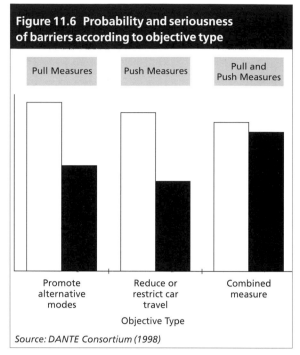

Figure 11.6 Probability and seriousness of barriers according to objective type

Source: DANTE Consortium (1998)

The most serious difficulties arise where the more complex combinations of strategies are proposed, so the most innovative policies may also be the most difficult to introduce in their entirety.

11.4 Barriers at the political level

It is easy to make an extensive list of barriers that occurred during the implementation of the traffic reduction strategies studied. Lack of financial resources is an obvious barrier which speaks for itself, and is almost always a result of political decision making. Politicians have to balance various interests and spend money accordingly. Also, as is shown in Figure 11.1, a scheme or measure does not stand alone. It is part of a wider policy or a package of measures which is aimed at a particular goal, such as sustainable development, and transport is only one element in that policy. To achieve sustainable development, methods of analysis have to be extended beyond single-sector analysis to include explicitly the effects of policy decisions. This lack of interaction between sectors is seen by Banister (1998a) as one of the main barriers to achieving urban sustainability. A second set of barriers mentioned by Banister relates to the responsibilities of the decision makers themselves. They do not seem to have a real political commitment to introduction of measures to address the key issues in a comprehensive and consistent approach.

In the latter case, it is difficult to implement the measure in the way originally intended, and it then becomes important to discuss the means by which the policy can be modified so that implementation can take place.

From Figure 11.6, it appears that measures that combine both promotion of alternatives and restriction of car travel have to cope with the most serious barriers, but that the overall probability of barriers occurring is slightly less than for either of the other two options. The differences between the three categories of measures (concerning the probability that barriers occur) are quite small. There is some evidence that measures which promote alternative modes of travel encounter the greatest resource barriers. These are mainly financial resources for investments in infrastructure for particular modes (e.g., public transport prioritisation). Measures that reduce or restrict car travel often have to cope with substantial social or cultural barriers most of which concern the lack of public support for the measure, particularly when it restricts car use or car parking. Examples include the design of neighbourhoods with few car parks, and the imposition of different taxes for parking, depending on the distance to the city centre.

Although there is a high probability that barriers will be present for all travel reduction strategies, the seriousness does vary between the different strategies. More importantly, the nature of the barriers differs substantially, so the means by which they can be overcome must also vary.

The points Banister raises can be illustrated by the case of Edinburgh, in Scotland. Edinburgh City Council has a commitment to travel reduction and pursues this goal by promoting a modal shift away from the car. The number of car journeys is to be reduced from 48% in 1991 to 46% by 2000, with a further reduction to 34% by 2010. The share of sustainable transport modes, meanwhile, is to be increased. Cycling is to account for 10% of all journeys by 2010 and public transport is to account for 39%. To turn these targets into reality, a number of concrete measures were implemented, ranging from bus lanes and car-free housing to car-sharing schemes. Some of these measures delivered considerable improvements but, according to Mittler (1999c), on the whole they are too piecemeal. Their impact is too small because they are rather small in scale or can deliver only local improvements. Also, many projects are too slow in their implementation to reverse the trend.

Mittler also points out that although the city council committed itself to a travel reduction policy, at the same time it has a commitment to economic growth. The current planning policy still encourages further traffic growth. Large out-of-town shopping and housing developments are still being planned and built. These developments inevitably generate further traffic and erase any advances made through the support of sustainable transport projects. In Edinburgh, this dichotomy of commitments is a key barrier to wide-scale implementation of a travel reduction policy.*

Moreover, four other barriers were identified by an expert Commission investigating sustainable development in Edinburgh (Mittler, 1999c):

- Lack of knowledge and awareness among the population: opinion polls show that only some 10% of the population know anything at all about sustainable development. Consequently, there is insufficient public pressure for change, and insufficient awareness of the need for everyday lifestyle changes.

- Financial constraints and funding arrangements: not only is the amount of money available for sustainable transport initiatives often insufficient, but its distribution among implementors of sustainable policies is also a concern. Groups have to compete against each other for central funds on a yearly basis. Sufficiently long-term planning is difficult under such conditions; often one sustainable transport mode competes against another or one city's sustainability 'victory' means that another city will lack the resources to implement change.

- Limitations of an institutional framework: the council has no scope for holistic policy making. This is an example of an institutional barrier in which different departments have different agendas and in the end do not support each other's goals.

The economic interests of the finance or economic development departments often override the concerns of the planning and environment sections of the Council.

- Existing regulations and legislation: unsustainable practices are favoured rather than being discouraged. Low fuel prices, for example, make the car the most economic way to travel for those who own one. Insufficient air-pollution regulation means that car drivers are not hindered in their mobility, even if excessive pollution levels are reached.

These four barriers illustrate the fact that obstacles to a sustainable transport policy are institutionalised into the economic and social system. This makes them difficult to overcome. However, this finding does not imply that sustainable transport policies should be abandoned – rather, we should learn from these obstacles and focus on the ways in which implementation can be improved.

One suggestion often made is that the awareness of all parties should be raised, to gain acceptance for policies that are perceived as negative. A clear example is the implementation of car restricting measures in the city centre of Enschede, in the Netherlands. At the beginning of the 1980s the main shopping streets were transformed into a pedestrian area. By 1989, it became clear that the number of cars entering the city centre had not been reduced and that the police were unable to enforce the traffic regulations. A plan was made by the Municipality for (partial) closure of the city centre to cars. Because of fierce resistance by local entrepreneurs, this plan was withdrawn. However, it was clear that something had to be done. Therefore, in 1990 the Municipality established a study group with the task of producing proposals to reduce car traffic in the city centre. In this group various parties were represented: shopkeepers, the police, local residents, cultural agencies, disabled persons and the economic development department of the Municipality.

In 1991, the initial proposal of the study group was discussed during a public hearing. After some adjustments of the plan, it was presented to the City Council, which agreed to a half-year trial period. During this period, a survey was conducted and another public hearing was held. The survey showed favourable results (a reduction in the number of cars) and both city centre residents and entrepreneurs were positive about the measure. By the end of 1992 the City Council decided to make the measure permanent. The most interesting aspect of this approach was that the measure in its final stage restricted the car access to the city centre more than the original plan, which had been withdrawn because of public resistance. The area and time period in which no cars are allowed were increased after the trial period.

* Elsewhere, Mittler also argues that a commitment to economic growth is inconsistent with a commitment to sustainable development (Mittler, 1999c).

In the Netherlands, this method of implementation is called interactive planning, while in the UK it is called community participation (Hathway, 1997). Interactive planning is not just implementation, but decision making and implementation together. Both the politicians and the general public are involved in decision making and implementation. This is done not by a formal public inquiry procedure, but by creating awareness and debate with all the parties involved. The goal of interactive planning is to bridge the gap between politics and citizens, to democratise decision making and to create public support.

11.5 Conclusion

We have argued that the success of travel reduction policies is vulnerable to the difference between policy intentions and behavioural outcomes. The implementation process must be taken into account when assessing the rate of success – a policy is no better than its implementation. This is especially true for policies that are aimed at sustainable development and the restriction of car use, because we still live in a car-dependent society.

This makes the success of a policy highly dependent on its implementation. If a potentially successful measure is badly implemented, it is unlikely that the measure will show its desired effect. Unforeseen effects may occur which are counter-productive and have impacts on unrelated areas of policy. Policy makers therefore need to pay attention to the feasibility of a policy alternative, at both strategic and operational levels. But even if the measure is successfully implemented and there is a favourable response by the public, it may be too limited in scale to have a measurable impact.

Policy makers should take account of the various barriers to implementation. When the barriers are not overcome, it may be preferable to abandon a particular policy, rather than to press on with a poorly thought out, partial implementation. This is especially true where there are substantial institutional, policy, legal and resource barriers. In most cases, these barriers can be foreseen and addressed. If a measure is innovative, it is advisable to implement a pilot measure first. Experiences are gathered through learning-by-doing and the measure takes shape during its implementation.

Another way to avoid bad implementation is to create awareness before introducing the measure. Even better is to get the people involved in the decision making itself, to increase public acceptability. This approach may be most worthwhile for individual measures, and less effective for the implementation of a policy as a whole. For a major change in implementing a sustainable transport policy in a wider context of spatial and economic development, a general political commitment is essential. Only then can the institutional barriers be overcome.

Barriers to Realising Travel Reduction Outcomes

12.1 Introduction

When implementing travel reduction strategies it is possible that the outcomes in terms of travel behaviour do not match the policy intentions. In Chapter 11, we have presented the barriers to implementation in terms of the problems of introducing policy changes (policy output). Here, the focus is on the behavioural outcomes, which again result in a different set of barriers (policy effect).

Certain situations can be identified which represent barriers to realising travel reduction outcomes. Those included in this analysis relate to ways in which measures have been unsuccessful (or only partially successful) in achieving the desired travel reduction. This does not preclude the possibility that these measures may have been successful in addressing other objectives, or might also be capable of reducing travel in different circumstances. In this chapter we shall therefore take a closer look at the reasons for these discrepancies between intentions and outcomes, and illustrate where and why these barriers might arise.

For this purpose, seven different types of barrier to realisation have been identified. These are first summarized briefly, then discussed in more detail in following sections of this chapter.

- *Non-complementary policies:* cases where measures have been unsuccessful because of a lack of complementary policies or the presence of directly conflicting policies.

- *Direct incentives to travel more:* cases in which a particular measure directly encourages more travel of some sort (while implicitly relying on other mechanisms to reduce travel overall). For example, subsidies may be devised to increase travel by particular modes but, unless there are any disincentives to travel by other modes, travel will simply increase.

- *Improving system efficiency:* cases where travel reduction is activated to some extent, but the very act of removing traffic or journeys liberates more roadspace or vehicles to be used by others. Thus, the initial travel reduction feeds back to generate a net increase in travel.

- *Contradictory outcomes:* cases where more travel was generated despite the intention of the measure to reduce travel.

- *Change without improvement:* cases where measures have achieved some change, but where no improvement in terms of travel reduction has been achieved, e.g., mode switching from bicycle to walking, or destination switching that does not reduce the trip distance.

- *Absence of evidence or impact negligible:* cases where the travel reduction impact of a measure is negligible, or the evidence is weak or inconclusive and effects cannot be attributed explicitly by the measure.

- *Non-acceptance or lack of uptake by users:* cases where the measures have not been used by the public.

The first three barriers equate with causes of the lack of realisation, due to conflicting objectives, inappropriate use of incentives and the generation effects of transport reduction measures. The remaining four barriers represent effects – contradictory outcomes, no improvement, measurement problems and non-acceptance.

12.2 Non-complementary policies

Even though a measure is aimed at travel reduction, its success may depend on certain other policies, activities or prerequisites. The effectiveness of a measure may be reduced if other related transport policies do not sufficiently reinforce, but rather detract from, the intended travel reduction. Also, some measures may not achieve the desired impact on travel reduction if they are in direct conflict with other policies or measures, which may be unrelated to transport policy. Examples of non-complementary policies in Edinburgh and Enschede are given in the case studies below.

Encouraging new travel generation: Edinburgh, UK

In Edinburgh, several effective travel reduction policies are being pursued (as described earlier, in Section 7.5). At the same time, however, there are a number of policies that facilitate further traffic generation. For example, in 1998 the City of Edinburgh Council consented to an IKEA store being built at a retail park to the south of the city. This store, the first IKEA in Scotland, will create significant amounts of additional traffic, most of which will travel on Edinburgh's already congested city bypass. The City Council is also promoting the development of a major new suburb known as the South East Wedge: 5,000 houses, most of them owner-occupied, are to be built on a greenfield site 8 km to the south of the centre. Although this development is meant to include bicycle lanes and some special provisions for public transport access, it is situated so close to the city bypass that it will inevitably be most accessible by car. Next to this suburb, the Council has agreed to a large new hospital, which will be relocated from a city centre site extremely well served by public transport. This new Royal Infirmary will cover an area of 125,000 m² (Figure 12.1) and will be fully operational by 2003. With the hospital geared to treating over 100,000 in-patients and day-case patients a year, more car traffic to and from the new site will be inevitable.

Even housing projects that are planned as 'sustainable inner city quarters' will generate more, rather than less traffic. In 1999, work began on the Waterfront Edinburgh scheme which will regenerate a vast area of currently derelict brownfield land in north-central Edinburgh. The project will house 4,000–8,000 people, at least some of whom, it is hoped, will find work locally in one of the 4,000 jobs to be created by the development. 'By building on … brownfield sites, land within the city boundaries will be brought back into use and pressure will be taken off the cities surrounding greenbelt', the project specification argues (Scottish Homes, 1999). At the same time, however, the project involves the building of four extra kilometres of road and is predicted to cause increases in traffic level in the surrounding neighbourhoods of at least 50%. The Waterfront development, therefore, will make any travel reduction across the whole city of Edinburgh even more difficult to achieve.

Improving public transport – building more roads: Enschede, Netherlands

In 1992–1993, the city of Enschede joined the Combi-route project. The aim of the measure was to promote the use of bicycles and public transport along the 10 km corridor between Enschede and Oldenzaal. Investment was made in various facilities such as bicycle parking, bicycle and bus priority, reconstruction of roads and bicycle lanes, and adaptation of bus stops. The measure was evaluated, by traffic counts, before and after implementation. Between 1991 and 1994 car traffic increased between 2 and 5%, which is more than average for provincial roads. This increase is attributed mainly to the construction of a new connection to the A1 motorway and the building of a new industrial park. Between 1991 and 1994, travel by bicycle fell by between 12 and 14%. This decrease in bicycle traffic is attributed mainly to the introduction of a free public transport ticket for students in 1991.

12.3 Direct incentives to travel more

Measures may be aimed at travel reduction through the promotion of alternative, more environmentally friendly modes. This could be achieved though substitution of motorised modes by non-motorised modes, or indirectly by switching trips from low-occupancy cars to high-occupancy public transport, thus reducing vehicle kilometres for the same number of passenger kilometres.

This may not be successful, however, in achieving actual travel reduction. Typically, by promoting alternative modes their attractiveness is increased, which in turn can increase overall mobility without necessarily reducing car travel; any reduction in car travel may be offset by general increases in travel by other modes.

Figure 12.1 Greenfield site for construction of Edinburgh's new Royal Infirmary, a development which is not complementary to the objectives of travel reduction

The following examples from Zürich and Bucharest illustrate the problems of increasing attractiveness of alternative modes with a resulting increase in overall mobility.

More go by public transport – but no fewer go by car: Zürich, Switzerland

In the early 1990s the city of Zürich made significant improvements to the public transport system, expanding the S-Bahn network. The promotion of public transport increased ridership significantly. However, there is no clear evidence so far of a parallel reduction in car traffic, either into or within the city of Zürich. Hence there is no indication of a switch between public and private transport, as the overall mobility has increased.

Free travel – more travel: Bucharest, Romania

The public transport subsidy in Bucharest (82% in 1997) contributes to maintaining a high level of public transport use in the city. This high level of patronage is no doubt assisted by successive increases in fuel prices but there is also direct evidence that the fare subsidy has led to increased travel. It has been estimated that the free passes granted to retired people have induced a growth in travel, and are perceived as an incentive to travel more. Indeed, it is clear that for any individuals who do not have access to a car, no 'positive' modal switching is possible. Any increased travel by public transport must be regarded as induced travel.

12.4 Improving system efficiency

A measure can be aimed at promoting conditions for certain favoured modes, but this may then result in capacity release or an overall improvement of the transport system efficiency, which in turn feeds back to generate more traffic. In some cases measures may be aimed at making improvements which either directly or indirectly influence all transport modes. In these cases, even though the purpose of the measures may be to speed up travel time by bus, and therefore promote the bus as an alternative to the car, such measures may also simultaneously improve conditions for cars. The following two examples from Bucharest illustrate this.

Improving bus flows – but all traffic benefits: Bucharest, Romania

The implementation of the Public Transport Roadspace project on Elisabeta Boulevard is part of the plan for reorganising the traffic system in the city centre which consists of a one-way traffic system, Park and Ride facilities and priority for public transport vehicles.

The design of public transport roadspace took the form of a contraflow bus lane to allow the bus routes to be retained, in conjunction with a one-way traffic system introduced to improve the general traffic flow. The significantly improved conditions for public transport on the boulevard were amplified by the introduction of one-way traffic.

Public transport roadspace encouraged public transport use because of the travel improvements it engendered: there was a 50% increase in travel speed and a 60% decrease in traffic collisions. As a result, the number of travellers increased by 39%. The general traffic on the boulevard decreased by 30% and it became more free-flowing.

The one-way traffic system also featured the introduction of one-way traffic flow on the streets adjacent to the boulevard. A side-effect of the system was the increase in travel on these adjoining streets, which are narrow and characteristic of the old city centre; they do not have sufficient capacity to absorb the traffic diverted from Elisabeta Boulevard. Overall, therefore, the amount of traffic in the area did not decrease, because it switched to the adjacent streets.

Fewer passenger trips – but more goods trips: Bucharest, Romania

Due to the introduction of new development at public transport nodes, the Militari area of the city functions more efficiently than in the past. The distance travelled and the number of journeys made by individuals has been reduced because the increased density of activities has allowed trips to the development for more than one purpose. The available capacity of public transport vehicles increased four-fold in seven years (1990–1997), the public transport traffic was augmented by 41% and the general traffic measures were implemented (i.e., traffic signals installation, rearrangement of two main crossings, prevention of on-street parking). A survey conducted in the area revealed the following:

- in 1997, 8% of car drivers used public transport more frequently than in 1996;

- 19% of car drivers are travelling both by car and by public transport.

However, there is a negative side-effect. The development of the commercial activities induced an increase in motorised traffic by 8–18%, especially cars, vans and trucks supplying goods to the new development.

12.5 Contradictory outcomes

Even though a measure may have been devised specifically to reduce travel, the direct outcome in terms of travel behaviour may be the opposite of that intended. This can happen when a measure successfully causes a substitution or switching of trips, but in a way that ultimately encourages more travel than in the original situation.

A contradictory outcome may arise when a measure has resulted in some form of capacity release, effectively creating room for additional traffic which more than offsets the benefits associated with the original measure. This situation is often the case when a measure is not aimed directly at travel reduction, but more at increasing efficiency of the travel flow in general. It is often argued that these measures have a positive environmental effect, because they reduce certain aspects of travel (e.g., congestion time, or the distance of trips in search of a parking place). Examples of such cases are parking information systems, and Park and Ride facilities, which are illustrated by the following two examples from Aalborg and Enschede.

Trip distance reduced – more trips made: Aalborg, Denmark

In the city centre of Aalborg a parking information system was implemented in 1995, which informed drivers of parking vacancies and the nearest vacant parking facility. The aim of the measure was to improve the parking conditions and reduce the distance travelled in search of parking spaces by traffic, thus contributing to an overall reduction of traffic in the city centre.

Although the overall effects of the parking information system were in line with what was expected by the city, in that it became easier to find a parking space, there are indications that more people now go to the city centre by car because of the improved conditions. This may offset the travel reduction benefits originally envisaged for this measure.

Residents switch to bicycles – visitors find parking: Enschede, the Netherlands

In 1991, restrictions on access by time and user were put in place in the centre of Enschede in order to improve traffic conditions and the liveability in the city centre. Although the share of cars decreased and the share of cyclists increased for the residents in Enschede, the modal share of visitors coming by car increased significantly. This was mainly due to the extra capacity in the city centre for weekend visitors coming by car.

A further example of contradictory outcomes occurs where the measure has succeeded in causing some form of switching, but this has resulted in more travel, either through longer trips or through the generation of a greater number of shorter trips. This is illustrated by the following Aalborg example, where route switching has resulted in longer trips.

Avoiding congestion, but travelling further: Aalborg, Denmark

In 1994, the National Roads Directorate of Denmark and the Municipality of Aalborg implemented a traffic information system and ran a field trial entitled 'QUO-VADIS'. The aim of the system was to improve the traffic flow at key points around the city, particularly around the Limfjord crossing tunnel. The system informs drivers of traffic conditions at key points and advises on alternatives routes in case of heavy traffic, congestion or incidents (Aalborg Kommune, 1994).

Even though the measure is aimed at improving the efficiency of the traffic flow, there is evidence that redirected vehicles have taken longer routes, and so the measure has had an opposite effect in terms of travel reduction.

12.6 Change without improvement

In some cases a measure may be successful in causing modal or destination switching to take place, but even so there may be no improvement in terms of achieving travel reduction. This is typically the case when modal switching occurs between two similarly 'favoured' modes (e.g., between walking and cycling), instead of from a less favoured mode (such as car) to a more favoured mode. Change without improvement is also seen when the measures induce a switch of route or destination, but the overall distance is not reduced, or any reduction in distance is offset by an increase in travel time because of the route is slower. The following examples from Enschede and Aalborg illustrate changes without improvement.

Cheaper fares – attract mostly cyclists: Enschede, the Netherlands

As part of the city policy to encourage citizens of Enschede to travel to the city centre by bus or bicycle, reduced off-peak fares to the city centre were introduced on the buses in 1997. These fares were valid on Saturdays from 09.00 to 18.00. As a result of their introduction, a long-term increase in passengers of 15% is expected. When a survey was carried out among the passengers on the city buses in 1995, it was found that 37% of the passengers used the new reduced fare ticket. However, 7.8% (26 passengers) stated that they only made the trip because of the new reduced fare ticket. Of these cases only nine made a switch away from the car, while 14 had switched away from the bicycle.

Switching to the bus – from other buses: Aalborg, Denmark

In early 1996 the Municipality of Aalborg implemented a bus priority system on the Citybus route (Figure 12.2), with the aims of increasing the attractiveness of the bus through reduced transit time, and reducing energy consumption. Even though the measure achieved modal switching by attracting additional passengers to the route, there was no contribution in terms of travel reduction. Only 8% of passengers had switched from the car, while 53% had previously used the bus, 38% had cycled and 1% had walked.

12.7 Absence of evidence or impact negligible

When evaluating travel reduction measures there is a multiplicity of problems in determining their impact.

The general problems are that there is either a lack of suitable data on the level of the individual measure, or that the effects are impossible to separate from aggregate effects, or that the impact of the measure is so small compared with overall measurements that the impact can be considered negligible.

Interactions between different policies and transport modes make it difficult to identify the impact of single policies. There is a lack of empirical research on the impacts of single travel reduction measures. Furthermore, travel reduction measures or strategies are often not well defined. For example, 'travel reduction' may in fact be

taken to mean a reduction in *car* traffic, combined possibly with an increase in public transport ridership. In many cases evaluation is complicated by the lack of a base for reference and a multiplicity of different indicators, resulting in a series of data with no evident structure or message.

Although, while the detection of travel is relatively straightforward – people and vehicles can easily be observed and counted – detecting reduction in travel is more difficult. This requires analysis of travel data, identification of any alternative behaviour that took place, and conclusions on cause and effect. It is therefore not simple or always necessarily possible to 'prove' that travel reduction has occurred, and hence whether travel reduction strategies have been indisputably successful (Chapter 9).

Cycling to work – but what about the cars? Bristol, UK

As part of the annual 'Don't Choke Bristol' campaign, the city coordinates a 'Bike to Work' day which targets the work-related segment of mobility for one day. The impacts of 'Bike to Work' day have been monitored by counting the cyclists on campaign and non campaign days. Although an increase in the number of cyclists was recorded, since the data are limited to counts on only one day per year and no information is available on reduction of car travel, it has been impossible to determine whether a shift from cars to bicycles has been achieved. For example, if one person cycles to work instead of taking the car, the vehicle may be available for another family member to use that day. Even if data were available showing a reduction in car use or overall traffic flows, it

Figure 12.2 Although the Citybus in Aalborg has increased patronage, relatively few passengers switched from car use

would be difficult to demonstrate that a simple switch from car to bike on that route had taken place. Moreover, it would be problematic to attribute this trend to a particular policy stimulus without further data on travel behaviour. In Bristol, the council are now monitoring the success of 'Bike to Work' day in terms of the number of local employers taking part in the event each year and requesting information on becoming a cycle-friendly employer.

Travel reduction schemes successful – but on a limited scale: Edinburgh, UK

In Edinburgh both the innovative car-free housing scheme (Section 5.6) and the car-sharing scheme (Section 2.3) are extremely small in scale. The car-free housing scheme will accommodate only 120 households, most of whom would probably not own a car even if they lived elsewhere. The car club has also replaced 30 cars, at most (assuming all founding members gave up their car to join). In a city which had 127,525 registered cars on its roads in 1991, this can hardly count as a major improvement. The limited impact of these two schemes (as with other cases elsewhere) is a serious policy issue: both schemes took up a considerable amount of council staff time. Much of political capital was expended by councillors, developers and civil society representatives to obtain approval for these projects. Could their time and effort have been better spent on different projects such as the extension of traffic-calming schemes or bicycle lanes? However, one should not underestimate the symbolic significance of these schemes, even if their immediate impact on traffic levels is limited. Both the car club and the car-free housing scheme were the first such projects to be implemented in the UK. Through their implementation, they have proved that such schemes are possible even within the current policy framework and political climate. They thus help indirectly to pave the way for similiar schemes elsewhere. Their wider impact is not exactly discernible (and may be measured in newspaper column inches rather than numbers of car trips), but nonetheless it must not be underestimated. The developers of the car-free housing scheme in Edinburgh, for example, have been approached by developers from across the UK investigating their options of imitating the scheme.

12.8 Non-acceptance or lack of uptake by users

Successful implementation of a measure does not automatically guarantee that it will achieve its objectives and reduce travel. For a measure to be successful a change of behaviour is typically required, but if users do not accept or use the measure, there will be no effects. There can be several reasons for non-acceptance or non-use, ranging from practical problems, through lack of political acceptance, to tradition.

Typically non-acceptance or non-usage problems are met when an attempt is made to achieve a modal switch to non-motorised or unconventional modes of transport, as illustrated in the examples from Zürich and Edinburgh below.

Non-use of bicycle lanes: Zürich, Switzerland

The non-acceptance of bicycle lanes in Zürich might have several reasons. Probably the most important is the excellent public transport supply, which competes not only with private traffic but also with non-motorised modes. This fact, together with the relatively cheap public transport (compared with the high average income), leads to high 'opportunity costs' for cycling: this is probably the most striking aspect concerning low bicycle use.

Other factors are as follows:

- only the inner city and some of the outskirts of Zürich are flat, so the hilly topography elsewhere is a deterrent to cycling;

- there is a lack of secure bicycle parking facilities;

- the bicycle network is currently incomplete;

- there is a high incidence of traffic signals and traffic-calming measures (e.g., speed humps) which apply to bicycles as well as to general traffic and so do not give bicycles any advantage.

It is often not worthwhile to take a bicycle instead of walking, because the short distances in the inner city make the average speed of cycling not much higher than that of walking. Note that non-acceptance or uptake may be related to social and cultural barriers (Section 11.3).

Poor response to pooling: Edinburgh, UK

In the early 1990s, Edinburgh attempted to set up a car pooling scheme, encouraging people to share cars on journeys to work. This scheme was widely publicised and attracted an excellent initial response. Several thousand people asked for help in identifying suitable car-sharing partners. In the end, however, the uptake for the scheme was less than 2%. It proved difficult for people to agree on the time of travelling to and from work. Many people could or would not give up the extra flexibility provided by having their own car always available. Car pooling has therefore been dropped in Edinburgh and a car club has been set up instead (Section 2.3).

12.9 Interplay of barriers

The various barriers to realisation discussed in this chapter do not act in isolation. This section explores how they may be related to each other as well as with the travel reduction mechanisms which are affected by them (Chapter 9), and the kinds of packaging of measures which may overcome them (Chapter 7).

The distinction between barriers associated with causes and those associated with effects has been suggested earlier. It can be seen that the three 'causal' barriers (non-complementary policies, direct incentives to travel more, and capacity release) may give rise directly to three of the four barrier 'effects'. These three barrier effects can be summarised as:

- *contradictory outcomes*: where there is actually a net increase in travel;
- *change without improvement*: where the amount of travel stays more or less the same, even though the measure activates a behavioural response on the part of the traveller;

- *lack of evidence or impact negligible:* where the measure appears to have had little or no effect on behaviour, and hence no effect on the amount of travel.

The interplay of barriers is shown in Table 12.1, with examples of measure cases which demonstrate the inter-relationships between cause and effect.

The fourth barrier 'effect', non-acceptance or uptake, does not relate so directly to the three barrier 'causes' (which equate with incomplete or inappropriate policy implementation), so much as to the public's response to what might otherwise be considered a worthy and consistent policy set. In this sense, non-acceptance or uptake of measures is more closely associated with the social or cultural barrier to implementation. Note also that the 'lack of evidence or impact negligible' barrier is also related to the complexities of evaluation as discussed in Chapter 9; these will be revisited in our conclusions (Chapter 13).

A key and recurring theme lying behind the barriers discussed in this chapter is capacity increase or release, which can be a factor in all three barrier 'causes':

- non-complementary policies may provide an increase in capacity for car traffic, which is likely to detract from the success of measures aimed at reducing car travel;

Table 12.1 Examples of interplay between barriers to realisation

'Cause' barrier	Contradictory outcome	'EFFECT' BARRIER	
		Change without improvement	Lack of evidence or effect negligible
Non-complementary policies	Promoting car travel for other travellers • Switch between residents' and visitors' parking (Enschede; Section12.5) Area Access Control (Enschede, Section 3.9)	Increasing road capacity • (Enschede; Section 12.2) HOV-bus lane (Madrid; Section 3.3) Promoting more traffic-generating development • (Edinburgh; Section 12.2)	Insufficient restraint of cars relative to promotion of bicycles • (Bristol; Section 12.8) Little evidence in area studied but traffic growth elsewhere • Traffic Calming (Bristol; Section 3.8)
Direct incentives to travel more	Promoting public transport but without inducing mode switching • S-Bahn, (Zürich; Section 4.4) Free travel (Bucharest; Section 12.3)	Mode switching from bicycle to subsidised bus, or between buses • (Enschede and Aalborg; Section 12.6)	Not applicable
Improving system efficiency	Reducing trip distance encouraging more trips • (Aalborg; Sections 6.3, 12.5) Short-term parking increasing turnover, but hence generating more trips • (Zürich, Section 4.3)	Promoting conditions for travel that benefit all modes • One-way traffic, (Bucharest; Section 12.4) HOV Lane, (Madrid; Section 3.3)	Efficiency benefits accrue to operator, but no evidence of travel reduction • Transport optimisation (Albertslund; Section 2.9)

- direct incentives to travel more may provide an increase in capacity for the favoured mode of travel although in the absence of switching or substitution this leads to an absolute increase in travel;
- improving system efficiency leads to capacity release since the travel-reducing component of the measure frees up capacity for more travel by others.

Capacity increase is a feature of measures which are not themselves inherently travel-reducing. However, capacity release potentially affects any measure that manages to have a travel-reducing effect: the measure may become a victim of its own success, in that the resulting system ends up accommodating more travel than previously – a contradictory outcome.

Capacity release can be manifested in various forms, for example:

- the freeing-up of roadspace (on a particular route or corridor not travelled);
- the freeing-up of parking spaces (at either end of a journey);
- the freeing-up of a vehicle (where a traveller switches mode or forgoes a trip altogether);
- the freeing-up of time (which may allow the traveller to make more trips).

These effects may be related both to the attempted travel reduction mechanisms and the barrier 'effects' that may result, as shown in Table 12.2.

These issues of capacity point to the importance of assembling measures in complementary packages. By packaging together measures that are complementary

towards travel reduction, it should be possible to mitigate the effects of capacity release. By removing roadspace (replacing a traffic lane with a bus lane) there is no new incentive to travel on that route by car. By removing parking spaces, there is greater incentive to leave the car at home. By encouraging a lower level of car ownership (through car-sharing schemes or car clubs), there is less likely to be a spare car available in which others then make trips that would not otherwise have been made.

Packaging options such as those discussed in Chapter 7 may address all three of the 'causal' barriers discussed in this chapter. Self-evidently, complementary packaging nullifies the barrier of non-complementary policies (Section 12.2). Packaging can also balance the direct incentives to travel more (Section 12.3) inherent in some otherwise travel-promoting types of measure. Finally, as discussed above, packaging can mitigate the effects of capacity release that are due to improved system efficiency (Section 12.4), and that would otherwise see travel reduction policies undone by their own success.

12.10 Conclusion

These last two chapters present the two main limitations to the achievement of travel reduction strategies. From the individual measures presented in Part I of this book, and from the means by which measures can be combined into packages, the problems of measurement and evaluation and the questions relating to transferability and compatibility covered in Part II, we come to reasonably optimistic conclusions. There are problems and unanswered questions, but these are not insurmountable.

Table 12.2 Forms of capacity release and their effects

Form of capacity release	Travel reduction mechanism	Effect of capacity release	Example of contradictory outcome
Freed-up roadspace	Mechanisms removing car trips (mode switching; substitution)	Incentive for others to use their car on that route or corridor	Improved traffic flows on boulevards; Bucharest (Section 12.4)
Freed-up parking space	Mechanisms removing car trips (mode switching; substitution)	Incentive for others to use their car to access that destination	Area access control, Enschede (Section 2.9) Parking turnover, Zürich (Section 4.3)
Freed-up vehicle	Mechanisms which specifically 'leave car at home' (mode switching; substitution by technology)	Incentives for others (e.g., family members) to make use of the car left at home	Netherlands teleworking experiment (Section 6.5)
Freed-up time	Mechanisms reducing travel time (time switching; switching to closer destination; substitution)	Incentives for that individual to use time gained to make more trips/travel more/further	Aalborg parking information (Sections 6.3 and 12.5)

Even the difficult questions of uniqueness can be addressed. However, when it comes to barriers to implementation and to realisation, a new level of complexity is presented.

In Chapter 11, we broke down the many barriers to implementation, and argued that travel reduction strategies can be introduced, even though the problems relating to the six barrier types may result in different solutions being introduced in different situations. The transferability analysis might suggest the same solution, but the situations may still not be compatible, so the solution may be similar or different. This flexibility is important, as the political context and the barriers are of different levels of importance in each city, whether the cases under consideration are in the same country or in other parts of Europe. The first objective is to introduce the most appropriate package of measures, given the local barriers. Supporting measures to increase political and public awareness are also valuable means by which new ideas and policy measures can be introduced to decision-makers. The presentational aspects and demonstration factors (from similar experience elsewhere) are also key components in the diffusion of new ideas.

Despite the strong intentions of some politicians, often supported by the professional planners and other public agencies, the policy package for travel reduction strategies may not be entirely consistent. There are obvious reasons. A city has other (more important) priorities, such as the maintenance and enhancement of its employment base and prosperity, so that it is seen as being a dynamic and competitive environment within which to live and work. Public funding agencies have other priorities – for resourcing health, education and housing projects – so investment in travel reduction strategies may come quite low on the political agenda.

Underlying all these questions is the intensely political nature of many transport decisions. Measures to restrict the use of the car are often seen as being politically dangerous, as the majority of the electorate are now (potential) car drivers. Policies seen as directly limiting freedom to use the car may result in loss of political power. Hence the great importance of an understanding of travel reduction strategies, their contribution to the quality of city life, and the clear social and environmental benefits must be recognised. It may only be when there are clear win–win strategies available that the political barriers will be overcome.

Even if successful implementation of travel reduction strategies does take place, the outcomes (Chapter 12) may be very different from the intentions (Chapter 11). In the analysis in this chapter we have tried to identify the seven different barriers to realisation where, for reasons that are often very good, the outcomes are at best neutral and at worst lead to increased travel. In some cases, disappointing outcomes are the result of poorly thought-through implementation – but we should learn from this experience so that, in future, better implementation takes place. In other cases, the policy has not been clearly explained to the traveller. Individuals are very resourceful in finding ways to avoid doing what the policy maker wants. When faced with a choice of whether to use their car or not, many people make the decision to continue using it, and increase their travel rather than decreasing it. The key issue here is that people (particularly car drivers) must support the travel reduction strategy and be prepared to cooperate in achieving its objectives. If it is seen as being another challenge to the car driver that must be resisted at all costs, then it is doomed to failure.

The implementation of travel reduction strategies is only the starting point for changes in travel behaviour. In parallel with the actual changes should be a strong and continuing programme of explanation and involvement – such as the Dutch integrative planning process, where there is a continuous process of debate and discussion between all the key actors.

The involvement process has usually been the weakest and least successful component of the implementation process. In most situations, the presentation of transport policies has been set in opposition to the transport user, particularly the car driver. To achieve successful implementation, the support of the car driver must be recognised and addressed. This means that all road users must accept that they are part of the problem and that they must also accept responsibility for contributing (in part) to the success of the solutions.

CHAPTER 13

Conclusions

13.1 Introduction

In this book, we have demonstrated that travel reduction can be achieved over a wide variety of circumstances and by a variety of means – through policies for restraining or promoting alternatives to car use, through land-use planning and technological solutions. Travel reduction has been demonstrated in all the countries studied and at all scales of application. Its attainment has also been shown through each of the six switching or substitution mechanisms identified. In this respect, the demonstration of travel reduction possibilities can be considered a success.

The nature and scale of travel reduction has therefore been observed in a variety of forms:

- Travel reduction results have included a high proportion of changes in behaviour, such as a 90% increase in use of public transport in one case in Zürich, and a 90% reduction in cars in the central zone of Enschede.

- Where individual instances of travel reduction may be modest, there can still be a large travel saving in aggregate. For example, the 115m saving in trip length attributed to the Aalborg parking information scheme adds up to a saving of 280,000 vehicle kilometres per year. Similarly, the cycle subsidy scheme in Aalborg resulted in 18,000 bicycle kilometres replacing car travel.

- Travel has been shown to be reduced even when some car use is still involved. For example, in the Netherlands, 55% of car poolers transferred from single-person car trips, and 31% of car sharers were previously car owners. In one case, car sharing resulted in a reduction of over 2,000 km per person per annum – a substantial and direct manifestation of travel reduction.

- Travel can be reduced through changed practices in daily life, as in a teleworking experiment in the Netherlands, which showed that on a teleworking day the number of trips was reduced to about half, travel time to about 40%, and the distance to less than 10%, compared with a normal working day.

In this concluding chapter, we focus on three of the main lessons that have emerged from this book. Firstly, 'travel reduction' is difficult to quantify, as it cannot be measured directly. Only travel itself can be measured, and hence it is necessary to make educated deductions as to whether observed changes in travel patterns indeed represent a reduction in travel. This can make the assessment of success, and hence justification, of travel reduction strategies difficult (see Section 13.2).

Secondly, a net reduction in travel may often be difficult to achieve in practice. Thus, while the amount of travel might be 'pinned down' in one case, it might be 'released' elsewhere. Efforts concentrated on reducing travel by a particular mode, or to a particular destination, may be offset by general growth in travel by other modes and to other destinations. Indeed, in some cases the act of reducing existing car traffic on a route effectively releases capacity, thus to encouraging travel by car on that route by other travellers not targeted by the travel reduction scheme. These considerations suggest that areawide approaches may be necessary (see Section 13.3).

Thirdly, the process of travel reduction is not instantaneous, but takes place over a period of time. Even the direct impacts of a set of new measures will not necessarily result in immediately measurable results that will not change over time. Responses to measures will be variable; they will be adjusted as a result of the reassessment process. More important over the longer period is the expectation that growing public support will lead to more fundamental changes in attitudes to the use of the car, particularly in areas where priority must be given to other users. The simple causality argument needs to be modified with a process of positive reaction, leading to a change in behaviour, and eventually being measurable as a travel reduction (see Chapter 9). In addition, there are strong social implications in the sense that certain locations, types of activities and modes can be more easily targeted (see Section 13.4).

Each of these issues is now discussed in greater detail; this is followed by a more general debate on the necessary conditions for the successful implementation of travel reduction strategies.

13.2 Measurement of reduction

Evaluation and measurement of travel reduction are complex processes. Prediction of travel reduction may be even more difficult, as an understanding of behavioural response is also necessary (see Section 13.5). Part of the problem relates to the availability of 'before' and 'after' data for the policy implementation (Chapter 9), but there are also important conceptual questions.

The overall picture of good practice in travel reduction is not yet complete. Although measures such as public transport priority and traffic calming have been applied over many years, policies devised to reduce travel *per se* have been implemented only relatively recently. It is only lately that the notion of trying to reduce travel has turned from being regarded as a rather radical proposition to a commonly adopted strategy. This means that evaluation data for travel reduction – which are not straightforward in the first place – are not readily available.

Indeed, there may be a data paradox. In some cases, the more diligently one looks for travel reduction, the less one finds. For example, if one simply assumes that a telecommuter stays at home and cuts out a work trip, then clearly travel is reduced. But if more data are found on non-work travel (e.g., more time being made available for leisure activities) and travel by other members of the household, making use of the freed-up vehicle, then they are likely to demonstrate the possibility that travel has actually increased. This example excludes any car trips generated as a result of the freed-up road capacity and the freed-up parking space at the workplace.

Several 'barriers to evaluation' have been identified with respect to the measurement of travel reduction:

- Absence of travel reduction data: data may not have been collected, since travel reduction has only recently become an explicit policy objective;
- Inability to measure travel reduction directly: it must be deduced, needing at least 'before' and 'after' data (two data points);
- Requirement, ideally, for a combination of aggregate (scale and volume-at-point) and disaggregate (causal) data: some of these (naturally) do not involve travel at all (e.g., time and place of work activity);
- Paradox of data resolution: in some cases, the more carefully you look for travel reduction, the less you may find;
- Complexity of behavioural response: travel behaviour is itself volatile, and short-term and long-term causes and effects are intertwined;
- Need to quantify the hypothetical: whereas detection of absolute travel reduction needs two data points, deduction of relative travel reduction needs three (Figure 13.1).

Travel reduction may have to be measured against what might have happened. To measure travel, say the patronage of a new light rail service, we need only measure flow now (one data point). To determine if there is an increase or decrease in patronage, we need two data points ('before' and 'after'). To prove or deduce that there has been a reduction in travel growth needs an estimate of what travel would have been, had the travel reduction policy not been implemented (Figure 13.1).

The simplest measurement of travel reduction would be an assessment of whether travel at time $t+1$ is less than that at point t (Y to D). From this logic, there has been an increase in travel at points A and B, whilst C represents a stabilisation of travel, and D represents travel reduction proper. But it is extremely unlikely that changes such as a reduction from Y to D will ever be found. So if these 'hard'

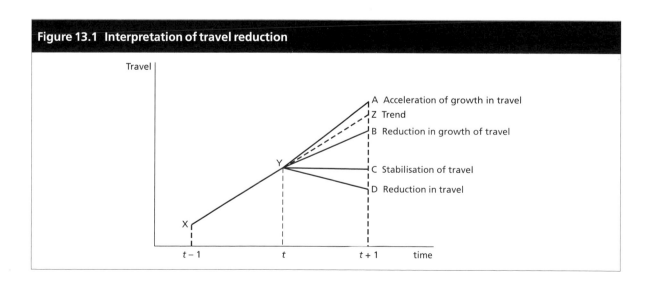

Figure 13.1 Interpretation of travel reduction

definitions of travel reduction are used, then travel reduction will never be found.

However, if three points are determined, then the historic trend from X $(t-1)$ through Y (t) to the future $(t+1)$ can be presented as variations around the trend or predicted position (Z). Point Z represents the result of a 'do nothing' situation and B now represents a reduction in the growth of travel. This could also be interpreted as achieving the aims of travel reduction. Positions C and D demonstrate substantial travel reduction. Point A now represents the negative outcome, where as a result of policy intervention, the growth of travel has been accelerated above the trend or predicted levels with no policy intervention.

This kind of deduction – evaluating travel reduction relative to a predicted future level of travel (Z) rather than the current level (C) – has to be allowed for, otherwise we will be resigned to failure, since the modest but steady increase in population, growing levels of affluence and general mobility will always tend to push up the base level of travel regardless of policy intervention.

Of course, point Z may be a rather hypothetical quantity, and the estimation of Z at a sufficiently high level will enable even travel increases of the order of Y–B to count as a relative 'reduction' in travel. Yet, when it comes to evaluating travel reduction success, there has to be some give and take, since it is difficult or impossible to judge what otherwise would have been the case – and point Z could as easily be set too low as too high. Therefore, we recommend some latitude in deducing whether travel reduction has actually taken place.

Equally, it is important to emphasise that if a particular policy has not resulted in a measurable reduction in travel in a city, it does not mean that the policy has 'failed'. This is related partly to the measurement problem discussed above, but also to the softer benefits of strategies which create a better quality urban environment. If there are fewer cars in the city centre, a more pleasant pedestrian environment, cleaner air, and a vibrant feel about the urban space, then it is a successful achievement of travel reduction – at least in the target area, namely the city centre.

13.3 Reduction and generation

There is unlikely to be any universality in the packages of measures best able to achieve travel reduction. We have explored at considerable length (see Chapters 8 and 10) the underlying mechanisms at work, as well as the difficult issues of transferability and compatibility. Our conclusions are that there is no magic solution as all cities are different, but that there are important lessons that can be learnt from the implementation of good practice. It is through building up that knowledge base and understanding the limitations of particular measures that more widespread implementation can take place.

A crucial element here is the packaging of measures in imaginative ways so that consistency and coherence of action is possible. Measures applied individually may not achieve stated policy objectives, but when combined they may begin to work. This means that the simple dichotomy used in this book between push and pull policies needs to be replaced by a composite approach that combines both push and pull policies; this approach would achieve two fundamental objectives, namely more effective travel reduction and political acceptability.

The achievement of travel reduction over the whole of a city region is extremely difficult (if not impossible), as it requires application of different packages of measures in different locations. Improvements in one location may be an incentive to travel further, or to switch destinations to locations further away to avoid the city centre. In the inner city area, most of the restrictive (push) policies have been applied – road closures, pedestrianisation, carriageway narrowing, parking controls, priority for particular users. The more positive measures (pull) have been applied in both the inner city and in suburban areas – public transport investment and priority, facilities for cycling and walking. Packaging of policies for the inner city can be effective in maintaining the vitality and accessibility of the centre. The objectives of the travel reduction policy are clear and there is a reasonable level of acceptance that something dramatic needs to be done (see Chapter 7).

However, in the outer city, the options are much less clear, as the problem is not perceived to be so great but, more importantly, the policies available seem to be much more limited. There are still the possibilities for investment in public transport and priority measures for green modes, but there is less support for restrictive measures on car use. In the surrounding region, there are even fewer opportunities, and if one car user switches to another mode, then the additional roadspace is quickly absorbed (Table 13.1). There are not the opportunities to package measures in the way that is possible for the city centre. Moreover, as the public does not perceive the problem as being so severe, the policy priority is much lower. The car is seen as being the most appropriate form of transport for nearly all activities.

It should not therefore be surprising to find that it is mainly in the inner city areas that traffic reduction (or at least, stabilisation) is realised. Thus, in Enschede, the level of traffic within the 'Singel' ring road has decreased by 8%, but the level of traffic outside it has increased by 25%. Travel has stabilised for residents, but increased for visitors. Similarly, in Zürich, traffic flows in the central area have stabilised, despite an increase in city employment and a general increase in mobility. The increase in mobility is manifested in the outer areas of the city, particularly on the motorways, and the area around the airport to the north of the city. In Bristol, the modal share of cars has been reduced and that of public transport has increased in the targeted corridors, but elsewhere in the city traffic growth continues. In Edinburgh, just as 250,000 extra passengers have used the (radial) Greenways bus routes in a six-month period, the edge-of-town Gyle centre has generated 200,000 extra car kilometres *per day*.

We can also see how the economic imperative is at work, from the lengths to which the cities go to maintain the accessibility of their centres. The restrictions on parking in the inner city are typically targeted at commuters. This frees up parking spaces for short-stay visitors (the economically valuable shoppers and tourists), from both the outer city and the external areas, who could choose to take their custom elsewhere. In Aalborg, automatic information systems direct shoppers to the most convenient parking areas, and in Enschede the police direct German visitors to the Park and Ride site to ease their passage to the town's shops and market on Bank Holidays.

Meanwhile, residents and local business people are to some extent exempted from the more punitive measures in the centre. Residents and business proprietors are able to drive to and park in the centre (as in Enschede, and Rome). As we have seen, in Zürich the residents' mobility by car has actually improved. The environment of the centre also improves, as roadspace is given over to the pedestrian or other landscape treatments.

The impression, then, is of city centres becoming carefully controlled 'fortresses' against traffic, safely enclosing ambulant, cash-dispensing shoppers and tourists, while outside the centre, the traffic and development are left to grow wild and, in the 'free market' of convenience, the car is the winner. We can see that inner-city residents benefit from a better local environment with less traffic (but still a parking place). For them, the compact, mixed-use city is a reality. They are able to access a wide range of services locally, on foot or by bicycle, and also find themselves at the hub of the public transport networks, with easy access to other towns and cities, and to the airport.

In the outer city, things continue much as before. The outer-city resident who works in the city may have to switch to public transport, at least for the inner-city part of their trip. Of those who already do not use a car in the

Table 13.1 The emerging pattern: policies and effects in the different parts of a city

	Inner City	Outer City	External
Policy			
Parking	Restricted, especially for commuters: shoppers welcome, residents exempt	No restrictions	No restrictions
Roads	Road narrowing, closures and pedestrianisation. Restricted access to cars: residents and businesses exempt	No significant restrictions on mobility by road	No restrictions
Public transport	*Improved public transport from centre outwards, particularly in a radial pattern, including access to airport*		
Walking and cycling	*Walking and cycling promoted in general in all areas*		
	Improvements concentrated in inner areas (more of a walk/cycle-friendly environment, shorter distances)	Improvements more diffuse and hindered by longer distances	
Effects			
Travel effects	Stabilisation of travel and traffic levels	Travel growth	Travel growth, especially long-distance car travel and travel by air

Source: Marshall (1999)

131

suburbs, there is not much improvement in terms of their own local access or in a contribution to overall travel reduction. As long as the new and improved public transport services are filled by existing public transport users, no travel reduction will materialise.

Bacon (1975) distinguishes between 'favourable' environments and 'hostile' environments. In the urban caricature envisioned in Figure 13.2, conditions become increasingly hostile for the driver towards the centre, but going outwards from the centre, conditions become increasingly hostile for the more sustainable modes. The 'favourable' environment to the driver – fast, wide roads and big car parks – is hostile to the walker, and difficult territory to reach by public transport. Conversely, the 'hostile' environment to the driver (congested streets, road closures, priority surrendered to others) is the 'favourable' environment to those who use public transport, cycling and walking as a means of getting about. The more closely the driver approaches the centre of the city, the greater the repulsion encountered, until ultimately travel there becomes impossible.

This is the great unresolved problem. We can think of exciting packages for the city centre, which have excellent implementation possibilities and measurable travel reduction (and other) benefits, but it is almost impossible to devise similar packages for the suburbs and the regions around the cities where most of the traffic growth is now taking place. If people continue to move out of the cities, then travel reduction may take place in the cities naturally without any policy intervention. Perhaps it is the non-city locations where good practice is now desperately needed.

13.4 Social and spatial implications

The policies under consideration may also be interpreted in the light of concepts of elasticity and dependence, which are both related to the notion of user choice. Travel reduction policies (packages of push and pull measures) tend to be directed at relatively easy targets, in relatively 'inelastic' situations (i.e., the user has little choice), whereas the more 'elastic' situations are addressed by 'pull' policies alone. Dependence relates to the necessity

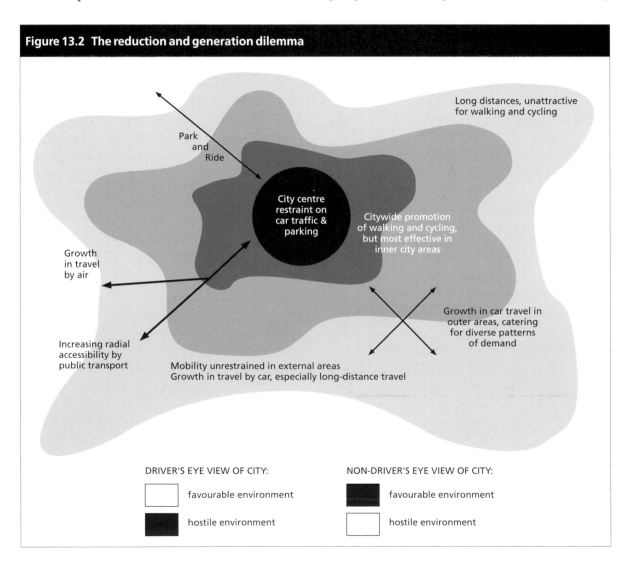

Figure 13.2 The reduction and generation dilemma

Long distances, unattractive for walking and cycling

Park and Ride

City centre restraint on car traffic & parking

Citywide promotion of walking and cycling, but most effective in inner city areas

Growth in travel by air

Growth in car travel in outer areas, catering for diverse patterns of demand

Increasing radial accessibility by public transport

Mobility unrestrained in external areas
Growth in travel by car, especially long-distance travel

DRIVER'S EYE VIEW OF CITY:
favourable environment
hostile environment

NON-DRIVER'S EYE VIEW OF CITY:
favourable environment
hostile environment

for reliance on the car and the availability of choice of alternatives (e.g., modes, destinations, times, substitutes).

Among users, then, city authorities can afford to be hard on commuters, who are obliged to go to work and cannot change their workplace very easily. However, they actively court the footloose shoppers and tourists who could easily take their custom elsewhere. Public transport schemes may also be directed more towards existing users of public transport (as in Aalborg), and do not necessarily address car drivers. Such an approach may meet general approval. Car drivers may favour public transport, if it puts off gridlock or more drastic action for another year.

Among locations, it is easiest to single out the city centre for tough targeting of car use, since the city centre has such a magnetic pull in the first place. It is most likely to be a distinct or unique location, which is not easily rivalled locally or regionally. It is also likely to be the most accessible destination by public transport, and convenient for walkers and cyclists. It can therefore afford the risk of restraint on cars, especially when the very removal of cars can enhance its distinctive qualities and hence its attraction.

By contrast, accessibility is often the sole distinguishing feature of developments around the outskirts of cities. Since they are so dependent on the car, restriction of car mobility could represent a terminal loss of accessibility. 'Big box' out-of-town developments with their car parks barred and converted to piazzas are not commonly observed (Figure 13.3). It can be concluded that policies to restrain car use (push policies) are generally only applied in the 'inelastic' cases, while the 'elastic' cases are better suited to accommodation of the car and promotion of the alternatives (pull policies) (Table 13.2).

Policy makers must be fully aware of the preferences of the public, so that their policies might succeed as planned. If the public are expected to pay more for something or sacrifice convenience, there must be a payback that relates in a meaningful way to their own aspirations. For the inner-city resident, it is clear enough that in return for vehicular access being slightly more difficult, and a parking space a little harder to find, there are distinct advantages to 'inner city living', such as less traffic, walkability and a generally improved environment (Figure 13.4). For the residents of outer areas, however, there will not necessarily be any convincing incentive to leave the car behind. With the exception of radial travel, where public transport may be a competitive alternative, all that the car user is really offered is a second-best option. In these circumstances, it would be optimistic to rely on invoking concern for the 'good of the planet' alone to change travel behaviour.

Figure 13.3 Kinnaird Park 'big box' car park, designed for the combination of cars and shopping, on the outskirts of Edinburgh

Table 13.2 Elasticities and policies

Case	User purpose	Business location	Policy
'Elastic'	Shopping, leisure	Local and peripheral functions	Pull policy only
'Inelastic'	Commuting	Central functions	Push (and pull) policy

This brings home the nature of car dependence. It is not the car, nor any car user, that is dependent. Anyone with a car is effectively *independent* of the form of the built environment. Rather, it is the suburban dweller who is dependent on a particular mode of transport. Conversely, it is the car-free individual who is dependent on the built environment, relying on the short distances and concentration of facilities available in the inner areas, and perhaps finding other areas of the city inaccessible.

As long as suburban dwellers are car-dependent, then, any attempt to force them out of their cars would be seen as disenfranchisement. In accessibility terms, it is the same sense of disenfranchisement that would be felt by the inner-city dweller if shops and services were closed and moved away from the traditional urban core. One would not expect either scenario to be tolerated without a fight from those affected. Suburban advocates of car use and the advocates of vital (traditional) town centres are all following the same argument – that of maintaining their *own* accessibility (Table 13.3).

The concepts of elasticity and dependence (both of which are related to the issues of user choice and location) help to explain the problems of implementation of travel

133

Figure 13.4 Portobello Road, London: the amenities and walkability of the inner city are appreciated by its residents as well as the ambulant, cash-dispensing shoppers and tourists

for enhancing measures and achieving political commitment from all the stakeholders, and it allows discussion and some assessment of the proposed visible impacts. Adverse impacts can be addressed and unintentional outcomes anticipated. In short, it is an essential prerequisite for successful policy implementation. These issues are further discussed in this section.

Encouraging travel reduction is not merely a matter for transport professionals. We have seen how both land-use planning and technological solutions can play a role in contributing to travel reduction. Nor is it merely a case for policy makers. National and local authorities can play a significant role in providing an important stimulus and an overall framework within which more local actions can be taken, together with necessary financial support. Involvement and responsibility for effecting travel reduction must be shared by a variety of actors.

Private companies and public utilities can also play a role in providing some of the services that are required by travel-reducing alternatives. Public transport operators can promote not only their own services but others – for example cycling, by providing bicycle parking and accommodation for bicycles on board where appropriate, and even bicycle hire. Similarly, the provision of utilities, such as telecommunications services, is required before some travel-reducing options become possible.

reduction policies. They also explain, to some extent, other important considerations in successful implementation. It is better to design travel reduction policies into the layout of city centres, peripheral locations and housing developments, so that they are clearly seen as part of the design process rather than just as good ideas that are retrofitted to the urban or peripheral location. Land-use strategies are equally important to traditional transport policies in reducing travel, since location policies, decisions on opening hours, and integration of land and transport all offer opportunities for packaging policies. The trip-making requirements of individuals must be seen as an entity. If only the origin or the destination is suitable for another mode or another location, then the car will still be used. Thus if non-central locations are involved, it is difficult to promote realistic alternatives to car drivers for their entire trip.

Employers have an important role to play, not only in directly encouraging particular commuting behaviour such as car pooling, but in allowing flexibility in the workplace that creates opportunities to travel off-peak, or to work at home. Provision of showers and facilities for cyclists would demonstrate the importance attached to a cycling promotion initiative, as would the direct provision of bicycles themselves; or laptop or home computers (perhaps in lieu of company car benefits) would encourage homeworking. Local and national authorities may take the lead in promoting travel reduction through example, as these authorities are both major local employers, and providers of public transport and other services.

13.5 Involvement

We have already discussed the importance of packaging as a means of presenting combinations of imaginative and attractive policy measures. It is also an essential process

Table 13.3 Dependency and policy

User mode	Dependency	User Location	
		Compact inner city (independent of any single mode)	*Outer city and beyond* (dependent on car, where available)
Car available	Independent of built form	Push policies	Pull policies
Car not available	Dependent on compact form	Pull policies	Pull policies

Finally, individuals themselves can take the initiative in altering their own travel patterns. Particularly important in this respect is the necessity for the travel reduction message to get through to the public and to command their support. We return here to some of the necessary conditions for travel reduction. In Chapter 1, we drew attention to the primary reasons for travel reduction, mentioning transport and environmental arguments, together with the necessity to obtain political and public support. Here, we expand on this last factor, by elaborating on certain key requirements for political and public acceptance of travel reduction strategies: this acceptance depends upon individuals' willingness to change their behaviour, their awareness of the benefits and of the importance of finding alternatives, effective publicity of the effects of travel decisions on lifestyle, and the ready availability of choices.

Willingness to change

Unless individuals understand the importance of travel reduction objectives, and the pressing need for these to mitigate the environmental consequences of unrestrained mobility, then the effectiveness of travel reduction measures will be lost. For example, if obstacles are put in the way of the drivers, they must also be convinced of the benefits of using an alternative mode of transport, or they may simply take evasive action that allows them to continue to use their cars. Such action may involve a longer route or entail spending more time in congestion, which are both contrary to the objectives of travel reduction.

Awareness of benefits

A change in behaviour can also be encouraged if, in addition recognising 'global' benefits of their action, individuals also see a direct personal benefit. Thus, where individuals were given bicycles by their employer (Aalborg company bicycle scheme; Section 4.2), this direct positive gain could be realised through participation and use. In such cases participants can feel that they are benefiting personally as well as helping the broader, indeed global, environment.

This sense of benefit need not be material, but may be realised through time and convenience. Thus, the urban structure of a settlement may be devised in such a way that routes on foot or by bicycle are more direct than those by car, enabling trips by the 'slower' modes to be made in times that are comparable with longer journeys by car. This case demonstrates how it is easy for the individual traveller to make the 'favoured' decision to

walk or cycle to the shops rather than taking the car. It is interesting to note that Houten (Section 5.5) has an above-average rate of car ownership, and yet car travel within the town is less than in comparable places. This suggests that travel within Houten is made by non-motorised modes by choice (not simply due to the non-availability of the car), and demonstrates that it is possible to combine the mobility of the car with mobility by alternative modes.

Finding alternatives

It is important to make individuals aware that they can make a difference, and that this difference can (and should) be made now. It is not some global problem that will only be solved at some remote time in the future. Thus, the schemes to raise awareness can make a point of encouraging even relatively minor or temporary changes in behaviour, as in Bristol's 'Cycle to Work' day or Enschede's campaign that 'the car can manage a day without you' (Section 2.7). Although the immediately tangible effects of a day not travelling by car may be slight, the willingness to participate in the scheme and the act of finding alternatives to the car are important. The latter includes overcoming the barrier of reluctance to try out unfamiliar travel modes, which may have an effect in the longer term – for example, when changes in individuals' lifestyles present new opportunities for alternative travel possibilities.

Travel decisions and lifestyle

Individuals make travel decisions within a wider context of activities and lifestyle (Figure 13.5). In particular, travel behaviour may become habitual for any given circumstances, and often the 'choice' to use a car on a particular occasion is not so much a positive decision, as merely the failure to consider the alternatives. Making those alternatives explicit, through publicity (information technology) and physical visibility (buses speeding past on dedicated lanes; clearly marked bicycle lanes, as in Figure 13.6), is therefore an important activity.

Moreover, as noted above, life-cycle changes can precipitate travel changes. For example, any location choice is effectively also a travel choice. Thus, the decision to move to the suburbs or out of town will imply particular travel consequences. Similarly, moving one's place of employment, or changes in household size, or an increase in income (the ability to purchase a car) can all precipitate changes in travel behaviour. Such changes provide an opportunity to take travel-reducing decisions rather than travel-increasing ones. In the case of business location in The Hague (Section 5.3), the siting of offices next to a railway node precipitated a modal shift away from the car to rail.

Similarly, individuals may have a fixed 'travel time budget': we may argue that the amount of travel (time) available is constant, and by providing choice we can make this travel less harmful. For example, we can encourage the use of slower modes over shorter distances, or we can use less fuel through travelling at more constant speeds outside peak periods.

Creation of choices

What the policy maker can do, therefore, is not so much force changes in behaviour, but rather create choices for people so that travel alternatives involving less travel become more desirable. By contrast, if the choice is not available – for example, to work at home, to have mixed-use development within a block, or to take the bicycle on the train – then travel reduction by these means is impossible from the outset.

13.6 Summary

It is possible to learn from the case studies and the wider travel reduction context to suggest a few principles or pointers, which may be used to summarise the messages of travel reduction emerging from this book. It has been seen that travel reduction is certainly possible in some

Figure 13.5 A residential neighbourhood in Zürich: individuals' travel choices must be recognised within the context of wider lifestyle choices

Figure 13.6 A highly visible bicycle strip in central London

cases, even if overall mobility nevertheless to continues increasing. Given this reality, the form of travel reduction to be targeted – who is encouraged to change some element of their mobility, and by what means – then becomes a political decision.

A simple example of a policy decision is whether the target reduction of a given number of vehicle kilometres is to be distributed between a few long-distance journeys or several shorter ones; or between a few public transport journeys or several low-occupancy car journeys. This kind of decision will be familiar to transport policy makers who are balancing objectives between different transport-related priorities.

However, policy decisions will also depend on what kind of city or environment we wish to live in (Figure 13.7). It is evident that for the same amount of mobility, some very different environments and travel regimes could result. An attractive urban environment, amenable to walking and cycling, may be contrasted with an urban environment which is more hostile to the pedestrian or cyclist (indeed, to people in general). In this hostile environment people choose to telecommute, living further away from the city and visiting it less frequently. Both possibilities might involve the same amount of travel, but very different environments result.

This is why it is important to pay attention to the wider policy context. For example, land-use and urban design policies can create a favourable urban environment, which can sustain urban vitality and services for a cross-section of society. In addition to making a contribution to travel reduction objectives, this design-based solution can also allow more or less unrestricted mobility on foot or by

Figure 13.7 Town houses in Notting Hill, London: the type of built environment desired determines the most appropriate form of travel reduction

bicycle. It is better to retain services and employment in central areas currently accessible to most people than to allow dispersal to peripheral locations, entailing longer distances and more travel by car, and then have to create commuter plans or road capacity reductions to mitigate these effects. In the former case, travel reduction is 'built in', but in the latter case special proactive or restrictive policies are required.

For the same amount of travel reduction success, we can operate with a different range of lifestyles, activity patterns and environments: the choice of travel modes and preferred environments becomes significant. Moreover, the equity implications of travel reduction policies become important, as does the issue of which individuals have that choice of modes, and these choices all influence the wider environment. In this sense we can choose to reduce travel not only for its own sake, but in ways which are complementary to wider social and environmental objectives, and hence contribute to sustainability in its widest interpretation.

References

Aalborg Kommune (1994) *Handlingsplan for trafik and Miljø*. Aalborg: Aalborg Kommune, p. 19.

Aalborg Kommune (1997) *Evaluering af forsog med firmacycler, arbejde-bolig-cykel-Projektet*. Aalborg: Vejdirektoratet og Aalborg Kommune.

Abraham, M and Rosenkrantz, V (1995) Transport, land use and urban structure – getting past the rhetoric. Short paper prepared for New South Wales Department of Transport.

Adams, J (1997) Can technology save us? In *The greening of urban transport*, ed. R Tolley. Chichester: John Wiley & Sons, pp. 81–98.

AGV (1996) *Deelauto: de stand van zaken*. Nijmegen: Adviesgroep voor Verkeer en Vervoer.

Anon. (1997) Antrag des Gemeinderates von Zürich über die Verordnung von Fahrzeugabstellplätzen. *Parkplatzverordnung*, 7 January 1997.

Avon County Council (1993) *Kingsdown traffic calming evaluation study*. Bristol: Avon County Council.

Avon County Council (1994a) *A4 Bath Road Park & Ride user survey*. Bristol: Avon County Council.

Avon County Council (1994b) TPP (Transport Policies and Programme) Submission 1995/1996, Avon County Council (July 1994): Appendix 1, Bus priority measures in Avon. Bristol: Avon County Council.

Bach, B (1996) Cycling planning and design. *Seminar Civil Engineering European Courses*, Athens (Spring Seminar on Transport, 27–28 May).

Bacon, E (1975) *The design of cities*. London: Thames and Hudson.

Banister, D (1994) *Transport planning*. London: E & FN Spon.

Banister, D (1997) Reducing the need to travel. In *Environment and Planning B: Planning and Design*, **24**, 437–49.

Banister, D (1998a) Barriers to implementation of urban sustainability. *International Journal of Environment and Pollution* **10**(1), 65–83.

Banister, D (1998b) *Transport policy and the environment*. London: E & FN Spon.

Banister, D and Steen, P (1999) Policy scenario building for sustainable mobility. Paper presented at ESF/NSF Transatlantic Research Conference on Social Change and Sustainable Transport (SCAST), University of California at Berkeley, March.

Banister, D, Watson, S and Wood, C (1997) Sustainable cities: transport, energy and urban form. *Environment and Planning B: Planning and Design*, **24**, 125-143.

Banister, D, Stead, D, Steen, P, Åkerman, J, Dreborg, K, Nijkamp, P and Schleicher-Tappeser, R (2000) *European transport policy and sustainable mobility*. London: E & FN Spon.

Begg, D. (1998) Plan for transport of delight. *Edinburgh Evening News*, 17 June.

Bentvelsen, Th, Papa, OA, Priemus, H, Spruyt, P and Van der Zon, F (1988) Enquête Bouwsubsidies, 5 Woningbouw-subsidies in de premiehuursector 1966–1986. *Tweede Kamer, vergaderjaar 1987–1988* **19623**(36). Den Haag: Staatsuitgeverij.

Birch, S (1999) Want to cut pollution, fight gridlock and save yourself 1500 pounds? *The Guardian*, 15 April.

Breheny, MJ (ed.) (1992) *Sustainable development and urban form*. London: Pion.

Bristol City Council (1996a) *Bike to Work day cycle counts*. Bristol: Bristol City Council.

Bristol City Council (1996b) *A4 Bath Road Park and Ride user survey*.Bristol: Bristol City Council.

Brükx, E, Meijer, J and de Jager, H (1993) Ruimtelijke inrichting en intern woon-winkelverkeer. *Verkeerskunde*, **44**(1), 22–25.

Cairns, S, Hass-Klau, C and Goodwin, P (1998) *Traffic impact of highway capacity reductions*. Report prepared for London Transport and the Department of the Environment, Transport and Regions, in conjunction with MVA Ltd. London: Landor.

CAPTURE Consortium (1998) Data from European Commission Directorate General VII (EU DG VII): CAPTURE project.

CBS (1996) *Geemente ol Maat 1996*, Enschede, Voorburg/Heerlan, Central Bureau voor de Statistiek.

CEC (1995) *Towards fair and efficient pricing in transport: policy options for internalising the external costs of transport in the European Union*. Brussels: CEC.

CEC (1997) Road pricing schemes in operation – practical examples. Paper presented at Conference on Making Road Pricing Work, Brussels, September 1997.

CEC (1998) *The Common Transport Policy. Sustainable mobility: perspectives for the future*. Communication from the Commission to the Council, the European Parliament, the Economic and Social Committee and the Committee of Regions. Brussels: Commission of the European Communities, December COM 716 Final.

Commune di Roma (1997) *Tempi ed Orari della Città di Roma: relazione consuntiva 1994–1997*. Rome: Commune di Roma.

Commune di Roma and CISPEL (1997) *Commune nuovo. La modernizzazione dei servizi: imprenditorialità, qualità, garanzie*. Rome: Commune di Roma.

DANTE Consortium (1997) *City strategies and measurement of their impact on avoiding the need to travel*, DANTE project Deliverable 2A, Report prepared for EU DG VII. Aarhus: PLS Consult.

DANTE Consortium (1998) *The implementation of city strategies and measures for reducing travel: barriers, potentials and transferability*, Report prepared for EU DG VII. Delft: OTB Research Institute for Housing, Urban and Mobility Studies, Delft University of Technology.

DANTE Consortium (1999) *Encouraging travel alternatives. A guide to good practice in reducing travel*, Report prepared for EU DG VII. London: Bartlett School of Planning, University College London.

De Borger, B, Mayeres, I, Proost, S and Wouter, S (1996) Optimal pricing of urban passenger transport: a simulation exercise for Belgium, *Journal of Transport Economics and Policy*, **30**(1), 31–54.

DeLucchi, M (1995) Original estimates of social costs of motor vehicle use. Paper presented at the Transportation Research Board, Washington DC, January.

DETR (1998a) *A new deal for transport – better for everyone*. London: The Stationery Office.

DETR (1998b) *Places, streets and movement. Companion guide to Design Bulletin 32, Residential roads and footpaths*. London: Department of the Environment, Transport and the Regions.

DETR (1999) Revision of PPG 13 Transport: Public Consultation Draft. London: Department of the Environment, Transport and the Regions.

DoE and DoT (1994) *PPG13: Planning policy guidance – transport*. London: HMSO.

DoE (1995) *PPG13: A Guide to Better Practice: Reducing the need to travel through land use and transport planning*. London: HMSO.

Geemente Enschede (1996) *Mobiliteitsplan Enschede 1996–2005* (Mobility Plan Enschede 1996–2005), Enschede: Bouw en Miliendienst, Geemente Enschede.

Giovenali, S (1995) Nuova Ipotesi di Gestione della Zona a Traffico Limitato dell'Area Centrale di Roma. Paper presented at Urbania Conference in Rome.

Goodwin, P, Hallet, S, Kenny, F and Stokes, G (1991) *Transport: the new realism*. Report presented to the Rees Jefferys Road Fund, Oxford.

Goodwin, P, Hass-Klau, C and Cairns, S (1998) Evidence on the effects of road capacity reduction on traffic levels, *Traffic Engineering and Control*, **39**(6), 348–54.

Graham, S and Marvin, S (1996) *Telecommunications and the city: electronic spaces, urban places*. London: Routledge.

Greaf, PAM (1995) *Onderzoek Parkeerbus Enschede*. Enschede: Gemeente Enschede.

Grubb, M, Vrolijk, C and Brack, D (1999) *The Kyoto Protocol: A Guide and Assessment*. London: The Royal Institution of International Affairs/Earthscan.

Hackney Borough Council (1996) *Supplementary Planning Guidance Note: Live work development*. London: Hackney Borough Council.

Hallsworth, A, Tolley, R and Black, C (1998) Transport policy-making: the curse of the uncomfortable consequence, *Journal of Transport Geography*, **6**(2) 159–66.

Hansen, A (1996) Jupiterprojektet-Parkeringsinformationssystemer. Paper presented at the Conference Trafikdage på Aalborg Universitet, Aalborg.

Hathway, T (1997) Successful community participation in local traffic proposals, *Journal of Advanced Transportation*, **31**(2), 201–13.

Hervik, A and Braathen, S (1994) Charging systems for the use of the urban infrastructure. Paper presented at The ECMT Round Table 97, Paris, pp. 5–54.

Hollander, B, Kruythoff, H and Teule, R (1996) *Woningbouw op Vinex-locaties: effect op het woonwerkverkeer in de Randstad*. Delft: Delft University Press.

Konings, JW, Kruythoff, HM, Maat, C (1996) *Woningdichtheid en mobiliteit. Woon-werk-verkeer op nieuwbouwlocaties in de provincie Noord-Brabant.* Delft: Delft University Press.

Kropman, H, Neeskens, J (1997) *Carpoolen, een kansrijk alternatief. segmentatie van het carpool potentieel in het woon-werkverkeer.* Nijmegen: Nijmegen University.

Langmyhr, T (1999) Understanding innovation: the case of road pricing, *Transport Reviews* 19(3), 255–72.

Lord Provost's Commission (1998) *Report to the Lord Provost.* Edinburgh: Lord Provost's Commission on Sustainable Development for the City of Edinburgh.

Maat, C (1998) The compact city and mobility. Paper presented at the 8th World Conference on Transport Research, Antwerp, July.

Maat, C (1999a) The compact city and mobility; a Dutch perspective. In *Transport and environment: in search of sustainable solutions,* eds ET Verhoef, E Feitelson. Cheltenham: Edward Elgar.

Maat, C (1999b) The compact city: conflicts of interest between housing and mobility objectives. Paper presented to the ESF/NSF Transatlantic Research Conference on Social Change and Sustainable Transport 10–13 March 1999, University of California at Berkeley.

Maat, C and Louw, E (1999) Mind the gap: pitfalls on measures to control mobility. *Built Environment,* 25(2) 151–61.

Maddison, D, Pearce, DW, Johansson, O, Calthrop, E, Litman, T and Verhoef, E (1996) *The true cost of road transport.* London: Earthscan, Blueprint 5.

Maeder, S (1993) *Kosten Wirksamkeit von Luftreinhalte- massnahmen.* Schellenberg Winterhur, Austria.

Marshall, S (1999) Restraining mobility while maintaining accessibility: an impression of the 'city of sustainable growth'. *Built Environment,* 25(2) 168–79.

Marshall, S and Banister, D (2000) Travel reduction strategies: intentions and outcomes, *Transportation Research (A).*

Marshall, S, Banister, D and McLellan, A (1997) A strategic assessment of travel trends and travel reduction strategies, *Innovation* 10(3), 289–304.

Massnahmenplan Lufthygiene Kanton Zürich (1988) Entwurf Teilplan Umsteigen, Uebersichtsplan der Korridore, Zürich.

Mathers, S (1999) Reducing travel in the City of Bristol – promoting bus use through complementary measures, *Built Environment,* 25(2), 94–105.

Meijs, M and Himmels, M (1994) *Bezoekers van de Enschedesche Binnenstad.* Enschede: Bureau Informatie & Onderzoek.

Mittler, D (1999a) Reducing travel!? A case study of Edinburgh, Scotland, *Built Environment,* 25(2) 106–17.

Mittler, D (1999b) Sustaining Edinburgh!? The Lord Provost's Commission on Sustainable Development for the City of Edinburgh, *Scottish Affairs,* 29(Autumn), 104–20.

Mittler, D (1999c) Environmental space and barriers to local sustainability. Evidence from Edinburgh, Scotland. Paper presented at Planning Patterns for Sustainable Development, International Conference, Padua, Italy, 30 September–3 October 1998; *Local Environment,* in press.

Molnar, H (1997) Samen in de auto. Over bezettigsgraden en carpoolen, *Maandstatistiek Verkeer en Vervoer,* 60(4), 6–11.

Mulder, H and Hillen, P (1991. *Evaluatie Afstuiting Binnenstad, Deel 1: Een Inventarisatie van Enkele Feitelijke Ontwikkelingen.* Enschede: Gemeente Enschede.

Mulder, H and Hillen, P (1992) *Evaluatie Afstuiting Binnenstad, Deel 1: Een Inventarisatie van Enkele Feitelijke Ontwikkelingen, Gedrag en Meningen.* Enschede: Gemeente Enschede.

Municipality of Rome (1996) *TRADE: an experiment of teleworking in public administration.* Rome: MoR.

Municipality of Rome (1997) Piano Generale Urbano del Traffico. In *Proceedings of the Telematics for Mobility Conference,* Rome.

MVROM (1994) *National Environmental Policy Plan 2 (Summary).* The Hague: Ministry of Housing, Physical Planning and Environment.

MVROM (1998) *Second Transport Structure Plan.* The Hague: Ministry of Transport, Public Works and Water Management.

Naber, AG (1994) Experiment GedragsbeVnvloeding Automobiliteit. Onderzoek naar de Effecten van een Wijkcampagne ter Vermindering van het Autogebruik, Zwolle (Natuur en Milieu Overijssel).

NCE (1999) Congestion: who cares? *New Civil Engineer,* 28 (January), p. 14.

Newbery, DM (1990) Pricing and congestion: economic principles relevant to road pricing, *Oxford Review of Economic Policy,* 6(1), 22–38.

Peirson, J and Vickerman, R (1998) The environment, efficient pricing and investment in transport: a model and some results for the UK. In *Transport policy and the environment*, ed. D Banister. London: E & FN Spon, pp. 161–75.

Pharoah, T and Apel, D (1995) *Transport concepts in European cities*. Avebury Studies in Green Research. Aldershot: Avebury Ashgate.

Planungsbüro Jud AG (1990) Parkierungsbeschränkungen zu Schutze der Wohnquartiere Pilotversuch Zürich Hottingen. *Im Auftrag der Stadtpolizei Zürich*.

POSSUM (1999) Project on policy scenarios for sustainable mobility, Deliverable 4, Final Report prepared for the EU DG VII Strategic Research Programme, Brussels.

Priemus, H and Maat, C (1998) *Ruimtelijk en Mobiliteitsbeleid: interactie van rijksinstrumenten. Stedelijke en Regionale Verkenningen 18*. Delft: Delft University Press.

PROED SA (1997) *Consultanta Privind Traficul Urban (Urban Traffic Consulting)*. Bucharest: City Traffic Department.

Quade, ES (1989) *Analysis for public decisions*. New York: North-Holland.

Rambøll, Anders Nyvig A/S and PLS Consult A/S (1997) *Transport, energi og miljø – visioner og virkemidler*. Aarhus: consultancy report by PLS Consult.

RATB (1996/1997a) *Sondaje de trafic 1996 & 1997*. Bucharest: RATB (Traffic Department).

RATB (1996/1997b) *Rapoarte trimestriale 1996 & 1997*. Bucharest: RATB (Traffic Department).

RATB (1997) *Serviciul exploatare-miscare, rapoarte trimestriale*. Bucharest: RATB (Traffic Department).

Ringeling, AB (1987) Beleidstheorieën en theorieën over beleid (Policy theories and theories about policy). In *Handboek beleidswetenschap*, eds PB Lehning, JBM Simonis. Amsterdam: Boom.

Royal Commission on Environmental Pollution (1994) *Transport and the environment*, 18th Report, Cmnd 2674. London: HMSO.

Royal Commission on Environmental Pollution (1997) *Transport and the environment – developments since 1994*, 20th Report, Cmnd 3752. London: HMSO.

SACTRA (1994) *Trunk roads and the generation of traffic*, Report of the Standing Advisory Committee on Trunk Road Appraisal, (chairman) D Wood. London: HMSO.

Salomon, I (1997) Transport and the environment. Paper presented to NECTAR seminar on Transport and the environment, Amsterdam, June 1997.

Salomon, I and Mokhtarian, PL (1997) Coping with congestion: understanding the gap between policy assumptions and behavior, *Transportation Research D*, **2**(2), 107–23.

Salomon, I, Bovy, P and Orfeuil, JP (1993) Introduction: can a billion trips be reduced to a few patterns. In *A billion trips a day. Tradition and transition in European travel patterns*, eds I Salomon, P Bovy, JP Orfeuil. Dordrecht: Kluwer Academic Publishers.

Schipper, L (1995) Determinants of automobile use and energy consumption in OECD countries, *Annual Review of Energy Environment*, **20**(4), 325–86.

Scottish Homes (1999) *Waterfront Edinburgh, Granton development framework – a vision for the future*. Edinburgh: Scottish Homes.

Small, KA and Kazimi, C (1995) On the costs of air pollution from motor vehicles, *Journal of Transport Economics and Policy*, **29**(1), 7–32.

Smith, T.B. (1973) The policy implementation process, *Policy Sciences*, **4**(2), 197–209.

Socialdata (1995) Mobilität in Zürich, Bauamt 1 dec Stadt Zürich, Institute für Verkehrs und Infrastrukturforschung, Hans Grässet-weg 1, D-18375, München 70.

Sorrell, S and Skea, J (eds) (1999) *Pollution for sale: emissions trading and joint implementation*. Cheltenham: Edward Elgar.

Stadelmann, H, Riedel, W, Vollenweider, K (1996) *Einführung in das Verkehrsregelkonzept der Stadt Zürich*, Sonderdruck aus Srassenverkehrstechnik 40. Bonn: Kirschbaumverlag.

Stadtplanungsamt Zürich (1991) *Parkierung 1991*. Zürich: Survey for the City of Zürich.

Statistische Berichte des Kantons Zürich (1995) *Fünf Jahre S-Bahn: SBB Fahrgastfrequenzen 1989–1994 im Züricher Verkehrsverbund*.

Statistische Berichte des Kantons Zürich (1996) *Die Verkehrsentwicklung im Kanton Zürich 1990–1995*.

Stead, D and Banister, D (1999) Transport futures planning. Paper presented at the RTPI Conference, University of Sheffield, March.

Stokes, G (1996) Alternative strategies to reduce car dependence. Paper presented to the CAPTURE Cities Conference, London.

Tolley, R (1997) Obstacles to walking and cycling. In *The greening of urban transport. Planning for walking and cycling in Western cities*, ed. R Tolley. Chichester: John Wiley & Sons, pp. 3–20.

TUD (1997) DANTE Project internal working paper. Delft: Technical University of Delft.

Urban Task Force (1999) *Towards an urban renaissance.* London: E & FN Spon.

Urban Villages Forum (1997) Crown Street, Glasgow – a mid-term review, *Urban Villages Forum*, Winter.

Wackernagel, M and Rees, W (1996) *Our ecological footprint: reducing human impact on the Earth.* Gabriola Island: New Society Publishers.

WCED (1987) *Our Common Future* (The Bruntland Report). The World Commission on Environment and Development. Oxford: Oxford University Press.

Weger, THD de (1987) Parkeerbus Enschede vlakt piek in parkeerprobleem af, *Verkeerskunde*, **38**(7/8), 328–32.

Wel, W van (1995) *Modal split van de centrumbezoekers in Enschede.* Enschede: Gemeente Enschede.

WSW, der pluspunkt (1998) Carriba! in der Großkundenbetreuung, Wuppertal, December 1998.

Züricher Verkehrsverbund (1995) *Der ZVV in Kürze 1995.* Zürich: City Transport Department.

Index

Page numbers in *italics* refer to illustrations (i.e. Figures).
Page numbers in **bold** indicate a main reference to the subject.

Spotlight
on FCE

Jon Naunton with John Hughes

Teacher's Book

HEINLE

Japan • Korea • Mexico • Singapore • Spain • United Kingdom • United States

Spotlight on FCE Teacher's Book
Jon Naunton with John Hughes

Publisher: Jason Mann

Development Editor: Amanda Cole

Marketing Manager: Ruth McAleavey

Senior Content Project Editor: Natalie Griffith

Art Editor: Amanda Cole

Production Controller: Denise Power

Cover Designer: Co Studio

Text Designer: Echelon Design

Compositor: Echelon Design and Parkwood Composition Service, Inc.

Illustrator: Michael Perrin

ISBN: 978-1-4240-1680-8

Cengage Learning EMEA
Cheriton House
North Way
Andover
SP10 5BE

Cengage Learning is a leading provider of customized learning solutions with office locations around the globe, including Singapore, the United Kingdom, Australia, Mexico, Brazil and Japan. Locate our local office at: **international.cengage.com/region**

Cengage Learning products are represented in Canada by Nelson Education, Ltd.

Visit Heinle online at **elt.heinle.com**
Visit our corporate website at **cengage.com**

Printed in China by R R Donnelley
3 4 5 6 7 8 9 10 – 15 14 13 12 11

Contents

Spotlight on First Certificate

	Teaching in Practice	Background	Spotlights
Unit 1 **Friends and family**	• Pair and group work • Opening up • 'Back-chaining' • Word definitions	• Soap operas	• State and dynamic verbs • Conversation • Listening for general meaning • Keeping a vocabulary notebook • Finding key words • Compulsory letter
Unit 2 **Jobs and work**	• Pronunciation • Demonstrating activities	• Raleigh International	• Multiple-choice cloze • Suffixes • Rules for comparing • Multiple matching • Two-way conversation
Unit 3 **Sport and leisure**	• Managing discussion in groups	• Eccentric sports	• Verb + noun collocations • Multiple matching • Gapped text • Sentence completion • Individual 'long turn'
Unit 4 **Nature and animals**	• The difference between transitive and intransitive verbs • Negative checking	• A dog's life?	• Adjectives + prepositions • Word formation • Useful expressions for describing photographs
Unit 5 **A good story**	• Pre-teaching vocabulary	• McCall Smith and Mma Ramotswe	• Multiple choice • Handling multiple choice questions • Verbs of manner • Sequencing • Gradable and non-gradable adjectives
Unit 6 **Transport and travel**	• Teaching monolingual/different nationalities • Pronunciation: phrasal verbs • Concept questions • Writing as a process	• Dream holidays	• Listening • Particles and meaning in phrasal verbs • Scanning • Report writing
Unit 7 **Technology**	• Clarifying tense with timelines • Showing interest	• Chinese inventions	• Verbs followed by the gerund or the infinitive • Exchanging ideas, expressing and justifying opinions
Unit 8 **Crime and social responsibility**	• Monolingual dictionaries	• The history of the police	• Defining and non-defining relative clauses • Informality and formality in relative clauses • Active listening

- Grammar: Phrasal verbs in context

- Pelmanism
- The Hacienda Club

- Speaking: correcting errors

- Find me a Nanny!
- In or Out? Balloon debate

- Listening: inventing more choices

- Information gap: The origin of two sports
- 'A new sport'
- Sporting Equipment

- Useful expressions: sentence correction
- Key word: phrases using *look*
- Writing: comprehension questions

- Phrasal verbs jigsaw
- Introductory expressions
- Letter writing: Pet problems

- Key word extension: phrases using *thing*

- Word search: A Good Story
- Picture composition:
  - But who ate the cake?
  - Harvey gets what he deserves …

- Listening: 'who says' questions

- Boardgame: Introducing your town
- Cued-dialogue

- Key word extension: phrases using *to*

- Talk show (student A and B)
- My FCE robot

- Getting started: punishment expressions
- Vocabulary: example sentences

- Debating society
- Who in the class…?

- Reading: stereotypes
- Speaking: describing photographs

- Phrasal verbs: Take that!
- Dinner party through the ages
- Cooking instructions: Recipe for success

- Key word: phrases using *seem*

- What's in Granny's attic?
- Archaeology role play: Lost worlds

- Vocabulary: spidergram
- Reading: synonyms

- Deal-makers
- Life after Debt?

- Getting started: paraphrasing idioms

- Weather idioms
- Role play: Winds of change

- Vocabulary: new 'news' pairs
- Photocopiable: Reporting the news

- The Daily FCE
- Reporting the news

- Speaking: topic cards
- Key word: vocabulary diary additions

- From sweats-shop to street brawl
- Chat show

- Getting started: introducing artwork
- Key word: phrases using *mind*
- Writing: multi-national reviews

- Do you hear what I see? Drawing picture dictation
- Do you hear what I hear? Talking picture dictation
- Just a minute! Vocabulary cards

- Vocabulary: negotiation
- Topic discussion: the future
- Writing: Exam practice
- Speaking: offering advice

- Arranging Your Room
- Our island world
- Post-FCE quiz

What are the differences between the old exam and the revised exam?

If you've taught FCE before, then you are probably wondering what the differences between the old and revised exam are. There are still five papers, but overall the exam has been reduced in length. A question type has been lost from each of Paper 1 (Reading) and Paper 3 (Use of English). The number of questions in each part may be slightly different, but essentially there are few differences between the old and the new exam.

Revised exam	Old exam
1 Paper One: Reading (1 hour) • Part 1 Multiple choice (8 questions) • Part 2 Gapped text sentences (7 questions) • Part 3 Multiple-matching (15 questions)	**1 hour 15 minutes** • There are now three rather than four parts (questions). • The matching exercise where candidates matched headings to paragraphs has disappeared.
2 Paper Two: Writing (1 hour 20 minutes) • Part 1 Compulsory letter or email (120–150 words) • Part 2 One question from four – Non-transactional letter, report, essay, review, story (110–180 words.) Question 5 based on set text.	**1 hour 30 minutes** • Students now write emails. • The word length for part 1 is now shorter. • Students can now write a 'Review' in part 2.
3 Paper Three: Use of English (45 minutes) • Part 1 Multiple choice lexical cloze (12 questions) • Part 2 Open cloze (12 questions) • Part 3 Word formation (10 questions) • Part 4 Key word transformations (8 questions)	**1 hour 15 minutes** • The number of questions has been reduced in parts 1, 2 and 4. • Old part 5, sentence correction, where students identified an extra and unnecessary word has disappeared.
4 Paper Four: Listening (approximately 40 minutes) • Part 1 A series of eight short unrelated extracts from monologues or exchanges between interacting speakers. There is one multiple choice question per extract. • Part 2 A monologue or text involving speakers. Sentence completion (10 questions). • Part 3 Five short unrelated monologues. Multiple matching (5 questions). • Part 4 A monologue or text involving interacting speakers. Multiple choice questions (7 questions).	**40 minutes (approximately)** • This paper is unchanged, however the old 'who said what' format of part 4 has disappeared. • Emphasis has been placed more on candidate's understanding of attitude and opinion.
5 Paper Five: Speaking (14 minutes) • Part 1 A conversation between interlocutor and each candidate (spoken questions). • Part 2 An individual 'long turn' for each candidate, with a brief response from the second candidate (visual and written stimuli, with spoken instructions). • Part 3 A two-conversation between the candidates (visual and written stimuli, with spoken instructions). • Part 4 A discussion on topics related to part 3 (spoken questions).	**14 minutes** • The only change is that there are now written prompts with the photos and pictures in parts 2 and 3 which students use when speaking.

Introduction

What will I find in this teacher's book?

In this introduction you will find an overview of the exam, key differences between the old and new version, and some remarks about the differences between general English teaching and teaching exam classes.

In the main body of this teacher's book you will find notes and guidance for each unit with an easy access answer key at the end. The notes often contain suggestions for alternative approaches and ideas and for handling pronunciation. Teaching tips figure in earlier units, but receive less emphasis as the course progresses and students are exposed to more and more examination-style practice. There are also tapescripts of all the listening passages. Lastly, each unit has at least two pages of photocopiable material. The first page usually practises the vocabulary that has appeared in the unit through a game or puzzle. The second page generally has an activity that provides the kind of freer speaking practice more common to general English classes.

Why do students do the exam?

Cambridge First Certificate is an internationally recognised qualification that has been a benchmark of achievement for many decades. Indeed, it is not unusual to find several generations of the same family who have all studied for and taken this exam! Students are attracted to it because it validates their knowledge and is an untarnished gold standard of competence that is recognised by employers and educational institutions around the world. It proves that the holder has a solid knowledge of grammar and vocabulary, and a corresponding level of ability across the skills. It also offers the promise that the successful student will have a reasonable level of communicative competence in most everyday situations. In today's terms, it is considered a B2 level by the Council of Europe.

What does FCE show?

Students who have successfully followed a First Certificate preparation course will finish with a useful and very solid knowledge of grammar, vocabulary and skills. It proves that students have achieved a useful level of competence and can end there. For others, it can act as an extremely solid foundation on which their more advanced studies can be based. Students with a good pass, pass A or B, might consider for instance embarking on a CAE programme.

What do students need to pass First Certificate?

To pass, students need:
- adequate language knowledge
- a clear understanding of how the exam works and how they will be tested
- skills practice
- exam skills
- regular and extensive practice of all the question types.

What's in a name?

We chose *Spotlight on FCE* as the name for our course because we believe in the importance of focusing and shedding light on the language and skills students need for success. We believe that for students to do well, they need precise information about language. We also wanted to emphasise important information about the exam, as we believe that students should know the exam format well.

WHAT ARE THE SPOTLIGHTS?

The spotlights throughout the course give these areas prominence by focusing on key areas of language and examination skills' development. They draw the student's attention to what is being tested and illuminate problem areas such as how to sequence ideas, how to make contrasts, and so on. They give authoritative and useful advice on grammar, vocabulary and skills that is then practised. Exam spotlights are particularly useful for teaching students about the nature of the exam and examination technique. They may help learners avoid common pitfalls and traps.

How does *Spotlight* help?

Spotlight helps by being thorough and challenging. It contains a lot of material and information and is not 'FCE-lite'. *Spotlight* helps with language by systematically revising and extending the main structures and language areas of English, and by teaching the additional structures that are often tested in the exam. There is a full First Certificate Grammar Reference and practice exercises at the back of the course book. Vocabulary is also prioritised. This is because we believe that students who wish to excel need as wide a vocabulary as possible. As well as dealing with lexical sets of topic vocabulary and phrasal verbs, *Spotlight* also focuses on a 'key word' in each unit. These are high frequency words notable for the phrases and expressions that are built around them and their collocation with other words.

To the new teacher: how is teaching an exam class different from general English?

If you haven't taught a First Certificate class before, it is probably best to think of it as an upper intermediate plus examination. A public examination inevitably affects the teaching that precedes it – this is known as the 'backwash effect'. The good news is that teaching for FCE doesn't require too many compromises. Indeed, its 'backwash effect' by and large benefits what happens in class. Teachers who are new to exam teaching often ask how they need to change their teaching style and approach from general English classes.

We need to consider the following points:
- the emphasis of a First Certificate class
- the content and balance of what we teach
- the way we teach and the demands that we place on our students.

Quite rightly, general English classes often focus on developing students' fluency and confidence and developing their overall communicative competence; that is, maximising successful communicative outcomes from what they know. In general English classes, teachers may prize fluency and spontaneity over accuracy and reflection. In a general English class there is always the temptation to allow speaking and discussion activities to run on as long as they need. In FCE classes we need to be much more vigilant and disciplined about our use of time.

Who are our students?

It is difficult to generalise about learners. Most people are a rich mix of differences and contradictions. The starting level of students will depend on their previous learning experience and individual differences. Students who have studied in a traditional educational system with an emphasis on grammar, reading and writing will often be stronger at these skills than at speaking. They may be more 'bookish' and academic. Speaking (in general) and communicative competence may be relatively weak. Conversely, learners who have acquired English from living in an English

speaking community, or who have studied in institutions where fluency and communicative competence are favoured over accuracy, may often be weaker at writing and formal grammar. In either case, the more extrovert and less self-conscious students are, the better communicators they appear to be, at least superficially.

What do students need?

To their good intermediate, or upper intermediate grammar, students need to add the grammar and vocabulary that are often tested in the First Certificate examination. This should be balanced across the four skills of listening, speaking, reading and writing. Be warned: students often have a frighteningly poor level of written English.

Finally, successful candidates will need total familiarity with all the aspects of the examination coupled with good exam technique.

TEACHING IN PRACTICE

A few tips:
- Be strict about time keeping and disciplined about how classroom time is spent. Don't allow speaking activities or discussion to drag on.
- Set homework after every lesson. Contact parents if it is not done.
- Set at least one piece of writing a week, and make sure it is corrected.
- Encourage students to be aware of their problems and to keep a record of their mistakes.
- Organise a full mock examination two thirds/three quarters through the course. Make sure that this is carried out following exam conditions. Give students individual tutorials telling them what they need to focus on.
- Use a lot of simulations of the Speaking Paper, as students often find this the most stressful part of the exam.

As the exam approaches, be more and more strict about respecting time limits and doing more work under examination conditions. Check out students' writing by getting them to produce a piece of writing straightaway. Writing is the 'Cinderella skill' – much ignored in general English classes. I am always shocked by how poor students' written work is at the beginning of a FCE programme.

'CAN DO' SUMMARY

Typical abilities	Listening and Speaking	Reading and Writing
General ability (overall)	Can follow a talk (on a familiar topic). Can maintain conversation on quite a wide range of topics.	Can scan texts for relevant information. Can make notes while someone is talking + write a letter with unusual requests.
Social/Tourist	Can ask for further explanation, and is likely to understand the answer. Can converse well.	Can read and understand texts quickly for meaning/information. Can express opinions + justify those opinions.
Work	Can ask for factual information + understand the answer. Can express own opinion + present arguments (to a limited extent).	Can understand general meaning and majority of content of letters. Can write a simple report (using evaluation, advice and so on).
Study	Can answer predictable/factual questions. Can check that instructions are understood.	Can make simple notes containing essence of information needed. Can present arguments using limited range of vocabulary and grammatical expressions.

Breakdown of the Exam: Paper by Paper

1 Paper One: Reading

This is divided into three parts.

Part 1 has a long text with multiple choice questions.

Answering text-based multiple choice questions often appears to have little to do with truly understanding the text for what it is, or the messages the writer wishes to transmit through it. This is why *Spotlight* always begins with questions that help the student obtain a general understanding and appreciation of the text before becoming engaged in exam-style practice. Students are made aware of how the multiple choice question works and are given tips on how to deal with it.

Part 2 is a text with gaps.

Students match missing sentences to gaps, although there is always one extra and unnecessary sentence. In order to answer this part well, students need to be aware of how cohesion is achieved in texts through the use of references, pronouns, lexical replacement and so on. *Spotlight* helps by highlighting what is required, showing how referencers help to hold a text together – and by providing a lot of practice of this question type.

Part 3 consists of four shorter texts where students have to match statements to the text concerned.

This mostly practises the reading skill of scanning for information, although the questions themselves often rely on paraphrasing the relevant part of the text in question. Again, *Spotlight* provides ample opportunity to practise this question type throughout the course.

2 Paper Two: Writing

This is divided into two parts.

Part 1 is a compulsory letter or email.

This is based around a task such as responding to another piece of writing (like a letter, email, advertisement, etc.) Here the students have to write a reply carefully, taking into account the notes and annotations that accompany the task. There is a word limit of 120–150 words for this.

Part 2 is a longer written piece.

Students have to write an answer to one question only. The choices include a non-transactional letter, a report, review, essay, story and a question on each of the set books. *Spotlight* helps by providing a thorough and extensive writing programme that includes:

- Model compositions and analysis for each question type (except for the set book).
- Teaching writing sub-skills e.g. linking clauses, contrasting ideas and sequencing.
- Helping with the writing process, such as gathering ideas, planning, drafting and execution.
- Providing plenty of opportunities for writing.

3 Paper Three: Use of English

This is divided into four parts.

Part 1 Multiple choice lexical cloze (12 questions)
Part 2 Open cloze (12 questions)
Part 3 Word formation (10 questions)
Part 4 Key word transformations (8 questions)

Spotlight helps because embedded in every unit there is the vocabulary and grammar that will help learners with these question types. *Spotlight* provides a resource of linguistically rich and roughly tuned input that gives learners a broad exposure to language. The end of each unit carries a dedicated review and Use of English section to practise each question type.

4 Paper Four: Listening

This is divided into four parts.

Part 1 is a series of eight extracts from unrelated monologues or exchanges between interacting speakers. There is one multiple choice question per extract.
Part 2 is a monologue or text involving interacting speakers. There is a sentence completion task with ten questions.
Part 3 is five short, unrelated monologues, with five multiple-matching questions.
Part 4 is a monologue or text involving interacting speakers, with seven multiple choice questions.

Spotlight treats listening as an holistic skill and does not focus on listening sub-skills that are often treated at lower levels. Instead *Spotlight* provides natural and challenging listening passages that replicate the level and nature of the examination. There is a variety of accents and the material is delivered at normal speed so includes features of natural and connected speech. However, unlike the exam where subject matter is varied and random, all the listening passages are on the unit theme. Further, *Spotlight* always has a more overall and general treatment the first time passages are heard. This bridges the gap between general English teaching and examination teaching.

5 Paper Five: Speaking

Due to its peculiar format, the Speaking Paper often seems to pose the most problems for inexperienced teachers. Candidates take the exam in pairs. There are two examiners. One examiner sits, listens and assesses, the second, the 'interlocutor', asks the questions and 'animates' the session. Remember that candidates take this paper in pairs (that is, with another student). However, each is assessed on solely his or her performance. The Speaking Paper is tightly organised and follows the following structure:

Part 1 The interlocutor gets to know each candidate in turn asking them questions.
Part 2 Candidates take it in turns to compare two photographs based around a written prompt.
Part 3 Interactive task: candidates work together to solve a problem or make choices based around visual prompts.
Part 4 The interlocutor asks each candidate follow-up questions based on and around the task.

Even though the whole procedure may appear contrived and unnatural, it does provide a real opportunity for candidates to show what they can do. While nobody could pretend that it reflects a natural, everyday use of English it is broader in scope than a straightforward one-to-one interview. The interlocutor system allows the second examiner to concentrate fully on listening to the candidates while marking them against detailed criteria. This all helps to make the examination as fair and as 'objective' as possible.

Pre-FCE Quiz

How much do you know about the FCE? Answer the following questions by choosing A, B, or C.

1 What does FCE stand for?

A First Certificate Examination

B First Certificate in English

C Full Certificate in English

2 What subject is the Certificate on?

A Mathematics

B French

C English

3 How many papers are there in the exam?

A Five

B Four

C Three

4 Which skills do the examinations cover?

A Reading, writing and listening

B Reading, writing and speaking

C Reading, writing, listening and speaking

5 What do the exams mainly test?

A the ability to think in English

B the ability to communicate in English

C the ability to write in English

6 When was the first FCE offered?

A 1901

B 1989

C 1939

7 What's the pass mark?

A More than 60%

B Less than 60%

C 80%

8 What's a good reason to take FCE?

A To travel

B To gain employment

C To pass the time

9 All FCE papers are worth the same in marks.

A True

B False

10 What is Paper 2?

A Reading

B Grammar

C Writing

11 How many questions do you have to answer in Paper 2, part 2?

A All of them

B None of them

C One of them

12 Is the grade D a fail?

A Yes

B No

C Maybe …

13 How many times a year is the examination offered?

A Once

B Three

C Twice

14 How many parts are in the Reading Paper?

A One

B Two

C Three

15 A multiple choice question means:

A The answer is supplied

B The answer isn't supplied

C There are no questions

16 In which of the papers do you have a partner?

A The Writing Paper

B The Listening Paper

C The Speaking Paper

17 Can you choose to do the Listening Paper on your own?

A Yes

B Sometimes

C No

18 Spelling should always be correct in the Use of English Paper.

A False

B True

19 How many parts are in the Listening Paper?

A One

B Ten

C Four

20 Your FCE class should be:

A Lots of fun and no work

B Lots of hard work and no fun

C A good mix of fun and work

Congratulations! You've now completed the Pre-FCE Quiz. Good luck with the rest of your course!

1   Friends and family

Before you begin

If you are starting your class with an entirely new group, you may want to begin by 'breaking the ice' and using different types of warm-up activity.

1 Ask students to line up in alphabetical order. To do this they will have to ask each other's names.

2 Go round the class: ask the first person's name and something that is interesting about them. The next person has to remember about the first person, and then add their own information, the third person the first two and so on.

> Hi, I'm Marcello and I am in the school basketball team.

> Hello, his name is Marcello and he is in the school basketball team. I'm Saskia and I have three dogs.

> OK. Erm, he's Marcello and he's in the school basketball team. Her name's Saskia and she has got three dogs. Me, my name is Roberta and I am planning to study in the States ... etc.

Topic: Friends and family

At the FCE level, a learner should be able to talk about 'everyday life'; to use appropriate communicative strategies in a variety of social situations. Talking about their relationships with friends and family members is also an excellent way to make learners feel at ease.

Unit 1 Wordlist:

acquaint/acquaintance	fall out
assist/help	fiancé(e)
boyfriend	friendly/friendship
break up with	friendly relationship
close/closeness	get back together
close relationship	get on with
cousins	go along with
difficult/difficulties	go out with

gossip	relatives
half-brother	request/ask for
hit it off	require/want
inform/tell	research/researcher
let down	siblings
look after	sisters-in-law
look up to	spouse
make up	stand by
mother-in-law	step-sister
offspring	strong relationship
personal/person/personality	strong/strength
put up with	take after
ran into	twin
receive/get	unavailable/busy
relation/relationship	verify/check

Getting started

Aim: To generate interest in the topic of the unit; to assess how good students are at answering personal questions.

Tell the class that in the introductory part of the Speaking Paper, the examiner will ask general questions such as these to find out about the candidate. Students may ask when we use *like to do/like doing*. Tell them that *like to do* is used more to describe habits; *like doing* is more for preferences. Students then report back to the class as a whole with the results of their questions. Insist on correctness.

TEACHING IN PRACTICE

Pair and group work

Pair and group work allows students to maximise their participation and the amount of time they can practise their English. It also allows the teacher to gauge the strengths and weaknesses of individual students, as well as the overall level of the class. Make a note of particularly well-formulated answers, and any obvious mistakes. We need to recognise that some students may be unfamiliar with working in pairs or groups. They may be more familiar and comfortable with a teacher-centred approach. This may be typical of the way they have already studied English and other subjects, or of education within their culture. Explain that working in pairs or groups allows them to maximise the amount they can participate and practise their English.

Reading: family soap operas

Generate interest in the text the students are about to read:

1   Conduct a quick survey to find out how many hours of TV students watch each day.

2   As a class, ask about the viewing habits of students and their favourite programmes. Check that students understand 'soap opera'. Lead a brief conversation about soaps. Common themes in all kinds of soaps are family relationships, infidelity and jealousy. It's safe to say that very few soaps reflect real life, even those that pretend to deal with the lives of ordinary people. Soaps that deal with the lives of rich oil barons or celebrities are more obviously pure fantasy. Soaps are often used to discuss hot topics.

TEACHING IN PRACTICE

Opening up
Sometimes a good way of getting students to open up and say something about themselves, is to be open oneself.

> Me, I watch about three hours of TV a day. I don't usually turn it on until after dinner in the evening, but then I watch the news, etc...

3   This exercise encourages a fairly rapid read through of the passages. Students discuss preferences in pairs and groups.

4   Students read the texts more carefully and answer the questions. Set a five minute time limit.

Vocabulary: family connections

1   Introduce exercise. Teach concept of 'odd one out'. Something which is the 'odd one out' doesn't belong in a group. In the following example, 'cow' is obviously the 'odd one out' because the other items are fruit. Example: *apple, banana, cow, orange.*

2   Students describe a family they know well. Listen in, and check that the students are using the vocabulary they have covered in the previous exercise.

Key word: *like*

Dictionary meaning:

1   Expressing similarity
2   Expressing preferences and wishes

This exercise compares *like* as a verb with *like* as a preposition with a similar meaning to *as*.
Synonyms: admire, appreciate, enjoy (verb); alike, comparable, similar (prepositions).
Antonyms: dislike, mind (verb).

Grammar: present tenses

Present simple and present continuous

1   If your students need to review these tenses, refer to Section 12.4 of the Grammar Reference before answering these questions.

2   Listen as your students work together and create sentences using the present continuous and the simple present.

3   Students work in pairs and correct the passage where necessary.

GRAMMAR SPOTLIGHT

State and dynamic verbs
Read through the grammar spotlight box on state verbs. Remember that state verbs usually occur in the simple form in all tenses. That is, state verbs are not usually used in continuous forms. 'States' occur in categories such as:
• feelings (*like, love,* etc);
• thinking/believing (*think, understand,* etc);
• wants and preferences (*prefer, want,* etc);
• perception and the senses (*hear, see* etc);
• *being/seeming/having/owning* (*appear, seem, belong, own* etc).
Remember that some verbs that we usually use statively can be used in the continuous with a change in meaning.
For example, what do you think about capital punishment? = what is your view?
What are you thinking about? = What is going on in your head?

6   🎧 Spot the errors. Play Listening 1.1 through and ask students to make a note of any errors. Alternatively, ask them to shout 'Stop!' each time they hear an error and correct it there and then.

Speaking: asking and answering questions

Conversation (Paper 5, part 1)
This is an important pay-off for all the work on simple and continuous forms, and the questionnaire activity from the 'Getting Started' section. Tell students that if they can make a good beginning with this first part of the exam, they will create an extremely favourable impression on the examiner.

Listening: talking about people

Aim: To assess how good students are at listening for general information as well as detail.

Listening for general meaning (Paper 4, part 1)
The eight questions in this part of the paper are presented both on the question paper and on the recording, so that candidates are led carefully through them. The testing focus is spelt out in each question. For example: *What is her job?* Make sure that your students are clear that there are only four questions in their first encounter with this part.

🎧 Checking 'Listening 1.2' answers: You can simply give students the correct answers or else you can ask them to 'self-check' by listening to the recording again and discussing their answers, or by asking them to check their answers against the tapescript. Of course, where necessary you may need to arbitrate and provide explanations.

Vocabulary: describing relationships

Phrasal verbs

This section focuses on a set of phrasal verbs on the topic of relationships.

Understanding words that are linked: it is important that students are able to identify and recognise when two words run together in connected speech. This exercise focuses on phrasal verbs where the stem ends with a consonant and the particle begins with a vowel. This linking, or liaison is an important feature of connected speech. The phrasal verbs most likely to sound like one word are: *run into; put up with; fall out; break up; look after;* and *get on with.*

'Back-chaining'
Some nationalities may have acquired the habit of putting a /h/ sound before the vowel of the particle.
For example: 'break hup'; not 'brea - kup'.
You can help them over this obstacle by drilling the phrase from the back.

> up
> kup
> break up

Keeping a vocabulary notebook
This section gives advice on keeping a vocabulary notebook. It focuses on phrasal verbs. This is an area that is often tested in parts 1 and 2 of the Use of English Paper, where the stem or the particle may be missing. Phrasal verbs may also be the object of a question in the Key word transformations exercise in the Use of English Paper.

2   Definitions of phrasal verbs:

Make up with: reconcile with someone.
Take after: resemble someone in appearance, behaviour or character.
Go along with: support or agree with a person/decision.
Look up to: respect and admire someone.

You could also provide your students with the phrasal verbs in context so that they can guess their meaning.
You could say to them:

> They had a terrible argument, but they made it up with each other the following day, and now they are the best of friends.

> She really takes after her mother; she has got the same eyes and mouth – she even has the same cheerful personality!

> His father always went along with his wife even if he secretly thought she was wrong.

Reading: gossip

Consider pre-teaching the key words for this reading:

Gossip:
1   A person (n) = *He's a terrible gossip.*
2   A concept (n) = *I heard some gossip/an interesting piece of gossip.*
3   An activity (n) = *I enjoy gossiping with my neighbour.* (Gossiping is talking about the lives of other people behind their backs. Usually, it involves scandalous or humiliating information they would like to keep secret.)

Chat: a casual conversation about nothing in particular, such as the weather or sport.

Moan: to complain = *'Stop moaning and carry on walking.'*

Word definitions

Consider using alternative ways to teach new words, such as demonstrating a word through a 'story'. See the example for 'gossip', and consider following the same format for 'chat' and 'moan'.

1   Discuss the question with the whole class. Elicit their views. This will help the students develop expectations about the text they are going to read which should, in turn, help them understand the meaning of the overall text.

> I heard an interesting story about Anna the other day. You'll never guess what I heard! If you promise to keep it a secret then I'll tell you ... So... my question is: What am I doing?
>
> Gossiping!

Finding key words

To answer questions such as part 2 of the reading paper, your students will need to be able to identify reference words and phrases that help position the various lines of reasoning within the given piece. Words that refer **backwards** may include: *after, afterwards, following, next, once, at a later time, subsequently.*

Words that refer **forwards** may include: *ahead, yet to come, beforehand, prior to, previous to.*

2   Gapped text sentences: This is a text from which sentences have been removed and placed in jumbled order after the text. In gapped text sentences there is an emphasis on text structure, cohesion and coherence, and candidates' ability to follow the development of a long text.

3–4 If your students need to revise adjectives, refer to Section 1–5 of the Grammar Guide before answering these questions.

Writing: a letter or an email

Aim: To practise writing transactional letters with both formal and informal registers.

Compulsory (transactional) letter (Paper 2, part 1)

This is a compulsory letter that involves a transaction. A transaction means getting something done or arranging something. (It is also possible to write a letter in part 2 of Paper 2, but this is generally more social and interactional.)

1 Make sure your students answer the four questions before the exam question.

> Exam Question: 120–150 words.
> You could lose marks for:
> - ungrammatical sentences
> - poor spelling and punctuation
> - inappropriate style.

Degree of difficulty

Decrease the level: If your students do not yet feel comfortable writing a longer transactional email, allow them to use letters A and B as templates (models). The writing checklist is also a useful aid and can be elaborated further to make the writing process easier.

Increase the level: If, however, your students are quite capable, then remove the temptation of the two example replies and see how they manage without being able to copy the structure. Once they have attempted the writing exercise, you could allow them to look at letters A and B, and see where their answers differed.

Photocopiable activity instructions

1 **Activity 1.1: Pelmanism (a memory card game)**

Aim: To recycle and reinforce vocabulary of family, and relationships

Instructions:

1 Paste the words onto card and cut them out so they look the same when they are turned over.

2 Students mix up the cards and turn them over so they can only see the blank side.

3 They then take it in turns to turn over two cards. If they make a match between a word and a definition they keep them, and have another go. The winner is the one who makes the most pairs.

2 **Activity 1.2: The Hacienda Club**

Aim: Fluency; practise of present tense forms for historic present; expressing likes and dislikes.

Instructions:

1 Lead into the activity by reminding students of the *Soap Opera* text.

2 Ask what topics they generally deal with, the surprises they introduce, etc.

3 Students work in groups and study the family trees and family profiles.

4 Get them to decide in their groups what the relationships are, the people who love/hate each other and why.

5 Students create summaries of the first three episodes and compare them with each other.

6 Alternatively, tell students that they have to write the plot for a special 'pilot' episode which will introduce the main characters and themes.

You could give your students the following instructions:

1 Read the profiles and study the family trees. Quickly decide what the connections are between the characters. Draw the lines of love, hate and jealousy/envy.

2 Think of two or three terrible or embarrassing secrets that the Marshals and the Esperanzas may want to hide.

3 Create summaries of the first few episodes. You will need to write these in the present tense.

SPOUSE	SIBLINGS	OFFSPRING	FIANCÉ(E)
DAUGHTER-IN-LAW	EX-HUSBAND	STEPMOTHER	NEPHEWS AND NIECES
NEIGHBOUR	RELATIONS	TWINS	EXTENDED FAMILY
LOOK AFTER	GET ON WITH	FALL OUT	STAND BY

UNIT 1 PHOTOCOPIABLE: PELMANISM

formal word: a husband or wife	formal word: brothers and sisters	formal word: children	a mother's son's wife
someone you are going to marry	the man a woman used to be married to	your father's new wife	the children of your brother/ sisters
someone who lives near you	parents, aunts, uncles, cousins, grandparents	two children born at the same time	several generations under the same roof
phrasal verb: take care of	phrasal verb: have a good relationship	phrasal verb: argue	phrasal verb: support

The Hacienda Club

New soap opera

Location: The *Hacienda* is an exclusive country club and casino for the rich of southern California. The Marshals and the Esperanzas own the club. The story focuses on their lives and loves...

Extras:
Ralph (50) and Benny Weiss (45) Brothers who are the head of a criminal gang.
Banjo the dog (8 months) Labrador who regularly spends time on club premises.

The Marshals:
• Senator: Bobby Marshal (65) Ex-marine colonel. Rich oil-man. 30% owner of the Hacienda country club. Married 3 times. First wife Dana (Rufus' mother) killed in a helicopter crash 28 years ago.
• Second wife: Loretta (50) Divorced from Bobby five years ago. Bobby junior's mother – her only child.
• Third wife: Bonny Marshal (35) ex-air hostess. Pregnant with first child.
• Oldest son: Rufus Marshal (34) The senator's son from his first marriage. The senator's heir apparent. 20% owner of the Hacienda.
• Daughter: Carly Marshal (34) Senator's estranged daughter, Rufus's twin sister.
• Daughter-in-Law: Anita Marshal (29) (née Schenker) Rufus's wife. Two children Hannah (6) and Paris (3).
• Son: Bobby junior (19) The senator's son from his second marriage. A playboy. Owns 5% of the Hacienda.
• Driver / Bodyguard: Bud Hunter (45) ex-marine sergeant.
• Maid: Stella Gomez (23).

The Esperanzas:
• Father: Pablo Esperanza (75) Bobby's business partner. 40% owner of the Hacienda.
• Wife: Lourdes (73). Married to Pablo for fifty years.
• Son: Jamie Esperanza. Missing, presumed deceased. May have disappeared due to company fraud.
• Daughter-in-law: Carmen (45) Jamie's widow. Lives in Miami.
• Granddaughter: Conchita (23) Manager of the Casino at the Hacienda club. Owns 5% of the Hacienda.

Staff at the Hacienda:
Tennis Coach: Pete Harriman (28).
Receptionist: Kate Merton (21).
Bartender: Jorge Gonzales (25).
Lifeguard/Swimming Instructor: Paolo Marinari (18).

Tapescript 1

Listening 1.1

Examiner:	First of all I'd like to know something about you. Where are you from?
Candidate:	I'm from Greece. I'm living in Piraeus. It's near Athens.
Examiner:	And how long have you lived there?
Candidate:	I am living there all my life. But at the moment I also look for a place at university. So maybe I'll move away. I don't know exactly.
Examiner:	What do you like about living in Piraeus?
Candidate:	Oh I enjoy to go to the beach and it's very easy to visit some of the islands by boat. My family has a boat so we often go sailing.
Examiner:	Do you prefer spending time on your own or with other people?
Candidate:	I think with my friends but I think it's important to be on your own also.
Examiner:	What's the most exciting thing you've ever done?
Candidate:	Oh, that's a difficult question ... hmmm .... I suppose when I been visiting London was fun. Every year my school visited a school in England and we have met English school children. So that's fun ...

Listening 1.2

One

B: What's the problem?

A: I don't know how long I can put up with her.

B: She seems OK to me.

A: Do you think so?

B: Well, she's very friendly. The other staff get on with her. And she's got some good ideas. She wants to move the office around but that's fine. It doesn't work the way things are at present.

A: You don't think she's a bit bossy? I mean, all these changes. She's only been here a week!

Two

A: I ran into Michelle's boyfriend, Nigel, the other day.

B: Really?

A: I didn't know he lives down the road from me. He was at the bus stop. How well do *you* know him?

B: Not very. I've met him a couple of times. I heard she wants to break up with him again.

A: Oh, that's a pity.

B: Don't worry. They always fall out over something then she leaves him and then a week later they get back together again!

Three

I've been watching this TV show for a few weeks now. It was one of those shows where people are really angry all the time and talk about their problems at home. It's stupid really but good fun to watch. So, anyway, this morning there was this mother and father who still look after their three children but these children are all in their thirties! Anyway, the mother and father were saying the 'kids' never do anything around the house and constantly let them down. Unbelievable! I couldn't understand why they just didn't ask them to go and find their own place!

Four

Yes, it's true. You know how he told his brother he would stand by him whatever happened? Well, not last night he didn't! He just walked out and said he didn't want to see him ever again. I can't wait to see what happens next week!

Answer key 1

Getting started p5
2 A 1, 6, 7, 11; B 1, 7; C 5, 6, 7, 11; D 8, 9, 10;
E 2, 12; F 3, 4, 5, 6

Reading p6
4 1B; 2C; 3A; 4B; 5D; 6A; 7C; 8A; 9D

Vocabulary p7
1 1 spouse
2 offspring
3 half-brother
4 stepsister
5 extended family
6 sisters-in-law
7 fiancé
8 extended family (relatives)
9 twins
10 cousins
11 mother-in law
12 siblings

Key word p7
1 1b; 2d; 3e; 4a; 5c

Grammar p8
1 1 1a 2b; 2 1b 2a; 3 1a 2b
3 ~~moves house~~ is moving
~~I'm hoping~~ I hope
~~always lands~~ lands
~~doesn't starting~~ doesn't start
~~he is looking~~ he looks
~~not having~~ don't have/haven't got
4 1 1b. Because *ago* denotes use of past simple.
It shows a finished action.; 2 1b 2a; 3 1a 2b
5 1 are you
2 live
3 have you lived
4 have lived
5 'm
6 studied
7 studied
8 do enjoy
9 like
10 go
11 've ever done
12 'm taking

6 ~~I'm living in Piraeus~~ I live in
~~I am living there~~ I have lived there
~~at the moment I also look for~~ I am looking for
~~I enjoy to go to~~ I enjoy going
~~when I been visiting London~~ when I visited
London
~~my school visited a school~~ visits a school
~~we have met~~ we meet

Listening p10
1 Speakers 1 and 2 have met the person;
3 and 4 have seen the person.
2 1C; 2C; 3C; 4B

Vocabulary p10
1 1 put up with
2 get on with
3 ran into
4 break up with
5 fall out
6 get back together
7 look after
8 let down
9 stand by

Reading p11
2 1B; 2C; 3E; 4A; 5D
3 close, friendly, strong
4 closeness; friendly; difficulty (difficulties);
strong
5 1 close
2 strong, difficult
3 friendship, difficulty

Writing p12
3 1 Thanks for your letter
2 I'm really sorry
3 He would be delighted
4 With regard to
5 You should …
6 I look forward to hearing from you
7 Speak to you soon
8 Yours sincerely
9 Best wishes
4 inform = tell
ask for = request

verify = check
busy = unavailable
receive = get
assist = help
require = want

Review p14
1 1 closeness
2 relationships
3 Psychologists
4 friendship
5 researchers
6 discovery
7 personal
8 dislikes
9 living
10 acquaintances
2 1 aunt
2 half-sister
3 twins
4 nephew
5 ex-fiancé
6 grandmother
7 cousin
8 mother-in-law
3 1 She looks just *like* her mother.
2 The two boys are *always* playing tricks on the
rest of the family.
3 I never really got *on* with my brother-in-law …
4 You've really let me *down* this time …
5 I'd say she's still *in* her twenties.
4 1 *with regard to* your
2 *look forward to seeing*
3 *recommend (that) you go*
4 *Further to your*
5 1 I like to play/playing tennis at the weekend.
2 I must learn English for my job.
3 My friends and I often have parties.
4 My family are the most important people to
me.
5 For my last holiday I went to America with my
family.
6 I'd rather spend time with my friends.
7 … I spend a lot of time with her.
8 I love snowboarding and I can also ski.
9 English is spoken all over the world …

SPOUSE	SIBLINGS	OFFSPRING	FIANCÉ(E)
DAUGHTER-IN-LAW	EX-HUSBAND	STEPMOTHER	NEPHEWS AND NIECES
NEIGHBOUR	RELATIONS	TWINS	EXTENDED FAMILY
LOOK AFTER	GET ON WITH	FALL OUT	STAND BY

UNIT 1 PHOTOCOPIABLE: PELMANISM

formal word: a husband or wife	formal word: brothers and sisters	formal word: children	someone you are going to marry
a mother's son's wife	the man a woman used to be married to	your father's new wife	the children of your brothers/sisters
someone who lives near you	parents, aunts, uncles, cousins, grandparents	two children born at the same time	several generations under the same roof
phrasal verb: take care of	phrasal verb: have a good relationship	phrasal verb: argue	phrasal verb: support

The Hacienda Club

New soap opera

Location: The <u>Hacienda</u> is an exclusive country club and casino for the rich of southern California. The Marshals and the Esperanzas own the club. The story focuses on their lives and loves...

Extras:

<u>Ralph</u> (50) and <u>Benny Weiss</u> (45) Brothers who are the head of a criminal gang.

<u>Banjo the dog</u> (8 months) Labrador who regularly spends time on club premises.

The Marshals:

- Senator: <u>Bobby Marshal</u> (65) Ex-marine colonel. Rich oil-man. 30% owner of the Hacienda country-club. Married 3 times. First wife Dana (Rufus' mother) killed in a helicopter crash 28 years ago.

- Second wife: <u>Loretta</u>. (50) Divorced from Bobby five years ago. Bobby Junior's mother – her only child.

- Third wife: Bonny <u>Marshal</u> (35) ex-air hostess. Pregnant with first child.

- Oldest son: <u>Rufus Marshal</u> (34) The senator's son from his first marriage. The senator's heir apparent. 20% owner of the Hacienda.

- Daughter: <u>Carly Marshal</u> (34) Senator's estranged daughter, Rufus's twin sister.

- Daughter-in-Law: <u>Anita Marshal</u> (27) (née Schenker) Rufus's wife. Two children Hannah (6) and Paris (3).

- Son: <u>Bobby junior</u> (19) The senator's son from his second marriage. A playboy. Owns 5% of the Hacienda.

- Driver / Bodyguard: <u>Bud Hunter</u> (45) ex-marine sergeant.

- Maid: <u>Stella Gomez</u> (23).

The Esperanzas:

- Father: <u>Pablo Esperanza</u> (75) Bobby's business partner. 40% owner of the Hacienda.

- Wife: <u>Lourdes</u> (73). Married to Pablo for fifty years.

- Son: <u>Jamie Esperanza</u>. Missing, presumed deceased. May have disappeared due to company fraud.

- Daughter-in-law: <u>Carmen</u> (45) Jamie's widow. Lives in Miami.

- Granddaughter: <u>Conchita</u> (23) Manager of the Casino at the Hacienda club. Owns 5% of the Hacienda.

Staff at the Hacienda:

Tennis Coach: <u>Pete Harriman</u> (28).

Receptionist: <u>Kate Merton</u> (21).

Bartender: <u>Jorge Gonzales</u> (25).

Lifeguard/Swimming Instructor: <u>Paolo Marinari</u> (18).

Before you begin

How you begin will depend on the age and interests of your class:

- With younger, teenage students ask if any have a part-time job or help around the home for pocket money. You could also find out what their ambitions are.

- For students in higher education or early on in their careers, ask what their ambitions, dream jobs are and whether what they are doing will help them to achieve their longer term aim.

- For older students ask what their ambitions were when they were younger. What kind of job did they dream about?

Topic: Jobs and work

At the FCE level, learners should be able to talk about jobs and work; they should be capable of describing their own and their family's jobs. They should also be able to talk about their education, qualities and qualifications and ambitions. They should be able to compare and contrast jobs, read job advertisements and produce a short application for a job.

Unit 2 Wordlist:

able/abilities	journalist
actor/actress	lay off (staff)
advertisement	look for
apply (for)	manager
artist	musician
assess/assessment	notice
assistant	opportunity
chance	organise/organisation
convenient	overtime
cook/chef	painter
deal with	possibility
doctor	qualifications
electrician	qualities
employee/employer/	recruit/recruitment
employment	(make sbdy) redundant
experience	refer/referee/references
experiment	resign
find out	sack
flexitime	salary
form	select/selection
formation	send off
hand in notice	success/successful

suitable	wages
teacher training	waiter/waitress
turn down (a job)	writer

Getting started

Ask your students to open their books and tell them that they are going to be studying the 'English of jobs and work'. Run through the menu with them so that they have an idea of what the unit contains. Next, read the rubric and set the scene.

1   Students work in groups and study the pictures and decide which job would suit them best. In other words, they should match the qualities and personality of the person concerned.

2   Put students into pairs or groups to list the advantages and disadvantages of being a butler or housekeeper.

Celebrity: a famous person, often from the world of show-business.

Bodyguard: a person employed to protect someone. (Should be: brave, tough, willing to take risks for their employer; prepared to stand in the way of an aggressor or bullet; someone who is able to be calm in emergencies, with quick reactions.)

Butler: the chief male servant in the house.

Housekeeper: the person employed to look after the cleaning and cooking of the house. (Both the butler and the housekeeper should be: well-organised, calm and polite; able to organise the household, greet guests, discreet; experience of good food and wine, how to lay table, serve drinks and take care of people would also help.)

Chauffeur: person whose job it is to drive and look after someone's car. Note: chauffeur can also be used as a verb. (Should be: a good driver; able to avoid paparazzi and protect employer; knows way around major cities; patient as chauffeurs have to wait around a lot!)

> 4   Suggested answers:
> Some of the disadvantages of this job include always having to be available; having to be polite even when dealing with rude people; wearing uncomfortable clothes when everyone around you is relaxing; and working while everyone else isn't.

5   Consider getting each of the pairs to draw up a table to
    display their responses:

I'll be able to ...	Yes but ...
• share my star's life	• you'll have no life of your own
• travel around the world	• you'll be stressed and exhausted
• borrow their jewellery and clothes	• you'll have to give them back/clothes won't fit!
• drive around in a limo	• you'll be squashed in a small seat
• have a luxury lifestyle	• you'll get fat!
• mix with the rich and famous	• they won't be interested in you
• go to opening and gala nights	• once a year if you're lucky!

TEACHING IN PRACTICE

Pronunciation

Question 5 provides a chance to practise the pronunciation of
'll in I'll /aɪl/ and you'll /juːl/. In English /l/ can be pronounced
two ways:

> Clear 'l' as in *leaf*
> as in *long*.

> Dark 'l' as in *tall*.
> as in *while*.

Note: In dark 'l', the back of the tongue is also raised.

Use of English: multiple-choice cloze

EXAM SPOTLIGHT

Multiple-choice cloze (Paper 3, part 1)

Check that students remember the number and titles of the
different examination papers. Paper 3 is 'Use of English'.
Remind them that a 'cloze' is a text with gaps. Read through
the explanation with the students. Emphasise that the answers
depend on having the right grammar.

Vocabulary: jobs and work

SPOTLIGHT ON VOCABULARY

Suffixes

Tell the class that we can build words using prefixes and
suffixes. Give a couple of examples, such as [un]*happy*
(prefix) and *care*[ful] (suffix).

Now say we can use suffixes to create job titles:

1 With the whole class, ask students to create job titles and
  professions by combining a word in the left-hand column
  with a suffix in the right-hand column. Draw attention to
  suffixes which denote job: *-er -ist, -ant, -or*. For example,
  someone who teaches is a teacher. Nowadays, it is

considered less 'sexist' to use gender-free job titles. For
example, using *firefighter* rather than *fireman*; *police
officer* rather than *policeman*.

2 Check pronunciation
  of the jobs and drill
  as required. Pay
  special attention to
  word stress.

> Highlight word stress by using
> bubbles for each syllable.
> A large bubble denotes the
> stressed syllable. e.g. musician
> → mu-**si**-cian → oOo

Topic vocabulary extension

Ask students to work in pairs or groups to decide which
three jobs are the best and the worst paid; the most
and the least useful; the most worthwhile, and the least
enjoyable.

TEACHING IN PRACTICE

Demonstrating activities

It is often better to demonstrate an activity than to explain to
students what they have to do. Choose a good student and
demonstrate the activity in question 4.

Next, choose two other students to perform the activity for
the rest of the class. Ask the class to work in pairs or groups
and take it in turns to ask and answer questions. Listen to
the students and where necessary help with questions and
answers. Light correction only.

5 Students work in pairs and decide which of the choices
  is correct. Then run quickly through the exercise, check
  meaning and pronunciation as appropriate.

> Amy, choose one of the jobs.
> Don't tell me which one it is. I
> am going to ask some questions...
> First, is it easy to get this job?

> Well, I wouldn't say it is easy. You
> have to be trained to do it, and
> really have a love for this kind of
> work. It's not the job for everyone.

> I see. Do you need special skills for this job?

> Well, yes. You have to be trained and
> know how to deal with people. Sometimes
> people are frightened or are in pain and
> you have to know how to help them.

> So you're a nurse.

> Yes–that's right.

Listening: talking about jobs

Aim: Question 1 encourages the students to listen all the way through for a general understanding, before focusing on the exam-style questions that follow. Even so, this is a challenging activity and may require you to play the recording more than once. Remind students that in the real examination the listening passages are not related by theme.

Degree of difficulty

Decrease the level: If you think your students will find the task hard, play the recording speaker by speaker, and answer the questions as you go along.

Increase the level: For question 2, ask students to support their answers by giving you evidence from what they have heard.

Reading: voluntary work

Aim: To practise scanning (and encourage students to read text quickly to extract information); to prepare students for Paper 1, part 3 (multiple matching).

BACKGROUND

Raleigh International
Raleigh International is an organisation that helps people from different backgrounds and nationalities discover their potential. This is achieved by sending them on a three-month expedition to foreign countries that have included Mongolia, Fiji, Namibia and Costa Rica. There are three main parts to each expedition: Adventure, Environment and Community. Prince William spent 10 weeks in Chile through Raleigh International. The original Sir Walter Raleigh (1552–1618) was a famous English sailor and explorer. He is famous for introducing tobacco and the potato to England.

1 Check students understand 'volunteer'. Remind them that
-*eer* = one who does: *auctioneer, engineer, volunteer. Vol*
= will: bene*vol*ent, in*vol*untary, *vol*unteer. Note that the stress is on the last syllable volunt**eer** ⟶ ooO.

> The word volunteer can be used as a noun: community volunteer, volunteer work, volunteer organisation.

> It can also be used as a verb: volunteer for a job, volunteer to help.

2 Generate interest in the text by discussing the photographs. One shows people who are volunteers; the other shows people doing their jobs. Explain that in some countries young people may have a 'gap year' between

school and university. Some may choose to do voluntary work. Next, explain that the class is going to read about a voluntary organisation called *Raleigh International*.

EXAM SPOTLIGHT

Multiple matching (Paper 1, part 3)
3 Study the first four questions which have already been answered. Ask the students to call out the parts of the texts that give them the correct answers. Then carry on and allow the class to answer the rest of the questions. Set a time limit of eight minutes to complete the task. If you wish, allow students to confer so that you can listen in to what they say. This will give you a better idea of how effectively they read and complete the task. A useful way of getting feedback to the task is to ask students to 'vote' for their answer. Write their choices on the board. This will give you a clearer overall idea of how they have performed. With answers that are incorrect, try to find out what made them go for the wrong choice.

4 Tell your students to read the questions and the texts quickly to find the answers in the texts. Set a time limit of two minutes to encourage a rapid reading of the text. Tell the students not to worry about the meaning of unknown words or expressions. Discourage them from reading slowly 'word by word'. Remind them to focus on the task.

5 Choose a student and ask them about their skills and qualifications. What do they think they could offer an organisation such as 'Operation Raleigh'? Ask the rest of the class to do the same in pairs or groups. With younger students, who have little or no experience or qualifications, ask them to imagine themselves in five years' time.

Grammar: making comparisons

Aim: To revise and extend the use of comparative and superlative sentences.

1 Ask students to read through the advertisements and discuss which job they would prefer. Get the students to work in pairs or groups. Without interrupting, listen carefully to what they have to say. See how well the class as a whole and individual students manage with comparative and superlative forms.

2 There are a number of different options here. Ask students for their answers and write them on the board. Accept anything that is correct. This will give you the opportunity to revise the different sentence patterns that can be used to say essentially the same thing.

Rules for comparing

Complete the rules with the students. This should be a quick and relatively easy revision exercise. Section 5 (p168) of the Grammar Reference covers comparisons.

6 This exercise practises the expressions from the earlier activities, and allows students to relate them to their own experience.

You may need to teach the following questions:
- How big is your family?
- When did you learn how to ride a bike?
- How tall are you?
- How long are your holidays?
- How far do you walk every day?

If your students are younger, consider adding:
- How much TV do you watch every day?
- How long do you spend doing your homework?

Demonstrate the activity by drawing a table on the board and selecting two students.

	Ana	Dimitri
Size of family	3	7
Age/learnt to ride a bike	5	4
Height	150 CM	180 CM

Ask the class to make statements about Ana and Dimitri using expressions which compare. Then ask students to work in pairs or groups to do the same.

Key word: *as*

As is both a preposition and a conjunction. It is used to compare appearances, actions, events, qualities and times (past and present).

1–2 Give students a minute to think about their own lives and experience using *as* constructions. Then, put them in pairs to compare and where necessary correct each other's sentences.

Speaking: comparing

Two-way conversation (Paper 5, part 3)

This section illustrates just how important it is to be able to make comparisons in the collaborative part of the Speaking Paper. In this part of the exam, students have to discuss a task which will usually involve comparing and contrasting different options and making choices.

1 Read the introduction and check that students understand the task.

Look at the illustrations and say what the different activities are: building cycle paths, creating a children's playground; creating trails through the woods and making a skateboard park. Choose a good student. Take the role of the other student and demonstrate the task in front of the rest of the class. Ask another student to time how long you speak.

> I like the idea of building a children's playground in the park.

> Yes, I do too! But I also think cycle paths are very important, especially where there may be a lot of traffic.

Make pairs of the rest of the class. Pair a stronger with a weaker student to work together. Tell them to carry out the task and to speak for about three minutes. To maximise practice, you could ask students to repeat the activity with two or three different partners. Listen to what the different pairs say, and note common errors or good points.

Speaking extension

After the activity, have a quick correction spot where you write major errors on the board and encourage students to correct them.

Writing: compulsory letter
(Paper 2, part 1)

Letter of application

Aim: to teach useful expressions for semi-formal letters; to raise awareness of what is required in this part of the exam.

Part 1 of Paper 2 is a compulsory letter based around a question and notes.

1 Tell students to work in pairs and match formal phrases 1–8 to their less formal equivalents A–H.

2 Tell the students to read the job advertisement and ask them what sort of qualities and skills they think successful candidates are likely to need.

3 Ask the students to read Becky's letter (on page 23) and the annotations which surround it. In groups, ask them to rewrite and improve Becky's letter. Decide if you want one piece of work from each pair or group, or separate pieces of writing from everyone.

Once students have finished, ask them to turn to Writing guide at the back of the coursebook. They can compare their letters with the model supplied on page 199.

p/c 2.1

4 Set up the final writing task. Either give it for homework or ask the students to do it in class. Pair any weak students with a stronger one.

Photocopiable activity instructions

Activity 2.1: Find me a Nanny!

Aim: To practise the letter writing skills needed for Paper 2, part 1.

Instructions:

1 Set up the situation about the Harrington family.
2 Read the introduction and discuss what kind of person they think would be suitable.
3 Ask the students to read the letters of introduction and to compare and contrast the candidates.
4 Consider dividing the class into interviewers and candidates. Role-play interviewing all three candidates or the two most likely candidates.

Activity 2.2: In or Out? Jobs and Work 'Balloon' debate

Aim: Promote fluency; develop self-confidence in speaking out.

Instructions:

1 Set the scene using the pictures, the example script, or demonstrate the activity in front of the class.
2 To make it fairer, allocate roles by putting them on separate pieces of paper which the students pick out.
3 Emphasise that their choice should depend on how persuasive each speaker is, not who their friends are!
    Here is a sample speech that you can share with your class:

> Hello, I am an English teacher and I am going to give you my reasons why I should be allowed to stay in the balloon. I know that some of you would love to throw a teacher out of a balloon, but I am going to tell you why I am essential for your survival. To begin with, as a teacher I am good at working with groups of people and understanding their problems. You will need me to help you to understand what other people are saying, so that there is no risk of giving the wrong message. Being a teacher is also about being a good communicator and a peace-maker. As a teacher, I have a sense of what is just and fair, and I am an expert at solving conflicts. When we eventually land on this island we will have to stay together as a group if we want to survive. We will have to be fair and share what we have as a community, and we'll have to get on well together. So to sum up, even though you might think it's fun to throw your teacher overboard, you would regret it. I will be essential for everyone's survival when we land!

Find me a Nanny!

Tapescript 2

Listening 2.1

Speaker 1: Actually, a friend from university who had gone straight into their graduate training programme originally told me that they were looking for people. But at the time I was working for a charity and I really wanted to finish the project I was working on. It was unpaid but I was getting good experience. Anyway, a few months later I noticed in the newspaper they were looking for someone, so I called my friend again. She said I had a good chance of getting the position, so I applied.

Speaker 2: I grew up on a farm so it's always been in my family. We had dogs and cats and of course lots of animals. The vets used to come out when there was a problem, so I knew what they did, so it made sense I did something related to the countryside. I suppose my parents had hoped I'd follow in their footsteps but farmers work hard and the money isn't anything like as much as a vet can earn. So I guess that was what convinced me in the end.

Speaker 3: I normally hate people asking me questions but at my last interview I was quite calm for a change. Actually I didn't really want the job that much but I thought I'd go along for the practice. There were two people interviewing and they were both very nice and asked me lots of questions about my other work and why I wanted to leave my current job. It turned out one of the interviewers knew my boss, but he was OK about it. Advertising and marketing is a small world and everyone knows everybody else. In the end I was short-listed and finally they offered me the job so I took it.

Speaker 4: A lot of people think being a journalist is quite a glamorous profession. They think we must all be meeting celebrities and interviewing world leaders every day of the week! Actually I deal with stuff from all the towns and villages in the area most of the time, like finding out which village team won the football or going to council meetings at the town hall. It really can be quite dull. It would be nice to report on something more interesting for a change!

Speaker 5: When people ask me about working in the police force I always say you need to have some experience of people and life – so don't join straight from school. Do something else for a few years first. They give you training before you start on the job, with dealing with difficult people and so on, which is great, but it isn't quite the same as being out there with the public. Of course when you do start in the job you have to learn quickly and the first two years of the job is walking round the streets and dealing with the public.

Speaker 6: Being the daughter of the owner was a bit difficult at first. Obviously it made it easier to get the job here but even though I'd been to university and got a degree in business studies I think some of the employees didn't think I could be a manager at first. They just thought I was in charge because it was my family's firm. Anyway, I'm responsible for administration and things are going really well now. I've built a good atmosphere in my office with a strong team. I always look forward to going in every morning.

Speaker 7: I know the company is going through a hard time – they've even laid some people off – so I do understand … but I've been here for two years now and I've never been sick. Last year was OK because there was plenty of extra work and I was able to work on Saturdays so that helped earn me a bit extra. But I haven't had any way to make more money in the last few months so I think it's about time I got one really.

Speaker 8: Lots of people say it must be great not to go out to work. And in general I do like it but I think they imagine you're sitting in front of the TV all day. Actually, being an artist means long periods of being on your own and really hard work. If I don't finish the painting I only have myself to blame. And if I don't paint I don't eat, or can't pay the rent. It can be hard.

Listening 2.2

A: Anything in the paper today?

B: Nothing much. Though there are a couple of jobs that might interest you.

A: Well, they can't be any worse than the others I've seen.

B: This one is for thirty thousand a year which is a bit more than your old job.

A: Well, I used to do a lot more overtime so actually that isn't anything like as much.

B: Oh it says here 'opportunities for overtime', so it's probably almost the same.

A: Yes. It sounds OK. What is it?

B: Receptionist and they provide training.

A: But my last job was far more responsible than that. And I know how to answer the phone and all that stuff.

B: Alright. I'm just trying to help.

A: Sorry, but it's just that I don't want to do something that isn't any more skilled than what I was doing before.

B: Well here's one … 'Personal Assistant. Forty five thousand', so it's easily as good as your last job and you have plenty of experience in planning and organising. Oh, and you get to travel …

Answer key 2

Use of English p16
2 3B; 4B; 5C; 6A; 7B; 8D; 9C; 10B; 11A; 12D

Vocabulary p16
1 waitress; journalist; teacher; actor/
actress; musician; assistant; employer/ee
2 conductor; manager; artist; painter;
writer; electrician
5 1 suitable; interview
2 qualities; qualifications
3 advertisement
4 flexitime
5 recruits/trainee
6 sack
7 resign
8 salary/perks
7 1 in (out)
2 with
3 for; on
4 in/off; back
5 off
6 down; out

Listening p17
1 1 Speakers 2, 4, 5, 6, 8; 2 1, 3, 6; 3 4, 5,
6, 8
2 1A; 2C; 3B; 4C; 5B; 6C; 7A; 8C

Reading p18
2 1 self confidence + leadership
2 high school diploma + university degree
3 She was a doctor.

4 team skills, leadership skills,
communication skills + listening skills
4 5A; 6B; 7A; 8B; 9B; 10A; 11C; 12B; 13D;
14D; 15B

Grammar p20
2 1 Incorrect: The receptionist is paid less
than the PA/the PA is paid more than …
2 Incorrect: The receptionist's holidays are
longer than/aren't as short as the PA's. The
PA's holidays are shorter/aren't as long as
the receptionist's.
3 Correct
4 Correct
5 Incorrect: The PA needs more experience
than the receptionist.
3 1 -er; 2 less; 3 as/as; 4 the; 5 more/less;
6 better
4 2 a bit more than
3 a lot more
4 anything like as
5 almost
6 far more
7 any more
8 as good as
5 a lot more/far more/isn't anything like as
much; a bit more/almost the same as; isn't
any more/as good as
7 1 more
2 deal
3 the
4 as

5 much
6 more
7 slightly
8 much
9 better
10 than

Key word p21
1 1a; 2d; 3e; 4c; 5b

Writing p22
1 1B; 2A; 3H; 4F; 5C; 6E; 7G; 8D

Review p24
1 resign; perk; title; designing;
giving notice
2 1 organisation
2 recruits
3 children
4 qualifications
5 ability
6 selection
7 application
8 assessment
9 successful
10 references
3 a in; b at; c for; d to; e about/on; f for;
g with; h up
4 1A; 2D; 3C; 4C; 5C; 6B; 7A; 8C; 9C; 10B;
11D; 12A

Find me a Nanny!

You work for an agency that specialises in finding au pairs for rich and famous people. Read the profile of the family and decide which two of the applicants you would like to call for interview.

Belinda Harrington

- Concert violinist
- 38 years-old
- Ms Harrington spends four months of the year away from her family.
- She is currently single. She has had two spouses, Markus Moritz (another musician); Hank Shafter (film actor).
- Children: Hattie 9 and Benji 7
- They have had a series of nannies and au pairs. They have the reputation of being very spoilt and naughty children, but this is probably partly due to the large number of changes they have had in their young lives.
- Benji is full of energy and dangerously adventurous.
- Hattie is quieter and loves drawing and making things.
- Both are learning to play musical instruments, although there is no pressure from their mother who wants them to learn at their own rate.

Dear Perfect Nannies,

I'm writing in reply to the ad I saw in Nanny and Au Pair World last week. Anyway, I am a twenty two year old psychology graduate from New Zealand and am currently working my round around the world. I come from a big family and get on very well with kids of all ages. I would like to work in a family where I would be considered as a big sister rather than some kind of old-fashioned authority figure.

I am also a keen musician – flute and guitar – although I am not very good. I am keen on arts and crafts and enjoy showing children how to make and decorate objects. When I go back to New Zealand in a year or two I hope to train as music therapist.

Hope to hear from you soon. You can get me on my mobile (number on CV).

Trina Scott

Dear Sir or Madam,

I am writing to enquire whether you have any vacancies for an experienced children's nanny and governess. I am thirty five years' old and have nine years' experience of working with the children of middle-eastern royal families and members of the diplomatic community. I received my training at the Blue Chip Nannies School where I received their diploma with distinction.

I shall shortly be returning to the UK following the successful completion of a three year contract. During my career I feel as though I have achieved some remarkable results with what had previously been considered difficult and unruly children. Clearly, a nanny is never a substitute for a child's mother but I feel that a combination of love and discipline can win a child's heart.

I am available for interview at your convenience and can supply references on request.

Yours faithfully,

Anne-Liese Newman.

Dear Perfect Nannies,

I am writing to see if you have any vacancies for male nannies or au pairs. Despite the prejudice that exists against men doing this kind of job, I think that younger children often benefit from the presence of a male figure. After leaving school I trained as a child-carer in Sweden where I have worked with a number of different families.

I am a twenty seven years old. I am also a qualified skiing instructor and climber. In the summer I often work in camps for disadvantaged children where we teach them how to kayak, camp and live in the forest.

Yours truly,

Piet Johansson

IN OR OUT?

Everyone has to speak for at least one minute to say why they should stay in the balloon.

Listen to each person speak. Concentrate on the quality of their English, and how convincing they are. Do you believe what they are saying? Fill out the table below. Write more notes to justify your decisions. Once you have heard everyone speak, decide who is 'in or out'!

Name	Job	Quality of Speech	Quality of Ideas	In or Out?
Suzanna	teacher	excellent!	poor	OUT
1				
2				
3				
4				
5				
6				
7				
8				
9				
10				
11				
12				
13				
14				
15				

PHOTOCOPIABLE 2.2

In or Out?

Situation: You went on a balloon trip with the other people in your class. Unfortunately there was a storm and you have been blown over a mysterious and uninhabited island towards a volcano. The balloon is too heavy so two people will have to be sacrificed to save the rest. Eventually, when the balloon lands, you will have to know how to survive until you are rescued.

PHOTOCOPIABLE 2.2

Before you begin

Ask your class what sports and activities they play and/or used to play.

If you have a multilingual group, find out:
• the national sport of their country of origin
• the success of their national and local teams.

> Table tennis is extremely popular in China.

With people who are not interested in sport, find out about other spare time activities. For example, do they play chess or watch films?

Topic: Sport and leisure

At First Certificate level, students need to be able to speak confidently about their free time activities, as well as their abilities, likes and dislikes. Questions on these topics often form a portion of Speaking Paper, part 1.

Unit 3 Wordlist:

archery	pastime
bat	pitch
beach volleyball	puck
chess	racquet or racket
compete/competition/	rival/rivalry
competitive	sailing
contest/contestant	satisfy/satisfaction
court	shuttlecock
croquet	snowboarding
darts	soccer
difficult/difficulty	spectator
fan	supporter
friend/friendship	synchronised swimming
game	tennis
golf	tenpin bowling
hobby	tug of war
hooligan	use/useless
hope/hopeless	win/winner
intelligent/intelligence	wrestling
karate	

Getting started

Aim: To generate interest in the topic; to pre-teach certain sports that are not immediately recognisable to students.

1   Students match the images in the collage to the words in the box. In feedback take the opportunity to do some work on pronunciation and word stress. See the suggestion in Unit 2 to use bubbles to denote the stressed syllable.

2   Demonstrate the activity. It allows you to show a well-shaped response which will set the standard for your class.

> I think that Frisbee should become an Olympic sport. It deserves this recognition because it is extremely skilful and requires perfect hand and eye coordination. It is also very athletic and requires high levels of fitness from players. It has the reputation as being a game you play in the park, or on the beach, but the same is true of many other sports which have Olympic recognition. Finally, there is nothing more beautiful than the sight of a Frisbee disk floating through the air and being caught by an expert player.

Vocabulary: sports and pastimes

1   This exercise deals with confusable words and collocations. Ask students to decide quickly which verbs go with which nouns.

SPOTLIGHT ON VOCABULARY

Verb + noun collocations
Ask students to think of collocations from their own languages. In *Spotlight* different kinds of collocations are studied as we progress through the book. Answers could include: **play** *croquet/beach-volleyball/darts/chess;* **go** *sailing/ten pin bowling/snowboarding;* and **practise** *wrestling/synchronised swimming/tug of war.*

3   Differences between definitions:

A **game** (n) is an activity usually involving skill, knowledge or chance, in which you follow fixed rules and usually try to win.	To **play** (v) means to participate in the game.

You use the definite article, *the*, in front of countable nouns to refer to a specific thing (in this case, his/her violin).	A **violin** (musical instrument with strings) is a countable noun, which means it needs a definite article in front of it.
A **hobby** (n) is something you enjoy doing in your spare time (synonyms: activity, craft, interest, pastime).	**Sports** (n) are games which need physical effort as well as skill.
To **pass** (v) the time means to spend it in that way.	To **spend** (v) time doing something means to use your time to do it. It is not used correctly in this sentence.
To **hit** (v) something is to strike it forcefully, in this case with an object in your hand.	To **kick** (v) is to hit something with your foot (not your racquet).
To **let in** (v) a goal means you didn't defend your goal net well enough to keep it out.	If a player **scores** (v) a goal, they gain a point.
Beating (v) someone means to do better than them.	You can use **winning** (adj before n) to describe a person or thing that wins something.
A **court** (n) is an area for playing tennis or squash.	A **pitch** (n) is an area of ground marked out for cricket, football or hockey.
Won is the past tense and past participle of win.	To **gain** (v) something is to obtain it. It is not specific enough in this sentence.
If you are a **fan** (n) of something, you actively admire it.	A **spectator** (n) is someone who watches something. It doesn't imply support.
Supporters (n) give support to help something, in this case their team, to succeed.	**Pitches** (n) is the plural form of pitch.
A **board game** (n) usually involves the use of a flat piece of board in order to play it.	A **pastime** (n) is a hobby. You can't use 'board pastimes' as a collocation.
To **play for** (v) a team means you are a part of it.	To **compete against** (prep) someone is to try and beat them.
To be **beaten** (v) means to lose.	**Lost** is the past tense and past participle of *lose*. It is not used correctly in this sentence.
To **practise** (v) is to do something regularly in order to do it better.	**Practice** (n) refers to something people do regularly to improve.

Vocabulary extension

Put the students into groups and ask them to brainstorm three or four collocations for each of the verbs:

Make	the dinner, a mistake, the bed, money, a suggestion
Do	one's best, the washing up, something for a living, 100 km/h, do Science (as a subject at school)
Take	advantage of something, care of, pride in
Have	a good time, a sleep, a party, the chance to do something
Go	shopping, go for a walk, away

Listening: free time

Multiple matching (Paper Four, part 3)

This introduces part 3 of the Listening examination. Candidates have to match speakers on a similar topic to sentences that describe what each person says. The main lesson to remember is that the answer is rarely overtly stated. Instead, candidates have to infer and construct meaning. In addition, there is sometimes 'misdirection' in this part of the examination, although we shall look at this in a later unit. Candidates may have to work hard for the answer. Often the correct answer may not be obvious. Finally, remind students that there is always an extra and unnecessary sentence. This means that they cannot decide which one is correct by making their other four choices.

1–2 Read through the questions and then the highlighted tapescript and annotations.

4 Put the students into pairs and ask them to refer to Listening 3.1 on page 208. If you prefer, divide the class into groups. Each group studies just one of the speakers to identify the clues which give the answers. Afterwards, ask a person from each group to tell the rest of the class what they have found.

Key word: time

There are many expressions and lexical phrases based around the word *time*. This exercise deals with just a few of them. Consider pre-teaching some of the phrases before doing the exercise. You could also refer your students to a good dictionary, for as you can see on the next page, there are many more phrases than the six in exercise 1.

Degree of difficulty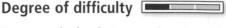

Decrease the level: For questions 1 and 2, allow weaker students to work in pairs first.

Increase the level: With a stronger class run through the exercise straight away. Consider extending the six phrases from question 1 with examples of your own, such as these time phrases below.

Ahead of your time / before your time: having new ideas before other people start to think similarly.
At one time: it was the case during a particular period in the past.
For the time being: something is the case only until something else becomes possible, or happens.
In time / on time: not late.
It is about time / it is high time: emphasises that something should be done now.
Of all time: of all that has ever been.
Take your time: to do something slowly and not hurry.

2   Notice that this exercise is similar, but not the same as part 4 of the Use of English Paper. In this case, *time* is the key word that would be used throughout. For exercise 2, you may wish to preview *it's time* + **pronoun** + **simple past**. For example: *It's time for us to leave* → *It's time we left.* This is a rule form students should know.

3   In groups, students personalise the expressions using *time*.

Reading: eccentric sports

Eccentric sports
Popular theory claims that the eccentric sport of Finnish wife-carrying began in the 19th century. A male grouping conducted raids on surrounding villages with the intention of carrying off someone else's partner. Nowadays the sport has been modified: the wives must all be returned, and the baggage must be older than 17. The course has been standardised to a 253.5 metre track made up of sand, grass and asphalt. Two dry and two water obstacles have been added, making it more a steeplechase than a marathon. Dropping wives is a serious breach of the rules and carries a deduction of 15 points and some well-deserved berating. Runners-up receive the spoils of mobile phones, US$170, and rye bread. The main winner receives the wife's weight in beer!

Before reading: Ask students what they think *Eccentric Sports* will be about. If something is **eccentric**, it is strange, unusual, 'out of the ordinary'... Then use the photographs to generate interest in the text students are about to read. Ask the class to compare and contrast them. Ask questions of the class.

> What is the aim of each sport?

> Which sport would be more fun to play? Which one would be more fun to watch?

1   By now students should be sufficiently motivated and intrigued enough to read the text through quickly to find the names of the sports in question.

2   Ask students to complete the rest of the exercise. They should use the words that have been highlighted in conjunction with the missing sentences. Students may find it useful to work in pairs to complete this. During feedback, make sure that students are able to justify their choices based on the words that have been highlighted. Finish off the section by asking some general questions about the text.

> Which sport or competition would you most like to watch? How successful would they be in your country?

> I want to see the Air Guitar Championships! I think they sound unusual.

Grammar: obligation and necessity

Here, we can assume that students are familiar with the ways of dealing with obligation and necessity. However, there may be residual confusion on when to use *must* and *have to*. Even at FCE level, there will be students who over-use *must*. In most classes there will be students who have problems with the past of *must/have to*. They may say 'we hadn't to do that' instead of 'we didn't have to do that'.

The use of *supposed to* when talking about rules which are not always respected may add a newer element to students' knowledge of this area.

The distinction between *didn't need to* and *needn't have done* is a subtle one that students at this level should understand.

1   Students work in pairs to match the beginnings of sentences to their endings. Otherwise, you can do this as a whole class activity. Choose students to match the halves of the sentences one by one. For weaker classes, provide a quick commentary as you go through the exercise in preparation for question 2. If you wish, you can combine feedback to this exercise with question 2. Remember to emphasise that an inappropriate use of *must* can be considered impolite or aggressive – this is particularly true when speaking to native speakers.

2   **Aim:** to address some basic difficulties with *must* and *have to*.
    Write the table on the board and ask students to give you the answers. Remind them that:
    • The past of *mustn't*, **isn't** *mustn't have*. *Mustn't have* is used for deductions in the past;
    • The past of *didn't have to* **isn't** *hadn't to*.

4   Students often get confused between *didn't need to do* and *needn't have done*.
    Consider breaking it down for weaker students:

1. In *didn't need to do* 'need' is used as a full verb and so needs the auxiliary 'do'. A Form   2. In *needn't have done* 'needn't have' is a modal auxiliary.

1. With *didn't need to do*, it isn't clear if someone performed an action or not. B Concept (meaning)   2. With *needn't have done* it is clear that the action was performed but that it wasn't necessary.

 C Pronunciation:

Needn't have is often said with a double contraction, which may make it difficult to understand – *needn't've*.

5   This is a further practice activity. In some instances, it may be possible to use more than one way of expressing obligation. Pause after each prompt to give the students time to respond.

7   This is a light-hearted freer practice activity. Students work in groups. Consider getting your students to give a demonstration of air guitar – or even air saxophone, air violin, air tuba … and so on!

Listening: the early history of football

1   Ask your class if anyone is a football fan. Which team do they support? Who is their favourite player? Talk through the quotations: check that students understand them.

2   Read the introduction. Allow students one minute to read through the questions. Reading the questions tells them what they will have to listen out for. Remind students that in the real examination they will have three choices to choose from. Play the recording all the way without stopping. Students confer/compare their answers in pairs and feedback to teacher. If necessary, play the recording again. Ask your students to ask you to stop each time they hear the information which enables them to answer the questions correctly.

Listening extension

Ask students to invent a third wrong choice for the questions they have just answered.

Example: *Q2 the Chinese game …*
              C was played only by royalty.

Sentence completion (Paper 4, part 2)
3 Tell students that in this part of the exam they have to complete notes using a few words for each of the gaps. Play the first part of the recording and ask the students to correct the answer. Students listen to the rest of part B and complete the notes. If necessary, play the recording a second time, pausing where the essential information appears.

Speaking: expressing ability

Can, could, was able to

This section examines ways of expressing ability. You may wish to lead into the section by examining some of the different uses of *could*. Ask students to give you some sentences that use *could* and write them on the board. Or mention these examples:

Could you open the door?   = a request/ polite order

The phone's ringing. It *could* be Anthea.   = an expression of possibility

She *could* tell you the names of all of the presidents of the USA.   = a conveying of ability

The point we need to make is that the same modal can have a number of quite different meanings.

1 The aim of this exercise is to make students aware of a common error. Students often confuse *could* and *was able*. *Was able* is used when we succeed in doing something <u>only</u> after a lot of effort has been expended. *Could* is used to describe a general ability in the past.

2 Students work in pairs. Emphasise that sometimes both answers are correct. Discuss why.

3 *Manage to* and *succeed* are both ways of describing ability and achievement.

Speaking: comparing photographs

EXAM SPOTLIGHT

Individual 'long turn' (Paper 5, part 2)
Explain the spotlight to your class. The photographs are linked by theme. This section aims to give students strategies for describing photographs and objects when they don't know the exact word. All five questions are designed to make students comfortably aware of how to answer, and how to improve on their answers, without making them feel threatened by the longer length.

Writing: a review

(Paper 2, part 2)

Remind students that in part 2 of the Writing Paper, students have a wide choice of question type. This can include a non-transactional letter, a narrative composition/story, a discursive, discussion-type essay, a report or a review. These questions focus on the review question.

1 Use the question and photographs to generate interest in the topic.

2 Adjectives can be used to bring a piece of writing to life. This exercise focuses on some key area of difficulty with participial adjectives.

3 Read through the adjectives in the box checking students' pronunciation. Drill where necessary. Put the students into groups and give each group four words from which to write sentences. Move around the class and provide help where provided. Quickly run through the sentences from each group to the whole class.

4 Complete the reviews with the adjectives. Make sure that a variety of adjectives are used.

Photocopiable activity instructions

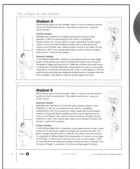

Activity 3.1: Information Gap: The Origin of Two Sports

Aim: Practise emphatic/shifting stress.

Instructions:
1 Put students into pairs.
2 Cut the versions on page 32 out. Hand them to your students, and ask them to read their incorrect version to their partner.
3 Their partner should correct their version, telling them where change is necessary.
4 They should be capable of explaining the differences to you / the class:
Student A *has the correct version of the early history of basketball; and an incorrect version of the history of rugby.*
Student B *has the incorrect version of the early history of basketball; and a correct version of the history of rugby.*

Activity 3.2: A New Sport

Aim: Fluency; to practise modals of obligations and vocabulary of sport.

Instructions:
1 Put students into groups and tell them they are going to create the rules of an entirely new sport.
2 Run through the table on page 33 and the illustrations and check that students know the names and pronunciations of the different objects. Use the questions as a way of structuring their discussion and choices.

    Answers for Sporting Equipment on page 34, from left to right, top to bottom: 12; 13; 8; 16; 6; 1; 3; 10; 9; 15; 11; 2; 7; 5; 4; 14.

Tapescript 3

Listening 3.1

Speaker 1: Well, when I was a kid my hobby was collecting football stickers. You know for the World Cup, or the league – you put them in an album and try and get all the players for all the teams. They sell them in packets - you've got half a dozen stickers in each one. There were always three or four I could never find. One year, there was just one player I needed – hmm … Roberto Carlos, that's right. Well in the end I got him by swapping fifteen of my spare stickers for just one of him – but it was worth it. I completed the whole album for the first and last time. Now and again, I look at it and feel the same pride.

Speaker 2: Once upon a time I used to play for fun, but now I take it very seriously and there is a lot of rivalry. At a top level you have to give the game one hundred per cent, the same as a physical sport. You have to be determined to win and can never show your opponent mercy. You must *look* calm and in control at all times. However, although players may look calm, under the surface their hearts are beating as fast as any athlete's! And of course, one bad move can mean you lose the game. There are things you mustn't do, like knocking over the board if you're losing; but believe me, there are ways your opponent can use to put you off – they can smile in a superior way, sigh impatiently, hum or tap the table. None of this is fair play, but I've seen it all in competitions.

Speaker 3: My family takes a lot of looking after. I don't get the chance for much exercise. All the same, I go to a keep-fit class once a week. My husband Jeremy leaves early on Thursdays so he can take care of the children when they get home from school. That will have to do for the time being. And from time to time, when we can get a babysitter we go to the theatre, or have a nice meal somewhere. I play the piano for a few minutes each day; it helps me to relax. The only other thing I do, I suppose, is every so often I help out with the homeless and serve meals and stuff, not that it makes me a saint or anything.

Speaker 4: Before you go you should have some lessons on a dry slope. I thought I didn't need to but when I got there I was hopeless. I wasn't even able to stand up without falling over. There were all these kids, three and four year-olds whizzing past me. After a couple of tries I decided it wasn't for me. Never again! I needn't have bought *any* equipment … the school supplied everything. Now I'll have to sell it all! It would have been a complete waste of time and money if someone hadn't told me about rackets, you know the kind you wear on your feet. In the end I just went off on my own and wandered through the forests – it was quite magical really – I had a great time.

Speaker 5: Most of the time I go up to my room and go online. My parents think that I am doing my homework. I like to download the latest music, surf the net, and email my friends. I also like chat rooms. I've met some really great people and formed some good friendships. You'd better not say anything to my mum and dad, though. They'll be furious if they find out!

Listening 3.2

One You are supervising an important examination. Tell the candidates that it is absolutely forbidden to whisper the answers to each other.

Two Tell your friend, Heidi, that she's going to have an accident if she doesn't drive more slowly.

Three You regret bringing towels and sandals to the spa because everything is provided.

Four Someone is smoking in the changing room. If the coach catches them he will be furious. Warn them!

Five One of the rules of the tennis club is that you can only wear white shirts and shorts. Tell a new member, but add that not everybody always respects this regulation!

Listening 3.3

Part A

Marcus: So, Jessica. How old is the game of football, then?

Jessica: Well, throughout history people have played games using their feet and a ball, but that doesn't mean that football has had a continuous history.

Marcus: What are some of the earliest versions of the game, then?

Jessica: Well, there is evidence that the ancient Egyptians had a pastime which involved kicking a ball around. And the Chinese had a sophisticated game where players scored by kicking a ball filled with feathers into a basket. Tsu Chu ('soo choo') I think it was called and it was part of a training exercise for soldiers.

Marcus: Wow, and I seem to remember hearing something about the Aztecs who played a kind of football. Is that right?

Jessica: Well, yes. It was, if you like, a mixture of volleyball, football and basketball. It was quite a complicated game. It was called tlatchi.

Marcus: Goodness, what a strange name! And how was it played?

Jessica: In an indoor court, away from the public. The only spectators were members of the nobility. Players kicked a heavy rubber ball from side to side – without letting it drop to the floor. It could travel at high speed and players wore protective clothing and helmets. The aim was to get it through a hoop, you know like a basket at the other end of the court. Few players were capable of doing this, and the game ended the moment someone was able to do it, which could be bad luck for the team that had been beaten.

Marcus: Why's that?

Jessica: Well, sometimes the losers were killed … you know … sacrificed to the gods.

Marcus: Wow. At least the worst you can get nowadays is a red card. And what happened to the winners? Were they rewarded, or did they get some kind of trophy?

Jessica: Well, the player who scored could claim all the clothes and jewellery of the spectators. So they were rich and famous.

Marcus: Just like today's soccer players!

Listening 3.4

Part B

Marcus: Just like today's soccer players! So, Jessica, you've told us something about some very early versions of football but what are the roots of the game we know today?

Jessica: Well, in various forms it was played across Europe from the Middle-Ages onwards. In Anglo-Saxon England in the tenth and eleventh centuries there was a game like football which was called 'Kicking the Dane's Head'. This would presumably have been the head of an invading Danish prince!

Marcus: Delightful!

Jessica: And a few hundred years later football became very popular because of the Italians. Florence had developed its version of the game called 'calcio'. That's C-A-L-C-I-O, which is what it's still called today, in fact.

Marcus: What were the differences between 'calcio' and the English version?

Jessica: Well, it was more organised than the English game. There were proper teams, and the players wore lovely costumes. In England it was far more disorganised: there were huge matches where entire villages used to play; anyone could join in.

Marcus: Gosh.

Listening 3.5

Part C

Marcus: Gosh.

Jessica : There were no rules about how many people could play and no time limit. It only ended when the ball was kicked into the house of the opposing team's captain. Sometimes, it ended in a draw because everyone was so exhausted or it was too dark to continue. It

used to get so violent that sometimes people were killed, and there are various periods in British history when the game of football was banned altogether. In the middle of the twelfth century, King Henry the second and the Lord Mayor of London became worried that his subjects were neglecting their compulsory archery practice. So, it was banned! The ban lasted for 400 years!

Marcus: I see! There always seems to have been violence associated with the sport. Some of the behaviour of these so-called supporters or fans is really shocking.

Jessica: Yes, you're right. But this has nothing to do with the sport itself – the sport is just a focus. Where there is rivalry you'll always find this. In Ancient Rome you had chariot-race hooligans who fought and actually killed each other in large numbers.

Listening 3.6

Interlocutor: In this part of the test I'm going to give each of you two photographs. I'd like you to talk about your photographs on your own for about a minute. It's your turn first, Kasia, here are your photographs. They show people participating in activities at festivals or at parties. I want you to compare the photographs and say how the different people are having fun.

Listening 3.7

Kasia: Right, well, let me see. They aren't exactly sports, but they are the kind of thing you can see at a festival or a children's party, you know, somewhere like that. Both photos look as though they were taken in the States. The people look American to me. Anyway, in the first one there's a sort of wall, the kind you put air in… and a person stuck on the wall! It looks strange. I think I understand … he has a suit with that sticky stuff, maybe. It is a game to see how high you can jump. It must be fun to do that, to jump up and see how high you can go!

The second picture is different, because it is a kind of competition between two children, I think. They are dressed in … big … suits … costumes. It is like that Japanese sport, the one those big, very fat men play. I don't like it really. I wouldn't find it fun. I don't think it is nice to encourage children to fight like that, even if it is meant to be fun.

Answer key 3

Vocabulary p26

1 play tennis/golf
go sailing/bowling
do karate/archery
3 1 game
2 the violin
3 hobby/pass
4 hit
5 let in
6 beating
7 court
8 won
9 fan
10 supporters
11 games
12 for
13 beaten
14 practise
4 1 tennis, badminton, soccer
2 pitch, court, field
3 chess, darts, backgammon
4 bat, racket, foot
5 shuttlecock, ball, puck

Listening p26

1 A2; B5; C1; D4; E spare; F3
2 C

Key word p27

1 1d; 2e; 3a; 4 f; 5b; 6c
2 1 first time I
2 waste of time
3 time to time
4 upon a time
5 spend your free time?
6 really good time

Reading p28

1 wife-carrying and mobile phone
throwing
2 A6; B3; C spare; D5; E2; F4; G7;
H1

Grammar p29

1 1e; 2c; 3g; 4d; 5a; 6f; 7b;
2 mustn't
be supposed to
don't have to/needn't
'd better (had better)
must
have to
must
3 1 She **has** to sell tickets. → She
had to sell tickets. → She**'ll have
to** sell tickets.
2 We **must** post that letter. → We
had to post that letter. → We'll
have to post that letter.
3 You **don't have to** come. → You
didn't have to come. → You **won't
have to** come.
4 1 didn't need to
2 needn't have done
5 1 I needn't have taken my lunch.
2 I didn't need to take my running
shoes.
6 1 You mustn't whisper the
answers.
2 You need to/You'd better slow
down otherwise you could have an
accident.
3 I needn't have brought towels
and sandals to the spa.
4 You're not supposed to/You
mustn't smoke in here.
5 You're supposed to wear white
shirts and shorts, but a lot of
people wear what they like.
7 • Absolutely compulsory:
invisible instrument; must be a
guitar; performance must last a
minute.
• Don't have to: know the notes
you are playing.
• Not permitted: No 'back-up'
bands; no other instrument other
than a guitar.

Listening p30

2 1B; 2B; 3A; 4A; 5B; 6B; 7A
3 1 the Middle Ages
2 the Dane's Head
3 calcio
4 teams
5 anyone
4 6 into the house
7 was too dark
8 wanted to ban
9 compulsory archery practice
10 chariot-race

Speaking p31

1 1a; 2b
2 1 was able to
2 could/were able to
3 couldn't/wasn't able to
4 was able to
3 1 *Manage* is followed by the
infinitive.
2 *Succeed* is followed by the
preposition *in* and the gerund.

Use of English p31

1 1 needn't have taken
2 had better
3 spends his free time building
4 aren't supposed to smoke
5 is good at walking
6 wasn't able

Speaking p32

1 The examiner wants the
candidate to compare the
photograph; talk for about a
minute; say how the different
people in the photographs are
having fun.
2 She handles it very well. She
speaks confidently and for the
right amount of time.
3 1 the kind of thing
2 sort of/kind

3 stuff
4 those big, very fat men
4 a sort of wall, the kind you put
air in.
sticky stuff
a kind of competition ... those big,
very fat men play

Writing p32

2 2 ~~exciting~~ excited
3 ~~enjoyed~~ enjoyable
4 correct
5 ~~various~~ varied
6 correct
7 ~~fun~~ funny
8 correct

Review p34

1 1 competitive
2 rivalry
3 useless
4 contestants
5 intelligence
6 competitions
7 hopeless
8 recognition
9 friendships
10 difficulties
11 satisfaction
12 winners
2 1 known
2 between
3 but/although
4 Having
5 less
6 their
7 case
8 whose
9 why
10 some
11 up
12 because

The origin of two sports

Student A

World famous sports can be invented! Take it in turns to read the incorrect version out loud to your partner. They need to correct you – using the correct version.

Correct version

Basketball was invented by a Canadian sports teacher called Dr James Naismith. In 1891 he was working for the YMCA in Springfield, Massachusetts, USA. He was asked to create a game that could be played indoors. He put two peach baskets at either end of a gymnasium and wrote a set of thirteen rules, twelve of which are still in use today. The big difference is that in the original game players weren't allowed to dribble with the ball. It could only be passed.

Incorrect version

In 1833 William Webb Ellis, a teacher at the famous school for boys, Rugby, picked up the ball during a game of football and kicked it down the pitch. The game of Rugby had been born! In 1846 the unofficial rules were written. In recognition of William Webb Ellis's achievement, his name is on the Rugby world shield. At that time the ball was still round, or olive-shaped. In 1851 the oval ball we know today was created by Richard Burton a craftsman from the town of Rugby. It was easier to hold an oval ball against the body.

Student B

World famous sports can be invented! Take it in turns to read the incorrect version out loud to your partner. They need to correct you – using the correct version.

Incorrect version

Basketball was invented by an American sports teacher called Dr James Goldsmith. In 1891 he was working for the YWCA in Springfield, Massachusetts, USA. He was asked to create a game that could be played outdoors. He put two banana baskets at either end of a gymnasium and wrote a set of fifteen rules, twelve of which are still in use today. The big difference is that in the original game players were allowed to dribble with the ball. It could only be passed.

Correct version

In 1823 William Webb Ellis, a schoolboy at the famous school for boys, Rugby, picked up the ball during a game of football and ran down the pitch. The game of Rugby had been born! In 1846 the first official rules were written. In recognition of William Webb Ellis's achievement, his name is on the Rugby world trophy. At that time the ball was still round, or plum-shaped. In 1851 the oval ball we know today was created by Richard Lindon a craftsman from the town of Rugby. It was easier to hold an oval ball against the body.

A new sport

You are going to invent a new sport. Who knows, in one hundred years time, millions of people could be playing it!
Fill out your answers below. Where necessary, circle your choice, or write in your response.

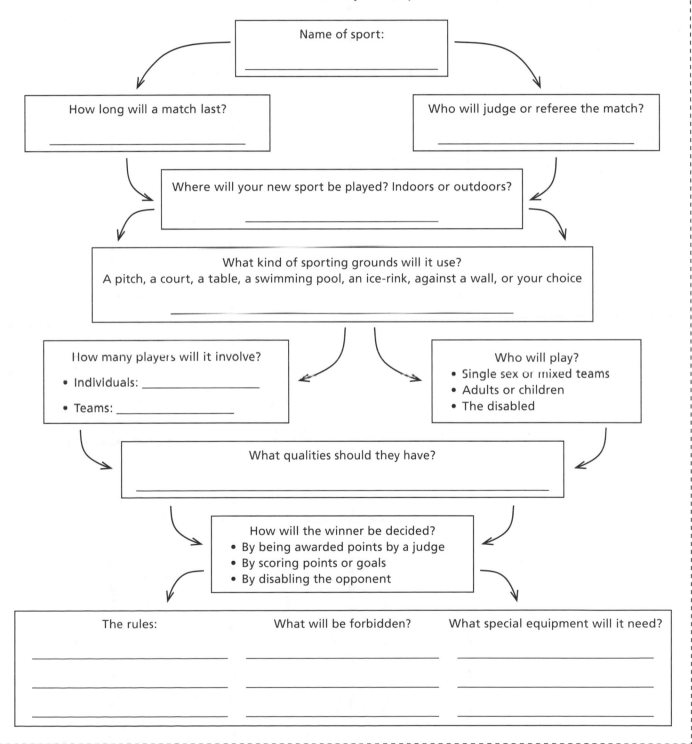

Name of sport:
_____

How long will a match last?
_____

Who will judge or referee the match?
_____

Where will your new sport be played? Indoors or outdoors?
_____

What kind of sporting grounds will it use?
A pitch, a court, a table, a swimming pool, an ice-rink, against a wall, or your choice
_____

How many players will it involve?
• Individuals: _____
• Teams: _____

Who will play?
• Single sex or mixed teams
• Adults or children
• The disabled

What qualities should they have?
_____

How will the winner be decided?
• By being awarded points by a judge
• By scoring points or goals
• By disabling the opponent

The rules:
_____
_____
_____

What will be forbidden?
_____
_____
_____

What special equipment will it need?
_____
_____
_____

Sporting Equipment

Label the following drawings with their correct name. Then choose at least THREE for your new sport.

1 hoop
2 length of rope
3 cone
4 hour-glass
5 goal
6 butterfly net
7 a football
8 a tennis ball
9 whistle
10 boxing glove
11 net
12 rugby ball
13 bells
14 shuttlecock
15 racquets
16 stick

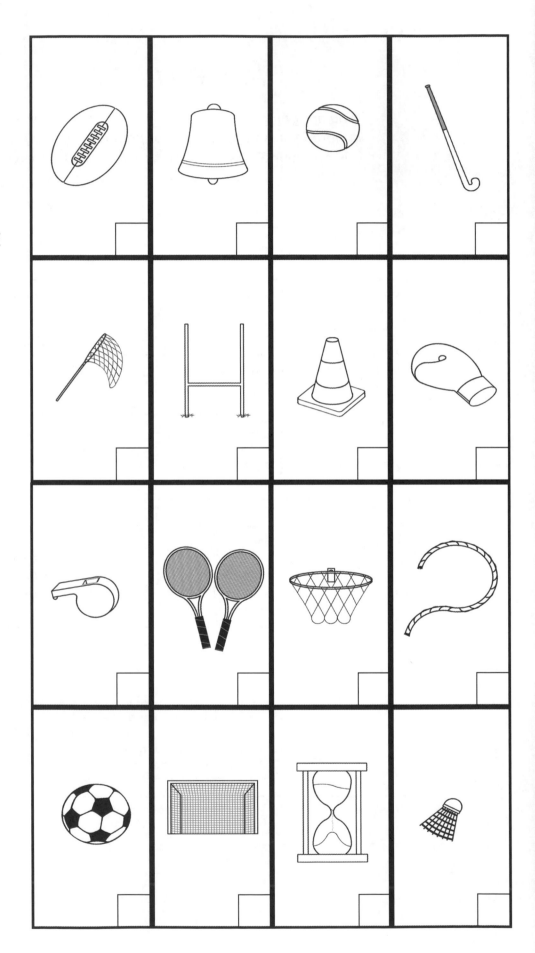

PHOTOCOPIABLE 3.2

4 Nature and animals

Before you begin

Generate interest in the topic by asking your students about their pets and favourite animals. A fun activity is to ask them to write down the names of their three favourite animals. Collect the results and then tell them what they mean:

1 *The first is what you would most like to be*
2 *The second is what people think you are*
3 *The third is what you really are!*

Topic: Nature and animals

This topic involves discussing animals, and the relationships that humans form with them. Most students will probably be interested in describing their pets, and hearing about other people's pets.

Unit 4 Wordlist:

appear/appearance	look down on
attack/attacker	look for
breed	look forward to
cage	look into
carry out	lucky/luckily
come across	mammal
come up with	mystery/mysterious
dead/deadly	pass away
die/death	pet
die out	pleasant/unpleasant
endangered	poison/poisonous
except/exception	prey
extinction	react/reaction
extreme/extremely	real/reality
find out	regular/irregular
go through	relation/relationship
habitat	success/(un)successful
harm/harmless	take in
imagine/imaginary	tame
instinct	terrify/terrified/terrifying
invent/invention	train
let down	watch out
live on	wild
look after	

Getting started

Aim: to generate curiosity and interest in the topic of animal behaviour.

1 Put students into pairs to quickly discuss their answers.

2 Give or elicit the following answers from the students:
1b; 2b; 3a; 4a; 5a.
Suggested answers. There are, of course, other theories.

1b Apparently, cows dislike eating wet grass.

2b Their owners laugh at their behaviour so the dog keeps chasing its tail for its master's approval. So this crazy behaviour is created by the owner and the people who find it funny.

3c Birds, in common with the majority of animals, can't recognise themselves in a mirror. They think that the bird in the mirror is a threat and try to fight it.

4a This is typical pre-attack behaviour.

5a When bees get together they instinctively know how many are needed to begin a new colony and hive.

Then lead a short all-class discussion about the results. Students may want to know where bees live (in a hive). The technical word for bees coming together is 'to swarm'.

3 Students produce other 'Why, oh why?' questions such as:

> Why don't the feet of a penguin freeze?

> It has a special blood supply system which prevents this.

Vocabulary: animals

1 This section deals with vocabulary on the topic of wild-life and nature. Run through the words in the box to check pronunciation and drill if necessary.

If something is **endangered** (v) it is at risk of being destroyed.
The **extinction** (n) of a species is the death of its remaining members.
To **breed** (v) is to produce offspring.
A **pet** (n) is an animal you keep in your home to give you company and pleasure.
An **instinct** (n) is the natural tendency to behave in a certain way.
Wild (adj) animals are in their natural habitats.
The **habitat** (n) is the natural environment where something (normally) lives.
To **train** (v) something is to teach it the skills you want it to know.
A bird of **prey** (n) is a bird which hunts and eats other animals.
If something is **tame** (n) it has been trained not to be afraid of humans.

Three-part (phrasal prepositional)	look forward to

However, teachers should be aware that here we only deal with the four basic types and that there are other variations and exceptions. See Section 12.3 Phrasal verbs in the Grammar Reference.

The difference between transitive and intransitive verbs (Section 17, Grammar Reference)

Before beginning this section you may need to check that your students understand:

1 The difference between the *subject*, *verb* and *direct object*, and *object pronoun*:

Jane likes chocolate.
Subject + verb + object

Jane likes it.
Subject + verb + object pronoun (it)

2 The differences between *transitive* and *intransitive* verbs: Intransitive verbs cannot be followed by a direct object; transitive verbs must be followed by a direct object. Many verbs can be used both transitively and intransitively. To show the difference, take two verbs which are similar in meaning, but which are grammatically different.
Check students know the verbs *rise* (*rise, rose, risen*), and *raise* (*raise, raised, raised*).

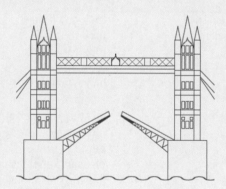

Draw a picture of London's Tower Bridge on the white-board. Show it opening up.
Write: The bridge rose.
Ask if we can add 'it' to the end of the sentence.
Answer 'no', because rise can't take an object – **it is intransitive**.
Write: The engineer raised.
Ask if this is correct.
Answer 'no' because raise must take an object – **it is transitive**.
The correct answer is: The engineer raised **the bridge**.

1 Students look at the definitions and the phrasal verbs in bold in context. We can often deduce the meaning of a phrasal verb from a close look at the context in which it appears. Students match meanings to verbs.

Adjectives + prepositions

The area of adjective + preposition collocations is an important one as it can be tested formally in the lexical cloze and open cloze questions of the exam. Here students may have to supply either the adjective or the correct preposition.

1 Students work together and match adjectives to prepositions.
2 Point out to students that if we want to say we don't like something, it is common to use the 'not keen on …' as a more polite formula.

> Would you like some Brussels sprouts?

> Actually, I'm not very keen on them.

Listening: animals and humans

(Paper 4, part 3)

In this part of the test, students match speakers to descriptions of what they say. Before they listen, ask students to read the descriptions A–F so they know what they are going to listen out for. You may need to pre-teach the word **greedy** (Someone who is greedy wants more of something than is necessary or fair.)

1 Play the recording all the way through, pausing if necessary after each speaker.

2 Although this is not an exam-specific task, it aims to encourage students to listen intensively for specific information. Students listen again for details and specific information. Deal with the sections one by one. Ask students for evidence to support their answers.

Grammar: phrasal verbs

Aim: While some students may be aware that phrasal verbs are governed by a particular grammar, this section formalises this knowledge by going into some of the differences in more depth.

p/c
4.1

Tell the students that you are going to look at the grammar of phrasal verbs. Check that they remember that: **phrasal verbs = verb + one or two particles**. The particle can either be a preposition, or an adverb, or in three-part phrasal verbs. A phrasal verb can have an idiomatic meaning that is often not clear from its constituent parts.

Type	Example
Intransitive	get on; to progress; have a (relationship)
Separable	let down
Transitive inseparable	break into

2   Now that the meanings of the phrasal verbs have been established, we can come to grips with their different grammar. The phrasal verbs in the exercise have been chosen as examples of the four different grammatical types. Essentially, the biggest problem faced by students is knowing when a phrasal verb is separable. With separable phrasal verbs, the object pronoun must come between the verb and its particle. If in doubt, they can nearly always put the full noun after the phrasal verb.

TEACHING IN PRACTICE

Negative checking

An effective way of making sure that our class is with us is to use the technique of 'negative checking'.

'He let her down'...
Is this sentence Ok?

Yes.

'He let down Sally'...
Is that Ok?

Yes.

'He let down her'
Is that Ok?

No.

So is *let down* separable or inseparable?

Separable.

So where do we have to put the object pronoun?

Between the verb and the particle.

Correct!

3   Students work in pairs or groups and search for the phrasal verbs in Listening 4.1 in the Tapescript. If time is short, tell some pairs/groups to search for answers 1–5, and the others to look for answers 6–10.

4   Go through the example then put students into pairs or groups to comment on the situations using the phrasal verbs from the exercises. Accept answers that use the phrasal verbs in a logical and correct way. Do not focus too much on errors away from this area.

Suggested answers:
1 You'll never guess what I came across in my grandmother's attic.
2 I'm really looking forward to seeing Annie again. I haven't seen her since …
3 You really shouldn't look down on other people just because they can't afford designer brands.

4 You have really let me down. I am so disappointed. I can't do my homework without …
5 I am sorry to tell you that Flopsie passed away the other day …
6 Well, I'm afraid that we were all taken in …
7 …I have come up with this really great idea …
8 … the polar bear will have died out, the only ones left …

Reading: a dog's life

BACKGROUND

A dog's life?

You may want to get your students thinking about what the title (and idiom) 'it's a dog's life' even means nowadays. Traditionally, most people would assume that the term refers to a miserable, unhappy existence – the hard life of the working dog. Nowadays, however, it has acquired a completely different meaning, implying instead a life of extreme pampering, where the individual may do as they please. Ask your class which definition is the most accurate today?

1   Generate interest in the topic of people and their dogs by asking one of the students to read the bumper sticker and take a vote in the class to see how many people agree with it. Alternatively, ask what evidence there is to support the idea that people choose dogs which look like them.

2   Multiple matching: This exercise provides exam-like practice of part 3. Get students to do the exercise. Perhaps negotiate a time limit with them. Ask them to support their answers with evidence from the texts. Note that in the examination students write A, B, C or D (here, it is just the first initial of the dog's name).

3   Lead a short all-class debate about the rights and wrongs of humanising pets.

Listening: points of view

Aim: to provide listening practice to a discussion between multiple speakers (which could appear in Paper 4, part 3); to revise/introduce some common ways of giving opinions and agreeing and disagreeing.

In this listening passage three friends discuss the article the students have just read.

1   Set the scene for listening and play the recording all the way through. Allow students to confer and then lead feedback. Remember that students will have another opportunity to listen to the recording in the next exercise.

2   Play the recording again, asking students to tick ✓ the expressions they hear. Go through the list and practise saying the introductory expressions aloud. Pay particular attention to the sentence stress of giving opinions. Remember, the stress should fall on the words in bold:

I think/believe   *As I see it.*

From my point of view   *In my opinion*

As far as I'm concerned…

3   Students add other expressions. They may come up with expressions such as:

> I couldn't agree more.

> Come off it Chi-Mai.

> You can't be serious.

> What (absolute) nonsense/rubbish!

Remind them that some ways of disagreeing can appear very offensive to native speakers, particularly from the mouths of a foreigner. Also, you should gently ignore any suggestions involving 'taboo' words.

Useful expressions extension

Sentence correction

It is sometimes useful to give students wrong sentences to correct. Write a and b on the board and ask what is wrong with each of the sentences:

Example 'wrong' sentences	Corrections:
a I am agree.	I agree (agree is a verb, not an adjective)
b According to me.	According to Jane (i.e. someone else)

Use of English: word formation

Word formation (Paper 3, part 3)
Run through the exam spotlight advice with your students. Emphasise the four steps. You should insist that they read the text all the way through as this will help them.
1 Students study the example and follow the reasoning carefully.
2 Students read the rest of the example and work backwards, deciding what the original root word was in each case.

---

3   Set a time limit of one minute for the class to read the story through for gist (global understanding).

4   Students complete the table and the text simultaneously.

Speaking: comparing photographs

Aim: To revisit part 2 of the Speaking Paper where candidates have to contrast a pair of photographs.

Quickly remind/elicit from the students what the different parts of the speaking exam consist of:

Part 1 Individual information

Part 2 Comparison of photographs

Part 3 Interactive task

Part 4 Discussion and individual follow-up questions.

Be sure to ask your students this exam-style question:

> What is the relationship between the dogs and the people in the two photographs?

1   Play the introduction and ask the students to make notes.

2   Students work together and list the similarities and differences between the photographs thus giving them a reason to listen.

3   Play the recording of Beate's answer and see what the class managed to predict. Remember that Beate is, in a sense, an 'idealised' candidate. Her performance is something students should aim for.

4   This focuses on the follow-up question asked by the interlocutor. It is important to remind students not to sit back and switch off while the other candidate is comparing his/her pair of photographs. The question the examiner asked Walter was: 'So Walter, which of the dogs do you think is happier?' He answers it well!

Useful expressions for describing photographs (Paper 5, part 2)
p/c 4.2
Run through the expressions with the class. Drill where appropriate, insisting on clear pronunciation, and a 'bright and light' delivery. Students refer to tapescript. Other expressions students could add for 'speculating' are: I *guess*; I *imagine* … However, tell your students not to overuse 'maybe' for speculating.

Key word: *look*

1   *Look* is at the heart of a number of expressions for describing and speculating.

Look is both a verb and a noun – you can *look for something*, or you can *have a look*. The grammar that surrounds *look* is quite complex and often poses problems for students. This section focuses on these expressions and their accurate use.

4 We revisit phrasal verbs here, focusing on *look*.

Key word extension

Consider drawing up a table, and asking students to offer an example sentence for each use of *look*.

Phrasal verb: *look* ...	Example sentence
look after	My grandparents love looking after me.
look (a)round	We went to look around the new house.
look back	Looking back, I feel foolish.
look down on	I really look down on people who don't work hard.
look forward to	She looks forward to meeting him.
look into	Dougal will look into the rumours.
look on	The neighbours looked on in silence.
look out for	Look out for the bus!
look through	Amelie looked through the magazine.
look to	The people look to the government for support.
look up	I looked up the definition/ Things are looking up!
look up to	A lot of the younger students look up to her.

Listening: almost human

1 Sentence completion (Paper 4, part 2): This question is to generate interest in the topic of the listening passages. A lot of people have anecdotes about animals they think show human characteristics. If students can't come up with any from their own experience, ask them to think about any animals which appear on TV.

2 Exploit the pictures and set the scene. Pre-teach the word **trunk**: it is an elephant's long nose. This exercise gives students practice in completing sentences to summarise what they have heard.

Listening extension

Exploit the drawings below question 2: ask your students what they think is going on. Elicit the words and phrases: *experiment, cup, guess where food is*.

Play the recording and ask students to choose their answers. Ask them to write down any key words or expressions that helped their choice.

Grammar: countable and uncountable determiners

1 This should be a quick revision exercise as students will be very familiar with these areas. See Section 7 of the Grammar Reference if students need to revise.

Writing: compulsory email

Aim: To provide another opportunity for students to gain practice in writing the compulsory letter.

Writing extension

If you want to guide the reading of the first letter more, put these comprehension questions on the board:

1 Jordan has emailed her old friend Ashley. Read the email and answer the questions.

2 Who are Miranda and Rick, and what do they want?

3 Why doesn't Jordan want to give in?

4 What are Ashley's comments, and what do you think of them?

2 Students read Ashley's reply and complete it using the words and phrases from the box.

3 Expressions used to ...

Ask for advice	Give advice	Consider and balance opinions
I need some advice	I think you should ...	Or else you could ...
What would you do if you were me?	If I were you ...	How about you ...

Degree of difficulty

Decrease the level: If you don't think your students are ready to write a complete reply, consider asking them instead to underline any expressions for asking for and giving advice.

Increase the level: See photocopiable activity

Photocopiable activity instructions

Activity 4.1: Phrasal verb jigsaw

Aim: To practise and consolidate phrasal verbs covered in Unit 4.

Instructions:

1   Photocopy and mix up a set of phrasal verb cards for each set of paired students, or small groups.
2   Students complete the jigsaw (stem, particle and definition) for each verb.
3   Ask them to test each other.
4   Finally, get students to create sentences of their own using the phrasal verbs that have been covered.

For example:

I'm really looking forward to my date with Ian tonight!

Activity 4.2: Introductory expressions

Aim: To practise introductory expressions for agreeing and disagreeing.

Instructions:

1   Divide class into groups.
2   Copy and distribute sets of expression cards to each group.
3   Suggest several topics that could be discussed, and ask your students to use the cards to introduce their opinions.

For example:

A: *I think cats are better pets than dogs.*

B: *I completely disagree because ...*

Activity 4.3: Pet problems

Aim: to provide letter-writing practice of the compulsory letter/email of Paper 2; to practise giving advice.

Instructions:

1   Ask your students to look at the two letters written to Dr Hope.
2   Discuss the comments made by Dr Hope. Make sure your students understand these annotations.
3   Ask your students to write Dr Hope's reply, using these comments. For a less-confident class, allow your students to work in pairs.

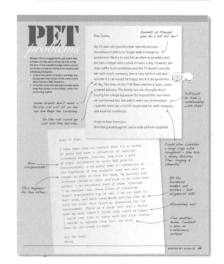

Tapescript 4

Listening 4.1

Speaker One: Well, I suppose we first noticed when I was about four. My mum and dad took me to the circus. I had really been **looking forward to it**. There were going to be lion-tamers, clowns and, best of all, horses. My parents knew that I was slightly allergic to dust, but they didn't want to **let me down** so off we went. Anyway, shortly after the show started in came the horses, you know with riders and acrobats, they came into the ring and started galloping around. And within a couple of minutes my eyes had gone red and I had started sneezing badly. When I started having trouble breathing, mum got really anxious about me and we had to go. So it was then that we discovered that although I was crazy about horses, they couldn't stand me!

Speaker Two: People **look down on** scorpions, but human beings have no need to feel superior. We are likely to become extinct, you know to **die out**, well before the scorpion. Scorpions have hardly changed in the past 350 million years. You can find them everywhere except Antarctica – so they are hardly an endangered species. Their habitat can be under rocks and in rainforests. You can even **come across** them between the bark of trees, so **watch out**! They can **live off** one meal for up to a year and their favourite snack is another scorpion! It has such strong pincers that it doesn't need to use its sting that often. It breaks its victim into little pieces and then spits its digestive juices onto the bits. Then, when these are nice and soft it'll suck them up. Bon appetit!

Speaker Three: I've never been very keen on guinea pigs – I mean they don't do much, do they? Anyway, we finally agreed to get a pair on condition that the girls looked after them, although I was usually the one who **ended up** taking care of them, I got really fed up with doing it. But then one morning, a few months after we'd had them, I went into the garage and one of them had **passed away**. Now you can imagine what a drama that was, we had to have a funeral for it – we buried it in a shoe box I remember and the girls were terribly upset. And then we had to **go through** the same thing a couple of months later for the other one. Never again!

Speaker Four: The study of ants or bees can really give us an insight into the collective intelligence they use to complete tasks. Many species can achieve a common goal without a leader. Each insect simply reacts to its immediate environment. Together they can achieve enormous results. Just think of beehives and ant heaps! Scientists who have **carried out** research into insect behaviour have realised that they can teach us some valuable lessons. They've **come up with** programmes which imitate this behaviour, which can, in turn, be used to understand big problems like traffic jams, and how to control crowds and so on.

Speaker Five: So this cat, Sid, had six, yes six different owners, and six different names! None of the owners was aware of anyone else. And in each place he lived he was given something to eat every night. That's why this story is called 'Six Dinner Sid'. Sid **took everyone in**; each person believed he or she was his one and only owner. Just look at how fat he got! But one day he got a cough and all of those people took him to the vet. In the end the vet said to himself, 'Hold on, I've seen this fat fellow with a cough already, today.' So he phoned around to all the owners and they each **found out** that they weren't the only one to think they 'owned' him! So, they started taking turns to give him a dinner once a week … one owner for each day! But, Sid was a six-dinner-a-day cat, so he moved to a new street and started again with six new owners!

Listening 4.2

Rebecca: Charlotte, did you see that article, the one about the owners who spend a fortune on their dogs?

Charlotte: Mm, yes. They look so lovely don't they, all clean and beautiful; their owners must be so proud of them.

Terry: Come on, Charlotte. Alright, so they look nice, but in my opinion they could spend their money far better … you know … in a much more sensible way.

Rebecca: I hear what you're saying, Terry. I know, for instance that there are a lot of kids out there who don't have anything to eat, but that doesn't mean that you can't give love to a pet either.

Charlotte: Yeah, I agree with you Rebecca. But, we don't know what else the owners do, do we? I mean they could be helping the homeless *too* for all we know.

Terry: I suppose so, but as far as I'm concerned it just goes completely against decent behaviour to spend so much on dogs – I'm sorry, Charlotte, but that's the way I feel.

Charlotte: I can see where you're coming from, but they aren't doing anything wrong as such, are they? It's not as if they were being cruel to animals or anything.

Rebecca: Mm, but I suppose Terry is right, Charlotte, it is rather unhealthy to be so obsessed with a pet, don't you think? And I'm not even sure that they are treating the dogs that kindly. As *I* see it dogs just want to be dogs and run around and enjoy themselves. I'm sure if they could speak they'd say how awful it was having to be dressed up and shown off all the time.

Charlotte: I see your point, but as far as I'm concerned it's up to the owners to choose. And if taking care of a pet is what pleases them, who are we to argue?

Listening 4.3

Interlocutor: Right, thank you. In the second part of the test, I'm going to give each of you two different pairs of photographs. I'd like you to talk about your photographs on your own for about a minute, and also to answer a short question about your partner's photographs. OK. So we'll start with you first, Beate. Here are your photographs. They show people and dogs interacting in different ways. What is the relationship between the animals and the humans in each picture?

Listening 4.4

Beate: Well, let me see. Both photographs show people working together with dogs. In the photo on the left there is a man ... hmm ... it *looks* like a policeman ... who is with a young-looking dog; it looks like a German shepherd, I think. Whereas in the second photo, the one on the right, there are a lot of dogs, huskies I think, and these dogs are pulling a sledge. It looks as though they are going be in a race, or maybe they have as the dogs look a little bit tired. The person in the sledge looks happy so maybe they have won. Anyway, going back to the first picture, I think that the man is trying to train the dog, you know, to be a police dog. Perhaps he is teaching it how to jump over things, and fences, yes? I think it takes a long time to train a dog to do this. The dogs in the other picture of course they must already be trained, but all they have to do is run and follow their leader. I imagine that this kind of dog is much wilder than the one in the first picture.

Listening 4.5

Interlocutor: Thank you, Beate. So, Walter, which of the dogs do you think is happier?

Walter: Which is happier? Well, I guess the ... huskies , they are in the open air and they can run and act more like dogs together, with other dogs like in nature, while the police dog ... I don't know if I would be satisfied with its life because it is going to be a bit like a slave for a human being, isn't it, and it will be lonely without other dogs.

Interlocutor: Thank you, Walter. Now I'd like you to look at this pair of photographs because now it's your turn to give a description.

Listening 4.6 Part A

Interviewer: The distinction between human beings and other animals is an artificial one isn't it? We live and breathe and take care of our young in a similar way, don't we?

Professor: Mm, well, yes, you're right. Biologically there is little difference between us – and chimpanzees – but there are a number of key distinctions which separate us from other mammals. There is language; then there is intelligence: the ability to think about things, if you like. Animals are driven by their instincts and how they react to sensation. And another important distinction is our capacity for self-awareness.

Interviewer: Self-awareness?

Professor: Mm, yes. You know if we see ourselves in the mirror, we know that it is us we are looking at.

Interviewer: But how can you know whether an animal is self-aware?

Professor: Quite simply by placing it in front of a mirror and seeing how it reacts. Hardly any animals are capable of recognising themselves, but there are a few exceptions to this. A small number of creatures including chimps, dolphins and elephants can do this.

Interviewer: Elephants! Really!

Professor: Yes, after some research at a zoo in New York, we can now add elephants to this group. Three elephants which were given the mirror test behaved in a way which showed that they understood the animal in the reflection was them.

Interviewer: So how did they react, then?

Professor: Well, they did several things like putting their trunks in their mouths and watching themselves in the mirror which show they're interested in themselves. One of the three, Happy, I think it

was, tried to remove a spot she was ashamed of, you know a mark which the researchers had put on her face.

Interviewer: Oh I see. And what about cats and dogs? Many people believe that they have an almost human intelligence too.

Professor: Mm, yes. But I'm afraid dogs and cats show no self-awareness at all. They are incapable of recognizing themselves. People who pretend otherwise are just fooling themselves.

Listening 4.7 Part B

Interviewer: If that's the case, how come dogs have such close relationships with human beings. They couldn't do that if they weren't self-aware, could they?

Professor: Well actually, this has nothing to do with self-awareness, basically it is all because dogs are brilliant at reading human expressions and gestures, and interpreting them. They are much better at this even than chimpanzees who are our closest relatives.

Interviewer: There is scientific proof of this, is there? Has anyone looked into this area?

Professor: Yes. There has been a great deal of research so scientists have gathered a large amount of evidence. There's another simple experiment where there are two cups. One has food underneath it, and the other is empty. Well, with dogs, if someone touches the cup, or even just glances at it, then a dog will pick up the signal and choose the one with the food every time. Chimps, would you believe, simply guess.

Interviewer: I see, and how did this come about ... the dog's ability to do this?

Professor: Good question. The most likely explanation is that it is a result of evolution. In domesticated dogs, you know, dogs which have been tamed and in human contact generation after generation, well, this ability to recognise human emotions and gestures has evolved.

Interviewer: So it wouldn't be developed in wild dogs, then?

Professor: Absolutely not. No ... wolves and so on, they're different from domesticated dogs.

Interviewer: Hold on, though, how can we be sure of that? You know ... that this ability to recognise human emotions is as a result of evolution?

Professor: Well, in another piece of research one scientist did the two cup experiment on a breed of dog called the New Guinea singing dog.

Interviewer: New Guinea singing dog? Weird.

Professor: It's called that because it's famous for its funny bark. When it howls it sounds like a cross between a wolf and a whale.

Interviewer: Bizarre.

Professor: Anyway. What is special about this breed is that once upon a time, many generations ago, it had been domesticated, you know tamed and trained how to live with humans. But then it returned to the wild and had no more human contact. This made it ideal to test the evolution theory.

Interviewer: So what happened when they carried out the experiment? How much importance does evolution really have?

Professor: Well, to cut a long story short, when they performed the cup test with these dogs, none of them were able to pick the cup with the food under it. They couldn't read human expressions or gestures any more. Any ability which had once evolved had been lost.

Interviewer: Fascinating.

Answer key 4

Vocabulary p36
1 1 endangered/extinction
2 breed
3 pet
4 instinct
5 wild/habitat
6 train/prey
7 tame
2 keen on; aware of; famous for; allergic to; fed up with; interested in
3 1 aware of
2 fed up with
3 famous for
4 interested in
5 allergic to
6 keen on

Listening p36
1 A4; B5; C3; D2; E Extra; F1
2 1a He was looking forward to it.
1b The horses
1c His eyes went red and he started sneezing.
2a 350 million years
2b Antarctica
2c Under rocks, in rain-forests, even between the bark of a tree
2d Break the victim up into pieces and then spit on it to dissolve it.
3a He/she isn't very keen on them
3b The girls would look after them, but they didn't.
3c The children were upset and so there was a special funeral for the pet.
4a Nobody, they achieve common goals without a leader.
4b Extremely, they can achieve enormous results.
4c Scientists can learn lessons and create programmes which copy their behaviour. This can help to solve problems such as traffic congestion and crowd control.
5a Six
5b Each of the owners took Sid to the vet.
5c Yes

Grammar p37
1 1c 2a 3d 4b
2 1b 2d 3a 4c
3 1 live off / intransitive
2 find out / separable
3 come up with / inseparable
4 go through / inseparable
5 carry out / separable
6 die out / intransitive
7 end up / intransitive
8 take in / separable
9 look down on / three part
10 watch out / inseparable

Reading p38
2 1L; 2B; 3N; 4B; 5N; 6L; 7D; 8B; 9D; 10L; 11N; 12D; 13L; 14N; 15D

Listening p39
1 1C 2T 3R 4C 5T 6R 7C
2 In my opinion; As far as I'm concerned; I hear/understand what you're saying.

Use of English p40
2 6 real
7 pleasant
8 pain
9 extreme
10 dead
3 1 reaction
2 successful
3 Luckily
4 attacker
5 poisonous
6 irregular
7 death
8 invention
9 appearance
10 mysterious
4
1 REACT; verb; noun; *reaction*
2 SUCCESS; noun; negative adjective; unsuccessful
3 LUCKY; adjective; adverb; luckily
4 ATTACK; verb; noun; attacker
5 POISON; verb/noun; adjective; poisonous

6 REGULAR; adjective; negative adjective; irregular
7 DIE; verb; noun; death
8 INVENT; verb; noun; invention
9 APPEAR; verb; noun; appearance
10 MYSTERY; noun; adjective; mysterious

Speaking p41
1 Here are your photographs. They show people and dogs interacting in different ways. What is the relationship between the animals and the humans in each picture?
2 Similarities: Both photographs show people working together with dogs; both photos show trained dogs.
Differences: one dog looks like a German shepherd, the others are huskies; the first dog looks like a police dog, the second dogs are pulling a sledge (it looks as though they are going be in a race); the huskies look wilder than the German shepherd.
4 Very well.

Key word p41
1 1 looks like
2 look a little bit
3 looks as though
2 1 Correct
2 The dog looks tired.
3 Correct
4 It looks like they are going to stop.
5 The photographs look similar.
3 forms: *looks* + adjective; *look/s like* + noun; *looks as though* + verb phrase
4 1 for
2 after
3 into
4 forward to
5 down

Listening p42
2 1 language
2 intelligence
3 for self-awareness
4 instincts
5 mirror
6 elephants and dolphins
7 New York
8 their trunks in
9 Happy
10 fooling themselves.
3 1C; 2B; 3A; 4A; 5C; 6B; 7C

Grammar p42
1 1 several; 2 All; 3 No; 4 little; 5 any; 6 deal; 7 much; 8 any; 9 a number; 10 amount

Writing p43
3 1 first
2 face it
3 Obviously
4 Basically
5 Or else
6 I were you
7 Believe
8 as for
9 Anyway
10 as far as

Review p44
1 1C; 2A; 3C; 4A; 5B; 6B; 7A; 8B; 9A; 10B; 11A; 12B
2 1 looking forward to seeing
2 you do if you were
3 take care of/care for
4 as I'm concerned,
5 little difference between
6 looks as if
7 disappointment that hardly anyone
8 come up with
3 1 If I were you
2 otherwise
3 Basically
4 as far as I'm concerned
5 All things considered
6 Anyway

Phrasal verb jigsaw

live	on	survive
find	out	discover information
come	up with	have an idea
come	across	find by chance
look	forward to	eagerly await
let	down	disappoint
carry	out	perform/execute
die	out	become extinct
end	up	finish
take	in	trick/deceive
watch	out	pay attention
get	on (with)	have a relationship
look	into	investigate
look	after	take care of
look	for	search

Introductory expressions

I think	I think	I think	I think
I believe	I believe	I believe	I believe
As I see it	As I see it	As I see it	As I see it
From my point of view	From my point of view	From my point of view	From my point of view
I quite agree	I quite agree	I quite agree	I quite agree
In my opinion	In my opinion	In my opinion	In my opinion
I totally/entirely agree	I totally/entirely agree	I totally/entirely agree	I totally/entirely agree
Absolutely	Absolutely	Absolutely	Absolutely
According to X … Y says/thinks (that) …	According to X … Y says/thinks (that) …	According to X … Y says/thinks (that) …	According to X … Y says/thinks (that) …
Yes but … I don't/I can't agree	Yes but … I don't/I can't agree	Yes but … I don't/I can't agree	Yes but … I don't/I can't agree
I (completely/totally) disagree	I (completely/totally) disagree	I (completely/totally) disagree	I (completely/totally) disagree
Yes but…I don't/I can't agree	Yes but…I don't/I can't agree	Yes but…I don't/I can't agree	Yes but…I don't/I can't agree
I hear what you're saying but …	I hear what you're saying but …	I hear what you're saying but …	I hear what you're saying but …
I understand/respect your point of view but …	I understand/respect your point of view but …	I understand/respect your point of view but …	I understand/respect your point of view but …

PET
problems

Modern Pet is a magazine for pet lovers that contains articles about choosing and caring for pets. It has a problem page where owners can write and ask for advice from experts and animal psychologists.

1 Look at the letters in today's postbag, and decide who the winner of this week's prize letter (worth £100) should be.
2 Using the notes that the psychologist Sasha Hope has written on the letters, write two convincing replies.

some breeds don't mind: a Persian cat will sit on her lap and keep her company.

So the cat could go out into the balcony.

Dear Sasha,

sounds as though you do a lot for her?

My 78-year-old grandmother recently became housebound and is no longer able to leave her apartment. We try to visit her as often as possible, and she has a helper who comes in twice a day. However, she does suffer from loneliness and the TV doesn't provide her with much company. She is very fond of cats but I wonder if a cat would be happy stuck in an apartment all day. She lives on the 11th floor and has a large, sunny, covered balcony. The family has also thought about buying her a large aquarium for tropical fish, but when we mentioned this she didn't seem very enthusiastic. I wonder what we could do to provide her with company and ease her loneliness.

Difficult to have a relationship with fish!

Hope to hear from you,
Worried granddaughter (name and address supplied)

Dear Dr Hope,

I have been keen on unusual pets for a number of years and have a collection of reptiles including snakes, turtles, and even a pair of small alligators my uncle Ted gave me. Unfortunately, I am going away to university at the beginning of the academic year and will no longer be able to care for them. My parents and brothers refuse to have anything to do with them either. I am extremely fond of them, although I do realise that these kinds of creatures aren't everybody's cup of tea. I do not want to hurt them, and have considered letting them go into the wild. This could be dangerous for the environment. There is a large lake and a forest near my home where I think they could be happy. I would just like to check with you first before I decide to release them into the wild. What do you think is best?

All the best,
Snaky

How irresponsible!

This happens far too often...

Could also consider a large cage with songbirds – she has a sunny balcony. Their singing is cheerful.

OK for harmless snakes and turtles – but alligators? NO!

Absolutely not.

Find another home. Contact a zoo, or a veterinary school.

5 A good story

Before you begin

Find out about your students' reading habits: how much do they read? What do they read? What kind of things do they read: websites and web-pages/blogs; newspapers and magazines; or books? A blog is short for web-log; a kind of open journal or diary that appears on the Internet.

Topic: A good story

This unit deals with storytelling in the form of different types of literature and films/TV programmes. It also focuses on writing narratives using a variety of tenses and the kind of descriptive vocabulary that helps to bring a narrative to life.

Unit 5 Wordlist:

angry	lovely
chapter	mortified
character	myth
classic	narrator
delighted	novel/novelist
devastated	playwright
dialogue	pleased
disappointed	plot
embarrassed	ridiculous
episode	scene
exhausted	scenery
fact	script
fiction	serial/serialise
frightened	series
furious	set in
gasp	shoot
gaze	sigh
ghastly	sip
giggle	slurp
glance	snigger
glare	stagger
gorgeous	stare
gulp	stroll
hero	stupid
heroine	terrified
legend	tired
limp	villain
location	yawn

Getting started

Aim: To generate interest in the theme of stories and literature. (There is an international choice of story and character. All of the stories have been adapted for children or 'Disneyfield' for the cinema-going public.)

1   Students work in pairs or teams and try to identify the characters shown.

2   Students listen and match the speakers to the characters, all of whom appear in the collage.

3   Lead a short, all-class discussion on the theme of original books, and adaptations for children and the screen.

4   Round off the section by asking students to think of two characters used on the Aladdin 'model'. Go round the class and make sure that students haven't all chosen the same characters. If students wish, they can choose some of the characters from the collage.

Vocabulary: books and films

1   Spend five minutes brainstorming some of the different types (genres) of literature. Put students into groups and consolidate what they say on the board.

2   Students complete the sentences with words from the box. If you wish, put them in pairs or groups to do this. Spend time dealing with the pronunciation and word stress of each item.

A **series** (n) is a basic story but may have different stories or characters in each episode. TV series can continue over many seasons.	A **serial** (n) is one story divided into a number of episodes. The last episode completes the story.
A **playwright** (n) is a person who writes plays.	A **novelist** (n) is a person who writes novels.
An **episode** (n) is one quantity of viewing in a serial.	A **chapter** (n) is one of the parts that a book is divided into.
A **classic** (n) is a piece of writing of high quality which has become a standard against which other works are judged.	**Mythology** (n) refers to the well-known stories made up in the past to explain natural events or to justify religious beliefs or social customs.

A **heroine** (n) is a female hero (main character with good qualities).	The **villain** (n) is the main bad character.
The **characters** (n) are the people in a book or film.	The **plot** (n) is the storyline.
A **script** (n) is the version of the novel that has been adapted for TV, radio or film.	A **novel** (n) is a book containing a long story about imaginary characters.
A **scene** (n) in a novel, film or play is part of it in which a series of events happen in the same place.	**Scenery** (n) is the land, water or plants that you can see around you.
The **location** (n) is the place where something is filmed.	If something is **set** (v) somewhere, it is located there.
The **narrator** (n) is the person whose voice tells the story.	**Fiction** (n) is stories about imaginary people or events.

3   Students in groups ask each other about favourite books and films.

Vocabulary extension

Question 3 can be taken further by getting your students to create a 'Favourite book/film questionnaire'. For example:

Faye's questionnaire	Student A	Student B
Title of book		
Author		
Name of main character		
Year it was written		
Setting		
Genre		

Note: Students who don't read books will probably read magazines or comic books or manga.

Listening: great adaptations

1   Check that students understand the meaning of adaptation. (An **adaptation** is when the story in a book is transformed into say a film or play.)

Pre-teaching vocabulary
We may need to pre-teach vocabulary:
- Students won't understand the overall meaning of a passage if the meaning of certain items of vocabulary is unknown.
- Texts are made more readable, and listening passages more comprehensible, when unknown words are clarified. If we just want students to know the meanings for the text or listening passage then a quick explanation or translation will be enough.

Multiple choice (Paper 4, part 4)
Read through the spotlight on listening with the class. The key message here is that students should not waste their time in the exam but use the pauses between each part to read the questions they have to answer next. This may also help them to make some predictions that they can test as they listen.

Aim: to create an expectation and bring to the surface what ideas students may already have about the topic.

1 Elicit ideas from students and write them on the whiteboard.

> What do you think the scriptwriter will talk about?

> Maybe there is less money for a TV adaptation?

> Perhaps there are fewer big scenes in TV series than in a film?

> The cinema can have more well-known stars than TV?

2   Play the recording all the way through and allow students to confer. Ask students to provide you with evidence for their answers. If necessary, play the recording again, pausing before each section where supporting evidence appears.

3   Warn the students that they may not hear everything in exact chronological order. That is, they won't be able to answer all the questions one after the other.

Key word: *thing*

A thing (n) is a physical object that is considered as having no life of its own.

1   All these expressions appear in the interview, as well as typical everyday English.

Reading: the bangle

McCall Smith and Mma Ramotswe

A professor of medical law, Alexander McCall Smith published *No. 1 Ladies Detective Agency* in 1998. He was born in Zimbabwe, but educated in Scotland. The series' debut started as a short story, and then grew into a set of stories. Finally it became a novel. The series currently boasts more than four million English copies in print. It is translated into twenty-nine additional languages. McCall's inspiration for the novel was seeing a woman chasing a chicken around her yard in Botswana. McCall reflected upon how she probably had a very interesting past, bringing up a number of children with very little money. Her yard and house were both respectable and clean – she was probably making a good life for herself, despite being so poor. This woman became Mma Ramotswe, who we read about in 'the bangle' excerpt.

Look at the photograph of the woman in a car, and ask the students to imagine where the story might be set. Explain that the photograph is from a TV adaptation of a story by the same author. Pre-teach market stall and bangle .

1   **Aim:** to encourage a quick skim read of the story for gist (overall meaning).

Set a time limit of five minutes for your class to read the text. Then allow them to confer in groups on what the best title might be. This should give you a clear idea of whether the class has understood the overall meaning of the passage and the humour of the end.

Handling multiple choice questions (Paper 1, part 1)

Read the advice with the students. Then, with the class, read the analysis of the first multiple choice question. Allow students ten minutes to read the text in more depth and answer the remaining questions.

3   Follow up the reading passage with a class discussion of the question.

Vocabulary: verbs of manner

Verbs of manner combine an action verb with an adverb all in one. They carry implicit information that tells us *how* an action is performed. Writers provide more precise descriptions by using verbs of manner. If students need a further example of this, write this example on the board: Walk (verb) in long determined steps (adverb/how the person walks) = stride.

1   Ask students to find the verbs in the context of the passage they have just read and to select the definition which matches it closely.

2   Allow students five minutes to work in pairs and categorise the verbs in italics.

3   Allocate two or three verbs to different groups and ask them to create short definitions.

Verb of manner	Definition
Sigh	to breathe outwards, often in sadness or disappointment.
Gaze	to look wide-eyed in wonder
Slurp	drink noisily
Giggle	laugh in a stupid, high-pitched way
Stagger	walk with difficulty and not a in a straight line, perhaps from carrying something heavy, or because you are ill or injured
Gulp	drink quickly in big mouthfuls
Glare	look with disapproval/anger
Stroll	walk slowly, taking pleasure in your company or surroundings
Snigger	laugh unpleasantly, often at someone else's misfortune, often behind their back
Limp	walk slowly and painfully because one of your feet hurts badly

4   Choose an extroverted student to mime one of the verbs of manner. Students guess and then work in groups taking it in turns to mime the different verbs.

Grammar: narrative tenses

1–4 Students should already be fully familiar with the range of narrative tenses. These exercises review and revise them. Some students may be uncertain when faced with a choice between different narrative tenses. The past continuous poses special problems, as it is used for scene setting as well as to describe actions that were in progress in the past. If you feel that students are uncertain about the basic uses of these three tenses, refer them to Section 12 of Grammar Reference.

5–6 This exercise is in three sections: the first gives students a clear choice between two tenses; the second asks students to make a choice within a context; the third section lets students make their own free choice.

7   Here is a possible ending to the story:

There was nothing for it but they had to climb onto the roof of the car before they were drowned. They watched as the bottle of champagne and the rest of their picnic floated off into the distance. Fortunately their cries managed to attract a group of fishermen who rescued them. After they and the car had been rescued Olivier spent all the following day cleaning and polishing it so that it looked as though nothing had happened. Everything was fine until his father opened the glove compartment next to the steering wheel and found it full of sand and seaweed. Isabelle and Olivier have both been terrified by their experience, but if anything it made them closer than before. Luckily for Olivier, he had managed to keep the ring in a safe place so it hadn't been lost. All that remained was for him to wait for another occasion to present itself.

There is a further adventure of Isabelle and Olivier in the back of the course book. See Section 12.1 of the Grammar Reference.

Writing: a short story

This section pulls together the work that has been done on narrative tenses and adverbs of manner to create a narrative composition. In the First Certificate, there is often a question that asks students to write a story. One variation of this is to ask candidates to begin or end their story with the words they are given.

To start, ask students to study the invitation. Ask them to say what kind of event they think it will be.

1   Introduce the concept of the narrative composition, and ask the students to read the passage and identify anything that may be wrong in the picture.

SPOTLIGHT ON WRITING

Sequencing
2 Tell your class that one of the biggest problems students have with narrative composition is sequencing events:

they overuse 'then' and make mistakes with 'before' and 'after'. Run through the information showing how two events may be sequenced. Remember: the biggest problem is often when students place 'after' between the two events. Unless we have prior knowledge, it is unclear which action happened first.

3   Put students into pairs or groups for this exercise. Tell them the object is to use different ways of putting events in sequence. Acceptable answers should 'contain elegant variation' and use a variety of sequencers accurately. A possible answer could be something like this:

After getting up late last Saturday morning, I took the train to Barcelona to do some shopping and meet some friends. While I was buying some shoes, I bumped into my old friend Aranxa, who I hadn't seen for ages. Next, I met up with my friends in Catalunya Square. Once everyone had arrived, we had lunch together in a tapas bar. Afterwards, we strolled down the Ramblas. From there we ended up going down to the sea, and finally saw a movie. Later, on my way home, I thought what a lovely day it had been!

SPOTLIGHT ON VOCABULARY

Gradable and non-gradable adjectives
4–5 Read the information in the spotlight. Students work in pairs and match gradable adjectives with their non-gradable counterparts. If you want to provide intensive practice of this through a drill, you could give students this as a model:

> Did you feel embarrassed at the reception?

> Embarrassed? I was absolutely mortified.

7 Emphasise to students that we can set our compositions apart through a more precise use of vocabulary.

Degree of difficulty

Increase the level: Consider setting the short story writing task for question 7 as a test or as homework. Make sure students can't share their ideas. Afterwards, choose the most creative/correct stories and share them with the class (anonymously if you feel students will be embarrassed).

Decrease the level: If you feel that your students are not ready to write a short story for question 7, consider handing out copies of texts which they can scan for further examples. You could prepare several examples of short stories, such as the one in the Writing Guide, or the next page.

Paragraph one: Set the scene. Say what happened before the focus of the story. Notice the use of 'used to' and the past perfect.

When I was small I used to fly on holiday with my family. Yet, by my twenties I had become absolutely terrified of flying – and the older I got, the worse it became. When my parents retired to Spain I realised I needed to do something. As if by magic, I read about a course that helped people like me.

absolutely terrified = non-gradable adjective

Paragraph two: The focus of the story.

On the big day, I drove to the airport and entered the seminar room where fifty other people of all ages were waiting nervously. First of all, an airline pilot – a kind-looking man in his fifties – welcomed us. Afterwards he explained how a plane worked and answered our questions.

Notice the use of *first of all*, *afterwards*, to put events in order.

Paragraph three: The climax of the story. The big event is the flight.

Over lunch, I talked to different people and realised I wasn't alone. By now, I was ready for our twenty minute flight. Even though it took all of my courage to board the plane, take off was as smooth as possible. When I glanced out of the window, I thought how wonderful it was.

flight, take off = good use of topic vocabulary

Notice the use of 'even though' to make a contrast.

glance = a verb of manner

Paragraph four: Conclusion, ending with the words we were given.

Nowadays I take planes everywhere and wonder why I had been so worried. I can honestly say that it was a day which changed my life for ever.

Photocopiable activity instructions

Activity 5.1: Word search: A Good Story

Aim: To revise consolidate vocabulary on topic of books and TV.

Instructions:

1   Give puzzle to students individually or in pairs.

2   Demonstrate activity by identifying two or three words in the word-square.

Activity 5.2: Picture composition: *But who ate the cake* and *Harvey gets what he deserves*

Aim: To practise narrative tenses.

Instructions:

1a   Treat the stories as a straightforward picture composition where students say what is going on in the pictures.

1b   Alternatively, mix the pictures up and ask the students to reorder them as they think fit. This could also be carried out as an information gap activity in pairs where students initially describe their picture and decide what is going on and in what order.

2   Either way, make sure that students use a wide range of narrative tenses and a variety of ways of ordering events.

Picture Composition One is in random order. You don't need to chop and change it before showing your students. It shows a woman who invites a relative over for a meal. The guests decide to bring a cake. When they arrive, the cake gets placed on a table near a window. After the meal, they realise the dog has eaten the cake, and is hiding in the bushes outside!

Picture Composition Two is in the correct order. If you want your students to work it out in order, you need to cut between the squares and hand out in a mixed-up fashion. It begins in 1970. It shows a young elephant performing at the circus. It then shows a couple of young boys taunting the elephant with a stick. It skips ahead to the year 2000, where it shows the same boy as an adult, at the circus. The elephant recognises the man as the boy who teased him 30 years earlier. The boy is now running for President. The elephant squirts water all over him. It makes national headlines.

'A Good Story' solution:

Tapescript 5

Listening 5.1

One I spent most of my time travelling around on a horse with my servant trying to rescue young ladies from dragons, and fighting giants. People said I was crazy.

Two I just wanted to be left alone but a horrible priest fell in love with me. I was rescued by a hunchback. He was a nice guy but so intense. He used to ring the bells at the cathedral, you know.

Three Well I came up with this great idea to trick the enemy. We got into Troy inside a wooden horse, and that was the end of the war. It took me another ten years to find my way home and I had lots of adventures and had to fight a giant.

Four I wasn't born as such – my dad, he wanted a son so badly that he made me from pieces of wood. I became just like any other little boy, but each time I told a lie (and I used to lie a *lot*) – my nose grew, and kept on growing.

Listening 5.2

Lorolei: So, Jacinta, how did you get into adapting books for the cinema?

Jacinta: Well, by accident really. I started off editing scripts for radio plays, then I had the chance to join a team writing for a TV series – a soap opera if you like. Then one day I was asked if I'd be interested in adapting a book by Thomas Hardy for the radio, and one thing led to another.

Lorolei: So tell me, how do you begin adapting a book, or a piece of literature for the screen? What do you need to know before you begin?

Jacinta: Well, there are two main things really. First of all what the story is, you know, if it's a long novel with hundreds of chapters, or a short story or play. And the second thing is the medium – is it going to be for the big screen, you know a movie for the cinema, or for TV.

Lorolei: And I know you've done both … adapt for both TV and the cinema … but which do you prefer?

Jacinta: Well, it may seem strange, but all things considered, I'd rather adapt a classic, say a novel by Dickens, for the small screen.

Lorolei: Why is that, then?

Jacinta: Well, even though the budget is smaller, you have more time to do justice to the original. For instance, instead of two hours to tell your tale you may have, six, ten, or even twelve one-hour episodes. In a long serial you can take it at a slower pace, and focus much more on the development of the personalities of the characters. Another thing is you can include some of the smaller characters and sub-plots which you would just have to cut for a film.

Lorolei: Is it just a question of time, or is there anything else?

Jacinta: Well, the other thing of course is that for most films, if you are making something for the cinema, you know for the big screen,

which has to appeal to a large audience, you have to introduce an element of spectacle.

Lorolei: Spectacle?

Jacinta: Yes, you know, breathtaking scenery, battle scenes, chariot races – the sort of thing which is going to fill the cinema screen. Something to make the audience say 'Wow!' I don't know if you've seen the recent big screen adaptation of *Pride and Prejudice*?

Lorolei: The one with Keira Knightley as the heroine, Elizabeth Bennett?

Jacinta: Yes, that's the one. Well, essentially the novel itself is a domestic drama, not the subject of a typical big budget movie. But the director made a really big thing of the big formal dances, the balls. And of course it looked magnificent and the attention to period detail was fabulous, you could only really appreciate it at a big cinema, but, of course, it took up a lot of time which could have been dedicated to other aspects of the story. I prefer the adaptation the BBC did a few years ago, but that's probably because I've got a thing for Colin Firth, the actor who played the hero, Mr Darcy.

Lorolei: I know what you mean! So, how free do you feel to change the story?

Jacinta: Well, I know some people take enormous liberties when they are adapting a book – you know they'll mess around with the plot or change the ending. Personally, I try to be as faithful to the original book as I can. In my view, if you want to do your own thing, that's fine, but then you should create something original.

Listening 5.3

Lorolei: But can film, and here I'm talking about TV as well as the cinema, can it ever be superior to the written word?

Jacinta: Mm … yes. It is much more economical in terms of time … you know … setting the scene and so on. With just a couple of seconds of camera work, you can set a scene which, in a classic novel, would take pages and pages of description. If you choose the right location, go to where the book was set with the right scenery, the effect is immediate.

Lorolei: So a picture is worth a thousand words. And is there anything that film or TV can't do?

Jacinta: Oh yes, lots. For me the biggest thing is the narrator, you know the storyteller's voice, if you like. Although it's easy to use dialogue straight from the page it's very difficult to do that with the narrator's voice, unless, that is, you are going to have voice-overs every few minutes.

Lorolei: Can you give me an example of that?

Jacinta: Well, the one which immediately comes to mind is *Vanity Fair*. Now *Vanity Fair* is a story about a young woman called Becky Sharp who will do anything to rise in society.

Lorolei: Yes, she's the ultimate social climber.

Jacinta: Absolutely – she is a terrible, heartless, ruthless young woman. Now in the original book by Thackeray, the narrator is always looking down on the action, you know making comments on what's going on. This, in my opinion, is what makes the book. But recently, when *Vanity Fair* was turned into a blockbuster, well this was missing. OK, it was wonderful to look at. There were some fabulous scenes and

the costumes were breathtaking. Yet, the thing is, *despite* having a huge budget, *despite* its cast of stars, there was something missing from the film, which made it rather empty, in my view.

Lorolei: And that 'thing' which was missing was the narrator's voice.

Jacinta: Exactly.

Answer key 5

Getting Started p45
1 From left to right, top to bottom: Esmeralda and the hunchback of Notre Dame; Romeo and Juliet; Alice in Wonderland; Don Quixote; Pinocchio; Sherlock Holmes; Aladdin; Odysseus.
2 Speaker 1: Don Quixote (by the Spanish author Cervantes).
Speaker 2 Esmeralda (from *The Hunchback of Notre Dame* by Victor Hugo).
Speaker 3 Odysseus/Ulysses (from *The Odyssey* by Homer).
Speaker 4 Pinocchio (from *The Adventures of Pinocchio* by Carlo Collodi).

Vocabulary p46
1 Genres: thrillers, crime and detective novels, spy stories, adventure, historical fiction, romances, (auto)biography, cartoon stories, comic books, fiction, classical literature, travel, horror, science fiction, fantasy, war stories.
2 1 series
2 playwright/novelist
3 serial/episodes
4 classic/chapters
5 heroine/characters
6 plots
7 script
8 narrator
9 scene
10 location/scenery
11 set
12 fiction/novel
13 villain
14 mythology

Listening p47
2 1B; 2B; 3C; 4B; 5A; 6B; 7C
3 1 more economical/quicker

2 many pages
3 location
4 narrator
5 dialogue
6 voice-overs
7 rise in society
8 going on
9 wonderful
10 narrator's voice

Key word p47
1 1f; 2c; 3e; 4a; 5b; 6d

Reading p48
1 'The last honest woman' is probably the best title, as everybody else in the story appears to be dishonest.
2 2D; 3C; 4C; 5D; 6A; 7A; 8C

Vocabulary p50
1 1a; 2b; 3b; 4b
2 a: 2, 3 (staring), 7; b: 3 (slurping), 6: c: 1; d: 5, 8, 10; e: 4, 9

Grammar p50
1 Simple past: went; glanced; sat; smiled; turned; thought; leaned; addressed.
2 Past continuous: were sipping
3 Past perfect: had witnessed; had not seen
2 1 simple past
2 past continuous
3 past perfect
3 1 while the trader was searching = past continuous
2 as she was leaving the café = past continuous
3 had been following everything = past perfect continuous
4 were looking at the stalls, traders were selling their goods ... Mma R was waiting = past continuous.

4 a4; b1; c3; d2
5 1 had been going
2 met
3 felt
4 bought
5 was
6 had prepared
7 picked
8 was waiting
9 had driven
10 made
11 had reached
12 driven
13 were sailing
14 dived
15 was
6 16 ate
17 had prepared
18 drank
19 was going to give
20 noticed
21 had already fallen asleep
22 yawned
23 was having
24 was woken
25 were having
26 had come in
27 was surrounding/had surrounded/surrounded

Writing p52
4 disappointed/devastated
pleased/delighted
embarrassed/mortified
tired/exhausted
frightened/terrified
stupid/ridiculous
lovely/gorgeous
bad/terrible
5 1 Yes, I felt mortified.
2 Yes, she was devastated.
3 Yes, I feel terrible.
4 Yes, they were delighted.
5 Yes, you look ridiculous!
6 a non-gradable adjectives: furious,

delighted, fabulous, gorgeous; mortified; ghastly.
b descriptive verbs: glanced, gasping, sipping, staggering
c adverbs of manner: nastily, admiringly desperately

Review p54
1 1C; 2B; 3C; 4A; 5D; 6C; 7B; 8A; 9C; 10A; 11D; 12C
2 1 than
2 by
3 on/about
4 little
5 asked
6 hardly
7 Instead/Rather
8 series/serial/programme
9 come/spring
10 so
11 despite
12 about
3 laughing: *giggle, snigger*
walking: *stagger, limp, stroll*
breathing: *sigh, gasp*
looking: *glance, gaze, glare, stare*
drinking: *slurp, sip, gulp*
4 1 limp
2 stare
3 glare
4 gasp
5 glance
6 stroll
7 sip
8 snigger
9 gaze
10 slurp
11 sigh
12 stagger
13 giggle
14 gulp
5 2 delighted
3 gorgeous
4 mortified
5 terrified

A Good Story

J	N	Q	N	J	E	Z	G	B	N	X	T	G	N	N	E	F	M	I	P
E	D	O	S	I	P	E	L	I	J	Z	S	E	Q	K	U	K	L	D	F
N	H	B	V	E	Y	V	A	I	R	P	P	E	C	J	G	W	A	K	A
F	O	H	H	E	W	L	T	S	A	C	C	B	R	U	O	T	P	H	H
S	Y	I	A	T	L	B	W	R	C	W	W	S	P	I	L	B	S	J	I
E	U	Q	T	I	Y	I	G	B	H	U	N	A	R	R	A	T	O	R	M
R	H	H	V	C	K	M	S	B	A	V	E	G	D	Z	I	L	V	D	E
I	Z	Y	R	T	I	C	Z	T	P	L	E	G	E	N	D	U	Q	O	N
E	X	I	O	E	U	F	G	S	T	J	F	T	S	Q	F	J	M	O	Q
S	G	H	I	P	T	T	A	U	E	V	F	O	K	Q	U	B	I	E	X
J	S	Y	S	Q	E	C	X	H	R	B	S	L	X	Y	N	T	G	N	R
T	H	G	I	R	W	Y	A	L	P	C	A	P	Q	J	A	H	P	I	V
I	G	F	I	U	Z	Y	W	R	E	J	Y	E	Y	C	A	P	U	O	T
U	Z	N	B	V	F	H	R	N	A	K	N	J	O	C	S	Q	C	R	G
O	X	Y	Z	W	A	A	E	U	P	H	I	L	O	O	Y	X	E	E	V
U	Q	R	Y	B	H	M	A	L	Q	G	C	S	O	M	V	X	C	H	P
L	K	C	M	I	P	D	N	S	E	T	T	Z	R	F	U	Z	I	K	B
W	Q	U	E	A	Z	O	N	A	F	U	N	Y	C	D	N	V	Y	F	O
K	U	M	S	G	M	V	S	I	M	E	J	O	U	A	E	H	O	G	F
E	T	H	R	G	M	M	F	E	T	C	Q	U	B	K	G	O	Y	F	R

CAST	HEROINE	PLOT
CHAPTER	LEGEND	SCENE
CHARACTER	LOCATION	SERIAL
COSTUME	MYTH	SERIES
DIALOGUE	NARRATOR	SET
EPISODE	NOVELIST	SHOT
FICTION	PLAYWRIGHT	VILLAIN

PHOTOCOPIABLE 5.1

But who ate the cake?

PHOTOCOPIABLE 5.2a

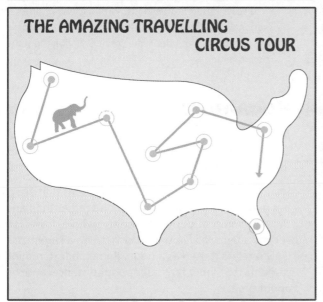

Harvey gets what he deserves ...

PHOTOCOPIABLE 5.2b

6 Transport and travel

Before you begin

Introduce the topic by asking students their opinions about different types of transport. Remind students that **transport** is both a noun and a verb. As a noun, it means the aeroplane or lorry, etc, which is used to move people or goods. As a verb, it means to transfer or convey from one place to another.

> Which type of transport is the most efficient? exciting? romantic? interesting? dangerous?

> I think that sailing a yacht at sunset is very romantic ...

Topic: Transport and travel

This unit deals with the theme of vehicle types, and travelling. At FCE level, students should be able to talk with ease about their travel plans and experiences. This unit also examines ways of expressing the future and a set of phrasal verbs associated with travel and transport.

Unit 6 Wordlist:

anguished	irresistible	spectacular
attendance	itinerary	spoilt/unspoilt
brochure	journey	stillness
celebration	meet up with	take off
check in	package holiday	take out
check out	pageant	timetable
commuter	pastures	tour
crossing	phone back	tourist/tourism
domination	pick up	travel around
drop off	popularity	travel(s)/traveller
endless	put up	trip
excursion	reminder	tunnel
ferry	resort	turn up
flea market	set off	unrivalled
flight	show around	voyage
gruelling	sightseeing	waxed
guide book	souvenir	waned
indigenous	spectacle/	wilderness

Getting started

1   Answers will depend on how far students have to travel to class. Make sure that they use the correct preposition: *on foot* (not by feet), *by car, train, bus,* etc. You could lead into a general discussion about public transport in your town/country.

2   Students identify the vehicles in question.

3   Pair a brighter, more creative student with a less imaginative one.

4   Remind candidates that these are similar to the kind of follow-up questions we find in the Speaking Paper, part 4.

TEACHING IN PRACTICE

Teaching monolingual/different nationalities
If you have a monolingual class, you could ask different pairs to discuss different questions. With a group of different nationalities, this is one of those rare occasions where we can have students from the same country working together to pool their ideas.

Vocabulary: confusable words

Aim: As this exercise focuses on confusable vocabulary, it allows a starting point for making sure students understand the differences between such words.

Students will be familiar with all the items that are covered, but may not know where to use one rather than another. We should remind students that on the whole, *travel* is used as a verb or adjectivally in words such as 'travel agent/travel card'. Only rarely is it used as a noun. Remember to remind your students that 'how far?' asks about distance, and 'how long?' about time.

Typical mistake learners make are:

> ~~Did you enjoy your travel?~~
> Did you enjoy your trip?

> ~~I'm going on a travel next month.~~
> I'm going on a journey next month.

2   Differences between definitions:

A **package holiday** is a holiday where everything, or nearly everything, is included in the price (flights, hotel, meals, etc).	A holiday **resort** is a popular tourist destination, which usually depends on the tourist industry for its existence and survival (like a ski-resort).

A **brochure**, or specifically travel brochure contains details about holidays and package tours.	A **guide book** gives us information about what to visit, where to eat and stay and so on when we travel as a tourist.
A **timetable** gives us the departure and arrival times of different forms of transport.	An **itinerary** is the travel programme for a particular trip.
A **commuter** is someone who works in the city and lives in the suburbs or the countryside. A commuter travels backwards and forwards to work – usually by train or public transport.	A **traveller** is simply someone who travels.
A **souvenir** is something you buy on holiday to remind yourself about the place you visited.	A **reminder** is something like a post-it note that you put on your fridge to remind yourself to do something.
When we talk about a country's national **heritage** we mean the things that belong to the whole nation such as museums and monuments.	**Sightseeing** is the activity of visiting such places.
A **trip** is usually a short visit to one place, such as a weekend trip to Stonehenge, or a business trip to Vienna.	An **excursion** is an organised visit to a place of interest. It is often by coach and includes a guided tour.

Listening: travel and visits

Degree of difficulty

Increase the level: If you feel you have a strong class, you could miss out this question and move directly on to the exam-style practice.

1 This first question encourages students to listen for gist. Note that the extracts contain various ways of expressing the future that will be examined in the grammar section.

2 Multiple choice: this is similar in style to part 1 of the Listening exam. Here, however, the extracts are linked by the topic of travel. Remind students that in the examination itself these extracts would be unrelated. Play the recording all the way through and allow students to confer. Listen in at a distance to get an overall idea of how well they have managed the questions. If necessary, play the recording again, pausing after each passage for answers and feedback.

Listening (Paper 4, part 1)
Sometimes questions focus on feelings, relationships and attitudes rather than simple facts. Ask students which of the questions they have just answered focus on these areas.

Vocabulary: travel

p/c 6.1

This section deals with a number of phrasal verbs commonly used in travel and tourism. Students match the phrasal verbs in the box with the highlighted words in Questions 1–12. Point out to the students that the dots between the verbs in the box (e.g. *put ... up*) show that the phrasal verb is separable. Refer students to Section 12.3 of the Grammar Reference if necessary. Do the first two questions as examples, then allow the students to do the rest on their own.

Pronunciation: phrasal verbs
In feedback to the exercise, make sure that you practise liaison between the consonants and the vowels of the particles that follow.
For example: e.g. set off, check in

4 This 'game' adds a competitive/fun element to the lesson. Make sure that the rules, such as one 'go' per team, are followed strictly – otherwise it could descend into undisciplined chaos!

Particles and meaning in phrasal verbs
It can be useful to focus on the particle of phrasal verbs: in certain situations, the particle may have an inherent meaning. A word of caution: we shouldn't search too hard to establish relationships between the inherent meaning of a particle and phrasal verbs as, unfortunately, this is often not at all clear!

Speaking: organising a schedule

Aim: to give students practice in interactive activities and 'problem solving'; to practise the vocabulary and phrasal verbs that have already been dealt with in the unit.

2 Ask the students to work in groups and come up with a programme that will suit the entire family. Appoint a spokesperson for each group to present their programme.

Grammar: expressing the future

This section provides a general revision of the different ways of expressing the future in English. The main problem students have is to over-use *will*. Even though *will* is a clear and unambiguous marker for the future, native speakers use it in a fairly limited fashion. If you want to give students an all-purpose way of expressing the future, tell them that *going to* is nearly always correct. It is a good alternative to *will*.

10 Put the students into pairs or groups for this exercise. Tell them that the aim is practise the different ways of expressing the future you have just covered. Pause after each prompt to give students time to formulate a response.

Suggested answers:

1 So, tell me, *what are you doing* for your holidays/ next summer/next year?

2 Excuse me, when does the next bus to Cambridge leave?
   Could you tell what time/when the next bus to Cambridge leaves?
   How long *does* it/the journey *take*? How long *does* it *take* to get there?

3 It's *likely* that China will win the most medals. China is bound to win.

4 I'll phone you as soon as I've heard something.

5 I'll be leaving/I'm leaving/planning to leave in about half an hour. I should be at your place by five. I will/should have arrived by five.

6 I'll have finished my studies. I'll be working as a nurse in a big hospital.

7 Don't blame me. I didn't know/ I had no idea it was going to be (so) awful. It's not my fault!

8 Oh dear, Marina should have been here by now. I wonder what can have happened. I hope she hasn't had an accident.

Listening: travel arrangements

1 Students look at the map and identify the different places mentioned. Check understanding (pre-teach) the words *ferry*, *tunnel* and *motorway*.

> What possible routes are available?

> What are the pros and cons of each route?

> Which route they would take?

> Where they are setting off from?

> What is their destination?

The main difficulty students are likely to have is distinguishing between the two male speakers, Loïc and Marco. Loïc has a light French accent, while Marco has a

light Italian one. The speed of the conversation could also pose problems.

2 Although not presented as such, this three-way conversation and 'who said what?' task *could* be the type of question to appear in part 4 of the Listening examination. Give students a minute to read through the questions. Remind them that this is an essential examination technique. Play the recording through. Allow students to compare answers then gather feedback.

Listening extension

If time allows, ask students to study the script and create three or four further 'who says' questions.

> Who doesn't mind driving?

> Loïc doesn't mind driving.

Speaking: discussing options

p/c 6.2

Aim: to provide students with ways of discussing options; to examine how the simple past is used to discuss unreal situations, and as a rule of form after the expressions *it's time/would rather* + pronoun.

1 Students work together and match examples of use to their definitions. Gather feedback, making sure that their pronunciation is accurate.

2 Check that they are clear that **'d better** is *had better* not *would better*. Focus on the stress of *always* when saying 'We could **always** hire a car...'

3 Compare the two pairs of sentences. Quite simply, this is a rule of form. If a noun or pronoun is used after *it's time* or *would rather* then the simple past is used. Point out that nevertheless the simple past is used with a present meaning! It is something that should be happening. For example, *leaving* isn't happening.

TEACHING IN PRACTICE

Concept questions
You could try using these concept questions:
It's time we left.
Teacher: Have we left?
Students: No.
Teacher: Are we leaving?
Students: No.
Teacher: But should we/is it a good idea to leave?
Students: Yes!

4 Put students in groups of three or four in separate parts of the classroom. If students are unable to choose a city, ask them to select one of the following: Paris, Shanghai, New York, Sydney, London, Venice, or Barcelona.

Reading: dream holidays

1   Lead into the topic with a brief all-class discussion.

Dream holidays

The four holidays in this reading text are set in very different, and quite remote, areas of the world. Your students may find the texts more interesting if you lead-in with some general knowledge regarding these places.

Anchorage: It is the largest city in the US state of Alaska (population approximately 250 000). It lies slightly farther north than St Petersburg. It has unpredictable weather, but often experiences large downfalls of snow in winter. Being so northern, its days are long in summer, and very short in winter. It was first established as railway construction port in 1914.

Buenos Aires: It is the capital city of the South American country Argentina (population 13 million). In English, the name means *Fair winds*. The city was established around 1530. Buenos Aires has a temperate climate, with average temperatures in January of about 30 degrees Celsius (86 degrees Fahrenheit).

Masai Mara: It is a large park reserve in south-western Kenya (population approximately 900 000). At approximately 1500 square kilometres, it is not the largest game park in Africa, but it is probably the most famous, and extends from the Mediterranean Sea to South Africa. It is inhabited by (now endangered) species of lion, cheetah, black rhinoceros, hippopotami and wildebeests. The Masai people have lived here for over 300 years. Europeans first arrived in the 1800s.

Rovaniemi: It is situated close to the Arctic circle, in Finland (population 60 000). The word *Rovaniemi* has often been considered to be of Lappish origin: 'roavve' in Sami denotes a forested ridge or hill or the site of an old forest fire. There has probably been continuous settlement in the area since the Stone Age. Besides Santa's village, the 'Northern Lights' also provide another reason to visit Rovaniemi.

Scanning

Even though students will probably be effective readers in their own languages, and scan texts effortlessly and efficiently to extract information, in a foreign language they may lose this skill and try to read word-by-word. They will often get stuck on unknown items. The aim of this exercise is to help them transfer skills they have in their own language (and their own 'virtuous' reading behaviour) to English. Set a time limit of between three and five minutes according to the age and abilities of your class. In feedback, focus on the information being correct; do not worry of they are grammatically inaccurate. The focus of this section is developing reading skills.

2   Give students thirty seconds to have a very quick look at the texts to put the destinations into a notional order.

3   Give students a further ten minutes to complete the exercise.

4   Students work in pairs or groups.

Vocabulary: words in context

This exercise gives students practice in deducing the meanings of words from their context. Demonstrate the activity by taking two or three definitions and finding the words with the whole class.

Speaking: discussing your travels

Aim: to give students some practice in everyday conversation and exchanges.

1   Run through the questions and comments. Sound lively and enthusiastic and where necessary drill. Choose a bright communicative student and demonstrate the activity to the whole class, taking it in turns to ask the questions and provide the answers. Ask students to make their choice of destination, either from the texts they have just read or from their personal experience and set the activity in motion. If space allows treat this as a milling activity where the class moves around and practises conversation with several different partners – this will give volumes of practice.

Key word: *just*

This exercise focuses on *just*, which has a number of different meanings in everyday conversation.

1   (adverb) use to indicate that something has happened very recently.
I just got married!

2   (adverb) use to imply that you are about to finish doing something very soon.
I'll just be another minute.

3   (adverb) use to indicate that something is no more important, interesting or difficult as you say it is.
Oh, it's just Ali on the phone …

4   (adverb) use to admit that it may be the case, but only slightly so.
Perhaps it is just a little over-cooked?

5   (adverb) use to mean exactly or precisely.
That's just perfect!

6   (adjective) use to describe a situation, action or idea as right or acceptable.
The judge's decision was quite just.

Writing: a report

One of the possible genre types for part two of the writing paper is producing a short report. This section focuses on areas students frequently find difficult:
• producing sub-headings
• introductory sentences
• comparing and contrasting ideas
• and writing conclusions.

Refer your students to this section in the Writing Guide if necessary.

TEACHING IN PRACTICE

Writing as a process

Students often do not know how to prepare and start a piece of written work. They may have the unrealistic expectation of passing directly from an essay title to the finished article. The reality is different. Even expert writers admit that they follow a process. First, we gather our ideas, select and reject those we wish to use, produce a plan, create a first draft, make changes and edit, find suitable subheadings, produce the final draft. It is important that we guide them and help them with this process, and show them how necessary it is.

3   This will probably work best as a whole class activity. Write the subheadings on the board and elicit ideas from the students to write beneath each heading.

How to answer question 5 thoroughly:

	Email	Report
Layout	Long continuous text	Shorter paragraphs with subheadings
Vocabulary	Less formal (e.g. *a lot of parents came*)	More formal (e.g. *the well-attended meeting*)
Expressions	Active and personal	Passive and impersonal

Note: The use of the passive means that the report says what was decided or suggested, but not who made the suggestion. In the report, the subject is also used in an impersonal way: *Those present* decided … *The next proposal was …*

Report writing (Paper 2, part 2)

6 Suggested answers:

a Introduction: Homelessness – a growing problem among young people.

b The results of family breakdown – divorce, new step parent, leave home, run away.

c Fear and friendship on the streets – safe to be in a group/gang.

d The dangers of street life: danger from criminals, drugs, prostitution; feelings of hopelessness.

Photocopiable activity instructions

Activity 6.1: Board game: Introducing your town

Aim: Fluency; to practise functional language and phrasal verbs.

Instructions:

1   Students move around the board according to the toss of the coins.

2   Monitor the activity from a distance, and note problem areas. If students are too inaccurate, then stop the activity and revise the language implicit in the answers. Ideally students should have an acceptable level of accuracy as well as being fluent.

Activity 6.2: Cued-dialogue (based around information files)

Aim: To practise question making; to consolidate the vocabulary of travel and tourism.

Instructions:

1   Put the students in two large groups (Students A and Students B).

2   Run through the information files with each group in turn and check that everyone understands the task.

3   Ask them to brainstorm what questions they will ask based on the prompts.

4   When you feel the students are ready, make pairs of A and B students taking one from each group.

5   Demonstrate the activity by running through an example with a bright and self-confident student.

6   Students work in their own pairs. If you want volume of practice, ask students to practise the activity with different partners.

Tapescript 6

Listening 6.1

One

Harry: Hi, Sophie. Nice to see you. You're going to university this autumn, aren't you?

Sophie: Hi, Uncle Harry. Well, actually I've decided not to go this year. I'm going to take a gap year and travel around the States. I'm planning to get a job as a nanny or waitress or something like that. Apparently even if you just turn up you can find something quite quickly. Otherwise, I might try and join a voluntary organisation … you know … do some work in Africa. Don't say anything to mum and dad though, will you, Uncle Harry? I haven't told them yet!

Two

Mark: Hello. This is Mark Wilson. I'm afraid I'm not able to take your call right now, but please leave a message after the beep.

Juan: Mark, hi it's Juan. Just to say that I'm setting off at three o'clock. The journey takes about three and a half to four hours which means I should get to the exhibition centre at around seven. Hope that's not too late. Anyway, will you, or somebody else from the office, be able to come and help me unload the van? There's a lot of stuff and I won't be able to do it on my own. Can you call me back on my mobile?

Three

Sharon: I hate the whole thing of organised holidays and excursions. I'm really into couch surfing. That's where you meet someone on the internet who will then put you up for a couple of days on their sofa and show you around. It's great, honest, for a short trip somewhere … who cares if it's a bit uncomfortable? I've just come back from Prague where I spent two nights on this guy's sofa. He showed me around places you'd never find in a guide book. It was brilliant. I've had some fascinating and unexpected experiences on my travels. You should give couch surfing a try, I'll mail you the website details.

Four

Blanka: Now, listen please … Professor Heron's flight takes off at three and lands at four fifteen; I'm going to meet him with Marika. A taxi is due to pick us up at the airport and drop us off at his hotel. Marika will help Professor Heron check in and make sure he knows the arrangements. Now, he'll be tired after the journey so he's bound to need some time to himself. If we plan to meet at around eight he'll have had time to freshen up and relax. We'll take him to the conference centre and show him where he's giving his talks. Remember, he likes everything to be perfectly organised so it's very, very important that *everything* goes smoothly. Afterwards we'll take him out for dinner at the new restaurant at the Hilton.

Five

Seb: Listen, everyone. Kate will be waiting at the station. She'll call as soon as Mum has left the station to say that she's on her way home. She's likely to be feeling a bit sad. Now, the lights are going to be off, and I want everyone to hide in the kitchen with the food and drink. The kids can go behind the sofa – *not a sound*, OK … so when Mum opens the door and walks into the sitting room, everyone will shout 'Happy retirement!' She really deserves it after twenty five years of commuting backwards and forwards to London.

Six

Kim: It's not a hotel; it's a building site! And we have to cross a main road to get to the beach. Someone is going to get hurt, I can see it happening. I wouldn't come here again if they were *giving* holidays away.

David: Well don't blame me. I didn't know it was going to be like this. It was supposed to be a package holiday in a *luxury* resort!

Kim: Well, you should have chosen a holiday from a *real* brochure, from a *proper* travel agent – not a so-called last minute bargain off the Internet. Next time we go away *I'm* in charge!

Seven

Dagmara: This evening we could go and visit the old town. We're very proud of our heritage here. There are some lovely squares and monuments and I could show you around a bit. What do you think? Later on we can meet up with some of the others from head office and eat out in a nice restaurant in the old town.

Roy: That sounds brilliant. I'd like to do a bit of sightseeing and maybe get a couple of souvenirs … you know … the kids always expect to me to buy them something when I'm away!

Eight

Waiter: Welcome signora. Are you ready to order?

Gemma: Yes, I think so. I'd like to try some of the local specialities. I'll begin with the artichokes and Parma ham.

Waiter: Yes madam, and for your main course?

Gemma: Can you tell me what the special is?

Waiter: Ah yes, it's baby cow, cooked in the milk of the mother.

Gemma: Mm, no thanks. That's enough to turn you into a vegetarian. I think I'll have the spaghetti bolognese, if that's OK.

Listening 6.2

One To present yourself and register at a hotel or airport.

Two To give somebody somewhere to sleep for the night.

Three To choose.

Four To entertain another person by taking them to, say, a bar or restaurant.

Five To leave on a trip or a journey.

Six To have a wash and change your clothes after a journey.

Seven To move from place to place.

Eight To take someone in your car and let them out at the destination.

Nine To arrive or present yourself somewhere; often late or without warning.

Ten To have a meal in a restaurant.

Eleven To give someone a guided tour of somewhere.

Twelve To have a rendezvous.

Thirteen To collect someone in your car.

Fourteen To give something free of charge.

Fifteen To take a break.

Sixteen To delay something until a later date.

Listening 6.3

One Tell each other about your plans for next weekend or your next major holiday.

Two You want to know the time of the next coach from Oxford to Cambridge. You would also like to know the journey time.

Three Make some predictions about the results of the next elections or your country's performance in the World Cup or Olympic Games.

Four A neighbour has telephoned to find out if your friend has had her baby. Promise to phone the moment you have some news.

Five You are phoning a friend to tell him or her about your travel plans. You are planning to leave your home in half an hour. Even though the traffic is heavy, you believe that you can be there by five o'clock if everything goes to plan.

Six You are in a job interview. One of the interviewers asks how you see yourself in five years' time. Make some predictions about your position in five years, and some of your achievements between now and then.

Seven You have just left the cinema. The film was awful and the people you are with are criticising you for having suggested it. Defend yourself!

Eight The roads are icy and you're starting to get worried. You expected your friend, Marina, to arrive half an hour ago. What do you say to yourself?

Listening 6.4

Tess: It's time we decided about our travel arrangements. I mean, if we leave it too late the prices will have rocketed.

Loïc: We'd better make up our minds then. I suppose we could take the tunnel and then drive all the way down.

Tess: What do you think, Marco?

Marco: It's a long way and the motorway charges will be high.

Loïc: Mm, I know what you mean, and we shouldn't forget the petrol.

Tess: We could fly, you know, take one of these low cost flights and then we could always hire a car if we need one when we get there. We should be able to afford that.

Loic: But wouldn't that end up just as expensive as driving?

Marco: Yes, but driving down could be part of the holiday, couldn't it? I don't mind spending a few days stopping off at different places.

Tess: OK, but personally I'd rather we got there as quickly as possible. We only have two weeks. I don't really want to spend a lot of time just getting there.

Loïc: I was just about to say the same thing. I just want to lie on a beach and relax.

Tess: I've got to say too I am a bit nervous about driving. I've never driven on the continent before.

Loïc: That doesn't bother me. I don't mind doing the driving.

Marco: And I could share it with you.

Tess: Not the way you drive, Marco! I tell you what, why don't I take the plane and meet you down there!

Loïc: Very funny. Hold on. I've just had an idea. There is another option. What if we took the ferry from Portsmouth, across to Brittany? It would make the journey at the other end a lot shorter.

Marco: And if we took a night crossing, it would give us a night's sleep and then we could get down there by the middle of the afternoon. We'll have gained an extra day.

Tess: The ferry. Mm, I like that idea. But before I look at prices, does anyone suffer from sea sickness?!

Answer key 6

Vocabulary p56

1 1 travel
2 travels
3 journey
4 trip
5 take
6 far
7 flight

Listening p56

1 1 Not very clear; she still isn't sure of the details.
2 Juan might be a salesperson or perhaps a van driver.
3 She uses the Internet to find free accommodation ('couchsurfing' – sleeping on people's sofas).
4 He is some kind of VIP. It sounds like he is quite a demanding person.
5 (i) Quite sad (she has just retired from her job).
(ii) Surprised and excited.
6 They are in a hotel room overlooking a building site.
7 Business
8 Gemma is not very adventurous.
2 1C; 2B; 3A; 4C; 5C; 6A; 7B; 8B

Vocabulary p57

1 1 drop you off
2 check in
3 set off
4 put me up
5 phone me back
6 pick you up
7 travel around
8 turn up
9 show you around
10 meeting up with
11 taken off
12 take you out
2 1 back
2 off
3 up
3 1 return money you have borrowed
2 start a match

3 begin something new
4 1 check in
2 put (someone) up
3 go for
4 take someone out
5 set off
6 freshen up
7 travel around
8 drop someone off
9 turn up
10 eat out
11 show around
12 meet up with
13 pick up
14 give away
15 get away
16 put off

Grammar p58

1 a present continuous
b present simple
c 'going to' future
d future simple
2 1a; 2c; 3d; 4b
3 1 shall we do
2 'll phone
3 shall we get/are we going to get
4 'll buy/going to buy
5 'll get/going to get
6 is going to buy
7 'm going to get
4 Predictions 1a, 2b, 3b
5 Advice: 2a, offer: 3a, intention: 1b
6 the future perfect – c
the future in the past – b
the future continuous – a
7 1a; 2b; 3c
8 1 will have sunk
2 will have already found
3 was going to break down
4 will be eating/(will) be watching
5 will have had
6 'll be waiting
7 was going to be
8 will have eaten
9 1c; 2b; 3a

Listening p59

2 1 Loïc; 2 Marco; 3 Tess; 4 Tess; 5 Tess; 6 Marco; 7 Tess

Speaking p59

1 a4; b1; c2; d3
2 a always; b had (*not* would)
3 1 The past simple
2 We have to follow the pronoun with the past simple.

Reading p60

3 1973: Year of the first Iditarod race.
$600,000: The total amount of prize money.
1,149 miles: The length of the race.
600,000: The number of letters Santa Claus receives each year in Lapland.
Serengeti: 'Endless plains' in the Masai language.
2,500 metres: The height of the balloon ride.
1935: The year of Carlos Gardel's death
El Viejo Almacén: Large dance hall where you can dance, or see the tango.
Plaza Dorrego: This is a flea market in Buenos Aires where you can see amateur dancers of the tango.
4 1D; 2A; 3C; 4B; 5B; 6C; 7B; 8D; 9A; 10A; 11A; 12B; 13D; 14A; 15C

Vocabulary p61

1 A: show up; gruelling; wilderness; cheer on
B: tormented; waxed and waned; dimly-lit; flea market
C: pageant; pasture; marvel; spectacular/awesome
D: indigenous; jovial; nominal fee; myriad
2 legendary; spectacular; remarkable; protected
3 unspoilt; unrivalled; irresistible; endless

4 stillness; celebration; attendance; popularity; domination; shipment

Key word p62

1 1e; 2b; 3a; 4d; 5c; 6f
2 1 My car is *just* as fast as yours.
2 I'm *just* about to switch this off.
3 You've *just* missed him I'm afraid.
4 Hold on, he's *just* walking through the door.
5 I'll *just* need a minute of your time, if that's OK.

Writing p62

2 a Four (sponsored bike ride, lorry pageant, boat race, sponsored walk)
b The sponsored walk
3 A5; B3; C4; D1; E2

Review p64

1 1 journey/take/far
2 last/need
3 trip/travel
2 1 time you found a
2 as soon as
3 time I've (ever) driven
4 long does it take
5 rather we went
6 You'd better
7 could always take
8 we made up our minds
3 1 teddies/bears
2 are
3 by
4 As
5 famous
6 be
7 where
8 addition
9 less
10 During
11 own
12 costs

Introducing your town

19 Recommend an excursion to somewhere in your town.

18

11 Recommend some shops where your visitor can buy souvenirs.

17 Ask about journey times between two places.

16 Ask for directions to the bus stop.

BUS STOP

Move forward two squares.

15 Your visitor wants to see live entertainment. Make a suggestion.

Have another go!

10 You want to book a restaurant for dinner. What do you say? [PV].

9

8 Tell your visitor about an important historical event in your town.

12 Talk about a famous monument in your town.

13 Tell your visitor about a typical dish from your town or country.

14

Introducing your town

Instructions:
heads + tails = go forward one square
heads + heads = go forward two squares
tails + tails = go forward three squares
Where you see PV, this means that you have to use an appropriate phrasal verb.

1 Start

2

7

6 Take your visitor to their hotel and help them check-in [PV].

THE GRAND HOTEL

5

3 You are greeting a visitor at the airport. What do you say? [PV]

4 You drive your visitor from the airport to town. Describe what you see.

Finish!

Say farewell to your visitor and wish them well!

37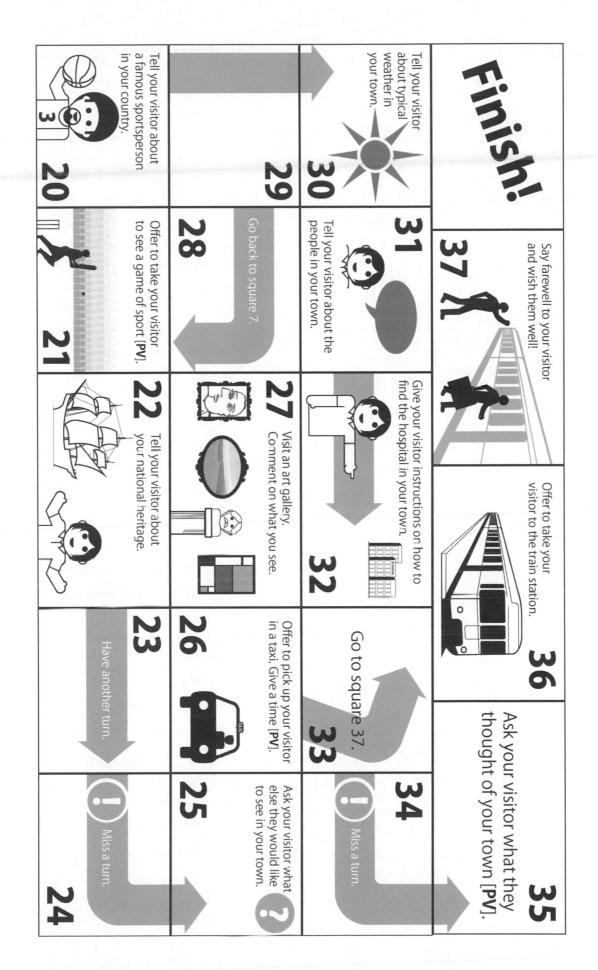

36 Offer to take your visitor to the train station.

35 Ask your visitor what they thought of your town [PV].

34 Miss a turn.

33 Go to square 37.

32 Give your visitor instructions on how to find the hospital in your town.

31 Tell your visitor about the people in your town.

30 Tell your visitor about typical weather in your town.

29

28 Offer to take your visitor to see a game of sport [PV].

Go back to square 7.

27 Visit an art gallery. Comment on what you see.

26 Offer to pick up your visitor in a taxi. Give a time [PV].

25 Ask your visitor what else they would like to see in your town.

20 Tell your visitor about a famous sportsperson in your country.

3

21

22 Tell your visitor about your national heritage.

23 Have another turn.

24 Miss a turn.

Student A

Situation one

> You have just bumped into your friend B in the street. You haven't seen him/her for a long time. You notice he/she has a nice sun-tan. You want to find out what they have been doing/where they have been.

Greet partner

Ask where they have been

Ask what time they stayed there

Ask about transport

Ask about travel time

Find out what they did

Ask if they had a good time

Ask about the most memorable thing

Ask about what they bought

Situation two

> You have just been to a travel agent's to organise a holiday. You meet B in the street.
>
> You are going on a Mediterranean cruise which lasts twelve days. You are going to fly to Barcelona and take the boat. The itinerary includes Tunis, Naples and Alexandria. After sightseeing in Tunis, you are going to take an excursion to the Oasis of Gabes by 4×4, and visit a crocodile farm! You are interested in the classical world and its ancient heritage. The next stop is Naples where you hope to have an excursion to the city of Pompeii. The final stop is Alexandria is Egypt. You plan to do a scuba diving course. You will then visit the underwater sites of shipwrecked roman vessels and the ruins of the lighthouse of Alexandria! You will fly back home from Alexandria. You hope to buy lots of souvenirs.

Respond to questions:

• Say you'll send a postcard

• Describe your excitement

• Take your leave

Student B

Situation one

> You meet A in the street. You have just been away on a long holiday. You were away five weeks. You have been on a safari holiday in Kenya. You flew to Nairobi. The flight took six hours. You travelled around by jeep. You even went on a flight in a hot air balloon. The thing you'll always remember is the animal migration in the Serengeti. You had a great time – the experience of a life-time. People were friendly and hospitable. You slept in tents with a guard. You could hear the wild animals outside. You bought some carved animals and a warrior's shield made of leather. You have a small present for your friend too!

Respond to the questions:

• Say you have a present for A

• Arrange a time to show your photos

• Take your leave

Situation two

> You meet A in the street. He/she is carrying some holiday brochures, and looks very excited. Ask what they are planning to do.

Greet partner

Ask where they are going

Ask when they are going

Ask about time they plan to be away

Ask about who is going

Ask about transport

Find out what they'll do

Ask about what they'll buy

Ask about cost

Cued dialogues

Technology

Before you begin

Ask the students to empty their pockets and bags and find out how many different items of technology they have with them. Encourage your students to talk about how technology, and their use of it, has changed over time.

> How many items would you have had five years ago?

> Well, five years ago I didn't own an MP3 player, but I did have a walkman...

> How often do you use your mobile?

> I can't live without it!

Topic: Technology

This unit focuses on innovation and invention. At First Certificate level, students need to be able to talk in general terms about technology and its impact on people's lives. This unit looks at the area of changes and improvements in the field, and more specifically at semi-technical computer language.

Unit 7 Wordlist:

attachment	log into
back up	made out of
brainchild	mouse
breakthrough	obsession
burdens	online
came up with	patent
carbon copy	pick up
click on	pioneers
come across	plug in
device	prototype
experiments	remote control
funding	revolution
hack into	salary
homepage	screen
imagination	set up
inbox	setbacks
inventors	subject
keyboard	tests
license	try out
links	world wide web

Getting started

Consider leading into this section by talking about one of your 'pet hates'.

> If I could 'un-invent' anything it would be the mobile phone. Young people waste too much time in empty conversation and do not pay attention to the world around them. There is nothing more annoying than having to listen into someone's stupid mobile phone conversation on a train or at a restaurant, except possibly the noise that leaks out of someone's supposedly 'personal' stereo.

Reading: robot revolution

BACKGROUND

Chinese inventions

As the title suggests, this reading focuses on Mr Wu's robot inventions. Nevertheless, it does mention a 'long list of Chinese inventions' – and this list may interest your students. Many people already know that the Chinese invented papermaking, printing, gunpowder, and the mariner's compass. In addition, however, the Chinese also invented modern agriculture, shipping, astronomical observatories, decimal mathematics, paper money, umbrellas, wheelbarrows, multi-stage rockets, brandy and whiskey, the game of chess, and much more. Mr Wu's robots have a lot to live up to!

1 These two questions might be a good opportunity to revise some of the ways of speculating and describing. Try to break the habit of students over-using 'maybe' to speculate or to express doubt/uncertainty.

> **Perhaps** this photo was taken in Japan, as the female passengers look like they are dressed in traditional clothes.

> **It could/might be** a new robot who has been invented to replace the man pulling the seat along?

At the end of the interaction, elicit the additional questions which students asked. Have a short correction spot focusing on two or three important errors.

Robot revolution: Quick definitions

Compass is an instrument that helps find the way by always indicating the direction of north.

A rubbish dump is a place where rubbish is taken to be buried, burnt or disposed of.

Gunpowder is the explosive mixture we find in fireworks, or used in guns.

A magnet attracts metal objects. People often put magnets on their fridges in the kitchen. If something is magnetised it has this property.

A rickshaw is a kind of two-wheeled carriage that is pulled by a man.

Scrap is the things that are thrown away because they are no longer useful. Scrap metal, for example, is metal that is recycled from broken cars and machinery.

Vocabulary: inventors and inventing

p/c 7.1b

2   This section studies phrasal verbs in context, and examines a lexical set of vocabulary on the topic of invention (see the definitions above if you need to clarify answers). Many of these words appear in the text that students have just read. Students work in pairs to complete the exercises.

Confusable pairs:

A **pioneer** (n) is an early developer or explorer of something.	A **prototype** (n) is an early version of something. When inventors develop something they usually move through a large number of prototypes before arriving at something.
Setbacks (n) are obstacles that block your progress or even send you backwards.	A **drawback** (n) is a disadvantage or negative consideration.
An **obsession** (n) is a preoccupation with a feeling or idea.	Your **imagination** (n) is your ability to form pictures or ideas in your mind of new, exciting, or imaginary things.
An **innovation** (n) is a new thing or method of doing something.	An **invention** (n) is a machine or system that has been invented by someone.
A **brainchild** (n) is the offspring/fruit of your imagination.	To have a **brainwave** (n) is to come up with a new idea.

A **test** (n) checks that something is of good quality, or works well.	An **experiment** (n) is a scientific test which is done to discover what happens in particular conditions.
A **breakthrough** (n) is an important development or achievement.	A **breakdown** (n) is the failure or ending of a system, plan or discussion.

Listening: intelligent robots

1   Before students listen to the interview, tell them to read through the notes carefully and think about what answers they feel able to predict.

2   Listening 7.1 Accept answers that fill in the gap correctly in terms of meaning. Allow spelling mistakes provided the intended meaning is clear.

3   Use this follow-up question to generate a short all-class discussion on the topic of intelligent robots. Some students may have seen the films *I, Robot* or *Blade Runner*, both of which deal with this topic.

Grammar: verbs followed by the gerund or the infinitive

Aim: To increase familiarity with verb changes that have an important shift in meaning.

Students will already know that there are verbs followed by the gerund and those that take the infinitive. They will also be aware that there is a class of verbs that may be followed by either form. Yet while they will most probably remember *to/-ing* they will probably be unfamiliar with other verbs where there is an important change in meaning.

1   This should mostly be a revision exercise. The forms are being compared and contrasted. Check that students understand the terms gerund and infinitive. It is confusing to call the gerund the *-ing* form. This is because students can get mixed up with the present participle.

Nigel is smoking.   Smoking is bad for you.
        ↑   ↑
present participle   gerund

Students may ask why 'look forward to' is followed by the gerund. This is because the preposition 'to' belongs to the phrasal verb, and prepositions are followed by the gerund, 'to' isn't part of the following verb.

Would like can only be followed by the full infinitive, unlike *like* which may be followed by both the gerund and the infinitive.

Verbs followed by the gerund or the infinitive
After reading through the Grammar spotlight with the class, ask them to categorise the verbs that have just been dealt with.

4   Timelines can be extremely useful for clarifying tenses. Pages 902–909 of the *Collins Cobuild Intermediate Dictionary* contain a number of timelines which explain tense in a simple but effective way. Alternatively, consider putting your own timelines on the whiteboard, as this TIP explains.

Clarifying tense with timelines
We can often make meaning clearer by creating a timeline on the whiteboard.

Now

The past   1   2   Future

1 *First* she remembered
2 *Next* she took her medicine
= She remembered to take her medicine.

Now

The past   1   2   Future

1 *First* she took a drink
2 *Then* she remembered
= She remembered taking a drink.
A general rule that students might find useful is that we use the infinitive when we refer to something *forward in time*, and the gerund when we are referring to *backwards in time*.

5   This is similar to the kind of exercise students will meet in the Use of English Paper. However, remind them that the real examination will test a broad range of structures and lexis.

Key word: *to*

To can be used
1 as preposition and an adverb;
2 before the base form of a verb.

Key word extension

As *to* may be used in a number of ways, consider providing an example of each way:
A phrase: If someone moves *to and fro*, they move repeatedly from one place to another.
An adverb: If you push a door *to*, you close it but don't entirely shut it.

A preposition: If you say *five to eight*, you mean five minutes before eight.
With an infinitive: If you say *I'm disappointed, to be honest*, you're commenting on your attitude or your intention.

Vocabulary: computers and technology

3   Students discuss websites. Some very young or older students may not have much of an idea about websites and the internet. It may be a good idea to go to your lesson armed with some examples of Internet home pages.

Showing interest
Encourage your students to show their interest by using words such as:

Oh really! That sounds interesting/fun/scary.

Lucky you! Fantastic! I'm really jealous.

Speaking: suggesting and recommending

1   The first exercise practises the skills of intensive listening and note-taking. Check that students understand the meaning of the computer-specific words in this exercise. The homepage is the first on-screen page of information we come to when we access a website.
Links are connections to other related websites.
An icon is a symbol or picture that represents an applications programme or file. You can access a programme by clicking onto the icon.

2   Lead a brief discussion about the speaker's recommendations and what makes a good website.

3   This is an important step: students need to know the underlying grammar of the expressions they use.

Exchanging ideas, expressing and justifying opinions (Paper 5, part 3)
p/c 7.1

This focuses on the importance of interacting appropriately with a partner during the collaborative task. Run through the expressions and ask which ones are used to agree and disagree. Students work in pairs and perform the collaborative task.

Writing: A review

1   Match a student who has played a computer game with one who hasn't. Then move into a brief all-class discussion about computer games.

2   Students often have problems with ideas. Here the ideas are provided, in order to be modified and included in the review that follows. From the reviewer's notes, students should conclude that the review is 'mixed'; they should say that she is enthusiastic about the graphics, but less keen on the theme, story and location. Nevertheless, the review should be generally positive.

3   Answer the first few questions as a class, then put students in groups to complete the rest of the task.

> The aim of the new computer game 'Goldfinder 3' is to find treasure and fight monsters which isn't very original! All the locations are in caves and mountains and really it should be be more varied and include, say, jungles and cities.
>
> Nevertheless, the graphics are fantastic and extremely realistic it's worth playing just because the monsters are so scary! One other thing I really like is that the game provides hours of fun even if it is the most expensive one currently in the shops.

4   Students quickly skim the reviews to see if they are positive or negative. Remind them that a positive comment that begins with *not*, or *not very* is negative.

Common phrases in reviews

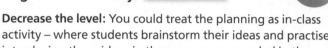

If a book is a **page turner** (+), it makes us want to turn the page. It is exciting.
If a story has **a (nice) twist** (+), it has an unexpected surprise or ending, which makes it interesting.
If a plot **keeps you guessing** (+), it maintains interest and suspense.
A **blockbuster** (+) is a big hit film with lots of stars.
If a film **keeps you on the edge of your seat** (+), it means you are leaning forward in anticipation and excitement. Notice that this example says it *isn't* like this (-).
If you are **wowed** (+), it means that you are pleasurably surprised or impressed by what you see.
Great special effects (+) means time and money have been spent on producing a visually exciting film.
Gripping (+) means just what it seems: it grabs your attention and won't let you look away. Notice that this film review states that it is *less than gripping* (-), which means it doesn't get your attention at all.
If a song is **catchy** (+), you find yourself singing it or humming it everywhere. Notice, however, that the review as a whole is unflattering – there's only *one* song that's worth listening to (-).

Something that **your grandmother might listen** (+) to implies that it is old-fashioned, out of date (generally a negative thing, especially among younger people).
An **easy to navigate** (+), webpage means the user isn't confused or lost while using it.
Retro (+ and -) means going back in time – it can be both a positive or negative term depending on how it is applied. Here, it is negative, for it suggests a out-of-date appearance (-).
Up-to-date (+) is a positive term meaning contemporary and relevant.

Degree of difficulty

Decrease the level: You could treat the planning as in-class activity – where students brainstorm their ideas and practise introducing these ideas in the ways recommended in the Exam spotlight on page 71.

Increase the level: Alternatively, set the task as homework or test. Stronger students usually enjoy an opportunity to get their opinion across.

Photocopiable Activity Instructions

Activity 7.1 Talk show presentation

Aim: to open discussion and practise making speeches.

1   Divide your class into Student A and Student B pairs.

2   Distribute handouts A and B accordingly.

3   Allow your students a fair amount of time to practise their roles.

4   Ask selected pairs to present their situation to the class.

Activity 7.2: My FCE Robot

Aim: to consolidate vocabulary in context and writing a review.

Instructions:

1   Ask each student to label their robot according to what features they think it should have.

2   Once each student has labelled at least ten items, allow them to write their review of their robot.

For example:
My robot, the Bondy, is a remarkable piece of machinery. It features ears which are capable of hearing noises from several kilometres away, and hands which can ...

Tapescript 7

Listening 7.1

Interviewer: We all remember watching those old black and white science fiction films at the cinema with androids and robots. As soon as you saw a robot you expected to see them go crazy and then they started attacking people. In reality there has never been a real case of robots attacking humans and robots have been used in manufacturing, especially car production, for years. And now robots are becoming part of our home life. In Japan for example, scientists are working on robots to be companions for elderly people. You might also have seen robot toys which children can control with their voices. Well, some manufacturers are looking at ways for such toys to look after children while their parents are at work. So, should we be worried? Do we risk having our day-to-day life controlled by machines that think for themselves? To discuss these questions I have Noel Witfield with me in the studio today. He's a professor of electronic engineering and is also a specialist in robot ethics. Professor Witfield, first of all, isn't all this talk of robots in the house a bit scary? Don't you think most people would prefer to communicate with a real person?

Professor: That's possibly true but you mentioned the work being done in Japan for example. The Japanese have succeeded in developing household robots for some time because they have an aging population. If they don't have robots, there won't be the people to take care of the elderly. Also I don't agree with your comment that we don't want to talk to machines. After all, we spend hours a day on our mobile phones and computers. But in fact a human being isn't designed to look at a screen all day. I'm actually better-suited to communicate with a computer which has a humanlike appearance – which is of course what a robot is. A computer with a face.

Interviewer: But we've also heard a lot about scientists who've managed to make robots with intelligence.

Professor: Well there I do think there's a potential problem with this and we need to look at this.

Interviewer: In what way?

Professor: Well, when we talk about intelligence, we're really talking about the fact that robots in the future will be able to make their own decisions. In the past robots have always been controlled by humans but we are giving them the abilities to make decisions and have some free will.

Interviewer: So do you think we should stop moving in this direction?

Professor: No, I wouldn't say stop it altogether but I would like to see a real public debate take place on how this will affect society in the future. And there's also the issue of safety and reliability. After all, some of the major work that is being done into robots is for military purposes. Governments should consider using robots ethically.

Listening 7.2

One We all remember watching those old black and white science fiction films at the cinema with androids and robots.

Two As soon as you saw a robot you expected to see them go crazy.

Three Do we risk having our day-to-day life controlled by machines that think for themselves?

Four Don't you think most people would prefer to communicate with a real person?

Five The Japanese have succeeded in developing household robots for some time.

Six A human being isn't designed to look at a screen all day …

Seven But we've also heard a lot about scientists who've managed to make robots with intelligence.

Eight I would like to see a real public debate take place on how this will affect society.

Nine Governments should consider using robots ethically.

Listening 7.3

Because it's so easy to use the internet these days, virtually anyone can think to themselves 'let's set up a website'. Maybe you want a home page for friends to look at, or how about advertising your local club? Perhaps you could even start an e-business and become a dot com millionaire. Before you begin, make sure you know why you want a website and what it's going to be for. It's also important to choose a good name early on and get an address for the web page. It should be a name that's easy to remember and the best ones are generally those which say what the site does or which get your attention.

Take the site www.milliondollarhomepage.com. Alex Tew, the student who came up with it, chose a name that said what it was about and it was also interesting because most people want to know about anything that mentions money. Another reason people visit sites is because they want information. So I strongly recommend that you include links to other sites. These need to be up-to-date and useful.

You might think that links to other sites will send people away but in fact if you can help users they will keep coming back to yours. Also, don't forget that links can take the form of words that you click on or they can be icons which are more visual and make the site colourful.

People also often ask me about things like having pictures and music. That's OK but it's also worth remembering that the more features and effects you have, the harder it will be to find what you want and it may take a long time to load the site. Visitors will get bored if they have to wait everytime they click on another page. It's a good idea to give a contact email so you can get feedback from visitors to the site.

Answer key 7

Reading p66

3 1E; 2C; 3F; 4A; 5B; 6H; 7G

Vocabulary p67

1 a pick up
b come up with
c trying out
d giving up
f comes across
2 1 pioneers
2 setbacks
3 obsession
4 innovation
5 brainwave
6 tests
7 breakthrough
3 1 drawbacks
2 breakdown
3 prototype
4 experiments
5 invention
6 imagination
7 brainchild

Listening p68

2 1 people
2 homes
3 the elderly and children
4 real person
5 machines
6 screen (all day)
7 intelligence
8 their own decisions
9 public debate/discussion
10 the ethics/morality

Grammar p68

1 3 having
4 to communicate
5 developing
6 to look
7 to make
8 to see
9 using

3 *Always take the gerund:* mind;
enjoy; finish.
Always take the infinitive: afford;
decide; want; seem
*Take either infinitive or gerund, with
little change in meaning:* like
*Take either infinitive or gerund, with
an important change in meaning:* try
Verbs followed by a preposition: look
forward to
*Sentences containing would/prefer
like to:* would like
4 1 A to take
B taking
2 A looking
B to look
3 A to tell
B telling
4 A thinking
B to think
5 A to be
B being
6 A to stop
B stopping
7 A to answer
B answering
5 1 stopped smoking in
2 Would you like
3 hate working late, don't
4 tried to answer
5 managed to get
6 went on to become
7 need to check your work
8 regret asking him

Key word p70

1 2 What are you listening to?
3 That's a terrible thing to say!
4 Is she old enough to ride a bike?
5 Remember to call me …
6 It's sure to rain.
7 Do you have to leave so soon?
8 We're afraid to go out in the
dark.
9 Let's get down to some work now.
10 I prefer talking face to face …

Vocabulary p70

1 1 log in
2 hacked into
3 click on
4 plug into
5 back up
6 set up
2 Hardware: keyboard, mouse,
screen
Email: attachment, subject, carbon
copy, inbox
Internet: links, world wide web,
online, homepage

Speaking p71

1 Name: Name and address, choose
a name that says what it does and
that's easy to remember.
Links: Include links to other sites,
must be up to date and useful.
Icons: Use for links. Should make
site colourful
Other features: Pictures and music
Contact: Give email address.
3 1g; 2f; 3e; 4b; 5i; 6j; 7a; 8d; 9c;
10h.
5 1 it's important to, it's a good
idea to
2 how about, it's also worth
3 let's

Writing p72

3 1 find treasure and fight
monsters
2 original
3 in caves and mountains
4 more varied
5 fantastic (very realistic)
6 are scary
7 many hours of fun
8 expensive
9 well above average
10 better than Goldfinder 1 and 2
4 1 A book (thriller or detective
novel)
2 A film

3 A CD
4 A website

Review p74

1 hacker, hacking; terrorism,
terrorist, terrorise; engineer;
management; government,
governor, governing; electrical,
electrician, electricity; consultant,
consulting; expertise.
2 1 hacking
2 government
3 computers
4 engineer
5 consultant
6 expertise
7 educators
8 terrorism
9 security
10 management
3 1 working
2 tried to
3 visiting
4 succeeded
5 making
6 asking
7 to do
8 remind
9 forget
10 trying
4 1 have
2 need
3 the
4 For
5 only
6 to
7 are
8 any
9 was/is
10 of

Student A

Situation one

You have invented a special pair of laser cutting scissors. You have been invited to take part in a TV programme about young entrepreneurs and inventors. You have brought along your invention to the show. Study your information, and feel free to add or invent anything else you think is important.

Background information:

– You were working for a fashion designer. Lots of the fabrics you worked with were extremely expensive and you were worried about the amount of waste. You found that many of your assistants couldn't cut a straight line.

– One day you saw a laser in a do-it-yourself shop. You had the idea of fixing this to a pair of scissors so that anyone could make a straight cut.

– You made a hundred prototypes using different pairs of scissors. The big problems were:
  • avoiding damaging people's eyes with the lasers
  • integrating the laser into the scissors
  • making sure that it was always reliable

– After five years and a hundred prototypes, you managed to develop a perfect pair of scissors.

– You spent a lot of money on patents to protect your invention.

– It became a commercial success. It is sold by mail order.

Situation two

You are the interviewer on a successful talk show. You are about to interview a young inventor.

Interviewer

Ask …
– the name of the invention
– what it is for
– what need does it satisfy
– how the person got the idea
– how it was developed
– what technical problems were encountered
– what problems they had
– if it is now a success

Student B

Situation one

You are the interviewer on a successful talk show. You are about to interview a young inventor.

Interviewer

Ask …
– the name of the invention
– what it is for
– what need does it satisfy
– how the person got the idea
– how it was developed
– what technical problems were encountered
– what problems they had
– if it is now a success

Situation two

You have invented a method of flood protection for homes. You have been invited to take part in a TV programme about young entrepreneurs and inventors. You have brought along your invention to the show. Study your information, and feel free to add or invent anything else you think is important.

Background information:

– With global warming there are far more floods than there used to be. Houses that once were safe are now vulnerable to floods.

– Your house was flooded twice. Water came through the doors and damaged the carpets and furniture.

– You went to your garden shed and experimented with lots of different ideas.

– The flood stop is an inflatable cushion that takes the shape of any opening. It fits perfectly and prevents water coming in from doors, windows or even corridors.

– You made a lot of prototypes. The problems were:
  • making it quick and easy to fit
  • finding a strong material that could expand

– You took your invention to show a manufacturer. The manufacturer tried to steal and copy your idea. You took that company to court and won.

– You borrowed lots of money to launch the product. It is now produced under licence in China and exported all round the world.

MY FCE ROBOT

You've just created your very own robot. Label the body parts and then write an imaginative description of what your invention can do.

Robot's name: _____

Dog's name: _____

_____
_____
_____
_____
_____
_____
_____
_____
_____
_____
_____
_____

Crime and social responsibility

Before you begin

Ask students if they have been the victim of any kind of crime in the past few months. Ask them if they think the situation is getting better or worse. Ask if they think there are any areas in their town or city, which are 'no go' areas (that is, places where it is too dangerous to venture).

Topic: Crime and social responsibility

This unit focuses on the topic of crime but also on ways of being more responsible citizens. At FCE level, students should be able to understand articles and programmes on social issues, and express their views on a range of current topics.

Unit 8 Wordlist:

accuse	judge
annoy	jury
arrest	kidnapping/kidnapper
arson/arsonist	legal/illegal
blackmail/blackmailer	mugger/mugging
blame	police officer
burglar/burglary	prison/prisoner/imprison
capture	probation
community service	prosecution
detective	punish/punishment
drug dealer/drug dealing	release
fine (noun)	robber/robbery
force	shoplifter/shoplifting
forgery/forger	smuggler/smuggling
get away (with)	speeding
get into	steal
get out	theft/thief
get up to	vandalism/vandals
hacking/hacker	

Getting started

1   Students will certainly recognise the different crimes, but may not know how to say them in English. Run through the pictures with students and make sure that they understand the nature of each of the crimes. You could encourage your students to practise the expressions they've been learning for Speaking Paper here:

> It looks like a **mugging**, a street robbery, or something like that.

> Perhaps these people are illegally accessing, or **hacking** into, computer databases.

> The person appears to be dropping litter, like wrapping from sweets and cigarette packets. It's very anti-social.

2   Either treat this as a whole class, or group activity. You may want to run through some of the definitions first.

Community service is where you have to do things like pick up litter, paint over graffiti.

A **fine** is money you have to pay as a punishment for something – it doesn't mean how you are feeling.

Probation is where you have to report to a probation officer on a regular basis to tell them what you have been doing.

Students decide which punishments best match each crime. Attitudes towards crime vary between cultures so be aware of not offending students' sensibilities!

3   Allow students to discuss their views about the topic. If feelings start to run too high, then defuse discussion by having a break or moving on to the reading passage.

Getting started extension

Explain the expression 'the punishment should fit the crime', or 'a fitting punishment' to your students. Discuss what they think about the concept.

Reading: crime and punishment

BACKGROUND

The history of the police

Police are legal and state agents or agencies who enforce the law. They are meant to encourage public and social order through the legitimate use of force. The word comes via French from the Latin *politia* (civil administration), which itself derives from the Ancient Greek for *polis* (city). The first police force comparable to the present-day police was established in 1667 under King Louis XIV in France, although modern police usually trace their origins to the 1829 establishment of the Metropolitan Police in London, the Glasgow Police, and the Napoleonic police of Paris. An alternative name for the police force is *the constabulary*.

1 Students speculate about kinds of crime being committed. Elicit their ideas. Use this as an opportunity to remind the class about different ways of speculating (rather than using *maybe* all the time):

> **It looks like** he is being arrested ... **although I wonder why** he is biting the policeman on the arm? **He could be** trying to escape, **or perhaps** he is just hungry!

2 Quickly pre-teach the words *gums* and *false teeth*. You may also wish to have a quick look at the title of text D – *A criminal whose bark was worse than his bite*. Barking is the noise dogs make. If we say 'someone's bark is worse than their bite', we mean that even though they may act aggressively, you have nothing to fear from them. Encourage a rapid read of the texts by setting a one minute read of each section.

3 Give students ten minutes to find answers to 1–15. Ask them to underline the evidence that gave them the correct answer.

Vocabulary: crime and criminals

1 Allow students two minutes to complete the table. Lead all class feedback. Insist on accurate pronunciation and word-stress.

2 Demonstrate the activity by showing the line between the crime and the definition. Consider finishing off the exercise by creating a grammar table on the whiteboard:

Noun	Verb	Person
arson	arson	arsonist
theft	steal	thief
forgery	forge	forger
kidnapping	kidnap	kidnapper
smuggling	smuggle	smuggler
blackmail	blackmail	blackmailer
mugging	mug	mugger
shoplifting	shoplift	shoplifter

Vocabulary extension

Consider asking your students to form example sentences of the words from the exercises so far. It is a good way to see whether they understand what the crime involves. For example:

> People often commit arson to wrongfully claim money from an insurance company.

Key word: get

The exercises in this section emphasise the importance of knowing replacements for *get* and *got*. Students should be capable of using an alternative wherever possible.

You may wish to spend some time teaching the following expressions:
I get it = I understand.
That gets to me = it annoys me.

1 Students work in pairs and substitute the words in the box for the forms of *get* in questions 1–10. If time permits, encourage the students to create sentences of their own using these forms of 'get' that you have just examined.

Listening: stopped by the police

1 Remind your students to read the choices before they listen. Ask them to listen out for evidence to support their choice.

Grammar: relative clauses

Great. So, what sort of relative clause is it?

Well, it has commas around it, and I don't think it is all that important in this sentence to know what he was trying to steal, which means it seems more like background material ... is it a non-defining relative clause?

Yes. Excellent!

3   When looking at this exercise, remind your students that punctuation *does* matter in the FCE.

Informality and formality in relative clauses

This grammar spotlight describes the difference between inserting a pronoun in some defining relative clauses, and excluding it. It is very useful for students to understand register; they need to realise how to sound more or less formal, and when. Consider conducting some roleplay scenarios in class where you see how your students would speak at, for example, a job interview compared to a private phone conversation with a close friend.

5   After the students read through the text, 'Man fined over Cigarette', ask them questions about it:

What was the man's 'crime'?

How fair was the punishment?

6   Encourage the students to expand the text using various relative clauses. Emphasise that there is no one correct answer. When they have finished, refer them to File 8.2 on page 230.

7   This exercise provides a good opportunity for you to encourage your students to take 'ownership' of their writing. You could demonstrate the task with several confident students:
• Write two versions of your three sentences on separate pieces of paper. The first version shouldn't use any relative clauses.
• Give this to Student A.
• The second version should contain a fair amount of description (within relative clauses). Give this version to Student B to keep for now.
• Once Student A has added their relative clauses into your sentence, ask them to read it aloud to the class.
• Then ask Student B to read your second version aloud.
• Compare the two versions. This should allow you to emphasise the many varieties of answer that are possible.

A man was arrested in Sydney yesterday afternoon.

A man was arrested in Sydney yesterday afternoon when he tried to climb the Harbour Bridge.

A man was arrested in Sydney, where the law is very strict, yesterday afternoon.

A man, who was wearing gold underwear on his head and nothing else, was arrested in Sydney yesterday afternoon.

Use of English: open cloze

1   Generate interest in the exercise by asking students to speculate about what's going on the page from the 'freegan' website. Before students begin the exercise, ask them what they understand from the word 'freegan'. Tell them that it is a new word. Ask them to read the passage all the way through without trying to fill the gaps and to tell you what 'freegans' stand for.

2   This is a prelude to a short discussion activity. Ask students to give their own opinion about freegans and freeganism by completing the sentences in their own words. Then allow them to compare answers or lead a short all-class discussion.

Listening: social responsibility

1   This listening passage compares the activities of two movements with similar, but not identical, aims. The first exercise allows the students to concentrate on overall meaning before doing exam-type practice.

2   Ask the students to go through the questions, and to try and answer them based on what they have already heard. Either play the recording all the way through or else pause the recording after each piece of key information.

Speaking: showing you're listening

1   Students listen to the recording again and decide on the order in which the words appear.

p/c 8.2

2   This gives students the opportunity to really practise some of the active listening and conversational techniques we have just examined. Instead of working in pairs, you could ask students to mill around the class asking and answering different people to maximise their practice.

Active listening

This spotlight emphasises the importance of active listening. Students need to know how to show interest in what the other person is saying. While the exercises concentrate on verbal strategies to do this, you may want to reinforce the message using body language as well. Remind students that while they are responding to the other speaker, they could also:

✓ Nod their heads when agreeing

✓ Smile when offering encouragement

✓ Shake their heads when disagreeing

✓ Frown when remonstrating someone

Of course, make sure your students realise that these actions are not meant to replace their spoken responses, but to accompany them.

Writing: an article

1   Your students should look closely at the article written in response to the advertisement. The candidate answers the questions well. Consider breaking the article down into its main features and writing these on the board. This will provide your students with a basic template, or skeleton, for them to echo in question 6.

Potential article plan

Paragraph one:
Rhetorical Question
Opening statement/Factual sentence

↓

Paragraph two:
Example one
Factual statement/rhetorical question
Example two
Factual statement
Example three
Factual statement

↓

Paragraph three:
Rhetorical questions
Concluding statement

2   This question provides good practice for your students in planning an article. Encourage students to summarise the points in their own words rather than directly copying those of the article's author.

Photocopiable activity instructions

Activity 8.1: Debating society

Aim: To practise the language of giving and enumerating opinions, agreeing and disagreeing.

Instructions:

1   You will need to choose a very strong student to act as the chairperson for this activity. Alternatively, you could take the role of chairperson. If you have a class that is large enough, you could have two debates running simultaneously in different halves of the room.

2   Explain the process of debating to your students.

3   Tell your students that they are going to hold a debate on one or more of these propositions:

This house believes that capital punishment is never justified.

This house believes that people are more worried about criminals than the victims of crime.

4   Then leave them in their groups to discuss their ideas. Facilitate occasionally, but let them attempt to work through it on their own.

Activity 8.2: Who in the class…?

Aim: To practise active listening while using relative clauses.

Instructions:

1   Copy and distribute the handout.

2   Encourage your students to mingle. Remind them of the tips given in the Active Listening spotlight. Keep a close eye on their use of relative clauses.

Tapescript 8

Listening 8.1

Speaker One I really don't know what we would have done if he hadn't arrived. We'd been driving round the same part of the city for at least an hour and I must have asked about five different people where to go. And it was all rather dark and scary. I even drove the wrong way down a one way street! *That* was when, suddenly, out of *nowhere* this policeman stopped us! Well, once I'd explained that I was completely lost he told us the way and we were able to ...

Speaker Two Have you seen that poster they're showing everyone? It has a man's face – he has a beard but he still looks like any number of other people. Anyway there were about three police officers asking people in the High Street if they saw anything strange outside the local supermarket last Thursday night at 8 o'clock. I suppose they spoke to *me* because I always walk past at that time of night, and, well, actually, when I started to think back it occurred to me that I *had* seen a couple of suspicious people in that street that goes down the side of the shops, who perhaps...

Speaker Three Believe me! I wouldn't want to be the *actual* attacker. I mean, the way they spoke to me was *really* scary! I even *felt* like a criminal by the time I left the police station. Even once they'd realised my name was spelt differently and I've never even *known* anyone called Rita, I still *never* got an apology. I couldn't believe it. I mean you'd think that if ...

Speaker Four The shopping bags were both sitting there and they were identical. I'd just grabbed them and put them in the trolley and I'd only gone halfway across the car park before a security guard was running and using his radio. The next thing I know is the police arrive to question me. I think they realised I'd just made a mistake and taken the wrong ones but that security guard was determined to get me! He really fancied himself as one of those detectives you see on TV! You know the ones ....

Speaker Five It was just my luck, wasn't it? I mean, I normally go through that area quite carefully because I know they wait there. But, well, I was in a rush that day to pick up Lionel from work and I wasn't thinking. Within seconds I saw the lights flashing and they'd pulled me over. The young man was very nice about it but it didn't stop him from giving me a fine! It just wasn't my day ...

Listening 8.2

Presenter: Today, we've got Connie Wicher on the phone and Connie has rung in to let listeners know about her new idea to recycle things in your home. Is that right, Connie?

Connie: That's right Geoff, though it isn't really *my* idea. It's part of something called Freecycling.

Presenter: OK. So tell us about it, Connie.

Connie: Well, the Freecycle Network, or 'Freecycling', began in 2003. There was a group of people who wanted to save the landscape around their town from having more landfills and being used for dumping trash – which you guys would call rubbish. So they set about finding ways of helping the town reduce its waste.

Presenter: I see, but didn't it cost them money to do something like that?

Connie: Well, no, it was absolutely free. It wasn't a government thing or anything like that ... just a bunch of people getting together and doing something about all the stuff being thrown away. It's all done in people's spare time.

Presenter: It sounds great. Now, people listening will be wondering how this is different to recycling.

Connie: It isn't *quite* the same as recycling because everything is just reused rather than taking it away for recycling. So, for example, if I have a fridge I don't want, I advertise to my local freecycling community and someone can have it for nothing. It's as simple as that.

Presenter: OK – I see. I had a look at the website earlier, Connie, and there are over *three* thousand of these communities around the world! That's a *lot* of people.

Connie: Yes ... I think the most recent number is three thousand, seven hundred and nineteen, with close to three million members in places all over the world, in countries including the USA and Germany ... all sharing their unwanted things.

Presenter: Wow! So tell our listeners how they can become freecyclers.

Connie: Just go the website www.freecycle.com and find your local group. You click 'join' and then you get an email telling you what to do. If you can't find a freecycler nearby then you can start your own in your local area.

Presenter: And what can people give away?

Connie: Literally anything. Chairs, fax machines, pianos. You name it! I gave away a door last week.

Presenter: Right. So pretty much everything, then!

Connie: Sure, as long as it's legal and free, you can freecycle it.

Presenter: Well thanks, Connie. And if you want to get in touch here's the website again. It's www.freecycle.com ...

Answer key 8

Reading p76
3 1C; 2D; 3A; 4A; 5D; 6B; 7A; 8A; 9D; 10B; 11C; 12C; 13B; 14B; 15D

Vocabulary p77
1 1 shoplifter
2 shops
3 vandalism
4 burglar
5 breaking and entering
6 hacking
7 computers (data bases)
2 1 arson: deliberately setting fire to property
2 theft: stealing, such as robbery or burglary
forgery: copying something such as money, important documents or paintings
kidnapping: taking someone and asking for money
smuggling: carrying and not declaring items
blackmail: threaten someone
mugging: attacking and stealing
3 A speeding
B release
C detective
D police officer
E blackmail

Key word p77
1 1 arrested
2 received
3 understand
4 arrived
5 manage
6 annoys
7 capture
8 met
9 forced
10 was
3 1 away
2 away with
3 up to
4 into
5 out

Listening p78
1 1E; 2C; 3D; 4F; 5B

Grammar p78
2 2 He's the one who (or that) was seen at the scene of the crime.
3 This is the shop where we said we'd meet.
4 Do you know the reason why he couldn't come?
5 Over there is the building which (or that) was destroyed by fire last night.
6 The woman whose car was stolen is waiting for you in reception.
7 Do you remember the time when you could walk down the streets safely at night?
3 1 The shoplifter, who had only been released from prison a week ago, was caught on camera.
2 The house, which had a security system, has been burgled three times.
3 The town, where over half a million people live, is one of the safest in the country.
4 A retired policeman, who had left the police force in 2005, was accused of forgery yesterday at the High Court.
5 The factory, which employs 200 people, caught fire in strange circumstances.
4 1 Which date was it when we all went to that club?
2 Do you understand the reasons for which you are going to prison?
3 The neighbour who (or whom) I mentioned is still causing problems.
4 Do you know the reason why she called?
5 The suspect says he was away on business the night on which the crime was committed.
8 1 whom 2 who 3 which 4 in 5 which 6 why 7 who 8 which

Use of English p80
1 1 to
2 whose
3 can/could
4 make
5 that
6 into
7 to
8 just/simply/only
9 through
10 are
11 on
12 for

Listening p80
2 1A; 2C; 3A; 4A; 5B; 6B; 7B

Speaking p81
1 1, 5, 6, 4, 3, 2

Writing p83
4 a2; b3; c1; d5; e4
5 a1; b3; c2; d2; e1; f1; g3; h2

Review p84
1 1B; 2C; 3D; 4D; 5B; 6A; 7D; 8A; 9B; 10C; 11B; 12B
2 1 where
2 why
3 who
4 where
5 which
6 when
3 1 are
2 into
3 some
4 that/the
5 They
6 of
7 went/searched
8 a/her
9 In
10 the
11 has
12 who
4 1 hackers
2 imprisoned
3 forged
4 kidnappers'
5 punishable
6 blackmailer
7 thief/thieves
8 illegal
9 smugglers
10 arsonists

DEBATING SOCIETY

A debate is a formal discussion about a subject on which people have different views. During a debate there is a motion (proposition) to be debated, a chairperson and two teams (for and against).

CHAIR

To start the debate:

We're here today to debate the motion: 'This house believes that …'

I now call on …………. who is going to speak on behalf of the motion.

You have two minutes left. I'm afraid that I have to stop you here.

Your time is up!

Opening debate to the floor:

I am now going to open the debate to the floor. Please address all your questions or comments through the chair.

Maintaining order:

Order, order! Keep quiet please! Do be quiet please!

Taking the vote:

I would now like us to pass to the vote.

All those in favour of the motion, please raise your hand.

All those against the motion please raise your hand.

All those who wish to abstain please raise your hand.

I (hereby) declare the motion carried/defeated by … votes to …

Thank you very much for a lively and interesting debate.

- opens and closes the debate
- indicates when and for how long the speakers can speak
- controls the noise level of the floor
- takes the vote, declares the winner and winds up meeting.

Thank you very much Mr/Madam chairperson …

I am going to speak in favour of/against the motion …

I have three main points to make …

First of all … Secondly/furthermore … Last but not least … To sum up … In conclusion …

SPEAKER

- speaks from notes only, not a prepared speech

Asking a speaker a question:

I'd like to ask … what he/she thinks about …

Don't you think that we/the government should be/are responsible/guilty of …

Commenting during the talk:

Hear hear! Absolutely!

How ridiculous/How absurd!

AUDIENCE

Making a contribution:

I'd just/simply like to say …

The point I'd like to make is …

I'd like to remind everyone …

We shouldn't forget that …

- makes comments and ask questions
- must always have the permission from the chairperson

WHO in the class ...?

... has a pet? (find out what sort and its name)	... has always wanted to be famous? (find out who their idol was when they were younger)
... has been abroad more than 3 times? (find out which foreign countries they have visited)	... has been in love more than twice? (find out who their first love was)
... thinks they are a good cook? (find out what their speciality dish is)	... has been on a diet before? (find out what sort of diet and how much weight they lost)
... reads a daily newspaper? (find out which one)	... has been punished at school? (find out what for and what the punishment was)
... likes reading books? (find out their favourite author)	... has changed a baby's nappy? (find out what they thought of it)
... usually goes to bed late? (find out what time)	... knows a joke in English? (ask them to tell it to you)
... plays a musical instrument? (find out which one)	... believes in love at first sight? (find out what sort of person they are attracted to)
... has cried watching a film? (find out which film and why)	... has lived at their present address for more than six years? (find out what they like about it)

PHOTOCOPIABLE 8.2

Before you begin

Find out from each member of the class what their favourite food is. What do they enjoy to eat? Do they prefer healthy or unhealthy food? If you suggested a list of 'top five foods', would they agree or disagree with you? Is there anything that they used to hate to eat, but now enjoy as they get older? The scope for discussion is endless!

> I'm a vegan – which means I don't eat any meat or any other animal products.

> I'm quite the opposite! I love meat – I think a big chunk of steak is delicious!

Topic: You are what you eat

This unit focuses on the topic of food, drink and eating out. At FCE level, students should be able to talk about food and cooking, as well as their culinary likes and dislikes.

Unit 9 Wordlist:

bitter	raw
bland	receipt
boil	recipe
bowl	roast
chop	slice
cook/cooker	sour
course	sparkling
diet	spicy
dry (for wine)	sprinkle
fast food	still
fry	stir
frying pan	sweet
grate	take advantage of
greedy	take care of someone
grill	take off (remove; imitate)
ingredients	take on (employ; challenge)
mild	take something for granted
mix	take something into account
peel	take the opportunity
put off (postpone; feel	tasteful/tasty
disgust)	well-done
rare (meat)	

Getting started

1   The photograph launches the topic of healthy eating and how eating habits have changed.

Super Size Me

The photograph is taken from a film called *Super Size Me*. It is a documentary that followed the progress of a man who ate nothing but food served at McDonalds for a month. If one of the servers asked him if he wanted to 'supersize' his meal (have extra fries and an extra large Coke) he had to accept. By the end of the experiment he had developed serious health problems, and gained a large amount of weight, which then took quite some time to shed.

2   Students match the comments to the questions.

3   Lead a quick all-class discussion asking how students would answer the questions.

Listening: eating out

1   Remind students that *to eat out* usually means to eat in a restaurant. There will probably be quite a lot of unfamiliar vocabulary in the recordings, so tell students just to focus on the listening task. The vocabulary will be dealt with afterwards.

2   Students listen and match pictures to speakers.

3   Ask students to read through the descriptions 1–6 carefully. See if they are able to match any of the speakers to the statements already.

Multiple matching

Occasionally, there are traps in the listening exam. Individual words that seem to give the right answer may misdirect the candidate. Ask students to find the words in question in the tapescript.

Vocabulary: food and drink

1   This first exercise shows that the opposite of an adjective often depends on the context. If you wish, use these examples before you begin:

a light colour	⟶	a dark colour
a light bag	⟶	a heavy bag
a dry day	⟶	a wet day
a dry wine	⟶	a sweet wine

2   If students have difficulties with this, refer them to Tapescript 9.1, where they can find the words in context.

3   Students quickly sort the words into the appropriate columns. Use mime to show what they mean. Students can then test each other by miming the actions where possible.

5   This exercise shows that the same word can be used in very different contexts with different meaning.

6   This exercise examines a set of easily confusable words. If you wish, contrast words like *cooking* with *kitchen* and *cuisine*.

When you **cook** (v), or are **cooking** a meal, you prepare and heat food so it can be eaten.	A **cooker** (n) is a large metal device used for cooking food using electricity or gas.
A **recipe** (n) is a list of ingredients and a set of instructions that tell you how to cook something.	A **receipt** (n) is a piece of paper that you get from someone as confirmation that they have been paid.
Your sense of **taste** (n) is your ability to recognise the flavour of things with your tongue.	Something **tasteful** (adj) is pleasing to the eye, like the way a room is decorated. Something **tasty** (adj) is pleasing to the taste-buds in your mouth. It has a strong and pleasant flavour that makes it good to eat.
Ingredients (n) are the raw materials we need to cook with.	**Greed** (noun) is a desire for more of something than is fair or necessary. **Greedy** (adj) describes the person who wants more than their fair share.

Speaking: expressing preferences

Aim: to focus on common errors with stating preferences; the use of *rather* as a verb.

If you **prefer** (verb) someone or something, you like that person or thing better than another. If you **would rather** do something, you would **prefer** to do it.

> I'd prefer to walk = formal   I'd rather walk = less formal

1   Students underline correct choices.

2   When *would rather* is followed by a pronoun, or noun, then the following verb takes the past simple. This is similar to the use of time. Consider: *It's time we left.*

For further information on this, refer students to Section 15 of the Grammar Reference.

3   This is similar to part 3 of the Speaking Paper where students have to carry out a communicative task. After the students have finished, ask them about their decision. You could also ask some follow up questions.

> Where do you usually go to eat out for a special occasion?

> How adventurous are you?

> Do you like foreign food?

> Would you rather drink tea or coffee?

p/c 9.2

Reading: all mouth

History of competitive eating
Competitive eating involves the consumption of large quantities of food in a fairly short amount of time (usually 15 minutes). Although food type varies, it is usually a dessert or type of junk food. Competitive eating is most popular in Japan and the United States. The International Federation of Competitive Eating hosts more than 100 Major League Eating events annually worldwide. This organisation first established eating as a sport in the 1990s.

1   Use the photographs to generate interest in the text. Ask the students to speculate about where the event is taking place and who the people in the pictures are.

> What kind of people would be successful competitors?

> Hmm. Perhaps people with very large stomachs?

2   This task is to encourage students to read the whole text through quickly for gist.

Gapped text (Paper 1, part 2)
Aim: to reaffirm the importance of good examination technique by contradicting the statements in the box. Show what students have to do by dealing with the first two statements as a class. Either treat this as pair work or continue it as a whole class activity.

Possible responses:

I never waste my time reading the text all the way through.
You shouldn't do that. If you read the text all the way through, you'll get a better global understanding.
I always trust my instinct and go for the sentence which feels right.
No, you must attack the questions carefully and logically.
I start matching sentences to gaps straight away.
It's never a good idea to rush. You need to check each sentence against each gap.
I always do the answers in order.
It's better to start with the easier sentences first, and leave the more difficult ones to the end.
I don't bother looking for pronouns and references.
You should always look for pronouns and references as they will often help you find the right answer.
I don't try to identify the extra sentence. At the end it's obvious.
You should always try to identify any sentence which is obviously wrong.
Never guess if you don't know.
Yes and no. Don't guess at the beginning. But you can guess at the end! There are no penalties for a wrong answer.

4   Give students 15 minutes to complete the exercise. In feedback, ask the students to **justify** the answers. They should be able to say something like this:

1A 'At the beginning Bill Simmons was *confidently* expecting to win...... *confidence* turned to disbelief ...' = A different part of speech.
2H 'Today she has come to Stockton...As usual she has eaten sparingly ...' = ... Next sentence matches with immediacy of topic.
3B '... if you're fat ...' = sentence contrasts with 'thin people' in previous sentence and 'no spare fat' of next sentence.
4E 'However, Sonya claims she is in good shape ...' = This contrasts with 'looks like a form of mass suicide' in the previous sentence.
5D 'In geographical and cultural terms ...' = matches with the pronoun reference of 'There ...' (which refers to South Korea in previous sentence).
6C '18 hot dogs' = is followed by 25 and 37 in sentences that follow.
7F Sonya has won = so it logically follows on that the crowd cheers and she raises an arm.

5   Allow different points of view from the class. Clearly, there must be risks involved in eating such huge amounts in such a short space of time.
6   Point out that *-ism*, *-ment*, *-tion* and *-ance* are four suffixes that indicate nouns. Ask students to think of other nouns with these endings. Examples could include:

Suffix	Noun
-ist	pessimist; cyclist; artist; socialist ...?
-ment	government; development; commitment ...?
-ion	abolition; condition; competition ...?
-ance	performance; clearance ...?

Reading extension

'Sonya the Black Widow' describes several stereotypes – for example, the idea that the obese truck driver would be the most likely winner of the competition – only to destroy this stereotype with a thin woman winning the competition instead.

- Discuss the idea of **stereotypes** with your students. A stereotype (n) is a preconceived idea.
- Give your students a topic and ask them to list as many stereotypes as they can think of.
- Then, in pairs, tell your students to decide whether the stereotype is accurate or inaccurate. Remember, some stereotypes can be offensive, so make sure your students are careful.

One stereotype is that all men can eat more than women.

But surely this is not always true!

Grammar: forms of *used to* and *would*

This section focuses on a minor grammatical area that often poses students with problems. They often confuse the forms and uses of *used to*. They are often unsure about when to choose between *used to do* and *would* for past actions.

Remember that the basic difference in grammar between the forms of *used to* is that it can either be used as an auxiliary (a 'semi-modal'), or as an adjective.

They *used to* be poor = *used to do* is a semi-modal auxiliary.

She is *used to* running around = *used* is an adjective and *to* a preposition, which is why it is followed by the gerund (*running*).

The mistakes students typically make are: *She is used to run around.*

She gets used to consuming = *get* = become; *used to* doing = adjective.

Do you smoke?

No I don't, but I used to.

Notice that *used to* appears in the short answer, not just *I used*.

Used to or *would*

The two essential points that students need to remember are:
A) We can only use *would* to talk about past habits, not past states.
Typical mistake: 'She would be fat when she was a baby'.
However, 'She would cry a lot when she was a baby' (habit) or 'She used to be fat when she was a baby' (state) are both OK.
B) *Used to* can't be used when we say how long we did something.
Typical mistake: 'I used to play tennis for three years'.
However, 'I used to play tennis every summer while I was growing up' is OK.

Speaking: talking about the past

Students work in pairs or groups. This exercise is an excellent opportunity to encourage your students to open up.

Speaking extension

Depending on your class, consider asking your students to bring in an old photograph which contains some meaning for them. Ask them to describe this photo to either a partner or the class. They can use it as a 'prop'. It may help them relate a personal anecdote based in the past to an audience.

> This is a photograph of me as a small child. I used to have very short hair. My mother would cut it for me every week.

Listening: in the dark

1   Use the photographs to generate interest in the listening passage. If you are wondering why the photographs look so well-lit, it is because they were taken using a camera with 'infra-red' film.

Words to pre-teach:

The ability to **cope** (n) means you can deal with a problem, task or difficult situation successfully.
A **glow** (n) is a dull, steady light.
If you **grope** (v) for something that you cannot see, you search for it using your hands.
If you **opt** (v) for something, you choose it.

2   Make sure that students read the questions before listening to the recording. Play the recording all the way through, then allow students to confer and compare their answers. If you think that they have by and large managed, go straight into feedback without listening to it a second time. Alternatively, play the recording again, stopping where important information comes up.

3   Elicit different opinions.

4   Students work in groups.

Key word: *take*

1   This exercise looks at lexical phrases using *take*. Tell students that this is something that could be tested in the 'key word transformations' part of the Use of English Paper. Students match beginnings and ends of sentences to create definitions of the phrases in question.

Take can be used with nouns describing actions; used in other verb and noun senses; used in phrases, and used as a phrasal verb.

Suggested answers:

1   I used to take my mother for granted/He used to take advantage of his mother!
2   I didn't take the petrol costs and motorway charges into account.
3   She takes advantage of her brother.
4   I took the opportunity to visit the Louvre/I took advantage of being in Paris to visit the Louvre.
5   My neighbour takes care of my plants when I go away.

Phrasal verbs and their different meanings

This section draws students' attention to the fact that the same phrasal verb can have very different meanings. Run through the information in the Spotlight and ask students to work in pairs to discuss their answers to exercise 6.

Writing: opinion essay

Aim: to show students that the production of a finished essay is the result of a process. This section focuses on the process of generating ideas, essay planning and execution.

1   This introduction should generate interest and act as a springboard for ideas. Elicit comments from the students.

> A lot of people might think that her parents are at fault for letting her have a mobile phone from the age of six, and for allowing her to spend so much time texting. Can a child of eight really have an active social life?

2   Allow students to work in groups. Next, choose a spokesperson from each group and write key ideas on the whiteboard.

3   Students read Melanie's answer and compare the points they came up with with Melanie's points.

4–5 In these two questions, students look at the work leading up to the composition:
– the spidergram: 'brainstorming of ideas'
– the composition plan.
Students need to realise that it is one thing to have ideas, but another to organise them into a linear plan.

6 This returns to the topic of food and drink. By now, students should have a lot of opinions about food, drink and health, as these have been recurring topics within the unit. The pre-writing discussion exercise 6 will help them to pool and compare these ideas.

7 Help students with the process of creating a spidergram and a linear plan.

9 Once your students have completed their essay, consider showing them several versions which contradict each other. This will reinforce the idea that an opinion essay can argue either side to an argument, as long as it contains a strong structure and relevant ideas.

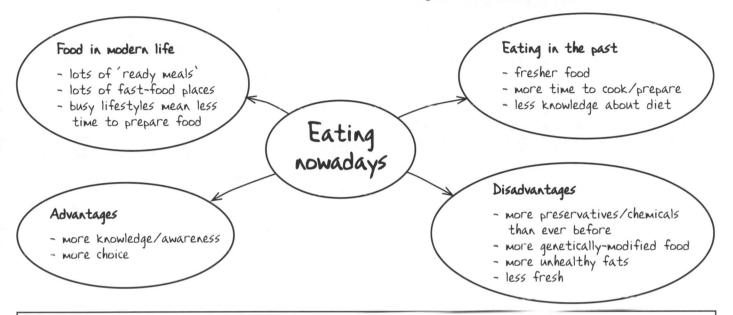

Food in modern life
- lots of 'ready meals'
- lots of fast-food places
- busy lifestyles mean less time to prepare food

Eating in the past
- fresher food
- more time to cook/prepare
- less knowledge about diet

Eating nowadays

Advantages
- more knowledge/awareness
- more choice

Disadvantages
- more preservatives/chemicals than ever before
- more genetically-modified food
- more unhealthy fats
- less fresh

Photocopiable activity instructions

Activity 9.1: Phrasal verb match-up: Take That!

Aim: to practise the key word *take* with its use in phrasal verb.

Instructions:

1 Copy handout and distribute.

2 Explain to your students that the phrasal verbs on the left (*take back, take apart,* etc …) should be matched with the phrasal verbs on the right.

3 If students find this difficult, allow them to work in pairs, or use a good dictionary/phrasal verbs dictionary.

4 Once each definition is matched up, students should be able to complete the sentences very easily.

5 A possible extension is to create similar worksheets with other unit key words.

Answer key: 1 take away; 2 take apart; 3 take on; 4 take off; 5 take in; 6 take up; 7 take back; 8 take in; 9 take off; 10 take on; 11 take out; 12 take to; 13 take after; 14 take over

Activity 9.2: Dinner Party through the Ages

Aim: To practise asking imaginative questions.

Instructions:

1 Copy handout and distribute.

2 Ask students to consider which famous person (dead or alive) they would invite to a dinner party.

3 Ask students (either on their own or in pairs) to come up with one question per guest.

Activity 9.3: Recipe for success

Aim: to practise topic vocabulary; to practise giving instructions using sequencers.

Instructions:

1 Copy handout and distribute.

2 The boxes show the preparation and cooking of a traditional burger. Ask your students first to glance over the steps, and then to tell you what they think is being prepared.

3 They then need to write each step down on the lines provided. They should be very specific. Eg. *First, you chop the onion. Secondly, you slice the tomato. Next, you…*

4 Finally, ask your students to draw their own favourite recipe in the boxes provided. Can they break it down into 7 steps? Insist on simplicity for clarity.

Tapescript 9

Listening 9.1

Speaker One I used to go there a lot, but the last time I ordered a steak, it was hardly cooked at all. Anyway, when I asked one of the staff if I could, you know, have it cooked a bit more he said that I'd asked for it rare – you know as though it was *my* fault. I told him it was more like *raw* than *rare*. Of course he took his revenge – when he brought it back it was so well-done I could hardly cut it. I won't be going *there* again.

Speaker Two It's often a problem when I go out because I'm not used to eating hot, spicy food. I prefer, you know, plain home cooking – if it's *too* spicy, well, it upsets my stomach. A Chinese takeaway, you know, sweet and sour, that's OK, but on the whole I'd rather have something plain and bland … you know … quite unadventurous. So, as I was telling you … we went to this Indian restaurant and I ordered the mildest curry on the menu but it was still far too hot for me. I couldn't eat it!

Speaker Three Well, I don't like to give away my secrets, but it's quite simple really. I prefer to use low fat cream for this. So what you do is … when the pasta is cooked, you mix in the egg and cream mix – it'll cook on its own without going back on the heat. Stir in the chopped up bacon pieces … like so. And *then* sprinkle on some fresh basil to decorate it. Food has got to *look* good too – tasty *and* tasteful – that's what I always say. We eat with our eyes as much as with our mouths! If you don't have basil you can use parsley – *only* use the leaves though because the rest is bitter.

Speaker Four Well, in those days they would work in the fields harvesting the corn by hand, and then they'd come in for a simple meal at lunchtime. It was a tradition that the farmer and workers ate *together*. The farmer used to sit here at the end of this long table. Meals were quick because they had to get back to work. Usually, there would be soup and bread and cheese. Anyway, once the farmer closed up his knife, well, that was the end of the meal. Everybody had to get up and get back to work – even if they hadn't finished eating! There were no arguments about that back then.

Speaker Five To begin with the waiter brought us a tasty salad, with locally produced cheese. Then there was fish and a fabulous stew. There was a different wine for each course – dry white with the fish, red with the meat. I drank lots of water. I always drink still – sparkling makes me too full. Finally, there was a delicious dessert with a sweet white wine. At the end I felt like, you know, one of those snakes which can swallow a whole sheep! All the same, I could get used to eating like that!

Listening 9.2

Roddy: So here in the studio we have Katrina, our food and restaurant critic. Now Katrina, what have you been up to since we last spoke?

Katrina: Well, I have had the most extraordinary eating out experience at a restaurant called In the Dark.

Roddy: In the Dark?

Katrina: Yes, it's precisely that – you eat in a pitch-dark restaurant where you can't see a thing.

Roddy: Well, OK, but what's the point of that?

Katrina: Well, first of all I should say it is run for the blind.

Roddy: Oh really? It's a kind of charity then is it?

Katrina: Mm, more than that. The idea is to give us, that is sighted people – those of us who can see, the sensation of what it must be like to be blind. It also provides work for blind people who are taken on as staff and some of the money it is true is donated to charities for the blind.

Roddy: So mainly it raises awareness among sighted people and provides jobs. And is it popular, as a concept I mean?

Katrina: Oh yes, it has really taken off – there are restaurants like it in major European cities, from Paris to Moscow. Anyway, the next thing is, once you've ordered your food from the menu and your drinks, blind serving staff lead you down the corridor towards the dining room. They took really good care of us.

Roddy: What, straight into the dark? That's scary.

Katrina: Not really, they let you get used to it bit by bit. There are a few red lights and then it gets darker and darker and you go through heavy drapes, you know … thick curtains … into the dining area where they help you sit down.

Roddy: How do they get it to be so dark – I mean in most situations a bit of light normally manages to penetrate the room, doesn't it?

Katrina: Mm, that's true. You have to leave things like matches and cigarette lighters with your stuff, and you aren't even allowed to take a mobile phone in with you, 'cos that could act as a source of light. Oh and another thing – you have to take off your watches as well … those which have a face which glows in the dark.

Roddy: I've got to say, I wouldn't be able to cope with it at all. I'm claustrophobic and I panic if I can't see anything. I always have to have a light on somewhere.

Katrina: So you wouldn't come with me? Not even if I held your hand?

Roddy: Not even. And what about the meal, how did you get on with that?

Katrina: Well, the practical aspects were quite difficult. You have to grope for everything – your knife and fork and so on, and your wine glass. So I found myself knocking into my neighbour and drinking his wine.

Roddy: Oh no!

Katrina: Yeah, but he took his revenge by pouring wine over my arm – so in the end we were even! At first everyone was nervous and giggly at the beginning but pouring wine over each other is a real ice-breaker. After that we got on really well. He had a lovely voice, although I never got to see his face.

Roddy: Shame. And how easy was it to eat?

Katrina: Well, let's say that good table manners go out of the window too. But you can take advantage of the dark to eat with your fingers.

Roddy: Gross! And how did you know what you were eating, then?

Katrina: Well, we had opted for the surprise menu so we had no idea what would be landing on our plates. I think we had meat.

Roddy: You think!

Katrina: Well, OK we could tell it was meat, but not what type. The same goes for most of the vegetables.

Roddy: So would you recommend it?

Katrina: Well, the food wasn't bad, but it was the overall experience, of course, which is memorable. So basically, yeah, I'd recommend it – I would. But if you do go, make sure you don't wear your best clothes.

Roddy: And what else did you get out of it – apart from, of course, an evening out?

Katrina: Well, it made me much more aware of what it must be like to be blind. Like most of us I've always taken my eyesight for granted – it made me realise how hard it must be to get by without one of your major senses.

Answer key 9

Getting started p85
2 1d; 2a; 3f; 4b; 5e; 6c

Listening p86
2 1E; 2C; 3B; 4D; 5A.
3 A2; B–; C5; D3; E1; F4

Vocabulary p86
1 sweet – sour
sweet – bitter
sweet – dry
still – sparkling (water)
hot – cold
rare – well-done (meat)
spicy – mild
raw – cooked
tasty – bland
2 1 still
2 sour
3 bland
4 cold
5 spicy/hot
6 bitter
7 tasty
8 well-done
9 dry
10 raw
3 Cutting: slice, chop, peel, grate.
Cooking: fry, boil, grill, roast, bake.
Other: sprinkle, mix, stir, add, pour.
5 1 course; 2 diet; 3 rare

Speaking p87
1 1 prefer
2 have
3 prefer
4 to go
5 prefer
2 When 'would rather' is followed by a pronoun, or noun, then the following verb takes the simple past.

Reading p88
2 1 What is surprising about her success is that she is a tiny, skinny woman who can eat more than her huge male competitors.
2 Yes. A 'black widow' is a female spider that kills and eats its mate ('husband'). Sonia is like a black widow because she destroys her male opponents (but of course she doesn't eat them!)
3 She doesn't eat very much in the days before the competition, but expands her stomach by drinking gallons of fizzy cola.
4 1A; 2H; 3B; 4E; 5D; 6C; 7F.
6 1 optimism
2 astonishment
3 concentration
4 appearance

Grammar p89
1 a2; b3; c1
2 1 sentence 1
2 sentences 2 and 3

3 They take the 'bare infinitive' (i.e. the infinitive without *to*)
4 1 No (state)
2 Yes (habit)
3 No (state) '
4 Yes (habit)
5 No (offer)
5 1 I used to be really fat when I was younger.
2 correct
3 ... where I used to go to school.
4 correct
5 I used to know your mother. We worked together for ten years; you used to have blond, curly hair.
6 ... she got used to living in London.

Listening p90
2 1B; 2A; 3B; 4B; 5C; 6A; 7C

Key word p91
1 a5; b3; c2; d1; e4
3 1a removed 1b become successful
2a hire 2b compete against
3a handling it 3b board

Use of English p91
1 1 Customers used to smoke in restaurants.
2 I'll never get used to eating with chopsticks.
3 I'd rather we stayed in and watched television.
4 Would you rather we cooked, or shall we order a takeaway?

5 They took her age into account before making their decision.
6 The food was awful, nevertheless we had a good time.
7 They turned us away despite the fact we had booked.
8 Don't take your parents for granted.

Review p94
1 a The Western diet
2 1 Until
2 their
3 little
4 an
5 which
6 much
7 some
8 on
9 were
10 found
11 still
12 take
3 1 more
2 out
3 lost
4 that
5 were
6 until
7 lost
8 broken
9 had
10 have
11 across
12 where

TAKE THAT!

Can you match the following phrasal verbs using 'take' with each definition? Draw a line between the correct matches. Once you're finished, create example sentences for each one.

Take back	Remove something from someone or somewhere. Brian will _____ the paperwork once he's finished with it.
Take in	Separate something into separate parts. Stuart will _____ the car engine to see why it's broken.
Take on	Accept a job or responsibility. John will _____ that higher position.
Take after	An aircraft leaves the ground and starts flying. The plane will _____ at 3pm.
Take in	Allow someone to stay in your house. The Jones will _____ that orphan for the weekend.
Take off	Accept an offer. Susan decided to _____ Bill's offer.
Take apart	Return something. I will _____ the dvds tonight.
Take off	Be deceived or fooled by someone. Wow, that con artist really managed to _____ his victims.
Take away	Remove something from your body. I want to _____ this hot jacket.
Take on	Give someone a job. The company will _____
Take to	You take someone to an enjoyable place, and pay for it. Mandy, let me _____ you _____ on Valentines day!
Take out	Liking someone immediately. I'm sure I will _____ your brother as soon as I meet him.
Take up	Looking or behaving like someone (usually a family member). April and Alison _____ their mother, mostly.
TAKE OVER	Gain control of something. I will _____ that company one day, just watch!

Dinner Party through the Ages

You can invite any five people from
history to a dinner party at your home.
Which five people would you invite and why?
You can ask **three** of them **one** question.
Decide what your question will be.

Recipe for Success

Look at the pictures. Write down the steps involved in making this meal. When you have finished, draw your own favourite recipe in seven easy steps inside the remaining boxes. Be sure to make your instructions very clear.

PHOTOCOPIABLE 9.3

10 Is it real?

Before you begin

The scope for discussion is wide and varied with a unit called 'Is it real?' Consider asking your students to browse through the ten pages of this unit, and cast their eyes over the images it contains. Photographs of possible unidentified flying objects (UFOs), alien activity, ghostly apparitions and fairy life will usually encourage discussion regardless of age or gender!

Topic: Is it real?

This unit looks at the paranormal and the unexplained. How do you explain the 'unexplainable'? **Paranormal** means beyond the range of normal experience or scientific explanation. Such a topic offers scope for speculation, guessing and deduction.

Unit 10 Wordlist:

ancient	metal/metallic
army	modern
beautiful	mysterious
bright	odd-looking
burial grounds	orange
circle/circular	paranormal
clear	phenomena
colour/colourful	plastic
community	rectangle/rectangular
cubes	rough
dark	round
deep/depth	rubber
diameter	shapeless
document	silver
frying	small
gardening	smooth/smoothness
ghost	soft/softness
glass	sort of
gorgeous	sparked off
green	spherical/sphere
hard	sports
heavy	sticky
height/high	swirling
intricate	tall
iron	thin
kind of	triangle/triangular
large	ugly
leather	universe
light	wide/width
long/length	wooden/wood
made of	

Getting started

1   Grab the students' attention by pretending to 'dowse' – that is, search for underground water. Take a couple of pencils and hold them together in front of you. Walk across the class and make the pencils appear to be drawn to the floor by an invisible force!

2   Run through the questionnaire and check that students understand all the questions. Treat this as a 'milling' activity. Students stand up and discuss their answers with different partners. Round off the activity with a brief all-class feedback session. Finish with a vote: who thinks that aliens and UFOs are 'out there'?

Listening: out of the blue

1   Generate interest in the listening passage by asking students to speculate about the photograph of the 'UFO' object running across the top of page 96. Encourage the students to speculate about the origins of the photograph (when and where it was taken).

2   Students listen to the recording all the way through and make notes about the boy and the object in the sky. Ask them who they think the boy is and where he comes from.

Vocabulary: describing objects

Aim: to improve students' understanding and use of adjectives.

2 Remind students that while the order of these answers may vary slightly, there is generally an accepted form which 'sounds' better.

3 This exercise should reinforce the importance of adjectives in describing something.

Avoiding too many adjectives

Transferring information somewhere else doesn't mean omitting it, or even necessarily starting a new sentence. As the example shows, it may be as simple as adding in a word such as *was* or *with*. Consider writing up several sentences, full of adjectives, on the whiteboard. Tell your students to verbally transfer the information elsewhere.

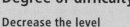

It was a crisp, sunny, sparkling and slightly breezy day.

> It was a crisp day, with a slight breeze and plenty of sparkling sunshine.

> The sparklingly sunny day was crisp and breezy.

Individual 'long turn'

Degree of difficulty

Decrease the level

As the spotlight suggests, allow your students to practise the Individual 'long turn' in pairs. Allow each student to write down their descriptions/use a dictionary to choose their adjectives before telling their partner.

Increase the level

By Unit 10, your class should be feeling much more comfortable with each other. Consider setting this as a mock exam. Allocate roles such as speaker and interlocutor, and allow students to mark each other.

Exam practice extension

Take activity 6 further than what the pages of the coursebook can allow. This will need a little preparation on your behalf, but it should be well-rewarded by the response of your students.

1 Using plain brown paper bags, place one item of fruit or vegetable (or any item of food really) inside. Items could include: an unwashed potato, a grape, an orange, a carrot, broccoli, a piece of chocolate, etc.

2 Give a bag to each student (or each pair of students, depending on class size and ability).

3 Making sure they don't use their eyes, ask each student to stick their hand inside the bag and feel their item. They need to write down at least five adjectives to describe what they touch.

4 Repeat the action, but this time, the student needs to use their nose and smell the item. Even if the item is odourless, they need to be able to describe what 'no smell' smells like!

5 Repeat the action, but allow each student to look at their object (still within the bag).

6 By now each student should have at least 15 adjectives written down. Ask them to write these into proper sentences.

7 Each student reads their sentences aloud to a partner. Each partner should then try to guess what the item is. If the partner guesses accurately, the student has been successful!

> It's quite round, or perhaps more of an oval, with an uneven surface. It has a rough, rather dirty feeling when you touch it. It doesn't seem to smell much, perhaps it has a slight smell of dirt or earth. It is about the size of your fist. It is brown, with patches of creamy white, and small dents here and there.

> Is it is a potato?

> Yes!

Reading: crop circles

Pre-teaching definitions:

A **crop** (n) is typically wheat or maize.
A **crop circle** (n) is some sort of pattern within the field of crops.
A **hoax** (n) (rhymes with jokes) is a kind of practical joke that often isn't very funny.
A **three-dimensional object** (n) is solid rather than flat, because it can usually be measured in height, depth and width. (Remind students that the 3-D in the title is short for three-dimensional.) Try to teach these words in context:

> The other day the police had to evacuate the university after a telephone call said there was a bomb in the building. In fact it was a hoax. It was a student who didn't want to take his examination.

Crop circles

Examples of crop circles can be found around the world. Various explanations have been offered to explain their formation. One possible explanation is that the circles are human-made hoaxes (a study in 2000 into circle hoaxing concluded that 80% of UK circles were definitely made by humans). Secondly, the circles may result from geological anomalies. Thirdly, paranormal explanations include formation by UFOs. In the 2005 film, *Chicken Little*, crop circles were created by aliens as they chase the main characters around in the crops.

1   Ask students to speculate about the origins of crop circles. Possible responses will probably deduce that crop circles could be made by people on tractors, members of a mysterious cult, or by aliens. The most likely explanation is that they are the result of a 'hoax' or practical joke.

2   Give students two minutes to quickly read the text and to try and find the answer. If you want to encourage another read through, this time scanning for specific information, ask them to find out what the following people believe/d:

> What does Steve Alexander believe?

> He thinks they seem totally original.

> What did the Bishop of Lyon believe?

> He thinks that they are an example of devil worship.

> And most of the inhabitants of Ashbury?

> They think the circle is a hoax.

3   Students match the words in bold in the text to the definitions.

4   Give students ten minutes to make their choices.

5   Students speculate about the hoaxes in the pictures: Loch Ness monster; fairies; ghost on stairs.

Loch Ness Monster

The Loch Ness Monster is an alleged animal claimed to inhabit Scotland's Loch Ness. It first came to the world's attention in 1933, when a tourist from London claimed to have seen a pre-historic animal, or dragon, near the Scottish Loch. Since then, evidence of its existence has been largely anecdotal (based on personal stories). Minimal and disputed photographic material and sonar readings do little to prove whether or not there is actually something in the loch. No physical evidence (skeletal remains, live animal capture, tissue samples or spoor) has, to date, been uncovered.

Listening: crop circles

Identifying the speaker's purpose

Talk through the spotlight. Once you have dealt with the multiple matching exercise that follows, ask students to identify which questions they think focus on one of the categories from the spotlight.

Speaking: guessing and speculating

Play the recording through again, pausing where necessary. Notice that this activity flows very neatly from the Listening task before it and the Key Word task after it.

Key word: seem

Seem is a very useful verb for speculating.

Key word extension

Consider putting these three definitions of *seem* on the whiteboard.

Seem

→ 1 (Link verb) Use to say that someone/something gives the impression of having a particular quality, or of happening in the way you describe.

→ 2 (Transitive verb) Use to describe your own thoughts/feelings, in order to make your statements less forceful.

→ 3 (Transitive verb) Use to say that you tried to do something and were unable to.

Then give your students three example sentences like the ones below, and ask them to match to them definitions 1, 2, or 3.

> A) I seem to remember that you promised to work hard.

> B) Everyone seems busy.

> C) I can't seem to stop talking.

Answers:
1B; 2A; 3C.

1–2 Drill the introductory phrases until students are comfortable and confident with using them. As a class, match the words in bold to the introductory expression. Students work in pairs and speculate about the second photograph.

Grammar: modal verbs for guessing, speculating and deducing

This section should largely be a matter of revision for most of the students in the class. If there is residual difficulty, refer them to Section 11 of the Grammar Reference.

3   Students speculate. Accept sentences that are logical and that practise the forms from the grammar section.

Writing: compulsory email

1   A lot can be deduced from reading other people's correspondence. After your students have read the 'informal exchange' between Michelle and Yvonne, discuss what it shows of their relationship. Through the emails, it appears that the two girls share a close, relaxed friendship, with similar hobbies and the ability to chat about holiday plans together.

2–3 Based on the emails in 1, your students should be able to annotate the Guidelines with something like this:

Guidelines for writing formal letters

1   Always start your letter with Dear …
    No, you can use Hi.

2   Always use sentences.
    Only where necessary.

3   Start a new line or use separate paragraphs where necessary.
    Yes, this should probably be true even in emails.

4   Avoid contracted forms such as I'll.
    No, contracted forms are much more relaxed.

5   Do not use exclamation marks.
    No, use them as much as your expression needs them.

6   Avoid direct questions
    The more direct questions, the more answers you'll get!

7   Spelling and punctuation must be accurate.
    Well, it isn't as strict, but both still help to make something easy to read.

8   End your letter with Yours sincerely or Best regards.
    Rather, use a casual expression that finishes off your sentiment, like See you on Friday!

Photocopiable activity instructions

Activity 10.1: Granny's Attic
Aim: To practise and consolidate vocabulary describing objects and adjective order.
Instructions:

1   Copy the large illustration of 'Granny's attic'. Hand out one copy per pair of students.

2   Ask the students to run through the objects one by one, and check their pronunciation. They should be able to recognise (from left to right): rugby ball; rocking horse*; painting with large frame; portable radio* toy rocket, teddy bear; Navy chest; record collection*; typewriter; 'lava' lamp*; army helmet; photograph album; gramophone*: suitcase: polka-dot dress; and doll.

* these items may be harder/require more pre-teaching, especially if you want a specific name such as 'gramophone' rather then 'record player'.

3   Next, demonstrate Kim's game by arranging the cut-out objects (second page of activity) on the table. Ask the students to study the arrangement of the objects carefully.

4   Then ask the students to avert their eyes.

5   Change the position of three of the objects.

6   Students turn round and name the moved objects.

> Let me see. Well, the sad old teddy bear with one eye has been moved. Before it was …

7   Hand each pair an envelope containing the cut-out objects. Ask them to continue on their own.

Activity 10.2: Lost World
Aim: To practise the language of making deductions and intelligent guesses.
Instructions:

1   Encourage your students to speculate on the societies in the pictures.

2   Divide your students into two large groups (A and B) to work on one of the pictures. Write the following topics up on the whiteboard:

1 religious practices	6 hunting
2 beliefs	7 transport
3 life after death	8 clothing
4 warfare	9 the role of women
5 agriculture	10 the role of children

3   Monitor the groups and where necessary help with ideas. When everyone is ready, put the students into pairs to exchange their ideas.

Tapescript 10

Listening 10.1

It was ten o'clock and I was supposed to have finished for the night. But then someone brought in an odd-looking, small boy. He couldn't have been much more than nine or ten. They said he'd been wandering down a lane about ten miles south of town. But he couldn't say a word – in *any* language. Anyway, we made him a bed in one of the cells at the station. Maybe someone would show up in the morning looking for him. He seemed surprisingly calm – not worried at all. There was nothing on him to say where he was from. The only thing that was strange was a triangular, blue metal badge on his jacket. It was a *deep* blue colour. It must have been special to him cos when I reached out to touch it he got kind of angry. I tried asking him about it but he didn't answer. His eyes just got big and more angry.

Anyway, I had kids of my own waiting at home so had to leave him with the other officers. Anyway, while I was driving home I was on the road out of town when I had to stop. I thought it was a car coming towards me. I flashed my car lights because his lights were so bright. But they weren't two lights like a *ordinary* car. First of all there was a beautiful orange light. Then it grew and became three, four, and then they changed colour!

I thought 'what is going on here?' so I switched my police lights on. I thought it's someone making fun of me. Then the lights rose above me and I could see it. It had a smooth round base like a mirror. I could see the lights changing colour on it and then realised it was the blue and red lights on the top of my car. Then suddenly it flew off and all I remember is a metal disc with a triangular shape across it. That was the second time I'd seen that blue triangle that day.

Listening 10.2

Speaker One It could be any number of things. We had some strong wind last night. It was blowing *really* hard and a tree fell down in my garden so it could have blown the corn over. Or maybe it was some kids playing around. We often get teenagers coming down from the city in the summer and they sleep out so they could quite easily have done it. I also read that helicopters can make shapes like this so it might have been as a result of some kind of flying machine. There's a military air force base about fifty miles away. Who knows? Perhaps a plane or something flew over last night.

Speaker Two I'm absolutely certain that aliens did it. I mean, there have been lots of UFO sightings round here. A friend of mine saw lights in the sky only last week. This triangle of lights flew past his house. It was sort of metal he said and moving really quite quickly. Anyway, he saw them land in the distance. So it seems to me that any spaceship would leave a mark on the ground like that.

Speaker Three Some crop circles are probably hoaxes and for fun but in this case it would have been impossible for someone to make something this complex in the middle of the night. They couldn't have done it all in seven hours! The farmer said he'd been to the field in the evening and saw nothing and then the next morning it appeared. It must have been something more mysterious. I know that some people have seen UFOs around here.

Speaker Four I can't believe all the fuss over this. In my opinion it's a complete hoax. For one thing, people are saying it's aliens. Well, aliens wouldn't come here and even if they did, why spend their time making circles in the corn? Surely they have better things to do! I *think* it's probably someone creating a story. It seems like the sort of thing a newspaper would set up because we have loads of journalists visiting the village all of a sudden. In my opinion they should all go home – leave us alone.

Speaker Five I can't seem to make my mind up on this. The fact is it's there and it is very clever, very beautiful in a way. Whoever did it was very artistic. I have heard that there are groups of people who travel round the country making these circles. They do it as a kind of hobby. But I live nearby and I didn't hear anything so ... I'm not really sure. Maybe it *was* aliens after all.

Answer key 10

Listening p96

3 1 at 10 pm
2 nine or ten
3 south of town
4 in the morning
5 surprisingly calm
6 triangular
7 towards
8 changed colour
9 a mirror
10 second time

Vocabulary p97

2 There are several possible answers to these questions. Suggested answers:
1 We saw a … a) long thin silver metal object in the sky b) long thin object made of silver c) metal object in the sky, it was long and thin.
2 … he would always wear a) an ancient shapeless army overcoat … and dark green rubber gardening boots/dark green gardening boots made of rubber.
3 My uncle always used a) a heavy old iron frying pan b) an old heavy frying pan made of iron.
4 They brought in a a) large mysterious rectangular wooden document box b) mysterious document box, it was large and rectangular.
5 Their own offices are in a modern, tall ugly/ugly tall building made of glass.
6 She turned up in a) a gorgeous bright red German sports car b) a gorgeous bright red sports car from/made in Germany.
3 Sticky tape; kites; ball.
5 long; wooden; wide; deep; high; triangular; hard; spherical; circular; soft; coloured/ful; metallic.

Reading p98

2 Reasons: a message left by aliens in a spaceship; a hoax created during the night; formed by helicopters.
3 1 hoax
2 community

3 cubes
4 diameter
5 burial grounds
6 sparked off
7 intricate
8 phenomena
9 paranormal
10 swirling
4 1C; 2C; 3C; 4D; 5A; 6D; 7B; 8D

Listening p100

1 1C; 2A; 3E; 4F; 5B.

Speaking p100

1 1 could be
2 maybe
3 might have been
4 certain
5 have been
6 couldn't
7 must
8 opinion
9 think
10 sure

Key word p100

1 1 appear to be
2 appear
3 in my opinion
4 I'm unsure
5 I'm fairly certain

Grammar p101

1 1b; 2a; 3b; 4a
2 Pairs 3 and 4
4 1 sure that it's/sure that's
2 was supposed to be
3 can't be
4 likely (that) she's waiting
5 'm certain it's not
6 must have used that
7 couldn't have been
8 possibly be/have been

Writing p102

2 1, 2, 4, 5, 6, 7, 8
4 b I'm sorry but/that …
c The good news is that …
d Why don't we …/Would you like …
e you should …
f Would you like to …/Why don't we …
g The bad news is that
h Thanks
i Is it OK
j until the end of the week at 'Shoeshine'
k They're plastic …
l See you soon
5 1b; 2f; 3h; 4a; 5i; 6g; 7e; 8k; 9j; 10l; 11c; 12d
7 1T; 2F; 3T; 4T

Review p104

1 1A; 2C; 3D; 4A; 5D; 6B; 7C; 8D; 9A; 10D; 11A; 12C
2 1 be
2 be
3 have been
4 be
5 can't
6 have cancelled
7 couldn't have been
8 it have been
9 seems
3 1 for
2 really/so/extremely
3 at
4 of
5 on
6 that
7 Why
8 by
9 do
10 while
11 me
12 forward

What's in Granny's Attic?

PHOTOCOPIABLE 10.1

PHOTOCOPIABLE 10.1

LOST WORLDS

Cave People

You are archaeologists who have found evidence of a long ago civilisation. Study the evidence and make some guesses about the kind of civilisation your evidence suggests. Say what they *must have/can't have/might have done* in their societies.

Ancient Egyptians

You are archaeologists who have found evidence of a long ago civilisation. Study the evidence and make some guesses about the kind of civilisation your evidence suggests. Say what they *must have/can't have/might have done* in their societies.

PHOTOCOPIABLE 10.2

Before you begin

Lead into the topic of shopping and money. Ask a few questions which will lead into discussion:

> Who likes shopping more, men or women?

> What are the different types of shopping that people do?

> How many people have tried shopping online?

Topic: Shopping and money

This unit looks at the topics of handling money, shopping and consumerism. While dictionaries just describe shopping as 'going to the shops and buying things', it is slightly more complex than this: in a culture where credit card limits are being exceeded every day, shopping is often considered a hobby, or even an art-form!

Unit 11 Wordlist:

afford	pay by
bargain	pay off (a loan)
borrow from	pocket money
brands	price
budget	refund
come to	repay
cost	save up
customers	set aside
deal	shop around
discount	special offer
get by	spend
in debt	splash out on
lend to	stay within
pay (a cheque) into (an account)	take something back
	whim

Getting started

Run through the questionnaire, taking care to check any unknown vocabulary. Consider teaching how these words can be used as either nouns or verbs:

Noun	Verb
A bargain is something which is good value for money, usually because it has been sold at a lower price than normal.	**To bargain** for something is the process of getting that something for a cheaper price.
A brand is a famous name associated with a product; e.g. *Nescafé* is a brand of instant coffee; *Reebok* is a brand of sportswear.	**To brand** someone as something, is to decide that the person is that thing.
A budget is the amount of money you have to spend.	**To budget** is the process of sticking to this amount of money.
A purchase is something that you buy.	**To purchase** is a more formal way of saying 'to buy'.
A shop is a building or part of a building where things are sold.	**To shop** is to go to the shops and buy things.

Vocabulary: shopping and consumerism

This series of exercises examines broad nouns, prepositions, verbs and phrasal verbs on the topic of money.

1   Refer students back to the text on the previous page. Remember:
    A **shopper** is simply a person who shops; a **customer** is someone who buys from a shop. **Consumer** is a term used more by economists; **consumerism** is an abstract noun that describes the phenomenon the desire to buy and acquire goods. If we buy something on a **whim**, we buy it on impulse.

2   Students complete the sentences with words in orange on the previous page.

> **TEACHING IN PRACTICE**

Pronunciation
Make sure that students are able to pronounce:
• *bargain* so that it rhymes with *hooligan*.
• *whim*: the 'h' is silent so it rhymes with *dim*.

3   The first few questions deal with the prepositions that commonly combine with verbs on areas to do with

money. The rest of the exercise contrasts confusable verbs of similar meaning. Students will certainly be familiar with all the words in the exercise but will probably make mistakes in using them correctly.

> The **cost** is the amount of money you have to pay to get something.

> The **price** is the amount of money at which something is sold.

4   Students join the split sentences to provide a clear, explanatory context for the phrasal verbs that are embedded within them. Integrate work on pronunciation and sentence stress. Practise consonant vowel liaisons.

Vocabulary extension

As a consolidation activity, you could ask students to create a spidergram on a large piece of paper. It should map all of the words that they have come across in this unit so far. You can then ask them to predict/think of other words that could be added to the spidergram, such as: *client, take out money, form an account, credit card, store card, withdraw, cash machine, to be overdrawn, overspend, be in the red* or *in the black*.

---

5   Use the questions for a short all-class discussion on the topic of borrowing and spending money, and on the ethics of advertising to children.

Listening: money habits

1   This section follows on from the topic of the previous pages. Students listen and decide which speakers are customers, which are selling something and which one is giving advice.

Degree of difficulty

Increase the level: If you want to treat the listening passage as straightforward examination practice, dispense with this question and move directly onto the multiple choice questions, playing the recording through twice without pause or commentary. Allow students to confer and compare their answers while listening in to what they say.

Decrease the level: On the basis of their answers decide whether to play it a third time. If you do choose to do this, remind your students that they will not have this option in the exam.

Grammar: conditionals

By this unit, students should be very familiar with conditionals and their different forms. The following exercises compare and contrast them.

1   Students listen and note the missing words. Check their answers and then refer them to Section 6 of the Grammar Reference. Alternatively, if you are fairly confident that students are already familiar with the forms and names of these tenses, ask them directly what they are. Remember that some students may have learnt these as *real* or *unreal conditionals.*

2   Students name the forms.

3   Students complete the sentences with the most likely conditional form.

4   This exercise tries to distinguish between natural consequences where one thing systematically follows another, and causal relationships where only a high degree of likelihood exists.

5   Take the first sentence and deal with it as an example eliciting suggestions from the class as a whole.

> If we didn't have cars we wouldn't be able to live out of town. If we weren't able to live out of town the cities would be much bigger ...

> If we had electric cars then there would probably be less pollution ... This would help against global warming.

Put the students into groups to create other chains of events from the prompts.

6   Students create sentences using the third conditional. In feedback remember to do intensive work on pronunciation, in particular contractions and weak forms (see the TIPs in earlier units).

Reading: pocket money

BACKGROUND

Money

Early traders used a system of barter which didn't involve money. Barter is a type of exchange: a farmer might trade a cow for a wooden cart. In China, India and Africa, cowrie shells (small, shiny oval shells) became a form of currency. The first coins were crude lumps of metal; circular coins appeared in China around 1500 BC. Around 560 BC, the Lydians (living in what is now known as Turkey) minted three types of coins: a gold, a silver, and a mixed metal coin. Their use spread through Asia Minor and Greece very quickly. In 1150 AD, the Chinese began to use paper bills for money.

1   Ask your students when – or if – they received pocket money. Elicit the type of thing they spent it on. Was it clothes, magazines, credit for mobile phones, holidays, music, or lunch money?

2   Set a ten minute time limit for this task, treating it as examination practice.

3   Put the students in groups to discuss their answers. Find out whether they had to do anything to earn money. Find out if your students have/used to have summer or part-time jobs. Alternatively divide the class into two groups: Western parents and Asian parents. Ask each group to brainstorm reasons for their point of view. Then place the students in pairs with a partner from the other group.

Reading vocabulary extension

Ask your students if they know of any other words synonymous with *money*. Answers could include: *capital*, *cash*, *currency*, *funds* or *wealth*. Some quirky personal terms may be brought up as well.

Key word: *if*

Remind your students of when to use if :

→ 1 (Conjunction) Use in conditional sentences to introduce the circumstances in which an event or situation might happen, or might have happened:
  She gets very upset **if** *we don't leave class on time.*

→ 2 (Conjunction) Use if in indirect questions when the answer is either 'yes' or 'no':
  I wonder **if** *anyone is listening today.*

→ 3 (Conjunction) Use to suggest that something might be slightly different from what you are stating in the main part of the sentence:
  What one quality, **if** *any, do you dislike about your teacher?*

1   Notice that this comes before alternatives to *if* (activity 5), so it's important that the position and uses of *if* are revised and consolidated. Students add *if* to the sentences. Move rapidly through the series of exercises 1–3.

TEACHING IN PRACTICE

Structures and functions

Explain to your students that when we talk about function we are primarily concerned with the communicative purpose of a form or expression. Of course, it is then important to examine the grammatical structure of these expressions so that students can use them creatively in different situations. Example: *How about going to the cinema?*
    → Function = making a suggestion
    → Underlying structure = *How about* + verb+ *-ing*
      (the gerund)

4   Students listen to the snippets again, or alternatively they can find them in the Tapescript on page 219 of their coursebook.

5   Remind students that *provided that* is used to introduce a formal or stricter condition. Students may not understand when we use *unless* and *otherwise*. Both have the idea of *if not* but come in different places in the sentence. *Unless* comes before the condition clause. *Otherwise* comes before the consequence clause.

> Unless you call to let me know, I'll meet you at the shop.

> Call to let me know, otherwise I'll meet you at the shop.

Grammar: mixed conditionals/*wish*

Mixed conditionals occur when we cut across the time boundaries between traditional conditional sentences. Functions: expressing regret, giving advice and making suggestions.

p/c 11.2

GRAMMAR SPOTLIGHT

Mixed conditionals

Play the recording, pausing after each sentence to allow students time to modify sentences. In feedback insist on emphatic stress on the strong condition: *so long as, provided*. Remind students that *in case* is followed by the present simple, not the future.
Typical mistake: *Take an umbrella in case it* ~~will~~ ~~rain~~.
          – *in case it rains.*

Speaking: regret, advice and suggestions

This activity uses the two photographs on page 111. The first photo shows a group of people standing around a broken-down car. The second photo shows people stuck in a (seemingly temporary) airport terminal. Answers could include:

	Broken-down car	Airport delay
Regret	I think they regret not checking the car engine before leaving home! I'm sure they wish it hadn't happened!	I'm sure they regret booking that plane. I wonder whether they wish they were on a train instead?
Advice	I would advise them to ring a mechanic. If I were them, I'd consider walking next time!	I would advise that they are patient and read a book while waiting. I think they should travel by train or bus in the future.

Note: don't forget to remind your students that there is a **Useful Expressions** list on page 227 of their coursebook.

Writing: an opinion essay

In part 2 of the Writing Paper there is often an opportunity to write an essay where candidates set out their opinions or contrast opposing opinions. Read through the Exam spotlight with your students.

4   Students underline the introductory phrases to the sentences they have just studied.

5   Better students will probably be capable of arriving at something like this:

On the one hand this could encourage students from poorer backgrounds to stay on at school and obtain better qualifications/provide students with a little pocket money.

However on the other, it could encourage disruptive students who have no interest in studying to stay on at school and make life difficult for other students and teachers.

Another argument for this is that by staying on at school it will broaden the educational level and outlook of students who stay on for an extra year, and favour those people who are so-called 'late developers'.

Nevertheless, for a few it could be a frustrating experience and a complete waste of time.

You could also argue that education is never wasted.

However, one big disadvantage of the idea is that it puts a price on 'good behaviour'. People should stay on at school

from a genuine love of study, not simply because they expect some kind of immediate reward.

6   Students select the ending that best accords with the essay they have written.

7   Students return to the titles from the beginning of the section.

Degree of difficulty

Increase the level: You could treat this as an individual exercise; perhaps set it for homework. Or, you could exploit it as an in-class timed essay.

Decrease the level: Alternatively, you could use it as a further instance of cooperative writing in pairs or groups. Encourage students to brainstorm and share their ideas. They could use some of the techniques which have already been introduced earlier in the course such as the use of 'spidergrams'.

Photocopiable activity instructions

Activity 11.1: Deal-makers

Aim: To practise the vocabulary of buying, selling and negotiating; to apply the first and second conditional.

Instructions:

1   Set up the situations with the class as a whole.

2   Divide the class into two large groups (A and B).

3   Monitor each group, and make sure that they fully understand the information on their role cards. Ask them what they would say in each situation and help them with ideas.

Activity 11.2: Life After Debt (reading and discussion)

Aim: To practise the third conditional; to apply ways of expressing regrets, wishes and lost opportunities.

Instructions:

1   Exploit the title *Life After Debt*: ask the students to predict what it might be about.

2   Run through the story and check that the students understand the story.

3   Students then read through the jigsaw pieces of the second page and work in groups to put the main actors in order of responsibility. Gently encourage students to formulate sentences using the third conditional and *wish* + past participle.

Tapescript 11

Listening 11.1

Speaker One Well, I'd say that I'm fairly good at staying within my budget. I mean I won't just buy stuff for the sake of it – like on a whim or anything. I go out with a certain amount of money in my purse and I won't go over that amount. Most of my friends have credit cards but they're always in debt so I just carry cash. That way if I suddenly see something I like, I either buy it or come back the following week with the money I need. And then if it's gone, it's gone but usually you find it still there.

Speaker Two I'm a bit of a bargain hunter. If I see something on special offer, I'll buy it but I'll never pay full price for anything. I don't go from shop to shop but what I will do is look it up on the Internet and compare prices of things. There are some great websites that will actually show you how much you can save depending on where you go. And besides, if you go to the same shop every time, they'll often give you a loyalty card so you save money when you shop there. And that's on top of any discounts.

Speaker Three I just can't make my mind up. It looks in good working order. It only has about thirty thousand kilometres on it and he says the last owner was an old couple who only drove it at weekends but he probably says that about every one in the showroom. I don't know. It's not like I've even looked at any others. Maybe if he reduced the price, I would be interested. After all it's only two years old. It seems like a good deal. Let's see what he says.

Speaker Four Well, it's funny you're asking for that 'cause if you had come in last week I would have had just what you were looking for. It was a green sofa and chairs that would have matched your wallpaper. I'd order you another but I'm pretty sure it was the last in that line. They said they'll be sending us the new catalogue for next year in the next couple of days and then I can tell you. Otherwise, all we have is what you can see here. Though one thing I can do is ring our other branch and see if they have any left in stock. Don't go away. I'll give them a call right now.

Speaker Five You don't have to decide now. If you want to take it home and see how it looks once you get it home, that's fine. There's a 28-day money-back guarantee on all our products so long as you bring it back within 28 days of purchase, that's fine. Oh, that's also provided that you have the receipt with it of course. So you could take it today with absolutely no obligation. All we ask is that you return it in the same condition as you bought it. You'd be amazed to see what some people bring back …

Speaker Six At the end of the day I think the main thing to remember is that whether you earn a lot or a little, it's really important to make sure you've got some left over for a rainy day. So there are three ways you can do this. There's short-term saving in case you have an emergency. Then there's medium-term saving which means money that you might need to use in about five or ten years' time. And finally, there are long-term things like pensions and the rule on that is you start paying into it as soon as you can. The younger the better, in fact.

Speaker Seven You know, I really wish we hadn't bothered. For one thing it's caused so much stress worrying about how much it's all going to cost and then they've changed the hotel twice. It isn't the one in the brochure anymore so I hope it's decent. Of course, I didn't want to go in the first place but Graham was with me and we went into the travel agent and the next thing I know, he's writing the cheque.

Speaker Eight I wish I could afford it but I can't borrow any more from my mum and dad. I already owe them money for my new bike. In fact it's a bit unfair because my sister got a bike for her birthday and so she has some money she's saving. But for me, my dad wants to know when I'm going to pay him back. Had I known, I wouldn't have bought it in the first place.

Listening 11.2

One … If I suddenly see something I like, I either buy it or come back the following week with the money I need.

Two … If you go to the same shop every time, they'll often give you a loyalty card so you save money when you shop there.

Three … Maybe if he reduced the price, I would be interested.

Four … If you had come in last week I would have had just what you were looking for.

Listening 11.3

One There's a 28-day money-back guarantee on all our products so long as you bring it back within 28 days of purchase, that's fine.

Two Oh, that's also provided that you have the receipt with it of course.

Three There's short-term saving in case you have an emergency.

Four Had I known, I wouldn't have bought it in the first place.

Answer key 11

Vocabulary p106

1 shopper, customer, consumer

2 1 bargain

2 logo; brands

3 whim:

4 budget

5 special offer

6 deal

7 discount

3 1 in

2 within

3 to

4 by; in

5 price

6 paid

7 broke; lend

8 cost

9 afford

10 buys

11 cost

12 pay

13 price

14 spend

15 refund

4 1e; 2c; 3j; 4h; 5b; 6a; 7i; 8f; 9g; 10d

Listening p107

1 1, 2, 3, 7, 8

2 4 and 5

3 6

2 before; guess; twice

3 1B; 2A; 3C; 4C; 5B; 6C; 7B; 8C

Grammar p107

1 1 see; buy; come

2 go; give

3 reduced; I would be

4 had come; would have had

2 1: zero

2: first

3: second

4: third

3 1 booked

2 brought

3 revises

4 had known

5 won't come

6 would have taken

7 get

8 don't hear

4 2 Likely

3 Likely

4 Likely

5 Certain

6 If he hadn't spent all his money he would have had some left.

If she had heard the alarm clock she wouldn't have been late for work. If she hadn't been late for work, her boss wouldn't have shouted at her.

If he hadn't failed his exams he could/would have gone to university.

Reading p108

2 1D; 2C; 3A; 4D; 5B; 6B; 7A; 8C; 9D; 10A; 11D; 12A; 13C; 14B; 15C

3 1 questions

2 texts

Key word p110

1 2 I wonder **if** they're ready yet.

3 What **if** you tried doing it this way?

4 Do you mind **if** she comes too?

5 I wouldn't do that **if** I were you.

6 I keep thinking **if** only Molly had come too. She would have loved it.

7 I'll do it, but only **if** he does too.

2 a3; b6; c2; d1; e1; f4; g5

4 1 so long as

2 provided that

3 in case

4 Had I known

5 1A; 2C; 3B; 4B; 5A; 6B

Grammar p110

1 1 hadn't gone

2 have informed

3 hadn't been caught

4 studied/be

5 would be wise

6 started; be expected

2 a1, 2, 5; b3, 4; c6

3 1 If only I'd saved my money instead of spending it.

2 If I'd studied medicine I would be a doctor now.

3 I wish (that) you had taken that job so that we could have more money now.

4 I wish I could speak Spanish./I wish I had learnt Spanish.

Writing p112

1 a2; b1; c3

2 As a result more people are in debt in the modern world than ever before.

So the question is whether we should have to work…

However, some people claim…

3 1e; 2b; 3d; 4a; 5c

Review p114

1 1 ~~borrow~~; lend

2 ~~at~~; to

3 ~~down~~; aside

4 ~~off~~; back

5 ~~budget~~; offer

6 ~~on~~; in

2 1 did the bank lend you

2 I wish hadn't spent

3 Should you change your

4 provided you have some

5 final bill comes to

6 enough I wouldn't be

7 Unless they change their

8 Do you mind if

1 A; 2C; 3B; 4D; 5A; 6C; 7D; 8A; 9C; 10B; 11A; 12D

DEAL MAKERS

Situation 1

Student A wants to buy a reliable second-hand scooter to get backwards and forwards to university. Student B is a scooter dealer.

When you are ready, negotiate a deal and write your final agreement here:

Price: _____

Guarantee: _____

_____

Extras: _____

_____

_____

_____

Situation 2

Student A, the owner of a shop selling expensive designer clothes, is recruiting an experienced shop assistant. Student B is the shop assistant. A has agreed to hire B, but you are meeting to agree the salary and conditions of the employment contract.

When you are ready, negotiate the contract and write an agreement that covers:

Contract length: _____

Salary/commission: _____

_____

Extras: _____

_____

_____

_____

PHOTOCOPIABLE 11.1

Student A

Situation One: Student scooter buyer

You are a student. Public transport is so unreliable in your town that you want to buy a good second-hand scooter. You have seen a model you like, but the dealer is asking €2250. But you want to get the lowest price, and the best deal possible. You have a total budget of €2000. You can pay cash for a good discount. The scooter has a six month guarantee and a helmet carrier.

Extras:

You would like the following extras:
- six months' extra guarantee. Other dealers give a year's guarantee.
- a free helmet.
- a big lock so you can chain your scooter up.

Situation Two: Shop owner

You are the owner of an expensive clothes' shop. Your shop sells designer fashions from Paris and Milan. You have decided to offer a job to an experienced shop assistant who works at a rival shop. You feel sure that that he/she will be good at the job.

Contract: To begin with, you want to give them a trial period of three months. Then if everything is OK, you'll give them a one year contract. If you are satisfied after a year, you'll give them a permanent contract.

Conditions: You expect the shop assistant to sell €500,000 worth of goods each year (This isn't difficult because your shop sells very expensive clothes and accessories; handbags cost €1000 each!)

Salary: You don't want to pay a basic salary, instead you want the shop assistant to work for a 5% commission. If he/she manages to meet the target of €500,000 there will be a €2000 bonus at the end of the year.

Extras: You give a 75% discount on any clothes they want to buy. You will pay for three hours of group English lessons a week at your cousin's language school.

Holidays: new staff have four weeks in their first year. This rises to six weeks after three years. Staff have to work three Saturdays a month. Your shop does most of its business on Saturdays.

Student B

Situation One: Scooter dealer

The scooter you are selling is only two years old. A new one would cost €3000 so you think this is a bargain. It has done 20,000 kilometres. You think 2000 is reasonable price (it cost you €1300 but don't tell A!)

Your lowest price is €1750, but you want be as close to €2250 as possible. The scooter is sold with six months' guarantee. You usually charge €150 for another six months' guarantee. You think that the machine you are selling is in good condition and that this brand of scooter is reliable and does not usually have problems for the first two years.

You are not interested in making a reduction for cash.

You sell helmets that cost between €100 and €150. You also have some second-hand helmets for €50. Chains and locks cost €80. These locks are almost unbreakable. It is important that people invest in a good lock because scooters are often stolen. The scooter you are selling also has a very good box for a helmet. This is an extra that usually costs €150 so the buyer is getting this for free!

Situation Two: Shop assistant

You are an experienced shop assistant. You have accepted a job with a rival shop owner, but before you accept it you want to make sure that the conditions are just right.

You want:

A permanent contract without a trial period. After all, you are experienced salesperson.

You expect a monthly salary of €1500 plus commission of 2% of everything you sell.

You also expect a generous bonus at the end of each year.

You want 6 weeks holiday a year. You would also like two Saturdays a month off.

You want to dress yourself with clothes from the store. In your last job you were given free samples from designers.

You would like to know what opportunities exist for training. You would like to learn English.

Life after Debt?

1 **Read the story about Katherine and David Thomas.**
How common is this type of story in your country?

Katherine Thomas lived a life that was the envy of her old friends and neighbours. Her husband David was a partner in a successful property company while Katherine worked as an interior designer with her rich golf-club friends as her clients. It was different from her past where she had lived in poverty, part of a large family. Now, her magnificent house was beautifully furnished and their kitchen full of the latest gadgets. She and her husband David each had a lovely new German car, and their gorgeous children Henry and Chloe were both at expensive private schools. The whole family belonged to an exclusive golf and country club. Even their dog, Mietta, was beautiful! Life looked perfect even though many people asked how they managed it all. Then, very quickly, this perfect world fell apart. The economy suddenly slowed down and people no longer wanted to build. Finally, one morning, David went to his business to find that his partner Derek had run away after emptying the safe. He then discovered a pile of unpaid bills and threatening letters from the bank. On returning home to tell Katherine, his wife told him that their beautiful home and lifestyle was built on a mountain of debt!

2 **A lot of different people and organisations played a part in the Thomas's downfall. On your own, read the pieces of the jigsaw and put them in order of responsibility.**

1 The most important: _____

2 _____

3 _____

4 _____

5 Important _____

6 _____

7 _____

8 _____

9 _____

10 Not as important _____

3 **In groups, discuss your answers.**

4 **In groups, decide what Katherine and David can do to turn their lives around.**

5 **Finally, imagine that you are the characters in the story. Use the expressions in the boxes to express how you feel.**

Useful expressions:

I think X is to blame.

I think it's Y's fault.

If X hadn't done Y then Z wouldn't have happened.

X shouldn't have done Y…

Express their regrets using:

I wish I had/hadn't…

If only I had/hadn't…

If I hadn't done X then Y wouldn't have happened.

Criticise other people using:

You shouldn't have _____ -ed

Why on earth did you do _____?

The shops

Each shop was happy to give Katherine a store card that allowed her to buy thousands of pounds worth of goods. These shops charge very high interest rates on goods that are bought this way. Now they want Katherine and David to pay back all the money they owe them.

Derek (David's business partner)

Derek has always been a risk-taker and it is thanks to him that the company grew and grew. He made a bad decision that he told David nothing about. He also has an internet gambling habit and has 'borrowed' tens of thousands of pounds from the company. He has had to run away because he has borrowed money from some 'mafia-like' money lenders.

The bank

When they discovered the state of the company's debts, they wanted their money back. David had signed a paper agreeing to guarantee any debts his business partnership created. This means he may have to sell the family home.

Advertising and the consumer society

Everywhere we look, there are images that encourage us to spend. Advertisers condition us to want things that we don't need.

David

As far as David was concerned, anything to do with the house and the family and paying bills was Katherine's concern. He had enough to do with the building side of the business. All the important financial decisions he left to his partner, Derek.

The government

A lot of people think that the government's mismanagement of the economy is the reason for the economic crisis. Interest rates are so high now that people are afraid to borrow money for projects such as building houses and buying cars. This is a disaster for the economy in general, and business in particular. The government has also been criticised for passing a law that has made it easy for internet gambling addictions to develop.

Katherine

Her extravagant shopping habits meant that she was putting the family further and further into debt. She was ashamed of her poor background and wants to be surrounded by beautiful things. She wanted a better life for her children and to buy them everything they desired.

Henry and Chloe

Henry and Chloe go to exclusive private schools. They refuse to go to state schools with ordinary children. Chloe has a pony, and Henry has expensive go-karting lessons with an ex-champion.

David's parents, Tony and Karen

They refuse to pay off their son's debts. They come from a generation that never borrowed money. Five years ago, David had to beg them for money because of his wife's spending. They think that David is a fool to have let Katherine have such a 'free hand', and to have trusted his business partner so completely. They think Katherine and David should sort out their own lives.

Katherine's father, Charles

Charles, Katherine's father, was widowed when Katherine was very young. He had to provide for Katherine and her six brothers and sisters without any help. As a baker, he worked long hours with often little return. He is not in a position to help his daughter, even though he wishes he could.

Before you begin

Find out from the class what their favourite season is, and why. Stimulate conversation by talking about seasonal expectations.

> What kind of weather would you expect in each season?

> I always expect summer to be very warm and sunny, so I can spend the holidays at the beach.

> And has the weather conformed to this expectation during the last few years?

> No! It rained almost every day last summer. I was very frustrated!

Topic: Forces of nature

This unit considers the weather both in terms of daily conditions as well as seasons. It looks into climatic conditions in countries around the world. It also considers natural disasters, such as tsunamis and hurricanes.

Unit 12 Wordlist:

breeze	meteorite
climate	mist
dribble	raining
drizzly	rainy
drought	shining
earthquake	snow
famine	storm/stormy
flood	sunny
fog	tempest
forecast	thunder
frozen	tidal wave
gale	tornado
hail	volcanic eruption
icy	weather
lightning	

Getting started

1 Find out how people start up conversations with people they don't know. With which subjects do they begin? Are there any subjects that you shouldn't talk about?

> Hi, nice to meet you. How are you?

> Me? No good. I'm really broke, I need to borrow some money. Even though we've just met, can you lend me some?

> !!!

2 Students match beginnings of sentences to their replies. Make pairs across the class for feedback.

Getting started extension

As a consolidation activity, you could ask students to paraphrase what the weather idioms mean:

Every cloud has a silver lining = even an unfortunate or unhappy event can have a positive side.

Under a cloud = with a damaged reputation.

Lightning doesn't strike/never strikes twice in the same place = if something bad happens somewhere, then it won't happen again.

Save some money for a rainy day = keep some money aside for when you really need it.

Feeling under the weather = feeling ill/unwell.

To have / not have the foggiest idea = to have no idea at all.

A storm in a teacup = an argument about nothing at all important.

3 Exploit the three photographs. Find out how your students think the people feel: the woman in the raincoat is smiling, but what about the people inside the snow-surrounded cars, or the man whose car has been trapped in flooded water? What does it tell us about the character/temperament of different nationalities? What effect has the weather and climate on their national character? For example, does it make them optimistic, or melancholic, or shy, or outgoing?

How the weather affects humans

Researchers believe that the weather affects our bodies and minds. The barometric pressure drops before a storm. The difference in pressure may change the flow of blood to the brain. Some people get migraines (intense headaches). In damp, humid weather people can have problems with arthritis. A sudden heat wave can produce heatstroke. People get seasonal affective disorder or SAD in the winter. They feel depressed during the short, gloomy days.

Vocabulary: weather and disasters

1   Run through the exercises.

Feedback on Pronunciation

2   In feedback, remember to integrate work on pronunciation during feedback. In particular:

- flood /flʌd/
- tornado /tɔːˈneɪdəʊ/
- earthquake /ˈɜːθkweɪk/
- meteorite /ˈmiːtɪəraɪt/
- famine /ˈfæmɪn/
- drought /draʊt/
- volcanic /vɒlˈkænɪk/
- tidal /ˈtaɪdəl/

3   This exercise contrasts confusable verbs whose main difference is that one of each pair is transitive (it takes a direct object) while the other is intransitive. As intransitive verbs have no object, they cannot be used in the passive.

4   In a multinational class, this should give a fairly wide use of the vocabulary just covered. The example allows students to personalise the vocabulary and relate it to their own country and experience. Obviously, be sensitive to students who are from regions that have recently suffered a natural disaster.

Listening: natural disasters

1   Run through the questions checking that the students understand the different choices.

Deadly means highly dangerous, causing death.

Fertile describes land able to produce lots of crops.

Remind students to beware of 'misdirection' (odd words that will lead them to choose the wrong answer in multiple matching).

2   Quickly decide the order in which the events occurred.

3   Students work in pairs or groups to decide which event they would have most liked to witness.

> I think it would have been amazing to have seen the volcano, Mount Pelée, erupt. There would have been smoke, and boiling hot lava!

> I would rather have witnessed a famine in Roman times. I can just see the goats trying to find grass in desert-like lands.

Speaking: criticising and complaining

1   Read the sentences to the students, making sure that you emphasise the words in bold in the sentences (sound annoyed or angry). Then ask the students under what circumstances they might hear them. Example explanations include:

> Perhaps this is someone complaining about a colleague who keeps taking his/her umbrella without permission.

> Well, maybe someone is angry because the other person didn't tell them there was going to be a storm. Perhaps they went out and got soaked through!

> This sounds like someone forgot to close the sun roof of the car and it rained. Now the inside of the car is wet.

> It is someone talking about a third person, who lives in an ideal climate, but who keeps on complaining about it.

2   Match sentences 1–4 with their descriptions of use.

3   Refer to the tapescript on page 219 to find further examples of these forms in context.

4   Students decide which of the words would be stressed.

5   Choose a strong student and act out the situation between Javier and Peter in front of the class. Just act out one or two of the prompts given in the arrows, and then let your students continue in pairs. Choose the best to perform in front of everyone else.

Reading: weather forecasts

The history of weather forecasting
People have tried to predict the weather for many thousands of years. The Babylonians, in 650 BC, used cloud patterns as well as astrology. However, it was not until the invention of the telegraph, in 1837, that the age of modern weather forecasting began. The telegraph allowed reports of weather conditions from a wide area to be received almost instantly. This meant that forecasters knew what the weather was like further 'upwind'.

1 The pictures show different ways of predicting the weather.

2 Ask students if there are any folk traditions for predicting the weather in their countries.

3 Remind students of the technique for handling gapped text questions:
   • First, with this type of question, remember to read the text all the way through for gist.
   • Next, don't jump to conclusions, but rather try every sentence in every gap.
   • Finally, write your choices on a piece of paper before transferring them to the answer sheet.

Contrast and concession
This section looks at how contrasting ideas can be balanced. Run through the section. Take care to highlight the grammar that follows the different forms, such as *despite* (noun/gerund) etc.

An alternative approach would be to write a single sentence on the board and to work your way through the different options, eliciting from the students all the time how you should continue each one.

Even though
↘
... the weather is hot, Jeanette feels quite refreshed.

Despite
↘
... feeling exhausted, Christine keeps on studying.

4 Suggested answers:

1 *Even though/Although/Despite the fact that* the pine cone was open it rained the rest of the day.
   Despite the pine cone *being* open...
   The pine cone was open, *however/nevertheless* it rained the rest of the day.

2 *Even though/Although/Despite the fact that* she knew nothing about the weather she learnt the basics quickly
   She knew nothing about the weather, *however/nevertheless* she learnt the basics quickly.

3 *Even though/Although/Despite the fact that* the weatherman had always had an excellent reputation. The weatherman had always had an excellent reputation. *However/nevertheless* he lost it overnight.

Listening: hurricanes

Ask the class to study the photograph of hurricane damage as a way of generating interest in the passage that follows. Then refer students to the Exam spotlight.

1 Tell students to read the notes through and to try and predict the words that might be missing.

Activating your knowledge
Ask your students to tell you what they already know about hurricanes and pool the knowledge of the class. Activating previous knowledge generally helps us understand what we are listening to.

2 This is the second half of the same interview in activity 1. This time your students need to choose the right answer from a selection of three. Remind them that both task types in activity 1 and 2 occur in the Listening Paper.

Key word: way

This section looks at a number of common expressions and lexical phrases that use the word *way*. **Way** can be a countable or unaccountable noun, as well as an adverb. It also occurs in many phrases. Here are the main uses of *way*:
1 (Noun) A *way* of doing something refers to how you can do it. *Another way of learning a language is to travel to the country.*
2 (Noun) You can refer to the way an action is done to indicate the quality that it has. *He smiled in a friendly way.*
3 (Noun) The ways of a person or a group of people are their customs or their usual behaviour. *They will never change their ways.*
4 (Adverb) You can use way to emphasise that something is a great distance away or very much above or below a particular level or amount. *Way down in the valley there's a goat farm.*

Students substitute the words in bold with the words and expressions from the box.

Grammar: the definite article

This should largely be a matter of revision. Many language groups will already have an implicit knowledge of the use of the definite article from their own mother tongue.

Writing: a discussion-type essay

In part 2 of the Writing Paper, students may have the opportunity to write an essay that discusses a topic and contrasts opposing points of view.

1 Possible answers include:

• When we have H_2O with CO_2 we are drinking fizzy water.

• **Fossils** are hardened remains or impressions of a prehistoric animal or plant inside a rock. **Fossil fuels** are fuels such as coal, oil, and natural gas. The problem with burning these fuels is that they are finite, and pollute the atmosphere.

• **A greenhouse** is a glass building in which you grow plants that need to be protected from bad weather. The **greenhouse effect** refers to the way in which, over the past 100 years, the average temperature around the globe has risen dramatically. Researchers believe that this global warming comes from added carbon dioxide and other gases in the atmosphere. With water vapour, the gases form a layer that holds in heat (hence the word *greenhouse*). Some natural causes of this warming may include increased solar radiation and tiny changes in the earth's orbit. However, human activities, such as deforestation, and the use of fossil fuels, seem to be an important cause.

4 Students decide where they could make breaks for paragraphs. Reassure students that there is nothing definitive about this. Allow students to make their own suggestions:
– after *individuals can take*
– after *from wind-turbines*
– after *gas guzzling vehicles off the roads.*

5 These exercises focus closely on the text the students have just read. The first question looks at how ideas can be sequenced. The second examines how 'cohesion' can be achieved through the use of pronouns and other reference devices.
• Words could be exchanged for more variety: but – *nevertheless*; and – *in addition, furthermore.*
• The ideas could be sequenced – *first of all, secondly.*

6 Examples of questions:
So what has caused this rise in temperature?
So what can we do on a personal level?
These questions help the writer by posing questions that can then be answered. (These are called rhetorical questions.)

7 Students examine the statistics and decide what is likely to happen to the elephants. If this trend continues, then the African elephant will become extinct; poachers will have wiped it out.

Run through the vocabulary:

A **ban** is to state officially that something cannot be done, shown or used.	A **penalty** is a punishment for doing something which is against a law or rule.
Ivory is the precious substance made from tusks. People use it to make ornaments and chess pieces.	**Resin** is a chemically produced substance used to make plastics.
A **poacher** is an illegal hunter.	**Poaching** is the activity of catching animals, fish or birds on someone else's property.
An **ornament** is an attractive object that you display in your house or garden.	**Tusks** are the long white pointed things that stick out of the front of the elephant (its nose is called its **trunk**).

TEACHING IN PRACTICE

Writing an essay
Writing an essay can be extremely intimidating for some students. Make sure they feel comfortable with the form. Some ways of helping students to feel comfortable with the form are to:
• explain that an essay is just a structured piece of non-fictional writing;
• show plenty of example essays (see the Writing Guide);
• encourage students to plan ahead, to map out the structure following a formula.

8 The notes are there to help the students with the content of the essay. This is less an exercise in imagination, and more an exercise of how to achieve cohesion and order ideas.

Degree of difficulty

Decrease the level: Take the notes about elephants and turn them into a flow chart on the whiteboard. Set up the use of sequencers for the students while doing so. They'll find it easier to form a complete essay by looking at the structure in this way.

Increase the level: Consider setting a research essay for homework. So far, students have had to stick quite closely to the topics we have chosen within each unit. Remove these boundaries by asking each student to write a well-balanced essay on a topic which interests them.

Photocopiable activity instructions

Activity 12.1: Weather idioms

Aim: To practise weather idioms and develop fluency.

Instructions:

1 Treat this as a 'milling' exercise. Get students to stand up and give each an idiom card and one of the explanation slips (below).

2 Students read out their half of the idiom until they find their partners. If you wish, you can do this several times.

3 Write on the board: **Conversation topics** 1 An unexpected event 2 Health problems 3 A pleasant/unpleasant surprise 4 A misunderstanding 5 Money and spending.

4 Now ask your students to engage in conversation around these topics.

12.1 Answers: *Any port in a storm* = In an emergency, any solution will do.
Cold light of day = Seeing things as they really are.
Get wind of = To hear or learn of something.
Steal someone's thunder = When someone takes the credit and praise for something they didn't do.
Bolt from the blue = When something happens unexpectedly and suddenly ...
Come rain or shine = Nothing will stop me from being there.
Greased lightning = To move very fast indeed.
Stem the tide = Trying to stop something unpleasant from getting worse, usually unsuccessfully.
Brighten up the day = When something happens that makes you feel positive and happy all day long.
Down in the doldrums = Feeling depressed and lacking energy.
Head is in the clouds = To have unrealistic, impractical ideas.
Storm in a teacup = To exaggerate a problem or make a small problem seem far greater than it really is.
Calm before the storm = A quiet time immediately before a period of violent activity or argument.
Dry spell = Being not as successful as normal.
Hit rough weather = To experience difficulties or problems.

Take a raincheck = Decline an offer now, suggesting you will accept it later.
Chase rainbows = Trying to do something that will never be achieved.
Every cloud has a silver lining = It is always possible to get something positive out of a situation, no matter how unpleasant, difficult or even painful it may seem.
It never rains but it pours = When things go wrong, they go very wrong.
Throw caution to the wind = To take a great risk.
Cloud nine = Feeling extremely happy.
Face like thunder = Looking like you are clearly angry or upset about something.
Right as rain = When everything is going well in your life.
Under the weather = Feeling a bit ill, sad or lacking energy.
Cloud of suspicion = An individual is not believed or are distrusted.
Fairweather friend = The type of friend who is always there for you when times are good, but forgets about you when things get difficult.
Shoot the breeze = Chat in a relaxed, breezy way.
Weather a storm = To get through a crisis or hard time.

Activity 12.2: Role play: Winds of change

Aims: Fluency; using topic vocabulary.

Instructions:

1 Lead into the topic of energy and sources of renewable energy (solar power, geothermic power, wind power and bio-fuels).

2 Elicit their respective advantages and disadvantages.

3 Then read the situation and allow the students to study the map.

4 Allocate roles to students. Make groups according to the size of your class.

Tapescript 12

Listening 12.1

One A fascinating new theory suggests that Britain was once connected to the rest of Europe, by hills which rose above what is now the English Channel. Then, three hundred thousand years ago, a violent flood swept them away and the link disappeared. Within twenty-four hours the hills had vanished and Britain became an island. This explains why Britain remained uninhabited for such a long time. Even though men had been present they had left for warmer climates. Once this new barrier appeared, it most probably prevented Neanderthal man from returning to the island.

Two While people say that weather forecasters are always getting it wrong the *opposite* is true. Yet it only takes one serious mistake for reputations to be affected as shown by Britain's most infamous weather forecast. Britain had been preparing itself for storms, but on the evening of October 15th 1987, even though someone telephoned the television station saying she'd heard there would be a hurricane during the night, the country's most eminent weatherman, Michael Fish, said that the expected gales would *not* reach disastrous speeds. When, during the night, many parts of the country were *devastated* by incredibly high winds, everyone pointed the finger at poor Mr Fish, accusing him of failing to make the public aware of what was about to happen. It was the country's worst storm since the Great Storm of 1703.

Three One of the biggest mysteries is the disappearance of the dinosaurs. For many decades scientists believed that they died out gradually due to climate change. Then the meteorite theory changed all that. A meteorite crashed into what is now the Gulf of Mexico and caused an immediate climate change, catastrophic to the dinosaurs which simply vanished. However, in the last few years geologists have raised objections to this theory – claiming that the meteorite occurred well before the dinosaurs came on the scene, so that it can't have been the cause of their extinction.

Four People are terrified of nuclear war, but the energy produced from a volcanic eruption can be even more catastrophic. Normally there is plenty of warning and in 1902 Mount Pelée, on the island of Martinique, had been showing signs that it was about to explode. Why on earth didn't people leave the island you might ask. The answer is depressingly simple. Even though the authorities should have evacuated the island's capital St Pierre, they chose to ignore the signs because an election was going to be held. Twenty eight thousand people were killed in the eruption. There were just two survivors: a shoemaker and a prisoner.

Five In Roman times the southern part of the Mediterranean was known as the granary of the Empire. If the harvest failed it led to shortages and famine elsewhere. Once the Romans left north Africa the land was taken over by nomads who let their goats eat all the vegetation. Over-feeding led to the gradual desertification of the region. Despite the obvious damage this caused, they kept on allowing them to eat everything in sight until hardly anything green was left. All the same, this doesn't fully explain the increase in the desert. Climate change and long periods of drought are probably as much to blame. And once fertile land is lost it is difficult to reverse the process.

Listening 12.2

Part A

Interviewer: Hurricanes have been more and more in the news ever since the destruction caused by Katrina in 2005. You'll remember that Katrina devastated the south east of the United States. Flooding covered an area the size of the UK. With me today is weather expert Dr Kate Jackson who is going tell us about hurricanes. So, Kate, perhaps we could begin by asking what causes them.

Kate: Certainly, Jamie. It's all rather technical but I'll try my best. Let's start with where they appear, shall we? Basically they form over the oceans in the warm zones we find either side of the equator.

Interviewer: OK. Why not over the equator itself?

Kate: Because over the equator the spin, the rotation of the earth, isn't great enough. It's the rotation of the earth which helps to generate the wind, you see.

Interviewer: Mm, I think so. Anyway, go on.

Kate: Well, what happens is that water vapour evaporates and forms clouds.

Interviewer: Just like for ordinary rain.

Kate: Exactly, except the wind, combined with the rise and fall of temperature sets up a kind of chain reaction, which eventually creates a hurricane.

Interviewer: So when does a strong wind turn into a hurricane?

Kate: Well, officially when it reaches a speed of 120 kph, but some of those we've seen recently have been much more powerful. Katrina got up to 280kph!

Interviewer: Wow, I understand that the wind caused a lot of destruction, but the southern states were flooded too, weren't they?

Kate: Indeed, they were. This is due to the surge – the increase in the height of the level of the sea caused by the hurricane. And, before you ask, the highest recorded surge happened a hundred years ago in Australia. People found fish and even dolphins on the top of cliffs. Oh and by the way, these cliff-tops were fifteen metres above the usual level of the sea.

Interviewer: Wow. Unbelievable. And what has been the most disastrous hurricane on record?

Kate: Economically, it was Katrina, but in terms of loss of life the worst so far was in Bangladesh in 1970. Half a million people died. Isn't that dreadful? With Katrina around one thousand eight hundred lives were lost.

Listening 12.3

Part B

Interviewer: One thousand eight hundred. How terrible. But what is the reason for the increased number of hurricanes these days? Is it tied up with global warming?

Kate: To my way of thinking all the evidence points to that, but it is almost impossible to be one hundred per cent certain. There are other factors too. For instance, each three or four years there's a warm water current called El Niño which appears in the eastern Pacific – El Niño is linked with increased hurricane activity.

Interviewer: OK – but going back to temperature levels, I know some people claim that the temperature of the oceans goes up and down naturally.

Kate: Mm, yes, there is some truth in that. In the early 1900s sea temperatures started to rise. But then they went down again only to rise again, and continue to rise from the 1970s.

Interviewer: So people who claim that rises and falls in temperature are natural have got a point?

Kate: Perhaps, but other scientists, myself included, think that atmospheric pollution was responsible for keeping temperatures down.

Interviewer: Atmospheric pollution?

Kate: Yes. Particles from factories actually helped to block out sunlight. But now, there is no question that world temperatures are rising all the time mostly because of CO_2 emissions. Burning fuels like coal and oil, the so-called 'fossil fuels' releases the carbon stored in them into the atmosphere.

Interviewer: Yes, I see that. So, how much CO_2 is actually in the atmosphere, then?

Kate: Well, there is 0.03 of a per cent. That's one part in 3300.

Interviewer: But that's absolutely minuscule. How can that possibly have any impact – I can't see what all the fuss is about.

Kate: Well, all I can say is that while it may seem very slight, just a tiny increase can have devastating consequences. If I had my way, I'd ban any car with a large engine.

Interviewer: Mm … if you say so. Right … and a couple of quick questions. First one. What is the difference between a hurricane and a typhoon?

Kate: Scientifically, none at all. They are just the names which have been used in different regions. Typhoon means, I think, 'big wind' in Japanese. We can also call them cyclones too. We shouldn't confuse them with tornadoes or twisters because *they* happen over land.

Interviewer: Right, like in the mid-west in the United States. And is there a difference between hurricanes or typhoons in the northern and southern hemispheres?

Kate: Yes, they rotate differently. It's all rather complicated, but basically a hurricane in the northern hemisphere rotates anti-clockwise, and one in the southern hemisphere goes the other way round.

Interviewer: I see. OK, well, thanks for being with us today. And now for a weather up-date …

Answer key 12

Getting started p115
1 1d; 2f; 3e; 4b/f; 5g; 6a; 7c

Vocabulary p116
1 1 climate
2 fog
3 forecast
4 icy
5 breeze
6 drizzles; poured
7 thunder; storm
8 hail
9 sunny
10 rainy
2 1 volcanic eruption
2 flood
3 tornado
4 tidal wave
5 earthquake
6 famine
7 meteorite
8 drought
3 1 raised
2 lost

3 risen
4 died
5 vanished
6 killed
7 raises
8 arisen

Listening p117
1 A3; B2; C5; D–; E4; F1
2 Storm of 1987
Mount Pele eruption
Desertification in North Africa
Formation of Britain
Disappearance of dinosaurs

Speaking p117
2 1 Sentences 2 and 3
2 Sentences 1 and 4
3 1 keeps; 2 earth; 3 should've; 4 always

Reading p118
3 1D; 2H; 3A; 4F; 5E; 6C; 7G

Listening p120
1 1 the UK
2 warm zones (we find)
3 isn't great enough
4 chain reaction
5 reach a speed of
6 280kph
7 of the sea
8 Australia
9 dolphins
10 fifteen metres
2 1A; 2B; 3C; 4C; 5B; 6B; 7A

Key word p121
1 keep out of Simon's way
2 tell me the way
3 come a long way
4 I had my way
5 By the way
6 has changed his ways
7 To my way of thinking
8 under way

Grammar p121
1 1e; 2b; 3a; 4c; 5f; 6d
2 1 a; 2 the; 3 Ø; 4 the; 5 a; 6 The; 7 the ; 8 a; 9 a; 10 The; 11 a; 12 a; 13 a; 14 Ø; 15 the; 16 a; 17 a; 18 the; 19 the; 20 the; 21 the; 22 Ø; 23 the; 24 the

Writing p122
3 1 T; 2 F; 3 F; 4 T; 5 T; 6 T; 7 T; 8 T
5 3 global warming; greenhouse gases; nuclear energy; of nuclear energy; China's Three Gorges Dam'; Brazil; the government

Review p124
1 1B; 2D; 3C; 4D; 5C; 6A; 7A; 8B; 9A; 10D; 11C; 12B
2 1 existed; 2 is/was; 3 have; 4 when; 5 able; 6 why; 7 its; 8 in; 9 had; 10 out; 11 be; 12 who

Weather idioms

Any port in a storm	Cold light of day	Get wind of	Steal someone's thunder
Bolt from the blue	Come rain or shine	Greased lightning	Stem the tide
Brighten up the day	Down in the doldrums	Head is in the clouds	Storm in a teacup
Calm before the storm	Dry spell	Hit rough weather	Take a raincheck
CHASE RAINBOWS	Every cloud has a silver lining	It never rains but it pours	Throw caution to the wind
Cloud nine	Face like thunder	Right as rain	Under the weather
Cloud of suspicion	Fairweather friend	Shoot the breeze	Weather a storm

In an emergency, any solution will do (even one that would normally be unacceptable).	Seeing things as they really are, not as you might want them to be.	To hear or learn about something, especially if it was meant to be secret.	When someone takes the credit and praise for something they didn't do.
When something happens unexpectedly and suddenly …	Nothing will stop me from being there.	To move very fast indeed.	Trying to stop something unpleasant from getting worse, usually unsuccessfully.
When something happens that makes you feel positive and happy all day long.	Feeling depressed and lacking energy.	To have unrealistic, impractical ideas.	To exaggerate a problem or make a small problem seem far greater than it really is.
A quiet time immediately before a period of violent activity or argument.	Being not as successful as normal.	To experience difficulties or problems.	Decline an offer now, suggesting you will accept it later.
Trying to do something that will never be achieved.	It is always possible to get something positive out of a situation, no matter how unpleasant, difficult or even painful it might seem.	When things go wrong, they go very wrong.	To take a great risk.
Feeling extremely happy.	Looking like you are clearly angry or upset about something.	When everything is going well in your life.	Feeling a bit ill, sad or lack energy, and under-performing.
An individual is not believed or are distrusted.	The type of friend who is always there when times are good but forgets about you when things get difficult.	To chat in a relaxed, breezy way.	To get through a crisis or hard time.

Winds of Change

1 Read the situation and find out what changes could affect Upton Mallet.

2 You are present at the meeting. Study the map and see where the projected wind turbines are likely to be built.

3 You will be given a role.

4 In your groups, you now need to argue for what you believe – as fluently as possible. Remember, your life and livelihood may depend on whether this wind farm goes ahead or not!

The village of Upper Mallet in Norfolk lies at the edge of a plain. It is a mostly agricultural community which has been undisturbed for hundreds of years. It is a small market town which has local services such as small shops, banks, pubs, restaurants and other services. Altogether there are five thousand people in the village and surrounding area.

Many of the people who live there are retired people. There are a couple of small factories, and a small psychiatric hospital for 60 patients. Other inhabitants mainly work from home or travel to work in Norwich or London once or twice a week. However, it has recently been revealed that now there are plans to destroy this calm!

Due to a European Union directive, all member states are being encouraged to provide at least 20% of their electricity needs by renewable sources by 2020. Experts consider that Upper Mallet is an ideal site for a wind farm of 10 to 15 wind turbines. Some local residents are for the wind farm; other residents think that it will spell disaster for the area. A meeting has been scheduled between the Mayor of Upper Mallet and interested parties.

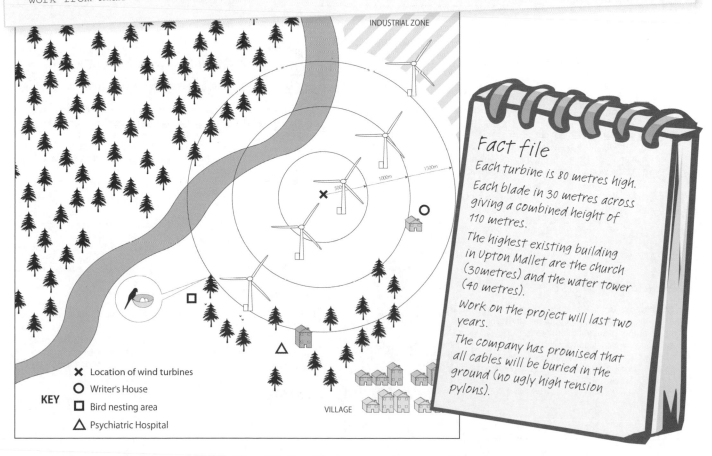

INDUSTRIAL ZONE

1000m   1500m

500

VILLAGE

KEY
X Location of wind turbines
O Writer's House
☐ Bird nesting area
△ Psychiatric Hospital

Fact file

Each turbine is 80 metres high.

Each blade in 30 metres across giving a combined height of 110 metres.

The highest existing building in Upton Mallet are the church (30metres) and the water tower (40 metres).

Work on the project will last two years.

The company has promised that all cables will be buried in the ground (no ugly high tension pylons).

Upton Mallet Residents

The mayor

You think the wind farm is a good idea because:
- it is a green way of creating electricity
- each turbine will provide local tax which will help with local projects
- extension of the primary school
- youth centre
- swimming pool

It would also encourage 'eco-tourism', as people and school children would come to visit the site. However, you also want to listen to the views of the people who will be affected.

The farmer

You think the wind far is a good idea because:
- it is a form of renewable energy
- you will receive €500 a month for each turbine on your land.
- farming is a difficult job and there is a lot of competition. This will help you continue with your farm and pay off bank loans.

'Wind of Anger' spokesperson

You are the spokesperson of an organisation that is against the wind-farm.

You are **not** against renewable energy such as wind farms.

The problem is that:
- the proposed turbines are too close to people's houses
- the turbines are too tall, you can see them for 20 kilometres, and too noisy
- nobody will be able to sell their property if the wind farm goes ahead, or else their houses will be worth a lot less
- medical evidence suggests that the sound waves from the turbine can cause illness

You don't want a wind turbine within 1500 metres of anyone's home.

Scientific expert 1

You are a scientific expert from the company that produces the turbines.

You think:
- we have a responsibility to our children and grandchildren to provide energy that doesn't produce CO_2, or problems with radiation or nuclear waste.
- that the turbines are perfectly safe.

Besides, you won't build a turbine within 500 metres of anyone's home.

Scientific expert 2

You used to believe in wind farms but now you think that they do not produce enough energy. You think that:
- wind farms are a waste of time, they do not produce enough energy
- wind-power is a passing fashion
- the future is with nuclear energy. Nuclear reactors nowadays are clean and safe and risk-free if they are well-managed
- the wind farm will upset people at the psychiatric hospital

Restaurant and hotel owner

You think that the wind farm is just what the village needs.
- It will attract a lot of visitors and there will be a big increase in trade in your hotel and restaurant.
- the money that it will provide in local tax will help develop the facilities in the local community.
- Upton Mallet is stuck in the past – the wind-farm equals progress.

Resident 1: artist

You moved to Upton Mallet for a quieter life. You are an artist who takes inspiration from the landscape. You do not want monstrous wind turbines to block your view. You spent a lot of money on your cottage and garden to make it perfect. It will become worthless if a wind farm is built nearby. If one is built, you want it as far away as possible from your home.

Resident 2: bird-watcher

You are a long-time resident of the village and a keen bird-watcher.

You believe that the wind farm will destroy the habitat of a rare and protected bird, the warbler. You think that nothing justifies the harm that the wind farm could do to the bird.

PHOTOCOPIABLE 12.2

13 In the news

Before you begin

Ask students how closely they follow the news. What are the biggest issues in the news at the moment? Which issues most concern them? Do they pay more attention to the local, national, or global news?

Topic: In the news

This unit discusses the news and media. It is a broad topic that allows for many discussions to spring up and new vocabulary to be used. It takes into account the fast-changing media which feeds the news into our daily lives. Note that, while *news* looks like a plural, it is an uncountable noun when it is used without the definite article: *good news spreads quickly.* You cannot say *a news* but you can say *a piece of news* when you are referring to a particular fact or message: *One of my students told me an exciting piece of news.* It is a singular noun when it is used as *the news: the six o'clock news.*

Unit 13 Wordlist:

bias	leak out
blog	local
break off	national
break up	news
breaking news	obituary
business	pack
celebrity	paparazzi
censor/censorship	photograph/photographer
circulation	politics
close the net on	prey
corner (v)	pull ahead
correspondent	pull out
cover up	quality newspaper
crossword	reporter
editor/editorial	science
fall out	scoop
front page	showbiz
go up	splash across
headline	sport
health	tabloid
hit the jackpot	thrill of the chase
horoscope	TV listings
item	weather
journalist	

Getting started

1   What is the main source of news for your students?

> Is there a TV programme anybody watches regularly?

> Or, is there a newspaper or magazine which any of you read regularly?

> Perhaps there is a radio station any of you listen to regularly?

> Yes, there's a radio programme called *Hack* – it's on every weekday, at 5.30pm. It discusses all the big news stories, but from an alternative, younger perspective ...

2   This examines students' attitudes to different sources. Are they 'media-savvy' in that they take everything 'with a pinch of salt' (i.e. they don't believe everything they see, hear or read)? Or are they more naïve?

3   This is a ranking exercise that gets students thinking about the kind of news that is shown, and the kind that they like to watch. A **blog** is an online journal that anyone can read on the internet. Many newspapers nowadays have blogs from their own journalists on the online version of the newspaper.

4   Run through the separate items and check that students understand each of the stories.

Consider using a follow-up activity like this one:

> Teacher: *Decide on a 'running order' for all seven items – that is, what order would you show the news items in?*
>
> Student A: I would show the emergency storm warning first, because ...
>
> Student B: No, I would show the celebrity gossip straight away, because ...
>
> Teacher: *Ok then. But how much time would you dedicate to each piece?*
>
> Student C: I would allow only 2 minutes for the weather, because ...

Vocabulary: news and newspapers

1   This question deals with the different sections readers find in a newspaper. Check that students understand the meanings of each section.

Newspaper section	Description
Business	covers work relating to the production, buying, and selling of goods and services
Classifieds	contains advertisements: cars, property for sale, job advertisements, etc
Crosswords	contains the word games in which you work out answers to clues, and write in answers
Editorial	has an article which gives the opinion of the editor/publisher on a particular topic
Health	discusses the condition and well-being of the body
Horoscopes	forecast of events, based on the position of the stars when you were born
News	contains information about a recently changed situation or a recent event
Obituaries	contains short biographies and appreciations of notable people who have recently died
Personals	requests from people looking for partners
Politics	discusses the actions or activities which people use to achieve power in a country
Science	discusses the study of the nature and behaviour of natural things and our knowledge
Showbiz	news about the entertainment industry
Sport	covers the games and other competitive activities which need physical effort and skill
TV listings	the programme of shows on the television channels available in an area
Weather	the section describing the condition of the atmosphere in an area at a particular time

TEACHING IN PRACTICE

Checking pronunciation
Run through the items checking pronunciation.
Check word stress on multi-syllable words.
For example: horoscope **Ooo**, obituaries **oOoo**.

2–4 These activities present a lexical set of vocabulary to do with the news and media. When you have completed the exercise ask students to brainstorm any other items they can think of to do with the same topic; e.g. controversy, burning issue.

Vocabulary extension

Can your students think of any words which pair up with news, and are in the media field? See if they can come up with words such as: newsagency – newsagent – newscaster – news conference – news group – newsletter – newspaper – news presenter – news print.

SPOTLIGHT ON VOCABULARY

Spidergrams
Spidergrams or 'mind-maps' are an excellent way of grouping vocabulary in a clear and memorable fashion. If your students aren't regularly using spidergrams by now, question 2 in activity 5 should reinforce the message.

Listening: a news report

EXAM SPOTLIGHT

Sentence completion
This spotlight reminds your students that they need to be aware of what each FCE paper involves. Forewarned is forearmed, as they say!

Grammar: reported speech

1   This section looks at some basic ways of dealing with reported speech. This should be a fairly straightforward revision exercise. The important thing to remember is to do with 'backshift'; i.e. how reported verbs tend to go one step further back into the past. Refer students to Section 14 of the Grammar Reference if necessary.

GRAMMAR SPOTLIGHT

Reporting spoken English
Students complete the rules based on the previous exercise. Don't be tempted to skip over activities such as these, as they are useful tools in reinforcing the essence of what the student should have learnt.

Speaking: reporting

1   Students should listen to, and then complete the expressions.

2   Ask students to brainstorm some recent news items. Divide them into groups and ask them to create sentences based around the item they have selected. They then form new groups and swap comments and stories.

Reading: The paparazzi

BACKGROUND

Paparazzi

Paparazzi is a plural term (paparazzo being the singular form) for photographers who take candid photographs of celebrities, usually by relentlessly shadowing them in their public and private activities. The expression *paparazzi* comes from the film character of Paparazzo in Federico Fellini's film *La Dolce Vita*. Paparazzo is an intrusive society photographer, who represents the swarm of insect-like photojournalists found around every passing celebrity, snapping away and jostling for the most exploitable shot.

Get students interested in the text by asking them what they know about Angelina Jolie.

> She is the famous actress from *Tomb Raider, Mr. and Mrs. Smith*, and other films. She is an international representative for the charity UNICEF. She is married to Brad Pitt, the actor who used to be married to Jennifer Aniston. Jolie and Pitt have established themselves as a family with adopted as well as biological children.

1   Find out why people are interested in the lives of these people. Elicit from students why people like to read about famous people in magazines and newspapers. You could find out who regularly reads magazines about celebrities and what motivates them to do so.

2   Give students three minutes to skim read the text and find answers to the questions.

3   Students match words from the article to the definitions in pairs or groups. The context of the text should help students pair up the definitions without using a dictionary.

4   Exploit the headline: **Behind the Scenes: Hot on the trail of Angelina Jolie.** Teach the word trail in the context of the headline: a hunter follows the trail left by an animal (usually in order to capture or shoot it).

Students complete the sentences with the highlighted words and expressions from the text. Tell students that texts often use the idea of a running metaphor. (Question 6, in exercise 5, returns to this idea as well.)

A metaphor is an imaginative way of describing something by referring to something else which has the qualities that you want to express: *The text sees the paparazzi as hunters, and the celebrities as animals.*

6   Students discuss their views. Perhaps ask if their views about the paparazzi have changed since reading the article.

Speaking: agreeing on what to watch

1   Suggested answers:
    The five photos show a variety of possible television programmes (each a 'Channel' from Listening 13.2). The first image is from Channel 3 (houses with 'for sale' signs). These signs, when coupled with the heading which warns of a slowdown in the economy, show a news or business programme. The second image is from Channel 4 (stars in the night sky, linked to form a constellation of a lion). This image represents a horoscope programme. The third picture is from Channel 1 (a man in a suit). It represents an interview with a chairman. The fourth image is from Channel 5 (a female presenter in front of a celebrity couple on the red carpet). This image relates to a showbiz, celebrity, programme. The fifth and final image is from Channel 2 (satellite/space shuttle). It is from a news programme describing a potential NASA landing.

Listening: what's on TV?

1   This activity refers to the photographs which were the topic of discussion in the Speaking activity.

Key words: *say* and *tell*

This exercise looks at two words that are frequently confused.

> With the verb *say*, if you want to mention the person who is being addressed, you should use the preposition *to*. *'What did she say you?'* is incorrect. *'What did she say to you?'* is correct.

> The verb *tell*, however, is usually followed by a direct object indicating the person who is being addressed. *'What did she tell to you'* is incorrect. *'What did she tell you?'* is correct.

Say is the most general verb for reporting the words that someone speaks. *Tell* is used to report information that is given to someone: *The manufacturer told me that … Tell* can also be used with a '*to*' infinitive to report an order or instruction: *My teacher told me to be quiet.*

1   This revises how we use both *say* and *tell* in reported speech and the verb patterns that follow them.

2   This looks at some of the common expressions that employ *say* and *tell*. Read the further lexical phrases and expressions that use *say* and *tell*.

Grammar: reporting verbs

1   Reporting verbs paraphrase what is said in direct speech. Use this as an example on the whiteboard:

Don't cross the road – there's a car coming!

= He warned her not to cross the road.

> What's the reporting verb here?
>
> *Warned!*

2   Do the first two questions as examples on the whiteboard and then ask the students to do the rest on their own.

GRAMMAR SPOTLIGHT

Suggest

If you suggest something, you put forward a plan or idea for someone to consider.

This grammar spotlight focuses on a reporting verb that often causes students a lot of difficulty because of the number of different sentence patterns that can follow it. Read through the box with the students and then ask them to transform the sentence given. If students still have trouble with the various patterns, work your way through the different forms on the whiteboard.

4   Clearly, there are a number of different ways in which this can be phrased. You can either leave students with an open choice, or, if you prefer a more structured activity, you could give them reporting verbs to go with each of the sentences and the witnesses.

One possible answer:

The policeman said that the driver was going too quickly which is why he didn't see him turning into his lane. He criticised the driver for not slowing down as he approached the junction. He also reminded us that as it was a foggy morning, drivers should have had their lights on.

The pedestrian told us she had been walking along when she heard a loud bang. She blamed the driver for what happened. She said he wasn't looking where he was going, so didn't see the other car coming up the road.

The lorry driver said he was sorry about the accident but criticised the other driver for not having his lights on.

Degree of difficulty

Increase the level: If you feel your students are able to accommodate a few more reporting verbs, you could add: *blame, claim,* or *maintain* to the list. Can your students think of any more?

Grammar extension

This activity can be built upon in a variety of ways:

a   Consider getting your students to report on any number of local events. In pairs, one student could write the notes, and the second student could report on the content of these notes.

b   Alternatively, bring in a print-out of a news story from an English website or newspaper, and ask students to change the story back to the notes with which the journalist must have begun.

Writing: checking and editing

It is important in the lead up to the examination that students become more exact with their spelling and punctuation.

TEACHING IN PRACTICE

Punctuation errors

Probably the punctuation mark that poses the most problems is the apostrophe.

The apostrophe: remind students that its two main uses are

1) to show that a letter is missing: she's = she is

2) to show possession: It's Jane's pen = It is Jane's pen = The pen belongs to Jane.

If students have difficulty with this, contrast the following on the board:

there's with theirs

whose with who's

it's with its

Remember that with nouns that end in 's' in the plural, the apostrophe denoting possession comes after the nouns.

• It's the boys' dog = the dog belonging to the boys.

With names ending with 's' we may have a choice.

• It's James' or it's James's.

2   Remind your students that spelling in FCE is important. The list of misspelt words here contain common mistakes. There are many sayings designed to help students remember the correct spelling of words. An example is: PIEce = a piece of PIE.

Ask your students to think of some more to help them.

6   This activity asks students to identify the errors in the letter. Remember, sometimes it's easier to identify other people's errors than your own!

Photocopiable activity instructions

Activity 13.1: The Daily FCE (headlines and stories)

Aim: To develop and extend the language of newspaper headlines and their 'grammar'.

Instructions:

1 In groups, get students to match headline words to their definitions.

2 Next, put the students in pairs to test each other.

3 Put students in groups of three or four to work out what the headlines mean and what the story behind them is.

4 Then distribute a mixture of headline words and ask students to create their own headlines and invent the stories behind them.

Activity 13.2: Reporting the news

Aims: To practise reported speech and the use of a variety of reporting verbs; to develop fluency and question making.

Instructions:

1 Depending on the size of your class divide them up equally between journalists and interviewees. There are two journalists and two 'witnesses' for each story. For smaller classes, you might wish to take just one of the stories so the journalists in story one are the witnesses in story two and vice versa.

2 Set the scene for each of the stories and then allow each journalist to interview his/her witness in separate parts of the class.

3 The journalists then come together to swap their version of the events and to create the story.

4 In the final phase of the activity, arrange a whole class 'broadcast' with the most thorough reports of each item.

D.I.Y. Furthering the activity

Depending on the size of your class, consider giving a third group a different story.

Possible additional material: Workers at a local factory have gone on strike because of rumours about the company moving production to a low-cost country. Up to two hundred jobs could be lost.

Student A (Journalist): Interview the manager of the factory. (Student C) Find out if the rumours are true.

Student B (Journalist): Interview the trade union representative who called for the strike.

Student C (Factory manager): The rumours are true, but will only affect 80 workers who work in production. Unfortunately, it has become too expensive to produce goods in your country so the firm has to find an alternative. It can't remain competitive otherwise. This is a problem of globalisation. Going on strike just makes things worse.

Student D (Trade union representative): You called a strike because the management refused to tell you anything about their plans. The director made lots of mysterious trips abroad, and this is what caused the rumours. You think that the company has the responsibility to keep jobs in the country and not to 'export' them. Going on strike is the only way of making the voice of the workers heard.

---

5 Once the students have completed their notes: ask the 'journalists' from each group to compare their stories together. They should then work together to prepare a short report for the evening news' bulletin.

Remind your students that they should report what they have discovered by using reporting verbs: *say, tell, ask, claim, maintain, suggest, deny* and so on.

Tapescript 13

Listening 13.1

Newswoman: Have you heard about a new report on education which says these are the worst results in over twenty years and one ex-headmaster said the situation is appalling. That's the verdict on the spelling ability of school children in Great Britain after the results of last year's national tests were released. The report reveals that pupils who were tested, aged 11 and 14, made more spelling errors last year than they did four years ago. Some of the most common errors among half of the eleven-year-olds were words such as 'change' and 'known', which were often spelt C-H-A-N-G and N-O-W-N'. In addition the word 'technique' caused problems for the majority of the 600,000 pupils taking the test! Well, we have Michael Bryant our education correspondent in the studio with us today. Michael, what are people saying about this report?

Michael: Well, one person who actually marked the tests told me that the report reveals that most errors had arisen because pupils had missed out letters, put the incorrect endings on words or used the wrong vowels altogether. The slip in spelling standards among 11 and 14 year-olds also comes as researchers found a decline in the ability to use basic punctuation correctly such as capital letters, full stops and commas.

Newswoman: One thing that surprised me was that the government has been telling us that it has spent more money on education than any previous government. Given the results of the survey it's amazing that this can be the case. It would be interesting to know more about how the government has responded to all this criticism.

Michael: Well, I asked the Minister for Education what she thought some of the reasons were and she responded to the findings by suggesting that teachers may be at fault. She said she'd sent schools a list of 600 words all children should know in their first year at secondary school, at age 11, and another list of 700 words that pupils should have mastered by 14.

Newswoman: Really? And how have teachers reacted?

Michael: Well, the teachers' union said it would be commenting later in the day once it had studied the report in more detail. In the past the union has welcomed government initiatives including the new-style English lessons which were introduced in schools last term and where teachers begin each lesson with ten minutes of spelling. The idea is that every department plays a role. For example maths teachers are meant to drill pupils in words connected with maths like 'geometrical', and sports teachers ensure pupils can spell 'athlete' and 'muscles', but the problem is that …

Listening 13.2

Channel 1

Interviewer: And if things weren't bad enough for the Prime Minister, today he came under fire again for his education policy.

Heads of schools and teachers' associations issued a joint statement speaking out against what they see as a lack of interest and understanding in the future generations of the country. In the studio with me today is Michael Woods, chairman of the headmasters' association who supported this statement. Mr Woods, good morning. What is the basis for this statement against the Prime Minister?

Woods: Well, it's quite simple. Year after year, this government has promised they would deliver on education but instead all we've seen is a cut in funding in both schools and resources.

Channel 2

Woman: Scientists at NASA are still looking for somewhere to land the space shuttle which is currently in orbit here, over Australia. The shuttle had been scheduled to land two days ago but poor weather conditions have prevented a safe landing. Freezing fog and heavy rain have caused the agency to look for an alternative or wait for the weather to clear. A spokesperson for NASA said the astronauts aboard the shuttle are all in good health. He added that the shuttle is able to remain in orbit for another ten days.

Channel 3

Woman: I don't think anyone would argue that the economy has done well this year but the outlook for next year is less predictable and the government needs to think its strategy through very carefully. I'd predict a slow down in house prices and I'd also expect inflation to rise by about half a per cent. The consumer will need to be a little more careful in the next twelve months and really start to watch their borrowing. Anyone with large credit card bills should pay them off as soon as possible otherwise they could really get caught out.

Channel 4

Woman/Man: This is a great week for you Leo's, with good news at work – maybe a pay rise or a promotion. Romance might be coming your way. It's a good week to take up a sport or something healthy. Maybe you've been eating a little too much and it would be a good idea to go jogging or perhaps eat a little less. You get on well with the star sign Libra at this time of year, so spend some free time with them. Perhaps you should take a trip to the cinema and relax a little. You've been working hard and I think you need to reward yourself.

Channel 5

Woman: Well, the news coming from Hollywood is that they might be thinking of taking their friendship further. Rumours that Mel and Christina, who met on the set of their recent film, are to get married seem to be spreading across Los Angeles. We haven't been able to get an official response from the publicity office of either star but one close friend of the couple said they wouldn't be surprised and described the couple as 'very close in recent weeks'. This news comes very soon after Mel's much publicised break up with his second wife.

Answer key 13

Vocabulary p126

2 business; sports; politics; news; news; horoscope; showbiz; business.

3 1 pull ahead
2 break off
3 fall out
4 pull out
5 go up
6 cover up
7 leak out
8 break up

4 1 scoop
2 celebrity
3 blog
4 circulation
5 front page news
6 censor
7 item
8 viewpoint
9 breaking news
10 editorial
11 paparazzi
12 tabloids

5 editor/correspondent – people
editorial – sections
national/local – types

Listening p127

1 1 yes; 2 one to three; 3 yes
2 1 twenty
2 headmaster
3 spelling
4 'technique'
5 pupils
6 the wrong vowels
7 full stops
8 Minister
9 union
10 muscles

Grammar p127

1 2 Mistakes arose/have arisen because students missed out letters.
3 What do you think some of the reasons are, Minister?
4 I have sent schools a list of 600 words all children should know.
5 We will/shall be commenting later.

2 a 2, 3, 4, 5; b 1; c 3
3 1 was going
2 could give
3 got home and could help
4 saw
5 do you do

Reading p128

2 1 excitement; money; only job capable of doing.
2 Good contacts and background knowledge; putting information together.
3 No, most of the time it is boring with lots of waiting around.
3 scoop 6
mundane 2
sources 1
uncanny 7
fetch upward 8
ethics 3
invading privacy 4
scum 5
4 1 thrill of the chase
2 pack
3 hitting the jackpot
4 splashed across
5 closing the net on; prey
6 have; cornered
5 1C; 2A; 3A; 4C; 5B; 6D; 7C; 8B

Listening p130

1 3, 4, 1, 5, 2
2 1D; 2F; 3B; 4E; 5A

Key word p131

1 1 tell; 2 said; 3 told; 4 said
2 1 tell; 2 saying; 3 tell; 4 say; 5 say; 6 tell

Grammar p131

1 remind 7
advise 5
invite 8
warn 4
recommend 2
apologise for 6
suggest 1
criticise 3

3 2 He recommended buying the new computer game.
3 The spokesperson criticised the new law.
4 His father warned them to be careful at that time of night.
5 She advised me to accept his offer.
6 Michael apologised for missing the party.
7 Mother reminded me to call her when I got there.
8 The neighbours invited her/him/them over for lunch.

Writing p132

1 ~~emergancy~~ – emergency
~~you no it makes sence~~ – you know it makes sense
~~studio's for rent~~ – studios for rent
~~employes only~~ – employees only
~~were closed~~ – we're closed
~~If your not~~ – If you're not …
~~when there gone, there gone~~ – when they're gone, they're gone
2 accommodation ✓
separate ✓
commitment ✓
dependent ✓
embarassed ✗ embarrassed
goverment ✗ government
business ✓
greatful ✗ grateful
recieve ✗ receive
advertisement ✓
wich ✗ which/witch
comftable ✗ comfortable
3 : colon
; semi-colon
! exclamation mark
' inverted commas
. full stop
' apostrophe
? question mark
, comma
4 1 It's your turn, I think.
2 How long have you been here?
3 The boy at the bus stop, who we'd seen earlier, was now crying.
4 The rabbit said to Alice, 'I'm late, I'm late'.

5 Please bring the following items with you to the exam: pens, pencils and an identity card.
6 Jesse was late as usual; it had always been the case since childhood.
7 My father shouted, 'Turn that music down!'
8 I look forward to hearing from you.

6 1 capital letter
2 a better adjective
3 full stop
4 better word
5 incorrect ending
6 conjunction needed
7 comma
8 problem with the pronoun
9 new paragraph needed
10 avoid repeating words
11 gerund needed
12 too informal

Review p134

1 1C; 2D; 3C; 4A; 5B; 6B; 7D; 8C; 9B; 10A; 11C; 12A
2 1 ~~is going~~ was going
2 They told me the latest …
3 He asked me if I'd like …
4 ~~will be~~ would be
5 ~~that~~
6 ~~to~~
7 ~~be~~ being
8 ~~us~~
9 The reporter wrote about the …
10 These days you can ~~receiving~~ receive your news online.
3 1 don't
2 are
3 of
4 which
5 their
6 more
7 has
8 the
9 to
10 and/so
11 said
12 read

The Daily FCE

SPECIAL SPOTLIGHT EDITION

£2

Newspaper headlines often use their own special vocabulary. Match the headline words in the box with the definitions below.

axe	crash	fishy	rift	rumour	snap	urge
blast	deny	fury	rock	quiz	star	wed
blaze	drama	quit	row	shock	talks	

1 encourage

_____

2 sudden fall

_____

3 great fire

_____

4 refuse to say something is true

_____

5 unofficial story

_____

6 important/exciting event

_____

7 suspicious

_____

8 division as a result of a disagreement/argument

_____

9 discussions/negotiations

_____

10 argue/argument

_____

11 get married

_____

12 upset/destabilize

_____

13 question/interrogate

_____

14 resign

_____

15 unexpected or surprising news

_____

16 anger

_____

17 (show business) celebrity

_____

18 cut

_____

19 explosion

_____

20 photograph

_____

Headlines have a grammar of their own.

• The present simple is often used to talk about the past:
MINISTER AXES HOSPITAL BUDGET
= The Minister of Health has cut the budget for hospitals.
• The infinitive is used to express the future:
DOC TO WED SOAP STAR
= A doctor is going to marry a soap opera actress.

Work in groups. What do you think the stories are behind these headlines?

1 STAR'S FURY OVER HOLIDAY SNAPS

_____

2 RUMOURS ROCK GOVERNMENT

_____

3 DOCTOR SACKED AFTER BLOOD SCANDAL

_____

4 SHOCK CRIME FIGURES – TOP COP QUITS

_____

5 MINISTERS URGES STRIKE TALKS

_____

6 BLAZE HERO TO MEET QUEEN

_____

7 PALACE DENIES ROYAL RIFT RUMOURS

_____

8 SHARES CRASH AFTER SAFETY ROW

_____

9 POLICE TO QUIZ REFINERY BLAST BOSS

_____

10 MODEL TO WED IN FISHY CIRCUMSTANCES

_____

Using the words below, create three headlines and stories to match. You can only use each word once.

AXE	DENY	HIT	ROCK	QUIZ	STAR	WED
BLAST	DRAMA	QUIT	ROW	SHOCK	TALKS	COVER UP
CRASH	FURY	RIFT	RUMOUR	SNAP	URGE	BREAK OFF

1 Headline _____

  Story _____

2 Headline _____

  Story _____

3 Headline _____

  Story _____

PHOTOCOPIABLE 13.1

Reporting the news

How possible is it to give a fair and unbiased account of events?

Story One

A show business celebrity has been involved in an accident.

Police have arrested two motorcycle paparazzi they claim are responsible for the accident. Everybody hates the paparazzi. You have been asked to go to the scene of the accident and find out the truth.

Student A (Journalist): Interview an eyewitness (Student C).

Student B (Journalist): Interview the driver of the star's car (Student D).

Students A and B: Prepare a short report for the evening news' bulletin. Remember to report what you discovered using reporting verbs: *say, tell, ask, claim, maintain, suggest, deny…* and so on. You will give your broadcast to the rest of the class.

Student C (The Eyewitness): You saw everything. You were just behind the star's car when it had the accident. It was going very fast and lost control. That's why the accident happened. The paparazzi arrived a minute later. They gave the star first aid and called the ambulance. The star was in the driver's seat!

Student D (The star's driver): You were driving the car when suddenly in your mirror you saw the paparazzi arriving. You accelerated into the tunnel. The motorcycle with the paparazzi came too close and forced you to crash

Notes

Golden rules of journalism: Never believe everything people tell you --- Never become personally involved. --- Always check the facts. --- Always listen to all sides of the story.

Story Two

An incident has occurred in a part of town which is well known for its problems between the police and youths (young men). Yesterday evening two youths were badly injured after being chased by the police.

Student A (Journalist): Interview the police spokesperson (Student C).

Student B (Journalist): Interview the café-owner witness (Student D).

Students A and B: Prepare a short report for the evening news' bulletin. Remember to report what you discovered using reporting verbs: *say, tell, ask, claim, maintain, suggest, deny…* and so on. You will give your broadcast to the rest of the class.

Student C (Police spokesperson): Police officers were following up a report of two youths tagging (painting graffiti) in the area. They found two suspects who matched the descriptions of the youths hiding in a café. Police officers chased the youths into a building site, where they climbed some scaffolding – but fell off it! Their bags contained spray paint.

Student D (Café owner): You know the boys well. They had been in your café all evening. You think they're good boys who never get involved in trouble. Youths in your area feel persecuted: there are too many controls. When the police burst into the café, the boys became scared and ran away.

Notes

Golden rules of journalism: Never believe everything people tell you --- Never become personally involved. --- Always check the facts. --- Always listen to all sides of the story.

PHOTOCOPIABLE 13.2

14 Fashion

Before you begin

Find out from students how important fashion is to them. Ask them where they think the fashion capital of the world is.

> Which nationality dresses the best?

> Who is the best dressed celebrity?

> Who is the worst dressed public figure?

Topic: Fashion

Fashion is the area of activity that involves styles of clothing and appearance. **A fashion** is a style of clothing or a way of behaving that is popular at a particular time. If something is **in fashion** (fashionable), it is a fashion at a particular time. If it is **out of fashion** (unfashionable), it is not. This unit will look at lasting and passing fads and fashions.

Unit 14 Wordlist:

accessory	faded	skinny
bare	fashion(able)	smart
brand	flair	stylish
cap	freckles	suit
clash	hang up/put on	suite
classic	have on	take in
classical	hungry/hunger	take off
cool	let out	think about
cosy	long/length	think back
cramped	loom	think through
craze	making a comeback	think up
cult	messy	trendy
designer	miserable/misery	try on
dimples	pigtails	turn up
do up	plump	uniform
dress up	poverty	wallpaper
elderly	put on	wardrobe
fad	retro	wrinkled
fade	scruffy	

Getting started

1   Students look at the photographs and pictures and discuss which period they come from. From left to right, the first photo is of an actress playing Queen Elizabeth I from the 16th century. The second picture shows an 18th century gentleman complete with wig and dog. The third image is of an early 20th century 1920s-style woman. The fourth picture shows a 19th century woman being laced into her corset (the binding garment beneath her dress). The fifth picture is of a 17th century lady sitting for her portrait. The final image is of a 1970s man wearing a suit.

2   Lead a quick class discussion about the benefits and dangers of cosmetic surgery. Remind students that while **cosmetics** are substances such as lipstick and face powder (make up), **cosmetic surgery** is surgery which alters the appearance of a person's body. Find out how popular it is in different students' countries.

3   Students complete the questionnaire and then compare answers. Alternatively, treat this as a whole class activity where students stand up and ask and answer.

4   Move into a general discussion about fashion and how much people are influenced by advertisements. You might want to talk about young women, and even men, copying 'size 0' models and their eventual problems with anorexia.

Vocabulary: fashion

1   Give students two minutes to make their choices and then move swiftly through the exercise. Make sure students understand the vocabulary used here, as the words will recur throughout Unit 14.

An **accessory** is a part added to something to make it more decorative (or, in the case of cars or bathrooms, for instance, more useful and functional).
A **brand** of a product is the version made by one particular manufacturer.
If one colour **clashes** with another, they look ugly together.
Classic designs or clothes are those cut for style rather than passing trends.
A **craze** is a fashion that is extremely popular for a short period of time, and which then quickly vanishes.

A **fad** is a temporary fashion.
If you have **flair**, it means you have a natural ability to do something well.
If you're **into** something, it means that something is your passion.
If something is **making a comeback**, it means it used to be fashionable, then it went out of fashion, but now has become fashionable once again.
Retro clothes, music and objects are based on the styles of the past.
Scruffy things or people are dirty or untidy.
Smart things or people are pleasantly neat or clean in appearance.
A **suit** is where the jacket and trousers, or skirt and jacket, are made from the same material.
A **suite** is a luxury apartment in a hotel, or a collection of matching furniture; i.e. sofa and matching armchairs
Trendy means of the latest fashion, whether it is flattering or not.
A **wardrobe** is both a place where we hang our clothes as well as referring to the selection of clothes we own.

Listening: crazes

This is full, exam-style practice. In the examination, the passages are not related by theme. Remind students to read the questions all the way through so they know what they have to listen out for. If you want to treat it as real exam-style practice, insist on examination conditions and play the recording twice without comment. Ask students to write their answers down on a piece of paper (like an answer sheet).

Grammar: *have something done*

1   This is also known as the causative *have*. We use it to talk about services that we have performed by someone else. Contrast the sentences you are given using the concept questions.

TEACHING IN PRACTICE

Constructing *have something done*
Note that the 'have something done' form takes the past participle. Consider writing the form of the construction on the whiteboard:

She had her face lifted

have + something + done

You could also refer your students to Section 12.2.4 of the Grammar Reference if necessary.

2   Give students two or three minutes to write the rest of the answers.

3   Students tick the things they have done and discuss their answers. The kind of things students have done will depend on where they live and their age.

> They had their kitchen repainted.

> She had her nose pierced.

Reading: fashion victim

BACKGROUND

Hair extensions
Since Egyptian times, men and women have worn wigs or hair-pieces according to the fashion of the day. Wigs, hair switches or hair-pieces have come in and out of fashion in just about every century. More recently, hairpieces have enjoyed a return to fashion in the form of hair extensions. They are usually used to lengthen short hair, or to improve hair that has poor texture. There are different ways of applying these hair extensions: you can either choose clip-on pieces, or have them fused to your scalp by a hairstylist.

1   Use the photographs to encourage students to speculate about the article they are going to read. Write a few of their predictions on the whiteboard.

> I think it will have something to do with hair, as that woman's long plait is very noticeable.

> Yes, I agree. The smaller photo shows women getting their heads shaved. The text must be about hair.

2   Set a short time limit to quickly read the first paragraph of the text to check their predictions.

3   These questions encourage the students to scan the text and extract specific information.

Degree of difficulty

Decrease the level: If you want to reduce the overall difficulty of the text you may wish to pre-teach some of these vocabulary items. These items should not stop students from answering the questions, but will make it easier to read.

Word/phrase	Explanation in context
red carpet	When someone important arrives, a red carpet is put down for them to walk along.
locks	A bunch of hair. Think of Goldi*locks* and the three bears.
pilgrim	Someone who visits a place of importance to their religion (e.g. each year millions of Muslim pilgrims travel to Mecca).
dowry	Money a bride's family gives to her husband; or vice-versa.
salon	A hairdresser's premises.
dye	To change the colour of something using a chemical or pigment.
black market	An illegal, unofficial market.
to prey on	To hunt, to select a victim.

4   Set a time limit of eight minutes for students to answer the questions.

5   The article will probably provoke some fairly strong reactions from the members of the class. Allow a short, all-class discussion on the topic.

EXAM SPOTLIGHT

Paper 1, part 1
This spotlight describes how this part of the Reading Paper may contain a 'global' question. It's important that your students are prepared for this question. In fact, you could extend your students' preparation by spending a portion of class time on this area.

Reading extension

Bring a series of short, unrelated texts to class. These texts don't have to be very long, perhaps just two or three paragraphs. Try and choose material which is opinionated and interesting. Ask students to describe, for each text, the author's overall attitude. Encourage students to start a table in their vocabulary book just for keeping a record of these texts which they have read.

Text topic	Author's overall attitude
Anti-fur protests at fashion show	Is furious and very opposed to people wearing fur.

GRAMMAR SPOTLIGHT

Homophones
Homophones are words that sound the same, even if they are written differently.
5   Questions 1 and 3 are homophones (that is, they sound the same), whereas 2 and 4 are slightly different. Can your students think of any more homophones from their wordlists so far?

Grammar: the passive

1   One of the main reasons we use the passive is to change the emphasis of an active sentence. Of course, we also use it when the agent (the person or thing performing an action is unknown).

3   Students identify examples of the passive from the text they have read.

4   Students decide if the statements are true or false.

5   This offers a chance to reinforce learning of tense as well as the passive.

Listening: school uniform

BACKGROUND

School uniform
School uniforms are common in many nations. Traditionally, school uniforms have been subdued and professional. Boys' uniforms often consist of dark trousers and light-coloured shirt with a tie. Girls' uniforms vary greatly between countries and schooling systems, but typically consist of a dress or blouse. These are worn with a skirt, trousers or under a pinafore. The use of a blazer (suit-like jacket) for either gender is also fairly common, especially in cold weather. Originally, school uniforms were introduced to hide the social differences between students. However, some students don't like uniforms because they do not have a choice in what they must wear.

1   Have a quick all-class discussion about the advantages and disadvantages of school uniform and take an informal vote. Find out how common school uniform is in their countries.

> I think school uniform is a dreadful idea! It takes away a person's individuality.

> No, I disagree. Look at the photograph of the girls in maroon uniform. They look very smart and neat!

Grammar: *make, let, allow and need*

If you think your class could be confused about the use of *make* (for obligation), write two sentences on the board and ask how *make* is used differently in each sentence.

make = prepare → She made him a sandwich.

make = force → She made him eat the sandwich.

1   Move into the first exercise, students decide which sentences are active, and which are passive. An important thing to note here is that the verb *let* cannot be used in the passive. For example: They let us take off our jackets = We were ~~let~~ allowed to take off our jackets.

2   Kickstart discussion by talking about your own experiences.

3   This focuses on the use of *need*. We can use *need* with a passive sense by following it with either the gerund (they *need taking up*) or the infinitive of *to be* + past participle (they *needed to be let out*). Students study the cartoons and decide what *needs doing/needs to be done*.

> In the first drawing, the tyre needs to be pumped/needs pumping.

> In the second drawing, the window needs to be fixed/needs fixing.

> In the third drawing, the dog's water bowl needs to be filled/needs filling.

> In the fourth drawing, the plant needs to be watered/needs watering.

Speaking: challenging

In conversation we may not simply want to disagree with what someone says. We may want to challenge their opinion more directly. We have to be careful that this does not appear aggressive. Work on stress and intonation with these introductory phrases; drill them until the students can use them confidently.

1   Remind students that in part 3 of the Speaking Paper, they have to carry out an interactive task with their partner. Remind them that the task is usually presented through pictures. In pairs, students carry out the task.

Speaking extension

Often students need a more tangible way of working.

1   Make cards of the introductory expressions.

2   Hand them out to the students.

3   When they successfully use one of the phrases, they put it on the table.

4   Remind students that after the interaction, the interlocutor (the examiner who asks the questions) discusses how the task went and what the candidates agreed. The interlocutor will then go on to ask a few 'follow up' questions. Ask students to practise asking and answering the follow up questions. If time allows, put them in groups to brainstorm further follow up questions that the interlocutor might ask.

Key word: *think*

Think is at the heart of a number of common expressions and lexical phrases. This is the kind of item that can be tested in the Use of English open or lexical cloze, or in the key word transformations part of this paper.

Think

1   If you think (v) that something is the case, you have the opinion that it is the case.

2   If you think (v) that something is true or will happen, you believe that it is true or will happen, although you are not certain of the facts.

3   If you think (v) highly of someone, you admire them.

4   When you think (v) about ideas or problems (or when you have a think about something), you make a mental effort to consider them or solve them.

5   When you think (v) of something, you remember it or it comes to mind.

6   Phrasal verbs which use *think*:
    If you **think back**, you remember things that happened in the past.
    If you **think something over**, you consider it carefully before making a decision.
    If you **think a problem or situation through**, you consider it thoroughly.
    If you **think something up**, for example an idea or plan, you invent it using mental effort.

Key word extension

Ask your students to add the following words to their Vocabulary diary. They need to remember that our key words should be used as a launch into improving their range of vocabulary:

believe	analyse	recall
consider	evaluate	remember
feel	meditate	forget
judge	reflect	understand

Writing: a descriptive essay

In Paper 2 of the exam, students may have the opportunity to write an essay that contains an element of description, either of a person, a place or both. This section focuses on the use of vocabulary in more creative writing, particularly the power of selecting words that carry a particular connotation. It will be of particular use to the stronger students in the class who are aiming for an A grade.

1   Students read the four short extracts and match them to the pictures.

2   Students look at the texts in more detail and assess the mood/atmosphere of each short piece.

3   The resulting table should look something like this:

Age	Height/build	Hair	Skin
early forties	smallish	untidy	wrinkled
elderly	plump	blonde	freckled
young	little	steel-grey	unhealthy
twenties	skinny	red	pale
	tall	pigtails	tattoo
		messy	
		dyed	

Degree of difficulty

Decrease the level:

4   Offer your students an example descriptive essay/story based on the prompt sentence: *'I'll never forget the time we...'* Here, we have pointed out the adjectives in the first paragraph. Consider preparing something similar, and asking students to identify the adjectives used throughout.

Age (adjective)
Colour (adjective)
Emotions (adjective)

I'll never forget the time we came home to find out that my Dad had accidentally slipped while sawing wood. My older sisters were at school. My Mum and I were out shopping. When we arrived home, all that was there was a trail of red blood. It led from the empty garage, down the driveway, and across the road. We were petrified! Where was Dad?

Mum raced across the road, and knocked on the green door of the neighbours. But nobody was home! So she tried the house next to them. Luckily, these neighbours were there. They explained that Dad had slipped while sawing, and chopped off the tip of his thumb! Feeling queasy and very dizzy, he had managed to walk to the nearest neighbours, and they had taken him to the hospital. It was very scary!

A few hours later, Dad returned home. He looked pale and shaken, but otherwise he was fine. The doctors had, thankfully, managed to sew his thumb back together. Now, all you can see is a thin silvery line across the tip. But what a scare! I'll never forget that horrible day!

Word connotations
The **connotations** of a word are the ideas or qualities it makes you think of:

The words 'sneaky' or 'sly' both have negative connotations ...

... while the words 'pleasant' and 'accommodating' both have positive connotations.

6 Connotations of these words are:

Cosy	=	warm and comfortable
Snap	=	speak sharply
Cramped	=	very small
Elderly	=	old
Glare	=	look aggressively/angrily
Lonely	=	sad and alone
Plump	=	slightly/pleasantly fat
Pretty	=	nice-looking
Stare	=	look fixedly

7   Suggested answers:

Affectionate/sympathetic: elderly

Welcoming/comforting: cosy

Negative/unattractive: messy, skinny, snap

Menacing/aggressive: glare, snap (again) loom

Small and uncomfortable: cramped

8   Sight = bright ...

Smell = sweet ...

Touch = sticky ...

Hearing = crackling ...

Note: Make sure your students work out that there is no direct reference to taste in the four pieces of writing. Ask them to add a sentence to one of the pieces which uses an adjective referring to taste.

Photocopiable activity instructions

Activity 14.1: From sweat-shop to street brawl: The story of the Spike Morrison shoe

Aim: To develop narrative composition skills and create an oral narrative using a variety of narrative tenses; to practise using the passive voice for describing processes; to use *make*, *allow*, and *need*.

Instructions:

1   You can either treat the story as a straightforward narrative, or you could copy and jumble up the pictures. Treat this as a whole class or activity in groups.

2   Once you have gone through the story, ask the students to imagine what the people said, and how they might have felt in each of the pictures.

3   Set the composition as a homework exercise. This is a good opportunity to practise narrative composition writing before the examination.

Activity 14.2: Chat show/role-play

Aim: to practise ways of agreeing and disagreeing and presenting points of view; to use the *have something done* form; to revise and recycle the vocabulary of fashion.

Instructions:

1   Lead in by asking about chat shows in the students' countries. Ask about different hosts: their popularity, what they do, and how the show is run.

2   Explain the concept of the activity to the students.

3   This activity can use up to seven people plus an audience of however many students you like. However, if possible, it is preferable to have the same activity going on simultaneously in a different part of the classroom, or a different room altogether. If you need to share a room, position tables and chairs in two distinct parts of the class and play some music. This gives everyone the opportunity to participate more fully.

4   Hand out the roleplay cards to each student. You should probably choose a confident student for the role of Sasha. Remember that you can copy the 'audience' square as many times as necessary.

5   If you have two groups, allow students a few minutes to prepare themselves by role (the hosts together, the psychiatrists together and so on) before setting up the main groups and principal actors.

Every day Sasha Prior has a chat show where she debates different topics and asks people to talk about their experiences. Today's topic is about fashion and looking good.

Tapescript 14

Listening 14.1

One

Daughter: Come on, Dad, you can't possibly wear that old-fashioned suit – it's so 70s.

Father: What do you mean? I've had this for years … I'm proud I can still get into it.

Daughter: Yeah, but it looks as though you've just come out of an old TV programme. It's just *so* weird. Two buttons are out, three are in.

Father: Two buttons, three buttons – I couldn't care less, I'm not into fashion. Anyway if I wait long enough two buttons will make a comeback.

Daughter: OK, but do you think you could change the shirt and tie. They don't go together at all. Those green stripes clash horribly with the pink.

Father: Do you really think so? Alright, if that makes you feel better, I will.

Two

Doctor: Yes, I perfectly understand, Hannah. In my opinion, the best way of losing weight is to follow a sensible balanced diet. Avoid fads like avoiding all carbohydrates or eliminating all fat from your diet. There are *no* miracle solutions. Take up some form of light exercise and then build up so that your body is getting a good workout for twenty minutes or so at least three times a week. Make sure you don't overdo it or you could get hurt, you know, tear a muscle or something like that. So avoid sports to start with which involve sharp violent movements like football or even tennis.

Three

Melissa: Well, finally, here comes Lulu.

Raymond: And about time too. And oh my goodness! Look at her! She looks like an orange.

Melissa: Yes, and just look at that permanent smile.

Raymond: Mmm, she has had her face lifted at least three times. But gravity always wins in the end.

Melissa: And she should think about getting her eyes done, those bags look awful.

Lulu: Sorry I'm late. I've just been to the tanning salon.

Raymond: Don't worry, darling. We were just saying how gorgeous you look.

Four

You're on a tight budget; you don't have to wear expensive brands or designer labels to be stylish. Let the real you come through and develop your own look. Accessories such as scarves and brooches can give you that something extra with a bit of flair.

Five

One of the latest crazes is flashmobbing. This is where a large group of young people, up to a couple of hundred, descend on a place they have agreed and decided on. They do something unexpected for a couple of minutes and then leave as quickly as they came. The meeting point is decided on the internet. They gather and then they get a set of instructions to follow. Then they'll do things like invade a sofa shop and sit on the sofas for five minutes, or go to a bookshop and ask for a non-existent book.

Six

Well, when I think back to when I was a kid, you know when everyone smoked, there was nothing cooler than one of those petrol lighters … Zippos, that's it … a Zippo lighter. Anyway, I guess what I'm trying to say is that each generation has its own set of cult objects – it's normal. My lighter was a lot cheaper than an iPod, that's for sure. But these new objects, some *do* become classics in the end. And do you know, the other day in the shopping centre, I saw this place which was selling flying jackets – you know the type of thing airmen wore in the second world war, with the fur collar and everything!? You can't get more retro than that, can you?

Seven

Well, here we go again. I know a lot of people will complain about it, because there are people living in poverty and dying of hunger, but people need to dream a little too, don't you think? To my way of thinking, there are of a lot of other things which are far more unethical – like the arms trade for instance. Fashion week doesn't hurt anyone. If anything it brightens up people's lives and makes them happier – and that can't be bad, can it?

Eight

Well, it certainly is a little bit behind the times, but it's a wonderful renovation project. And if a few things need doing to it then it will be a good investment. True, the kitchen and bathroom need to be modernized but it has great potential. And it's an up-and-coming area; there are a few new and trendy restaurants starting to appear and I would say that in a couple of years this area will be as fashionable as Hampstead or Islington.

Listening 14.2

Philip: Is that you in that photograph, Florence?

Florence: Mm, yes, it is, Philip. It was the first time I'd worn my new school uniform. I was so proud of myself.

Damien: You look so cute with your hair in pigtails!

Florence: That's sweet of you, Damien. I'm in the summer uniform there. I've got a straw hat, see. But in the winter we had a coat with lots of buttons and a funny-looking hat. It was like a nightcap ... you know, red with a long bit hanging down.

Philip: Oh no! You poor thing!

Florence: Yeah, people used to tease us ... they called us 'Santa's little helpers'! It was complete misery. I don't know who thought the uniform up. I hated that hat, but we were made to wear it.

Damien: I know how you feel. We had to wear our school cap on the way to *and* from school. Things are a lot less strict nowadays!

Philip: I'm glad to hear it. I loathed wearing a uniform.

Damien: I didn't exactly like it either, but the great thing about a uniform is it's so easy. What I mean is you just get up and put it on.

Philip: Yes, but don't you think that kids should be allowed to wear what they want? After all it's a way of expressing themselves.

Damien: You say that, Philip, but kids end up putting on a kind of uniform of their own – you know designer jeans and trainers. Don't you think that leads to a lot of unhealthy competitive dressing? *You* know ... who is wearing the most *fashionable* brands, and so on.

Florence: Not to mention all the hours which are wasted gelling their hair to make it spiky or worrying about looking cool.

Philip: I suppose so, but I don't care what you say. That's still better than school uniform! You know, in the summer, we weren't allowed to take off our jackets! Our teachers didn't even let us take off our ties. It was torture.

Florence: I agree with you Philip. I don't see the point of making people uncomfortable. All the same, in a uniform at least everyone is the same. What I mean is there are no differences between the kids and it makes everyone look equal. It looks smart too.

Philip: Well, you say that, and at the beginning of the year it's true, but it soon gets scruffy – and when they grow they have a jacket which is far too small for them.

Damien: Philip has got a point. He's thought it through. When I was at school the uniform was really expensive so my family couldn't afford to let me have a new one every year. So my trousers always needed taking up for the first four months of the school year because they were too long. The next four months it was OK but then for the last four months of the year they were too short and needed to be let down. In the end they looked awful!

Florence: All the same, I still think uniform is a good idea as it is much less trouble for parents.

Damien: I agree. After all, parents have enough stress as it is. Having their children complaining about not having *exactly* the perfect clothing for school and saying their friends have got better clothes than them is just more stress for them!

Philip: Maybe.

Answer key 14

Vocabulary p136

1 1 accessory
2 making
3 clash/go
4 into
5 cult
6 cool/designer
7 trendy
8 brands
9 fads
10 classic/wardrobe
11 flair
12 craze
13 designer
14 suit
15 scruffy
2 1 fashionable
2 fashioned
3 out of fashion
3 1d; 2g; 3b; 4f; 5a; 6e; 7c
4 1 let it out
2 take them in
3 turn them up
4 take off
5 put on
6 dress up
7 have on/try on
8 do up
5 1 Someone inviting another
person to a party
2 A shop assistant
3 Boss to employee
4 Mother to son
5 Friend to friend
6 Shop assistant
7 Customer to shop assistant

Listening p137

1 1A; 2C; 3A; 4B; 5C; 6B; 7A; 8A

Grammar p137

1 a someone did it for her
b she did it herself.
2 1 had his car sprayed in his
team's colours.
2 their new home in the mountains
built by a local firm.
3 having/going to have their
wedding photographs taken by a
professional photographer.

4 having her wedding dress
made …
5 is going to have his teeth
whitened for the occasion.
6 are having their hair done by the
best hairdresser in town.

Reading p138

3 1 **Lakshmi:** A beautiful 21-year-
old woman.
Vishnu: the Hindu God that
farmers make sacrifices to.
Vered: The owner of a hair
extension salon.
Shri E.V.K.S. Elangovan: An
Indian trade minister.
2 **Tirupati:** the name of the hills
where the temple is sited.
Melrose Avenue: Los Angeles'
most fashionable shopping street.
3 **£500:** the price of a set of hair
extensions
$120 million: the annual cost of
maintaining the temple site.
4,000: the number of women who
have their heads shaved each day.
six months: the length of time
an ordinary Indian family could
live for the price of a set of hair
extensions.
4 1B; 2C; 3B; 4B; 5A; 6D; 7A; 8B
8 1 weighs
2 preys
3 lightning
4 rites
5 dye
6 sight

Grammar p139

1 active a; passive b
2 Sentence a. emphasises the
people; sentence b. the hair.
4 1F; 2T; 3T
5 2 Form: present continuous
The labels are being sewn onto
designer clothes.
3 Form: past simple
Eighty million pairs of trainers
were sold last year (by them).

4 Form: present perfect
Japanese designs have been taken
as their inspiration.
5 Form: 'going to' future
Their new range of swimwear
is going to be presented at the
Olympic pool.
6 Form: past perfect
My favourite shoes were destroyed
by our new puppy.
7 Form: past perfect
Hundreds of holes had been made
in the clothes in the wardrobe.
8 Form: future perfect
The costumes will have been
finished by next weekend.
9 Form: modal in the present
Action should be taken …
10 Form: modal perfect
The trade should have been
banned …
6 1 by (+ agent); 2 with
(+ instrument)

Listening p140

2 1 Damien
2 Florence
3 Damien
4 Philip
5 Florence
6 Philip
7 Damien
3 1B; 2C; 3A; 4B; 5C

Grammar p141

1 force/oblige b prepare a
2 Active 1b, 2a; Passive 1a, 2b
4 1 and 2

Speaking p141

1 1 Yes, but don't you think that …
2 that kids should be allowed to …
3 … but I don't care what you say …
4 … there are no differences
between the kids …
5 … I still think uniform is a good
idea
6 … parents have enough stress
as it is
2 a4; b1; c6; d2; e5; f3

Key word p142

1 1 Do you think you could …
2 Don't you think we should …
3 thinking about …
4 … think so?
5 thought up …
6 … think things through.
7 think back to …
8 To my way of thinking …

Review p144

1 1 hunger
2 lengths
3 fashionable
4 choice
5 widening
6 exploitation
7 designer
8 ethically
9 poverty
10 employment
2 1 wasn't allowed to have
2 kitchen was decorated by
3 was made to have
4 skinny by
5 is quite shocked
6 had her tattoo removed
7 needs to have
8 are going to get hurt
3 1 like
2 place
3 for
4 where
5 were
6 its
7 for
8 just/only/about
9 Since
10 somewhere
11 the/this
12 quickly

PHOTOCOPIABLE 14.1

Chat show

Sasha Prior

You are the chat show host. It is your job to run the show and manage the guests. Introduce the topic of today's show and invite guests to take it in turns to speak. Choose the order, and invite guests to comment on what each other says. Remember, you want to create a lively and entertaining debate.

There are six main guests on today's show.

Kevin Bond: A psychologist and expert on eating disorders.
Sam Hoskins: Someone who has had seven major cosmetic surgery operations.
Annette Zisser: Anti-fashion activist.
Kobskii Ha: Fashion expert and magazine editor.
Ruth Dolton: a plastic (cosmetic) surgeon.
Lynette Walford : Managing director of 'Strike Out' fashions.

Kevin Bond

You are a psychiatrist who specialises in helping people with eating disorders. You think that fashion magazines are partly responsible for the problems faced by lots of teenagers. Skinny models make girls, and even boys, feel as though they are too fat. This is often the start of anorexia. Anorexia and eating disorders are big problems and can even result in death. When an anorexic looks in the mirror he/she sees an obese person looking back. You think that magazines should be made to have images of ordinary people with ordinary bodies. People should learn to accept themselves as they are. You do not agree with plastic surgery, unless there is a real reason for it. People can become plastic surgery addicts.

Sam Hoskins

You are famous for having had lots of different operations to improve your appearance. You had a miserable childhood because you felt that you were ugly and never had any friends. You have had seven different operations to make yourself look beautiful. You have spent over £50 000 on these operations and you think it is money well spent. You have had your eyes and nose redone. You feel that you look much better now. Before you had no self-confidence and were afraid to go out in public. Now you have lots of friends and have far fewer complexes about your appearance. You don't care what other people think and you are going to continue having these operations until you are absolutely perfect.

Annette Zisser

You are an anti-fashion activist. You think that fashion is a waste of time and organize demonstrations outside fashion shows. You think that there are millions of people in the world who are starving and that people in the fashion business should be doing something that is more worthwhile for humanity. You feel that fashion is nothing but a long story of exploitation. Animals are murdered for their leather and their fur. (You only wear shoes made from wood or plastic.) The farmers who grow the cotton for a pair of denim only get a few cents for their are exploited by fashion companies. Thousands of people, mainly young women are exploited in sweat shops to make the items. Lots of fashion items are made by young children working in awful conditions. The people who buy them are exploited by advertising and big business. They are encouraged to buy things they don't need. You think it is disgusting that people buy torn jeans, when there are millions of people who *have* to wear rags.

Kobskii Ha

You are a fashion expert and editor of a fashion magazine. You think fashion is a wonderful thing – an 'art-form', like painting, music or literature.

Without fashion society would stay stuck the way it is, or would start going backwards! Fashion is one of the ways that each generation has of expressing itself and breaking with the past. It is a healthy and natural expression of change. It also creates and maintains millions numbers of jobs in manufacturing and retail. You also think that models and fashion designers do more than almost anyone else to help the poor and developing countries. You are always going to fashion shows that are in benefit of the poor or the starving.

Ruth Dolton

You are a cosmetic surgeon, a doctor who helps people change their appearance. You think that what you do is a socially worthwhile and necessary job. You help people re-create themselves and lead happier lives. Before you operate, you always interview your patients and tell them whether you think an operation would be helpful. Where something is unnecessary you always try to convince the patient not to go ahead with the operation. You also work in a hospital where you operate on people who have had accidents, or burns. Every year you spend two or three weeks in a developing country performing operations on hundreds of patients free of charge.

Lynette Walford

You are the managing director of a big brand jeans manufacturer. You think that a lot of the accusations that people make about your brand and others are unfair. You always do your best to make sure that the workers who produce your goods are well treated, although you admit that it is impossible to visit every factory in the world that does work for you. People should remember that developing countries are grateful for factories that are set up in their countries. They provide jobs and wealth and help with development. You make sure that children under the age of fourteen are not employed in any of your factories. You help employees with literacy and training. Your firm has recently started making jeans from 'free-trade' cotton that guarantees farmers a better price. Many customers are prepared to pay more for this.

Audience Member

You are attending today's chat show because you are very interested in this topic of the price of fashion. You have not decided yet what you think about the industry, and hope that today's presenters will make you decided. You plan to ask at least one question about one of the issues involved.

PHOTOCOPIABLE 14.2

Before you begin

Ask students how important tradition is. By **tradition**, we mean customs or beliefs which have existed for a long time. What traditions do they have in their families? Schools? Places of work? Villages?

> Where I work it's a tradition that when it's your birthday you buy coffee and cakes for everyone.

> My family has a tradition of going to the beach every summer holiday.

> The village where I live has a tradition of having a Christmas tree in the town centre every year.

Topic: New traditions

This unit looks at the topics of culture in general, art and festivals. At FCE level students should be able to speak with confidence about their country's cultural heritage and be able to describe the unfolding of an event such as a festival.

Unit 15 Wordlist:

ancient	heritage	priceless
auction	historic	set out
ceremony	historical	sight
custom	infamous	site
event	invaluable	statue
exhibition	landscape	sword
expedition	middle-aged	take in
fake	Middle Ages	take off
famous	monumental	tradition
festival	museum	turn out
find out	notorious	turn up
gallery	pass off	worthless
go through	persuade/	worthwhile
habit	persuasive	youth/youthful
heartless	pike	
heirloom	portrait	

Getting started

This launches one of the main themes of the unit which is artwork. The two paintings were chosen because of their richness of detail. They are also appropriate given the topic of 'New' Traditions. Although these paintings may appear fairly old, they are actually relatively young. Each painter, however, looked back on a rich, folkloric traditional past. Their works are reminiscent of the Middle Ages, the mythic King Arthur, and the Renaissance.

1   Run through the Useful Expressions and put students in pairs or groups to describe the similarities and differences between the photographs in as much detail as possible. Encourage your students to avoid looking at Information Files 15.1 and 15.2 until after they've considered the paintings without any aid.

Getting started extension

Bring in a large poster of an interesting artwork, and allow your students to take it in turns to present it as though they were a guide in an art gallery. Many of the works by van Gogh or Chagall are likely to inspire discussion, and it provides excellent speaking practice for the students. It's also a welcome change from the photographs that students have been describing throughout their FCE study.

Listening: statues

1   Exploit the photograph to generate interest in the theme of statues. The person is obviously imitating a historical figure. He looks quite successful. Surely, however, the person must get bored, and their body begin to ache?

Is there a place in your students' town where tourists gather to watch such 'human statues'? Have your students ever been to such a place? Circular Quay in Sydney is quite well-known as one such location.

2   This provides exam-style practice. If you wish, you could play the recording through a first time asking students to match the speaker to the pictures in the collage on page 47.

3   Students say what materials are mentioned.

4   Pause after each speaker to allow your students time to decide whether the statement is true or false.

Vocabulary: culture and heritage

1 This section deals with confusable pairs of words on the topic of culture and heritage. Students will have already met the majority of these words, but will need reminding of them and the differences between them.

Confusable pairs

Correct word choice	Incorrect word choice
An **exhibition** is an event at which objects of interest are displayed in a public place.	An **expedition** is a journey made for a particular purpose such as exploration.
A **gallery** is a place that has permanent exhibitions of art in it.	A **museum** is a public building where interesting and valuable objects are kept and displayed.
A **tradition** is a custom or belief that has existed for a long time.	A **habit** is something that you do often or regularly.
A **site** is a piece of ground used for a particular purpose.	Your **sight** is your ability to see.
A country's **heritage** consists of all the qualities and traditions that have continued over many years, especially when they are considered to be of historical importance.	An **heirloom** is an object which has been passed on from generation to generation. Note: heirloom is pronounced with a silent 'h' – more like air-loom.
A **statue** is a large sculpture of a person or animal, made of stone, bronze, or some other hard material.	**Monumental** is used to emphasise the size or extent of something.
Ancient means very old, or having existed for a long time.	Something that is **old-fashioned** is no longer used, done, or believed by most people, because it has been replaced by something that is more modern.
A(n) **historic** event is important in history, or likely to be considered important at some time in the future.	**Historical** people, situations, or things existed in the past and are considered to be part of history.
A **memorial** is a structure built in order to remind people of a famous person or event.	A **souvenir** is something which you buy or keep to remind you of a holiday, place or event.
A **ceremony** is a formal event such as a wedding or a coronation.	An **event** is something that happens.

To take place means to occur, to happen.	**To take part** is to take a share in an event.
To be notorious means to be famous for something bad.	To be **famous** is to be well-known.
The **landscape** is everything you can see when you look across an area of land, including hills, rivers, buildings and trees.	A **portrait** is a painting, drawing or photograph of a person.
A **custom** is an activity, a way of behaving, or an event which is usual or traditional in a particular society or in particular circumstances.	A **customer** is someone who buys goods or services.
A **festival** is an organised series of events and performances.	**First of all** means the first thing (and is often mixed up with festival because of its pronunciation).
Worthless means of no real use or value.	**Priceless** means of immense value.
If you describe something as **invaluable**, you mean that it is extremely useful.	If something is **worthwhile**, it is enjoyable or useful, and worth the time, money or effort spent on it.
The **Middle Ages** is a period of history.	**Middle-aged** people are between the ages of 40 and 60.
Infamous people or things are well-known because of something bad.	Something or someone who is **well-known** is famous or familiar.

2 A time-saving way of handling this exercise will be to divide the students into groups and allocate a few of the words in the exercise to each group.

Reading: genuine fakes

Art forgery

Art forgery refers to creating and, in particular, selling works of art that are falsely attributed to be the work of another, usually more famous, artist. Art forgery is extremely lucrative (makes a lot of money). Art forgery dates back more than two thousand years. Roman sculptors produced copies of Greek sculptures. During the Renaissance, apprentices were trained to copy the works of the masters, with often little interest in whether it was an original or a replica. The practice was usually considered a tribute to the first artist. Lately, however, modern dating and analysis techniques have made the identification of forged artwork much simpler.

1 The title is obviously a **paradox**. A paradox is a situation which involves two or more facts or qualities which seem to contradict each other. Use this question to generate interest in the theme. Usually, if we approach a text with some kind of expectation, it will help us read it more effectively. First of all, deal with the title: ask how something that is 'fake' (a false copy) can be 'genuine' (real). Make sure that there is an imaginative student in each of the groups! Elicit some ideas and write these on the whiteboard.

2 Give students two or three minutes only to skim read the text to see if any of their predictions were correct.

3 Now move into exam-like practice. Set a time limit of 10–15 minutes to complete the task.

4 Use the follow-up questions for a short all-class discussion.

Grammar: inversion

This section looks at inversion: where the subject and the auxiliary of the main verb are reversed. Inversion is often used for dramatic effect and emphasis. It is more common in writing or when you are telling a story. Make sure that your students place emphatic stress on the words in italics. Refer students to Section 10 of the Grammar Reference if necessary.

Vocabulary: phrasal verbs

1–2 Warn students that they may *think* they know the meanings of the phrasal verbs, but that the same phrasal verb can have a number of different meanings. At this point, you may want to refer the students to the Grammar spotlight at the bottom of the column. Note: you may want to remind students of the photocopiable activity, 'Take that', from Unit 9.

p/c
9.1

GRAMMAR SPOTLIGHT

Different meanings of phrasal verbs
Phrasal verbs often have more than one meaning, so it is important for students that they look closely at the context in which a phrasal verb appears before coming to a premature conclusion. Remind students that a good dictionary will give them the different meanings of phrasal verbs.
When your students have run through the spotlight, make them take careful note that the same phrasal verb may have a different grammar. Notice that *take off* can be both transitive and intransitive with a change in meaning.

Listening: living traditions

BACKGROUND

The English Civil War
The English Civil War consisted of a series of armed conflicts and political machinations that took place between Parliamentarians and Royalists between 1642 and 1651. The first and second civil wars placed the supporters of King Charles I against the supporters of the Long Parliament. The third war saw fighting between the King's supporters and supporters of the Rump Parliament. The Civil War ended with the Parliamentary victory at the Battle of Worcester in 1651. The Civil War led to the trial and execution of Charles I as well as the exile (forced exclusion) of his son, Charles II. It also led to the replacement of the English monarchy with a protectorate led by Oliver Cromwell. The English Civil Wars established that British monarchs could not govern without the consent (permission) of Parliament.

1–2 Read the information in the box with the students. Check that they understand the meaning of **civil war**. It means a war between the people of the same country. Exploit the pictures to identify the key characters. Establish the character of Kelly Foster and her unusual hobby. Ask the class if it reminds them of similar organisations in their own country.

2 Elicit possible questions from the class and write them on the whiteboard.

Why did you start this hobby?

Is it something women can do too?

Is it ever dangerous?

3 Ask students what examination technique they should use before listening to the passage. Remind them that they should read all the questions through carefully so that they know what they will be listening out for. Check any unknown vocabulary. An **outcome** means a result. Play the recording and walk round the class checking the students' answers. If you think they need to hear the passage again, play it through, pausing where answers to the questions appear.

Key word: mind

Mind has three principal meanings:
1 Thinking (your ability to reason)
2 Expressing opinion (your ability to state what you think)
3 Care (to warn someone to be careful or to look after something).

Key word extension

Consider furthering the two key word questions by asking your students to consider the various phrases which use *mind*. For example, what do the following phrases mean?

1 The idea never crossed my mind.
2 I can see it in my mind's eye right now.
3 Keep me in mind for the job.
4 It's really playing on my mind.
5 I have an open mind about it.
6 It really took my mind off the problem.

Answers:
1 The idea hadn't occurred to me.
2 I can visualise it / see it.
3 Think of me for the job.
4 I'm thinking about it a lot.
5 I am quite flexible / easy-going about it.
6 I forgot about it / was distracted from it.

Speaking: adverbs in conversation

This section looks at ways students can make their English sound more natural and conversational.

1 Students read the information in the box and then find examples of how these adverbs are used in the tapescript of the interview they have just heard. Allow students to practise these forms in pairs or groups.

Degree of difficulty

Increase the level: Tell your students that they cannot refer to the tapescript. Instead, ask them to listen again. How do they go without that written prompt helping them?

Reading: festivals

TIP: Pre-reading activity

Ask your students to look at the four photographs of each country's festivals. Can they describe them? The colours and people are quite striking. What do they first notice? And then, on second glance, what kind of expectations do these photos create about the reading texts?

1 Students skim read the texts and order the festivals in level of interest. Allow a short all class discussion. There is no 'right' answer.

TIP: Post-reading activity

Ask your students to 'prove' their answers to questions 1–15. That is, ask them to provide the example sentence that demonstrates the basis of the answer.
Example:
Which festival ...?
2 is the earliest in the year?

A N'cwala, in Zambia, is held each February.

Writing: an article

1 Generate interest in the model text by exploiting the photograph.

2 This exercise tries to address the problem students have with putting events in order, and tries to compare and contrast easily confusable forms.

3 Ask your students to re-read the text and complete the table. Tell them not to worry if they can't find a lot to write after each heading. The table will provide a clear idea of how their own article can be structured.

Name and origins	Day of the dead
When it takes place	1st November
What it celebrates	one's ancestors
Its purpose	to help us remember the dead
Its origins	the Aztecs/it used to last all of August
What it is like nowadays	just one day: 'All Saints' Day' in Christian calendar
Preparations	clean and tidy graves, create an altar, decorate the altar with flowers and food
Costumes	no real costumes just your best clothes
Special food/drink	sweets in the form of skulls and tequila
Characters/personages	Catrina, the Lady of the Dead
Bizarre/interesting facts	read satirical poetry about the dead person!
What happens during the festival: - beginning	put on best clothes
- middle	go to the cemetery and say prayers
- end	go home!

Writing extension

If you have the advantage of a multinational class, you could have two or three students from the same country produce a joint piece of work. Ask them to illustrate it with ideas taken from the Internet or their own drawings. If you have a number of different pieces of work, use them to decorate the classroom or hold a small exhibition.

What: El Gran Pader
La Fiesta del Señor Jesús del Gran Poder
When: late May / early June
Where: primarily in La Paz, Bolivia
Originally started: late 1930s

Photocopiable activity instructions

Activity 15.1a: Do you hear what I see? (picture dictation)

Aim: To practise close description/comparison of pictures in preparation for the second part of the Speaking Paper; to practise prepositions of place, positioning, the language of description and comparison.

Instructions:

1   Students work in pairs.

2   Give Student A the complete picture, and Student B the incomplete picture.

First version:

3   Student A should help Student B to finish the drawing by telling him/her what to draw and where. Student A can look at Student B's drawing but cannot touch it or point to anywhere. Student A should not let Student B see the complete drawing until they have finished.

Alternate first version:

3   Student B needs to ask Student A questions, such as: 'Is there a house?' 'Yes'. 'Is it on the left or the right?'

4   Once both have finished they compare their results.

Activity 15.1b: Do you hear what I hear?

1   Copy and distribute one page per pair.

2   Tell your students that there are six differences between a view of an apartment building.

3   Ask Student A and Student B to take it in turns to tell each other what is happening in each room. They should try and identify what is different between the apartments.

Activity 15.2: Just a minute!

Aim: Fluency; to practise and recycle vocabulary on topic of culture and heritage; to apply a range of functional expressions.

Instructions:

1   Prepare a set of cards for each three or four students and mix up each set. Explain something like this to your class:

A minute can seem very long when you have to talk about something. Work in groups of three or four. Mix up the cards and put them face down on a table. Take it in turns to pick up a card and talk for a minute about the topic on the card. If a member of the group runs out of things to say, then someone else in the group can take up the subject.

2   Demonstrate the activity:
a) place cards face down and pick up the first card.
b) try to speak for a minute on the topic. Pretend to hesitate to allow other students to break in and continue the topic.

3   If you wish, you can have a 'quiz-master/mistress' for each group who deals with the timing. The game can also be played with the quizmaster/mistress awarding points.

4   Change your speakers if there is too much hesitation, repetition or the speaker simply runs out of things to say!

There is a **point** scheme of one point for the person who is speaking at the end of the minute.

There's a bonus point for the speaker if they experience an unfair or invalid interruption/challenge!

Tapescript 15

Listening 15.1

Speaker One And finally, guards at the terracotta army museum in Xi'an, China couldn't believe their eyes when they saw a man jump into the pit and disguise himself as one of the warriors. German art student, Paul Wendel, who was studying in China, decided to join the warriors he admired. These remarkable ancient terracotta soldiers are over two thousand two hundred years old, and an important part of China's heritage. They were created to accompany their emperor in the afterlife. Wendel pretended he was one of them and stood as still as he could until the guards lifted him away. Apparently he stayed frozen in his pose as the guards lifted him out.

Speaker Two In Britain, November the 5th is 'Bonfire Night'. It celebrates the discovery of a plot to kill King James the first, by blowing up the Houses of Parliament. Before Bonfire Night there's a tradition that children make a 'Guy' – a life-size doll of Guy Fawkes the infamous conspirator. They'll take some old clothes and fill them up with newspaper. Then they'll make a head and draw a face on it, and perhaps stick on a beard. A few days before Bonfire Night, they'll display the Guy outside supermarkets and train stations saying "A penny for the Guy". Of course, nowadays what they mean is 'at least 50p!' Then they'll use this money to buy fireworks or sweets for the celebrations on the 5th.

Speaker Three I enjoyed visiting well known sights such as Red Square in Moscow and going to the Hermitage museum in St Petersburg, but, to tell you the truth the thing that most moved me was a short visit I made to Volgograd and seeing an absolutely awesome statue that some people call 'Mother Russia'. Volgograd used to be called Stalingrad and was the site of the terrible siege and historic battle which proved to be the turning point of the war. Anyway, the statue, which is made of concrete, stands outside Volgograd, overlooking the city. It is, for sure, the tallest statue in Europe and is a memorial which commemorates the struggle and sacrifices made by the people of Stalingrad and the Red Army.

Speaker Four One of my favourite TV shows used to be with those rubber puppets. They were real works of art – you could immediately see who they were supposed to be. I used to like the way they made fun of politicians or famous or notorious personalities from show-business and so on. And the actors who took them off, sounded like the real thing. I don't know why they don't show it any more – I suppose they thought it was old-fashioned. The one thing I didn't appreciate, though was the way they mocked the royal family – I mean, that's totally unfair, I think.

Speaker Five Sometimes we should rely on our first impressions. For instance, the Getty Museum spent $10m on a fake statue which was supposed to come from ancient Greece. Now, everything about it seemed perfect, and museum officials managed to talk themselves into thinking it was real, but other experts knew the second that they looked at it that the statue was a fake. Years of examining hundreds of examples of the real thing simply told them that the Getty museum had been taken in by a clever imitation.

Listening 15.2

Part A

Betty: So would you mind telling us how you got into these, the re-enactments?

Kelly: Well, basically it was a way of getting to know people. I moved from London to this small town where I didn't know anyone. I hesitated a bit at first, 'cos I thought, you know, that there would be lots of weirdos, but I finally made up my mind to join and have been involved ever since.

Betty: Right, so basically you joined to make new friends. It wasn't because you were interested in history or anything like that?

Kelly: Actually, I wasn't that keen on history when I was at school. Mind you, since joining the society I have discovered a real love for history and our heritage.

Betty: And which side are you on?

Kelly: Well, I'm in a Royalist regiment, one which supports the king. You see, in the *real* war, in the 17th century … there was a local gentleman who established a regiment loyal to the king in my town. So the regiment I am in is a tribute to the original one. Anyway, I've always preferred the Cavaliers.

Betty: Me too. They had long hair, and lovely clothes and hats with feathers and all the rest. The Roundheads must have been a miserable-looking crowd, I think, in the brown and black they always wore! You can't imagine them having a good time, can you? So tell me, what happens in these re-enactments?

Kelly: Well, basically, we form a little army with other Royalist regiments then we re-enact battles and other historic events against Roundhead regiments – of course the outcome of the battle is decided at the planning stage, so we just act the story out like a play on a large scale. We do try to keep the suspense going as much as possible for the spectators.

Betty: Goodness. So how many people can be involved?

Kelly: Well, sometimes there can be several hundred participants on each side, not counting the thousands of people who come along to watch.

Betty: And do you do this on a stage or somewhere like that?

Kelly: No, not at all. We travel to the original battlefields and camp there for the weekend of the re-enactment battle. We may have to travel hundreds of miles. There is usually a farmer who will let us park or put our tents up on his land.

Listening 15.3

Part B

Betty: I hope you don't mind my mentioning this, fighting isn't a very lady-like activity is it?

Kelly: Well, there are more lady-like roles. At first I was one of the women-folk. I was a cook. But when I realised that the soldiers were having more fun I changed my mind and became a soldier too! Although this does mean dressing up as a man – there weren't women soldiers in those days as such.

Betty: So there's nothing to stop women from playing a full part in the fighting?

Kelly: No, anyone can wave a sword around. But I can't manage the pikes, those very long spears – well, they're five metres long and impossible for most of the women to handle! But there's nothing to stop a girl being a musketeer either, you know, firing a gun, or even joining the cavalry. Oh, and it almost slipped my mind, girls can be drummers too.

Betty: But isn't it dangerous? I mean taking part in a battle, even if it's a pretend one?

Kelly: No, not really, although people sometimes have small injuries. You have to mind where you stand – it hurts if a horse steps on your foot – it *really* hurts.

Betty: What was your first battle like?

Kelly: Great fun, although I did say to myself, 'you must be out of your mind, girl'. The noise and the smell of gunpowder are unimaginable.

Betty: Mm, goodness knows what the real thing must have been like. And what do you do other than this?

Kelly: Well, the social life is absolutely fantastic. You meet like-minded people from all walks of life and there are banquets … you know … *big* meals … for all the regiment. And dances! Every year we go to London to commemorate the execution of King Charles in 1649. There's a parade to where his head was cut off at the Mansion House.

Answer key 15

Listening p146
2 1C; 2F; 3A; 4B; 5D
3 terracotta; old clothes; newspaper; concrete; rubber
4 1F; 2F; 3T; 4T; 5F; 6T; 7F; 8F; 9T; 10T; 11T; 12F; 13T; 14T; 15F

Vocabulary p147
1 1 exhibition
2 galleries
3 site
4 tradition
5 heritage
6 statue
7 ancient
8 historic
9 memorial
10 ceremony
11 place
12 notorious
13 landscape
14 custom
15 festival
16 worthless
17 invaluable
18 Middle Ages; infamous

Reading p148
3 1H; 2C; 3E; 4G; 5A; 6D; 7B

Grammar p149
1 1c; 2a; 3d; 4b
2 The auxiliary verb and the subject are inverted (the auxiliary comes before the subject). 1–4 are more emphatic.

3 1 Not only did he produce work by impressionists, he also produced work by surrealist artists (too/ as well).
2 No sooner/Hardly had he left jail than he got an important phone call.
3 Not only did the officer who (had) arrested him ask for a personal portrait, but a member of the prosecuting counsel did too.
4 No longer does he pretend that his paintings are works of art by famous artists.
5 No sooner had Myatt recognised his letter to Drewe than he realised the game was over.
6 Not only does he read everything about the artist but he also tries to hypnotise himself with their work.
4 1 No sooner/Hardly had I closed the door to my flat than I realised I had left my keys inside.
2 Not only did they/had they eaten everything in the fridge but (also) the cat food too.
3 No longer do they employ 13-year-old children, now they only employ adults.

Vocabulary p150
1 1 look after
2 set out
3 turn out
4 turn up
5 take in
6 find out

7 pass off
8 go through
9 take off
2 1a deceived; 1b gave her a home; 1c understand
2a produce; 2b finally became apparent; 2c asked everyone to leave
3a arrived without warning; 3b increase; 3c reduce the length of something, e.g. jeans, a dress

Listening p150
3 1A; 2B; 3C; 4C; 5B; 6B; 7A
4 1 cook, one of the women-folk
2 more fun
3 dress up
4 drummer
5 pikes
6 five metres
7 horses
8 absolutely fantastic
9 banquets
10 execution/death

Key word p151
1 1 Mind
2 changing his
3 slipped my
4 out of her/lost her
5 make up
6 like-minded
7 reminder
2 1 I hope you don't mind my mentioning this, but you're wearing different socks!
2 Do you mind closing the window? It's terribly cold in here.

Reading p152
1 1D; 2B; 3B; 4D; 5B; 6C; 7C; 8C; 9D; 10B; 11A; 12A; 13B; 14D; 15A

Writing p153
2 1 At first
2 Once upon a time
3 Nowadays
4 Once
5 Before
6 First of all
7 after that
8 Afterwards
9 Eventually
10 In the end
4 sad; scary; moving; memorable; slightly shocked; most beautiful places; wonderful memories

Review p154
1 1 persuasive
2 Afterwards
3 infamous
4 heartless
5 relationship
6 mysteriously
7 remarkable
8 forgiveness
9 discovery
10 youthful
2 1 made up your mind
2 takes place in
3 only does she speak Chinese
4 would you mind opening
5 in taking us in
6 sooner did we turn
7 taking part
8 on turning

Do you hear what I see?

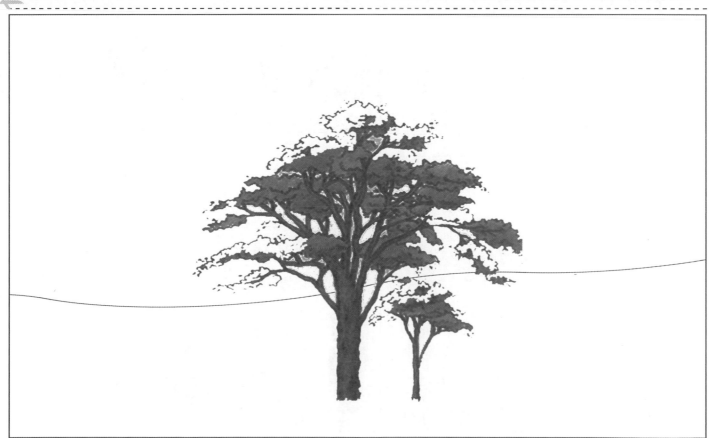

PHOTOCOPIABLE 15.1a

Do you hear what I hear?

Find the seven differences in your view of this apartment block without showing your partner what you see.

Just a minute!

Talk for a minute cards	**Talk for a minute about:** the most important tourist sight in your town or region.	**Talk for a minute about:** a terrible event associated with your town or region.	**Talk for a minute about:** a typical dish from your town or region	**Talk for a minute about:** a place of exceptional natural beauty in your town or region
Talk for a minute about: a sporting hero associated with your town or region	**Talk for a minute about:** the best way of getting around your town or region.	**Talk for a minute about:** a famous writer or poet from your town or region.	**Talk for a minute about:** a folk tradition associated with your town or region.	**Talk for a minute about:** an historic occasion or event associated with your town or region.
Talk for a minute about: the geographical position and characteristics of your town or region.	**Talk for a minute about:** a myth, legend or folk tale associated with your town or region.	**Talk for a minute about:** the origins of some street or place names in your town or region.	**Talk for a minute about:** a festival or celebration that takes place each year in your town or region.	**Talk for a minute about:** what a visitor should buy as a souvenir of your town or region.
Talk for a minute about: a famous drink from your town or region.	**Talk for a minute about:** an important historical figure from your town or region.	**Talk for a minute about:** typical products made in your town or region.	**Talk for a minute about:** a famous composer or musician from your town or region.	**Talk for a minute about:** a local custom or tradition from your town or region.
Talk for a minute about: a statue, monument or memorial in your town or region.	**Talk for a minute about:** a famous artist from your town or region.	**Talk for a minute about:** the most important agriculture and/or industry in your town or region.	**Talk for a minute about:** a sporting team or event you are proud of in your town or region.	**Talk for a minute about:** something to do on a Saturday night in your town or region.
Talk for a minute about: a local hero from your town or region.	**Talk for a minute about:** the best places to eat out in your town or region.	**Talk for a minute about:** a notorious criminal or historical character from your town or region.	**Talk for a minute about:** three pieces of important advice you would give a visitor to your town or region.	**Talk for a minute about:** the main shopping area in your town or region.

PHOTOCOPIABLE 15.2

Before you begin

Ask your students what their favourite colours are. Point out observations you can make concerning the colour of their clothes, jewellery, and accessories such as bags, belts, pens and work folders. For older students, ask them about the interior and exterior colours of their homes. For the younger class, ask them about their bedrooms, and how these are decorated.

> My entire house is painted white. I have chocolate brown furniture, and beige carpet. It is a very modern, comfortable style.

> Well, my bedroom is quite different to that. It is painted a warm, happy yellow, which always reminds me of sunshine, even in the middle of winter!

Topic: A colourful world

This final unit discusses colours, and how they affect us. It contains plenty of description material: adjectives to describe places as well as emotions and moods. Further, it consolidates and revises what the students have learnt so far.

Unit 16 Wordlist:

bare	exotic	pick out
brighten up	greeny	run down
brownish	homely	stand out
cheerful	impersonal	strong
cluttered	keep up	suburban
cold	let go	terraced
cosy	mix up	traditional
dark light	modern	turn into
detached	north/south-	warm
do up	facing	well-cared for
dreary	pale	

Getting started

1   Ask students to look at the colours and the shapes and to choose the one they like the best. Tell them to make their choice quickly. It should be spontaneous.

2   Put students into pair`s or groups to discuss their answers. Find out whether choice of colour is determined by

fashion or deeper feelings. Colour choices can be culturally dependent. Be sensitive to these choices: many cultures have a particular colour for mourning, as well as one that is associated with good fortune or bad luck. Remember to turn to Information File 16.1 at the back of the coursebook to read an explanation behind the colour choices.

Listening: design and colour psychology

1   Exploit the three photographs and the questions to move into a discussion about how colour affects mood. Before listening to 16.1, you may want to pre-teach the following vocabulary items:

Crucial (adj) means essential, indispensable, of great importance.

A **lid** (n) is the metal top of a jar (of jam, for example).

If you do something in **moderation** (n) you don't do it too much.

A **neutral** (adj) colour matches (or blends in) with most other colours.

You describe things in your house as **practical** (adj) when they are useful rather than just fashionable or decorative.

Shade (n) is a variation of a colour. Note: students may know the word *shade* in the context of staying in the shade to protect yourself from the sun (shade is protective shadow), but they probably won't know the meaning of shade for colour. For example:

> I think we should choose a different shade of pink, this one is too dark. ✓

> It's so hot and sunny – can we sit in the shade please? ✗

To **stimulate** something means to encourage it.

2   Students listen to the passage and complete the table.

3   Before students listen, ask them to remind you of the procedure they should follow for this part of the examination. Play the recording all the way through again. Ask students to listen out for evidence to support their answers.

Vocabulary: colour and decoration

1   Students work in pairs to choose which answer best completes the sentences they are given.

A **run-down** property has been allowed to grow shabby because it hasn't been looked after.	A **well-cared for** property is maintained well and isn't neglected.
A room that faces the **north** can expect less sun than a south or west-facing room.	A room that faces **south** can expect more sunshine than a north-facing room.
A **suburban** house is located in the suburbs (outer edges) of a city.	A **terraced** house is one of a row of similar houses joined together by their side walls. They are usually found in the city, where space is limited.
A **pale** colour is a light shade, neither strong nor bright.	A **strong** colour, flavour, smell, sound or light is intense and easily noticed.
Cheerful things are pleasant and make you feel happy.	If something is **dreary** it is so dull that it makes you feel bored or depressed.
A **bare** room is quite empty.	**Clutter** is a lot of unnecessary or useless things in an untidy state.

4   Students substitute the synonyms for phrasal verbs. Only the phrasal verb 'stand out' is intransitive.

5   Students work together to complete the task.

p/c 16.1

> ## Vocabulary extension
>
> If you wish, allocate roles within groups. This should practise negotiation and discussion.
>
> Student 1 = interior designer
>
> Student 2 = homeowner who likes contemporary decoration
>
> Student 3 = homeowner who has more traditional tastes.

6   Students compare their schemes. Round off with a short discussion about the many TV programmes now that look at giving homes a 'makeover'. A makeover means to improve the appearance of a property. This may involve complete renovation, or perhaps just new accessories.

Reading: a dream island

BACKGROUND

Island utopias

Utopia is a term for an ideal society. It's been used to describe both intentional communities that have tried to create an ideal society, and fictional societies described in writing. The term *utopia* is sometimes used in a negative sense, in reference to an unrealistic ideal that is impossible to achieve. It is taken from Sir Thomas More's fictional island in the Atlantic Ocean. This island was supposed to possess a perfect social and legal system. Environmental (eco) utopias first started appearing in the nineteenth century, but are becoming more and more popular now, as environmental issues become increasingly important globally.

1   Lead into the topic with a short all class discussion about 'dream homes'.

TEACHING IN PRACTICE

Using prompts

If your students have problems with ideas, give them some prompts:

A tree house in the Amazonian forest

A New York loft

A luxury campervan

A haunted castle in Scotland

An island in the Caribbean

Perhaps ask students who they would like to share it with.

Read through the Exam spotlight. By now examination technique should be second nature (come easily) for your students.

2   Set a time limit of 12 minutes to complete the task. During feedback, ask students to give you evidence from the text, and an explanation of how they arrived at their choices.

> The answer to Q2 is B, *a little envious*. This is because the writer admits to thinking how 'lucky' Reishee must be to live there.

> The answer to Q5 is D, *never gives up*. This is because Reishee experienced many problems and setbacks, but he overcame all of them.

Grammar: cleft sentences

p/c 16.2

GRAMMAR SPOTLIGHT

Cleft sentences are an important way of changing the emphasis of a sentence. Students will have certainly come across hundreds of examples of cleft sentences without having looked at them formally. Run through the Grammar spotlight carefully. With a less confident class, do question 1 as a whole class activity: write the answers on the whiteboard and highlight the cleft sentences.

2   Students work in pairs and create further cleft sentences using the text they have read for ideas. In feedback, make sure that the answers accord with the text, as well as being grammatically correct.

Use of English: multiple-choice cloze

1   Exploit the photographs. They show a wind turbine, solar panels on a roof, a water storage unit, an energy saving light-bulb, and a standby switch on an electronic product. Alternatively, move directly to the exercise using it as straightforward examination practice.

> ### Topic discussion extension
>
> Lead a short all-class discussion on what the class thinks the house of the future will be like. There are houses that don't use energy at all, and use smart shutters that control the amount of light and heat that can enter.

Grammar: so/such/too/enough

Aim: to examine the relationship between these forms that are often tested in parts 1, 2, and 3 of the Use of English Paper.

Degree of difficulty

Decrease the level: Consider lowering the level by running through a pair of example transformations before looking at the Grammar spotlight.

Such/so:	Too/enough:
She had such a tiring day that she went straight to bed. such + (adj) + noun	He was too young to join the army. too + adj + infinitive
She was so tired that she went straight to bed. so + adj	He wasn't old enough to join the army. negative + adj + enough +infinitive
It was so tiring a day that she went straight to bed. However, this is rarely, if ever, tested.	

2–3 Even at this point, students may still be having basic problems with:
   • Confusing *very* and *too*. Point out that *very* = a lot; *too* = excessive.
   • Putting *enough* after nouns. Point out to students that *enough* comes before the noun, but after the adjective.

   Now run through the Grammar spotlight.

Writing: an email

This is a good exam type task, an ideal way to reinforce the writing skills that your students have learnt so far.

> ### Writing extension
>
> Set this activity as an exam task. Allow individual work only, and set a time limit of 20 minutes.

Speaking: paper 5

The Speaking test
Aim: to revise the Speaking Paper in its entirety.
This spotlight uses two genuine FCE students. One is from Colombia; the other from Switzerland. Tell students that the English they will hear won't be perfect.
1 Put students into pairs to say which part of the test the sentences might come from. Don't forget to ask students to also say whether the interlocutor or the student said the sentence (and then write C or I in the brackets after the sentence).
2 There are four small photographs on page 163 for this task. Alternatively, the same photographs are available in larger form in the Speaking Files (pages 188–90), as well as the photographs of the second pair of students.
3 This checklist allows your students to judge the candidates which they just listened to. Monitor their responses – you'll probably find that some students are very harsh critics, while others are much too lenient. Encourage your students to be moderate.

> ### Speaking extension
>
> Given that your students have previously just written an email of advice, and have now 'judged' two FCE candidates on their Speaking Paper, why not ask your students to offer advice to these two candidates? What would they advise them to do differently? What do they think they excelled at?
>
> I would encourage the first candidate to ...
>
> Really? I would recommend that instead ...

4   This final question of the unit (excluding the review page) offers an excellent opportunity for Speaking Paper practice. Speaking Files 2 and 3 will complete your students' Paper 5 preparation.

Photocopiable activity instructions

Activity 16.1: Arranging Your Room

Aim: To practise imperatives and prepositions of place within the topic.

Instructions:

1 Divide the class into groups of four. Give each group one copy of the blank room and furniture key. Make an extra copy for yourself and draw the furniture on your copy.

2 Put your copy of the finished room on your desk. Allow one student from each group to come and look at this finished layout for one minute.

3 They then go back to their group and tell their group where to draw the furniture.

4 After a few minutes, allow a different student to come and look at the layout for one minute.

5 Continue this activity until all four students have had a turn at looking at the finished layout.

6 Mark each group out of ten depending on how accurate they were at arranging the furniture.

Alternatively:

1 Divide your class into groups of six. Give each group a copy of the blank layout, and the group cards. Each student should get one card.

2 Working as a team, each student needs to arrange the room according to the information on their card. They are not allowed to show anyone their written card, but instead must tell a point at a time.

3 Set a time limit, and then mark out of ten.

Activity 16.2: Our Island World

Aim: To promote discussion and fluency.

Instructions:

1 Remind students about Reishee Sowa.

> Reishee Sowa has made an island from recycled materials. He thinks that human-made islands are a possible answer to the population explosion.

2 After a brief discussion, tell your students that they have a chance to create a new society, but that (in common with all societies) there have to be rules!

Activity 16.3: Post-FCE test

1 Remind students about the Pre-FCE test they were given at the beginning of the course.

2 Copy and distribute the Post-FCE test.

3 Set a time limit depending on the ability of your class.

4 Mark as a class so that you can clarify the correct answers together. This allows a last opportunity to discuss the exam.

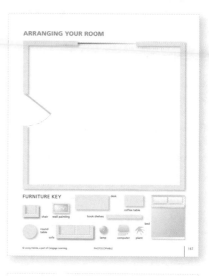

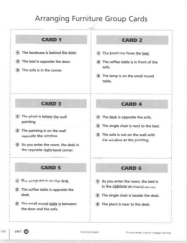

Tapescript 16

Listening 16.1

Presenter: Good morning and this week on 'Home help' we're looking at colour in the home. Now for many of us when we think of decorating the first thing we think about is things like curtains, paintings and furniture and quite often the colour of the walls comes after but in fact colour should be the starting point. And joining us this week is the design expert Laurence Cooper-Stafford to tell us why.

Laurence: Good morning.

Presenter: So Laurence, tell us why colour is so important.

Laurence: Basically it makes a statement about who we are to anyone coming into the house. It also says what the purpose of a room is.

Presenter: How do you mean?

Laurence: Well, I don't think people realise how much colour can affect our mood or how comfortable a visitor might feel.

Presenter: I see. So, imagine I've bought a new house and I'm getting ready to make it a home. Where do I start with colour?

Laurence: Well, one of the most exciting things about decorating any room is that moment when you first take the lid off the tin and start to paint. And the days when the choice was either white or something neutral are well over. These days people almost can't decide what colour to use because of the *huge* range available nowadays. But what happens as a result is that people cover their walls and then they realise it won't match the shade of their furniture or they find that bright red in the bedroom actually stops them from sleeping. So planning all your colours is crucial.

Presenter: But how do you know? I mean, most of us will find it quite difficult to imagine how it will look.

Laurence: It's true that interior designers often seem to have a built-in instinct for what goes with what but actually a great deal of their skill comes from years of working with different colours and learning to follow some basic principles.

Presenter: I see. Like what for example?

Laurence: Well, for example red looks great in dining rooms because it makes people feel social and stimulates an appetite. On the other hand you wouldn't use it in a nursery or baby's room.

Presenter: What colour would you use?

Laurence: Pink is restful though boys may find this a bit 'girlie' so blue is probably a better choice. They also say it prevents nightmares.

Presenter: Isn't blue a cold colour though? Not very welcoming.

Laurence: True but you can find warm tones of blue. Actually bedrooms are somewhere where purple can also work well. Downstairs you might choose yellows or something bright for the kitchen. These types of colours also help make north-facing rooms more cheerful. Brown is another very practical colour for kitchens or living rooms where you spend a lot of time during the day.

Presenter: And I guess black is a real no-no.

Laurence: In moderation black's OK. It can create a sense of drama if that's what you're looking for. But often it's the sort of thing you might see in a teenager's bedroom. But having said all that about rules and principles people should also rely on their own instincts and playing around with colour is one of the best ways of learning …

Listening 16.2

I = Interlocutor   J = Julian   A = Adrian

I: So good morning, my name's John Hughes, and this is my colleague, Richard Webb. He'll be listening to us today. And your name is?

J: Julian.

A: And I'm Adrian.

I: OK, thank you. Can I have your mark-sheets first of all? Thanks. OK first of all we'd like to know something about you. So, Julian where are you from?

J: I'm from Colombia. Medellin, naturally.

I: And you?

A: And I come from Switzerland.

I: And what do you like about living in Colombia?

J: Well, Colombia is a great country. I think the most I like of living in Colombia is the people … the people and the weather of course. Actually, real nice weather.

I: And what about Switzerland?

A: I live in a small village, near the Lake of Constance, so I like the lake there, and it is quiet in my village but with also some cities not too far away, so we have both nature and cities, and that's what I like most.

I: So, Julian do you prefer spending time at home or do you like to go out in your free time?

J: I prefer to go out with my friends to see people, talk, speak with other people, other things. And I don't know … actually, sometimes it's nice to be at home too, watching TV and just relaxing.

I: Do you like to do cooking in your spare time?

J: Mm, sometimes it's nice. For example, I like to food to cook breakfast. It's nice. Eggs, that kind of food.

I: And what's your favourite food?

J: My favourite food, maybe Chinese food and Mexican food – I like a lot Mexican food and Chinese food.

I: And Adrian, do you prefer to spend time on your own or with other people?

A: I need both. Sometimes I like to be alone at home, for example, doing something on my computer or read a book, or a newspaper, watch a movie. And then on the other hand I need my friends. I like to do sports and play volleyball or go out with my friends.

I: Can you tell me about a day that you've enjoyed recently?

A: Yes, for example, there was this weekend here in London. My girlfriend visited me and we had a really great day in London. We did some sightseeing, went to a musical as well … yes, I really enjoyed this day.

I: Who are the most important people in your life?

A: There are maybe three categories, I would say my family, my parents and my brothers and sisters. Then my girlfriend, of course, and I would say two of my friends.

I: OK, good. In the next part of the test, I'm going to give each of you two photographs. I'd like you to talk about your photographs on your own for a minute, and also to answer a short question about your partner's photographs. Julian, it's your turn first, here are your photographs. They show people living in different types of homes. I'd like you to compare the photographs and say why you think people choose to live in these types of homes, alright?

J: Perfect. Well, at first we can see … three people joined together. It's a urban landscape. They are on a ship in a river. And the second photograph we can see, like a family, maybe five people, with their own beds or maybe animals for food, and it's very isolate landscape, but it's in the countryside. They seem like they take their own food for example for the animals they have there. Maybe they choose to live there, for example for the first photograph, they choose to live in there because they have their friends near to them, and maybe they like the city. And the second photograph, maybe they all just need is their family.

I: Would you like to live in either of these homes, Adrian?

A: Not really, to be honest. I'd prefer … a proper house … bigger as well.

I: Thank you. Now here are your photographs, OK, they show people spending free time in the countryside. I'd like you to compare the photographs and say which you think is the best way to enjoy the countryside, and why.

A: Yes, on the first picture you can see four people skiing, I guess it's winter, and they are skiing in the forest, whereas on the picture below, there are some, some friends around a fire. Maybe it's a late summer day. One boy is playing the guitar, and maybe the others around him are singing. I would prefer to spend my free time with sports, for example skiing as on this picture, and because I like to have some activity, and to have some activity with my friends together, and yeah, that's the main reason why I'd prefer to spend my free time with sport … I like the second picture as well, because sometimes it is nice to be on a lake, and to sit around a fire and talk to friends.

I: Thank you. Now which kind of activity would you prefer to do in the countryside, Julian?

J: I'd prefer being, for example, singing with my friends, and playing maybe guitar and some instruments and near to the fire wood, all around, all joined together. I'd prefer that kind of activity, maybe with a barbecue.

I: Now I'd like you to talk about something together for about three minutes. I'd like you to imagine that your local town is five hundred years old and is planning events to celebrate the anniversary. First, talk to each other about how successful these suggestions might be

for the events. And then decide which two might appeal to the most people within the town, alright?

J: In the first stage, or the first activity, it's a puppet show and it would be nice, but only for children, I think.

A: Yes, exactly, it might be something for children or families. The second picture seems like a concert. The woman is playing the violin there. And I think it would be very nice especially if you maybe have an artist from the local town or area.

J: A famous artist from the local town.

A: Yeah, maybe.

J: The third one, we can see maybe, it's a kind of food festival, maybe with typical food of the local city. It could be nice because they can put join people together. They can enjoy the special typical food of the region.

A: Maybe you could combine the third picture as you described with the fourth picture where there is a party or a disco. People are dancing there. Maybe you could have a dinner in the beginning of the evening then later make a little party and listen to music. Maybe dance.

J: It would be a nice mix. Or in the fifth stage, or fifth activity would be a photographic exhibition.

J: It would be nice, for example, for a child that doesn't know the old buildings of the city. Maybe they want to see how was the city before they were born so it would be nice, for example, as a cultural activity.

A: Yeah I like this point and this exhibition. I think it's a good idea. Then we have free rides around the town with horses and it could be a good ideas for families and children to see the whole city. Maybe you have to abandon cars from the city during this day. I don't really like this idea because you can see the city by your own and you don't necessarily need a horse to do this.

J: That's right, that's right. And the last activity we can choose is… maybe a fireworks display. It would be nice as a finish a good finish for the activity for the day. So, I don't know. Maybe we can choose we can mix the food festival

A: Yeah, together with the dancing, clubbing …

J: … Dancing, maybe that two activities at the end of the day, afternoon and night.

A: Yes, yes.

J: And in the morning the photographic exhibition, with the history of the town yes.

A: Yeah, I think a photographic exhibition, and then the dancing and food festival would be nice.

J: Yeah, I agree.

I: OK thank you. Have you ever been to these kind of events in your town, Julian?

J: Yeah, actually in my city, in Medellin, there are a lot of festivals. For example we have one week in August. It's a *feria de las flores*. There's fireworks all days. There are all the clubs open from Monday to Sunday all days. There are food festivals … typical food festival. This kind of maybe puppets shows, so I've been in that kind of festivals and that kind of activities.

I: What about in your town, Adrian?

A: We have a firework every year basically and in a city near where I live, so we celebrate like the end of the summer there. There's every year a huge firework, and there a lot of people there. When I was a child for example I like to go to puppet theatres and also to play by myself to invent new theatres.

I: What do you think is important, Adrian when choosing where you're going to live?

A: I think for me it is important that, my work is not too far away, so maybe within one hour by public transport. Then there has to be a good infrastructure so good public transport system, some sports' facilities. Maybe a lake and a forest so the nature is important as well for me and, yes as I've said an infrastructure is quite important and maybe you have to consider as well taxes and cost of living there.

I: Do you agree, Julian?

J: Well, I agree for example, if I had my family near to my home for example I think it's very important to have job opportunities, nice job opportunities. Of course we have to think about all that things that Adrian said before so I agree with Adrian

I: As many people can work from home with computers do you think more of us will move away from cities in the future?

J: Well, I think in this moment with all the opportunities and all the tech advances that we can see it's very easy to work away from the office. Internet and network can give us all that kind of facilities, so it would be nice if we can work away from the office 'cos the office may, can , maybe be I don't know stressful, I mean stressful. It would be nice to work in a relaxing environment.

I: Would you prefer to work from home, Adrian?

A: Sometimes, maybe, but I think I'd prefer to have a work on a separate place than where I live because I think it's important to work outside my home and when I've finished or have finished my work then I'd like to be at home and don't think about my work so for me this separation is quite important.

I: OK, thank you very much. That's the end of the examination.

Answer key 16

Listening p156
2 Red: dining rooms/is social + stimulates appetite
Purple: bedrooms
Pink: baby's room/is restful
Blue: bedrooms
Yellow: downstairs + kitchens/is cheerful
Brown: rooms where you spend a lot of time; practical colour
Black: dramatic; in moderation OK
3 1B; 2B; 3C; 4A; 5C; 6C; 7A

Vocabulary p157
1 1 a bit run down
2 south
3 suburban
4 strong
5 cosy
6 dreary-looking
7 bare
2 colour: pale, strong
style: run down, well cared for, cosy, impersonal, cheerful, dreary, bare, cluttered
type: north-facing, south-facing, suburban, terraced
4 1 redecorate
2 not care for (appearance)
3 continue

4 combine/match
5 select
6 be (more) visible
7 transform
8 make light and cheerful

Reading p158
2 Places: England and Puerto Aventuras
Problems: Storms; waves; legal problems
Advantages: Recycling; model for environmentally friendly living; peace and quiet; allows him to travel.
3 1A; 2B; 3A; 4C; 5D 6C; 7B; 8D

Grammar p159
1 1 Michael who broke
2 is the woman
3 he did was
4 happened next was
5 wasn't until I
2 1 ... live on a desert island.
2 ... encouraged Reishee to continue.
3 ... he succeeded.
4 ... Reishee wanted.
5 ... could solve over-population problems.

Use of English p160
2 1B; 2D; 3A; 4B; 5D; 6A; 7C; 8A; 9B; 10C; 11C; 12A
3 solar energy; wind turbines; low energy light bulbs; turning off the standby button on the TV; a generator that uses bio-diesel fuel.

Grammar p161
1 1 too
2 enough
3 so
4 such
2 1 too much
2 such
3 so
4 so
5 enough
6 so
3 1 enough
2 such
3 too
4 so/too

Speaking p162
1 1 (I); 2 (C); 1 (C); 2 (C); 1 (I); 4 (I); 3 (C); 1 (I); 4 (I); 2 (I); 2 (I); 4 (I); 4 (C); 3 (I); 4 (C); 1 (I)

Review p164
1 1 urban
2 down
3 cellar
4 facing
5 appliances
6 such
7 do
8 pale
9 orchard
2 1 designers
2 environmentally
3 neighbourhood
4 generator
5 homely
6 cheerful
7 greenish
8 powered
3 1 from
2 in
3 the
4 has
5 as
6 take
7 after
8 What
9 cost
10 that
11 how
12 who

ARRANGING YOUR ROOM

FURNITURE KEY

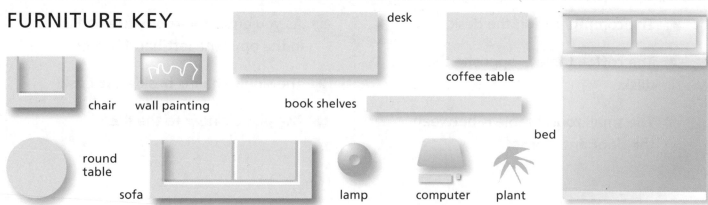

chair   wall painting

desk

book shelves

coffee table

round table

sofa

lamp

computer   plant

bed

Arranging Furniture Group Cards

CARD 1

1. The bookcase is behind the door.

2. The bed is opposite the door.

3. The sofa is in the corner.

CARD 2

1. The bookcase faces the bed.

2. The coffee table is in front of the sofa.

3. The lamp is on the small round table.

CARD 3

1. The plant is below the wall painting.

2. The painting is on the wall opposite the window.

3. As you enter the room, the desk is in the opposite right-hand corner.

CARD 4

1. The desk is opposite the sofa.

2. The single chair is next to the bed.

3. The sofa is not on the wall with the window or the painting.

CARD 5

1. The computer is on the desk.

2. The coffee table is opposite the desk.

3. The small round table is between the door and the sofa.

CARD 6

1. As you enter the room, the bed is in the opposite left-hand corner.

2. The single chair is beside the desk.

3. The plant is near to the desk.

Our Island World

Imagine
that you and your
classmates have built an enormous
island. You can move it from place to place
– anywhere in the world. Like any new society, you
need to decide on the rules and regulations that will
govern the behaviour of the island's new population.

In groups, decide on the rules and constitution of the new island.

1 What will you call your island?

2 Will it be a republic or a monarchy? If you have a president, how will he/she be elected and for how many years will he/she govern?

3 What will your flag look like? Describe its patterns and colours.

4 What will the island's official flower and animal be?

5 Where will you 'park' your island? How will this change during the year?

6 How will your island move? What kind of energy will you use?

7 Will you have a state religion?

8 What will your immigration policy be? Who will be able to come and live on the island?

9 What will your official language/s be?

10 Who will be able to vote and from what age?

11 Will you have an army or a navy? If so, will military service be compulsory?

12 Will you have prisons on the island? How will you punish wrong-doers? Will you have capital punishment?

13 Will people be allowed to smoke in public places?

14 How will people travel around? Will they be allowed to have cars?

15 What side of the road will people drive on? Will helmets and seat-belts be obligatory?

16 Will marriage exist?

17 What will your policy on social issues such as euthanasia be?

18 Will you have censorship or a totally free press?

19 At what ages will citizens of the island be able to drive, get married, or vote?

20 Will you have a police force? Will they allowed to carry guns?

**Now that you've finished, present your decisions to the class as a whole.
If you can, agree a constitution and a set of rules that you can all live with.**

Post-FCE Quiz

Are you prepared?

Paper One: Reading

1. How long does Paper One last?
   - **A** one hour
   - **B** an hour and a quarter
   - **C** an hour an a half

2. Where do candidates write their answers?
   - **A** On the question paper
   - **B** On a plain sheet
   - **C** On a special answer sheet

3. You write your answers in …
   - **A** ink.
   - **B** biro.
   - **C** pencil.

4. How many parts does it have?
   - **A** two
   - **B** three
   - **C** four

5. Match the part to the type of question.
   - **1** Part 1   **a** gapped-text sentences
   - **2** Part 2   **b** multiple matching
   - **3** Part 3   **c** multiple choice

6. How many questions does each part have?
   - **Part 1**   **A** 6   **B** 7   **C** 8
   - **Part 2**   **A** 6   **B** 7   **C** 8
   - **Part 3**   **A** 10   **B** 12   **C** 15

7. How many marks do you lose for a wrong answer?
   - **A** zero
   - **B** one
   - **C** two

Paper Two: Writing

8. How long does Paper Two last?
   - **A** 60 minutes
   - **B** 70 minutes
   - **C** 80 minutes

9. In Part 1, how many words are you supposed to write for your answer?
   - **A** 120–150
   - **B** 140–180
   - **C** 160–200

10. What is the maximum length of answers in Part 2?
    - **A** 150 words
    - **B** 180 words
    - **C** 200 words

11. You don't have to answer the question in Part 1.
    True ☐ False ☐

12. In Part 1 you have three choices to choose from.
    True ☐ False ☐

13. In Part 1 you have to take notes and annotations into account.
    True ☐ False ☐

14. It's possible to write a letter in each part of the paper.
    True ☐ False ☐

15. Addresses are included in the number of words required.
    True ☐ False ☐

16. Examiners will give you extra marks for a clear plan.
    True ☐ False ☐

17. You should write your answers in pencil.
    True ☐ False ☐

18. You can answer more than one question in Part 2.
    True ☐ False ☐

19. You always have the chance to write a story in Part 2.
    True ☐ False ☐

20. Question 5 of Part 2 is on a set text.
    True ☐ False ☐

Paper Three: Use of English

21. How long does Paper three last?
    - **A** 45 minutes
    - **B** 60 minutes
    - **C** 75 minutes

22. How many parts are there in this paper?
    _____
    What are they?
    _____

23. Where do you write your answers?
    - **A** On a sheet of paper
    - **B** On the question paper
    - **C** On a special answer sheet

24. How many questions do Parts 1 and 2 each have? _____

25. What changes can you make to the 'key word' in the 'key word' sentences transformations?
    _____
    _____

Paper Four: Listening

26. How many times are you allowed to listen to each part? _____

27. Match the part of the exam to the description.
    - **Part 1**   5 multiple matching questions
    - **Part 2**   8 multiple choice questions
    - **Part 3**   7 multiple choice question
    - **Part 4**   10 sentence completion questions

28. In which part of Paper Four do you:
    a listen to different speakers on the same topic? Part _____
    b complete notes with a few words? Part _____
    c answer multiple choice questions based on an interview or monologue? Part _____
    d listen to a number of different speakers on unrelated topics? Part _____

Paper Five: Speaking

29. How many examiners are in the examination room during Paper Five? _____

30. The examiner who asks the questions is called …
    - **A** the invigilator.
    - **B** the inquisitor.
    - **C** the interlocutor.

31. There are four parts to Paper Five. In which part do the candidates interact on a collaborative task? Part _____

32. In which part does each candidate compare and contrast a pair of photographs? Part _____

33. In which part do the candidates engage in a three way conversation with one of the examiners? Part _____

34. In which part do candidates take it in turns to interact and use social language with one of the examiners? Part _____

35. Can you expect the examiner to encourage or praise you during the speaking exam? _____

PHOTOCOPIABLE 16.3

Grammar reference key

1 Adjectives p165
1 There were four green cars in front of their house.
2 That watch looks expensive.
3 You look lovely today.
4 Correct
5 The government should look after the poor.
6 There was a baby lying asleep in its pram.

1.1 Participial adjectives p165
1 worried
2 boring
3 embarrassing
4 exhausted
5 disgusting
6 fascinating

1.2 Adjective order p165
1 She put a long black plastic snake on her teacher's chair.
2 He was given an expensive Swiss diver's watch for his eighteenth birthday.
3 She was wearing a lovely shiny Japanese dressing-gown made of silk.
4 Correct
5 They have a gorgeous big fat grey Siamese cat.
6 Last night I watched a fascinating new Swedish documentary on TV.

1.3 Gradable and non-gradable adjectives p166
1B delighted
2B furious
3B gorgeous
4B terrible/dreadful/awful
5B exhausted/starving
6B devastated

2.1 Adverbs of frequency p166
1 We nearly always take ...
2 ... the cinema from time to time.

3 We hardly seem to eat out these days.
4 ... he is always borrowing my clothes ...
5 ... always used to play tennis on Sunday mornings / they hardly ever have time.
6 I only see my parents once in a while.

2.3 Adverbs of manner p167
1 very well
2 very hard
3 beautifully
4 carefully
5 happily do that for you
6 extremely persuasively

2.5 Meaning shifts from adjectives to adverbs p167
1 hardly breathing
2 recently
3 Hopefully we'll ...
4 Unfortunately we ...
5 ... shortly.
6 Obviously ...
7 Well, basically ...

3.3 Articles p168
1 The; Ø; Ø
2 a; the
3 the; the; The; the; the
4 A; the; a
5 a; Ø; the
6 a; a; the; the; the; a; the
7 The; Ø; Ø; Ø; Ø; The; the; the
8 Ø; Ø; Ø; a; a
9 the; Ø; Ø
10 The; Ø

4 Cleft sentences p168
1 It was at nine o'clock in the evening when her last concert began.
2 What they did was take the legs off the piano and carry it through the window.
3 What happened was she slipped on the ice and broke her arm.

4 What you ought to try is a dating agency, I think.
5 What annoys me in restaurants is loud music.
6 What happened was our car was broken into while we/they were at the beach.

5.3 Comparative adverbs p169
1 1 ... the most delicious
2 the best; the worst
3 happier/most successful and richest
4 closest
5 better
6 easy as/difficult as
7 better
8 beautifully
9 faster/as quickly
10 Nobody works as hard as Xu, he has learnt all the irregular verbs, even the hardest.
2 1 the most tired I have
2 well as
3 worst flight I have
4 go as fast as
5 most recent
6 I read books the more

6.6 Conditionals p170
1 1 take/does
2 what would you do/won
3 you say/I will tell
4 hadn't missed/wouldn't be
5 gave up; would improve
6 have arrived/will you call me
7 Would you have given/had known
8 was/were
9 had known/would have thought twice
10 had remembered to/wouldn't have been stolen
2 1 Unless you hurry up, we'll miss the beginning of the film.
2 You'd better not leave your car there, otherwise you'll get a parking ticket.
3 You can borrow my car provided you fill it up afterwards. / Provided you fill it up afterwards, you can borrow my car.

4 If you don't give me a sweet I'll tell your sister what you did.
5 I'll lend you my ipod as long as you promise to take care of it.
6 Unless he drives more carefully he'll have an accident.

6.7 Contrasting ideas p171
1 1 Incorrect
2 Incorrect
3 Correct
4 Correct
5 Incorrect
2 1 Even though she came from a poor family she became prime minister.
2 In spite of the time we didn't feel too tired.
3 The sea was rough but nevertheless the sailors managed to reach port.
4 We had a lovely evening despite the fact that it was raining.
3 1 Despite (her) having lots of money, she never spends it.
2 It was cold, nevertheless he refused to wear a coat.
3 She still won the race despite the fact she had hurt her foot. / Despite the fact she had hurt her foot, she still won the race.
4 He still drove through the night, even though he felt tired. / Even though he felt tired, he still drove through the night.

7.4 Determiners with countable and uncountable nouns p172
1 a/a/ a
2 any
3 some/some/any
4 some/any
5 any/a/ any
6 a/any
7 any/some
8 a or any
9 some or a/a
10 a thing/anyone

7.4 Determiners with countable and uncountable nouns p173

1 much; many; 2 many; 3 deal; 4 little; 5 several; 6 lots; 7 many; a few; 8 loads; 9 few; 10 deal 11 much; 12 loads

8.6 Adjectives with a future meaning p174

1 1 I'm going to visit
2 I will bring
3 I'm going to study
4 I will answer (I'll)
5 is going to play
6 I will give
2 1 Are you doing
2 I'm going
3 are you getting
4 are going to take
5 leaves
6 is going to take
7 is going to look after
8 was going to
9 I'll
10 are you coming
11 should
12 will
13 are going to be
14 I'll drop
15 I'll be waiting
16 have taken

9.3 Gerund or infinitive p175

1 1 to open
2 playing
3 to tell
4 checking
5 going
6 telling
7 to keep
8 crying
9 phoning
10 to post
11 come round
12 saying
13 to upset
14 climbing; to have
15 to take
16 going
2 1 must remember to take my passport.
2 me forget to record that programme.
3 so looking forward to going to Canada.
4 you mind closing the window, please?

5 in order to lose.
6 you like to go
7 in spite of / despite not having a ticket.

10 Inversion p176

1 1c; 2f; 3b; 4e; 5a; 6d
2 1 Hardly had he finished one job than his boss gave him another.
2 No sooner had I got the exam results than I phoned my parents.
3 Never have I seen such an untidy bedroom!
4 Not only does she speak Italian, but also Chinese and Japanese too.
5 Had I seen him, I would have told him.

11 Modals p178

1 1 have to/must
2 needn't have bought
3 I'll
4 might
5 shall
6 ought to
7 could you
2 1 Should
2 ought to
3 can't have been happy
4 could
5 have
6 have left earlier

12.1 Past tense p179

1 gone by
2 decided
3 tried
4 heard
5 hung up
6 had
7 had received
8 would go/were going
9 wasn't able/was unable
10 borrowed
11 wore
12 had never looked
13 were driving
14 appeared
15 could not/couldn't
16 went into
17 did not/didn't do
18 knew
19 had happened
20 pushed
21 were doing
22 broke
23 had to
24 had finished
25 were
26 heard

27 had woken up
28 jumped
29 watched
30 destroyed
31 arrived
32 had to
33 got

12.2 The passive p180

1 has been turned into luxury apartments
2 is going to be opened by
3 ask someone to show her/Sally should be shown
4 was being written
5 going to have my photograph taken (by a photographer)
6 be hidden before she sees it.
7 apartment broken into
8 was opened by (the use of)
9 said to be the best restaurant
10 allowed (by his parents) to

12.3 Phrasal verbs p181

1 Correct; 2 Correct; 3 Incorrect;
4 Correct 5 Incorrect; 6 Correct;
7 Incorrect; 8 Incorrect 9 Incorrect;
10 Incorrect; 11 Correct;
12 Incorrect

12.4 Present tenses p182

1 leave
2 is being
3 do you do
4 is actually falling
5 tastes
6 have worked
7 been revising
8 hasn't stopped
9 redecorated
10 been painting

13.2 Non-defining relative clauses p182

1 who; 2 whom/who; 3 which;
4 when; 5 why; 6 who; 7 where;
8 that

14 Reported speech and reporting verbs p183

1 1 Paul told me to call this number.
2 Melinda said she felt tired.
3 Marissa told Kevin to be careful/ Marissa said to Kevin to be careful.
4 He told me the story.
5 She asked what time the train left.

6 Howard wanted to know where we had bought the flowers.
2 1 Romain to apply for the job.
2 Derek not to walk round that part of town after dark.
3 we should visit/we visited the ruins the next/following day.
4 Kim for being late two days earlier.
5 to collect his prescription from the chemist's.
6 he hadn't called her the night before (because) he couldn't find her new number.
7 Mr Rossi to go to bed earlier.
8 Nick for bringing up the subject.

15 *Will/Would and used to* p184

1 will; 2 would; 3 used to; 4 would

16 So and such; too and enough p184

1 1 She didn't have enough time to finish the exam.
2 The film was so funny that it made me laugh all day.
3 They were too poor to take their children on holiday.
4 He cried all day because he was so sad.
5 Rupert was in such a bad mood that he refused to speak to me.
6 Unfortunately Lucy wasn't fit enough to play in the final.
2 1 It was such a tiring journey that we went straight to bed.
2 She isn't old enough to travel on her own.
3 His parents were so disappointed with his exam results.
4 The suitcase is too big for the space.

17 Transitive and intransitive verbs p185

1 Correct
2 Incorrect
3 Correct
4 Incorrect
5 Correct
6 Incorrect
7 Correct
8 Correct

18 Wish p185

1e; 2c; 3a; 4f; 5b; 6d

Photocopiable activity instructions

Activity GR1: Add in the adjectives and adverbs
Aim: to practise understanding and positioning of adjectives and adverbs.
Instructions:
1   Copy one sheet per student (or per pair if students are not confident enough).
2   Explain the examples.
3   Set a time limit for a more advanced class.
4   Mark collectively.

Activity GR2: Word cross
Aim: to practise irregular verbs
Instructions:
1   Copy the page once for every two students.
2   Pair up your students.
3   Give each pair a matching crossword.
4   Ask your students to take it in turns to ask each other for a verb that is missing. The other student needs to answer according to their crossword.
5   Once finished, each pair needs to check each other's crossword and see how they went.

> What's three across?
> It's the past tense of ring.

Activity GR3: Countable and uncountable nouns
Aim: to practise recognising countable and uncountable nouns.
Instructions:
1   Copy one sheet per student.
2   Ask your students to decide whether each noun is countable or uncountable.
3   Mark collectively.

Activity GR4: Preposition dominoes
Aim: to practise various prepositions after verbs and adjectives.
Instructions:
1   Copy page 173 and shuffle the cards.
2   Divide the class into two groups with 30 cards each.
3   Toss a coin to see which group gets to place one card on a table between the two groups.
4   The other group need to match this card with a verb, adjective or preposition.

D.I.Y. activity instructions

5 Irregular verb matching
Aim: to familiarise students with irregular verbs
Material needed: paper/cardboard, scissors
1   Make cards of the irregular verbs list (pages 238–239 of coursebook).
2   Divide your class into groups of students.
3   Ask each group to match up the infinitive form with the simple past and past participle.
    For example: fly – flew – flown

6 Article without articles
Aim: to practise using the correct adverb
Material needed: magazine article, correction fluid (white-out)
1   Find a magazine or newspaper article which will interest your students.
2   Using correction fluid, delete every single article in the piece.
3   Photocopy and distribute to your students.
4   Ask them to work either individually or in pairs, and fill in each missing article.

7 Making comparisons: similarities and differences
Aim: to practise using comparatives/superlatives
Materials needed: paper and/or whiteboard

1   Create ten sets of words which will allow your students to find similarities and differences. For example:
Set 1: bull – tiger – cat – spider – rat – dolphin – horse – goldfish
2   Ask your students to describe what each of the words in a set share and don't share.

> A tiger is very similar to a cat, except bigger.
> Oh, but a cat is usually tame, whereas a tiger is wilder and more ferocious.

8 Make up a story: using narrative tenses
Aim: to practise using the correct narrative tense.
Materials: paper
1   Create 50 or so cards which each contain a word or several words, such as birthday / wet / angrily / yesterday
2   Copy and distribute to your students.
3   Ask your students to write a story using the words they have just received. Remind them to look at section 12 of the Grammar reference if they need any reminder.

Add in the adjectives and adverbs

1   I read three Internet blogs. (*regularly, interesting*)

_____

2   I enjoy class. It's boring. (*usually, never*)

_____

3   He drove a car to work. (*usually, red, old*)

_____

4   It's a warm day. Let's go to the beach. (*sunny, bright*)

_____

5   I'm searching for a new house. (*modern, large, furnished*)

_____

6   He's very good-looking with brown hair. (*tall, dark, handsome*)

_____

7   I ring my parents on the weekend. (*sometimes*)

_____

8   Mandy and Ian don't argue. (*often*)

_____

9   She has six brothers. They're married. (*all*)

_____

10 They bought a sofa. (*navy, soft, new*)

_____

11 A watch was stolen. (*silver, expensive, definitely*)

_____

12 What a teacher she is! (*clever, cheerful*)

_____

13 Who was that man at the supermarket? (*annoying, talkative, crowded*)

_____

14 I play football. (*occasionally*)

_____

15 I disagree with your views. (*completely, old-fashioned*)

_____

16 I haven't done my homework. I have two questions to go. (*still, yet*)

_____

17 I was drinking a mug of coffee. (*hot, large, strong*)

_____

18 Christine's not very brave. She hasn't travelled overseas. (*even*)

_____

19 Mike's a good drawer and he sings. (*also, well*)

_____

20 I've got two sisters and they're older than me. (*both*)

_____

21 We walked down a street to the river. (*long, narrow, run-down*)

_____

22 Maria's baby has big eyes and a friendly smile. (*green, happy*)

_____

23 I bought a new dress! (*just, black, sequinned*)

_____

24 There's a new film on in town. (*interesting, action*)

_____

25 I go swimming these days. There's enough time. (*rarely, never*)

_____

Crossword: Irregular verbs A (across)

This crossword is only half filled in. Your partner has the other half. Take it in turns to give clues for your partner to work out what the missing verbs are. They are all in past tense.

Crossword: Irregular verbs B (down)

This crossword is only half filled in. Your partner has the other half. Take it in turns to give clues for your partner to work out what the missing verbs are. They are all in past tense.

Countable and uncountable nouns

Decide whether each of the following nouns is countable or uncountable. Place it in the correct column.

animal	**equipment**	**excitement**	*banana*
suitcase	advice	job	*gold*
luggage	competition	happiness	milk
handbag	hair	SADNESS	cheese
brochure	scenery	*key*	house
television	*chair*	**family**	*magazine*
city	**traffic**	NEWS	**potato**
coin	weather	**bottle**	**WATER**

Countable	Uncountable

PHOTOCOPIABLE GR3

Preposition dominoes

for	from	the age of	keen	play
against	advance	famous	take	for
think	in	translate	care	into
about	on	ashamed	at	dream
by	of	on	holiday	nightmare
accident	to	by	believe	about
bus	fire	with	in	with
die	with	allergic	sorry	pride
for	disagree	to	about	look forward
example	hope	to	infamous	disappointed
wait	arrest	insist	happy	feel
escape	at	on	well-known	look

PHOTOCOPIABLE GR4

Exam Booster key

Unit 1

Reading p6
1 1C; 2B; 3A; 4C; 5D; 6 B; 7C; 8A; 9D; 10B
2 1 expecting
2 dilemma
3 heritage
4 thrilled
5 overseas
6 bullying
7 Practically
8 grow up

Vocabulary p8
1 1 fiancé; 4 spouse; 6 twins; 7 inlaw; 2 cousin; 3 relatives; 4 siblings; 5 extended
2 1d; 2c; 3b; 4a
3 1b; 2f; 3e; 4a; 5d; 6c

Grammar p9
1 1 are growing
2 eats
3 is changing
4 speaks
5 Do you usually send
6 she is playing
7 are getting
2 1 owns (state verb)
2 are thinking (active verb)
3 doesn't believe (state verb)
4 is having (active verb)
5 like (state verb)
6 tastes (state verb)
3 1 She has written five letters.
2 She has been jogging.
3 She has been cleaning the house.
4 She has broken a plate.
5 She has made a cake.
6 She has been working on the computer.

Spelling p10
1 1 periodically
2 Tragically
3 logically
4 Economically
5 genetically
6 sympathetically

Listening p10
1 1C; 2B; 3B; 4A; 5C; 6B; 7A; 8C

Use of English p11
1 1 normal
2 cultural
3 professional
4 sponsorship
5 membership
6 eventually
7 restlessness
8 personal
9 length
10 strength
2 1 which/that; 2 have; 3 Her; 4 at; 5 because; 6 of; 7 is; 8 their; 9 for; 10 well; 11 so; 12 a; 13 When; 14 in; 15 with

Writing p12
1 1, 3, 4, 6, 8
2 (Possible answers)
Paragraph 1: Your general impressions of the trip.
Paragraph 2: A description of interesting locations that you went to. A description of your trip to the capital city.
Paragraph 3: What your accommodation was like. A description of some food.
3 a3; b5; c4; d7; e2; f6; g1

Speaking p13
1 1 Julieta says she lives with her parents.
2 Julieta says she comes from a normal family: four people (Julieta, her parents and her sister). Philippe says he comes from a small family. He doesn't have any brothers and sisters.
3 Philippe's father is a teacher and his mother is a doctor.
2 1 There are four of us in my family.
2 I have one older sister, Ana, who is twenty-four.
3 I don't have any brothers and sisters.

4 My father is a teacher and my mother works as a doctor.

Pronunciation p13
2 Question 3 has a different pronunciation. The intonation falls at the end of the question because this is a question made without a question word. Questions made with a question word (*who, which, why, when,* etc.) have a rising intonation.
3 1 rises; 2 falls; 3 rises; 4 falls; 5 rises; 6 rises; 7 falls

Unit 2

Reading p14
1 1C; 2D; 3A; 4B; 5A; 6B; 7D; 8C; 9A; 10D; 11B; 12C; 13A; 14D; 15C
2 1e; 2d; 3b; 4g; 5c; 6h; 7a; 8f

Vocabulary p16
1 1 qualities
2 redundant
3 deal
4 letter
5 overtime
6 flexitime
7 payrise
8 cv
9 sack
10 recruit
11 resign
12 notice
13 training
14 perks
2 1e; 2a; 3c; 4f; 5d; 6b
3 a1, 6; b2; c4, 5; d3

Spelling p17
1 1 illustrator
2 sailor
3 director
4 translator
5 decorator
6 editor
7 ski instructor
8 doctor

Grammar p17
1 1 the quicker.
2 as interesting as
3 correct
4 We're busier
5 the most expensive
6 correct
7 is more difficult than
2 1 It's a bit more complicated
2 as good as the old one
3 do a lot more overtime
4 My job is far too easy/job with far more responsibility.
5 the money is almost the same.
6 It isn't anything like the project
7 a journalist is any more difficult

Listening p18
1 1A; 2B; 3A; 4C; 5A; 6C; 7B; 8A

Pronunciation p18
2 underline = stress, *italics* = schwa
org*a*nis*a*tion
poss*e*ssions
int*er*national
inform*a*tion
qualific*a*tion
p*o*werful
cert*i*ficate
comp*u*ter
3 The word in italics is pronounced with the schwa in the b sentences.
4 1 the first example of *to*
2 *have*
3 the second example of *you*
4 *a*

Use of English p19
1 1 a assessment
b improvement
2 a application
b communication
3 a successful
b doubtful
4 a reference
b existence
5 a ability
b similarity
2 1A; 2D; 3D; 4A; 5A; 6C; 7C; 8D; 9A; 10D; 11B; 12D

Writing p20

1 1B; 2A; 3B; 4C; 5A; 6C

2 a2; b5; c1; d3; e4; f6

Speaking p21

2 They forget to talk about the job delivering pizzas.

3 1 start; 2 it; 3 so; 4 compare; 5 think; 6 for

Unit 3

Reading p22

1 1H; 2B; 3E; 4A; 5G; 6C; 7F

2 1 demanding
2 talisman
3 bout
4 one-sided
5 bulk up
6 stew
7 soles
8 grip
9 sacred
10 trace back

Vocabulary p24

1 1 golf
2 sailing
3 darts
4 wrestling
5 chess
6 croquet
2 1 archery
2 volleyball
3 synchronised swimming
4 table tennis
5 American football
6 tennis
7 badminton
8 tenpin bowling
9 snowboarding
10 karate (also judo)
3 1 I like board games
2 correct
3 a grass court
4 Sarah beat me!
5 play for Juventus
6 correct
7 the pitch was terrible
8 favourite game

Grammar p25

1 1c; 2f; 3b; 4e; 5a; 6d

2 1 Laura could ride a bike
2 needn't have brought
3 You don't need to
4 You are supposed to wear
5 able to beat Suzanne
6 You had better start
7 Andy wasn't able to

Spelling

Across: delightful, eventful, powerful, graceful
Down: beautiful, grateful, hopeful, forgetful, colourful
Diagonal: wonderful

Listening p26

1 a1, 2; b3, 4, 6, 7; c10; d 5, 8, 9

2 1 two
2 three
3 court
4 Brazil
5 warm up
6 the States/USA
7 beach
8 photographs
9 the Olympic Games
10 competitive

Pronunciation p26

1 a5; b3; c6; d2; e4; f1

4 bending, best, van, bars, vote, buyer, very

Use of English p27

1 1 mustn't go / must not go
2 is good at
3 weren't able to / were not able to
4 from time to time
5 had better tell
6 aren't supposed to / are not supposed to or 're not supposed to / don't have to / do not have to
8 keeps beating
2 1 contestants
2 inhabitants
3 intelligence
4 correspondence
5 entrants/entries
6 patience
7 difficulty
8 expensive
9 impressive
10 competitive

Writing p28

1 1 excited
2 exciting
3 amazing
4 amazed
5 boring
6 bored
7 disappointing
8 disappointed

Speaking p29

1 Julieta (candidate 1)

2 1 whereas
2 Although
3 show

4 type
5 looks

Pronunciation p29

1 /ɑːʒ/: camouflage, collage, espionage, garage (US English), massage
/eɪdʒ/: cage, enrage, stage
/ɪdʒ/: cottage, courage, damage, encourage, garage (UK English), heritage, image, manage, message, village

Unit 4

Reading p30

1 1D; 2B; 3C; 4A; 5D; 6B; 7C; 8B; 9A; 10D; 11A; 12D; 13A; 14B; 15C

2 1e; 2g; 3a; 4c; 5f; 6j; 7h; 8b; 9d; 10i

Vocabulary p32

1 1 wild; 2 tame; 3 breed; 4 instinct; 5 endangered; 6 pet; 7 prey; 8 train; 9 habitat; 10 extinction

2 1 of; 2 to; 3 on; 4 with; 5 in; 6 for; 7of

Spelling p32

1 1a; 2c; 3b; 4a; 5b; 6c; 7a; 8b; 9a; 10c; 11b; 12c

Grammar p33

1 1 Mark and Steve get on well together.
2 I was so poor that I lived off rice.
3 I wonder how they found it out.
4 correct
5 I want you to carry out.
6 You shouldn't look down on environmental
7 correct
8 are coming across new species all the time
2 1 a
2 much
3 any
4 Few
5 Hardly
6 number
7 little
8 Each/Every

Use of English p33

1 1C; 2C; 3A; 4D; 5A; 6C; 7B; 8D; 9A; 10C; 11B; 12D

Writing p34

1 You must say whether you enjoyed your trip to the rescue centre. You need to say whether the trip is suitable for young children (there is a play park, but seeing the injured birds might upset children). You need to suggest somewhere to stay (a local bed and breakfast).

2 1d; 2b; 3g; 4c; 5a; 6h; 7e; 8f

Listening p35

1 A3; B1; C5; D2; F4

Pronunciation p35

1 1 grew up is linked with /w/ and larger and larger is linked with /r/
2 see a is linked with /j/
2 1 /r/; 2 /w/; 3 /w/; 4 /j/; 5 /j/; 6 /r/
3 Sentences 1, 3, and 5 make the linking sound from a letter which is already in one of the words. Sentences 2, 4, and 6 add a linking sound.
4 1 too old /w/, for a /r/, two-hour /w/
2 there another /r/, way of /j/
3 tea and /j/, Tina and /r/

Use of English p36

1 1 terrifying
2 breathe
3 imagination
4 harmless
5 successful
6 mysterious
7 majority
8 extremely
9 nervous
10 attacker

Speaking p36

1 a, b, c, d, f, i

Pronunciation p37

1 1 white
2 right/write
3 rail
4 wail/whale
5 ring
6 wing
2 1a; 2a; 3b; 4b

Unit 5

Reading p38

1 1B; 2D; 3D; 4A; 5B; 6C; 7B; 8D

Vocabulary p40

1 1 classic
2 chapter
3 villain
4 heroine
5 narrator
6 fiction
7 plot
8 series
9 scenery

2 1 mortified
2 ridiculous
3 terrified
4 furious
5 devastated
6 exhausted
7 delighted
3 1 slurp
2 limping
3 glared
4 giggling
5 gasping
6 slipped
7 strolled
8 sighs

Grammar p41
1 1f; 2a; 3e; 4c; 5b; 6d
2 1 it had disappeared
2 the audience were clapping for ten minutes
3 had been writing all night
4 I was working in the garden
5 I was reading a novel
6 it had been stolen

Spelling p41
1 1 furious
2 gorgeous
3 correct
4 curious
5 vicious
6 nervous
7 correct
8 victorious
9 unconscious
10 religious
11 correct
12 delicious

Listening p42
1 1C; 2A; 3A; 4C; 5B; 6A; 7B

Pronunciation p42
2 Words with stress on the second syllable from the end: appearances, experienced, characteristic: disappearance, disappointment, realistic, sympathetic, retirement
Exceptions: appropriate, embarrassment, enthusiasm, mysterious, necessarily, personality, professional, centimetre, characteristic, disappearance, disappointment, realistic, sympathetic
3 The stress in the adjectives that end -ic is on the penultimate syllable (one from the end).
4 When a word ends in -ion, the stress is on the penultimate syllable (one from the end).

Use of English p43
1 1 in; 2 by; 3 fact; 4 it; 5 the; 6 who; 7 had; 8 down/along; 9 not/never; 10 whose; 11 more; 12 as
2 1C; 2D; 3C; 4B; 5A; 6A; 7D; 8C; 9B; 10B; 11D; 12A

Writing p44
1 1 Yes; 2 No; 3 No: The story does not include the sentence 'I suddenly realised that I was lost';
4 Yes; 5 Yes
2 ~~vilage~~ village
~~Strangly~~ Strangely
~~alredy~~ already
~~comftable~~ comfortable
~~feel~~ fell
~~wich~~ which
~~panik~~ panic.
~~middle~~ middle

Speaking p45
1 They choose to invite famous authors to speak to schools and to have a national competition with prizes for the best book review.
2 1 which appeal to different
2 I can't stand reading
3 It's not an obvious choice
4 Something that would appeal to me
5 Personally, I think
6 Yes, I quite agree.
3 1d; 2f; 3b; 4a; 5c; 6e

Unit 6

Reading p46
1 1B; 2C; 3D; 4A; 5D; 6C; 7B; 8A; 9C; 10D; 11A; 12D; 13B; 14C; 15B
2 1 a number of
2 all to yourself
3 The highlight
4 a treat
5 Eventually
6 even so
7 like something out of
8 nothing short of
9 nowhere more so
10 even by its standards

Vocabulary p48
1 1 correct
2 checking in to
3 show you around
4 meeting up with
5 correct
6 setting off
7 turned up

8 kicking off
2 1 off; 2 up; 3 off; 4 back; 5 up; 6 back

Grammar p48
1 1d; 2c; 3f; 4a; 5b; 6e
2 1 due
2 to receive
3 'll just answer
4 Shall
5 have gone
6 is driving
7 be flying … be going

Spelling p49
1 British English   American English
-our, e.g. rumour   -or, e.g. rumor
-ise, e.g. realise   -ize, e.g. realize
-re, e.g. centre   -er, e.g. center
-ogue, e.g. catalogue   -og, e.g. catalog
Note that -ize is becoming increasingly common in British English.
2 British
3 2 American
3 British
4 American
5 American
6 British
7 British
8 American
9 American
10 British
11 American
12 British
13 British
14 British
15 American

Listening p50
1 1B; 2A; 3C; 4B; 5B; 6C; 7A; 8C

Pronunciation p50
2 1 /dʒ/
2 /tʃ/
3 /j/
4 /dʒ/
5 /tʃ/
6 /j/
3 church, you'll, gin, yet, general, use, chair, jaw

Use of English p51
1 1 what; 2 is; 3 from; 4 by; 5 be; 6 during; 7 addition; 8 have; 9 of; 10 If; 11 Take; 12 could/can
2 1 would rather go
2 time we bought or time to buy
3 had better book

4 could always go
5 the first time (that)
6 does it take or will it take
7 as soon as I get
8 if we didn't eat / if we did not eat

Writing p52
1 1 You are writing a report on the transport system of your home town.
2 To discuss how to get to your home town from the nearest airport and how to travel around.
3 A language school/Other foreign students.
2 The following report outlines:
It aims to
One suggestion when travelling by metro is to write down
Alternatively
Another possibility is
On the one hand
on the other
To sum up

Speaking p53
2 1 together
2 listen
3 imagine
4 decide
5 each
6 way
7 worry
8 hear
3 They choose the speedboat.
4 1 we would have to build
2 But if we delivered the post
3 bound to want more money
4 could always deliver the post
5 We had better make up
6 I think it would be very
7 wouldn't be able to deliver

Unit 7

Reading p54
1 1F; 2G; 3A; 4H; 5E; 6B; 7D
2 1 barely
2 warriors
3 paced
4 to hold their own
5 signed
6 narrowly
7 void
8 narrowing

Vocabulary p56
1 1 obsession
2 screen
3 setbacks

4 homepage
5 links
6 innovation
7 brainchild
8 pioneer
9 prototype
10 mouse
11 imagination
12 attachment
2 1 into; 2 on; 3 up; 4 into; 5 in; 6 up
3 1 with; 2 out; 3 of; 4 to; 5 up; 6 forward; 7 from
4 a look up to
b look forward to
c stand up to
d keep out of
e get away from
f come up with
g run out of

Grammar p57
1 1 forgotten to tell Mika
2 like to see what
3 correct
4 remember visiting the
5 correct
6 mean to stop you
7 It needs replacing.
8 went on reading the
2 1 in developing
2 to look after
3 to see
4 having
5 to think
6 telling

Spelling p57
1 Note that judgement can also be spelt as judgment.
2 1 environment 2 argument

Listening p58
2 IT, scientists, assembly line, pre-programmed, breakthrough, innovation, developers, prototype, potential
3 1 assembly lines *or* an assembly line
2 a banana
3 fragile objects
4 human eyes
5 voice
6 three years
7 prototype
8 elderly people
9 agriculture
10 a car manufacturer

Pronunciation p59
1 a3; b1; c2; d5; e6; f4

Use of English p59
1 1 connection
2 technological
3 argument
4 security
5 shopping
6 criticism
7 wider
8 drawing
9 consultant
10 natural

Writing p60
1 1d; 2h; 3b; 4f; 5a; 6g; 7c; 8e
2 1 cutting edge
2 scene
3 lifelike
4 villain
5 downside
6 All in all

Use of English p61
1 1 didn't remember to buy / did not remember to buy
2 went on playing
3 looking forward (to going) to
4 regret deleting
5 tried to fix
6 needs to be checked *or* needs checking
7 stopped using
8 succeeded in solving

Speaking p61
1 Pair 1: e; Pair 2: g; Pair 3: a; Pair 4: d; Pair 5: c
2 1 very useful
2 you mean
3 know about
4 That's a
5 so too
6 this is the best
7 could also
8 at all
9 of thing
10 a bad idea

Unit 8

Reading p62
1 1B; 2A; 3D; 4B; 5C; 6A; 7D; 8B; 9A; 10D; 11C; 12A; 13C; 14D; 15B
2 1 numerous
2 an institution
3 forced to
4 the state
5 colossal
6 within
7 run-down
8 bail

Vocabulary p64
1 Across: 1 speeding
6 prosecution
8 fine
9 vandal
11 probation
Down: 1 shoplifter
2 detective
3 thief
4 forgery
5 jury
7 service
10 arson

Grammar p64
1 2 This is the hotel where the murderer was caught.
3 The police want to speak to the man whose car was parked outside the bank during the robbery.
4 Three people were working in the jewellery store on Wednesday when several watches and pairs of sunglasses were stolen.
5 The police interviewed five people who had reported the vandalism in the railway station.
6 No one knew the reason why the crime had taken place.
7 These are the keys which/that were stolen last night at 11pm.
2 1 No commas needed.
2 The police released the man, who then sold his story to the newspapers.
3 My father, who you met last year, is now writing a detective novel.
4 Our head office, which is being decorated at the moment, is on the top floor of this building.
5 No commas needed.
6 Matt Damon starred in *The Bourne Ultimatum*, which was directed by Paul Greengrass.
3 1 This is the building which was built by Sir Norman Foster. *or* This is the building that was built by Sir Norman Foster.
2 That is the man whose dog is outside.
3 correct
4 correct
5 Denise is the woman who comes from France. *or* Denise is the woman that comes from France.
6 Do you know the name of the man who is working here tomorrow? *or* Do you know the name of the man that is working here tomorrow?
7 correct
8 I think November 19th is the day when we are having the party. *or* I think November 19th is the day on which we are having the party.
4 1 to; 2 on; 3 in/at; 4 for

Spelling p65
1 1 irresponsible
2 immature
3 inaccurate
4 illogical
5 irrelevant
6 immoral
7 irregular
8 improbable
9 inappropriate
10 illiterate
11 imprecise
12 immortal
13 irresistible
14 incapable
15 impolite

Listening p66
1 1 the fire brigade, matches
2 a shelf, a store, a till
3 to break, to scratch
4 a bag, to hit, a knife, a wallet
5 a bank statement, to clone, a credit card, the number
6 to break in, the front door, holiday, a window
2 1F; 2D; 3C; 4B; 5E

Pronunciation p66
1 1 a noun; b verb
2 a noun b verb
3 a verb; b noun
4 a noun; b verb
5 a noun; b verb
6 a verb; b noun
2 2 a re<u>jects</u>; b re<u>jects</u>
3 a <u>con</u>duct; b con<u>duct</u>
4 a <u>rec</u>ord; b re<u>cord</u>
5 a <u>pro</u>duce; b pro<u>duce</u>
6 a <u>pro</u>ject; b pro<u>ject</u>

Use of English p67
1 1 to; 2 to; 3 when; 4 them; 5 a; 6 the; 7 will; 8 who/that; 9 in; 10 of; 11 is; 12 and/while
2 1C; 2B; 3A; 4B; 5C; 6C; 7B; 8D; 9 A; 10C; 11D; 12B

Writing p68
1 1g; 2e; 3d; 4f; 5i; 6a; 7b; 8h; 9c

Speaking p69
1 Extract 1: D; Extract 2: A; Extract 3: B; Extract 4: E; Extract 5: C

2 1 That's right.

2 completely with you

3 Exactly … Absolutely … That's it

4 Is it … Sure … Right

5 I see

6 I see what … That's true … OK

7 Good point … Maybe … True

Unit 9

Reading p70

1 1D; 2B; 3E; 4A; 5H; 6C; 7F

2 1 buzzwords

2 originate from

3 a wide range of

4 Originally

5 dominates

6 to domesticate

Vocabulary p72

1 1 boil; 2 sprinkle; 3 slice; 4 grill;
5 chop; 6 fry; 7 stir; 8 roast

2 1 spicy; 2 salty; 3 well-done;
4 dry; 5 sparkling; 6 raw; 7 sour;
8 bland

Pronunciation p72

1 answer; island; sandwich; calm;
knight; sword; castle; knitting;
vegetable; chocolate; palm;
Wednesday; cupboard; pneumonia;
whole; guardian; psychiatrist;
yacht; guess; salmon

Grammar p73

1 1 used to love

2 get

3 used to

4 are

5 got

6 aren't used to eating

2 1 My father worked for the post
office for five years.

2 correct

3 I studied at Bristol University
from 1993 to 1996.

4 correct

5 Bill Clinton was President of the
USA for eight years.

6 We travelled across Asia from
January to June 2003.

3 1 Not possible to change.

2 My family would always eat lunch
together on a Sunday.

3 We would always go on holiday to
the same seaside village.

4 Not possible to change.

5 Not possible to change.

Spelling p73

1 noisy; stony; garlicky; tasty;
smoky; juicy; spicy; icy; nosy

2 Garlicky. A k is added to the
word garlic before the -y ending.

Writing p74

1 Fast food restaurants are good
for society: 1, 4

Fast food restaurants are bad for
society: 2, 3, 5

2 1 That must be

2 It is clear that

3 This results in

4 It is said

5 this is the case

6 It is important therefore that
people

7 On balance it seems

8 The main problem is that

9 There is some truth in the
statement

10 It depends on what is meant by

Listening p75

1 1F; 2B; 3A; 4D; 5C

Vocabulary p75

1 1e; 2a; 3c; 4b; 5d

2 1 Keep, up

2 spice, up

3 breaking up

4 chop, up

5 ate, up

Use of English p76

1 1 take care of

2 got used to driving

3 take his inexperience into
account or take into account his
inexperience

4 put off

5 take her for granted

6 used to spend

7 is Martina getting on

8 we ate

2 1 a; 2 without; 3 at/in; 4 have; 5
on; 6 the; 7 which/that; 8 much; 9
that/the; 10 in; 11 for; 12 so

Speaking p77

1 1d; 2a; 3b; 4e; 5f; 6c

2 1P; 2J; 3J; 4P; 5J; 6P

Unit 10

Reading p78

1 1C; 2C; 3A; 4D; 5C; 6B; 7A; 8C

Vocabulary p80

1 1 round/ circular

2 triangular

3 square

4 rectangular

2 1 spherical

2 width

3 height

4 correct

5 softness

6 colourful

7 length

8 correct

3 1d; 2f; 3e; 4a; 5b; 6c

4 1 off; 2 down; 3 down; 4 off;
5 off; 6 down; 7 down; 8 off

Grammar p81

1 1 It could be important

2 He must have been

3 she might not be from France

4 It may not have been the
postman.

5 You can't have seen Diana

6 he must be from the police

2 1 must have been

2 can't have been

3 might have made

4 might have sent

5 must have happened

6 must have found

7 must have run

8 can't have done

9 must have been

Note that you can use *couldn't have*
instead of *can't have* in sentences
2 and 8.

Writing p82

1 You must include 2, 4, 6, 7, 8.

2 1f; 2e; 3a; 4b; 5c; 6g; 7h; 8d

3 The writer forgot to say how to
get the tickets.

Spelling p83

1 1 friend

2 experience

3 receipt

4 review

5 perceive

6 deceive

7 chief

8 inconceivable

2 1 neither

2 ancient

3 efficient

4 neighbour

5 foreign

6 proficient

7 weird

8 protein

9 species

10 height

11 science

Listening p83

1 1 amateur

2 Computer Science

3 neighbour

4 bed and breakfast

5 curtains

6 four friends / some friends

7 nothing (at all)

8 Your Weird Events

9 (their own) ghost stories

10 foreign countries

Use of English p84

1 1 doesn't seem that / does not
seem that

2 seems that *or* seems like *or* seems
as though

3 might have forgotten

4 is rare to see

5 give a reason for

6 have no idea

7 apart from

8 no point (in) telling

2 1C; 2B; 3A; 4A; 5C; 6B; 7B; 8D;
9B; 10A; 11D; 12D

Speaking p85

1 Could you repeat the question
please?

2 1 first one

2 called

3 like

4 like that

5 The question

6 certainly

7 the thing is

8 really

9 much

10 lot more

11 the two

3 certainly, really, much, a lot
more, definitely

Pronunciation p85

2 1 aQ bC; 2 aQ bC; 3 aC bQ;
4 aC bQ; 5 aQ bC; 6 aC bQ

Unit 11

Reading p86

1 1B; 2C; 3D; 4A; 5D; 6C; 7B; 8D;
9A; 10B; 11C; 12C; 13A; 14D; 15B

2 Sabine: on the spot

Dirk: instantly

Amandine: right then and there

Walter: just like that

2 1c; 2f; 3a; 4b; 5d; 6e

Vocabulary p88

1 1 discount
2 budget
3 brands
4 out
5 offer
6 whim
7 deal
8 bargain
2 1 off; 2 around; 3 by; 4 up; 5 to;
6 aside

Grammar p88

1 1 I wish I had studied harder
2 If I had a million euros
3 If it rains tomorrow
4 correct
5 If my boss hadn't left
6 correct
7 If you worked in
2 1 I will buy them.
2 I would get the DVDs online if I were you.
3 If I had known that you can only cook this dessert …
4 Customers can return products to the store provided that they are not damaged in any way.
5 I'll go to the shop as long as you do the washing up.
6 Should I see Eric, I'll ask him to call you.
7 Don't buy anything unless you really want to.
3 1a; 2b; 3a; 4a; 5b; 6a

Spelling p89

1 1h; 2k; 3e; 4m; 5c; 6i; 7b; 8g; 9f;
10d; 11l; 12a; 13j

Listening p90

1 1B; 2B; 3A; 4C; 5A; 6A; 7C; 8A

Pronunciation p90

1 1e; 2c; 3g; 4f; 5b; 6a; 7d
2 The stress could be placed in six different places:
WE don't want to watch the concert tomorrow.
We DON'T want to watch the concert tomorrow.
We don't WANT to watch the concert tomorrow.
We don't want to WATCH the concert tomorrow.
We don't want to watch the CONCERT tomorrow.
We don't want to watch the concert TOMORROW.

Use of English p91

1 1 wish I had helped
2 did the bank lend you
3 you mind if I tell
4 wish I hadn't told / wish I had not told
5 would go or could go
6 comes to
7 unless you phone
8 if I were you
5 1A; 2D; 3B; 4C; 5A; 6B; 7D; 8D;
9B; 10C; 11A; 12C

Writing p92

1 1f; 2b; 3d; 4g; 5a; 6e; 7c

Speaking p93

1 Picture 1: department store, a special deal, included in the price, a guarantee, special features, shop assistant
Picture 2: to try, spices, to taste, sacks, merchant, to haggle
2 1 What the pictures have in common is that they show customers talking to salesmen.
2 Both the salesmen seem to be very friendly.
3 These pictures show very similar situations.
4 One thing that is the same in the pictures is that the customers are really going to buy something.
5 We can see the same thing happening: the customers are asking questions.
6 In each picture the salesman looks very friendly.
7 There isn't a big difference here: we can see people thinking about buying something.
8 The pictures show the same sort of thing.

Unit 12

Reading p94

1 1C; 2D; 3F; 4A; 5H; 6G; 7E
2 1d; 2f; 3g; 4a; 5c; 6h; 7b; 8e

Vocabulary p96

1 2 drought
3 earthquake
4 flood
5 tornado
6 volcanic eruption
7 famine
8 tidal wave
2 1 storm
5 drizzle
7 forecast
2 thunder
3 gale
4 climate
6 mist
3 1 died
2 raised
3 rose
4 was killed
5 devastated
6 was destroyed
7 was lost
8 disappeared

Grammar p97

1 1 knowing
2 Despite
3 even
4 fact
5 Although
6 Nevertheless
2 1 a; 2 The; 3 a; 4 Ø; 5 the; 6 the;
7 Ø; 8 the

Spelling p97

1 -os: radios, videos, studios
-oes: potatoes, tomatoes, heroes
-os/-oes: mangos/mangoes, dominos/dominoes, volcanos/volcanoes

Listening p98

1 1B; 2A; 3B; 4C; 5C; 6A; 7B

Pronunciation p98

1 1 the answer /ðiː/ the question /ðə/
2 the end /ðiː/ the book /ðə/
3 the orange /ðiː/ the banana /ðə/
2 1 /ðiː/; 2 /ðə/; 3 /ðə/; 4 /ðə/;
5 /ðiː/; 6 /ðə/

Use of English p99

1 1 a business b blindness
2 a catastrophic b energetic
3 a drinkable b believable
4 a recovery b bravery
5 a survivors b demonstrator
2 1C; 2D; 3A; 4A; 5D; 6A; 7B; 8C;
9D; 10B; 11D; 12D

Writing p100

1 1 this problem
2 these places
3 this
4 They
5 In this case
6 their
7 even though
8 Instead
9 this
10 it
2 paragraph 2: information, batteries, special
paragraph 3: elderly, heavy
paragraph 4: Finally, available, separated

Speaking p101

1 a3; b2; c5; d1; e4
2 Pair 1: 1; Pair 2: 3; Pair 3: 5;
Pair 4: 2
3 1 I don't think this is a good idea **at all**.
2 This doesn't work **for** me.
3 I don't see the point **of doing** this.
4 This is not **an** effective solution to the problem.
5 In this **case** I don't think this is the best option.
6 I don't think it's a bad idea, but I think some of the other **ones** are better.
7 Does this really work? I**'m not** sure.
8 **What** if nobody comes to the event?

Unit 13

Reading p102

1 1C; 2A; 3B; 4C; 5A; 6D; 7A; 8C

Vocabulary p104

1 across: 1 health
2 weekly
6 obituary
7 journalist
9 headline
10 showbiz
11 correspondent
Down: 1 horoscope
3 editorial
4 paparazzi
5 politics
8 weather
2 1 going; 2 broke; 3 out; 4 ahead;
5 up; 6 out; 7 up; 8 leak

Grammar p105

1 2 Rich said that he hadn't seen Tina.
3 Maria asked if I was going to buy a newspaper. *or* Maria asked if we were going to buy a newspaper.
4 The schoolteacher said that it would be a nice day tomorrow/the following day.
5 The policeman said that no one could go in the building.

6 Katy asked if Simon had heard the news.

7 Joe said that they had been asking him questions.

2 1 our parents warned us not to speak

2 Gemma advised me to compare

3 His sister reminded him to post the letter.

4 apologise for arriving late

5 he suggested we do an exam

6 the people who didn't

7 I recommended he ask for

Spelling p105

1 1a; 2a; 3b; 4b; 5b; 6a; 7a; 8b; 9a; 10a

2 -able: advisable, believable, notable

-eable: changeable, knowledgeable, manageable

Listening p106

1 1 prime minister

2 politics and news

3 college newspaper

4 nothing

5 office junior

6 editorials

7 the town name

8 a (famous) singer

9 hospital

10 a music magazine

Pronunciation p106

1 1b; 2b; 3b; 4a; 5b; 6a; 7b; 8a; 9b; 10a; 11b; 12a

Use of English p107

1 1 by; 2 a; 3 for; 4 as; 5 able; 6 own; 7 it; 8 much; 9 of; 10 to; 11 who; 12 which

2 1B; 2A; 3C; 4C; 5A; 6A; 7D; 8C; 9C; 10A; 11D; 12A

Writing p108

1 1d; 2f; 3a; 4b; 5e; 6c

2 1 I saw Mike. He was running to the station.

2 There is a Canadian student in the class who speaks English and French.

3 The person that they are looking for isn't here.

4 I worked in Switzerland for six months.

5 'Can anyone see my pen?' he asked.

6 It cost me 1,999.99!

3 1 I think that's Gary's wife's car.

2 Eight students' answers were right.

3 Tina's brothers go to the same school as me.

4 correct

5 I couldn't find Charles' phone anywhere.

6 We were surprised by people's response to the questionnaire.

7 correct

8 Everybody's answer is wrong.

4

Hi Anders

I'm really pleased that you're coming to London to study English.

I think that you will have a great time when you are over here.

In your last email, you asked me to help you find some accommodation. The good news is that you will be able to stay in James' room while you are here, because he is going to Madrid to learn Spanish over the summer. The bad news is that you will have to leave the room in September when he comes back, but it will be easy to find somewhere else then.

You also asked me how to get to the house from Heathrow Airport. The best way is to get a Travelcard, which you can buy at the station. It costs £6.70. I was planning to meet you at the airport, but unfortunately, on that day my university puts up a notice with all the students' exam results and I need to go and see it. Anyway, I'm really looking forward to seeing you in a fortnight!

Speak soon,

Tony

Speaking p109

1 1f; 2b; 3a; 4e; 5d; 6c

3 a It really depends.

b I have to think about this one.

c Personally

d I absolutely love it.

e I've not really thought about this before.

f That's an interesting question.

Unit 14

Reading p110

1 1B; 2C; 3A; 4D; 5C; 6C; 7A; 8A

Vocabulary p112

1 1 fade; 2 craze; 3 cool; 4 trendy; 5 fads; 6 clash; 7 retro; 8 flair; 9 stylish

2 1 hang; 2 turn; 3 try; 4 do; 5 take; 6 let; 7 dress; 8 take

Grammar p112

1 1 The city was destroyed by a volcanic eruption.

2 I couldn't believe that he was being questioned by the police.

3 correct

4 Many synthetic fibres, like nylon and polyester, are used in clothes manufacture.

5 *The Name of the Rose* was written by Umberto Eco.

6 The window had been opened with a screwdriver.

7 The washing machine has ruined my new shirt!

2 1 had their heads shaved

2 had her windows cleaned

3 has her shopping delivered

4 are having the walls painted *or* are going to have the walls painted

5 had it repaired

6 is having his eyes tested

Listening p113

1 1C; 2C; 3B; 4A; 5C; 6A; 7B; 8A

Spelling p114

1 1 flower; 2 jeans; 3 dye; 4 site; 5 complements; 6 hole; 7 heels

2 1 sight; 2 flour; 3 genes; 4 whole; 5 compliments; 6 heals

Speaking p114

1 They disagree because Claudio thinks it is not a problem to spend too much money on clothes because you need to buy brand names to get good quality. Eleni thinks that there are better things to spend money on when you are young.

2 1 don't you think

2 After all

3 I mean is

4 but we're

5 suppose not

6 the same

7 suppose

3 b

Use of English p115

1 1 made him wear

2 let me leave

3 allow us to wear

4 need to be watered *or* need watering

5 has to be given *or* must be given

6 am having mine repaired *or* am having my car repaired

7 has his house cleaned

8 were being designed by

2 1 a hunger, b anger

2 a fashionable, b miserable

3 a trendy, b handy

4 a width, b depth

5 a exploitation, b imagination

Writing p116

1 The first student is writing about a village. The second student is writing about a town.

2 A I spend a lot of time walking down the country lanes.

B One problem is that it's quite noisy especially in the morning as you can hear all the commuters driving to work.

C The house is a really traditional little place close to the sea

D There are large numbers of red-brick houses all around

E There is a little shop nearby which is covered in ivy,

F a view of the river.

3 2 wrinkles

3 skinny

4 freckles

5 messy

6 dyed

Pronunciation p117

1 1c; 2b; 3b; 4a; 5c

Unit 15

Reading p118

1 1D; 2A; 3H; 4C; 5F; 6B; 7G

2 1g; 2d; 3a; 4f; 5b; 6h; 7e; 8c

Vocabulary p120

1 Across: 1 ceremony

3 portrait

7 landscape

9 galleries

Down: 1 custom

2 memorial

4 festival

5 museum

6 statue

8 sites

2 1 out; 2 off; 3 after; 4 up; 5 out;
6 out; 7 through; 8 off; 9 in

Grammar p121
1 1 No sooner had he given
2 Not only did he break
3 Hardly had they sent the email
4 No longer does the government
5 the room than the whole class
6 Not only had he not done
7 but they also refused to pay
2 1 … than Maria walked out of
the room.
2 correct
3 No sooner had the police arrived
than he admitted …
4 correct
5 Not only did she break the vase
…
6 correct
7 Hardly had I arrived at work than
the telephone started ringing.
8 correct

Spelling p121
1 1 a dairy b diary
2 a lose b loose
3 a trial b Trail
4 a exiting b exciting
5 a desert b dessert
6 a choose b chose
7 a assurance b insurance
8 a quite b quiet

Listening p122
1 1C; 2F; 3A; 4E; 5B

Pronunciation p122
1 1 Unfortunately
2 Basically
3 Surprisingly
4 Actually
5 however
6 Amazingly
7 nevertheless
8 Anyway
9 interestingly
2 They pause after the sentence
adverb in sentences 1, 2, 3, 4, 6,
7 and 8. They pause before the
sentence adverb in sentence 5.
They pause both before and after
the sentence adverb in sentence 9.
3 2 He didn't tell anyone the bad
news, | surprisingly.

3 They did not ask the cost of the
painting, | however, | because they
weren't interested in buying it.
4 This is a very dangerous
expedition. Nevertheless, | I want
to be involved in it.
5 Basically, | they weren't really
interested in art.
6 Actually, | I have a degree in
History of Art.

Use of English p123
1 1 don't mind if / do not mind if
2 make up your mind / make your
mind up
3 you mind working
4 sooner had I told
5 only did he
6 took me in
7 going through
8 take part in
2 1 relationship
2 remarkable
3 infamous
4 discovery
5 unlikely
6 recently
7 impressive
8 building
9 historical
10 explanation

Writing p124
1 1b; 2e; 3c; 4g; 5a; 6d; 7f
2 1 fancy dress
2 It was crowded
3 huge procession
4 invited to our party
5 It's a tradition in carnival/It's
traditional in carnival
6 city goes crazy

Speaking p125
1 Student 1: c; Student 2: a
2 1 let
2 foreground, background
3 Regarding
4 while
5 both
6 going

Unit 16

Reading p126
1 1B; 2D; 3A; 4A; 5C; 6D; 7B; 8A

Grammar p128
1 1f; 2h; 3c; 4a; 5e; 6g; 7b; 8d
2 1 such; 2 too; 3 enough; 4 such;
5 so; 6 too; 7 enough; 8 so
3 1 I thought Denis was the person
that sent the email.
2 What he had done was to paint
the house green.
3 It's Fiona and Jurgen who are
moving house.
4 correct
5 What I dream of doing is sailing
around the world.
6 What he did was to ask everyone
for money.
7 correct

Pronunciation p129
1 2 A quiet house in the country |
is my lifelong dream.
3 Buying the paint for the whole
house | is what Pilar was worried
about.
4 One person who I really enjoyed
meeting | was the design expert.
5 It wasn't Tony. It was Ricardo |
who moved to London.
6 What you will need to do | is go
on the Internet and find examples
of the house design you want.
7 What happened next | was very
surprising.
8 It wasn't until Andrea looked at
her phone | that she realised Dino
had been trying to call her.

Vocabulary p129
1 1 dreary; 2 cluttered; 3 terraced;
4 facing; 5 strong; 6 cheerful;
7 pale; 8 bare
2 1 up; 2 doing; 3 up; 4 turned;
5 picked; 6 let; 7 out; 8 brighten

Listening p130
1 1B; 2A; 3B; 4B; 5C; 6C; 7A

Spelling p130
1 1 lengthen; 2 heighten; 3 widen;
4 lessen; 5 strengthen; 6 worsen;
7 soften; 8 lighten; 9 straighten;
10 sadden

Use of English p131
1 1A; 2B; 3C; 4C; 5A; 6D; 7C; 8A;
9C; 10B; 11C; 12B

2 1 neighbourhood
2 homely
3 environmentally
4 generator
5 powered
6 likelihood
7 designer
8 ambitious
9 unsuccessful
10 enthusiastic

Writing p132
1 You must explain that you are
sharing a house with people from
five different countries and to
describe them. You must describe
your room: it's small but nice. You
need to describe your view, which
is of the park. You need to explain
that you decorated the room last
week. You need to explain that
Katie can visit you but not until
September when the room is free.
2 Possible answers:
1 received/got/read
2 hear
3 asked
4 There
5 As
6 was/seemed/felt/looked
7 which/that
8 mentioned/said
9 welcome
10 care
3 She forgot to mention the view
of the park.

Speaking p133
1 1 something
2 living
3 prefer
4 recently
5 important
6 living
7 free
8 why
9 type
10 successful, appeal
11 events
12 choosing
13 move
14 much, differences
2 1F; 2T; 3F; 4F; 5T; 6T; 7T; 8F; 9T;
10F

Practice Test

PAPER 1: READING

Part 1

1 D [these characteristics are not all unique to our species: ... and although an opposable thumb is a useful thing to have, it doesn't seem much on which to base a sense of superiority.]

2 B [We believe we are the sharpest knife in the drawer. ... The trouble is that the more we learn about other animals, the more we are forced to question how unique our intelligence is.]

3 A [Scientists argue amongst themselves whether these animals demonstrate 'real' language in the way humans do.]

4 C [And of course, dogs are smart. After all, they can be trained to do all manner of useful things. Yet our egos are not threatened by the fact.]

5 B [Stupid people are often described as bird-brains, but ... Alex ... could count to six, identify colours and had a vocabulary of 150 words. He had the intelligence of a five-year-old and the communication skills of a two-year-old.]

6 D [they take them to crossroads and junctions where they wait until the traffic lights change and it is safe to cross the road. They drop the walnuts on the tarmac and wait for vehicles to drive over them and crack the hard outer shells. When the lights change again, the crows join the pedestrians and pick up the nut.]

7 D [If you show a chicken an object and then hide it, it doesn't forget all about the object. ... it is capable of understanding that the object has not stopped existing simply because it is out of sight.]

8 A

Part 2

9B; 10D; 11A; 12G; 13F; 14C; 15H

Part 3

16 A [The boulevard is all that separates the hotel from the sandy beach, which is visible from all rooms in the hotel.]

17 B [these beautiful villas are surrounded by a thick hedge which screens the complex completely from the main road.]

18 C [Visitors who wish to take advantage of what the area has to offer are advised to hire a car.]

19 D [This fantastic hotel is located in the heart of a nature reserve that stretches for kilometres along the coast.]

20 A [The water is safe for swimmers, but only within the designated area: poisonous jellyfish are a problem in the summer months.]

21 C [A twenty-minute drive will bring you to several beaches that are excellent for swimming, water-skiing and surfing.]

22 D [saltwater crocodiles are a constant threat in the waters around here and these enormous reptiles have been known to attack and even kill.]

23 A [fascinating galleries that exhibit and sell the work of local artists, some of whose works the visitor can see in the lobby of the hotel.]

24 B [All areas within the grounds have wheelchair access, and the villas themselves have been carefully designed to be safe for people with reduced mobility and vision.]

25 A [Families with babies are welcome and there is twenty-four-hour childcare so parents can relax.]

26 C [Canecutter's Lodge is situated twenty kilometres inland.]

27 B [There is also a swimming pool and fully-equipped barbecue area for those visitors who prefer to dine out of doors.]

28 C [This unusual hotel was once the home of a plantation owner and much of the character of the original building has been preserved.]

29 D [Alternatively, you can remain in the hotel grounds and watch the creatures that come to feed on the fruit and seeds that the staff put out for them.]

30 C [Canecutter's Lodge has a reputation for its excellent cuisine and many of the ingredients are gathered fresh daily from the property itself: guavas, mangoes, granadillas, papayas, bananas and avocadoes.]

PAPER 3: USE OF ENGLISH

Part 1

1B; 2D; 3A; 4B; 5B; 6C; 7A; 8B; 9D; 10A; 11B; 12D

Part 2

13 few; 14 because; 15 with; 16 to; 17 there; 18 by; 19 the; 20 finally/lastly; 21 more; 22 where; 23 have/need; 24 your

Part 3

25 musician
26 wealthy
27 independent
28 loss
29 totally
30 ability/invaluable
31 deafness
32 historical
33 valuable
34 personality

Part 4

(|| shows where the answer is split into two parts for marking purposes)

35 delivered the package || on/in **time**
36 was interviewed || **by**
37 (that) he || didn't **need**
38 are || hardly **any**
39 is || **too** cold
40 **must** be || turned/switched
41 **unless** it rains
42 should/ought to || **set** up

PAPER 4: LISTENING

Part 1

1B; 2C; 3A; 4A; 5A; 6C; 7B; 8B

Part 2

9 emotional
10 fifty/50
11 friendly
12 (full-time) employees
13 twenty/20
14 how to ride
15 the Town Hall
16 full-time
17 14 to 16
18 birth certificate

Part 3

19C; 20E; 21F; 22A; 23D

Part 4

24 C [It means 'car' in Chichewa – that's a language spoken in south central Africa. But it also refers to a type of toy.]

25 A [kids make their own out of the things others throw away: wire, tin cans, bits of rubber, things like that]

26 C [They're lovely – made with such care and love for detail. I once watched a child making a bicycle using wire. ... And I thought: these aren't just toys, they're works of art!]

27 B [There are toys from Malawi, Zimbabwe and South Africa, but other African countries are represented too.]

28 B [There will also be daily morning workshops where children can make toys themselves out of wire.]

29 A [The documentary will be broadcast on television later this year. If you miss it, you can order the DVD from our gallery's web site.]

30 B [Actually, I believe kids everywhere are creative, but in richer countries, they don't know the joy that comes from making things themselves. I mean, why make a toy when your bedroom is already full of toys from a shop? I think toys are like chocolate: a little is delicious, but too much makes you sick.]

Spotlight on teaching FCE

Using the Spotlight on teaching FCE worksheets

These worksheets accompany seven short videos looking at each of the five papers on the FCE exam and two recordings of students taking the speaking examination. The videos include extracts from classrooms and interviews with the teachers. The lessons take place with students using materials from the Spotlight on FCE student's book. These films can be watched at:
http://elt.heinle.com/emea/en_uk/index.html

Who are the Spotlight on teaching FCE videos and worksheets for?

They are especially useful if you are new to teaching the FCE exam as they give you tips on teaching FCE exam classes and how to prepare students for the final exam. However, more experienced teachers will also find it helpful to reflect on how we teach FCE and to contrast their own knowledge with the teachers in the films.

How do I use the worksheets?

There are three ways to work with the videos and worksheets:

Individuals
Watch them on your own and answer the questions on each page. Then check your ideas by reading the answer key and commentary on page 190.

With other teachers
Meet with other teachers and watch the videos and complete the tasks together. After finishing, compare and discuss your answers with your colleagues.

For teacher training sessions
Directors of studies or teacher trainers can make use of the material as part of their teacher training programmes.

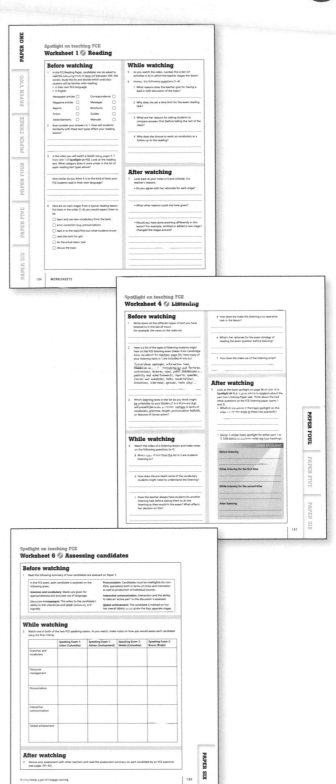

Spotlight on teaching FCE
Worksheet 1 💿 Reading

Before watching

1   In the FCE Reading Paper, candidates can be asked to read the following kinds of texts (of between 550–700 words). Study the list and decide which ones your students will be familiar with reading:
   • in their own first language
   • in English

   Newspaper articles ☐   Correspondence ☐

   Magazine articles ☐   Messages ☐

   Reports ☐   Brochures ☐

   Fiction ☐   Guides ☐

   Advertisements ☐   Manuals ☐

2   Now consider your answers in 1. How will students' familiarity with these text types affect your reading lessons?

   _____

   _____

   _____

3   In the video you will watch a lesson using pages 6–7 from Unit 1 of **Spotlight on FCE**. Look at the reading text. What category does it come under in the list of exam reading text types above?

   _____

   How similar do you think it is to the kind of texts your FCE students read in their own language?

   _____

   _____

   _____

4   Here are six main stages from a typical reading lesson. Put them in the order (1–6) you would expect them to be.

   ☐ learn and use new vocabulary from the texts

   ☐ error correction (e.g. pronunciation)

   ☐ lead in to the topic/find out what students know

   ☐ read the texts for gist

   ☐ do the actual exam task

   ☐ discuss the topic

While watching

5   As you watch the video, number the order (of activities in 4) in which the teacher stages the lesson.

6   Answer the following questions (1–4):

   1   What reasons does the teacher give for having a lead in with discussion of the topic?

   _____

   2   Why does she set a time limit for the exam reading task?

   _____

   3   What are her reasons for asking students to compare answers first (before telling the rest of the class)?

   _____

   4   Why does she choose to work on vocabulary as a follow up to the reading?

   _____

   _____

After watching

7   Look back at your notes in 6 and consider the teacher's reasons.

   • Do you agree with her rationale for each stage?

   _____

   • What other reasons could she have given?

   _____

   _____

   • Would you have done anything differently in this lesson? For example, omitted or added a new stage? Changed the stages around?

   _____

   _____

   _____

   _____

   _____

   _____

Worksheet 2 💿 Writing

Before watching

1   Read these statements about writing for the FCE. Do you agree with them? Why? Why not?

   a 'Students can write at home so it isn't a good idea to ask them to do it during class time.'

   _____

   b 'It's helpful to show students model answers of what's required for the exam.'

   _____

   c 'Writing is one of the hardest FCE papers because students don't usually write texts like articles, stories or reports.'

   _____

   d 'FCE writing isn't very communicative so my students tend to work alone in writing lessons.'

   _____

   e 'When I mark their writing, I tend to concentrate on the grammar the most.'

   _____

   f 'The ten minutes students spend planning their answer beforehand is probably the most important ten minutes of the time they need for answering the question.'

   _____

   g 'I like students to be creative so I avoid showing them examples of other people's writing.'

   _____

2   Study pages 82–83 from Unit 8 of **Spotlight on FCE**. From looking at these pages, which of the statements above do you think the authors would probably agree with?

   _____

   _____

While watching

3   Watch the video of a writing lesson. Which of the statements a–g in exercise 1 do you think Karen, the teacher, would probably agree with?

   _____

   _____

4   As you watch, make notes from the video on each of these questions:

   a What does Karen say can happen if students don't plan?

   _____

   b How does Karen focus the students on the structure and coherence of the text?

   _____

   c What reason does she give for showing students model versions?

   _____

   d What techniques does she use to help students think about the content for the essay?

   _____

   e What's her approach to checking work afterwards?

   _____

After watching

5   Imagine you are going to mark a student's piece of FCE writing. What would you give good marks for? Make a list of items. For example, *correct grammar, useful linking words….*

   _____

   _____

   _____

6   Now read this description from the *Cambridge ESOL FCE handbook for teachers* (page 28). It describes the minimum level a student must attain in the writing paper. Did your list in 5 include all the items mentioned in this description?

   'All the content points required in the task are included. Ideas are organised adequately, with the use of simple linking devices and an adequate range of structure and vocabulary. A number of errors may be present, but they do not impede communication. A reasonable, if not always successful, attempt is made at register and format which is appropriate to the purpose of the task and the audience.'

PAPER TWO
PAPER THREE
PAPER FOUR
PAPER FIVE
PAPER SIX

Worksheet 3 💿 Use of English

Before watching

1   Read comments a–d from teachers preparing students for the FCE exam.
   • If you've taught the exam before, think about if you have ever felt the same.
   • How do you think a teacher can address these issues?

   a 'I have to prepare students for the exam questions but the students don't have enough knowledge of the grammar yet.'

   b 'Students want to try exam questions but then find it very de-motivating when they get so many wrong.'

   c 'Sometimes students make mistakes not because they don't know the grammar, but because they don't understand how the question works.'

   d 'Sometimes I feel like I'm teaching the exam rather than the language…'

2   Here is some advice on preparing students for the FCE Use of English paper.
   • Did you mention any of these points in 1?
   • Which advice might address the issues in comments a–d? Write the letter in the box provided.

   'Spend plenty of time making sure students understand the task and what it is testing.' ☐

   'Teach strategies that will apply to the questions. For example, read the whole text first before answering individual questions.' ☐

   'To balance the need for development of language and exam skills, do what you would normally do in a language lesson but then point out moments when you are working on exam skills.' ☐

   'You can use exercises which are written in the same style of the exam question but are designed to target particular grammar points.' ☐

   'Students need to realise that when they start the course, they will make lots of mistakes.' ☐

While watching

3   Now watch part of an FCE lesson. The teacher is preparing students for Paper 3, part 1. As you watch, which of the advice in 2 does she follow?

4   Answer the following questions (a–e):

   a Which parts of the Use of English Paper does the teacher say share certain characteristics?

   b The teacher doesn't start work immediately on the Use of English question. What activities does she do first? What do you think her reasons are for this?

   c She sets the following tasks. Number them in the order she sets them:

   ☐ Students give answers and give their reasons.

   ☐ Students discuss what types of words are missing.

   ☐ Students choose the correct words.

   d How does the teacher suggest you can use incorrect answers?

   e What other type of activity does she set students?

After watching

5   In the lesson, the teacher had obviously trained students to be confident with terminology so they could talk about language. For example, students explained that words such as *prepositions* or *collocations* were missing. What are some ways to help students do this? How does **Spotlight on FCE** address this issue on page 16 of Unit 2?

6   In the lesson, she says that parts 1, 2 and 3 are similar so some of the exam strategies are similar. Look at part 4 of the Use of English paper. What kind of strategies or activities could you give students to help them with this question? (You might want to look at the Exam spotlights in **Spotlight on FCE** relating to this question to help you answer this.)

PAPER THREE
PAPER FOUR
PAPER FIVE
PAPER SIX

Worksheet 4 ● Listening

Before watching

1   Write down all the different types of text you have listened to in the last 24 hours.
For example, the news on the radio etc.

_____   _____

_____   _____

2   Here is a list of the types of listening students might hear on the FCE listening exam (taken from *Cambridge ESOL Handbook for teachers*, page 53). How many of your listening texts in 1 are included in this list?

'Answerphone messages, information lines, commentaries, radio documentaries and features, instructions, lectures, news, public announcements, publicity and advertisements, reports, speeches, stories and anecdotes, talks, conversations, discussions, interviews, quizzes, radio plays ...'

_____   _____

_____   _____

3   Which listening texts in the list do you think might be unfamiliar to your students? Are there any that will present particular problems, perhaps in terms of vocabulary, grammar, length, pronunciation features, or features of conversation?

_____

_____

_____

While watching

4   Watch the video of a listening lesson and make notes on the following questions (a–f):

a   Which type of text from the list in 2 are students listening to?

_____

_____

b   How does she pre-teach some of the vocabulary students might need to understand the listening?

_____

_____

_____

c   Does the teacher always have students do another listening task before asking them to do the listening as they would in the exam? What affects her decision on this?

_____

_____

_____

d   How does she make the listening a co-operative task in the lesson?

_____

_____

_____

e   What's her rationale for the exam strategy of reading the exam question before listening?

_____

_____

_____

f   How does she make use of the listening script?

_____

_____

_____

After watching

5   Look at the Exam spotlight on page 96 of Unit 10 in **Spotlight on FCE**. It gives advice to students about the part two Listening Paper task. Think about the two other questions on the FCE listening paper (parts 1 and 3).

• Which of the advice in the Exam spotlight on this page would also apply to these two questions?

_____

_____

_____

• Design a similar Exam spotlight for either part 1 or 3. Give advice to students under the four headings:

EXAM SPOTLIGHT

Before listening

_____

_____

While listening for the first time

_____

_____

While listening for the second time

_____

_____

After listening

_____

_____

_____

PAPER FOUR

PAPER FIVE

PAPER SIX

Worksheet 5 💿 Speaking

Before watching

1 Here are the four stages of the FCE speaking exam.

Stage 1: a conversation in which the interlocutor asks the candidate questions about topics such as friends or free time activities

Stage 2: the candidate compares and talk about two photographs for 1 minute

Stage 3: the two candidates talk about some visual prompts and then make a final decision

Stage 4: a discussion relating to the third stage with the interlocutor and both candidates taking part.

Which stage seems most authentic? Which seem least authentic?

_____

_____

Which stage do you think your students would find easiest to do?

_____

_____

2 Here are three pairs of opposing opinions (A and B) on how to prepare students for the speaking exam. Compare the opinions and decide which you tend to agree with most. Does it depend on certain factors? (e.g. *level of students, the stage in the course etc*).

1 A 'I think it's useful to give students fixed expressions for the different stages of the exam.'

B 'If you give students fixed expressions to use, they can often sound unnatural.'

2 A 'I provide students with recordings of examples and model versions of what they are expected to produce.'

B 'I let students answer in their own way and develop their own personal style.'

3 A 'Students need to spend most of their speaking time in class using actual exam materials.'

B 'It's easy to combine the kind of speaking tasks you do in a normal lesson with the demands of the FCE speaking exam.'

_____

_____

While watching

3 Now watch part of a lesson preparing students for part 2 of the Speaking Paper. Make notes on the following:

a Which of the opinions in 2 are reflected in this particular lesson?

_____

_____

b What is the purpose of the two listenings in this lesson?

_____

_____

c What speaking tasks do students have during the lesson? How authentic are they?

_____

_____

d The teacher suggests you can input expressions and useful language either before or after the task. Which approach does he use in this lesson? What are the pros and cons of both approaches?

_____

_____

After watching

4 You only watched extracts of the speaking lesson. Here are four more parts of the lesson plan we didn't see. When do you think they would be included? Watch the video again if necessary to say when you think they would occur (note there may be more than one possibility):

A Listen again and comment on what the candidate did well and pick out any useful language.

_____

B Role-play the exam with students working in groups of three (one student playing the part of the interlocutor and two being candidates)

_____

C Feedback and error correction stage

_____

D Provide strategies for when you don't know the name of something in the picture

_____

5 Imagine you are introducing the students to stage 3 of the Speaking Paper for the first time. How could you structure the lesson?

Worksheet 6 💿 Assessing candidates

Before watching

1 Read the following summary of how candidates are assessed on Paper 5.

In the FCE exam, each candidate is assessed on the following areas:

Grammar and vocabulary: Marks are given for appropriateness and accurate use of language.

Discourse management: This refers to the candidate's ability to link utterances and speak cohesively and logically.

Pronunciation: Candidates must be intelligible (to non-ESOL specialists) both in terms of stress and intonation as well as production of individual sounds.

Interactive communication: Interaction and the ability to take an 'active part' in the discussion is assessed.

Global achievement: The candidate is marked on his/her overall ability to complete the four separate stages.

While watching

2 Watch one or both of the two FCE speaking exams. As you watch, make notes on how you would assess each candidate using the five criteria.

	Speaking Exam 1: Julian (Columbia)	Speaking Exam 1: Adrian (Switzerland)	Speaking Exam 2: Waldo (Columbia)	Speaking Exam 2: Bruno (Brazil)
Grammar and vocabulary				
Discourse management				
Pronunciation				
Interactive communication				
Global achievement				

After watching

3 Discuss your assessment with other teachers and read the assessment summary on each candidate by an FCE examiner (see pages 191–92).

Worksheet key and commentary

Note: Answers and commentary are given for most of the questions. However, in some cases no answer is given because responses will vary a great deal and depend on your situation and teaching context.

Worksheet 1: Reading

1 In many cases students will be familiar with reading texts such as newspaper articles but less familiar with guides or manuals. For younger students, their experience of different text types may be even more limited.

2 If students are unfamiliar with texts in their own language, it means you will need to spend more time getting them used to reading them and knowing how they are structured and what kind of vocabulary they are likely to meet.

3 The text used in the lesson is about soap operas and is authentic material taken from a TV magazine.

4 The teacher follows these stages:

1 lead in to the topic/find out what students know; 2 discuss the topic; 3 read the texts for gist; 4 do the actual exam task; 5 learn and use new vocabulary from the texts; 6 error correction (e.g. pronunciation)

6 1 She has a lead-in order to set the scene and so students think about what the text contains. It also gets them speaking in response to questions which is useful practice for the speaking exam.

2 To reflect the time pressure of the exam.

3 So that students listen to each other and explain their answers.

4 Because the FCE readings have high vocabulary loads and students need to develop strategies for dealing with unknown words.

Worksheet 2: Writing

1 There is no right or wrong answer to this first task. Teachers' opinions will vary.

2 From what is in the book, the authors probably agree with statements b (they provide an example answer) and f (they provide work on planning). It's unlikely they would agree with statements a (as writing is one of the exercises) d (students are encouraged to work with each other in the book) and g (they want students to read examples in the book but also each other's work).

3 Based on what we see of her lesson, the teacher seems to agree with the answer to 2 (see above).

4 a Students' writing can lack coherence.

b By giving students a mixed-up text to reform it cohesively. She also asks them to think about important phrases that help the structure.

c To give them a basic idea of what is expected.

d She brainstorms ideas with the whole class on the board to illustrate the idea behind the initial planning stage.

e Before she collects in the writing she encourages students to evaluate each other's work and they can also use the writing checklists in Spotlight on FCE.

Worksheet 3: Use of English

1–2 The statements highlight the problem of balancing the teaching of language and the teaching of exam skills. Teaching exam classes requires you to do both with classes who may have different needs. There are no single correct answers but all the advice in 2 will be helpful to remember.

3 From what we see, the teacher seems to follow three pieces of advice:

'Spend plenty of time making sure students understand the task and what it is testing.' She devotes plenty of time to introducing students to the exam question and encourages them to identify the type of language which is missing.

'Teach strategies that will apply to the questions. For example, read the whole text first before answering individual questions.' She clearly does this.

'To balance the need for development of language and exam skills, do what you would normally do in a language lesson but then point out moments when you are working on exam skills.' Even though it's an exam class, she still uses techniques such as a lead-in to find out what students know about the topic.

4 a 1, 2 and 3. (They are all continuous texts.)

b She leads into the topic and gets students thinking about it. This generates key vocabulary. It also provides some motivational fun which will help with the difficult Use of English task that follows.

c 1 Students discuss what types of words are missing; 2 Students choose the correct words; 3 Students give answers and give their reasons.

d Rewrite the text or sentences using the incorrect words.

e Students create their own exam questions to test each other.

Worksheet 4: Listening

3 This will vary according to factors such as age and ability of the class. However, if a student isn't used to lectures, for example, you might need to play recordings of quite lengthy monologues. Students may also need help focusing on key words and becoming used to different accents.

4 a It is an anecdote in which a police officer describes an encounter with a strange boy and a UFO.

b She shows students a flying saucer and asks questions about it to elicit the vocabulary of shape and material.

c Not always. She says that as she gets nearer to the final exam, students will only do the exam task.

d Students listen and then share their ideas and answers as a group.

e Reading the exam question before listening helps students to predict the type of words they need to listen out for.

f Students can check their answers in the listening script and she also uses the script for follow-up vocabulary work.

5 Much of the advice in the Exam spotlight is true for all three parts of the listening. However, some can be varied according to the question type and length of listening.

Worksheet 5: Speaking

1 Stage 1 requires quite an authentic response from students as they talk about themselves. Stages 2 and 3 are less authentic because students respond to pictures. Usually, stage 1 of the exam is the easiest to prepare students for as it is quite predictable and many of the questions are typical of everyday conversation.

2 The opinions in A reflect the view that we need to prepare students for the exam in quite a formulaic way. Opinion B is that students still need plenty of work on their general language skills. Clearly, which view we follow may depend on factors such as how soon the exam is or if the level of the students' English is already ready for FCE but they don't know how the exam works. Note also that weaker students in particular often benefit from having some useful phrases to help them structure their language.

3 a In this lesson, the teacher seems to reflect the opinions in A as the lesson is focusing on the exam itself rather than any improvement of students' overall language.

b In both cases the listening is to illustrate what happens in the exam. The second listening also offers a model version of what candidates are expected to produce.

c Students compare pictures twice. The task in itself isn't authentic but the students' responses clearly are.

d The teacher in this lesson appears to input expressions and useful language after the speaking task. Presumably he then goes on to have students practise using the expressions. This is commonly referred to as 'task-based teaching'; the advantage of this approach is that the teacher responds to the needs of the students rather than presenting language beforehand which they may not need. However, input given before speaking can be equally effective, especially with less confident students.

4 The teacher may have done A after students have heard the listening for the first time. The role play (B) would follow on from the end of the film so that students can practise using expressions. This would then be followed by C assuming the teacher monitored the role play and took notes on any errors. Stage D could occur when students are thinking what they might say about the pictures or if they were unable to talk about the pictures in the role play.

5 See the sections in Spotlight on FCE where students are introduced to stage 3 for more ideas on this.

Worksheet 6: Assessing candidates

2-3 Compare your assessment with those of an FCE examiner below:

Checklist of advice
Session 1: Julian

In part 1 ...	score
• talk about general topics.	1 (2) 3
• make sure you answer the examiner's questions clearly.	(1) 2 3
In part 2 ...	
• briefly describe each photograph.	1 (2) 3
• compare and contrast the two photographs.	1 (2) 3
• answer the question with the two photographs.	(1) 2 3
• clearly answer the examiner's supplementary question.	(1) 2 3
In part 3 ...	
• discuss the pros and cons for each suggestion.	(1) 2 3
• compare and contrast some of the suggestions.	(1) 2 3
• ask for your partner's opinion.	(1) 2 3
• show you are listening to your partner.	(1) 2 3
• discuss and give a final answer to the question or questions with the suggestions.	(1) 2 3
In part 4 ...	
• answer the examiner's questions.	1 (2) 3
• give opinions.	1 2 (3)

Checklist of advice
Session 1: Adrian

In part 1 ...	score
• talk about general topics.	(1) 2 3
• make sure you answer the examiner's questions clearly.	(1) 2 3
In part 2 ...	
• briefly describe each photograph.	(1) 2 3
• compare and contrast the two photographs.	(1) 2 3
• answer the question with the two photographs.	(1) 2 3
• clearly answer the examiner's supplementary question.	(1) 2 3
In part 3 ...	
• discuss the pros and cons for each suggestion.	(1) 2 3
• compare and contrast some of the suggestions.	(1) 2 3
• ask for your partner's opinion.	(1) 2 3
• show you are listening to your partner.	(1) 2 3
• discuss and give a final answer to the question or questions with the suggestions.	(1) 2 3
In part 4 ...	
• answer the examiner's questions.	(1) 2 3
• give opinions.	(1) 2 3

Session 1 Interview

Candidate's name: Julian

Julian appears to be an above average FCE candidate.

His grammar is mainly accurate, although he uses a limited range of structures. His vocabulary is sufficient to deal with communication in everyday situations, despite a few errors (eg *near to the firewood, could join people together*). He is generally able to maintain the flow of language without much hesitation or any need for prompting by the examiner. He also communicates well with his partner in part 3.

However, Julian needs to develop the linguistic skills to express opinions and describe qualities, as he tends to describe everything as *nice*.

Although his pronunciation is clear enough to understand, it is occasionally inappropriate and in need of improvement. He mispronounces certain sounds, eg *th* in weather (*wedder*) and *three* (*tree*), confuses *ch* with *sh* in *choose, children* and *ship*, plus the *i* in *ship* (*cheep*) and *v* in *river* (*reeber*). The word *urban* was also difficult to distinguish.

Session 2 Interview

Candidate's name: Waldo

Waldo appears to be an average FCE candidate.

He has a limited command of grammar, relying on simple structures. Despite basic errors (eg *they decides, it attract*), this is sufficient to convey his intended meaning. However, he would benefit from further study of grammar before taking the exam. His vocabulary is accurate enough to respond to the examiner's questions and his contributions are usually coherent, relevant, and of appropriate length. Nevertheless, he does respond well to the examiner's supplementary question in Part 2.

Although he has difficulty with certain sounds (eg *i* becomes *ee*, *ch* becomes *sh*), most of the time his pronunciation and use of stress are appropriate to convey meanings. However, at times, notably in Part 4, his word stress obscures the meaning (eg *aunt* maybe '*virnment = and maybe the environment*).

Waldo also appears to be feeling nervous and would be well-advised to have further speaking practice and development of his linguistic resources to improve his speaking skills and confidence level before the exam.

Session 1 Interview

Candidate's name: Adrian

Adrian is a very strong FCE candidate.

He responds well to the examiner's questions, giving extended answers with reasons and examples. He also interacts well with his partner in Part 3, speculating on what may happen before or after the events and developing the discussion. He uses a wide range of grammatical structures and vocabulary with only rare errors (eg *abandon* (= ban) cars from the city, *invent new theatres* (= write new plays?), *a huge firework* (= fireworks display).

There are two minor points which he could improve on. First, his use of prepositions (eg *spend time with sports, rides with horses, by your own*) is possibly impeded by translation from his first language. Secondly, he makes rare pronunciation errors, eg *th* in *with* (*wiv*) and *the* (*de*), and has a little difficulty with *v* in *village* (*willage*).

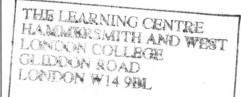
Session 2 Interview

Candidate's name: Bruno

Bruno appears to be a weak FCE candidate.

He appears to understand all the examiner's questions and attempts to respond in all parts of the exam. However, his grammar and vocabulary are too limited to handle communication at this level.

In part 1, he responds to the examiner's questions, but seldom answers in complete sentences and makes frequent errors (eg *is really too nice, to met my friends, from the stressful citizen*). In Part 3, he responded automatically to his partner with *I agree* although his partner had just made a point disagreeing with Bruno's previous statement.

Bruno's stress of some individual words is inappropriate (eg *stressed, bored*) and his pronunciation of some words occasionally makes him to difficult to understand. (eg *coun(t)rysides* [in Part 1], *mountain, the man(y) of them, three flights (flats?) in one house*).

He hesitates frequently throughout the entire interview, giving the impression that he has to search for vocabulary. Therefore, Bruno would be more likely to do better in the exam after further study and practice.

WORKSHEET KEY